Comprehensive Literacy Resource

for Grades 3–6 Teachers

Senior Author

Miriam P. Trehearne
National Literacy Consultant
Thomson Nelson

Authors

Dr. Roz Doctorow
Educational Consultant
Toronto, Ontario

Dr. Christine J. Gordon
University of Calgary
Calgary, Alberta

Charmaine Graves
Learning Supervisor, Languages and Social Sciences
Thames Valley District School Board
London, Ontario

Lynne Hemming Healy
Speech-Language Pathologist/Literacy Specialist
Halifax Regional School Board
Halifax, Nova Scotia

Sue Jackson
Learning Coordinator, Languages JK-6, Early Years, EQAO
Thames Valley District School Board
London, Ontario

Deidre McConnell
Consultant
Calgary Board of Education
Calgary, Alberta

THOMSON
NELSON

Australia   Canada   Mexico   Singapore   Spain   United Kingdom   United States

LA-P
T217
2006

Comprehensive Literacy Resource for Grades 3-6 Teachers
Miriam P. Trehearne
Roz Doctorow
Christine J. Gordon
Charmaine Graves
Lynne Hemming Healy
Sue Jackson
Deidre McConnell

Director of Publishing
Beverley Buxton

General Manager, Literacy, Reference, & International
Kevin Martindale

Director of Publishing, Literacy & Reference
Joe Banel

Senior Product Manager, Literacy, Reference, & International
Mark Cressman

Executive Managing Editor, Development
Darleen Rotozinski

Program Manager
Evelyn Maksimovich

Developmental Editors
Evelyn Maksimovich, Kate Revington

Editorial Assistant
Charlotte Martin

Executive Managing Editor, Production
Nicola Balfour

Senior Production Editor
Deborah Lonergan

Copy Editor
Gilda Mekler

Proofreader
Linda Szostak

Indexer
Noeline Bridge

Senior Production Coordinator
Helen Locsin

Production Coordinator
Cathy Deak

Creative Director
Angela Cluer

Design Director
Ken Phipps

Art Director
Suzanne Peden

Cover Design
Johanna Liburd

Cover Image
Ray Boudreau

Illustrators
Johanna Liburd, Deborah Crowle, Steve Corrigan

Compositor
Janet Zanette

Permissions
Patricia Buckley

Printer
Transcontinental Printing Inc.

Reviewers
James Coulter, Toronto DSB, ON
Dianne Dillabough, Peel DSB, ON
Cynthia Hatt, School District 6, NB
Phyllis Hildebrandt, Lakeshore School Division, MB
Leisa Holmes Albert, Department of Education, PEI
Andrew Mildenberger, Toronto DSB, ON
Janice Moore, St. Thomas University, NB
Bev Nugent, Elk Island District School Board, AB
Linda O'Reilly, Vancouver School Board, BC
Ann Varty, Trillium Lakelands DSB, ON

Acknowledgments
The authors wish to thank the staff and students at the following schools for their contributions:

Janice Churchill Elementary School, Martha J. Norris Elementary School, Serpentine Heights Elementary School, Chantrelle Elementary School, Maple Green Elementary School, and Betty Huff School of the Surrey District School Board; Lord Kitchener School, Vancouver School Board; Crossfield Elementary School and R.J. Hawkey Elementary School, Rockyview School District; Akiva Academy, Calgary;

Earl Grey Elementary School, Calgary Board of Education; Abbott School, Edmonton School Board; Fultonvale Elementary/Junior High School, Saskatchewan Christian School, and Crochester Elementary School, Elk Island District School Board; Dorset Elementary School, Lester B. Pearson School Board; Kindree Public School, Peel District School Board

Special thanks to Darcy Dycha, Jane Hutchison, and Louise Towill

Library and Archives Canada Cataloguing in Publication

Comprehensive literacy resource : for grades 3-6 teachers /
Miriam Trehearne ... [et al.].

Includes bibliographical references and index.
ISBN-13: 978-0-17-627030-8
ISBN-10: 0-17-627030-2

1. Language arts (Elementary). 2. Reading (Elementary). 3. English language—Study and teaching (Elementary). I. Trehearne, Miriam

LB1576.C646 2005   372.6'044   C2005-903438-6

TABLE OF CONTENTS

Introduction

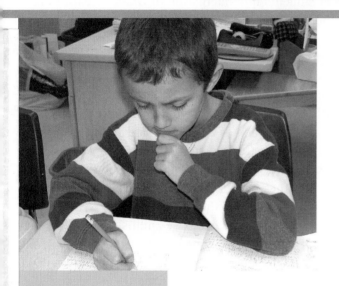 

A POWERFUL LANGUAGE ARTS RESOURCE FOR GRADES 3 TO 6— DEVELOPED BY TEACHERS ... FOR TEACHERS

"Elementary schools have but one overriding mission: to foster the development of independent literacy in all students so that each becomes literate for a lifetime." Learning to read and write is fundamentally essential to success in school and in society.

Allington and Cunningham 1996, viii

Why a Comprehensive Literacy Resource for Grades 3 to 6?

It is often said that students in kindergarten to Grade 2 learn to read and write, while those in Grades 3 to 6 read and write to learn. In fact, all students should be doing both simultaneously and continuously.

Students in the intermediate or upper elementary grades still have much to learn about reading and writing. With much more content-area reading and more complex texts, they face new challenges. They do not automatically know how to effectively manage such text. They need to learn how to keep track of characters and how to persevere when a text doesn't grab them immediately. They also need to become more thoughtful, to learn to think more critically. They need to learn how to summarize, synthesize, and infer. Many technical, abstract, and literary words now appear in their reading materials. Students need to continually expand their vocabulary and background knowledge to make sense of such text. They need to learn how to read and write different genres and modes. Most importantly, they must see reading and writing as purposeful and must see themselves as successful literacy learners across all subject areas.

Students develop these skills, strategies, and dispositions to literacy learning from working with knowledgeable teachers and parents. Teaching reading and writing is not the sole responsibility of early elementary teachers. *All teachers,* at all grades, teaching all subject matter, must see themselves as *teachers of literacy.*

The Fourth-, Fifth-, or Sixth-Grade Slump

The research of Jeanne Chall (2000), among others, indicates that many students, especially those from less economically advantaged backgrounds, become less effective readers as they move from the early to upper elementary grades. In other words, there is a slump in their reading. Many students can decode text at a high level but comprehend very little. To avoid or at least lessen this slump, all teachers in Grades 3 to 6 must focus on students'

- reading attitudes, motivation, interest, and time truly engaged in reading
- vocabulary, world knowledge, and comprehension
- fluency in both reading and writing
- ability and interest in reading and writing different genres and modes
- understanding and use of the strategies used by effective readers and writers
- frequent opportunities for talk/conversations and written response
- time spent reading and writing, which should be substantial
- development as thoughtful literacy learners

In the *Literacy Dictionary*, reading fluency is defined as "freedom from word recognition problems that might hinder comprehension" (Harris and Hodges 1995, 85). More recent definitions of fluency involve "reading smoothly, without hesitation and with comprehension" (Klenk and Kibby 2000, 672). In most instances in this resource, fluency is defined as encompassing comprehension, as described by Klenk and Kibby.

A Message to Grades 3 to 6 Teachers: Critical Elements for Success

Teachers want to know how they can best support student literacy. This resource responds to the following frequently asked questions:

- What are developmentally appropriate literacy expectations or goals for students in Grades 3 to 6?
- What is fluency and how can teachers support its development?
- What is thoughtful literacy and how is it best supported?
- What is critical literacy? Is it the same as critical thinking?
- What is visual literacy and how can it be supported?
- How can teachers support literacy learning across all subjects, across the day?

Teaching Methods

- How can teachers help their students reach literacy goals?
- What researched-based strategies support reading comprehension?
- What is a comprehensive literacy program? What does it look like in the classroom?

"The ability to read and write does not develop naturally without careful planning and instruction."
INTERNATIONAL READING ASSOCIATION 1998, 6

"The majority of students ... asked for more teacher read-alouds and more time to read independently in school. The majority wanted to hear about good books from teachers, to have teachers introduce books that students would like, and to read segments 'to get us interested.'"
WORTHY 2002, 568

For purposes of this publication, the word "parents" represents a parent, two parents, guardians, and other essential caregivers.

- How can teachers effectively support oral language and vocabulary development?
- Which literacy assessments should teachers use and how do these assessments drive instruction?
- What does the language arts block look like?
- What mini-lessons are effective for teaching writing?
- How can teachers effectively assess and teach word work and spelling? Which spelling strategies work?
- How many sight words should students know? Which words are they?
- How can teachers combine the writing process, writing modes and genres, and writing traits or characteristics during writing workshop?

Interventions and Motivation

- How do teachers help struggling students? What does effective intervention look like?
- How can teachers motivate reluctant readers and/or writers?

Organizing Classrooms and Schedules

- How much time should be allocated for language arts each day? How can teachers fit it all in?
- How can teachers effectively organize the classroom?
- When working with small groups, or doing guided reading, what are the other students doing?
- What classroom materials are needed and how should they be organized?
- How can technology support literacy learning in the classroom?

Home Connections

- What role can parents realistically play in support of literacy learning, and how can teachers enhance this home–school connection?
- What literacy homework is worthwhile?

The Teacher Makes the Difference

The curriculum and standards for student literacy learning are assigned by school boards and ministries. But it is teachers, with input and support from parents, who make the crucial decisions about what each student needs to become a successful literacy learner. Teachers organize the classroom and deliver programs. **Teachers make the difference**.

Teachers already know a great deal about teaching and learning. This resource is intended to help teachers construct and clarify their own ideas about teaching practices that work best for them and for their students, using a strong research base.

When working with at-risk literacy learners, teachers must focus on effective teaching to accelerate the learning and to close the gap. Teachers need to revise their instruction, not their expectations for learning, when children are not progressing (McGill-Franzen 1992, 57–58).

To sum up, today's educators want a manageable, affordable language resource that

- meets the needs of all students
- is congruent with provincial literacy curricula
- focuses on comprehensive (balanced) literacy and effective intervention
- demonstrates developmentally appropriate practices
- helps teachers meet the needs of diverse literacy learners
- provides tools for assessment, evaluation, and reporting
- is diagnostic and responsive to student needs
- facilitates communication with parents
- has strong teacher support

Thomson Nelson produced this comprehensive teacher's resource in response to these concerns and with the assistance of many educators—teachers, principals, and consultants. This truly is a language arts resource written by teachers for teachers.

Effective literacy instruction does not follow the "flavour of the month." Pendulum swings disenfranchise many learners.

Essential Elements of an Effective Literacy Program

Literacy learning is too important to be dealt with haphazardly. To be most effective, teachers must base their teaching on sound research verified by carefully examined classroom practice. Rather than constantly reinventing the wheel, effective teachers use what has been proven to work.

Research indicates that the essential elements of effective Grades 3 to 6 literacy programs are beliefs and understandings, time, engagement, instruction, materials, comprehensive literacy programs, effective intervention, and partnerships with home, school, and community.

Beliefs and Understandings

Teachers' beliefs drive thinking, planning, and action.

The most effective teachers believe

- that literacy learning is foundational knowledge and is the priority focus in elementary school
- that students in Grades 3 to 6 are still learning to read and write and not just reading and writing to learn
- that students need to be supported to improve their understanding, strategies, and skills
- that all teachers, no matter the content area, are teachers of literacy
- that virtually all students will become successful literacy learners
- that *they* can be effective literacy teachers
- that meaning making (comprehension) is the goal of all learning
- that students learn best when involved in activities that are meaningful and relevant, challenging but achievable
- that oral language is the foundation of all literacy learning

"Star teachers believe that, regardless of life conditions their students face, they as teachers bear primary responsibility for sparking their students' desire to learn."

ALLINGTON AND JOHNSTON 2001, 154, CITING HABERMAN 1995

Time

Teachers who allocate more time to reading and language arts are the teachers whose students show the greatest gains in literacy development (Allington 2001).

Students need to spend at least two hours daily focused on language arts. Long blocks of uninterrupted time are most beneficial. Reading deeply and writing thoughtfully take time. It takes time to lose yourself in a book. But how can a teacher fit it all into the day? The key is integrating subjects, time, and topics. Allington and Johnston (2001) found that this approach not only made the instructional day more coherent, but it also fostered motivation and engagement.

"In classrooms of effective teachers, students talk more than in typical classrooms. The talk is respectful, supportive, and productive. The teachers not only model the kinds of conversations that they expect, but creating these conversational communities becomes a focus throughout the year."

CLOSE 2001

Engagement

"The amount of time students are truly engaged in learning is the most potent predictor of literacy learning" (Allington and Cunningham 1996, 118). But what engages students? Interesting activities that they find worthwhile and that are at the right level of difficulty (see Chapter 5: In the Classroom: Making It Work). The project approach, which allows in-depth study of real-world topics, such as pollution, can provide this interest and sense of purpose.

Focused Teaching

Focused teaching is important. It is teaching that has a focus and that is matched to the learning needs of each student. This is easy to say but often challenging to do. Focused teaching involves moving to the "radical middle." Constructivism and direct teaching are not mutually exclusive. Students are given many opportunities to construct knowledge with the scaffolding provided by teachers, volunteers, paraprofessionals, parents, and peers.

"Students need more structured modeling, demonstrating and coaching, and less assigning" (Allington and Cunningham 1996, 45). This developmentally appropriate teaching involves much work with small flexible groups based on student needs and interests.

Materials

A print-rich environment is crucial. Books, magazines, and newspapers should be abundant. Students in classrooms with library centres read about 50 percent more than other students without such centres (Allington and Cunningham, 1996). Students need to read works of many different genres that tie in with their curriculum and interests. Because achievement levels vary more than in the primary grades, books must represent a wider range of levels of difficulty. The classroom needs hundreds of books for guided, shared, independent, read-aloud, and home reading. In fact, Allington (2001) found that the most successful teachers had about 1500 books in their classrooms.

Environmental print is also important. Posters, charts, and word walls should be everywhere. But having the print there is not enough. It remains simply decorative unless students are engaged with it in daily activities, with teacher guidance.

Comprehensive Literacy Programs

Comprehensive literacy programs involve a wide variety of activities, provided consistently:

- reading and writing *modelled for* students
- reading and writing done *with* students
- reading and writing done *by* students
- word work

"There is wide agreement among literacy researchers that students who read more become more proficient in reading fluency and comprehension, as well as general vocabulary and cognitive development."

WORTHY 2002, 568, CITING STANOVICH 1986

"One of the best ways to increase student thinking is to make sure you have a curriculum that provides kids with things worth thinking about and that offers kids enough depth that they can actually think."

PRELLER 2000, 1, CITING ALLINGTON

"Thoughtful literacy is more than remembering what the text said. It is engaging the ideas in texts, challenging those ideas, reflecting on them, and so on. It is responding to a story with giggles, goosebumps, anger and revulsion."

ALLINGTON 2001, 106

In exemplary classrooms "constant instruction took place ... although the teachers were only occasionally in front of the class."

ALLINGTON AND JOHNSTON 2001, 160

Students spend most of their language arts block actively engaged in authentic reading and writing.

"We need to get enticing, just-right books into each student's hands."

ALLINGTON AND CUNNINGHAM 1996, 4

- visual literacy
- oral language and numerous forms of representing knowledge and understanding

Such programs involve a balance of direct versus indirect instruction; whole-class, small-group, and individual activities; and intervention for students who need it. Many educators refer to this as a *balanced* literacy program. However, as Regie Routman comments, this term is often misused to represent "the belief that learning proceeds in a skills-based hierarchy (usually determined by a published program), a view not supported by research" (2000, 15). Thus, in this resource, where there is no page-by-page script to follow, the term *comprehensive literacy program* is used instead.

Effective Intervention

A research-based, proven form of intervention is crucial, involving much reading, rereading, and writing (see Chapter 6: Supporting Struggling and Reluctant Readers). Some students need intensive one-on-one support. Others do not. The intervention should be coordinated with effective classroom practice.

Summary of Features Associated with Exemplary Teachers

The chart that follows shows the beliefs, attitudes, and interpersonal and instructional skills associated with exemplary teachers. It is important to note that particular programs and materials are not mentioned in this list of characteristics.

Personal characteristics	Studies
Emotional and physical stamina, stress resistance, persistence, and self-control	H, SS
Warm, caring, flexible, concern for individuals as persons as well as academics	R, H
Supportive, encouraging, and friendly	S, SS
Have interests and hobbies—and assume others do	H
Enthusiastic, enjoys work	H, SS
Genuinely likes people and has positive expectations of them	SS
A sense of agency (also confidence)—the feeling that what one does makes a difference	H
Accurate self-assessment	SS
Expands professional expertise	SS, R
Beliefs, attitudes, and expectations	
Expects diversity and expects to manage it	H
All children can learn to read and write—believes in children's potential	T, SS, H
Learning is social	T
Ownership is necessary for learning; students need choice	T
Error is a place to learn	H, SS
Modelling is important	T, H
Respect and trust	H, R

Instructional practice	Studies
Organized and planful	H, R
Classroom routines; behavior, movement, lessons	S, Pb
Diverse instructional groupings	Pa,b
Arranges for student ownership	H, R, T
Believes students learn to read and write by reading and writing a lot	K, S, Pa,b
Integrates reading, writing, and subjects	K, T, Pa,b
Daily guided, shared, and independent reading	T
Listens and observes to adapt instruction	T, SS
High demands, but sensitive to individual needs and motivations—challenges and involves students	R, S
Flexible response to individual needs and interests	SS, H
Instruction is personally relevant, activities are stimulating	R, S
Explicit instruction, particularly of strategies	S, Pa
Displays student work along with much other print	T, S
Instructional talk	
Many constructive teacher–student exchanges	S
Discussion	K
Collaborative learning	T, Pa,b
Emphasizes strategic and critical thinking	R

Key: H= Haberman (1995); K= Knapp (1995); Pa= Pressley, Yokoi, Rankin, Wharton-McDonald, and Mistretta (1996); Pb= Pressley, Wharton-McDonald, Mistretta-Hampston, and Echevarria (1998); R= Ruddell (1997); S= Snow, Barnes, Chandler, Goodman, and Hemphill (1991); SS= Spencer and Spencer (1993); T= Thomas and Barksdale-Ladd (1995)

(Allington and Johnston 2001, 157)

Partnerships with Home, School, and Community

Studies show that students perform better in school if their parents are involved in their education. Yet too often, home–school connections diminish in Grades 3 to 6. This book offers many suggestions and resources for keeping those at home involved and informed, including

- newsletters with suggestions on how parents can reinforce classroom instruction and encourage a love of literacy
- recording, assessment, and tracking tools for parents, which help in conferencing

The most important thing is to make families feel welcome and encourage them to talk about and contribute to their children's learning.

Literacy Assessment

Making Meaning

Love of Literacy
Power of Language

Assessment is the way teachers monitor changes in students' growing awareness and competence. It involves regularly collecting and recording information on student learning and reviewing it in relation to the individual student. This information is used to identify the next goal for a student's learning, to plan interventions, to identify the need for alternative resources or techniques, to encourage students to reflect on their learning, and to show them how much progress they have made.

Assessment is based on learning objectives. There are three key goals in the literacy development of students in Grades 3 to 6:

- to create effective readers, writers, speakers, listeners, and viewers who can derive explicit and implicit meaning from text
- to foster a love of reading and writing
- to expose students to a wide range of genres and text forms so that they appreciate the power of the printed and spoken word

Literacy Skills in Grades 3 to 6

Students become effective literacy learners when they

- understand that reading, writing, speaking, listening, and viewing are active, thinking processes
- use a well-developed vocabulary, prior knowledge, and personal experiences to comprehend text and as a springboard for writing, speaking, and representing
- know their purpose for reading, writing, speaking, listening, and viewing, and their audience for writing, speaking, and representing
- read, write, speak, listen, and view for a variety of purposes and on a wide range of topics
- monitor and adjust their reading, listening, and viewing to facilitate comprehension and apply a variety of strategies to help them make meaning of texts
- think critically before, during, and after reading, writing, speaking listening, and viewing

Evidence of students' growth can be collected in four ways: by observing what they do, by listening to what they say, by reviewing the products they develop, and through feedback from parents. This resource provides a variety of assessment tools and strategies for diagnostic, formative, and summative assessment, tools to

- help match students with appropriate instruction
- encourage self-assessment
- identify students who may benefit from intervention
- chart the progress of individual students
- share information between school and home

Diagnostic Assessment

Diagnostic assessment gauges

- oral language: speaking and listening
- writing
- literacy learning across the curriculum
- attitudes toward reading and writing
- reading and writing habits and interests
- students' reading behaviours (strategy use)
- fluent reading
- reading comprehension

Formative Assessment Tools

Keeping anecdotal records from observations and student work samples helps teachers identify behaviour patterns and judge educational needs. For example, this resource includes tools for collecting writing samples for different genres and modes, the six traits, and writing across the curriculum.

Summative Assessment Tools

Tracking individual student achievement over time allows the teacher to gauge progress and is invaluable when conferencing with parents. Class records of assessment provide a class profile, identifying areas of strength and need, and suggesting responsive large-group, small-group, and individual support.

With this resource, teachers have all the tools needed to implement a comprehensive literacy program that can turn every student into a thoughtful and enthusiastic literacy learner.

ME I AM

by Jack Prelutsky

I am the only ME I AM
who qualifies as me;
no ME I AM has been before,
and none will ever be.

No other ME I AM can feel
the feelings I've within;
no other ME I AM can fit
precisely in my skin.

There is no other ME I AM
who thinks the thoughts I do;
the world contains one ME I AM,
there is no room for two.

I am the only ME I AM
this earth shall ever see;
that ME I AM I always am
is no one else but ME!

Chapter 1

ORAL LANGUAGE: SPEAKING, LISTENING, AND LEARNING

Lynne Healy

"Reading and writing should float on a sea of talk."*

"Talk is as essential to thought as exercise is to health."**

* Wilhelm 2001, 139
** O'Keefe 1995, 14

Find Out More About Oral Language

Allen, L. *First Steps Oral Language Resource Book.* Toronto: Irwin, 1994.

Beck, I., M. McKeown, and L. Kucan. *Bringing Words to Life: Robust Vocabulary Instruction.* New York: The Guilford Press, 2004.

Beck, I., M. McKeown, and L. Kucan. "Taking Delight in Words." *American Educator* (Spring 2003): 36–47.

Beers, Kylene. *When Kids Can't Read, What Teachers Can Do.* Portsmouth, NH: Heinemann, 2003.

Bell, Nanci. *Visualizing and Verbalizing for Language Comprehension and Thinking.* Paso Robles, CA: Academy of Reading Publications, 1991.

Booth, David. *Classroom Voices.* Toronto: Harcourt Brace, 1994.

Brownlie, F., C. Feniak, and V. McCarthy. *Instruction and Assessment of ESL Learners.* Winnipeg: Portage and Main Press, 2004.

Creaghead, Nancy. "Classroom Interactional Analysis/Script Analysis." In *Best Practices in School Speech–Language Pathology, Descriptive/Nonstandardized Language Assessment*, edited by Wayne A. Secord, 65–72. New York: The Psychological Corporation, Harcourt Brace Jovanovich, 1992.

Dodge, Ellen Pritchard. *CommunicationLab 1.* E. Moline, IL: LinguiSystems, 1994.

Essex, G., and B. Raban. *Teaching Speakers and Listeners in the Classroom, Stage 3, Early Years Literacy Program.* Melbourne: State of Victoria Department of Education/Pearson Education Australia, 2000.

Fay, K., and S. Whaley. *Becoming One Community: Reading and Writing with English Language Learners.* Portland, ME: Stenhouse Publishers, 2004.

Gajewski, N., P. Hirn, and P. Mayo. *SSS: Social Skill Strategies (Book A)*, 1st edition. Eau Claire, WI: Thinking Publications, 1989.

Johnston, Peter. *Choice Words: How Our Language Affects Children's Learning.* Portland, ME: Stenhouse Publishers, 2004.

O'Keefe, V. *Speaking to Think, Thinking to Speak: The Importance of Talk in the Learning Process.* Portsmouth, NH: Heinemann, 1995.

Smith, Patricia G., ed. *Talking Classrooms.* Newark, DE: International Reading Association, 2001.

Westby, Carol. "Learning to Talk—Talking to Learn: Oral Literate Language Differences." In *Communication Skills and Classroom Success*, edited by C. Simon, 334–55. Eau Claire, WI: Thinking Publications, 1991.

Research on Oral Language

Instruction in oral language continues to be a fundamental component of the Grades 3 to 6 curriculum because

- oral language is key to developing reading and writing proficiency—it forms the foundation of literacy
- the language of school, which is different from everyday conversational language, is integral to literacy and to learning

Developing oral language to support success in school requires intentional, contextualized, and scaffolded teaching.

This chapter

- provides key research that supports the teaching of oral language for school success
- describes the components of oral language and how to assess them in the classroom context
- outlines specific instructional strategies that support the development of oral language and its links to literacy

Oral Language in the Classroom

Speaking and listening are key components of the curriculum in Grades 3 to 6 classrooms. Talk is the bridge that helps students make connections between what they know and what they are coming to know (Booth 1994). Students use language to monitor and reflect on experience and to reason about, plan, and predict experiences, both orally and in print (Westby 1991, 334–55). They need well-developed oral language skills in order to use talk across the curriculum to develop strategies, problem solve, clarify ideas, and ask questions. Effective oral language skills form the foundation for all learning.

Oral language and literacy development are linked as students connect what they know about the purpose, meaning, structure, and sound of language to what they see or create in print. In Grades 3 to 6, students are asked to read and write fiction and nonfiction texts with increasingly complex language. To achieve further success in literacy and in learning, students need many opportunities to write and talk about their writing; to read and listen to others read; and to engage in purposeful activities in which speaking, listening, reading, writing, viewing, and representing are interrelated (Evans 1994).

Students learn about language as they use it for real purposes, in a social environment. Today's classrooms need to provide multiple opportunities for students to learn and practise effective speaking and listening skills through interaction with others. Students need to know how to

- talk to their peers to solve problems, give instructions, share experiences, discuss concepts, and elaborate on their thinking
- talk to adults to clarify or get new information, to question, and to access help
- work cooperatively in a small group to complete a project or assignment, engage in inquiry, and understand a text

- understand and follow the expectations for communication in a whole-class setting to obtain directions, listen to a strategy lesson, and share information with others

Developing this language knowledge allows students to communicate effectively in a variety of social situations for different purposes. Knowing how to be a competent communicator who can use language flexibly for a variety of purposes is important for success in school.

Language of School

"Learning in school depends on the use of one's own language knowledge for purposes of acquiring more language, concepts and information."

MERRITT AND CULATTA 1998, 11

When children enter school, communication demands change and they have to learn to use language in new ways. Language is not only used as a tool for personal communication, but also as a tool for learning and acquiring print literacy.

Although it may reflect aspects of home talk, school talk

- usually has different purposes and structures
- may be about unfamiliar topics or based on knowledge that is not shared among the participants
- has different expectations for speakers and listeners
- uses vocabulary and sentence structure that may be unfamiliar or more complex than students are used to

Understanding the different communication demands of school language helps teachers focus more effectively on classroom instruction to develop oral language that will enhance student learning. Teachers need to establish classroom environments, provide language models, and structure activities that help students

- further develop the language skills required for social interaction for an increasing variety of purposes
- use language to refine their thinking through effective questioning, self-reflection, and inquiry
- make connections between the known and the new to develop vocabulary and concept knowledge and to enhance both listening and reading comprehension across the curriculum
- expand the complexity of language used in reading, writing, and spelling across a variety of genres
- use knowledge of language structure and text structure to read and write increasingly complex fiction and nonfiction texts

Learning the Classroom Script

Part of learning the language of school is learning the language of instruction. What students know about how to act and interact in school is part of their script for school. This script enables them to determine what is appropriate to say and do during different aspects of the school day (Creaghead 1992, 65–72).

By Grade 3 most students use their knowledge of how school works to effectively interpret both the implicit and explicit language of the teacher and their peers. They also understand how to respond appropriately, both in speech and behaviour. However, some students may

still need help in understanding the cues the teacher uses. Examples of this implicit classroom script include

- how teachers signal they want the class to be quiet
- when students can move within and outside the classroom
- when questions can be asked during different classroom activities
- how students signal that they want to say something
- using figurative and indirect language in giving directions
- classroom routines

When students appear to misunderstand, it is good practice for teachers to consider whether they have used figurative or indirect language, and whether they need to rephrase or explain the intended meaning.

Sometimes students who struggle with classroom routines or who appear to have behavioural problems may not understand what is expected of them in particular aspects of classroom life. It is important not to assume that expectations for classroom behaviours are obvious to all students, particularly **ESL** students. These students may have had a different type of school experience or possibly no prior school experience.

Figurative language can be interpreted in more than one way. Some students understand this language literally and misinterpret the intended meaning. For example, on hearing "get a move on," students may think they have to move out of their chairs.

When **indirect language** is used, a directive is often presented as a question or a statement. Students may not understand that they are being asked to do something. For example, if they hear, "Would you like to put that away?" they may assume that they have a choice and reply "No."

Classroom Scripts

It is important to give some thought to the explicit and implicit language you use to give directions, set expectations, and organize routines. Jotting down examples of the language used throughout the day will reveal

- indirect language use
- common expressions that can be interpreted both literally and figuratively
- the script used for various classroom activities

THE FAMILY CIRCUS   By Bil Keane

"Yep. Whenever Mrs. Clarke raises her eyebrows at me."

"Strategic readers address their thinking in an inner conversation that helps them make sense of what they read."

HARVEY AND GOUDVIS 2000, 5

Check It Out!

Stephanie Harvey and Anne Goudvis. *Strategies That Work: Teaching Comprehension to Enhance Understanding* (York, ME: Stenhouse Publishers, 2000).

Ellin Keene and Susan Zimmermann. *Mosaic of Thought: Teaching Comprehension in a Reader's Workshop* (Portsmouth, NH: Heinemann, 1997).

These resources provide more information about specific strategies for maintaining comprehension and constructing meaning.

- how transitions are signalled between activities
- classroom routines that are implied rather than explicitly stated

One Grade 4 teacher realized that her classroom script was not as obvious as she thought. She always taught math after recess and by January most students automatically got out their math books at this time. She was becoming increasingly frustrated with four students who were never ready with their math books when she wanted to begin the lesson. They did not understand the implicit classroom routine. After she realized that they had not intuitively made the connection between "math time" and "after recess," she made this expectation explicit for them, which alleviated the problem.

Oral Language That Supports Comprehension

"Once thought of as the natural result of decoding plus oral language, comprehension is now viewed as a much more complex process involving knowledge, experience, thinking and teaching" (Harvey and Goudvis 2000, 6). Allington (2001) highlights the importance of talk to foster this process of "thoughtful literacy." Language is the tool that links students' knowledge, experience, and thinking. Students use different aspects of language to build their understanding of texts, and thinking and talking about texts develops their language skills.

Teachers need to provide explicit instruction in oral language skills and strategies, as well as teach how to use that language to develop the thinking strategies that enable students to understand what they hear, see, and read. (See Linking Assessment to Instruction later in this chapter and Chapter 2: Reading Comprehension: Strategies That Work.) Developing language to talk about such strategies helps readers use these thinking strategies more effectively.

Teachers need to explicitly model how to think about texts, demonstrating language that describes the reading process; they need to share their questions, their connections, and their thinking strategies. They also need to provide students with guided practice in how to talk about texts and to provide many opportunities for students to talk with one another meaningfully about what they have read, listened to, or viewed. These classroom conversations need to reflect the real connections students make between personal experiences and background knowledge, and what was heard, seen, or read; they need to consist of more than just answering questions or remembering and repeating information about a text. When teachers encourage students to listen closely to one another, consider multiple interpretations of text, and recognize different perspectives, students develop oral language and deepen their understanding of texts.

The Teacher's Role in Supporting Oral Language Development

Through informed assessment teachers gain a clearer picture of their students' speaking and listening abilities. Teachers then use this information to provide the appropriate contexts to support students' learning, and to group students for explicit teaching to meet their learning needs (Essex and Raban 1991). Informed assessment implies that the teacher understands the role of oral language in supporting learning and the development of literacy and uses this knowledge to monitor students' progress. Teachers support students' oral language development when they

- encourage purposeful talk in the classroom within the context of a comprehensive literacy framework
- structure specific opportunities to foster oral language development
- provide models of language use
- explicitly teach the strategies students need to build their oral language skills and provide opportunities for guided practice

Effective teachers monitor the type of discourse that occurs in the classroom, modelling and facilitating oral language that fosters greater student input and engagement. (See Teacher Talk: The Teacher's Role later in this chapter.) Traditionally, classroom discourse focused on asking questions, getting a response, and evaluating that response (interrogation sequences). When teachers engage students in conversations about texts, strategies, and students' learning, they ask

Check It Out!

For an excellent discussion of the role of teacher language in shaping the learning environment and influencing students as learners, see Peter Johnston, *Choice Words: How Our Language Affects Children's Learning* (Portland, ME: Stenhouse Publishers, 2004).

"The critical form of assisting learners is through dialogue, through the questioning and sharing of ideas and knowledge that happens in instructional conversations.... To truly teach, one must converse, to converse is to teach."

THARP 1994, QUOTED IN WILKINSON AND SILLIMAN 2001, 4

questions that encourage multiple and diverse responses (instructional conversations). Students' responses reflect their ability to actively construct meaning and monitor understanding (Palincsar and Klenk 1992, 221–225, 229).

Teachers need to consciously move from interrogation sequences to instructional conversations.

Interrogation Sequence	Instructional Conversation
T: What is the capital of Canada? S: Ottawa. T: Right, Mark. And Sarika, what is the name of an important building in Ottawa? S: Parliament Hill. T: Right. Why is it important?	T: We've been reading about our government and what happens in Ottawa. We are going to record what we have learned on a web. Who has an idea to share? S1: Ottawa is the capital city of Canada. S2: The Parliament Buildings are there. S3: That's where the government does business. T: Tell me more about that.

"The way we interact with children and arrange for them to interact shows them what kind of people we think they are and gives them opportunities to practice being those kinds of people."

JOHNSTON 2004, 79

Teacher talk shapes the classroom environment and the students' learning experiences. "How we say what we say shapes our students' views of themselves as learners" (Johnston 2004, 46). If the language used in the classroom encourages students to see themselves as thinkers and problem solvers, capable of making choices and figuring things out for themselves, they become independent learners who take responsibility for their learning.

Oral Language and English as a Second Language (ESL)

Students for whom English is a second language have specific needs when it comes to developing oral language. Most of these students have developed oral language in their home language, but require additional support in the classroom to understand and speak English. Although learning English is critical for school success for ESL students, sometimes speaking their first language in the classroom serves as a bridge between their thinking and learning (Fay and Whaley 2004).

Providing frequent opportunities for purposeful communication helps all students develop oral language, but is especially important for students learning English as a second language. Classrooms that support whole-class, small-group, and paired activities provide many opportunities for students to engage in meaningful conversations.

Although students learning English as a second language may become fluent in conversational English, effective teachers do not assume that these students understand the more complex and often implicit language of the classroom. They consider the subtle messages of classroom language and provide more explicit language models and demonstrations when needed.

Check It Out!

An excellent resource is Kathleen Fay and Suzanne Whaley, *Becoming One Community: Reading and Writing with English Language Learners* (Portland, ME: Stenhouse Publishers, 2004), especially Chapter 12: Making Home–School Connections.

Classroom literacy activities provide meaningful opportunities to teach vocabulary and to develop students' understanding of English language structure. ESL students also benefit from reading and writing opportunities as they learn oral English (Fitzgerald 1993, 638–47).

ESL students may be unfamiliar with the cultural and social expectations of school. They may also bring different cultural experiences and values to the classroom. Teachers need to be sensitive to these differences to help bridge the gap between home and school (Fitzgerald 1993, 638–47). Developing a strong home–school connection is important. Bringing the home language into the classroom signals acceptance and helps give ESL students a sense of belonging. This feeling enhances the development of a classroom community that supports risk taking and caring, which are essential to learning a new language.

"We need to realize that these children [ESL students] will continue to think and wonder and ask questions while reading books (or looking at illustrations) in the classroom, even if they are not yet speaking much English."

FAY AND WHALEY 2004, 41

Assessment

In classrooms where purposeful talk is valued, there are many opportunities to assess students' oral language development. Accurate assessment of a student's oral language depends on the teacher having

- knowledge of the components of language
- a clear understanding of language development
- an appreciation of the impact of context on language understanding and use
- an awareness of personal assumptions concerning what students know and understand about language and how it is used in the classroom

Students demonstrate their language knowledge in a variety of contexts throughout the school day. Effective teachers monitor how students understand and use language during whole-class, small-group, and paired interactions in the daily routines and activities of the classroom. For example, they may

- observe student interactions with peers
- listen to the language that students use in responding to open-ended questions or in reflecting on their learning during sharing time or one-on-one conferences
- review the products students develop (e.g., stories, role-plays, self-assessments, portfolios, and reports)
- listen to student discussions about, and responses to, books (See Book Clubs in Chapter 2: Reading Comprehension: Strategies That Work and Literature Circles in Chapter 5: In the Classroom: Making It Work.)
- observe students' use of language strategies to support reading and writing

Through informed observations over time, teachers determine which aspects of language are developing and which need additional support. Having a clear picture of students' language competence enables teachers to develop appropriate program goals that can be integrated into the ongoing activities of a comprehensive literacy program.

This section includes an explanation of the four components of language, how they function in the classroom to support learning and literacy development, and ways to assess them in daily classroom activities. Assessment BLM 1: Oral Language Checklist is a useful tool for organizing observations in each of the four components of oral language:

- speaking and listening behaviours (pragmatics)
- knowledge of language meaning (semantics)
- knowledge of sentence structure (syntax)
- knowledge of the sound structure of language (phonology)

Information gathered on Assessment BLM 1 might then be summarized on Assessment BLM 2: Oral Language Summary Sheet.

Assessment BLM 1: Oral Language Checklist

Assessment BLM 2: Oral Language Summary Sheet

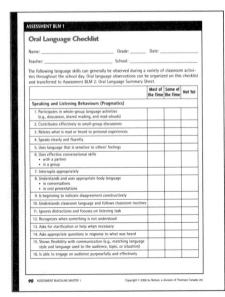

Understanding Language

When observing students' language use, it is important for the class-room teacher to consider four interrelated aspects of language:

- purpose (pragmatics)
- meaning (semantics)
- sentence structure (syntax)
- sound structure (phonology)

Although these components work together for effective communication, each area will be discussed separately for the purpose of assessment.

Purpose (Pragmatics)

Pragmatics refers to the language "know-how" that supports effective communication with different people, in a variety of situations, for various purposes. It can be observed through the speaking and listening behaviours communicators use. It involves understanding how to use language appropriately, both orally and in print, depending on the audience; in other words, knowing how to speak depending on whom you are talking to, what you are talking about, and why you are talking.

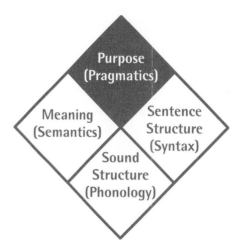

For students, pragmatics would include the difference in how they talk

- to a peer or a teacher
- on the playground about a game or in the classroom about a math problem
- when solving a problem or telling a story

Pragmatics also takes into account the difference in language use between different genres of written texts, including whether the text is narrative or informational.

Pragmatics provides the how-to framework for successful communication. Teachers need to recognize that cultures vary in terms of the language behaviours that are considered appropriate in different contexts. For example, in some cultures, looking directly at the speaker is a sign of disrespect. As well, the pragmatics of school language is often different from that of home language, and students may not understand the implicit rules of classroom communication. (See the box titled Classroom Scripts earlier in this chapter.) To assess pragmatics, it is important to understand the roles of speaker and listener in informal conversation, as well as within the broader context of the classroom.

Assessing Speaking

Oral communication generally involves a speaker and a listener who work together to ensure that conversation continues. As students in Grades 3 to 6 classrooms engage in a variety of interactions for learning, their understanding of speaking and listening needs to be assessed. These communication skills are central to the development of effective oral language.

Effective speakers know how to
- send a clear message
- begin and end a conversation
- interrupt appropriately
- take a turn and stay on topic
- clear up confusions

When assessing a student's ability to fulfill the role of the speaker in a communication exchange, the teacher observes how the student uses social conventions. These include understanding
- why sending a clear message is important and how to do this
- how to begin and end a conversation
- how to interrupt appropriately
- when and how to take a turn as a speaker
- when and how to clarify or rephrase if the listener is confused

Assessing a student's skill as a speaker also involves determining how effectively the student uses more subtle cues, such as
- body language, or nonverbal cues (e.g., eye contact, proximity to the listener, and gestures)
- volume and tone of voice that is appropriate for the situation
- language that is sensitive to the feelings of others

As teachers explicitly teach students how to be more effective speakers, they may ask students to complete Assessment BLM 3: My Speaking Skills.

Assessment BLM 3: My Speaking Skills

Teachers also need to consider the flexible nature of communication and whether students can change their speaking style appropriately. For example, how does their style vary in these instances?
- speaking with a teacher, parent, or peer
- speaking in the classroom or schoolyard
- sharing information with an individual, in a small group, or in front of the whole class
- giving and following directions
- using language to negotiate or resolve conflict situations
- using language to think, reflect, or problem solve

(Adapted from Trehearne et al. 2004, 33–34)

Assessing Listening

Teachers frequently comment on their students' poor listening skills. Effective listening is a complex process that involves more than sitting still while someone speaks. Students need to understand that listeners take an active role in communication.

Good hearing does not guarantee effective listening. Hearing occurs at a physical level; listening is a mental activity. Students need to learn how to listen. Being told to listen is not enough.

The listener needs to know
- how to listen for different purposes
- how to listen in a way that shows respect for the speaker
- when and how to switch to the role of speaker
- how to recognize when the message is unclear
- how to ask for clarification when the message is confusing

When assessing students' listening behaviours, effective teachers consider the complexity of the listening process and the variables that affect how well students listen, such as

- the situation (whole class, small group, pairs)
- the speaker (peer, teacher, guest)
- the purpose (for enjoyment, to ask or answer questions, to respond to a peer's presentation or a story, for specific information, to follow directions)

Distractions may also affect a student's ability to listen effectively. External distracters include background noise, a very quiet speaker, and other students talking. Internal distracters include hunger, cold, and anxiety. Students need to recognize which distracters affect their ability to listen and, when possible, to develop strategies to minimize their effect. (See Developing Listening Skills later in this chapter.)

Teachers need to keep in mind that students listen effectively in different ways. Some students keep their brains active for listening by sitting still with hands folded in their laps. Other students listen and understand better when they also see a model, picture, or gestures. Some students may need to move in order to keep their brains alert so they can listen and process the information. As these students do not appear to be listening, teachers are often surprised that they can answer questions or recount what they heard. Their movement may distract others, though, so teachers need to help students recognize and develop strategies to manage their activity and listening behaviours.

Listening Fatigue

Teachers also need to keep in mind that listening is hard work. Students may experience listening fatigue if they have to sit and listen for long periods of time. This condition may also occur when the demands of processing the information require increased listening energy. Perhaps the person speaks too quickly, mumbles, or talks with an unfamiliar accent. Students sometimes say they "can't listen fast enough." This reaction may be more a factor of what they are listening to, rather than the rate of presentation. An unfamiliar topic, new vocabulary, and the use of complex or unfamiliar sentence structures will affect processing. Students may tire quickly when their brains have to work overtime to listen and understand.

Think about your own experiences with listening fatigue, perhaps in a professional development session or university lecture. Have you listened to a discussion or a presentation that made frequent use of new terminology or unfamiliar acronyms? How did the vocabulary affect your ability to actively listen and process the information? What did you do? Share these experiences with your students. They may be surprised to know that everyone has difficulty listening at times.

If teachers are particularly concerned about a student's listening skills, Assessment BLM 4: Listening Skills Checklist allows for a more focused observation of listening.

Effective listeners know

- what to listen for
- how to show respect for the speaker
- when and how to take their turn to speak
- when and how to ask for clarification

Students listen more effectively when they know what they are listening for and when they connect what they are hearing to their own experiences.

Oral Language: Speaking, Listening, and Learning |

As teachers explicitly teach students how to be more effective listeners, they might have students complete Assessment BLM 5: My Listening Skills.

Assessment BLM 4: Listening Skills Checklist
Assessment BLM 5: My Listening Skills

Communication Behaviours

By Grade 3 many students are aware that they need to change their communication style and language use depending on the situation, purpose, audience, and topic. As the classroom demands for communicating effectively in a variety of contexts and for different purposes grow, students continue to need specific instruction on how to do so. Assessing these communication behaviours will provide important information for determining what instruction will help students learn the sharing and cooperation skills necessary for success both within and outside the classroom.

For specific suggestions for developing speaking and listening skills in the classroom, see Developing Oral Language for Social Interaction later in this chapter. Included are ideas for

- developing listening skills
- teaching about body language
- teaching how to interrupt effectively
- teaching language that promotes effective group work

Language Activities for Oral Reporting, later in this chapter, also supports the development of speaking and listening skills.

Pragmatics and Diversity

Different cultures approach social interaction in different ways. The implicit rules of communication for the teacher's culture may not be shared by all students in the classroom, whether they are **ESL** students or students from different social or economic backgrounds. It is

important for teachers to question their assumptions when students do not respond in expected ways. The teacher's language—verbal or nonverbal—may have a different interpretation in a student's experience. Even the language of politeness and respect differs from culture to culture. For example, at home, students may be expected to be silent during adult conversation; at school, they are expected to converse and share ideas with peers and the teacher.

Pragmatics and the Language of Print

Communication through print is also affected by pragmatics. Different texts (e.g., poetry, stories, letters, e-mail, and Internet chat messages) have different structures and conventions. The ability to understand a text relates to knowing about its structure. Even in kindergarten, students begin to recognize certain commonalities.

- Language is used differently in books than in conversation.
- Different types of books have different structures and purposes. (Consider stories, poetry, and informational texts.)
- Stories have a very similar structure (e.g., characters, settings, problems, and solutions).
- Informational texts have a variety of text features that signal important information to support comprehension. These include headings, subheadings, font size, bold print, captions, graphs, diagrams, and labels. (See Chapter 2: Reading Comprehension: Strategies That Work and Chapter 4: Literacy Learning Across the Curriculum.)

Recognizing the role of text structure becomes even more critical in Grades 3 to 6 as students read and write longer, more complex narratives and nonfiction texts. Learning the language of different genres supports students' ability to read and comprehend, as well as write in the genres more effectively. They learn to "read as a writer" and "write as a reader." The teacher assesses how students use the pragmatics of print to predict and create meaning during daily literacy experiences in the classroom.

The Speaking and Listening Behaviours (Pragmatics) section of Assessment BLM 1: Oral Language Checklist can be used to record observations of students' understanding and use of pragmatics as students interact with the teacher and peers in one-on-one conferences, small groups, and whole-class situations.

Assessment BLM 1: Oral Language Checklist

Meaning (Semantics)

Semantics focuses primarily on the meaning of language. Although all four components of language—purpose, language meaning, sentence structure, and sound structure—contribute to the creation of overall meaning, semantics refers specifically to the vocabulary, concepts, and background knowledge that the student brings to the learning experience. The following section highlights specific areas of concept development that teachers need to understand in order to assess students' semantic knowledge effectively.

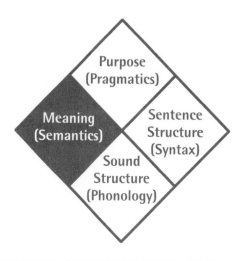

Three Types of Connections	
text to self	
text to text	
text to world	

Check It Out!

For a more detailed description of the three types of connections that support understanding, see Ellin Keene and Susan Zimmermann, *Mosaic of Thought* (Portsmouth, NH: Heinemann, 1997); Richard L. Allington, *What Really Matters for Struggling Readers* (New York: Longman, 2001); or Stephanie Harvey and Anne Goudvis, *Strategies That Work* (York, ME: Stenhouse Publishers, 2000).

Schema and Background Knowledge

A **schema** is a rich set of understandings around a particular topic (Wilhelm, Baker, and Dube 2001). It is part of the knowledge base that students draw on to make meaning when they listen, speak, read, write, and view. Keene and Zimmermann (1997) refer to this as "activating mental files." Making connections to other words and concepts is an important part of understanding what a word means. These connections help build the web of ideas, or schema, which the student has for that word or concept.

Students activate background knowledge in order to understand what they hear, see, and read. Connecting new information to something already known or experienced is critical to understanding and remembering it. For example, a book about basketball is easier to understand if you have played the game. Students need to learn to use what they already know about the world to make predictions, ask questions, and draw inferences about texts.

There are three types of connections that support understanding:

- text to self (How does it relate to something I have experienced?)
- text to text (How does it relate to something I have read or seen?)
- text to world (How does it relate to something I know about the world?)

These connections are part of the semantic knowledge that students are developing. Students make these connections using language such as

- "That reminds me of the time I ... " (text to self)
- "The same thing happened in the book (movie, TV show) ... " or "That's just like the book ... " (text to text)
- On reading a book about endangered animals: "I know that gorillas are also endangered." (text to world)

(See also Chapter 2: Reading Comprehension: Strategies That Work.)

Concept Development

Schemas develop through the growth of concept knowledge and the specific vocabulary that represent those concepts. New vocabulary is learned from encountering words used in context (oral or written) and discussing connections, rather than from memorizing a definition. Context is important because a word's meaning shifts depending on the way it is used. For example, the meaning of the word "window" changes depending on the context—a picture window, a window in a jail cell, a window of opportunity.

Word knowledge develops not only through context, but also through understanding a word in terms of

- how it is categorized (hammer—tool)
- what its attributes are (hammer—heavy, made of wood or metal, has a handle, a head, teeth, comes in different sizes)
- what its function is (hammer—to pound nails in wood or pull them out)
- how it relates to words that are similar in meaning (other tools)

Understanding Schema

To better understand what is meant by *schema*, write down all the words or ideas that you can think of related to the word "run." Look at the kinds of connections you make—its use as a noun or as a verb, different kinds of runs, multiple meanings of the word, its use in figurative expressions, related words, and ideas. That is your schema for the word. Ask a colleague to do the same activity, and see how your schemas are similar and different.

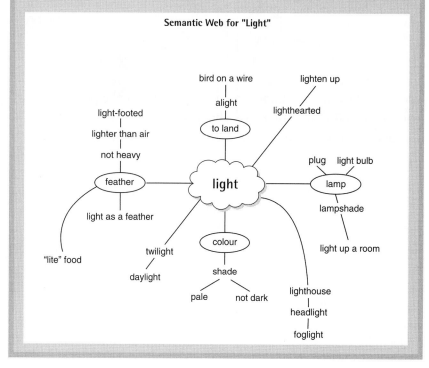

Semantic Web for "Light"

"New knowledge or new kinds of texts can sometimes be like the slick backside of Scotch tape—unless there is something to attach new knowledge to, unfamiliar concepts probably won't stick."

WILHELM, BAKER, AND DUBE 2001, 97

- how it relates to words that mean the opposite
- recognizing how it can have more than one meaning
    - homophones: *plain* and *plane*
    - homographs: *lead* (to guide) and *lead* (a metal)
- how it is used in figurative language such as metaphors (hammer out an agreement)

The teacher assesses students' understanding of words through their vocabulary use in conversations in the classroom, as well as in specific responses to vocabulary activities. (See Language Activities for Concept Development later in this chapter.) For example, BLM 1: Words in Context will assist students with expanding their understanding of a word. Students discuss and then record what they know about the different features of a word. (See Words in Context later in this chapter.)

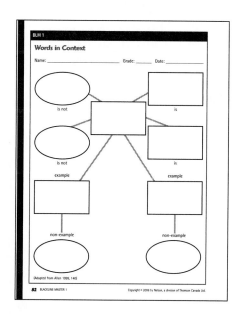

BLM 1: Words in Context

What Was Said? What Was Heard?

When students hear new vocabulary, they try to connect it with what they know. Unusual and sometimes humorous interpretations of what the teacher has said may result.

Born Loser © reprinted by permission of Newspaper Enterprise Association, Inc.

"In the classroom, reading comprehension and vocabulary are best served by spending extended time on reading and listening to texts on the same topic and discussing the facts and ideas in them.... These texts and topics must be compelling enough that both the teacher and the children want to talk about what they read, and deep enough that there is enough reason to revisit the topic."

HIRSCH 2003, 28

These misinterpretations have the potential to seriously compromise students' ability to understand a concept and to make the appropriate connections as they build their schema. Teachers observing any confusion during classroom discussions or in written work clarify the meaning for students. However, students also need to learn how to monitor their own understanding to recognize when something doesn't make sense and to ask for clarification. **ESL** students who have a limited English vocabulary are particularly prone to these misunderstandings. Seeing the word written down sometimes helps to avoid these confusions.

Sound-Alike Words in Math

This confusion of similar-sounding words occurs in all curriculum areas. Take a moment to think about possible confusions that students might experience with the sound and meaning of the words below. Consider how these confusions would compromise students' ability to understand math.

Mathematics Word	Everyday Word
altitude	attitude
sphere	spear
tenths	tents
half	have
cents	sense

(Adams 2003, 791)

Teachers may want to make a note of confusions they observe and create their own lists for other subjects, such as science and social studies. Ensure that students are clear about which word is being used.

Multiple-Meaning Language

Although they may not always know the alternative meanings, by Grade 3 most students understand that words and expressions sometimes mean more than one thing. Students' understanding of multiple-meaning language, such as homonyms, idioms, and figurative expressions, needs to be assessed and explicitly explained in the context of what is being read and discussed in class. Teachers need to observe how flexible students are with such language, paying particular attention to **ESL** students. Because this type of language occurs across the curriculum, students' inability to make the necessary shift in meaning can affect their understanding of the subject.

"Seventy percent of the most frequently used common words have multiple meanings. Students need a mindset that alerts them to this."
BROMLEY, IRA CONFERENCE, 2004

Multiple-Meaning Language in Math

Word	Mathematical Meaning	Everyday Meaning
volume	amount of space taken up by an object	noise level of electronic equipment
product	result of multiplying numbers	items produced by a company
ruler	tool for measuring length	person in authority
plot	to locate and make a point on a grid	place to build a house
mass	amount of matter in an object	a church service
count	to enumerate	to rely or depend on
face	flat surface on a solid	the front of something
fair	equal chance of happening	a temporary amusement park
range	numerical difference between two values	cooking equipment (stove)

(Adapted from Adams 2003, Table 1, 789)

Multiple-meaning language is also important for humour. By Grade 3 many students understand how to play with language to tell jokes and are beginning to understand puns. Teachers may observe students' responses to cartoons, riddle and joke books, or books that use figurative language (e.g., the Amelia Bedelia series) to assess the development of this type of language. They may also observe how students use this language as they create their own cartoons or joke books, which could be added to the classroom library. This creative activity provides students with an excellent opportunity to visually represent their understanding of word meanings.

Because so much of our humour is language and culturally based, **ESL** students may need help understanding when and how humour is used—in the classroom, on the playground, and in texts.

Semantic Knowledge for Different Purposes

The development of semantic knowledge in Grades 3 to 6 reflects the growth in vocabulary necessary to use language for a variety of purposes across the curriculum. Teachers observe this development as students discuss, problem solve, and interact throughout the school day. Some of these purposes of language use follow.

- sharing information
  - using the vocabulary of *who, what, where, when, why, how,* and *if* effectively to describe experiences

- using descriptive language effectively
- using language to persuade
- beginning to understand the difference between fact and opinion

• giving and following directions effectively
  - knowing how much information to give and being specific in word choice
  - listening for key words that indicate directions
  - understanding and using words that convey sequence

• retelling information from a story or information text (orally, visually, or in print)
  - describing the characters, setting, important events, problem, and conclusion of a story
  - maintaining meaning from chapter to chapter in a novel
  - discerning the main idea and relevant details in informational text
  - developing an awareness of how text features and text structure support an understanding of key ideas in informational text, including recognizing and using transition words when reading and writing (See Chapter 2: Reading Comprehension: Strategies That Work and Chapter 4: Literacy Learning Across the Curriculum.)

• learning new concepts and words related to different curriculum areas
  - developing vocabulary related to specific subjects, such as science, social studies, and math, which is critical to understanding and being able to talk about the subject
  - developing an increasing understanding of more abstract concepts

• using language to predict, confirm, and infer
  - making predictions about a story or informational text to set a purpose for reading and then confirming whether or not the prediction was accurate (using language like "I *think* … is going to happen"; "I *thought* she was going to … but she … instead. That surprised me"; "From the headings I thought this was going to be about … and I was right! But I also learned …")
  - continuing to develop the ability to "read between the lines" (infer) by connecting what is read, seen, or heard in the text with personal or world experience ("I *wonder* if he is sad because … "; "When the author says ' … ' that makes me think about … and I think the character acted that way because … "; "It doesn't say … but I can see that in the picture and I saw it in a TV show.")

• asking thoughtful questions
  - developing an understanding of the role of questioning as a strategy for comprehending spoken and written texts
  - using prior knowledge and the information in the text to ask thoughtful questions and set a purpose for reading, listening, or viewing

- using questions to generate interesting and meaningful investigations of nonfiction texts and topics
- using questions to clarify understanding

- using language to reflect on learning ("I learned that ... "; "It reminds me of ... "; "Next time I need to ... "). This type of abstract thinking needs to be modelled and taught, but is critical for self-assessment.

- using language for problem solving
  - in relation to the curriculum ("If I do ... , then ... happens.")
  - in personal conflicts, using "I" language ("Next time I can ... ": "I don't like it when ... ")

Monitoring Understanding

Students in Grades 3 to 6 need to actively monitor their understanding of what they hear, read, write, and view. Recognizing when they have not understood something is difficult for some of them, but monitoring comprehension is a critical strategy for listening and speaking, as well as for reading, writing, and viewing development. Through think-alouds, the teacher provides explicit modelling and instruction in monitoring comprehension, and helps students develop "fix-up" strategies. (For more information on think-alouds, see Chapter 2: Reading Comprehension: Strategies That Work.) Students also need to learn how and when to ask for clarification or help. They are most likely to do this in a classroom environment where they feel comfortable about taking risks.

Students show evidence of self-monitoring when they ask the teacher or a peer to repeat instructions or when they ask questions to get more information. In reading, self-monitoring is evident when students hesitate or notice that something they have read does not sound or look right or make sense. It leads to fix-up strategies, such as rereading and self-correction while reading or revision in writing. Effective teachers consciously model monitoring for meaning during classroom experiences, prompt students to use monitoring strategies, and observe and comment when students use them independently.

The Knowledge of Language Meaning (Semantics) section of Assessment BLM 1: Oral Language Checklist can be used to record observations of students' concept development and ability to use this knowledge to create meaning across the curriculum.

Before students are willing to ask for help, they need to be in a classroom environment where they feel safe enough to take risks. This is especially important for **ESL** students. Establishing this comfort level is important in building a classroom community. (See Chapter 5: In the Classroom: Making It Work.)

ESL students, who often have less vocabulary knowledge in English, may need extra support to develop vocabulary, make connections, and recognize when text makes (or doesn't make) sense.

Assessment BLM 1: Oral Language Checklist

Sentence Structure (Syntax)

Syntax refers to the form of language, or sentence structure, that is governed by the rules of grammar for that language. It supports effective communication in both oral and written language. When people speak a language, they have a shared knowledge of how words should be ordered to create meaning and foster understanding. These expectations for word order and word use support comprehension in listening and prediction in reading. For example, an expected sentence would be, "I'm going to play with my friend." Someone hearing

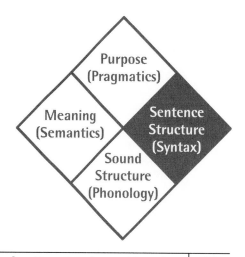

or reading "Going I to am play friend with my" would be confused. The natural flow of language established by grammar and syntax—that intuitive sense of what sounds right in the English language—helps students predict as they read.

Knowing how to use the appropriate words and word endings to indicate such meanings as plurals (car*s*), tenses, (*is* play*ing*, play*ed*), and possession (the girl*'s*) is another aspect of grammar. Students move from an intuitive understanding of these forms in their oral language to reading them in text and using them in their writing.

Understanding the syntactic relationships in a sentence is important as students become exposed to more complex sentences in conversation, classroom discussion, instructions, and books. Some students, among them **ESL** students, become confused by instructions because they focus on the first command given or the order of presentation rather than on the intended meaning. For example, when hearing "Before you go to recess, put your books and pencils away," students may think they have been told to go to recess and leave without putting anything away.

ESL readers may have difficulty using their knowledge of syntax if their first language has a different grammar or sentence structure. Books provide an excellent opportunity to practise working with English language structure, but ESL students may not have that intuitive sense of how English sounds to use for prediction and monitoring.

Phrases and Clauses

A **phrase** is a group of words that act together.

noun phrase   verb phrase   prepositional phrase
The little boy / walked quickly / down the dark street.

Clauses are formed when a noun is linked with a verb. They always tell what the subject—a noun or pronoun—is doing or being (the verb). The main or independent clause can be a sentence on its own. Subordinate or dependent clauses add extra meaning to a main clause and cannot stand alone.

dependent clause   main clause
Although he was late for the meeting, he decided to stop for some coffee.

Students first understand and use **simple** sentences such as "The boy is playing with his friend." They then begin to use **compound** sentences where two ideas are joined by conjunctions such as *and*, *but*, and *or* as in "The boy is playing with his friend *and* they are building a tower." **Complex** sentences have a main clause and one or more dependent clauses. The words used to join the clauses—the conjunctions—are important in determining this relationship and the meaning implied.

I bought a new coat *when* it was on sale.

I bought a new coat *after* I lost my other one.

I bought a new coat *although* I couldn't really afford it.

Words commonly used to join ideas in complex sentences (subordinating conjunctions) include *because, when, before, after, if,* and *although.*

Making Connections Within and Between Sentences

In reading, students need to transfer what they know about more complex sentences to help them make connections within and between sentences. Initially, sentences beginning with a phrase or clause may confuse students as they lack the benefit of the meaning and structure information in the main part of the sentences. Learning to recognize these phrases and clauses as sentence structures they have to deal with differently will help them predict for meaning. Scanning ahead to the main part of the sentence will set the context for the phrase or clause.

Phrase: *After supper*, the girls went to the playground.

The girls went to the playground *after supper*.

Clause: *Because he was afraid of the dark*, he kept his light on all night.

He kept his light on all night, *because he was afraid of the dark*.

As students deal with longer or more complex texts, as in informational text and the fiction texts of transitional and fluent readers, this knowledge of sentence structure will enable them to negotiate meaning.

Read the following excerpt from *The Canadian Shield*.

The ready and affordable supply of hydroelectricity in the Canadian Shield attracted some large industries to the region after the 1920s. In the early days of hydroelectricity, power could not travel as efficiently over long distances as it can today, so industries located near hydroelectric dams (Andrew et al. 2004, 32).

Read it again and think about the information expressed in the phrases and clauses in each sentence. Reading the text phrase by phrase reveals the complexity of the information presented in only one paragraph. Also, consider how the author references ideas within and between sentences and how making these connections is essential for comprehension.

The Canadian Shield; the region
After the 1920s; in the early days
Attracted some large industries to the region; so industries located near the hydroelectric dams

By Grade 3, students are typically able to use complete and correct grammatical form in their oral language. Exceptions are students who have dialectal differences in their home language or are learning English as a second language. Students who have had multiple exposures to the more complex language of books are also more likely to bring this knowledge to their literacy experiences. They benefit from hearing how sentence structure is used in a variety of texts through read-alouds, shared, guided, and independent reading. This exposure supports their ability to use syntactic knowledge effectively in their oral language as well as for prediction and comprehension as they read, and to express their ideas when they write. The teacher assesses students' syntactic knowledge in all of these areas. The section titled Knowledge of Sentence Structure (Syntax) on Assessment BLM 1: Oral Language Checklist can be used for this purpose.

Assessment BLM 1: Oral Language Checklist

Sound Structure (Phonology)

Phonology, or the sound structure of a language, refers to the sounds used in that language and the rules that determine how these sounds can be combined to make words. For example, English has the sound /th/; French does not. English allows the combination of some consonant sounds in blends but not others. *Scream* is an English word, but not *fkream* because *fkr* is not an initial consonant blend in English.

Children learn to speak the sounds of the language they hear. As they learn to read and write, they make connections between the sounds they say when they speak and the letters that represent those sounds when they are written down. In order to make these connections most effectively, students need to develop phonological awareness. By Grade 3 students likely have well-developed phonological awareness and use this oral language skill to support word solving in reading and spelling.

Phonological Awareness

Phonological awareness is the ability to think about the sounds in a word rather than just what the word means. It is a key oral language skill that supports the development of literacy, particularly word solving in reading and spelling. Phonological awareness involves recognizing what is meant by a word and realizing that a word consists of syllables, onsets and rimes, and individual sounds. Students with this language knowledge have the ability to "notice, mentally grab ahold of, and manipulate these smallest chunks of speech" (Yopp and Yopp 2000, 130).

Students need to be able to segment (break apart), blend, delete, and substitute word parts in order to effectively use word-solving strategies as they read and write. If students in Grades 3 to 6 are struggling with word solving, effective teachers assess their phonological awareness to determine whether it is a factor. These students may need specific support to develop this language skill.

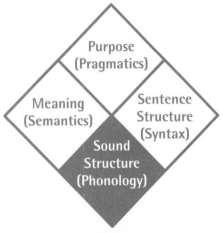

The English language has about 16 vowel sounds and 25 consonant sounds, although these numbers may vary depending on local dialects.

By the time students enter Grade 3, most can easily make all the sounds in English, although a few may have difficulty pronouncing a sound like /r/. The majority of students whose first language is English will be easy to understand.

> **Phonological awareness** = oral language skill = segment, blend, and manipulate the parts of words (syllables, onsets/rimes, sounds)
>
> **Phonemic awareness** = oral language skill = segment, blend, and manipulate individual sounds in words (sounds being one component of phonological awareness)

> **Phonics** = written language skill = knowledge of the relationship between letters and sounds for reading and writing
>
> Students need phonological awareness in order to use phonics effectively and efficiently.

Assessment in phonological awareness focuses on the student's ability to manipulate the sounds in oral language.

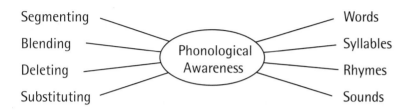

Use of Phonological Awareness in Grades 3 to 6

Syllable Awareness: segmenting and blending words by syllables, including prefixes, suffixes, and root words, to read and spell words with multiple syllables

Rhyme Awareness: using knowledge of rhyming to make analogies between words for reading and spelling (e.g., students being able to read or spell the word "green" because they recognize the onset /gr/ sound from the word "grow" and the rime /een/ sound from the word "seen")

Sound (Phonemic) Awareness: segmenting and blending words by individual sounds when "sounding out" in word solving for reading and spelling

Teachers need to remember that English does not always have one-to-one correspondence between letters and sounds.

- knock = 5 letters; 3 sounds /n/ /o/ /k/
- fix = 3 letters; 4 sounds /f/ /i/ /k/ /s/
- thought = 7 letters; 3 sounds /th/ /o/ /t/

Although students sometimes need to be able to segment and blend words sound by sound (phonemic awareness), it is usually more efficient to recognize and utilize larger chunks of words—syllables and rimes.

Words can be divided into onsets and rimes. **Onset** refers to the sounds before the vowel; **rime** is the sounds from the vowel to the end of the word. It is the part usually referred to as the *word base* or *word family*. For example,

	Onset	Rime
man	m	an
stop	st	op
sprinkle	spr	inkle

The word "rime" is the linguistic term for the part of the word that rhymes, the part that sounds the same in rhyming words.

Check It Out!

For more information on the assessment of phonological awareness, see Miriam Trehearne et al., *Nelson Language Arts Grades 1–2 Teacher's Resource Book* (Toronto: Thomson Nelson, 2004).

Rhyming is an oral language skill. Students need to be able to *hear* how words rhyme. When students connect what they hear with familiar spelling patterns, their word solving becomes more efficient and effective.

Although students gain a foundation in phonological awareness in kindergarten through Grade 2, they continue to apply their phonological awareness skills in Grade 3 and beyond. They

- segment multisyllable words when reading and spelling (e.g., ad • ven • tur • ous)

- fluently generate rhyme and use knowledge of onsets and rimes to decode and spell new words (e.g., "If I know the word 'at', I can use it when I read and write the words 'cat', 'splatter', and 'atmosphere.'")
- segment, blend, delete, and substitute sounds in words of increasing length
- isolate and substitute vowel sounds in words (e.g., f**un**, f**in**, f**an**, f**ine**)
- use these phonological awareness skills with increasing automaticity in reading and spelling

Classroom literacy activities, including word study, provide many opportunities to assess and teach these skills. (See Developing Phonological Awareness Through Word Study later in this chapter as well as specific word study activities in Chapter 5: In the Classroom: Making It Work.) Teachers may use the Knowledge of the Sound Structure of Language (Phonology) section of Assessment BLM 1: Oral Language Checklist with their students.

Students develop their knowledge of conventional spelling patterns as they explore words through word study activities; however, they need to be able to segment, blend, delete, and substitute sounds in words in order to use these patterns as they read and spell.

Check It Out!

For more information on the assessment of oral language, see P. Giffin and P. Smith, "Assessing Student Language Growth: Kirsten's Profile," in *Talking Classrooms*, edited by Patricia G. Smith (Newark, DE: International Reading Association, 2001).

Assessment BLM 1: Oral Language Checklist

Student Self-Assessment

Student portfolios are used as part of a comprehensive assessment plan in many classrooms. Effective teachers ensure that self-assessment of oral language skills is one component of these portfolios. The information gathered from these self-assessments can be used in developing personal goals to improve speaking and listening behaviours in the classroom. (For more information on the use of portfolios, see Chapters 3 through 5.)

Assessment BLM 3: My Speaking Skills

Assessment BLM 5: My Listening Skills

Teacher Self-Assessment

The language that teachers use in Grades 3 to 6 classrooms is critical to students' development of oral language. Teachers demonstrate

- how to use language effectively in various contexts for different purposes
- how to use language to problem solve through a think-aloud
- how to use current knowledge to understand a new experience through comparison and contrast
- what language structure is appropriate and how to use more complex language to enhance communication
- how to listen actively and effectively
- how to use questions effectively in different contexts, from simply seeking clarification to extending ideas or challenging assumptions

Teachers' self-assessment of oral language in the classroom focuses on two areas:

- their own language use (See the Teacher Talk sections in Linking Assessment to Instruction later in this chapter.)
- their oral language curriculum

Self-assessment enables teachers to more effectively contribute to the development of students' speaking and listening skills by determining when and how to provide additional language experiences or language use in different contexts.

"The speaking and listening behaviors of teachers have a powerful influence on students, acting as a model for them as teachers talk with students about their work, how they want them to proceed with activities, and how they generate criteria for judging success."

Smith 2001, 32

Reflecting on My Oral Language Program

The following checklist will guide teachers in reflecting on their oral language program. It will also help them set specific goals for areas they want to change. Reflections could be dated to serve as a record of how the classroom oral language program is developing.

❑ Do I provide opportunities for students to listen and talk to others for a variety of purposes and on a range of subjects?

❑ Do I explicitly plan opportunities to model and teach oral communication skills in meaningful contexts?

❑ Do I embed oral language instruction and use across the curriculum?

❑ Do I use oral communication effectively to support reading and writing tasks?

❑ Do I engage students in hands-on activities to develop and consolidate word study concepts and generalizations?

❑ Do I provide my students with multiple opportunities to actively engage in developing vocabulary and background knowledge?

❑ Do I provide students with ongoing assessment and feedback to enable them to improve their oral communication skills?

❑ Do I provide opportunities for students to assess themselves and their peers?

❑ Do I involve parents in developing students' oral language?

It is also important for teachers to reflect on

- what they are doing well
- what they need to focus on next
- what plans they have to achieve their goal(s)

Assessment Considerations for ESL Students

The following provides a summary of the particular issues that face teachers when assessing the oral language of ESL students.

Pragmatics and ESL

Students learning English as a second language may not understand or use the same social conventions for communication as native speakers of English. ESL students may need explicit instruction in expected communication behaviours. Teachers also need to be aware that certain behaviours express different meanings in diverse cultures.

Semantics and ESL

The challenge of developing vocabulary knowledge to support communication in social and instructional contexts is significant, but native speakers of English draw on one context to support the other. ESL students do not have this advantage. As well, with its many figurative expressions and multiple-meaning words, English is, at times, a very confusing language. ESL students will often miss more subtle language cues. Even English speakers from different nations may do this because constructing meaning from language is culturally based. For example, someone from one culture may fail to understand the cartoons or humour of a different culture.

Syntax and ESL

Every language has its own rules for grammar and sentence structure. ESL students may have a very different sentence structure in their home language that does not translate easily into English. Some new English speakers, for example, tend to omit function words (*the, an, of, to*), using mostly content words to get their meaning across. Other languages also have different ways of expressing tenses, plurals, and possessives.

Phonology and ESL

Students may not recognize or may be unable to pronounce particular English sounds that are not phonemes in their home language. For example, in English *sh* and *ch* are different phonemes, so the words "shop" and "chop" have distinct meanings. In Spanish, however, the two sounds are processed as the same phoneme.

ESL students may become confused about which word is being said because they do not have the same understanding of the sound structure as native speakers of English. Their understanding of sounds also affects which sounds they use in spoken English and which sounds and letters they use in reading and writing. The language itself may be the key as not all languages are based on an alphabetic system. For example, Chinese and Japanese writing is based on a combination of ideographs and characters representing syllables. Some languages, such as Vietnamese, signal meaning changes through shifting intonations. ESL students may be developing phonological awareness in their first language, but may have difficulty demonstrating it in English due to these varied sound structures.

Teachers of ESL students need to gather as much information as possible about their students' language use and to assess their oral language skills in English carefully.

While ESL students may be able to understand and speak English fairly competently within the first three years of exposure, their academic skills in English are not likely to progress at the same rate. Although they may be able to participate in many oral language activities as they are learning English, it is not reasonable to expect them to perform at the same level in reading and writing English (CIERA 2001).

Assessment BLMs

Assessment BLM 1: Oral Language Checklist

Assessment BLM 2: Oral Language Summary Sheet

Assessment BLM 3: My Speaking Skills

Assessment BLM 4: Listening Skills Checklist

Assessment BLM 5: My Listening Skills

Linking Assessment to Instruction

Speaking and listening are the foundations of literacy development and academic success, and students need many opportunities to develop these skills in Grades 3 to 6. Teachers focus on oral language skills throughout the school day when talk becomes an integral part of the classroom curriculum. From their informed observations of how students speak and listen, effective teachers plan classroom programs that support the development of

- language for social interaction
- background knowledge, and the ability to use this knowledge to make connections across the curriculum
- language for thinking and problem solving
- language for personal reflection and self-monitoring
- reading and writing, by helping students connect their knowledge of oral language to the reading and writing process

Teachers foster the development of oral language skills through whole-class, small-group, or paired activities, as well as through individual instruction and independent work. They view all classroom activities as opportunities to model, practise, and specifically teach language.

The Importance of Talk in the Classroom

As teachers consider how to support the development of students' oral language, they need to look at their own use of language and how they structure their classrooms to facilitate peer conversations that enhance learning.

Teacher Talk: The Teacher's Role

Teacher talk fosters the development of oral language skills for school-based social interaction, literacy development, and learning. Teachers often assume that students have the language knowledge they need to be successful in the classroom. However, teacher talk makes the implicit explicit for students. Teachers' awareness of what language they use and how they use it is critical.

Teacher talk provides an opportunity to

- demonstrate vocabulary, sentence structure, and language use appropriate to different contexts and purposes
- model respectful language and conversational skills
- use language that identifies classroom scripts (the implicit rules for classroom behaviour) and supports the development of the classroom as a community of learners
- demonstrate active listening, including how to give positive feedback, ask appropriate questions, and respond in a way that reflects an understanding of what was said

  "Let's see if I got this right. What I hear you saying is ..."

- extend student thinking through the use of statements and open-ended questions that invite further responses

  "What did you notice?"

  "What puzzled you about that?"

  "Is there anything else that surprised you?"

- model language to support reflective thinking and self-assessment

  "What did you try?"

  "What was the problem? How did you solve it?"

  "What did you learn?"

- use think-alouds to model language that demonstrates thinking and fosters problem solving and strategy use

  "Maybe ... "

  "I'm thinking that ..."

  "I'm wondering if ... "

Think-alouds can also be used to model language specific to different strategies, such as those that follow.

Predicting: "What do I already know about ... "; "What might happen next?"

Connecting: "That reminds me of the time ... "; "That makes me think about what I did when ... "; "That's just like ... "

Visualizing: "Let me get a picture in my head. Tell me that again." Or "I'm going to read that again so I can picture it."

Problem solving: "I don't get this. Let me see. I could ... "

Synthesizing: "I was thinking ... but now I think ... "

For more information about think-alouds, see Chapter 2: Reading Comprehension: Strategies That Work.

- use language that students need to talk about or describe language (noun, verb, sentence, phrase, infer, predict, and so on) in the context of daily literacy instruction. This shared vocabulary enhances classroom discussions and strategy use as students engage in literacy activities across the curriculum.

"Extended thinking time is related to more student talk, more sustained talk, and more 'higher order' thinking."

JOHNSTON 2004, 56

Establishing "Thinking Time"

In order to keep things moving in the classroom, teachers often wait only three or four seconds for a student to respond to a question; however, many students need more time to process the question or comment and then think of an appropriate response. Effective teachers know how to use silence to give students thinking time and to invite them to speak.

One way of increasing thinking time is to establish a longer wait time as part of the classroom routine. For example, after a student asks a question or offers an opinion the teacher could say, "That's a great question (idea). Let's take a moment to think about that before we comment" thereby pausing the discussion. Teachers would need to discuss this routine with students, model their own thinking with reflective pauses ("Hmm, let me think about that for a minute"), and teach students not to jump in with their comments or to answer for someone else.

Another option, if students need more time, would be to say, "I know thinking takes time. Let me know when you're ready with your answer (question, comment) by … (raising a hand, holding up two fingers, holding up a fist)." The teacher may ask another student to respond and then go back to the first student when he or she is ready.

Teacher talk shapes the nature of classroom discourse—how students and teachers interact and engage in conversation socially and for learning. The nature of this discourse is an important aspect of developing a classroom community of learners. (See Chapter 5: In the Classroom: Making It Work.)

Students benefit when teachers ask themselves these questions:

- Who controls the discourse in the classroom? Is it teacher driven, or is it shared?
- Who decides who speaks and for how long?
- Who does most of the speaking? most of the listening?
- Who asks most of the questions? Who gives the answers?
- Do I listen only for the "right answer" (mine) or do I listen carefully to what the student says and provide opportunities for clarification?
- Do I "shut students down" or am I open to multiple interpretations?
- Whose responses are valued? Do all students have a voice?

(Adapted from Gordon 2001, 72)

Peer Talk: Conversations to Support Learning

Students need many opportunities throughout the day to talk with peers in large-group, small-group, or paired activities. Purposeful and productive conversations support learning across the curriculum.

The sharing of ideas generated by conversations helps students to

- clarify their thinking
- deepen their comprehension
- develop new interpretations of what they hear, read, or see
- make connections between what they are learning and what they personally know

Talk supports reading and writing development as students learn how to respond to texts and how to create texts of their own. Conversations allow students to practise social skills, such as negotiating and collaborating.

Teachers plan opportunities for conversations. These may take place during language arts activities such as book clubs or literature circles, or during small-group investigations in content-area subjects. Book talks are also excellent forums for developing social communication skills. (See Chapter 2: Reading Comprehension: Strategies That Work.)

Small-Group Sharing

An excellent format for encouraging and supporting focused peer conversations is **compass group four-way sharing**. Students sit in groups of four with one student assigned to each point of the compass. The teacher indicates which student (point of the compass) initiates the conversation and then after five minutes asks those students to finish their sentences. The conversation then passes to the next person in a clockwise direction. After about 25 minutes, all students have shared their thinking and led the discussion. This format ensures that even reticent speakers have the opportunity to speak (Harvey and Goudvis 2000). Depending on the focus of the conversation, students may bring sticky notes, graphic organizers, visual responses, and so on, to support their comments.

Partner Sharing

In partner sharing, teachers create informal talk time by providing opportunities for students to talk to partners during any large-group activity during which students share their thinking. They might make a prediction, ask a question, confirm what they have learned, or suggest a solution.

Implementing Partner Sharing

1. The teacher has the students number off as 1s and 2s.
2. The teacher asks the 1s to raise their hands and then turn to their partners to talk for 30 seconds.
3. Once the teacher regains student attention, the 2s share their thinking.
4. One option is to then have some students share their thinking in the large group.

Once students know how this technique works, teachers can simply ask them to turn to a partner and share their thinking. Students may be familiar with this activity from earlier grades in the form of Eye to Eye and Knee to Knee.

Think-Pair-Share

In a Think–Pair–Share format, students are given time to think through a question or problem independently and then to discuss their ideas with a partner. The teacher then invites the students to share and compare their ideas in small groups or to return to a large-group discussion. This activity provides students with the opportunity to formulate their ideas before being asked to discuss them with a peer. It ensures that all students have a chance to voice their opinion and supports students who may be reluctant to speak in a large group.

Sharing ideas through oral language may be difficult for **ESL** students. Provide these students with the opportunity to create a quick sketch of what they are thinking and to label it using their home language before sharing it with others. If necessary, let them speak in their home language first and then in English. This strategy is helpful for any student who struggles with expressing ideas.

Developing Oral Language for Social Interaction

In a classroom that focuses on interaction and conversation as the medium for learning, it is important that students develop the social language skills that will enable them to work well independently, with a partner, in a small group, and in the whole-class setting. Teachers set the framework for this early in the school year as they develop expectations and establish routines with students for working and learning as a classroom community. This orientation enables students to manage themselves as they move through the various components of the comprehensive literacy classroom. (See Chapter 5: In the Classroom: Making It Work.)

To promote listening skills, the teacher may ask students to report back on what their partner said, rather than on their own ideas.

Students also need to learn how to converse effectively. Teachers teach conversational skills explicitly through focused lessons, and implicitly through the modelling they provide in their daily interactions with students. The focus is teaching students the civility of conversation. Students adopt the language of conversation they hear modelled in the classroom by the teacher, and learn to apply it in their interactions with one another (Miller 2002, 18–20).

Developing Listening Skills

Students need to know why they should listen, what they are listening for, and how to listen effectively.

Teaching the Importance of Listening

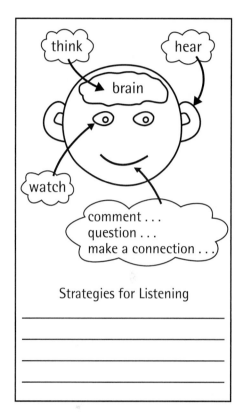

Strategies for Listening

_____

_____

_____

_____

1. The teacher brainstorms with students why they need to listen in class, charting their ideas. Reasons for listening might include, "so we know what we have to do," "to learn something new," "to answer a question," or "to keep a conversation going."

2. The class discusses how listening requires them to use their ears (to hear), their eyes (to watch the speaker), their brains (to think), and their mouths (to respond when it is their turn to speak). The teacher draws these on the chart as visual reminders.

3. The teacher and students discuss the cues for listening used in the classroom, such as raising a hand, flicking the lights on and off, ringing a bell, calling out a student's name, counting to three, or tapping a student on the shoulder.

4. Students brainstorm things that interfere with listening. The teacher encourages them to think about

   • speaker problems (coughing, covering mouth, standing too far away, talking too quietly)

   • listener problems (not watching, talking to someone, thinking about something else)

   • background problems (too many people talking, noise in the hallway)

5. Students role-play some of the difficulties and then problem solve what could be done to improve the listening.

6. The teacher prompts students to identify what makes listening easy or difficult for them and what strategies they could adopt to be better listeners.

7. The teacher charts the strategies and reviews them with students as needed.

Identifying a Purpose for Listening

Listening skills improve when students know what they are listening for. Before doing something that requires students to listen, it is important to have students identify whether their purpose for listening is to

   • be entertained (listening to a story)

   • gain information (to get directions or learn something new about a topic)

- provide a specific response (to comment on or ask a question about what a classmate or invited speaker has shared)
- develop a personal response

Listening can be affected by
- knowledge about the topic
- interest in the topic
- language skills
- memory skills
- hunger, thirst, fatigue, and anxiety

Listening Fatigue and Distractions

Listening effectively is difficult for many people, adults and students alike. Language and memory skills, as well as prior knowledge about, and personal interest in, the topic can affect the ability to listen effectively, as can internal factors such as hunger, thirst, fatigue, and anxiety. Some students who find listening very demanding will tire easily if they have to concentrate or listen for long periods of time. The length of time varies depending on the student. When teachers are aware of listening fatigue, they arrange instruction so that students experience shorter periods of listening followed by activity. This approach is helpful for all students.

Teaching Effective Listening Behaviours

Students also need to learn how to listen. Effective teachers call attention to their own listening behaviours or comment when they see students use appropriate listening behaviours. For example:

> "What did you notice about my body language when Lee was speaking?"

> "Emily is showing effective listening body language. See how she is nodding her head as Marco is speaking?"

> "Did anyone notice how Mei showed she was listening?"

Teachers may reinforce listening behaviours through student role-plays of effective and ineffective listening, or through discussions during group activities or sharing time. When the language to talk about effective listening has been explicitly taught, students are more likely to reflect on their own listening or take note of other people's listening behaviours. Assessment BLM 5: My Listening Skills will facilitate student self-assessment.

Assessment BLM 5: My Listening Skills

Effective listening includes

- using body language, such as nodding your head, maintaining eye contact, and leaning forward
- acknowledging the speaker through expressions such as "uh-huh" or "really"
- paraphrasing the speaker's message
- asking for clarification ("I'm not sure what you meant when you said ... "; "Can you tell me more about that?")
- waiting for the speaker to finish before commenting

Ways for students to reflect on their listening include asking themselves if they are

- keeping the purpose of listening in mind
- making connections between what the speaker says and what they already know
- asking questions about what is being said
- actively monitoring their listening

Actively monitoring their listening is an example of **metacognition,** or thinking about their own thinking. (See Chapter 2: Reading Comprehension: Strategies That Work and Chapter 4: Literacy Learning Across the Curriculum for more information on metacognition.)

In turn, teachers model how to support listeners by

- monitoring and varying their rate of speech
- using phrasing to highlight meaningful units of language
- using emphasis and transition words to highlight key ideas
- using visuals and gestures to augment what is being said

Effective teachers then explicitly teach these behaviours to their students.

Teaching About Body Language

The teacher models body language by sending nonverbal messages such as "Hi," "Come here," and "Stop." Students talk about what the message was and how the meaning was conveyed. The teacher then distributes separate index cards with the following messages for students to convey through body language only. Students could work in pairs or in small groups, or volunteers could demonstrate in front of the whole class.

bored	surprised	hot
in a hurry	shocked	hungry
worried	impatient	happy
afraid	frustrated	daydreaming
excited	cold	

Students guess what message is being conveyed and discuss how their peers used body language to convey it.

Students need to be aware that people sometimes misread body language. If they are unsure about someone's body language, they should ask the person. They also need to recognize that they sometimes send a message with their body language that they didn't intend. For example, scowling when someone asks a question may

Check It Out!

For more information about listening and activities to teach it, see Michael F. Opitz and Matthew D. Zbaracki, *Listen Hear! 25 Effective Listening Comprehension Strategies* (Portsmouth, NH: Heinemann, 2004).

mistakenly suggest that they are angry. It is important that students learn to monitor their own body language to ensure that it is sending the intended message.

(Adapted from Dodge 1994, 63–73).

As an extension activity, the teacher may have students watch TV shows and movies to see how actors use body language to convey emotions. Students may also transfer this awareness to their writing to describe how characters act and feel.

Body language and tone of voice are excellent tools for communicating with **ESL** students. Students may consciously use these tools themselves and also learn to tune in to the nonverbal messages of students who speak English less proficiently.

Teaching How to Interrupt Effectively

One social language skill that is particularly useful both in and out of the classroom is knowing how to interrupt effectively. Although many students in upper elementary classrooms have developed techniques for interrupting, explicit lessons will help students learn to do this in the least disruptive way.

Implementing the GAG Technique

1. The teacher brainstorms with students what it means to interrupt someone.

2. On a chart, using situations from both within and outside the classroom, the teacher writes when it is important to interrupt and when it is not.

3. Students think about times when they interrupted and categorize those interruptions as important or unimportant. Working with the "important to interrupt" side first, the teacher talks about how to interrupt effectively.

4. The acronym GAG, is explained.
   - **G**et the person's attention.
   - **A**pologize for interrupting.
   - **G**ive the reason for interrupting.

5. The teacher explains to students that the acronym spells the word "gag"—something put over the mouth so the person can't talk. This serves as a reminder that students need to stop (as if they had a gag over their mouths) and think before they interrupt.

6. The teacher discusses what a person might do and say during each step of GAG, and then has students role-play the situation. For example:
   - **Get the person's attention.** (Establish eye contact, say "Excuse me," stand close to the person, and wait.) Students also role-play inappropriate ways to get the person's attention. (Talk over the other person; yell the person's name loudly.)
   - **Apologize for interrupting.** ("I'm sorry to interrupt.")
   - **Give the reason for interrupting.** ("Could you help me with this?" "There is someone to see you." "I have something to add to what you said.")

Check It Out!

For practical suggestions for teaching students how to be effective communicators, see Ellen Pritchard Dodge, *CommunicationLab 1* (E. Moline, IL: LinguiSystems, 1994).

7. Next, the teacher discusses when it is important for students to avoid interrupting in the classroom. Students are asked to identify strategies to use in those situations, for example, during reading or writing conferences. If students are unsure about what to do, the teacher reminds them of these options:

- asking a peer
- asking someone else in their group
- checking the board (where instructions or symbols for directions are posted)
- raising their hand
- writing their name on the HELP board
- waiting for a break in the conversation

(Adapted from Gajewski, Hirn, and Mayo, 1989, 132–33)

Another option is to establish a classroom note board. Some teachers designate a specific place on the board or a wall, or use a special notebook. If students have questions or comments or want to meet with the teacher, but it is inappropriate to interrupt, they write their concerns on sticky notes or in the notebook. The students have often solved their problems by the time the teacher checks in with them, but communicating in this way may enable them to continue working.

At times in the classroom, interruptions, except for true emergencies, are not acceptable. Teachers adopt different signals for these times, often when they are working with a small group or doing individual conferences. They may wear a special button or sit at a special table. Students need to recognize these situations and to respect the expectations around them, but they also need strategies to solve problems when they arise. Discussing these strategies with students helps them to work more independently.

Teaching Language That Promotes Discussion and Effective Group Work

Teachers often ask students to work in groups without teaching them how to communicate effectively in that situation. Students need explicit instruction in the kinds of speaking and listening activities that lead to effective group discussions. Although the responsibility for contributing ideas is shared among group participants, providing students with specific roles and teaching them language to use within those roles develops more effective group interaction. The type of language used is determined in part by the focus of the group activity: to share ideas (e.g., book talk); to reach a common understanding of a text or a topic; or to complete a specific project or product.

Working effectively in a group is a complex process. Students need language to do the following:

- promote group cohesion
  - giving praise and encouragement
  - inviting individual group members to comment (and allowing them not to comment if that is their choice)
  - joking and using humour appropriately

The HELP board is a designated area on the chalkboard where students sign their names when they have a question or need help with an assignment. Teachers or students assigned as peer helpers check the board and provide help as needed.

Teachers may also discuss with their colleagues which routines or signals have worked with the students in earlier grades.

- asking for or offering help (e.g., "I understand this ... but I need some help with ... "; "Do you need help with ... or are you OK on your own?")
- coordinate group activities
  - calling for group attention
  - planning (e.g., "I think that first we need to ... and then ... "; "Are there any other suggestions about what we need to do?")
  - giving instructions
  - negotiating roles (e.g., "I wanted to be the manager today, but I could do that next time we meet"; "I think that Marnie would be a good reporter today. She is great at sharing ideas in a large group.")
  - offering feedback and summarizing comments
- explore topics creatively
  - offering ideas and opinions
  - elaborating on another's idea (e.g., "That was a great idea. Can you tell us more about that?")
  - disagreeing, challenging (e.g., "I agree with your point about ... but I'm not sure about ... "; "I'm not sure I agree. Can you explain it a bit more?" "That's a good point, but I think that ... ")
  - asking for clarification
  - explaining, justifying (e.g., "I think ... and the evidence from the book is ... "; "I think ... because my friend [mom, neighbour] told me ... "; "I think ... and I saw that on a TV show ... ")
- encourage resolution and consensus
  - appealing to rules established in the classroom
  - persuading
  - agreeing
  - suggesting compromise (e.g., "Well that might work, but what if we ... as well [instead].")

Teacher Talk: Modelling Respectful Interactions

Teachers listen for effective language use in their own group interactions and share what works with their students. In whole-group situations, such as sharing time at the end of the language arts block, they model the language needed for respectful interactions.

For example, effective teachers consider how they
- invite students to speak
- call for group attention
- use humour to keep everyone on track
- use language to support negotiation about making choices
- model specific feedback
- use body language
- ask students to elaborate on their ideas
- challenge a student's ideas

They also consider whether they are

- explicitly asking students to notice what they said or did to promote respectful interactions
- hearing their words in the conversations students have with one another

Activities such as literature circles also provide opportunities for students to develop expertise in a variety of roles and to practise group interaction skills. (See Chapter 5: In the Classroom: Making It Work for more on literature circles.)

The following are possible roles within a group. These roles may change depending on the nature of the task.

Role	Description	Example
Manager	watches the time, ensures that everyone understands and stays on task, and summarizes the discussion	"Does everyone understand?" "We've finished that one and have five minutes left."
Encourager	makes sure everyone is having a turn, asks people to share ideas or opinions, and provides appropriate praise and feedback	"Hey, it's your turn now." "That's a good idea. Let's make sure we write that one down." "That's really good thinking."
Recorder	writes down the group's ideas and asks questions for clarification	"One at a time, please." "How do you write that?"
Reporter	reports the group's ideas back to the class	"What can I say about this part?" "Is there anything else I need to say?"
Observer	monitors and comments on how the group is functioning	"I think we're on task today." "We need to make sure everyone gets a chance to talk."
Illustrator	provides a visual representation of the group's ideas	"How do I show that?" "Have I forgotten anything?"

(Adapted from Allen 1994, 23–31)

Teachers may introduce students to these roles in simple conversational tasks to enable them to develop some competence not only in the roles but also with group interactions. It is also helpful when students practise one role before learning a new one. Students benefit from the opportunity to reflect on their group work, talking about how they use language differently depending on their role, the nature of the task, and the way the group functioned. They might ask themselves these questions:

- What did I do to help the group?
- What did I notice others doing that helped the group?
- What do I need to work on next time we meet?
- What will I do differently?
- Was there a problem in the group today? How could it be solved?

Have students role-play or model group interactions while other students critique and offer suggestions. Ask specific students to focus on particular aspects of the group functioning, commenting on what they noticed—what they saw, heard, or felt. Taking this approach is better than having all students trying to focus on all aspects of group dynamics.

(Adapted from Allen 1994, 23–31)

Developing Oral Language Before, During, and After Reading

Oral language development occurs during all three phases of reading instruction: before, during, and after. Many of the activities outlined in this section will work at any stage of the reading process, depending on the focus of instruction.

Before Reading

The Before Reading phase provides an excellent opportunity to activate and build background knowledge, broaden vocabulary knowledge, and model the use of questions to gather and extend knowledge. Teacher-led discussions, as well as small-group and individual explorations, engage students in using oral language to set the stage for successful reading, writing, speaking, listening, viewing, and thinking.

Book Introductions

Book introductions serve many purposes. They provide an opportunity to create interest in a new book and help students activate prior knowledge before they read. Teachers model how to make connections between the text and personal experiences, and students share similar experiences. Reading a few sentences from the book also allows teachers to introduce unfamiliar concepts, including new vocabulary or multiple-meaning expressions, and any complex sentence structures used in the text. This helps set the stage for better comprehension as students listen to the text in a read-aloud or read the text later independently.

Before I Read, I Can ...

For this independent reading activity, students use a cue card that lists several before-reading activities. They complete all the steps or a particular number, depending on the book or the student. Sharing the activity with a partner provides an excellent opportunity to develop oral language. Here is what the cue card might say:

- Read the title and book covers.
- Use the Three-Finger Rule to see if the book is "just right."
- Make predictions about what might happen.
- Write down three things you know about the topic.
- Talk about the pictures or chapter headings.
- Read the headings, subheadings, bold print, captions, and diagrams if the text is informational.
- Think about questions that the book raises for you.

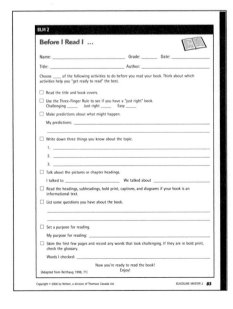

- Set a purpose for reading.
- Skim the first few pages and record any words that look challenging. If they are in bold print, check the glossary.
- Now you're ready to read the book!

Teachers may provide students with BLM 2: Before I Read I ... to prompt them to record their predictions, questions, connections, and so on. Students do not typically complete all the activities for one book or use this blackline master each time they read. It is worthwhile to encourage students to reflect on which activities they find most helpful as they get ready to read.

To remind students of before-reading strategies, teachers could copy BLM 3: Before I Read I ... Bookmark on card stock and have students place the bookmarks in their reading folders. (For more information on using the Three-Finger Rule to select "just right" materials, see Independent Reading in Chapter 5: In the Classroom: Making it Work.)

(Adapted from Reithaug 1998)

See Miriam Trehearne et al., *Nelson Language Arts Grades 1–2 Teacher's Resource Book* (Toronto: Thomson Nelson, 2004), page 96, for a simpler Before I Read blackline master.

BLM 2: Before I Read I ...
BLM 3: Before I Read I ... Bookmark

Visual Sort and Predict

Prediction activities such as Vocabulary Prediction (Let's Predict) and Sort and Predict (see Chapter 2: Reading Comprehension: Strategies That Work) provide excellent opportunities for students working in pairs or small groups to have purposeful conversations. Students may gain new understandings of word meanings as a result of these discussions, which may be of particular benefit to **ESL** students.

For the Visual Sort and Predict activity, students work in small groups. The teacher provides copies of six to eight illustrations or teacher-made drawings based on scenes from the text. Students cut out the drawings, discuss what might be happening in each one, and determine where it might fit sequentially in the story. Each group then presents its predictions in the form of a story.

One student from the group might tell the story to the rest of the class, or the group members might share in the storytelling. After the original story is read, students compare and contrast their predictions with the events in the story.

(Adapted from Brownlie, Feniak, and McCarthy 2004, 60–61)

This activity is particularly helpful for students with limited English, who may have difficulty making predictions about a story based on a series of words.

Teacher Talk: Using Questions and Comments to Build Conversational Skills

During the Before Reading phase, teachers want students to activate prior knowledge, make predictions, and generate questions about a text. As they model these strategies, teachers try to use language that will extend students' thinking and develop conversational skills.

Sometimes the questions teachers ask require only a simple "yes" or "no" answer, or a one- or two-word response. The use of open-ended questions, such as those that follow, is more effective in getting students to activate their prior knowledge, elaborate on their ideas, and give detailed responses.

- What does that remind you of ... ?
- What happened when you ... ?
- How did you ... ?
- Why do you think that?

Responding to a student's comment with a statement that elaborates on what was said provides an excellent language model and also encourages students to continue to think about their ideas and make additional comments. Sometimes questions discourage conversation, while comments allow students to build on previous ideas. Carefully chosen comments and open-ended questions help students make connections between the text and their experiences and predictions.

"Yes" or "No" Questions
S: I saw a show about tornadoes last night.
T: Did you see how a tornado is formed?
S: Yes.
T: Was it scary?
S: No.

Open-Ended Questions and Comments
S: I saw a show about tornadoes last night.
T: That must have been interesting. What did you learn about how tornadoes are formed?
S: They come from big thunderstorms.
T: Tornadoes can be very powerful. I think they have numbers for different strengths.
S: Yeah, a Force 0 is the weakest and a Force 5 is the strongest. It can tear a house off its foundation and throw a car 100 metres into the air.
T: What can people do to protect themselves from a tornado?
S: They have to take shelter, like under a desk. Some people build places in the ground, as I saw in the movie *Twister*.
T: I wouldn't like to be in the middle of a tornado.
S: It would be really scary with everything blowing around. Sometimes the wind is so strong it can blow you right off your feet.

As teachers model the use of open-ended questions and comments, students will begin to use this speaking style during their discussions with classmates and in their own thinking about texts.

Paraprofessionals and volunteers who work with students need to be aware of the importance of

- using statements to encourage student response
- using open-ended rather than "yes" or "no" questions

Teachers may find that commenting and asking open-ended questions is sometimes more difficult than they think. A good idea is to tape-record an interaction with students during a before-reading discussion or during the introduction to a new topic in science or social studies. A reflective teacher might ask, "What kind of questions did I ask? Did I use comments to extend students' thinking? How did students respond? What will I do next time?"

During Reading

The During Reading phase occurs when the teacher is reading in a read-aloud or shared reading activity, or when the students are working in guided reading groups, reading with a partner, or reading independently. During Reading is a critical time for teachers to support the development of reading strategies and students' ability to use the sources of information: meaning (semantics), structure (syntax), sound patterns (phonology), and text cues (e.g., headings, lists).

Teachers' comments and suggestions help students determine when and how to use reading strategies, and their prompts help students use their language knowledge to problem solve while reading. Students who share a common understanding of reading strategies and a common language to describe them effectively support one another. Rather than just telling peers the "tricky word," they provide helpful prompts during reading.

When paraprofessionals, volunteers, parents, and reading buddies also learn and use the language associated with reading strategies, students gain more opportunities to practise strategies and talk about them.

Questioning Web

Learning to ask and answer questions about a text is an important thinking process and reading strategy linked to students' oral language skills. Teachers demonstrate effective questioning when they stop during reading and ask authentic questions that puzzle them about a text. Through this process, they demonstrate that some questions can be answered from the text; some need to be inferred from the text, background knowledge, or an outside source; some questions are left to a reader's interpretation; and some questions may not be answered. (See Question–Answer Relationships in Chapter 2: Reading Comprehension: Strategies That Work.) As well, effective teachers teach students to think about which of their questions are central to understanding the text.

"As my questions became less literal and more sophisticated, so did the children's; as I began to think more about my reading and learning so did they; and as I began to ask questions that truly mattered to me, they did, too."

MILLER 2002, 124

One strategy that supports both questioning and language development is the Questioning Web (Harvey and Goudvis 2000). The teacher models its use initially as part of a read-aloud. Students then practise it in small-group settings and eventually use it independently to support their thinking both in and out of the classroom.

Students determine a question that is particularly puzzling about a text and place it in the centre of the web. They then draw lines radiating out from the centre where they write possible answers to the question or information related to it. When they reach a conclusion, they may write it at the bottom of the sheet (I'm thinking ...). Teachers need to resist the temptation to influence students' thinking toward one right answer or interpretation (Miller 2002). It is the process of constructing meaning that is critical. Students need the opportunity to think through the possibilities using their knowledge of the text and their own experiences. Having students choose a question and discuss it with others is a great opportunity for them to learn the benefit of sharing and building on ideas from others.

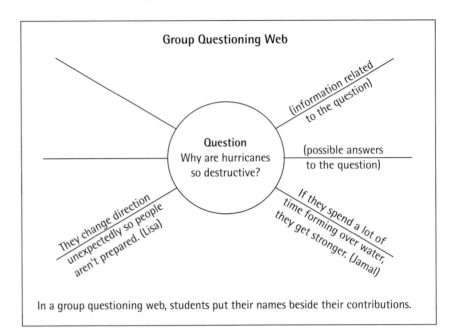

Group Questioning Web

Question
Why are hurricanes so destructive?

(information related to the question)

(possible answers to the question)

They change direction unexpectedly so people aren't prepared. (Lisa)

If they spend a lot of time forming over water, they get stronger. (Jamal)

In a group questioning web, students put their names beside their contributions.

Using Language to Infer (Syntax Surgery)

Students infer all the time in daily life, but are often not aware of when and how they do it. Many students apply this strategy intuitively to support their reading comprehension; however, some students have difficulty transferring this thinking skill to reading. Effective teachers explicitly show students how to use their oral language—their understanding of pragmatics, background knowledge, and sentence structure—to make connections between what they know and what they read in a text.

Kylene Beers, in *When Kids Can't Read, What Teachers Can Do*, uses a think-aloud process to show students how she makes inferences as she reads. The technique, outlined below, is called Syntax Surgery.

Implementing the Syntax Surgery Technique

1. The teacher copies a piece of text and puts it up on an overhead.
2. The class works through the piece, with the teacher uncovering one sentence at a time.
3. The teacher engages students in a discussion of the text while thinking aloud, demonstrating how to
   - determine pronoun reference
   - figure out the context of the story
   - use context to figure out unknown words

- determine the relationships among the characters
- develop conclusions based on the facts in the text and background knowledge

Read the following sample paragraph and think about what might be happening in this text.

> She drove quickly down the road. She needed more milk because he had finished the last of it. She knew that she had to hurry back before he began to cry. Fred was going to go, but he had fallen asleep. She looked at the woman and sighed as she reached the counter and realized she had forgotten something important.

How did you figure out what it was about? Who are the characters? Did you change your mind as you read on? Were there any confusing parts?

What follows is a sample think-aloud based on the preceding sample.

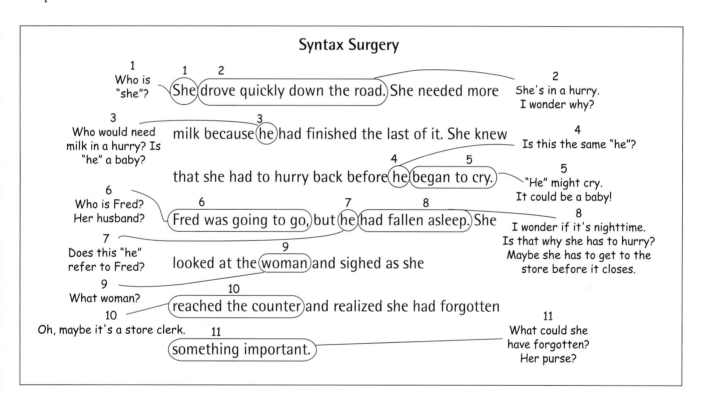

Syntax Surgery

1 Who is "she"?

She drove quickly down the road. She needed more

2 She's in a hurry. I wonder why?

3 Who would need milk in a hurry? Is "he" a baby?

milk because he had finished the last of it. She knew

4 Is this the same "he"?

that she had to hurry back before he began to cry.

5 "He" might cry. It could be a baby!

6 Who is Fred? Her husband?

Fred was going to go, but he had fallen asleep. She

8 I wonder if it's nighttime. Is that why she has to hurry? Maybe she has to get to the store before it closes.

7 Does this "he" refer to Fred?

looked at the woman and sighed as she

9 What woman?

reached the counter and realized she had forgotten

10 Oh, maybe it's a store clerk.

something important.

11 What could she have forgotten? Her purse?

Beers shares a list of possible inferences that skilled readers make. She suggests posting them on a chart as they are introduced to students and encouraging students to add to the chart as they discover other ways they infer. She also provides prompts that teachers might use to help students make certain types of inferences. (See the chart that follows on the next page.)

Skilled readers...	Teacher prompts
1. recognize the antecedents for pronouns 2. figure out the meaning of unknown words from context clues 3. figure out the grammatical function of an unknown word 4. understand intonation of characters' words 5. identify characters' beliefs, personalities, and motivations 6. understand characters' relationships to one another 7. provide details about the setting 8. provide explanations for events or ideas that are presented in the text 9. offer details for events or their own explanations of the events presented in the text 10. understand the author's view of the world 11. recognize the author's biases 12. relate what is happening in the text to their own knowledge of the world 13. offer conclusions from facts presented in the text	• "Look for pronouns and figure out what to connect them to." • "Figure out explanations for these events." • "Think about the setting and see what details you can add." • "Think about something that you know about this (insert topic) and see how that fits with what's in the text." • "After you read this section, see if you can explain why the character acted this way." • "Look at how the character said (insert a specific quote). How would you have interpreted what that character said if he had said (change how it was said or stress different words)?" • "Look for words you don't know and see if any of the other words in the sentence or surrounding sentences can give you an idea of what those unknown words mean." • "As you read this section, look for clues that would tell you how the author might feel about (insert a topic or character's name)."

(Beers 2003, Figs. 5.2 and 5.3, 65)

Pronoun Reference

Pronoun reference refers to the ability to understand who or what the pronouns in a text (oral or written) are referring to. Most listeners and readers keep track of this information intuitively. However, when doing this poses difficulty, it can greatly affect comprehension.

Sometimes the pronoun refers to the immediately preceding noun, and students who struggle with this skill often use this as their default strategy. But the pronoun can refer to a person, place, or event that occurs earlier in the sentence, later in the sentence, in a preceding sentence, or even in a preceding paragraph. Students need to learn to pay attention to these words and note when they are getting confused. They then need to stop and carefully consider what the pronoun is referring to.

Note how pronoun reference is used in the following paragraph from "Akla Gives Chase" by James Houston.

> Together **they** hurried away, trying to hide **themselves** from Long Claws in the heavy ice fog. **They** walked and walked until **they** came to a riverbed that seemed familiar to **them.** Violent

winds had blown one bank free of snow, but in the swirling fog **they** could not tell where **it** would lead **them.** Pitohok struggled up onto the stones **that** formed the bank of the frozen river. **His** sister had to help **him** by pushing at **his** back. (1998, 158)

In this passage, students have to read to the end of the paragraph to understand that "they," "themselves," and "them" refer to Pitohok and his sister. The word "it" refers to the bank free of snow and the word "that" refers to the stones.

One way to demonstrate pronoun reference is to work with a short section from a story or informational text that students might find confusing. The teacher talks about the connections between nouns or phrases and the pronouns, using arrows to demonstrate the connections. It is helpful to remind students to think about pronoun reference as a fix-up strategy if their reading does not make sense.

Teachers also discuss pronoun reference during revision in writing. Using pronouns without clear references can make a piece of writing difficult to understand.

After Reading

The After Reading phase is the time for both personal and critical response. Students need the opportunity to talk about what they read using literate conversations. Talking about a book in either formal or informal conversations, with the teacher or peers, or both, provides a forum for making personal connections, questioning understanding, extending concepts, and exploring text meaning. It also provides the opportunity to debrief and discuss how prereading and during-reading strategies were used.

This reflection time includes response activities that require students to think about and discuss particular aspects of texts. These response activities provide students with opportunities to discuss, write, or in other ways represent their understanding, reflect on their learning, and in turn, extend their reading to other texts. Many of the response activities outlined in Chapter 2: Reading Comprehension: Strategies That Work, Chapter 3: Writing: The Reading–Writing Connection, and Chapter 4: Literacy Learning Across the Curriculum provide excellent opportunities for students to develop their social and oral language skills.

Parents also support the development of oral language through the conversations they have with their children as they read and write. BLM 4: How Families Can Support the "Talking" to "Reading and Writing" Connection offers specific suggestions for parents on ways to talk with their children before, during, and after reading and writing.

BLM 4: Literacy Home Links: How Families Can Support the "Talking" to "Reading and Writing" Connection

Developing Oral Language Across the Curriculum

The development of oral language is a critical component of all areas of the curriculum. In particular, students need to learn strategies to support the development of background knowledge and vocabulary related to specific subject areas. Their interest in informational texts may be used to develop their speaking and listening skills through oral reporting. Drama, including role-plays and Readers Theatre, can be used to effectively engage students in the learning process and develop their oral language skills.

Language Activities for Concept Development

The development of vocabulary and concept knowledge is key to success in reading, writing, and thinking, particularly in content-area subjects such as science and social studies. Building schema for a wide variety of topics is critical to effective listening, reading, and viewing comprehension. Effective instruction in concept development gives students the opportunity to talk about what they know and what they are learning in order to make connections, remember information long term, and build broad background and world knowledge.

Immersion in language that introduces new words and concepts in a variety of contexts enables students to develop a rich understanding of word meanings, relationships, and connotations. At all grade levels, a read-aloud or shared reading provides this opportunity. It allows students to hear new and interesting words, or familiar words used in new contexts. Discussion or specific activities that actively engage students in talking about words helps them develop meaning. Vocabulary instruction is no longer a matter of "assign and define."

The teacher may provide specific instruction in vocabulary before, during, and after reading. Sometimes vocabulary instruction involves teaching new labels for familiar concepts. (Students may know the concept of fair/unfair, but may not know how it relates to honest, scrupulous, reputable, and virtuous.) At other times the students need to learn the concept as well as the labels associated with it.

Vocabulary Instruction Through Read-Alouds and Shared Reading

Read-alouds and shared reading experiences provide excellent opportunities for contextual vocabulary instruction. Teachers talk about words from the text or use sophisticated words to refer to the text. For example, the word "preposterous" may not have appeared in the story, but the teacher uses it to describe something that happened in the text. Effective teachers build this sophistication of language into any text they read.

It is important to remember, however, that frequent interruptions during read-alouds or shared reading experiences can have a negative impact on comprehension. Effective teachers usually embed this vocabulary instruction before and after reading.

Parents often have a wealth of knowledge on topics that will be read about or studied, and sharing some of this knowledge enriches students' background knowledge.

"Indeed, being curious about the meaning of an unknown word that one encounters and about how it relates to other words is a hallmark of those who develop large vocabularies."

BECK, MCKEOWN, AND KUCAN 2003, 46

Suggested Steps for Discussing Words from a Read-Aloud or Shared Reading

1. Refer to the word in the context of the text.

2. Have students say the word to establish its phonological representation.

3. Define the word in student-friendly, everyday language.

4. Provide other contexts that further explain the word meaning.

5. Have students give examples of how the word might be used.

6. Provide students with other examples and have them decide whether the use of the word is appropriate given the context.

7. Have students think of related words: antonyms, synonyms, homonyms, words in the same category, and so on.

8. Chart the words and have students keep track of when they occur in other texts or could be applied to other texts.

(Adapted from Beck, McKeown, and Kucan 2003, 36–39, 41, 45–46)

Students need to see and hear a word in an authentic, meaningful context as many as 10 times before they "own" its meaning. They also need to use a new word immediately. Talking about a word and sharing what it means in the context of personal experience helps to clarify and reinforce its meaning.

Words in Context

The Words in Context graphic organizer is another tool for focusing on vocabulary before or after reading. One of its strengths is that it helps students think about both what the word *is* and *is not*. It also provides the opportunity to explore antonyms and synonyms in a meaningful context. (See BLM 1: Words in Context.)

Teachers initially model how to use this graphic organizer through whole-class instruction. Before students are asked to complete this organizer independently, they benefit from working in pairs or small groups. Teachers might also partially complete the organizer and then have students provide an additional synonym, antonym, or example.

The word being studied is placed in the middle box and a synonym is placed above it. The boxes on the side are used to give additional synonyms and antonyms. At the bottom of the graphic organizer, students list examples and non-examples. (See an example of the Words in Context graphic organizer on the next page.)

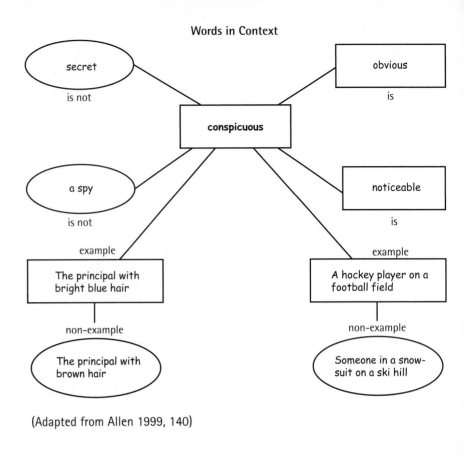

Words in Context

secret — is not
obvious — is

conspicuous

a spy — is not
noticeable — is

example — The principal with bright blue hair

example — A hockey player on a football field

non-example — The principal with brown hair

non-example — Someone in a snow-suit on a ski hill

(Adapted from Allen 1999, 140)

BLM 1: Words in Context

How Well Do I Know These Words?

This activity occurs before reading. Teachers choose key vocabulary from the story. The words are read aloud (or students read them silently) and then the students determine how well they know the words. For each word, students decide if they

- are completely unfamiliar with it
- have seen or heard it before, but don't know the meaning of it
- think they know the meaning of it
- know a meaning for it

Working with partners, the students talk about the words to extend understanding. Students then discuss their findings in small groups. The teacher asks students to identify words that they didn't know. These words can then be addressed through specific vocabulary activities.

An extension of this activity is to provide the word in the context of its use in the text. The teacher reads the word in the sentence from the text and students try to figure out the meaning from the context. Students are encouraged to write in the appropriate column what they think the word means.

(Adapted from Allen 1999)

BLM 5: How Well Do I Know These Words?

Semantic Webs

As the basis of a brainstorming activity, semantic webs allow students to share what they know about a topic. Using webs helps students predict what might be in the text or summarize what was read. (See Chapter 2: Reading Comprehension: Strategies That Work.) Software programs such as Kidspiration and Inspiration are useful tools for developing a variety of semantic webs.

Recognizing that words can have more than one meaning becomes increasingly important as students deal with more complex fiction and nonfiction texts in Grades 3 to 6. A multiple-meaning word web illustrates how some words mean more than one thing. Students work in small groups to develop their webs based on words they discover in their reading, writing, listening, or viewing.

Multiple-meaning words pose particular difficulty for **ESL** students or students with language problems. Using books or illustrations can help make the meanings more concrete.

Multiple-Meaning Word Web

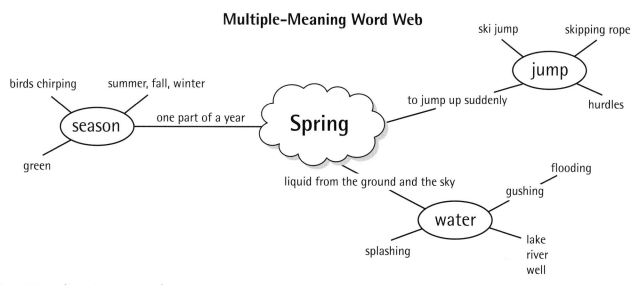

Adapted from (Bromley 2002, 106)

Books with Multiple-Meaning Language

Books with multiple-meaning language are great additions to classroom libraries as they serve as springboards for discussion of how some words have more than one meaning. Two examples by Fred Gwynne are *The King Who Rained* (Simon and Schuster, 1994) and *A Chocolate Moose for Dinner* (Prentice Hall, 1987).

Students will also enjoy the Clarion wordplay books by Marvin Terban (New York: Houghton-Mifflin Company). The book *Eight Ate* in this series introduces homophones through fun and engaging riddles.

Concept Ladder

The Concept Ladder is another graphic organizer that teachers may use to help students expand their understanding of words. As students answer a variety of questions related to the concept, they have an opportunity to talk about the characteristics of a specific word, such as

- how it is similar or opposite in meaning to another word
- what category it belongs to ("It is a kind of ...")
- what it's made of
- its parts
- its function
- its description (what it looks, feels, sounds, and smells like)
- what else it can mean

BLM 6: Concept Ladder might initially be used as a focus for a whole-class discussion about a concept. As students become familiar with the format, the teacher may have them work in small groups to complete a ladder. Different groups could work with the same word or the teacher may choose to have groups discuss different words from the same text. These can then be shared with the rest of the class and other students can add information. This sharing also provides students with an opportunity to talk about the word, an important part of truly understanding its meaning.

The features of the word to be discussed may vary depending on the word. Since the blackline master is blank, teachers can insert the appropriate questions for the words they choose.

Concept Ladder for "Bog"

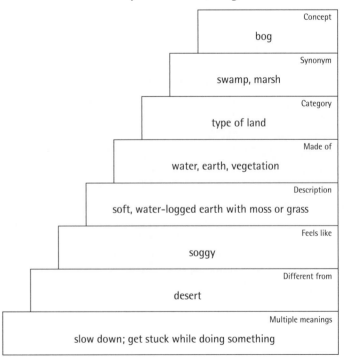

Concept	bog
Synonym	swamp, marsh
Category	type of land
Made of	water, earth, vegetation
Description	soft, water-logged earth with moss or grass
Feels like	soggy
Different from	desert
Multiple meanings	slow down; get stuck while doing something

(Adapted from Allen 1999, 131)

BLM 6: Concept Ladder

Vocabulary Anchor

The Vocabulary Anchor is an excellent activity for helping students, including **ESL** students, make connections between a concept that is new to them and what they already know. In the same way that a boat anchor keeps a boat from drifting away, students can "anchor" something new to something they already know. After setting the context, here is how the teacher might introduce the activity to students.

Implementing the Vocabulary Anchor Technique

1. The teacher draws a simple boat and writes a term already familiar to students on the boat.

2. Then, the teacher chooses a related word that students know and writes it in the anchor.

3. The next step is to connect the boat and anchor with a line to represent the rope.

4. The class talks about similarities between the words, and the teacher writes their responses to the left of the anchor, labelling each with a plus sign (+).

5. They also talk about characteristics that set the words apart and the teacher writes these ideas to the right of the anchor, labelling each with a tilde sign (~).

6. The teacher discusses a memorable experience prompted by the word, captures the memory in a few words or phrases, and then writes them in the sail at the top of the boat.

7. The teacher summarizes by reviewing the drawing and talking about what the words mean and why they are not interchangeable.

8. Once students are familiar with the structure of a vocabulary anchor, the teacher may choose words from a read-aloud or content-area topic.

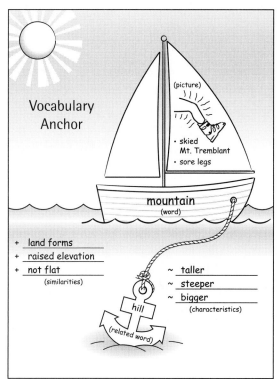

(Adapted from Bromley 2002, 12)

Oral Language: Speaking, Listening, and Learning |

List-Group-Label

List-Group-Label is an excellent activity to discover what students already know about a concept and the words related to it. It also helps students organize their thinking about the topic. The teacher reviews the results of this activity to determine what vocabulary may need to be taught.

Implementing the List-Group-Label Technique

1. Students brainstorm words related to a topic or target word.
2. Students then sort their words into categories and decide on a label for the category.
3. The teacher may suggest additional words and prompt the students to sort them into an appropriate category.
4. Students share their categories and discuss which words were most common across categories. Although there is no right or wrong answer, students need to be able to explain why they placed the words in the various categories and how they chose the labels.

See also Identifying, Categorizing, and Sorting in Chapter 2: Reading Comprehension: Strategies That Work.

Developing Background Knowledge: How Parents Can Help

There are many ways that parents can help their children develop background knowledge. Teachers may want to share the suggestions that follow with their students' families.

- Inform parents of upcoming topics in science, social studies, and health. Provide books on the topics that parents can read to or with their child. Teachers might provide parents with a list of suggested titles, or send students home with library books or classroom resources.

- Work with public or curriculum libraries to provide videos on these topics that parents and their children can watch and discuss.

- Develop a list of Web sites that parents and their children can visit and discuss, or TV shows, such as those on the Discovery channel, that provide valuable information on a wide range of topics.

- Ask students and parents about their special areas of interest. Have them share their expertise with the class.

- Encourage parents to talk to their children about what interests them. Provide parents with leading questions that will help their children develop the thinking strategies they need for reading and writing success. They will find it easier to apply these strategies to topics they know a lot about.

- Encourage students to share with their parents the graphic organizers they develop in class on particular topics or words. Talking about them helps deepen understanding.
- Remind parents that students truly benefit from the opportunity to share what they're learning. When students are excited and engaged in learning, they will be eager to share their discoveries at home.

Language Activities for Oral Reporting

An important component of the literacy program is the students' ability to share information with others. There are many opportunities for informal sharing during the day, but students also need to learn strategies for more formal reporting.

Extemporaneous Speeches

Students benefit from giving informal extemporaneous speeches. These may focus on topics of interest related to personal experiences, favourite movies, hobbies, sports, vacations, and so on. Setting specific time limits is a good idea. Teachers also need to model speeches for students and discuss what is expected. Students learn to

- state the topic at the beginning
- provide an opening statement that catches the audience's interest
- stay on topic
- take one idea and elaborate on it
- use humour to engage the audience
- summarize what was said
- pause and check that the audience is understanding
- answer questions from the audience
- end with an effective conclusion

Teachers provide students with opportunities to plan their speeches and teach them ways to give appropriate feedback to their peers about what went well and what could be improved. Providing simple checklists is helpful. A good practice is for different students to focus on different skills for feedback: it can be difficult to monitor several speaking skills at once. Many of the skills practised in these speeches can be integrated into report writing. (See Chapter 4: Literacy Learning Across the Curriculum.)

Oral Reports

Oral reports provide one way to respond to reading across the curriculum. Initially, students structure oral reports using questions (e.g., who, what, where, when, why, and how). Teachers model these questions with reference to the stories or informational texts that the students are reading in whole-group or small-group lessons. Posting these questions allows students to refer to them during discussions in social studies, science, or health. As students are brainstorming information about a new topic, they could check to see if these questions have been addressed. They could also refer to them when generating questions for a K-W-L-M chart or creating a semantic web. Teachers will want students to expand their reports beyond these questions, but they provide a good starting point. (For more on questioning, see earlier in this chapter as well as Chapter 2: Reading Comprehension: Strategies That Work, Chapter 4: Literacy Learning Across the Curriculum, and Chapter 6: Supporting Struggling and Reluctant Readers.)

Students in Grades 3 to 6 benefit from giving reports that reflect the variety of informational text structures they are reading. These structures include description, sequence (including timelines and procedural text on how to make something), question and answer, compare and contrast, cause and effect, and problem and solution. Using graphic organizers that represent the text structures helps students organize and plan their presentations. (For more on text structures and graphic organizers, see Chapter 2: Reading Comprehension: Strategies That Work. For information on report writing, see Chapter 3: Writing: The Reading–Writing Connection and Chapter 4: Literacy Learning Across the Curriculum.)

Other oral reports may consist of brief, informal presentations that address specific questions students have been researching. For example, after reading an informational text, students may generate a variety of questions requiring further investigation. They research these questions either individually or in small groups, and then present their information to the whole class.

Book talks are another form of oral report that give students the opportunity to share information in a group setting. (See Chapter 2: Reading Comprehension: Strategies That Work.)

Although oral reports provide one way of sharing information with classmates, some students benefit from the opportunity to draw their ideas, while others may be more comfortable writing fuller texts. Students in Grades 3 to 6 also need experience with more formal presentations for which they may prepare cue cards, present visual displays, and use props.

Nelson Language Arts 5, Making a Difference provides specific suggestions on preparing and delivering an oral report.

Persuasive Reports

In persuasive reports the focus is on convincing an audience to agree with a particular point of view. These reports include

- an introduction, in which the main idea of the report and the presenter's point of view are clearly stated
- a number of arguments backed up by facts and reasons
- an effective conclusion that summarizes the point of view

Students need to hear examples of persuasive texts, such as advertisements, movie reviews, and speeches. They also need to understand the difference between a fact and an opinion. Practising and evaluating persuasive reports is a step toward persuasive writing. (See Chapter 3: Writing: The Reading–Writing Connection for more information on persuasive writing.)

Computer-based multimedia projects allow students to present information through sound and visual images with minimal text. Students working in pairs or in small groups to develop these presentations practise their oral language, problem-solving, and group interaction skills.

Fact	Opinion
Only male humpback whales sing.	The songs are strange and beautiful.

Oral Presentation Skills

Students need to understand the skills required for effective oral presentations. Key skills include the following:

- Speak clearly and slowly.
- Use intonation to highlight key information.
- Use transition words to highlight important ideas.
- Look at the audience.
- Present ideas in a logical order.
- Use visuals effectively.
- Use gestures to support and clarify.
- Avoid fidgeting, which can distract the audience.

Effective teachers develop checklists and rubrics with students to assess oral presentation skills. These can be placed in the students' portfolios and used to generate specific goals for improvement.

ESL students who cannot yet write a lot about a topic can produce oral reports using pictures and a few key words. This option enables them to participate even when they have difficulty with reading and writing.

Encouraging students to use transition words in their oral language will facilitate their understanding of them in reading and writing.

Supporting Oral Language Development Through Drama

Role-Plays

In Grades 3 to 6, role-plays provide an excellent vehicle to help students identify what effective communicators do. Through role-plays, students practise

- taking the roles of speaker and listener
- solving problems in group interactions

Check It Out!

For additional suggestions about how to use drama to develop comprehension, see J. Wilhelm, *Action Strategies for Deepening Comprehension: Role Plays, Text Structure Tableaux, Talking Statues, and Other Enrichment Techniques That Engage Students with Text* (Toronto: Scholastic, 2002).

- conveying meaning through facial expression, tone of voice, and other body language
- beginning a conversation
- interrupting and taking turns appropriately
- giving and receiving praise
- providing appropriate feedback or critical comments without put-downs

During or following the role-play, the teacher might call "freeze" and ask students to talk about what worked well in the situation, how the communication made people feel, and what could be done differently to improve the communication.

Role-plays also enable teachers to demonstrate and prompt discussion about how to set up and run class meetings, serve in group roles (see Teaching Language That Promotes Discussion and Effective Group Work earlier in this chapter), and problem solve issues in the classroom. Role-plays make the experiences concrete and provide explicit models of what to do and what not to do.

Readers Theatre

Readers Theatre scripts are not limited to fiction. Teachers and students can create scripts based on informational text across the curriculum. These scripts often provide easily accessible texts to teach key concepts in science, social studies, and health.

Readers Theatre provides students with the opportunity to practise fluency and oral expression in a safe, manageable environment. Students perform published Readers Theatre scripts or create their own. No costumes or sets are needed and students read from scripts rather than memorizing lines. In addition to enhancing oral expression and helping students refine their speaking skills, Readers Theatre develops group social skills: students are required to work cooperatively to plan and present their script.

Some publishers now include Readers Theatre scripts in their classroom collections. There are also a number of Readers Theatre Web sites that offer teaching tips and downloadable scripts. Many of these sites provide information on how to adapt texts for Readers Theatre.

See Chapter 5: In the Classroom: Making It Work for more information on Readers Theatre.

Assessment BLM 12: Readers Theatre Script Rubric in Chapter 5
Assessment BLM 13: Readers Theatre Performance in Chapter 5

Speakers Theatre

Speakers Theatre is a variation of Readers Theatre, but there is no script. Instead, students show what they understand about the major elements or events of a text through storytelling or oral presentation.

Implementing Speakers Theatre

1. A short text or a portion of a longer text is read by the students.
2. Students work in a small group, rereading, summarizing, and discussing how to best convey the "story" or information to the audience.
3. If necessary, the teacher provides an outline to help students decide what information they need to convey.

Check It Out!

When searching the Internet for information on Readers Theatre, it is best to type *Readers Theatre* in the search engine. The spelling of *Readers Theatre* may vary (Reader's Theater, Readers' Theatre), but the related sites are usually found as well. Recommended Web sites:

- www.scriptsforschools.com
- www.aaronshep.com
- www.teachingheart.net/ readerstheater.htm
- www.stemnet.nf.ca/CITE/ langrt.htm

4. The text is then divided into sections. Each member of the group takes one section to retell (rather than share the text as a skit with dialogue and actions). Students are encouraged to paraphrase, improvise, and weave their own knowledge and personality into the telling.

5. Students practise their retellings in the group to develop a coherent, smoothly flowing story. They may employ gestures, body language, and a few minor actions to enhance their voices.

6. The performers usually sit and then stand when it is time to perform their section. Alternatively, they may stand and step forward when it is their turn.

(Adapted from Arrington 2004)

Suggested texts for Speakers Theatre include newspaper articles, short stories, or informational texts about historical events. Different groups of students can also read and present different sections of a longer text.

Step into the Story

In this activity teachers choose from a book an action scene that has particular significance to the story. They make an overhead of an illustration from a picture book or a drawing of the scene, and project it on a screen or wall. Students take on the roles of the characters, "step into the story," and act out the scene. This brings the story to life for the students and gives them an opportunity to reflect on how the characters felt.

Teachers determine students' understanding of the story and their ability to infer information as the scene unfolds. Discussing the scene with the whole class helps clarify misunderstandings and deepens connections to the story.

To extend the activity, students might write about the scene, develop dialogue, write from the perspective of different characters, or prepare alternative endings.

Incorporating such varied literacies as visual arts, music, and drama into the classroom structure enables ESL students to participate and demonstrate their knowledge and understanding without having to rely on English or language (Fay and Whaley 2004).

Developing Oral Language Through Writing

During the writing component of a comprehensive literacy program, teachers focus on the links between oral language and print. They help students use their background knowledge as they begin to write and extend their thinking by asking appropriate questions.

Through mini-lessons and student conferences, effective teachers address specific features of language (for example, parts of speech, sentence structure, and descriptive language) in addition to modelling spelling and printing. In particular, they help students recognize the power of language for communication as they highlight reading-writing connections.

Students need to view writing as another tool for communication. Just as talking about their thinking helps students understand what they read, it also helps them write. They need many opportunities to talk to their peers as they write—to get ideas, clarify their thinking, obtain feedback, refine their writing, and problem solve in spelling.

Although writing programs with word prediction software, such as *Co-Writer* and *Write Out Loud*, may typically be used with students who struggle with writing, many students benefit from the added language support these programs provide.

Teacher responses serve to extend students' ideas when they are writing in personal journals or learning logs and during writing workshops. These responses, oral or written, might include a comment on the student's topic, a question to direct the student's thinking, or a connection between student writing and some aspect of the curriculum.

See Chapter 3: Writing: The Reading–Writing Connection for additional suggestions on linking talk to the development of writing.

Developing Phonological Awareness Through Word Study

Although most students have developed phonological awareness by Grades 3 to 6, continued practice with syllables, rhyme, and sounds through language play supports students' ability to use this knowledge. Poetry and song lyrics help students develop an ear for the rhythm of language. Word study provides an opportunity for more in-depth analysis of word parts.

The following word study activities provide opportunities to segment, blend, and manipulate word parts in the context of developing reading and spelling skills.

Content Word Boards

Content Word Boards are charts that can be used to collect and investigate multisyllable words to look for common prefixes, suffixes, base words, and root words. Students need to know how to segment and blend by syllables and sounds in order to benefit from this activity.

Implementing Content Word Boards

1. The teacher selects a topic under investigation in science or social studies.
2. Gradually, the teacher adds words associated with the topic to a chart and prompts students to add words as they discover them in their reading.
3. Students look for patterns of syllables, prefixes, suffixes, base words, and root words, as well as sound patterns, as part of word study.

Students may then use the chart as a reference when writing about the topic.

(Adapted from Cunningham 1995, 124–27)

Making Big Words

Making Big Words is another excellent activity that uses students' ability to segment and blend by syllable, rhyme, and sound. The word sorting component highlights the importance of reading and spelling by word analogy. (See Chapter 6: Supporting Struggling and Reluctant Readers for details.)

Weather	
temperature	humidity
thermometer	velocity
barometer	visibility
anemometer	cycle
centimetre	cyclone
condensation	absorption
twister	direction
blustery	precipitation
atmosphere	

Possible patterns for word study in the list of weather words above include *tion, er, ity, meter,* and *cycle.*

Word Webs

Word webs, used to investigate common prefixes, suffixes, and root words, help students see how words are connected by meaning and foster an awareness of syllables and word patterns. Developing word webs extends vocabulary knowledge, builds an interest in words and word meanings, and provides a purpose for learning dictionary skills.

Implementing Word Webs

1. The teacher chooses a word that has three or four syllables, has a word part for students to explore and, if desired, reflects an area of the content curriculum.

2. The teacher writes the word in the middle of a piece of chart paper and invites students to suggest possible places to start (syllables, prefixes, suffixes, small words).

3. Students are also invited to think of words that share that spelling pattern. The teacher draws a line from that part of the word, writes the new word, and then continues building on the word (e.g., trans–).

4. After a few examples, the class starts building from another part of the word (e.g., –tion).

5. Students work in small groups to develop their own webs, with the teacher encouraging them to check classroom resources when necessary in order to spell the words correctly.

6. The teacher brings the class together and they compare the webs.

7. The class discusses what they noticed and learned about words from the activity.

Check It Out!

For lists of prefixes, suffixes, and associated meanings, see Kylene Beers, *When Children Can't Read, What Teachers Can Do* (Portsmouth, NH: Heinemann, 2003), and Mary Tarasoff, *Reading Instruction That Makes Sense* (Victoria, BC: Active Learning Institute, 1997).

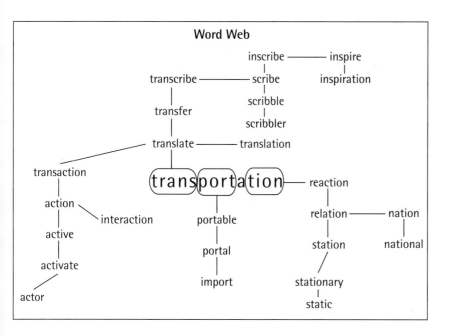

Word Web

Word Sorts

"Word sorting helps students form hypotheses about the properties of written words and make connections between words."

Fountas and Pinnell 2001, 377

When doing a word- or sound-sorting activity, a Does Not Fit column is helpful for words that the students cannot match to the intended key words.

In word sorts, students compare and contrast words according to specific features and sort them under different category headings. They form hypotheses or generalizations about the commonalities and differences of the words and use that knowledge to link new words to ones they already read and spell.

Talk is a key component of word sorts. Teachers encourage students to say the words out loud and to discuss why they have sorted the words a certain way. They ask questions such as, "How are all these words alike?" "Why did you put this word in this column?" "Why did you leave these words over here?"

Through conversation, students revise and refine their thinking. They are often asked to write what they have learned on chart paper to share with the class or to record the sorts and observations in spelling journals.

Word sorts can be closed or open. In a closed sort, the teacher decides how the words will be sorted and the categories are predetermined. There are key words for each category.

Closed Word Sort—Long *a* Sound

Words for sort:

grace	age	eight	pay	plate
aim	wait	gave	gain	rail
weigh	stay	take	lame	way
play	raid	bay	tray	

Key word:

name	rain	sleigh	say
grace	raid	weigh	bay
age	aim	eight	stay
take	wait		play
gave	gain		way
lame	rail		pay
plate			tray

What I Learned: I can spell the long *a* sound at least four ways: *a_e, ai, eigh,* and *ay*. The *a_e* and *ay* patterns seem to be most common, but I'm going to keep collecting words with those patterns to see which occur the most.

In an open sort, students categorize the words according to their own criteria; however, they must be able to explain their rationale for sorting the words in a particular way.

When doing a word- or sound-sorting activity, a Does Not Fit column is helpful for words that the students cannot match to the intended key words or chosen categories.

Open Word Sort

Words for sort:

watch	butcher	catcher	pitch
peach	pooch	reach	teacher
rich	stitch	such	fetching
wretched	munch	lunches	starch

Student sort #1:

One Syllable		Two Syllables
watch	munch	wretched
peach	reach	butcher
rich	such	catcher
pooch	pitch	lunches
stitch	starch	teacher
		fetching

Student sort #2:

Short Vowel + tch	Long Vowel + ch	Consonant + ch	Does Not Fit
watch	peach	munch	rich
stitch	pooch	starch	such
pitch	teacher	lunches	
wretched	reach		
butcher			
catcher			
fetching			

Sorts can be completed as a whole-class activity, in small groups, in pairs, or independently. It is best to introduce them in a whole-class setting where the teacher demonstrates the process and scaffolds students' participation. Some students will need additional guided practice before they are able to complete word sorts independently.

See the next page for resources on word sorts.

When wall charts are used to record sorts and generalizations, they become handy references for students when they write. They also serve as ready reminders that spelling is about making connections between words.

Check It Out!

For specific instructional activities for students who are experiencing difficulty with phonological awareness, see Miriam Trehearne et al., *Nelson Language Arts Kindergarten Teacher's Resource Book* (Toronto: Nelson Thomson Learning, 2000) and *Nelson Language Arts Grades 1–2 Teacher's Resource Book* (Toronto: Thomson Nelson, 2004).

Resources on Word Sorts

The following books provide more information on word sorts, including specific examples and suggested sorts:

- D. Bear, M. Invernizzi, S. Templeton, and F. Johnston. *Words Their Way: Word Study for Phonics, Vocabulary and Spelling Instruction,* 3rd ed. (Englewood Cliffs, NJ: Prentice Hall, 2004).

- I.C. Fountas and G.S. Pinnell. *Guiding Readers and Writers 3–6* (Portsmouth, NH: Heinemann, 2001).

- I.C. Fountas and G.S. Pinnell, eds. *Voices on Word Matters* (Portsmouth, NH: Heinemann, 1999).

- K. Ganske. *Word Journeys* (New York: The Guilford Press, 2000).

- R. McQuirter Scott and S. Siamon. *Spelling: Connecting the Pieces* (Toronto: Gage Learning Corporation, 2004).

- G.S. Pinnell and I.C. Fountas. *Word Matters* (Portsmouth, NH: Heinemann, 1998).

- D. Snowball and F. Bolton. *Spelling K–8* (York, ME: Stenhouse Publishers, 1999).

Supporting ESL Students

Students learning English as a second language benefit from the same instructional practices that support oral language development for all learners. Language is learned in a social, collaborative environment. Teachers need to build on the knowledge of language and communication that students bring from their first language as they learn the sounds, sentence structure, and vocabulary of English. The literacy activities of Grades 3 to 6 classrooms provide ongoing opportunities for students to speak, listen, read, and write English.

Like all students, ESL students benefit from repeated exposure to new vocabulary and sentence structure in activities that involve them in using language for real purposes. Their understanding of language is supported by the use of visual aids (pictures, gestures, or symbols). Learning classroom routines helps students cope in the classroom, even when they may not yet understand all the language used.

Teachers need to recognize the difficulties faced by students learning a new language and enable them to use their new skills in a safe environment. These students may be more comfortable using English in a paired or small-group activity than speaking in front of the whole class. Making connections to their home language, culture, and community helps students feel welcomed and valued, whether they speak a language that is non-English or a dialect that is non-standard English.

Students learning English as a second language need
- frequent opportunities to talk
- multiple opportunities to explore ideas and concepts
- daily literacy routines
- connections that link school with their home language, culture, and community

Fay and Whaley (2004, 5) note that ESL students also need classrooms where teachers
- listen with heightened sensitivity
- refuse to make assumptions about what a student can or cannot do
- design lessons that are accessible to all
- recognize that for all the time their English-proficient students need to grow, their ESL students need that amount of time and much, much more

Volunteers and Paraprofessionals

Paraprofessionals and volunteers may help ESL students develop oral language by providing immediate feedback to what they say. For example,

- by revising the student's comment to a more conventional form

    S: He not gonna come.

    V: No, he's not going to come today.

- by elaborating on what the student said

    V: But I think he will be here tomorrow.

When feedback is provided, the intention is not that the student repeat the conventional form, as this disrupts the flow of the conversation.

Check It Out!

For more ideas on supporting ESL students, see the following resources: L. Allen. *First Steps Oral Language Resource Book* (Toronto: Irwin Publishing, 1994). This book has an excellent section titled "Supporting Diversity Through Oral Language" (191–204). It provides considerations for assessment, as well as suggestions for classroom practice.
K. Fay and S. Whaley. *Becoming One Community: Reading and Writing with English Language Learners* (Portland, ME: Stenhouse Publishers, 2004).

Closing Thoughts

Oral language is a cornerstone to success in school. Classrooms are language-rich environments where students need to be able to communicate effectively to learn. Students continue to develop their language knowledge as they collaborate with others, expand what they know about the world, and learn to read and write.

It is important that teachers consciously consider how they are developing students' oral language skills in the context of classroom literacy activities. Effective teachers consider these questions:

- What opportunities do students have to develop skills for social interaction and to learn to use language for different purposes?
- Are students expanding their vocabulary and schema knowledge by making connections between what they already know and what they hear, see, read, and write?
- Are they learning to understand and use more complex sentence structures as they read and write both fiction and nonfiction texts?
- Are they using what they know about the sound structure of words to investigate multisyllable words, looking for common prefixes, suffixes, base and root words?
- How are they using this knowledge to read and spell the words in their ever-increasing vocabulary?

See Reflecting on My Oral Language Program earlier in this chapter for further reflection prompts.

Grades 3 to 6 classrooms that provide opportunities for interaction and collaboration ensure multiple opportunities for language learning to occur. Students continue to benefit from frequent opportunities to talk, listen, and share their experiences. This chapter has provided several suggestions for supporting language development in the classroom. In Chapter 2: Reading Comprehension: Strategies That Work, as well as in later chapters that focus on writing and literacy learning across the curriculum and school day, teachers will find many links between the development of oral language skills and the development of literacy in the Grades 3 to 6 classroom curriculum.

Chapter 1

BLACKLINE MASTERS

BLM 1: Words in Context

BLM 2: Before I Read I ...

BLM 3: Before I Read I ... Bookmark

BLM 4: Literacy Home Links: How Families Can Support the "Talking" to "Reading and Writing" Connection

BLM 5: How Well Do I Know These Words?

BLM 6: Concept Ladder

Words in Context

Name: _____   Grade: _____   Date: _____

is not

is

is not

is

example

example

non-example

non-example

(Adapted from Allen 1999, 140)

Before I Read I ...

Name: _____ Grade: _____ Date: _____

Title: _____ Author: _____

Choose _____ of the following activities to do before you read your book. Think about which activities help you "get ready to read" the best.

☐ Read the title and book covers.

☐ Use the Three-Finger Rule to see if you have a "just right" book.
Challenging _____   Just right _____   Easy _____

☐ Make predictions about what might happen.

My predictions: _____

_____

☐ Write down three things you know about the topic.

1. _____

2. _____

3. _____

☐ Talk about the pictures or chapter headings.

I talked to _____ We talked about _____

☐ Read the headings, subheadings, bold print, captions, and diagrams if your book is an informational text.

☐ List some questions you have about the book.

_____

_____

☐ Set a purpose for reading.

My purpose for reading: _____

☐ Skim the first few pages and record any words that look challenging. If they are in bold print, check the glossary.

Words I checked: _____

Now you're ready to read the book!
Enjoy!

(Adapted from Reithaug 1998, 71)

Before I Read I ... Bookmark

Before I Read I ...

- Read the title and book covers.
- Use the Three-Finger Rule.

- Make predictions.

- Make connections (What do I know about the topic?).
- Talk about the pictures or chapter headings with a friend.
- Read the headings, subheadings, bold print, captions, and diagrams.

- Think about questions I have about the book.
- Set a purpose for reading.
- Skim the first few pages and record any challenging words. If they are in bold print, I check the glossary.

  Now I'm ready to read the book!

Before I Read I ...

- Read the title and book covers.
- Use the Three-Finger Rule.

- Make predictions.

- Make connections (What do I know about the topic?).
- Talk about the pictures or chapter headings with a friend.
- Read the headings, subheadings, bold print, captions, and diagrams.

- Think about questions I have about the book.
- Set a purpose for reading.
- Skim the first few pages and record any challenging words. If they are in bold print, I check the glossary.

  Now I'm ready to read the book!

(Adapted from Reithaug 1998, 71)

How Families Can Support the "Talking" to "Reading and Writing" Connection

Children learn to read and write by using the same language skills they use when they talk— the words they know and their ability to put their ideas into sentences. The background knowledge they use develops from the experiences they have had, the texts they have read (books, articles, poetry, and so on), and the conversations in which they have taken part. Families can help their children improve their language, reading, and writing skills through conversations as their children read and write.

What to Do Before, During, and After Reading

Talk about the text selection **before** your child reads it ...

- Look at the title, the cover, and any pictures, headings, diagrams, and so on.
- Talk about what it might be about (making a prediction).
- Think about what words might be in the text (based on the topic).
- Discuss questions that the selection might answer.
- When reading a chapter book, briefly talk about what has happened so far, before reading the next chapter.

Talk about the text selection **while** your child reads it ...

- Does it remind your child of a similar personal experience? How was the experience the same or different?
- How do your child's original predictions change?
- What surprises your child while reading? (Example: I didn't know that; I didn't think that would happen.)
- What does your child ask or wonder about while reading?

(In fiction, it is important not to stop too often as too many interruptions can undermine your child's understanding.)

Talk about the text selection **after** your child reads it ...

- "How did this text selection match what you predicted?"
- "How did the text answer questions you had about the topic?"
- "What questions do you have about the text or the topic now?"
- "Did the text selection remind you of anything in your own life?"

What to Do About Writing

- Encourage your child to write letters, cards, or e-mails to family members.
- Talk about what your child is going to write, whether for the purpose of a school assignment or personal communication, so that you can help expand the ideas and language used.

How Well Do I Know These Words?

Name: _____ Grade: _____ Date: _____

Title: _____ Author: _____

Directions: First, read the words at the bottom of the page silently. After you read each one, write the words from the bottom of this page in the column that best describes what you know about each one.

Don't Know at All	Have Seen or Heard—Don't Know Meaning	I Think I Know the Meaning	I Know a Meaning

(Allen 1999, 19)

Concept Ladder

Name: _____ Grade: _____ Date: _____

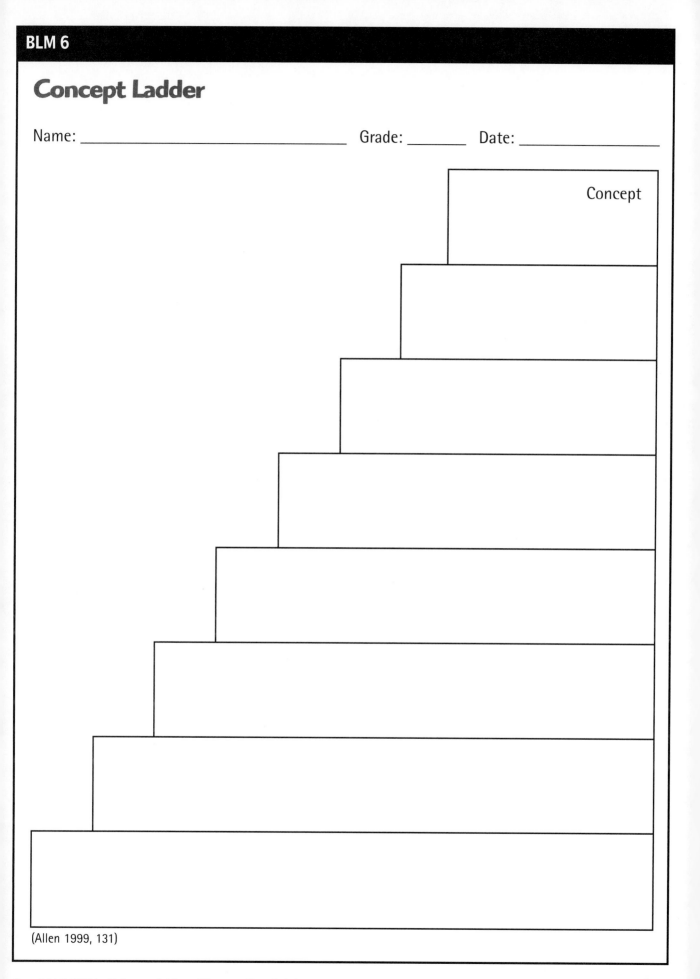

Concept

(Allen 1999, 131)

Chapter 1

ASSESSMENT BLACKLINE MASTERS

Assessment BLM 1: Oral Language Checklist
Assessment BLM 2: Oral Language Summary Sheet
Assessment BLM 3: Self-Assessment—My Speaking Skills
Assessment BLM 4: Listening Skills Checklist
Assessment BLM 5: Self-Assessment—My Listening Skills

Oral Language Checklist

Name: _____ Grade: _____ Date: _____

Teacher: _____ School: _____

The following language skills can generally be observed during a variety of classroom activities throughout the school day. Oral language observations can be organized on this checklist and transferred to Assessment BLM 2: Oral Language Summary Sheet.

	Most of the Time	Some of the Time	Not Yet
Speaking and Listening Behaviours (Pragmatics)			
1. Participates in whole-group language activities (e.g., discussion, shared reading, and read-alouds)			
2. Contributes effectively to small-group discussions			
3. Relates what is read or heard to personal experiences			
4. Speaks clearly and fluently			
5. Uses language that is sensitive to others' feelings			
6. Uses effective conversational skills • with a partner • in a group			
7. Interrupts appropriately			
8. Understands and uses appropriate body language • in conversations • in oral presentations			
9. Is beginning to indicate disagreement constructively			
10. Understands classroom language and follows classroom routines			
11. Ignores distractions and focuses on listening task			
12. Recognizes when something is not understood			
13. Asks for clarification or help when necessary			
14. Asks appropriate questions in response to what was heard			
15. Shows flexibility with communication (e.g., matching language style and language used to the audience, topic, or situation)			
16. Is able to engage an audience purposefully and effectively			

	Most of the Time	Some of the Time	Not Yet
Knowledge of Language Meaning (Semantics)			
17. Is developing broader understanding of vocabulary			
18. Uses descriptive language effectively			
19. Uses compare-and-contrast language to tell how items and ideas are the same and different			
20. Understands and uses figurative and multiple-meaning language appropriately			
21. Gives and follows multistep directions			
22. Retells story information, including characters and key story events			
23. Is able to talk about the main idea and supporting details in fiction and nonfiction texts			
24. Makes appropriate inferences from what is read			
25. Uses language effectively to explain and justify opinions and points of view			
26. Uses language for self-reflection and self-assessment			
Knowledge of Sentence Structure (Syntax)			
27. Uses complete sentences when speaking			
28. Uses compound sentences (e.g., joining ideas with *and, or,* or *but*)			
29. Uses complex sentences (e.g., joining ideas with *because, if, when, after, before,* and *although*)			
Knowledge of the Sound Structure of Language (Phonology)			
30. Uses all sounds correctly in oral language			
31. Identifies syllables, rimes, and sounds in spoken words			
32. Manipulates word parts (syllables, rimes, and sounds) to make word analogies			
33. Uses phonological awareness skills effectively for word solving in reading and writing			

Oral Language Summary Sheet

Teacher: _____

Grade: _____

Date: _____

School: _____

Transfer all results from Assessment BLM 1: Oral Language Checklist to this summary sheet using the key that follows.

Key

M = Most of the Time

S = Some of the Time

N = Not Yet

- Is an active participant in classroom language activities (1, 2)
- Shares personal experiences and feelings related to classroom topics and book discussions (3)
- Generally speaks clearly and fluently (4)
- Understands and uses appropriate social conventions for conversations (5, 6, 7, 8, 9)
- Understands classroom language and follows classroom routines (10, 11)
- Monitors comprehension (12, 13)
- Asks appropriate questions (14)
- Adjusts communication style to audience and topic (15, 16)
- Understands and uses a wide vocabulary (17, 18, 19)
- Understands and uses figurative and multiple-meaning language (20)
- Understands and follows multistep directions (21)
- Can retell a story and give information about a topic (22, 23)
- Uses language to explain, justify, infer, and reflect (24, 25, 26)
- Understands and uses appropriate sentence structure (27, 28, 29)
- Uses speech that is understandable, producing speech sounds correctly (30)
- Demonstrates phonological awareness skills (31, 32, 33)

Students' Names

Self-Assessment—My Speaking Skills

Name: _____ Grade: _____ Date: _____

	Most of the Time	Some of the Time	Not Yet
• I look at the person I'm speaking to.			
• I speak clearly and at an appropriate rate.			
• I speak loudly enough, but not too loud.			
• I know how to take a speaking turn.			
• I know how to stay on the same topic.			
• I know how to change topics smoothly.			
• I recognize and use body language effectively.			
• I let the person know when I am finished speaking.			
• I interrupt appropriately.			

Two things I do well as a speaker: _____

_____

_____

_____

_____

_____

One thing I need to improve: _____

_____

_____

_____

_____

_____

_____

_____

Listening Skills Checklist

Name: _____ Grade: _____ Date: _____

Teacher: _____ School: _____

Hearing History	Yes	No
Student has a history of hearing loss		
Student has a history of middle ear infections		
Student has had a recent hearing assessment		

	Most of the Time	Some of the Time	Not Yet
Listening Environment			
• Listens effectively one-to-one			
• Listens effectively in small-group situations			
• Listens effectively in whole-class activities			
• Recognizes classroom cues for listening			
List specific cues used to signal "time to listen."			
• Responds to specific cues to focus listening behaviour			
List specific cues used to signal "focus."			
Purpose for Listening			
• Identifies purpose for listening			
• Listens effectively when			
– listening to a story			
– listening to factual information			
– listening to instructions			
Listening Behaviours			
• Looks at speaker			
• Uses appropriate body language (e.g., nodding, leaning in)			
• Acknowledges speaker (e.g., says "uh, huh" or "hmm")			
• Responds by offering a comment or question			
• Identifies listening distractions			
• Has strategies to deal with listening distractions			

Self-Assessment—My Listening Skills

Name: _____ Grade: _____ Date: _____

	Most of the Time	Some of the Time	Not Yet
• I look at the speaker.			
• I think about what is being said.			
• I know what I'm listening for (my purpose).			
• I ask when I don't understand something.			
• I know the things that distract me when I listen.			
• I know how to handle the distractions.			
• I use body language that shows I am listening.			
• I show respect to the speaker.			

I listen best when ... _____

_____

_____

Two things I do well as a listener: _____

_____

_____

_____

_____

One thing I need to improve: _____

_____

_____

_____

_____

Chapter 2

READING COMPREHENSION: STRATEGIES THAT WORK

Miriam Trehearne
Roz Doctorow

"As teachers of literacy ... we must have as an instructional goal, regardless of age, grade, or achievement level, the development of students as purposeful, engaged, and ultimately independent comprehenders.... No matter what grade level you teach, no matter what content you teach, no matter what texts you teach with, your goal is to improve students' comprehension and understanding."*

"How important it is to remember that comprehension is the essence of reading and that it has to be taught and cannot be left to chance!"**

* Rasinski et al. 2000, 1
** Opitz and Eldridge 2004, 772

Find Out More About Reading Comprehension

Beck, I.L., M.G. McKeown, R.L. Hamilton, and L. Kucan. *Questioning the Author: An Approach for Enhancing Student Engagement with Text.* Newark, DE: International Reading Association, 1997.

Bergman, Janet L. "SAIL—A Way to Success and Independence for Low-Achieving Readers." *The Reading Teacher* 45(8): 598–602.

Center for Advancement of Learning. Learning Strategies Database: Background Information on Reading Comprehension. Available from http://www.muskingum.edu/~cal/database/general/reading.html#Background.

Cornett, Claudia E. "Beyond Retelling the Plot: Student-Led Discussions." In *Teaching Comprehension and Exploring Multiple Literacies.* Edited by T. Rasinski et al., 56–58. Newark, DE: International Reading Association, 2000.

Daniels, H. *Literature Circles: Voice and Choice in the Student-Centered Classroom.* Portland, ME: Stenhouse Publishing, 1994.

Davey, B. "Think Aloud: Modeling the Cognitive Processes of Reading Comprehension." *The Journal of Reading* 27(1): 44–47.

Duke, Nell K., and P. David Pearson. "Effective Practices for Developing Reading Comprehension." In *What Research Has to Say About Reading Instruction.* Edited by A.E. Farstrup and S.J. Samuels, 205–42. Newark, DE: International Reading Association, 2002.

Evans, Karen S. *Literature Discussion Groups in the Intermediate Grades: Dilemmas and Possibilities.* Newark, DE: International Reading Association, 2001.

Fehring, Heather, and Pam Green, eds. *Critical Literacy A Collection of Articles from the Australian Literacy Educators' Association.* Newark, DE: International Reading Association, 2001.

Harvey, Stephanie, and Anne Goudvis. *Strategies That Work: Teaching Comprehension to Enhance Understanding.* Portland, ME: Stenhouse Publishers, 2000.

Hirsch, E.D., Jr. "Reading Comprehension Requires Knowledge of Words and the World." *The American Educator* (Spring 2003): 10–29.

Hoyt, Linda. "Many Ways of Knowing: Using Drama, Oral Interactions and the Visual Arts to Enhance Reading Comprehension." *The Reading Teacher* 45(8): 580–84.

Keene, Ellin, and Susan Zimmermann. *Mosaic of Thought: Teaching Comprehension in a Reader's Workshop.* Portsmouth, NH: Heinemann, 1997.

McLaughlin, Maureen, and Mary Beth Allen. *Guided Comprehension in Action Lessons for Grades 3–8.* Newark, DE: International Reading Association, 2002.

Oczkus, Lori D. *Reciprocal Teaching at Work Strategies for Improving Reading Comprehension.* Newark, DE: International Reading Association, 2003.

Palincsar, A.S., and A.L. Brown. "Reciprocal Teaching of Comprehension: Fostering and Monitoring Activities." In *Cognition and Instruction 1.* 117–75. Mahwah, NJ: Lawrence Erlbaum Associates Inc., 1984.

Planet Book Club at http://www.planetbookclub.com.

Pressley, Michael. "Metacognition and Self-Regulated Comprehension." In *What Research Has to Say About Reading Instruction.* 3rd ed. Edited by Alan E. Farstrup and S. Jay Samuels, 291–309. Newark, DE: International Reading Association, 2002.

Pressley, Michael. "What Should Comprehension Instruction Be the Instruction Of?" In *Handbook of Reading Research, Volume III.* Edited by Michael L. Kamil et al., 545–61. Mahwah, NJ: Lawrence Erlbaum Associates, 2000.

Raphael, T. "Teaching Question and Answer Relationships, Revisited." *Reading Teacher* 39(6): 516–22.

Snow, C. *Reading for Understanding: Toward an R&D Program in Reading Comprehension.* Prepared for the RAND Education Office of Educational Research and Improvement, Santa Monica, CA: U.S. Department of Education, 2002.

Wilhelm, Jeffrey D. *Improving Comprehension with Think-Aloud Strategies.* Portsmouth, NH: Heinemann, 2001.

Research on Reading Comprehension

Reading is comprehension. "Comprehension involves what the reader knows as well as the nature of the text itself. It involves the type of text to be read—narrative, expository, poetry, etc. It involves the purpose for reading" (Rasinski et al. 2000, 1). The sociocultural context at home and at school also affects comprehension and all other learning.

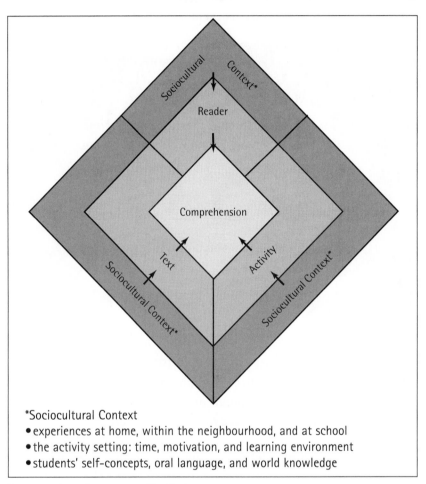

*Sociocultural Context
• experiences at home, within the neighbourhood, and at school
• the activity setting: time, motivation, and learning environment
• students' self-concepts, oral language, and world knowledge

(Adapted from Snow 2002, Fig. S-1)

Reading without comprehension is simply word calling. Effective comprehenders not only make sense of the text, but are also able to use the information it contains. They are able to think thoughtfully or deeply and to make personal connections as they analyze and question what they are reading, hearing, and seeing. Evidence from the National Assessment of Educational Progress (2000), however, indicates that most students' reading comprehension scores remain low despite many years of concentrated efforts to improve instruction (Hirsch 2003). However, this need not be the case.

> Reading without understanding is like eating without digesting.

Comprehension: Thoughtful Literacy

To teach comprehension is to teach thoughtful literacy. **Thoughtful literacy** is not a separate kind of literacy, but the umbrella for all literacy learning across the curriculum. Literacy is much more than being able to read a menu, fill in a simple form, or recall details from fiction or nonfiction text. It is about making connections with the text. Students who have mastered thoughtful literacy can do more than merely regurgitate the text: they can read, write, listen, speak, view, and represent in complex ways. Teachers whose focus is thoughtful literacy will invariably help their students to be critically literate: to question the attitudes, values, and beliefs that lie beneath the surface of written, spoken, and visual texts. Their students become aware that all texts are created from a certain perspective or bias and examine each text to see how it positions them as they read, listen, or view.

Why Is Teaching Critical Literacy So Important?

Many people read or listen to texts without questioning or analyzing the author's viewpoint, position, or purpose. They simply accept what is presented to them, especially what appears in print, as fact. Now, with more and more avenues for accessing information (e.g., computers, online networks, electronic games, the media, and music), it is crucial that students learn to question information. They need to be aware that all texts are written from a perspective and that it is important to examine the texts (including words, diagrams, photos, graphs, and charts) for issues of bias, stereotyping, and social justice.

Critical Thinking and Critical Literacy: Are They the Same?

Critical thinking and critical literacy are not the same, although they are related. Critical thinking involves logical and reflective thinking and reasoning, which helps one decide what to believe or do. A person who thinks critically asks appropriate questions, gathers and sorts through relevant information, reasons logically, and makes decisions as to how to think and live in the world. Critical literacy requires critical thinking with a specific focus on social issues and social justice.

Teachers, too, must be critical thinkers to develop critical literacy skills, especially in the area of educational research. When examining educational research, teachers will benefit from asking some key questions.

"Being a 'critical' citizen means questioning what one hears or reads and evaluating those texts for accuracy.... Analytic skills are essential for looking 'below the surface' to determine what a writer is trying to do. And critiquing skills are necessary for the reader to evaluate what the text is saying."

FOUNTAS AND PINNELL 2001, 368

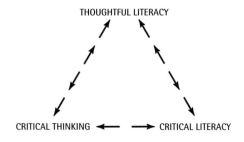

Knowing how to think thoughtfully (rather than *what* to think) is the key to all learning. Effective teachers set up a classroom environment that promotes critical thinking and critical literacy as students read, write, listen, speak, view, and represent across all subject areas across the day.

Critical literacy does not happen by osmosis or chance.

See Developing Critically Literate Students later in this chapter, as well as Chapter 3: Writing: The Reading–Writing Connection and Chapter 4: Literacy Learning Across the Curriculum for more information on critical literacy.

Effective Comprehension Teaching and Learning

Research offers guidance to teachers on how best to support their students' reading comprehension. The four key features of comprehension instruction are the amount of time engaged in reading, explicit strategy instruction, rich talk (discussion), and writing. Students not only need to read a great deal, but they also need to be taught a small number of effective comprehension strategies. In addition, students require many opportunities to solidify comprehension by discussing and writing about what they are reading, hearing, and seeing.

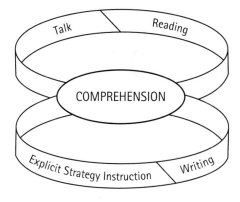

A research study conducted at the end of the 1970s (Durkin 1978–79, 481–533) found that from Grade 3 onward students received very little instruction in reading comprehension. Instead, teachers focused on comprehension testing. Once a reading was completed, students were often required to respond to questions based on what was read.

Researchers observed this same practice at the end of the 1990s. "Given the large volume of research on the topic in the past quarter century, there has been the potential for a revolution in schools with respect to comprehension instruction. Even so, no revolution has occurred. For example, when my colleagues and I observed fourth- and fifth-grade classrooms in the late 1990s, we, too, saw little comprehension instruction but many teachers posing post reading comprehension questions" (Pressley 2001). In other words, comprehension was more often assessed than taught.

Why Is So Little Comprehension Instruction Occurring in Classrooms?

The Language Arts curriculum (and indeed other curricula) is full, even stretched. Teachers often have a difficult time "fitting it all in." Also, it is often faster and easier to teach students to decode than to try to get inside their heads to improve understanding. For example, teaching a student to infer or summarize is generally more challenging than teaching a word family, prefix, or suffix. "Sometimes ... comprehension instruction is delayed until the later elementary grades, even though a focus on comprehension is desirable from the very beginning of reading instruction" (Snow 2002, 5).

Many students (including **ESL** students) may be able to decode at very high levels. However, effective decoding and comprehension are not always synonymous. It is important for teachers to distinguish the word callers from the fluent readers.

Finally, teachers are often unsure which of the many comprehension strategies will make a difference. Effective teachers now know, however, that a few—and only a few—research-based strategies have consistently proven their worth. And, since reading is comprehension, students' reading will improve with more selective and effective comprehension strategy instruction.

Factors That Affect Reading Comprehension

Research indicates that many students, especially those who come from economically disadvantaged backgrounds, become less effective readers as they move from the early to the upper-elementary grades (Chall, Jacobs, and Baldwin 1990). In other words, there is a slump in their reading beginning around the fourth grade and often increasing through high school. To understand the causes of the "fourth-grade slump," it is important to examine the factors that affect reading comprehension in general.

Key factors that influence reading comprehension are

- students' reading attitudes (motivation and interests)
- time truly engaged in reading
- effective comprehension strategy instruction across all subject areas
- vocabulary and world knowledge
- fluency
- type of text or genre
- opportunities for rich talk and written response
- understanding and implementing the strategies used by effective readers

Students' Reading Attitudes

Attitudes strongly influence motivation and affect achievement in reading. Students who see themselves as readers have positive attitudes toward reading. They are motivated to read and they read for a variety of purposes (e.g., for enjoyment, to escape, to obtain new

---

"Comprehension instruction is best when it focuses on a few well-taught, well-learned strategies."

DUKE AND PEARSON 2002, 236

To reduce the effect of the fourth-, fifth-, or sixth-grade slump, teachers must begin in the early elementary grades.

"Research has shown that many children who read at the third-grade level in grade 3 will not automatically become proficient comprehenders in later grades."

SNOW 2002, XVII

information, to gain understanding of issues, to learn about themselves). These students also set goals for their reading and are engaged with texts. In short, they are more likely to read!

Some students, however, reach the upper elementary grades with the attitude or belief that reading is more about word calling than making meaning. Other students may know how to read effectively but choose not to. These students are often described as aliterate.

Students with poor attitudes toward reading will usually read only when they have to and will often "fake it" during independent reading. Due to their lack of reading experience, they will likely not be able to comprehend complex texts beyond a literal level.

Time Truly Engaged in Reading

In an extensive study of independent reading, Anderson, Wilson, and Fielding (1988) investigated a broad array of activities and their relationship to reading achievement and growth in reading. They found that the amount of time students spent in independent reading was the best predictor of reading achievement gain between Grades 2 and 5. Stanovich (1986) found that students who are able to read generally read more. As they read, they become better readers, improve their vocabularies, and enhance their knowledge of the language structure. Reluctant readers, most of whom are struggling, read very little and fall further and further behind. Stanovich calls this the Matthew Effect, and it is a likely contributing factor to the "fourth-grade slump."

However, there is a caution: "Not all students automatically improve their reading just because we give them time to read. If students are reading mostly difficult books, if they don't understand what they read, if no one is monitoring their progress, not much changes. I have been in far too many classrooms where students are staring at books they cannot and do not read and where sustained silent/independent reading is largely a waste of time" (Routman 2002, 84).

Effective Comprehension Strategy Instruction Across All Subject Areas

As mentioned earlier, there is little comprehension instruction occurring in most Language Arts classrooms. In addition, there tends to be less emphasis on comprehension instruction in subject-specific classrooms where teachers are focused on content (Snow 2002). It is important for all teachers to see themselves as reading teachers. (See Chapter 4: Literacy Learning Across the Curriculum for more information.)

Vocabulary and World Knowledge

The texts in Grades 4 through 8 tend to contain words and ideas that are beyond the students' own language and knowledge of the world. Jeanne Chall found that although students' language seemed to be sufficient for the first three grades, students were not prepared for the greater number of abstract, technical, and literary words encountered in the upper elementary grades. The language gap is yet another suggested contributing factor to the fourth-grade slump and the "chief cause of the achievement gap between socioeconomic groups" (Hirsch 2003, 10).

"Any reading program that substantially increases the amount of reading students do will impact their reading achievement."
Routman 2002, 83

Check It Out!

The study by Anderson, Wilson, and Fielding can also be found at http://www.eduplace.com/rdg/res/literacy/in_read1.html

"A great deal of research suggests that vocabulary and comprehension are inextricably linked. Thus, strategies related to ascertaining the meaning of unknown words, as well as general vocabulary building, are also essential to a strong program in comprehension instruction."

DUKE AND PEARSON 2002, 14

Check It Out!

Research from Nell Duke and David Pearson is available from http://www.scholastic.com/dodea/Module_1/resources/dodea_m1_pa_duke.pdf

"One possible reason for the fourth-grade slump may stem from lack of fluency and automaticity.... Lack of fluency tends to result, ultimately, in children's reading less and avoiding more difficult materials."

CHALL AND JACOBS 2003

"Although skilled and eventually fluent word recognition certainly facilitates comprehension, it is not enough."

PRESSLEY 2001

Research has demonstrated that comprehension improves as a function of vocabulary instruction (Pressley 2001). For vocabulary teaching to be effective, it needs to be explicit. Although students may learn vocabulary incidentally, without planned opportunities for vocabulary instruction, they may not have the breadth of experience to derive the meaning of new words in unknown contexts. The more exposure students have to a new word, the more their vocabulary knowledge increases. Although reading frequently is important, it is not enough to increase vocabulary knowledge. To really learn the meaning of a new word, students must repeatedly encounter and use the word.

Another important component of reading comprehension is world knowledge, particularly background knowledge that is relevant to the topic of the text. Researchers at the Center for the Study of Reading at the University of Illinois (among others) found that reading comprehension can be enhanced by a developing reader's prior knowledge. One way to do this is to provide readers with high-quality, information-rich texts, and then to help them relate what they already know to the texts. "[O]ne of the most effective ways to improve comprehension is to 'activate mental files' before reading" (Keene and Zimmermann 1997, 51). But some readers will need these mental files supported.

See also Chapter 1: Oral Language: Speaking, Listening, and Learning, for more on vocabulary development and activating prior knowledge.

Fluency

Fluent readers read smoothly, without hesitation, and with expression. Generally, this allows them to focus on meaning making, or comprehension.

To be able to understand what they read, students first need to be able to decode the words on the page. The goal is to have students develop the capacity to have automatic word recognition (automaticity) in order to help them become good comprehenders. "A first recommendation to educators who want to improve students' comprehension skills is to teach them to decode well.... Word-recognition skills must be developed to the point of fluency if comprehension benefits are to be maximized" (Pressley 2001).

Reading fluently and at a rate appropriate for the text enables effective readers to gain meaning from what they are reading. When readers focus on the mechanics of reading and read word by word, their comprehension is limited. They are often so concerned with saying all the words correctly that they lose track of what the words mean. "If decoding does not happen quickly, the decoded material will be forgotten before it is understood" (Hirsch 2003, 12).

Fluent readers incorporate a variety of reading strategies to understand what they are reading. Students with strong vocabulary and background knowledge more easily use syntax (grammar) and semantics (meaning) to help them figure out the words and read fluently. Phrasing and reading the punctuation also support comprehension. Additionally, fluent readers adjust the rate of their reading based on their purpose for reading, the form of text, and their interest in and background knowledge about the text. However, some students read too quickly, which can lessen comprehension.

Type of Text or Genre

Most students in Grades 3 to 6 are interested in and need opportunities to read a variety of different genres. Beyond novels, short stories, and poetry, they read content from textbooks, articles, the Internet, and other resource materials in school. They also read magazines, comics, trading cards, recipes, advertisements, environmental print, and online material (Doctorow, Bodiam, and McGowan 2003). Students read about music, movies, fashion, sports, and technology. They read about the environment, animals, inventions, and people living in other places. When students read for pleasure, they make choices based on a variety of criteria, including the difficulty of the text. "The results of the 1992 National Assessment of Educational Progress (NAEP) revealed that fourth graders who reported reading not only stories but also magazines and information books had the highest [reading] achievement" (Dreher 2000, 18).

See also Using Various Text Types and Genres in the Content Areas in Chapter 4: Literacy Learning Across the Curriculum.

By learning to recognize the structures of different types of texts, students will be better able to comprehend what they are reading. At some point around the fourth grade there is an abrupt move from reading and writing mainly narrative texts to reading and writing expository texts. As students advance through the grades, expository text plays an increasing role in their learning. The fourth-grade slump has been attributed, at least in part, to children not having enough exposure to expository text during the third grade. Topics must be compelling enough that both teachers and students want to talk about what they read.

The main goal is to develop students who want to read. Hooking them is the key. Magazines, a popular choice for adult readers, are one good option. Statistics show that 57 percent of Canadians read a magazine at least once a week (Canadian Magazine Publishers Association 2005).

"[We] need to place a far greater emphasis on nonfiction in early language-arts classes. This emphasis is essential for children to learn the words and concepts they need to understand newspapers, magazines, and books addressed to the general public."

CHALL IN HIRSCH 2003, 21

Factors That Affect Comprehension

Fiction	Nonfiction
• Tells a story	• Provides information
• Vocabulary is more familiar	• Vocabulary is specialized and technical
• Reader needs to connect with characters	• Reader needs to interact with subject matter
• Holds reader's attention with plot	• Holds reader's attention by the structure, organization, and content of the text
• Usually bases themes on reader's experiences	• Often shares unfamiliar abstract concepts that are concisely presented
• Has a distinctive writing style	• Has concise content-laden writing
• Is mainly intended to entertain	• Presents material to expand knowledge and solve problems
• Allows fairly rapid reading	• Requires slower, more flexible rate, and constant need to adjust rate
• Conveys meaning mainly through words	• Often uses graphic aids (graphs, charts, tables, maps)
• Is more personal	• Often written in third person

(Adapted from State of Wisconsin, Wisconsin Governor's Literary Education and Reading Network Source)

"*Children's comprehension of text and topics, as well as their repertoires of strategies, grow as a result of conversations about text.*"

CIERA 1998, 4

Opportunities for Rich Talk and Written Response

Talk is the cornerstone for reading comprehension, especially for students in Grades 3 to 6, because they are spending more time reading for information and for learning. Talk with adults and other students plays a critical role in helping students clarify meaning and extend their understanding of texts that contain new concepts, ideas, and information.

It is important that students make personal connections to texts, not simply recall or summarize them; group discussions and conversations help students to do this. Students must explain how they know and make sense of the passages being discussed. Sharing their understanding through talk enables students to learn thinking strategies.

Teachers encourage talk by developing classroom discussions that focus on interpretation or constructing ideas rather than on giving right or wrong answers. In this kind of discussion, teachers assume that listeners have something to say beyond the answers teachers already know. Student-led book clubs and book talks offer authentic ways for discussion to occur. (See later in this chapter for more on these topics, as well as Chapter 1: Oral Language: Speaking, Listening, and Learning.) Research indicates that cooperative learning activities for students with mixed levels of reading ability can help students to improve their comprehension, specifically higher-level reasoning (Klinger, Vaughan, and Shumm 1998).

Writing also supports comprehension and helps students reveal what they comprehend.

How Writing Supports Comprehension

As a prereading activity, writing helps students to

- call up background knowledge
- relate the new knowledge from their writing task to their prior experience
- make predictions

As a during-reading activity, writing helps students to

- keep track of characters
- follow a story line
- make predictions

As a post-reading activity, writing helps students to

- elaborate on the text and their understanding of it
- become more sensitive to different topics or characteristics of text
- understand the text more deeply
- retain what they have read

See Chapter 3: Writing: The Reading–Writing Connection for more on how writing can support comprehension.

Understanding and Implementing the Strategies Used by Effective Readers

Many studies over the past 20 years have come to be known as "proficient reader research." This research set out to identify the reading strategies used most frequently by successful readers. What follows are the general characteristics exhibited by more proficient readers and less proficient readers.

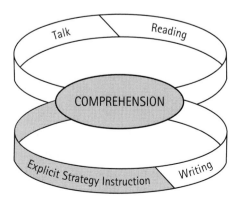

Characteristics of More Proficient and Less Proficient Readers

Before reading, more proficient readers ...	Before reading, less proficient readers ...
• have goals in mind and know their purpose for reading	• do not know why they are reading
• preview text (title, pictures, headings, drawings)	• start reading without thinking about the topic
• reflect (and often share) what they know about the topic	• do not preview the text
• make predictions about the text	• do not make predictions
• use various strategies to suit the text (e.g., fiction and nonfiction)	• read all text (e.g., fiction and nonfiction) the same way
• may decide to read all, some, or none of the text	• do not think about how much they will read
During reading, more proficient readers ...	**During reading, less proficient readers ...**
• continue to reflect on the text, anticipate, and make predictions	• may not know whether or not they understand the text
• confirm or correct predictions	• do not confirm or correct predictions
• monitor comprehension	• do not monitor their own comprehension
• use fix-up strategies when comprehension breaks down	• seldom use fix-up strategies
• read selectively by deciding what to read carefully or quickly, what not to read, and what to reread	• often give up or read on without understanding meaning, and do not revisit the text
• use text structures and text features to support meaning	• may not use text structures and text features to support meaning
• generate questions about text	• rarely generate questions about text
• react intellectually and emotionally to text (reader response)	• frequently do not make personal connections to the text
After reading, more proficient readers ...	**After reading, less proficient readers ...**
• decide if goals were achieved	• do not know what they have read
• reflect on how text matched or did not match predictions	• do not confirm or correct predictions
• compare characters, incidents, content (nonfiction) to self, other texts, the world	• do not make personal connections
• summarize major idea(s)	• do not summarize major ideas
• may seek additional information	• do not seek additional information
• react to text intellectually and/or emotionally (reader response)	• frequently do not react to text intellectually and/or emotionally

"Surprisingly, many of the studies that examined the thinking of proficient readers pointed to only seven or eight thinking strategies used consistently by proficient readers. Even more surprisingly, the researchers described the same seven or eight strategies in their findings."

<small>KEENE AND ZIMMERMANN 1997, 21</small>

The studies found that the most critical and overarching comprehension strategy is for students to be mindful of their thinking as they read. For example, when effective readers are having difficulty understanding what a piece of text means, they stop reading, think about why they might be having trouble understanding, and then try a fix-up strategy to help them understand before continuing. They monitor their comprehension. In other words, students need to learn how to think *metacognitively* in order to become proficient and thoughtful comprehenders of any kind of text.

Effective Comprehension Strategies

Students who enter third or fourth grade with limited exposure to effective comprehension strategies will likely experience a reading slump. For most students, it is imperative that teachers provide strategy instruction by modelling, demonstrating, and explaining, often through think-alouds. Students then need to apply these strategies through much shared, guided, and independent reading. (See The Think-Aloud—The Best Way to Teach Strategies and Gradual Release of Responsibility later in this chapter.)

Metacognition, or thinking about one's own thinking, is an umbrella term given to the following eight strategies for improving text comprehension. Each thinking strategy is a variation of metacognition (Keene and Zimmermann 1997).

- monitoring comprehension
- using narrative and expository text structures
- visually representing text using graphic and semantic organizers
- retelling, summarizing, synthesizing, inferring
- generating questions
- answering questions
- using prior knowledge/predicting
- using mental imagery (visualizing)

Use of these strategies requires students to think about their thinking and will assist them with improving their listening and viewing comprehension as well.

Using metacognitive (or thinking) strategies improves reading, listening, and viewing comprehension.

Monitoring Comprehension—The Number One Strategy

When students monitor their comprehension (or metacomprehend) as they read, they determine how well they are making sense of the text and what to do when their comprehension breaks down.

Weak comprehenders often don't realize where or when they don't understand. They just keep reading! Students need to know that reading must *always* make sense. When comprehension breaks down, it is important to use appropriate fix-up strategies. Students need to determine if a word has been incorrectly decoded or if a word or sentence has been misunderstood given the context. They also need to review whether they understand how the text is organized. Loss of interest or concentration also affects comprehension.

For more information, refer to Monitoring Comprehension—The Number One Strategy under Linking Assessment to Instruction later in this chapter.

Monitoring comprehension means

- being aware of what is understood
- being aware of where and when understanding breaks down
- using appropriate fix-up strategies to restore comprehension

Using Narrative and Expository Text Structures

Different kinds of texts are organized in different ways. The organization of most fiction texts is familiar to students in Grades 3 to 6. They know that the story will have a beginning, a middle, and an end. It will have at least one problem and solution and will involve one or more characters. The students know about setting, plot, and main idea.

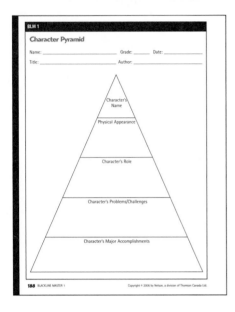

However, by the time students are in Grades 3 to 6, they are exposed to many more forms of writing, including poetry, content-area textbooks, magazines, and information from the Internet. Many nonfiction texts reflect a variety of text features, which may include different levels of headings, words in bold or italicized print, diagrams, graphics, tables of contents, indexes, and glossaries. Text is often presented in a nonlinear format, particularly on the Internet where text is hotlinked.

To become successful, proficient readers, students need to be exposed to, and learn about, a variety of text formats.

See also Using Narrative and Expository Text Structures under Linking Assessment to Instruction later in this chapter.

Visually Representing Text Using Graphic and Semantic Organizers

Graphic and semantic organizers help readers remember what they have read. They are an effective way to help students represent information from both narrative and informational texts and to concretely manage, retain, and recall abstract information. English as a Second Language (**ESL**) students, or other English Language Learners (ELL) and students with learning disabilities particularly benefit from their use. The visual representation of text content is an effective, non-verbal approach to interpreting what has been read. It is important, however, not to bombard students with organizers; rather, help them learn how and where to strategically use a few organizers effectively.

Students need to be able to strategically select an appropriate organizer to help them comprehend the text they are reading. Organizers include semantic maps or webs, story and character maps, Venn diagrams, and KWLM charts.

For more information, see Visually Representing Text Using Graphic and Semantic Organizers under Linking Assessment to Instruction later in this chapter.

BLM 1: Character Pyramid
BLM 2: Character Trait Map
BLM 8: Story Grammar
BLM 10: Plot Organizer
BLM 11: Main Idea and Supporting Details

Retelling, Summarizing, Synthesizing, Inferring

Retelling and summarizing are important strategies for developing student comprehension and oral language proficiency. Retelling is not, however, simply a listing of events from memory. Rather, it is an opportunity for students to select what was important to them from the text, make personal connections, and share that information either orally or in writing. When students retell, they

- identify what is important from what they have read
- provide the information in a succinct, logical order

- provide only essential information, often through synthesis
- relate what they have read to their personal experiences

A retelling is often described as a personal summary.

Summarizing is a step beyond retelling; it often involves condensing a portion of the text into a manageable chunk (Zwiers 2004) and is an important study skill technique. A summary provides the gist or essence of what has been read or heard, and may consist of only a sentence or two. Summarizing helps students to improve their grasp of the main idea, an important skill in comprehension, but it may also include making references to personal experiences or other texts.

Retelling and summarizing also incorporate students' ability to infer—that is, to read between the lines—in order to provide a more insightful, synthesized summary. When students infer, they go beyond the literal meaning to what is implied. They use their own experiences and background knowledge to help them make sense of, and gain deeper insights into, the text. Readers might make inferences about the deeper, underlying meaning of a text character's emotions and feelings, the significance of various events, and lessons that the author may be trying to teach. Retelling and summarizing also reveal to the teacher what students understand: information that can then be used to guide instruction.

Synthesis at a Glance

Synthesis involves combining different sources of information in a way that makes sense. Readers incorporate what they know about the topic from previous texts or experiences and make **text-to-text**, **text-to-self**, or **text-to-world** connections. Whenever students retell or summarize a text, they put their own spin on the information, synthesizing it.

Synthesis at work is described in this way:

- Readers monitor overall meaning, important concepts, and themes in text as they read, understanding that their thinking evolves in the process.
- Readers retell what they have read as a way of synthesizing.
- Readers capitalize on opportunities to share, recommend, and criticize books they have read.
- Readers extend their synthesis of the literal meaning of a text to the inferential level.
- Readers synthesize to understand more clearly what they have read.

(Miller 2002, 171)

See Retelling, Summarizing, Synthesizing, Inferring under Linking Assessment to Instruction later in this chapter.

Generating Questions

Generating or asking questions about a text helps students clarify their thinking and better understand what they are reading. Effective readers are always asking themselves questions; less effective readers rarely question. Questioning can occur before, during, and after reading. The kind of questions asked often depends on the genre of the text.

Readers ask questions to

- clarify meaning
- speculate about text yet to be read
- determine an author's style, intent, content, or format
- focus attention on specific components of the text
- locate a specific answer in the text
- consider rhetorical questions inspired by the text

(Miller 2002, 126)

Answering Questions

Students benefit from responding to questions that they, their peers, or the teacher generates before, occasionally during, and after they read. When reading fiction aloud to students, few questions should be asked during the read-aloud so as not to interrupt the flow and meaning making of the text.

Thinking about answers and listening to others explain their answers help students understand the text. It is important for students to not only be asked questions, but also to be taught how to find the answers. When higher-order responses are required, students learn to pay attention to more than just factual details. Higher-order thinking questions require students to analyze, infer, generalize, and synthesize what they are reading. Students learn that not all questions have one answer, and some answers are not found in the text.

See Generating Questions, Answering Questions under Linking Assessment to Instruction later in this chapter for much more information.

Remember: The kinds of answers you get depend on the questions you ask.

Using Prior Knowledge/Predicting

Predicting happens before, during, and after reading. Students use information from their own knowledge base to make sense of what they're reading. This base includes personal knowledge, knowledge of reading, and world knowledge. By making connections with what they already know, students are better able to understand new ideas and information presented in a text. Since students' life experiences are diverse, all students bring their own ideas to the text being read. This diversity of backgrounds accounts for differences in students' understanding of the same text. Each reader "personalizes" the text. (See Using Prior Knowledge/Predicting under Linking Assessment to Instruction later in this chapter.)

Using Mental Imagery (Visualizing)

By visualizing, or making mental images, students are able to relate what they are reading (abstract) to something concrete—a visual image, a feeling, a sound, a smell, or a taste. This ability to "image" helps anchor new ideas in the students' minds and enables them to recall the ideas in a visual way when appropriate. (See Using Mental Imagery (Visualizing) under Linking Assessment to Instruction later in this chapter.)

"The strategy of visualizing refers to the mind's capacity to imagine what is being suggested by the words on a page."

STATE OF WISCONSIN, WISCONSIN GOVERNOR'S LITERARY EDUCATION AND READING NETWORK SOURCE

Check It Out!

Michael Pressley. "What Should Comprehension Instruction Be the Instruction Of?" In *Handbook of Reading Research, Volume III.* Edited by Michael L. Kamil et al. (Mahwah, NJ: Lawrence Erlbaum Associates, 2000), 545–61.

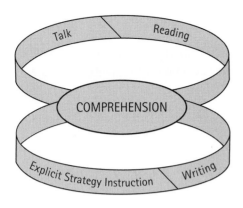

"Research indicates that using longer instructional blocks often results in productive and complicated student work being achieved."

Allington and Cunningham 2002, 122

Check It Out!

L.G. Katz and S.C. Chard, *Engaging Children's Minds: The Project Approach.* 2nd ed. (Westport, CT: Ablex, 2000).

Take Time to Teach Reading in Grades 3 to 6

Students in Grades 3 to 6 have spent their early years in school learning about texts and how they work. Unfortunately, many of them have had decoding emphasized at the expense of comprehension. Although upper elementary students know a great deal about reading, they need to be taught comprehension strategies across all subject areas. They also need to be provided with many opportunities to read and to make sense of what they read (hear or view) as they write and discuss.

The goal of the reading program for students in Grades 3 to 6 is to help them become thoughtful, independent readers who choose to read from a wide range of texts for a wide variety of purposes. To achieve this goal, students need long blocks of time devoted to language arts on a daily basis. At least two hours a day results in less time lost in transitions and more opportunities for students to integrate their learning as they read, write, speak, listen, view, and represent.

Students in upper elementary school need more time to read more complex texts and to respond to them. They also need more opportunities to integrate their knowledge across subject areas. A Social Studies or Science-based read-aloud and any form of response (e.g., dramatic, discussion, art) allow students to see that the same strategies taught in language arts are also used across the day. In addition, integration, especially using the project approach and lasting four to six weeks, allows teachers to "fit it all in" in a meaningful way. The project approach allows for an in-depth investigation of a real-world topic, such as pollution. Students delve deeper (rather than broader) into their learning.

Instructional approaches to support a comprehensive language arts program include oral language (talk); read-alouds; shared, guided, and independent reading; word study; and shared, guided, and independent writing. These approaches are brought to life in Chapter 4: Literacy Learning Across the Curriculum and in Chapter 5: In the Classroom: Making It Work.

Assessment

Assessing Reading Comprehension

A student's level of listening comprehension is generally a good predictor of reading comprehension potential. If students do not understand what they have heard, it is unlikely that they will be able to comprehend the same words in written text. Students' word and world (background) knowledge strongly affect their ability to both decode and comprehend. Therefore, it is a good idea to begin by assessing their level of listening comprehension (see Chapter 1: Oral Language: Speaking, Listening, and Learning).

Virtually all methods of assessing reading are indirect, even those that claim to directly assess reading processes. Teachers cannot see the processes involved; they can only infer how students have comprehended or what strategies they used

- by what they say (language), such as discussions
- by what they do (actions), such as dramatic presentations
- by what they make (products), such as drawings

If readers don't understand a word when they hear it, then they will not be able to comprehend it when they encounter it during reading (Hirsch 2003).

Learning Through Representing

Representation of Knowledge

Actions

Doing

Thinking and Learning

Saying — Language

Making — Products

Forms of Representation
(possible sources of evidence for assessment)

Actions	Language	Products
movement	dialogue	written work
dance	discussion	2-D and 3-D models
story drama	oral presentations	graphs, charts, maps
interactions	self-evaluations	webs, semantic maps
gestures, signs	conferences	drawings, paintings
		collages
		songs
		musical compositions

(British Columbia Ministry of Education 2000)

"Our ways of measuring reading are limited to what we observe when students read aloud, ... what they say or write after reading, and what they say or write about the way they read."

FOUNTAS AND PINNELL 2001, 488

Assessment of reading comprehension and of the factors that affect it is an ongoing process that helps teachers identify the individual and collective strengths and needs of students. However, to be useful and time efficient, most assessments should be integral to, and supportive of, instruction.

There are many ways to assess students, including

- using surveys, inventories, and interviews
- retelling and summarizing (oral and written)
- listening to students read and respond aloud
  - Informal Reading Inventories (IRI)
  - running records or miscue analyses
  - think-alouds
  - fluency assessments
  - reading conferences (having one-on-one or group conversations)
- having students respond in writing
  - written responses, such as reader response journals and reading logs
  - cloze assessments
- having students create dramatic or visual arts responses to text
- listening in on discussions such as those generated in book clubs, literature circles, and book talks
- using student self-assessments

Assessing Using Surveys, Inventories, and Interviews

To effectively support comprehension, teachers need to get to know their students. Students' attitudes toward reading, their beliefs and understanding about what makes a good reader, and their reading interests are reflected through

- reading attitude surveys
- reading interests inventories
- reading interviews

Reading Attitude Survey

Reading is pivotal to learning, so assessing students' attitudes toward reading is often a first step in analyzing reading progress. Too often a negative attitude toward reading leads students to choose not to read which, in turn, affects their work in all school subjects.

The Reading Attitude Survey is a good beginning-of-the-year self-assessment. It helps teachers identify those students with negative or indifferent attitudes toward reading. Follow-up enables teachers to implement strategies that encourage students to develop positive attitudes toward reading. It's important for students to understand that there are no right or wrong answers to the survey questions. The purpose of the survey is to find out how they feel about reading.

Assessment BLM 1: Reading Attitude Survey
Assessment BLM 2: Attitude Survey in Chapter 5

Reading Interests Inventory

Engaging Grades 3 to 6 students in reading often depends on the selection of reading materials in the classroom and the school library. A Reading Interests Inventory helps teachers find books that reflect the

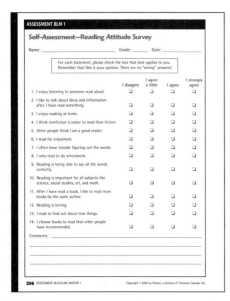

students' reading interests. The inventory can be completed by the whole class or individually. Tallying the reading interests of all the students provides a useful summary of what would likely interest students.

The Reading Interests Inventory is a useful assessment tool, especially for the beginning and the middle of the school year. It helps teachers make important decisions about grouping students, developing themes, and focusing lessons.

Assessment BLM 2: Reading Interests Inventory (Student)

Assessment BLM 3: Reading Interests Inventory (Class Tally)

Assessment BLM 3: Interest Inventory in Chapter 5

Reading Interview

One-on-one reading interviews early in the school year help teachers pinpoint a student's beliefs about reading (what reading is and what good readers do). In addition, ongoing interviews help teachers understand each student's approach to reading, reading strengths, interests, and possible reading difficulties. By discussing the results of the interviews, teachers help students understand personal reading strategies. This awareness will help students to think about their thinking, or exercise metacognition.

Assessment BLM 4: Reading Interview

Assessment BLM 10: Informal Reading Conference

Assessment BLM 4: Informal Reading Conference in Chapter 5

Assessing Comprehension Using Retelling and Summarizing

Retelling and summarizing require an ability to recall the text and to identify the important details of what has been read. A summary provides the gist of what has been read, heard, or viewed, perhaps in a sentence or two. A summary for this book might be, "This teacher professional resource book provides the research base, assessment tools, and practical instructional strategies to support effective teaching and learning in Grades 3 to 6."

When students retell and summarize, they synthesize what they have read. They select the most important information from the text and put it together in a logical, coherent way. In addition, retelling and summarizing encompass the ability to read between the lines, to get to the inferential level. In a retell or summary, students make sense of the text by relating what they have read to their own personal knowledge and experiences.

Students can retell or summarize either orally or in writing. One way of assessing a retell is to use a retell scale. Such a tool assesses the student's ability to

- provide an unaided retelling (some students may require prompts)
- state the main idea
- retell key ideas and supporting details (nonfiction)

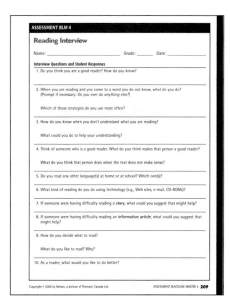

"Synthesis is the ... uniquely human trait that permits us to sift through a myriad of details and focus on those pieces we need to know and remember. It is the ability to collect a disparate array of facts and connect them to a central theme or idea.... It is a complex process in which children, even the youngest, engage very naturally every day."

KEENE AND ZIMMERMANN 1997, 169

- explain concepts from the passage (nonfiction)
- identify the character, problem, major events, climax, and solution (fiction)
- retell the story in sequence (fiction)
- make personal connections to the text

Summarizing can be assessed using a rubric. Typical criteria include

- selecting and describing relevant information and ideas
- inferring meaning
- interpreting, analyzing, and synthesizing information from the text
- connecting what has been read to personal knowledge and experiences

Retelling and summarizing skills need to be taught directly and explicitly to help ensure that students fully comprehend what they are reading. Too often students are assessed on their ability to retell or summarize without first being taught how to do it. They need to understand what a retelling or summary entails, to see it modelled, and to have guided practice prior to assessment.

Assessment BLM 5: Fiction Retelling Scale
Assessment BLM 6: Nonfiction Retelling Scale
Assessment BLM 7: Reading Response or Summarizing Rubric
Assessment BLM 6: Retelling/Interpreting Checklist—Narrative Text in Chapter 5
Assessment BLM 7: Retelling/Interpreting Checklist—Informational Text in Chapter 5

Assessing Comprehension Using Read-Alouds and Oral Responses

By listening to students read aloud (either in person or on an audiotape), teachers can determine whether students' decoding skills (or lack thereof) and fluency may be affecting their ability to comprehend what they are reading.

Informal Reading Inventories (IRI)

Informal Reading Inventories (IRI)—levelled reading passages read aloud by students—are useful tools to determine students' reading strengths and needs. When administering an IRI, the teacher assumes the role of neutral observer. This is not a teaching time; it is a time to observe what strategies the student uses without support. The errors (miscues) and self-corrections made by students are particularly informative. If the student appeals for help, an effective teacher may respond with "You try it" or "Give it a go." If the student is really stuck, it is best to tell the student the word so that the reading can continue (Trehearne et al. 2004).

Questioning students after reading or asking them to retell or summarize the text will reveal their level of comprehension. Even a simple conversation reveals a great deal about the connections the student is or is not making.

"We learn about students' processing strategies by observing oral reading behavior. As you listen to students read, you record the rate of reading and the accuracy level; judge the fluency; and note behavior that indicates they are using meaning, language structure or syntax, and visual information."

FOUNTAS AND PINNELL 2001, 488

"Informal Reading Inventories provide useful information to students about their progress, to parents about achievement and skills that need improvement and to teachers about instruction and texts to provide."

PARIS AND CARPENTER 2003, 579

Running Records or Miscue Analyses

By completing a running record or a modified miscue analysis during either a one-on-one IRI or a reading conference, teachers determine students' reading strategies and how well they self-monitor while they read a text aloud. This diagnostic assessment tool helps identify strategies that the student uses, overuses, and does not use.

"A miscue is any departure from the text. Analyze the miscues to determine how they may affect the student's understanding of the passage. Determine whether the reader was using cues from

- the meaning of the message (semantic cueing system)
- the structure of the sentence (syntactic cueing system)
- the letter–sound relationships (graphophonic cueing system)
- the features or characteristics of different kinds of texts, such as a letter, newspaper, recipe (pragmatic cueing system)"

(Doctorow, Bodiam, and McGowan 2003, 8)

An analysis of the following running record reveals that the student used graphophonics but did not consider whether the word "does" made sense (semantics) or fit grammatically (syntax). Even though the reading didn't make sense, the reader kept on going.

"On the walk in the woods we saw seven does [read as *duz*] coming up the path."

Steps for Taking a Running Record

1. The teacher sits next to the student, who holds the passage of text.

2. As the student reads the text aloud, the teacher records the reading behaviour (what the student says and does) on either a running record form or a blank sheet of paper.

3. To **score the errors**, the teacher
   - counts any substitutions, omissions, insertions, or "tolds" for a word as one error
   - counts repetitions as one error (in other words, multiple attempts at the same word are counted as one error)
   - self-corrections are **not** counted as errors

4. To **determine the accuracy rate**, the teacher
   - counts the number of words in the passage (excluding the title)

Modified Miscue Analysis Conventions

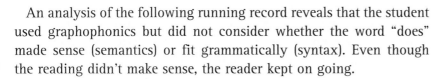

- Accurate reading (optional)   ✓ ✓ ✓ ✓

- Substitution $\dfrac{\text{went}}{\text{want}}$

- Repetition (R)   R or ✓ ✓R

- Self-correction (SC) $\dfrac{\text{went}}{\text{want}}$ SC

- Omission   (very)

- Insertion   little ∧

- Told (T)   thought [T]

- Appeal (A)   sometimes [A]

(Doctorow, Bodiam, and McGowan 2003, 40)

- counts the number of words that the student read correctly (including accurate self-corrections)

- divides the number of words read correctly by the number of words in the passage, and then multiplies by 100 to get a percentage

$$\frac{\text{number of words read correctly}}{\text{number of words in the passage}} \times 100 = \% \text{ accuracy}$$

Running records reveal how students problem solve and monitor their own reading. The accuracy rate can help the teacher to determine whether the text is appropriate for the student. (All students should be reading with at least 90 percent accuracy and comprehension; for independent reading, the accuracy rate and comprehension should be between 95 and 100 percent.) The accuracy rate also helps the teacher to group students effectively for guided reading. Using a particular level of text that is "right" for a group of students will work even if each student processes text differently (Fountas and Pinnell 1996).

Student Think-Alouds

Teachers use think-alouds to model strategies to make sense of a text. Students benefit when teachers model all reading strategies, such as activating prior knowledge, summarizing, clarifying, using fix-ups, and visualizing.

When students think aloud, they reveal to teachers what comprehension strategies they are using. Sometimes students will spontaneously think aloud when reading aloud. For example: "He is so ridiculous" or "I don't know the word so I am going to skip it." In a more formal think-aloud assessment, teachers ask students to pause during the reading to describe the strategies they are using and to share their understanding of the text. This assessment technique reveals what strategies students are (or are not) using, what they are thinking about as they read, and how they are feeling as they read. It is important for teachers to model think-alouds frequently before using the procedure as an assessment tool.

Implementing a Student Think-Aloud Assessment

1. The teacher chooses a short text that is at the student's instructional level (90 to 95 percent fluency).

2. The teacher then divides the text into four parts.

3. The student reads the first part of the text silently or aloud and stops.

4. The teacher asks the student, "What is happening?" or "What is this about?" or "What are you thinking about now?" or "What do you predict will happen next?" Another great open-ended prompt—"Say something" (Harste 1988)—simply encourages the student to respond to the text in any manner.

5. Once the student responds, the teacher may prompt with one of the following questions:
   - "What made you think that?"
   - "What clues made you think that?"
   - "What information made you think that?"

6. If the student does not respond to the initial question, "What is happening?" (perhaps he or she doesn't know or is a non-risk taker), the teacher might prompt with, "How about giving me your best guess" or "Describe for me what is going on in the text."

7. If the student is really stuck, the teacher explains his or her understanding of the text and what prompted that thinking.

8. The procedure is repeated for parts 2 through 4 of the text.

9. After completing the think-aloud, the teacher analyzes the student's level of comprehension (e.g., Did he or she realize when comprehension broke down and use a fix-up strategy? Did he or she infer?).

10. The teacher groups students together for comprehension strategy mini-lessons as needed.

Assessment BLM 8: Think-Aloud Summary Sheet

Written think-alouds may also be used to assess reading comprehension and strategy use. They are similar to oral think-alouds except that as the students read the text silently, they stop after each section to record their understandings and reasons for their thinking. The teacher explains to the student, "You are going to be doing exactly what you just did out loud, but this time you are going to write down your thoughts. This will help me understand your thinking." It is important to explicitly convey to students that this is a purposeful activity.

Assessment BLM 9: Thinking Aloud

Fluency

Fluent reading involves the students' ability to decode quickly and automatically. Fluency rate often affects comprehension, but not always. As stated earlier, many students read smoothly and sometimes with expression, but still don't understand.

Research indicates that training in think-aloud improves students' ability to monitor their comprehension during reading (Duke and Pearson 2002).

"Think-alouds in the research literature require informants to speak aloud into a tape recorder. In my classroom, I simply have students write down what they are thinking, feeling, noticing, seeing and doing as they read ... the written protocols are more useful, in that they provide an immediate record of internal reading activity that can be shared, evaluated, and worked on."

WILHELM 2001, 30

Scale for Oral Reading Fluency

Level 4 The student reads with expression throughout most of the text, reading in larger, meaningful phrase groups. Repetitions, hesitations, or mistakes are rare. The student appears to be very comfortable reading the text.

Level 3 The student reads primarily in longer phrases that preserve the author's syntax. Although there may be occasional hesitations, repetitions, and miscues, most words are identified or decoded automatically. The student is beginning to read with expression and more comfort.

Level 2 The student is beginning to identify more words automatically and to read in short phrases. Some word-by-word reading continues. The student reads with little or no expression, and there may be long pauses and frustration with unfamiliar words.

Level 1 The student reads slowly and word by word, with many pauses and with little or no expression. Few words are identified automatically. The student may seem frustrated.

(Adapted from the National Center for Education Statistics 1995 and Worthy, Broaddus, and Ivey 2001, 141)

Reading Conferences—Having a Conversation!

During a reading conference, the teacher focuses on an individual or a small group of students to find out how well they comprehend what they are reading. Through conversations, students are prompted to think about as well as recall what they have read. Having a conversation is a more authentic form of comprehension assessment.

"Outside school we rely on the richness of a person's conversation about texts to judge how well they understood it…. In school we typically rely on the flat recitation of events or information to make that same judgment" (Allington 2001, 89). A teacher may simply sit down beside a student during independent reading time and have the student share personal thoughts on the text. The conversation may begin in any of the following ways:

- "Tell me what the book is about so far."
- "What have you learned so far from what you have read?"
- "What do you remember so far about what you have read?"

Students may then be asked to talk about

- their reactions to the text
- connections between the text and their own lives (text to self)
- connections between the text they are reading and other texts they have read (text to text)
- how the author uses language to paint a picture
- how the characters are portrayed and why
- concepts the author has included
- the author's purpose for writing
- aspects of the topic that have been omitted and why

Three great prompts to support comprehension assessment

"Outside of school settings we engage in conversations about the adequacy of texts and authors to inform, engage, and entertain us. In school we engage in interrogations around what was 'in the text.'"

ALLINGTON 2001, 89

Assessment BLM 10: Informal Reading Conference
Assessment BLM 4: Informal Reading Conference in Chapter 5

Assessing Comprehension Using Written Responses

Much of a student's day in Grades 3 to 6 is spent reading and then responding to what has been read. Reading is required to complete tasks and assignments in all content areas, not only in the language arts curriculum.

Teachers may use various kinds of writing to help identify how well students understand what they read. They need to determine whether students are able to interpret and understand concepts they encounter, as they read more independently in all subject areas. Writing also helps students to make better sense of what they are reading and often leads to understanding.

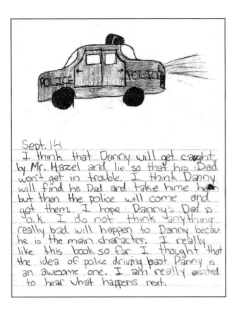

Sept. 14
I think that Danny will get caught by Mr. Hazel and lie so that his Dad won't get in trouble. I think Danny will find his Dad and take him home but then the police will come and get them. I hope Danny's Dad is o.k. I do not think anything really bad will happen to Danny because he is the main character. I really like this book so far. I thought that the idea of police driving past Danny is an awesome one. I am really excited to hear what happens next.

Reader Response Journals

When students respond in writing to a text, they reflect on what they are reading and often record their thoughts in a journal format. These reflections might be in the form of questions or responses that reveal text-to-self, text-to-text, or text-to-world connections. From these responses, teachers gain insight into how well students understand what they are reading and how deeply they are responding to a text.

Journal entries are generally free flowing and completely determined by the student. Occasionally, teachers may ask students to respond to specific prompts.

Reading Logs

Reading logs help students keep track of the texts they have read (or gave up on) and the genres of those texts. This form of record keeping helps students think about their reading and helps teachers and parents monitor students' reading interests and behaviours.

BLM 3: Keeping Track

Question-Based Responses to Text

The types of personal-response questions effective readers ask themselves as they read fall into three main categories. These types of questions may also serve as useful prompts for oral or written responses to a text.

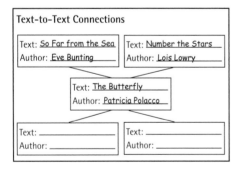

Text-to-Text Connections

Text: So Far from the Sea   Text: Number the Stars
Author: Eve Bunting   Author: Lois Lowry

Text: The Butterfly
Author: Patricia Polacco

Text: _____   Text: _____
Author: _____   Author: _____

Connection	Description	Sample Question/Prompt
Text to Self	questions that involve relating the text to personal experiences or knowledge	**Question:** I wonder what I would have done if I had been in her shoes? **Prompt:** If you were the main character, what would you have done and why?
Text to Text	questions connecting one text to another (comparing characters, settings, problems, and so on)	**Question:** The art in these two folktales is very different. Which version do I like better? **Prompt:** The art in these two folktales is very different. Which do you like better? Why?
Text to World	questions connecting the text and issues in the world (possibly social and moral issues)	**Question:** The author makes seal hunting sound so bad. Why didn't he tell the other side of the story as well? **Prompt:** If you were writing a story on seal hunting, what point of view would you take?

(Miller 2002)

As noted earlier, one effective way to assess students' written responses is to use a rubric that provides criteria for the responses. Assessment BLM 7 in this chapter is one example. Another method for assessing and developing reading comprehension is to use a questioning framework. (See Question–Answer Relationships (QAR) later in this chapter.)

Supporting Responses

Students need to learn how to support their responses with evidence from the text and from their own background knowledge. Through mini-lessons conducted over time, students will learn to support their responses by

- supplying facts or information from specific text pages
- identifying passages in the text that contain evidence
- citing facts or information that has been inferred but not stated
- applying background knowledge or personal experiences
- using "because" statements
- providing details and examples

Assessment BLM 7: Reading Response or Summarizing Rubric

Assessment BLM 11: Making Connections

Cloze Assessments

The cloze procedure involves reading a text from which certain words have been omitted. As a form of assessment, cloze reveals how well students understand what they read and what strategies they are using. It may also be used to determine a student's reading level and the appropriateness of reading materials chosen for guided or independent reading.

Cloze assessments enable teachers to identify how well students

- use context to help identify unfamiliar words or concepts
- predict
- use language structure to help them read
- use a variety of strategies to decode unfamiliar words

To create a cloze passage, teachers first decide what they want to assess. For example, to assess how effectively students use syntax (grammar), teachers omit structure words such as pronouns, prepositions, and conjunctions. To assess semantics (meaning), teachers omit content words—nouns, verbs, adjectives, and so on. To assess content and syntax, teachers omit every fifth word—the traditional cloze method. It is important for teachers to first model the cloze and then complete a cloze activity with students before implementing it as an assessment tool.

I do it. ⟶ We do it. ⟶ You do it.

Implementing a Cloze Assessment

1. The teacher selects a reading passage 10 to 15 sentences long deemed to be at the student's instructional or independent reading level*.

2. The teacher omits words based on the purpose of the assessment, making all the blanks the same length. The first and last sentences remain unchanged.

3. The student then fills in the blanks.

4. The teacher determines how many correct words the student was able to insert. (Synonyms for the omitted word are acceptable as long as they make sense in the context of both the sentence and the passage.)

5. The teacher then calculates the number of correct words as a percentage of the number of blanks.

6. If 40 to 60 percent of the blanks are filled in with exactly the same words as those that were deleted, then the text is within the student's instructional level. However, it is more important to consider whether the chosen words make sense in the context of both the sentence and the passage. The primary focus is not whether the student completes the text with the identical word, but rather, with a defensible word! If synonyms are accepted, then a rate of 70 to 80 percent correct indicates an instructional level, and more than 85 percent an independent level.

   * Instructional Level = 90 to 94 percent accuracy and comprehension

     Independent Level = 95 to 100 percent accuracy and comprehension

(Adapted from Rhodes and Shanklin 1993, 190–91)

To assess comprehension of content-area material (e.g., Social Studies or Science) key vocabulary words are omitted.

How Are People and Goods Transported in the Arctic Today?

Traditional methods of travel, such as by dogsled and kayak, continue to be used in the Arctic. Today, however, a variety of other _____ methods are also used.

Most people travelling to and from the Arctic go by _____ . Almost every community has a small _____ or all-weather landing strip. There are regular _____ flights into the Arctic from _____ such as Montreal, Ottawa, and Edmonton. Large _____ planes bring fresh food and many _____ each week.

Smaller planes, called _____ planes, move people and goods between _____ in the Arctic. The planes can be fitted with skis, _____ , or soft balloon tires so they can land on _____ , water, _____ , or landing strips. Helicopters can reach places where it is difficult for planes to land.

(Andrew, Griffin, and Mader 2004, 44)

Assessing Comprehension Using Arts-Based Responses to Text

Students' understanding of reading can be assessed through responses involving dramatic or visual arts. This form of assessment enables students to demonstrate their thinking in a way many feel is low-risk.

Dramatic Arts Responses

By observing students' dramatic responses to a text, teachers determine how well the students understood what they have read. Dramatic responses to text can take various forms, such as

- interviews of characters or conversations among characters
- dramatizations of selected scenes or situations
- production of commercials
- pretend walks through the story's setting or the characters' neighbourhoods

Visual Arts Responses

When students respond to literature visually, they translate and synthesize their reading experiences to show their understanding through an arts-based medium. They might draw or paint the setting or interesting characters in the story, or create a model of a scientific concept they've been studying.

Assessing Comprehension by Listening In

One of the best ways to get a sense of students' levels of comprehension is to listen in while partners or small groups discuss what they have read. These discussions may take the form of a book talk, a book club, or a literature circle. (More information on book talks and book clubs can be found later in this chapter. Information on literature circles is provided in Chapter 5: In the Classroom: Making It Work.)

When teachers are "kid watching" (observing students) or listening in, there are certain indicators to look for when assessing comprehension.

Comprehension Indicators During Literature Discussions

Does the student

❏ use background knowledge to construct meaning?

❏ make reasonable predictions?

❏ use the text to support predictions?

❏ visualize?

❏ personally identify or make connections with the text (text to self)?

❏ evaluate or analyze characters?

❏ question the author (to identify what was said or not said, implied or inferred, and why)?

❏ connect the book with other texts (text to text)?

❏ connect the book to what is understood in the world (text to world)?

❏ ask questions to further understand?

❏ use vocabulary effectively?

❏ infer?

❏ retell/summarize?

❏ use context to identify unknown vocabulary?

❏ mention the book's theme?

(Adapted from Evans 2001, 105)

Assessment BLM 12: Comprehension Indicators During Literature Discussions

> *"Self-reflection offers students an opportunity to be actively involved in internal conversations while offering teachers an insider's view of the learning and the student's perception of self as learner."*
>
> HOYT AND AMES 1997, 19

Assessing Comprehension Using Self-Assessment

Students should be encouraged to assess how much focus and time they give to independent reading. Assessment BLM 13: Independent Reading will help them to do this.

In addition, it is important for students to assess their reading comprehension through reflection. Self-reflection permits students to focus on what they have learned and how they feel about their learning (Cooper and Kiger 2001), encouraging them to become strategic learners and metacognitive thinkers. To foster self-reflection, teachers provide students with time and prompts that assist them with thinking about their learning.

I Know I Understand What I Am Reading When I Can ...

❏ get the gist of the text even if I can't read or interpret every word and idea

❏ retell the text orally or in writing so that another person understands my re-creation

❏ connect or relate what I'm reading to what I already know, have read, or experienced

❏ reread a portion of text and clear up confusions

❏ use my knowledge of the subject or author to think and evaluate more deeply and critically—for example, to question, agree, or disagree with the text

❏ take clear notes that demonstrate my insights and learning

❏ use my notes to help me as I read or reread

❏ summarize or paraphrase what I've read

❏ use what I've read to think about other contexts and texts

❏ recognize gaps in my understanding and attempt to understand better by rereading, listing or highlighting key words or phrases, figuring out the meaning of unfamiliar words, writing notes to myself, asking pertinent questions, conversing with others

❏ consider multiple meanings

❏ recognize and use the characteristics of the genre to help me comprehend

❏ consider and understand comments of others

❏ make new meaning

(Routman 2002, 125)

Assessment BLM 13: Independent Reading

Assessment BLM 14: When I Read

Linking Assessment to Instruction

"Being asked to think about the text you've just read is different from being asked to recall the text you've just read."

ALLINGTON 2001, 87

Ongoing assessment as an integral part of instruction must drive ongoing instruction. The goal of all comprehension assessment and instruction is to develop thoughtful literacy learners. "Thoughtful literacy is more than remembering what the text said. It is engaging the ideas in texts, challenging those ideas, reflecting on them, and so on. It is responding to a story with giggles, goose bumps, anger, or revulsion" (Allington 2001, 106).

"Students need an opportunity to voice their reactions to, feelings about, and interpretations of the texts they read. Being able to choose oral, written, even hands-on methods allows different types of readers to express their understanding in ways that match their learning styles.... The goal is to create readers who can demonstrate both a breadth and a depth of reading skills."

THOMPSON 1999

Developing Critically Literate Students

Critical literacy is a way of thinking that helps to uncover social inequalities and injustices. These discoveries might ultimately lead to social change. This way of thinking occurs as students are taught to question and challenge attitudes, values, and beliefs that lie beneath the surface as they read, listen, and view. Questioning to promote discussion and writing lies at the heart of a critical literacy program. It is through talk and writing that students develop new ideas. To become critically literate, students must learn to

- examine meaning within text
- consider the text creator's purpose and motive
- identify the audience to whom the text is intended to appeal
- understand that texts are not neutral, that they represent particular views, silence other points of view, and influence people's ideas and ways of thinking
- notice what has been intentionally left out of the text and what is inferred (between the lines) but not stated in order to present a certain belief or perspective

- question and challenge the ways in which texts have been constructed
- respond to what they hear, see, and view (e.g., by taking a stance on an issue, considering social action, and so on)

(Adapted from Government of Tasmania 2004)

As students talk and write about a text they have heard, read, or viewed, they understand more deeply and become more sensitive to different types of texts, characteristics of texts, and how authors get across their personal values or perspectives. (For examples of writing activities that support critical literacy, see Chapter 3: Writing: The Reading–Writing Connection.)

Introducing Critical Literacy

Providing students with multiple perspectives on the same event or topic is a great way to demonstrate that text reflects an author's personal viewpoints and values. What follows is an example based on a reading of the award-winning book *Voices in the Park* by Anthony Browne.

1. The teacher reads aloud *Voices in the Park*, in which the same park experience is told from four different perspectives, that of two parents and two children.

2. There is a class discussion, with the teacher using various questions to prompt students' thoughts about perspective.

> Questions on Perspective (*Voices in the Park*)
> - "Think about each of the four characters. What kind of person do you think each character is portraying?"
> - "What view of the world do you think each character has?"
> - "Why do you think the author wrote this book using four voices?"
> - "Why these four voices?"

3. The discussion continues with a focus on student experiences involving different perspectives. For example, have any of them had a disagreement with someone and described the incident

Check It Out!

Here are some great children's texts for demonstrating perspective on the following social justice issues:

Age Stereotyping

How Does It Feel to Be Old? by Norma Farber (New York: Dutton, 1979).

"The Little Boy and the Old Man," in *A Light in the Attic* by Shel Silverstein (New York: HarperCollins, 1981).

Wilfrid Gordon McDonald Partridge by Mem Fox (La Jolla, CA: Kane/Miller, 1985).

Displacement/Forced Relocation

The Butterfly by Patricia Polacco (New York: Philomel, 2000).

Number the Stars by Lois Lowry (New York: Houghton Mifflin, 1989).

So Far from the Sea by Eve Bunting (Boston: Clarion Books, 1998).

quite differently than the other person involved? Did anyone who witnessed the disagreement have yet another perspective?

In teaching students to become critical literacy learners, it is equally important to enhance their awareness of perspective as it relates to social justice or human rights issues. Here is one approach to exploring author values. The teacher shares three texts with the class dealing with the same social or human rights issue, but told from different perspectives:

1. For example, *Wilfrid Gordon McDonald Partridge* by Mem Fox (La Jolla, CA: Kane/Miller Book Publishers, 1995) is a wonderful read-aloud book that promotes much discussion about age stereotyping.

   Wilfrid Gordon McDonald Partridge describes the adventures of a young boy who befriends six senior citizens living in a nursing home next to his home. Each senior is portrayed as unique, but Miss Nancy is the boy's favourite.

   Miss Nancy is losing her memory, which is a stereotypical view of many seniors. In his search for what a memory is, Wilfrid is able to help Miss Nancy recover some of her memory. At first the story line seems simple, but it is not!

Questions Promoting Critical Literacy (*Wilfrid Gordon McDonald Partridge*)

- "How does the author portray the child and adults?"
- "Why do you think the child and the adults are portrayed in this way?"
- "What is the topic, focus, or theme?"
- "What is the story trying to make you think or feel?"
- "What wasn't said about the topic and why?"
- "Whose voices and perspectives are not expressed?"
- "What words did the author use to make the character [fill in character's name] funny, scary?"
- "Why do you think the author chose this setting?"
- "How do you feel toward people over 60 years of age? Please explain."

---

2. *How Does It Feel to Be Old?* by Norma Farber and the poem "The Little Boy and the Old Man" by Shel Silverstein are great follow-up texts to *Wilfrid Gordon McDonald Partridge* and provide other perspectives on the issue of age stereotyping. After reading these texts, students compare and contrast all three authors' perspectives on ageism. What values do students believe each author is promoting?

For extension activities, see Chapter 3: Writing: The Reading–Writing Connection.

Further Explorations of Perspective and Social Justice

Yet another effective way to explore perspective is to share with students the same story presented in at least two different media, such as a print and video version. Students may be asked to respond to the various versions of the same story in different ways. The questions and activities that follow are some suggestions for comparing and contrasting the authors' perspectives.

- How are the versions the same and yet different?

- How does each author present his or her perspective?

- Describe how each of the characters is portrayed in each version. Provide one example of both a similarity and a difference. Students might use a Venn diagram to show how the stories compare/contrast. (For more on Venn diagrams, see later in this chapter.)

- Are there any differences in the story line? Provide examples. Which story line do you prefer and why?

- How does the video (or audio) version differ from the print version? Which version do you prefer? Why do you think the author of the video or audio version chose to make these changes?

- If you were writing your own version of the text, how might you change the story line? Consider creating a story map comic strip. (More information on story map comic strips is provided later in this chapter.)

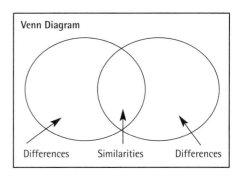

Check It Out!

Find the tools to create story map comic strips by visiting ReadWriteThink at http://www.readwritethink.org/lessons/lesson_view.asp?id=236

Books dealing with social justice issues generally help students to make emotional connections to the text. *Flying Solo* by Ralph Fletcher (New York: Dell Yearling, 1998) is such a book. The story, especially suitable for students in Grades 5 and 6, describes a sixth-grade class in which the substitute teacher never shows up. The students decide not to report that they are alone and instead run the

Flying Solo by Ralph Fletcher (New York: Dell Yearling, 1998) is a great book to stimulate discussion of playground politics: **teasing**, **name calling**, and **bullying**.

Check It Out!

Other great books that deal with **bullying**, **name calling**, and **teasing** include these:

Crow Boy by Taro Yashima (New York: Puffin, 1976) focuses on a young boy who is ostracized until Grade 6, when a teacher helps him to share his special talent.

Thank You, Mr. Falker by Patricia Polacco (New York: Philomel, 1998) is a moving account of the pain and ridicule felt by a girl struggling to learn to read from kindergarten to Grade 5.

Creativity by John Steptoe (New York: Clarion, 1997) describes a new Grade 6 student who is teased because his clothes aren't "cool."

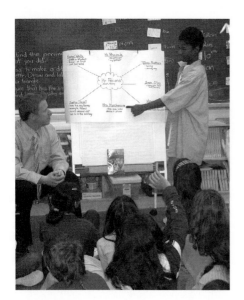

class themselves. At least six of the student characters are clearly portrayed and each one has private issues to contend with. Rachel is a selective mute; Bastian's Air Force family has to move again; Sean's father is an alcoholic.

Near the end of the book, the class comes together in how they deal with feelings of guilt, grief, and sorrow over their treatment of a developmentally challenged classmate (Tommy Feathers), who has since died. The book provides a great balance of emotions—happiness, sadness, guilt, and more.

Teaching Students to Persevere with Text

It is not uncommon for texts that increase in difficulty as the story line unfolds to begin rather slowly. *Flying Solo* is an ideal book for demonstrating this writing style and for teaching students the value of persevering.

For some readers, the major challenge of *Flying Solo* is that the issue of the substitute teacher not showing up is not presented until page 26. The first 25 pages set the stage for what is to come by dedicating a brief chapter to each of the major characters. Many students simply do not want to persevere through so many pages to get to the action; also, some students have trouble keeping track of each of the characters.

Flying Solo can be used to

- promote critical literacy regarding the social issue of bullying/name calling
- encourage students to realize that sometimes persevering with texts that start out slowly can be worthwhile
- demonstrate the value of using a semantic map to keep track of characters
- stimulate conversation with questions such as the following:
  - "Is this text realistic? Why or why not?"
  - "Is there anything you doubt about this text?"
  - "Whose voices do you hear?"

For extension activities related to *Flying Solo*, see Chapter 3: Writing: The Reading–Writing Connection.

BLM 3: Keeping Track

Features of Classroom Instruction That Support Comprehension

Several factors support effective literacy teaching and learning in upper elementary school. These include

- maximizing opportunities to read
- allowing for opportunities to discuss what is read
- focusing on meaning and ways of constructing meaning
- modelling
- providing explicit strategy instruction

- using small-group lessons and one-on-one conferences
- using diverse assessment tools
- integrating reading and writing with other subject areas

Reasons to Teach an Integrated Curriculum

- Unless teachers have 50 hours a day to teach, they'll never get it all in.
- An integrated curriculum allows science and social studies to frame reading, writing, and math.
- The brain thrives on connections.
- Life is not divided into neat little blocks of time called science, math, reading, writing, social studies, and recess.
- Problem-solving skills soar when knowledge and higher-level thinking from all curriculum areas are tapped.
- Real literature in real books provides an authentic diving board into learning all subjects. Award-winning literature provides models for problem solving, peer relationships, character development, and skill building. Students are captivated by exciting adventures with realistic characters who go through problems very much like their own or problems (like war) from which they will learn historical truths.
- Group interaction and team building inherent in an integrated curriculum depend on using various strengths and skills to create bridges to understanding.
- Inspiring students to think, to love learning, and to put their learning to work in authentic ways will equip them for whatever curves they might be thrown ... on standardized tests and in life!
- Students love an integrated curriculum and thrive on its challenges!

(Adapted from Red 2003)

"Children in classrooms with library centres read about 50% more books than children in classrooms without such centres."

ALLINGTON AND CUNNINGHAM 1996, 97

The characteristics of effective classrooms are demonstrated in these areas of instruction that support comprehension:

- reading
- talk and writing
- explicit strategy instruction

Reading

Students who are truly engaged in reading and read extensively will improve not only their vocabulary and background knowledge, but also their comprehension. Because reading is so vital to comprehension instruction, it is important for teachers to

- provide time for independent reading
- hook students on reading

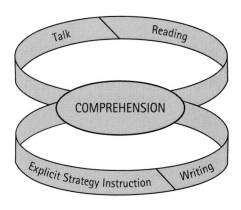

- develop a classroom reading collection
- conduct reading conferences
- provide many reading opportunities
- promote home reading
- model fluency by reading aloud
- use repeated reading

Provide Time for Independent Reading

"Kids need to read a lot to become proficient readers. They need books in their hands that they can read—accurately and fluently. They need books that are of interest to them" (Allington 2001, 110). Teachers must encourage student reading both in and out of the classroom.

Classroom independent reading time goes under many different names: DEAR (Drop Everything and Read), SSR (Sustained Silent Reading), SQUIRT (Sustained Quiet Uninterrupted Independent Reading Time). But whatever it's called, the purpose is the same: to provide time in the school day for students to select, read, and enjoy the books that they have selected. Independent reading is an important classroom routine. Providing time for students to practise reading quietly helps them to develop fluency, establish a reading habit, and learn to value reading. When teachers intentionally schedule time for reading, at the same time every day, it conveys a message that reading for pleasure is important.

Hook Students on Reading

Recent research by Jo Worthy (2002), among others, describes classrooms in which students in the upper elementary grades *want* to read. Interviews with students revealed that what hooked them on reading was

- having lots of time to "just read"
- teacher enthusiasm during read-alouds

- an extensive choice and variety of reading materials

Some students do not really read during independent reading time. They may be simply flipping through books that are too difficult for them. For these students, a portion of their time may be better spent reading to an adult or peer, or reading less challenging books aloud to younger students. Fluency is developed through practice with reading easier texts.

Assessment BLM 13: Independent Reading will help students self-assess their degree of reading engagement and their choice of "just right" texts.

Assessment BLM 13: Independent Reading

Develop a Classroom Reading Collection

Classrooms need hundreds and hundreds of books in addition to other types of reading materials. The reality is that most classrooms don't have the quantity and the quality of books needed. It is recommended that at least 400 books be made available to students in each Grades 4 to 6 classroom, with early elementary-grade classrooms having even more (Allington and Cunningham 1996). In addition, classroom collections should

- provide a range of content to match the students' interests, including cross-curricular texts such as social studies, math, and science
- feature high-interest, motivating reading material
- comprise texts of varying levels of difficulty so that all students will be able to experience success
- contain books that reflect a variety of multicultural perspectives
- offer a balance of different genres, including fiction, nonfiction, and poetry

Check It Out!

See "Getting Started: The First 20 Days" in *Guiding Readers and Writers: Grades 3–6* by Irene Fountas and Gay Su Pinnell (Portsmouth, NH: Heinemann, 2001), 142–62.

Genres to Include in a Classroom Library

❑ Adventure	❑ Humour
❑ Autobiography	❑ Informational books
❑ Biography	❑ Legends and folktales
❑ Classics	❑ Memoir
❑ Comics	❑ Mystery
❑ Fables	❑ Picture books
❑ Fairy tales	❑ Poetry
❑ Fantasy	❑ Realistic fiction
❑ Historical fiction	❑ Science fiction
❑ Horror	❑ Sports

It is important to provide a variety of formats, including books, magazines, and comics. The main goal of creating a well-stocked classroom reading centre is to motivate students to read, and comics are an acceptable reading choice.

For many more ideas on assembling a classroom reading collection, see Materials in Chapter 5: In the Classroom: Making It Work.

Conduct Reading Conferences

Holding regular reading conferences with individual students is crucial. Effective teachers use these conferences as opportunities to help students develop strategies for choosing "just right" books. They also monitor the difficulty level of each student's reading materials to ensure that the materials are appropriate. They offer encouragement and reinforcement, and help students to develop self-monitoring and other comprehension strategies. Most importantly, teachers have conversations with the students about their reading. It is through conversations that the teacher develops some sense of a student's interest in, and comprehension of, a text.

Provide Many Reading Opportunities

Effective teachers provide many varied opportunities for students to read, enjoy books, and talk about their reading. They

- read aloud daily to the class a variety of texts (including fiction, and poetry) linked to students' interests and often with cross-curricular, integrated ties. They also read from different formats, including magazines, comics, and texts on the overhead.
- encourage students to share background knowledge about given topics of interest
- listen to and value students' contributions to discussions
- provide opportunities for partnered reading with other students, classes, or with paraprofessionals and volunteers
- acknowledge that discussion is important
- encourage discussion through literature circles and book clubs
- arrange for students to read aloud to adults and receive feedback, which is especially crucial for struggling readers and those with weak vocabulary or oral language skills. This time is in addition to small-group time spent with the teacher.
- encourage students to read and share material that interests them
- provide opportunities for guided reading daily, with a focus on comprehension
- promote "family reading" events at home and at school

Promote Home Reading

When students see themselves as readers, they recognize that reading is done all the time, not just within the school walls. Teachers have a role to play in encouraging students to read outside formal school hours. It's important for teachers to emphasize to parents that, even though their child can read, they, as parents, still have an important role to play. Ideally, parents set aside after-school time for their children to read—whether novels, information books, information on the Internet, magazines, comics, or trading cards. They also spend time talking to their children about what they are reading.

Ways to Promote Home Reading

To encourage student reading at home, effective teachers

- send home a letter at the beginning of the school year outlining the home reading program and expectations for it. For those parents unable to read English, a conversation is equally effective.

- help parents to understand that they have a role to play in monitoring what their children read, listening for fluency, monitoring comprehension, and coaching their children as they read and talk about texts. Again, for parents unable to read English, other ways to help are suggested, such as discussion, sharing pictures, and reading to their children in another language.

- ensure that students have books from the classroom or school library that they may take home to read and exchange for new ones regularly

---

BLM 4: Literacy Home Links: Home Reading

BLM 5: Literacy Home Links: Choosing "Just Right" Books

> The most important factor in home reading is that the students are truly engaged in the activity.

Model Fluency by Reading Aloud

Many students struggle with comprehension because of a lack of fluency. Some students, for example, read right through the punctuation, not realizing what effect this has on meaning.

Students need to hear and understand what fluent reading sounds like in order to read fluently themselves. Teachers model fluency by reading aloud to students. They also "think aloud" to help students understand the strategies that they use to read fluently (e.g., "Did you hear my voice go up when I read this question?" or "Listen to how I read this in phrases, not word by word."). Students also benefit when they read to a group or a partner and give each other feedback on their reading fluency.

For more information on reading fluency, see Chapter 6: Supporting Struggling and Reluctant Readers.

Use Repeated Reading

This strategy helps to improve students' reading fluency. When the same passage is read over and over, the number of word recognition errors decreases, reading speed increases, and oral reading expression improves (Samuels 2002). Repeated reading can be carried out individually, with partners, in small groups, or with the whole class. (See Chapter 6: Supporting Struggling and Reluctant Readers for more on repeated reading.)

Talk and Writing

Talk and writing are crucial in supporting vocabulary development and comprehension. Research on effective classrooms shows that students in such classrooms spend a great deal of time engaged in real conversations with teachers, peers, and others. Students make sense of what they read, hear, and view through sharing their ideas with others and through gaining new ideas and vocabulary from others, whether orally or in writing. In this resource alone, two chapters have been devoted to talk and writing–Chapter 1: Oral Language: Speaking, Listening, and Learning, and Chapter 3: Writing: The Reading–Writing Connection.

Here are several effective ways to support comprehension through talk and writing:

- book clubs
- book talks, reviews, and recommendations
- written or oral cloze activities
- reading logs and journals
- literature circles (see Chapter 5: In the Classroom: Making It Work)

Book Clubs

Just as adults enjoy coming together to share information about books, so do students. Discussions about texts give students an opportunity to understand what they have read. As they talk about their books, they return to the text to clarify and support their ideas. Talking about books allows students to expand connections (text to self, text to text, text to world), vocabulary, and concept development. It also promotes listening skills.

Students meet regularly in groups to talk about books they have read. One structure is to organize clubs according to different fiction and nonfiction genres: novels, plays, autobiographies, and so on.

Implementing a Classroom Book Club

1. Groups of three to five students read the same "just right" book, selected by them or by the teacher. It's important that the book contains rich ideas and information that inspire students to think, ask questions, and make connections to their own lives, other texts, and the world around them.

2. As they read, students record responses in their reading journals.

3. Students meet after finishing the book, or an agreed-upon section of the book, to share the ideas and questions they have recorded in their journals. Teachers may also have book clubs meet after a guided reading lesson.

Book Talks, Reviews, and Recommendations

"The reading experiences of children can be extended by what other people reveal to them about their reading and what they reveal to others about their reading" (Booth 1996, 39). Book talks, reviews, and recommendations promote and encourage reading and offer ways of extending students' experiences.

Providing opportunities for students to talk about and report on books to others allows them to

- encourage or discourage others from reading the same book
- engage in authentic talk about texts
- share a broader range of texts than they would likely read on their own

Although book talks are oral, book reviews may be presented in written form (see BLM 6: Book Review); as a dramatic response, in which students re-enact parts of the text; or as a visual response, where they create a collage, poster, or book cover.

Students may recommend books through posters or short speeches that provide book summaries. When students recommend books, they encourage others to read what they have read; however, they may also discourage reading of a title. What one person recommends, another will not—this can lead to discussion and debate.

BLM 6: Book Review

Implementing a Book Talk

1. The teacher first explains that in a book talk or review, students respond personally to what they have read.

2. The teacher then models a book talk for the class. Good ideas include providing some information about the author or illustrator, reading aloud a brief excerpt from an interesting or special part of the book, and commenting on whether the book is worth reading and why or why not.

3. Students prepare talks during or after the reading of a book.

"I think it helps me because sometimes when I read I get lost and I just keep on reading and then after I stop (and discuss), it helps me to remember what happened."

GRADE 5 STUDENT IN EVANS 2001, VIII

Check It Out!

Planet Book Club:
http://www.planetbookclub.com

Ways We Choose Books

- interesting title
- picture on front cover
- back cover information
- characters we liked in other books
- favourite series
- great illustrations
- author we know and like
- recommended by a friend or teacher
- books that are movies
- type of book (genre) we like to read
- read the beginning or some of the middle
- heard it read aloud
- sequel to a book we've read
- read it before and enjoyed it
- won an award

4. The teacher reminds the students that not all books are winners. It is all right not to like a book or to discourage someone from reading it, as long as the reason is shared. (See Persuasive Writing in Chapter 3: Writing: The Reading–Writing Connection.)

5. Students present their talks to a small group or to the whole class.

6. The listeners participate by asking questions or adding to the response if someone else has also read the book.

Implementing a One-Minute Book Talk

1. Students select a book they have read. In a one-minute time frame, they provide an overview and share their opinion of the book.

2. Alternatively, students may prepare and tape-record or videotape a 30-second radio or TV advertisement that recommends a book that they have read and think others will enjoy.

BLM 7: Planning My One-Minute Book Talk

Written or Oral Cloze Activities

A cloze procedure is a useful technique for helping students improve their vocabularies and apply fix-up strategies (e.g., reading forward and back), thus increasing comprehension. Using cloze with fiction and nonfiction texts is a good check to see how well students have learned and understood the concepts being taught or the story being told.

Implementing a Cloze Activity

1. The teacher omits selected words from a written passage. Omitted words may be randomly chosen to target parts of speech, such as nouns, verbs, and prepositions; or chosen based on a pattern, such as every fifth word. The words chosen might also be specific to content vocabulary, for example, to social studies or science content.

2. The teacher models how to effectively complete a cloze before assigning this activity to students.

3. Students use context clues, prior knowledge, and fix-up strategies to predict the missing words.

4. The teacher monitors students' understanding by asking them to give reasons for their word choices. Other students may be asked to "judge" the words chosen. Do they sound right and make sense in the context of both the sentence and the passage?

5. The teacher lets students read the original passage to compare their word choices to the original text. Which words do they prefer and why? This is where the real vocabulary learning occurs.

> **How to Complete a Cloze**
> 1. Read the entire passage before completing any blanks.
> 2. Use only one word in each blank.
> 3. Skip blanks that you are stuck on. Try them again when you are finished.

Reading Logs and Journals

Keeping a reading log allows students to easily track what they read, how much they read, and any information they'd like to remember. When students incorporate additional components, the record becomes a journal where they respond in a variety of ways to their reading.

Making Reading Logs and Journals Work

1. The teacher ensures that students have a place to keep their log or journal entries, such as a notebook, binder, or jot pad.

2. Students are encouraged to record personal thoughts, descriptions, questions, and reflections about their reading. Their reflections may take the form of prose, point-form notes, diagrams, drawings, and so on.

3. Although the best writing usually comes from a spontaneous text-to-self, text-to-text, or text-to-world connection, the teacher may provide occasional prompts, such as those that follow.

Students should not have to respond to their reading each and every time that they read.

"Do we have to have journal entries every time we read?"
Worthy 2002, 568

Reading Comprehension: Strategies That Work | **143**

- "Explain how the story might have ended if a key character or incident were changed."
- "Write about how the story made you feel. What made you feel that way?"
- "Write about any new, interesting, or challenging ideas you learned from your reading."
- "Explain why you think this book will or will not be read in the next century. Give your reason."
- "List at least five questions that you think anyone who reads this book [text piece] will be able to answer. Are any of them 'thick' questions?" (See Thick and Thin Questions later in this chapter.)

4. The teacher monitors the logs or journals (see Assessment BLM 7: Reading Response or Summarizing Rubric).

Explicit Strategy Instruction

Much research over the past 20 years indicates that the Gradual Release of Responsibility Model (Pearson and Gallagher 1983) is a highly effective instructional framework. Teachers focus on one strategy at a time, first explaining and then modelling its use through think-alouds. Students are then provided with many opportunities to develop each strategy through repeated application. The goal is for students to apply each strategy automatically.

Gradual Release of Responsibility

As students gain experience and expertise using the strategies that support comprehension, effective teachers gradually give them more responsibility for using each strategy independently in authentic situations across the curriculum. Teachers continue to release responsibility to students until students demonstrate during independent practice that they are able to consistently use the strategies on their own. Nevertheless, teachers continue to monitor student strategy use. The ultimate goal is for students to make these strategies their own and to know how, when, and why to apply them to help them make meaning from what they are reading, hearing, or viewing.

Reading Log
Name: _____ Grade: _____ Date Completed: _____
Title: _____ Author: _____ Genre: _____
Rating (circle one): (low) 1 2 3 4 5 6 7 8 9 10 (high)
Favourite or Most Interesting Part: _____
_____
New Words and New Ideas: _____

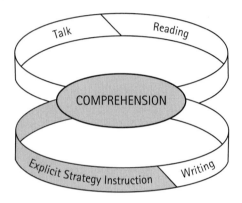

"Reading comprehension is a skill with a knowledge base just like all of the elements that support it, and as such, it can and should be taught explicitly."

SEDL 2000

"Good comprehension instruction includes both explicit instruction in specific comprehension strategies and a great deal of time and opportunity for actual reading, writing, and discussion of text."

DUKE AND PEARSON 2002, 2

Elements of the Gradual Release of Responsibility Model

- Explicit description of the strategy and when it should be used
- Teacher or student modelling of the strategy in action
- Collaborative use of the strategy in action
- Guided practice using the strategy with gradual release of responsibility: For example, the students may read silently, but are stopped every few pages to apply the strategy; they might be asked, "What do you think will happen next?" (prediction)
- Independent strategy use

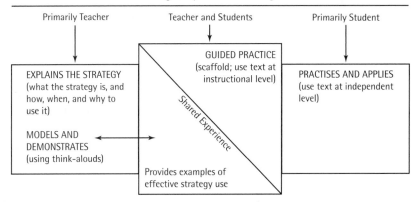

Primarily Teacher   Teacher and Students   Primarily Student

EXPLAINS THE STRATEGY
(what the strategy is, and
how, when, and why to
use it)

GUIDED PRACTICE
(scaffold; use text at
instructional level)

PRACTISES AND APPLIES
(use text at independent
level)

Shared Experience

MODELS AND
DEMONSTRATES
(using think-alouds)

Provides examples of
effective strategy use

(Adapted from Pearson and Fielding 1991, 815–60)

See Chapter 6: Supporting Struggling and Reluctant Readers for more information on the Gradual Release of Responsibility instructional framework.

BLM 5: Intervention Lesson Framework: Reading Comprehension in Chapter 6

The Think-Aloud—The Best Way to Teach Strategies

The single most effective method of teaching comprehension strategies is the think-aloud.

Thinking aloud is a technique modelled by teachers and practised by students to improve comprehension. It involves orally identifying strategies being used while reading. When students apply this strategy with a partner or a group, they are using a metacognitive process to help them understand the comprehension process that is taking place inside their heads as they read, listen, or view.

Think-alouds remove the cloak of mystery surrounding how one comprehends. They make thinking public.

Implementing Think-Alouds

1. The teacher selects a shared reading or read-aloud passage and begins reading it aloud.

2. The teacher models the think-aloud process by stopping periodically and talking about the thought processes taking place. For example: "The title of this story makes me think that the story will be about a child who is unhappy to be moving. I'll read some more to find out ... I'm not sure what this word means, but I'll read on to see if I can figure it out ... Oh! Here's some new information about looking for a new house. It makes me think my prediction was correct."

3. In guided practice, students in small groups or on their own read silently or aloud and identify elements that made it difficult or easy to read and understand the text.

4. Students identify either orally (thinking aloud) or in writing the fix-up strategies that they used.

Key Think-Aloud Techniques to Model

- Making, checking, and modifying predictions
- Making mind pictures (visualizing in your head)
- Making connections; linking new information with previous knowledge (e.g., "This is like when ...")
- Monitoring comprehension (e.g., "This doesn't make sense ..."); demonstrating fix-up strategies (e.g., "I am going to reread this part" or "I will skip over it now ...")

(Adapted from Davey 1983, 44–47)

See also Student Think-Alouds earlier in this chapter.

Strategies Used by Effective Comprehenders

As noted earlier, research has established that effective readers, listeners, and viewers use the following strategies to make meaning from texts:

- monitoring comprehension
- using narrative and expository text structures
- visually representing text using graphic and semantic organizers
- retelling, summarizing, synthesizing, inferring
- generating questions
- answering questions
- using prior knowledge/predicting
- using mental imagery (visualizing)

As students become more proficient at selecting and using the comprehension strategies listed above, they should also be introduced to

strategies for applying their comprehension skills in a more integrated way. (See Combining Strategies toward the end of this chapter.)

A Strategy Caution

Strategies are options to help learners construct meaning. They are a means to an end, rather than an end in and of themselves. Having students complete numerous graphic organizers will not necessarily improve their comprehension. Students have to understand the purpose of a particular graphic organizer, why using the graphic organizer will help them, and when and how to use it. Teachers must balance how much time is spent completing graphic organizers and responding in other ways versus more time reading.

"Students can 'know' lots of strategies and also document their use of particular strategies. But being able to complete a strategy exercise is not the same as knowing how and when to use and apply a strategy in the act of reading to gain understanding.... We teachers need to give explicit demonstrations not just on how to use a strategy in isolation but also on how to make the strategy a part of our unconscious reading process, so that students are able to combine any number of strategies to problem solve before, during, and after they read" (Routman 2002, 129).

"Metacognition—thinking about one's own thinking—is the umbrella under which all other strategies fall. Each strategy is a variation of metacognition" (Keene and Zimmermann 1997, 25).

Monitoring Comprehension—The Number One Strategy

Effective readers constantly check to see if what they are reading makes sense to them. Students who monitor their comprehension know when their reading does and does not make sense. These students also self-correct to ensure that they understand the text. Conversely, many less proficient readers are often unaware of when and where their comprehension has broken down.

When students pay attention to the text to determine whether it makes sense, they understand that reading is a meaning-making activity. Using the appropriate strategies will help students become better at monitoring their own reading comprehension. These same strategies will assist students with monitoring their listening and viewing comprehension as well.

Self-monitoring comprehension teaches students to

- be aware of what they understand

- identify what they do not understand

- use appropriate fix-up strategies to resolve their comprehension problems

"Before students can monitor themselves and apply 'fix-up' strategies, they need to know what understanding entails. That is, when they understand what they are reading, what are they doing, what's happening inside their head? And do they recognize when meaning breaks down, when they no longer understand what they are reading? Too many of our students don't have this awareness. We need to teach our students to ask themselves, as they read:

- *Does this make sense?*

- *Does this sound like language?*

- *Do I know what is happening in the text?"*

ROUTMAN 2002, 125

Click and Clunk

To help students self-monitor their comprehension, teachers may introduce the click and clunk technique. A *click* is a part of the text that is understood; a *clunk* is a part of the text that is not understood and causes the reader, listener, or viewer to stop. Through think-alouds, teachers model the technique. They then explain to students that as long as their reading makes sense, everything clicks and rolls along smoothly. When there is a "clunk," the student's comprehension is halted—something is broken, not quite right.

The click and clunk technique enables students to create both an auditory response (click and clunk) and a visual image—a car clicking along and then breaking down (clunk!). Teachers note the clunks using question marks placed on sticky notes. Once students find that their comprehension has broken down, it's time to use a fix-up strategy.

Encourage students to use the click and clunk technique during guided reading.

Fix-up Strategies

Effective comprehenders use fix-up strategies when they cannot readily understand what they are reading, hearing, or viewing. Not all students automatically use these strategies, though, so it's important for teachers to identify them, model them, and teach students how and when to use them.

Teachers instruct students in these strategies:

- Skip what is not understood and move on. Clarification of the meaning may come as the student reads further in the text.

- Slow down or speed up. Slowing down when reading a difficult text sometimes helps students make more sense of their reading. Reading faster, to look ahead, sometimes gives the reader clues to the meaning of the text.

- Delay judgement about what the text means. When students keep reading, they may find that the writer fills in gaps in their understanding.

- Make an educated guess about the meaning of the word, sentence, or paragraph that may be unclear. By keeping these "hypothesized" meanings in mind as they read, students can determine if their guesses make sense.

- Reread the sentence or an earlier part of the text. Often, rereading text quietly aloud helps. By rereading a difficult sentence or a larger piece of previously read text, students may gain the information they need to incorporate the meaning of the new sentence.

- Use pictures, graphs, and charts to help.

- Try to make a mental picture of what is happening.

- Explain to someone else what is understood so far.

- Consult a dictionary, thesaurus, or another student to help or clarify understanding.

- Ask for help, consulting the teacher only as a last resort.

When to Use a Fix-up Strategy

You know you need a fix-up strategy when ...

❏ the pictures inside your mind stop forming

❏ you cannot answer your own questions

❏ your mind wanders from the text; you read it, but are thinking about something else

❏ the page you are now reading has nothing to do with what you thought the text was about

❏ you cannot explain what you have just read

❏ characters appear and you cannot remember who they are

(Adapted from Zwiers 2004, 134)

Say Something

"Say something" (Harste 1988) is a simple technique that forces students to stop, reflect, share their thoughts, and thereby monitor their comprehension and learn from others.

Implementing the "Say Something" Technique

1. The teacher begins by reading aloud a passage from a text. A non-fiction text that promotes much discussion is often good to start with.

2. At a logical and enticing point, the teacher stops and asks the students to each turn to a partner and "say something" about what they just heard.

3. A few students share their thoughts with the large group. Were most of their comments similar? Were any very different?

4. The process continues until the text is complete.

Teachers may use this same technique during shared and guided reading. In the case of guided reading, it is necessary to designate a stopping point ahead of time so that the students know where to stop.

(Adapted from McLaughlin and Allen 2002, 132)

Self-Monitoring Using Questions

Asking themselves questions as they read, view, or listen to a text will help students self-monitor their comprehension. This is what effective comprehenders do. The questions in the chart on the facing page may prove useful.

Questions to Ask When Reading, Listening, or Viewing Fiction	
To get the gist of what I'm reading, hearing, or viewing	What is the story about? What is the problem? What is the solution? What do I need to know more about?
To predict / verify / decide	What's going to happen next? Is my prediction still a good one? Do I need to change my prediction? What makes me think so?
To visualize / verify / decide	What does this (person, place, or thing) look like? Is the picture in my mind still good? Do I need to change the picture? What makes me think so?
To summarize	What's happened so far? Who did what? What makes me think so?
To think aloud	What am I thinking right now? Why?
To solve problems when I don't understand	Should I ... • stop and review? • reread or look back? • ignore and move on? Why?

(Adapted from Allington 2001, 105)

It is important for students to understand and remember that comprehension is something done during not just after reading, listening, or viewing! Asking themselves self-monitoring questions helps students to make this a reality.

Summarizing Mini-Lesson

The purpose of this mini-lesson is to help students get into the habit of taking time to stop as they read, listen, or view to make sure that the text is making sense. Weak comprehenders rarely stop and reflect, but instead continue on whether the text makes sense or not.

It is important that students are stopped at natural breaks and only occasionally (once or twice in a short text and four or five times in a long text). Stopping too frequently, especially with fiction text, often decreases comprehension as the flow is disrupted.

Implementing a Summarizing Mini-Lesson

1. The teacher previews the text with the students. The class looks at
   - the front cover (and sometimes the back cover) of the text
   - information about the author and illustrator
   - a few pictures or other visuals in the text

   Students then predict what the text will be about.

2. The teacher reads the text aloud to the students and stops every page or two, or at the end of a section, to provide a summary by thinking aloud (e.g., "So far the text is about.... I know this because...." Do the students agree or disagree?)

Fig Pudding by Ralph Fletcher is a great read-aloud, with chapters ideally suited to summarizing. This moving book describes the antics of a family with six children and offers many opportunities for students to make personal connections. The book is also useful for teaching study skills, such as note taking and monitoring comprehension.

3. The teacher reads the next section aloud and stops. The students are given time to summarize in their heads.

4. Students may then make one of two choices:

   • Verbalize their summaries with a partner. Their summaries consist of two parts: a summary statement and a statement explaining "I know this because...." This statement may share evidence from the text or simply be something inferred. Some summaries may then be shared with the large group for discussion or debate.

   • Write down their summaries, which will become a written record or outline of the text.

5. The teacher continues reading subsequent sections until the entire text is completed.

6. Students write overall summaries of the whole text (one or two sentences), which may then be shared orally with a partner, a small group, or the entire class. Alternatively, students' summary statements may be submitted to the teacher for review.

Skimming and Scanning

Skimming is a technique readers use when they want a quick and general sense of what is covered by a text, whether it is fiction or nonfiction. The reader looks for key words (character names, subject-specific vocabulary, and so on), headings, diagrams, pictures, words in bold print, and opening and closing paragraphs. The purpose of skimming is to identify the author's main ideas at a high rate of speed.

Scanning is another reading technique used to quickly locate something specific in a text. The reader glances through the text, focusing on key words and sentences that relate to the information being sought. A reader may scan a text such as a phone book to find a phone number, a recipe to see what ingredients are needed, or a reading passage to identify the setting or the name of a character.

My Summary

Name: _____ Grade: _____
Title: _____ Author: _____

Summary	Date	I know this because . . .
Part 1, page ___ to ___		
Part 2, page ___ to ___		
Part 3, page ___ to ___		

Skimming for Key Words

1. The teacher provides the class with a short reading passage on chart paper or an overhead, or distributes individual copies to students.

2. The teacher then explains the term *skimming* (see the previous page). Students are asked to read the passage quickly, without stopping, to read every word, and to note any key words that help them understand what the passage is about. The teacher explains that often these words are found in headings, diagrams, pictures, and words in bold type.

3. Students identify the key words that helped them understand the passage.

4. The group discusses how these key words were found and in what way they facilitated understanding.

Scanning to Locate Specific Information

1. The teacher provides the class with a short reading passage on chart paper or an overhead, or distributes individual copies to students. The topic that the students will be learning about is introduced (e.g., recycling).

2. The teacher explains the term *scanning* to the students (see the previous page).

3. Students find key words in the passage that provide specific information about the topic. They may want to highlight or underline these key words if they have their own copies of the passage. Alternatively, the teacher asks students to scan the text to find a specific word or sentence (e.g., "On page 44, find another word for *garbage* [waste] that is used in the text.").

4. The group discusses how they found these key words and how these words helped them find the information they needed.

SMART

SMART, an acronym for Self-Monitoring Approach to Reading and Thinking, is a metacognitive technique that helps students think about how their reading is going and what strategies they may need to use. It is about students talking to themselves as readers. When students use the SMART technique, they know what questions they need to ask as they read, listen to, or view a text in order to gain meaning. They use this technique to recognize what they understand and do not understand—the basis of effective comprehension. The SMART technique

- provides students with a system for monitoring their reading success
- allows students to verbalize what they do and do not understand about a text
- encourages students to persist until a text is understood
- provides clear steps to resolve misunderstandings
- involves students in summarizing the text in their own words
- helps students to remember key ideas in a text

S
M
A
R
T

Check It Out!

More information on the SMART technique can be found at My Read: http://www.myread.org/guide_stages.htm

Implementing the SMART Technique

1. The teacher models the technique for students during shared reading by choosing several paragraphs with a few words or ideas that the students might find challenging. The teacher stops at the confusing part, places a sticky note with a question mark in the margin, and then thinks aloud about which fix-up strategy to use. One or two are tried.

2. Working in small groups (guided reading) or with a partner, students silently read a text. Students may place a check mark on a sticky note at the end of each paragraph or page if they understand it, or a question mark if they do not (some teachers prefer to use only the question mark).

3. Students reread the text with question marks after they have finished reading the paragraph or section. They then try fix-up strategies.

4. If they are still confused, students determine what might be the problem (e.g., vocabulary or concepts). They discuss the confusing part with their partner or small group, and then together determine how to solve the problem (e.g., use a dictionary).

5. After the problem is solved, the question mark is changed to a check mark or the sticky note is removed.

(Adapted from Rhodes and Shanklin 1993, 256)

The steps in this technique can be outlined on a large wall chart, much like the sample on the facing page.

See also the Click and Clunk technique earlier in this section and the INSERT Strategy in Chapter 4: Literacy Learning Across the Curriculum.

Using Narrative and Expository Text Structures

The majority of reading and writing that adults do is nonfiction and much of the content is informational. In fact, the era in which we now live is known as the Information Age. The Internet is increasingly used as the resource of choice for finding out information, and most of the sites are expository in form. As students move into Grade 3 and beyond, their academic achievement in a wide range of subjects depends, in large part, on their ability to read and write informational text.

Students' ability to comprehend a text often depends on the type of text and the particular characteristics of that text. Students need to pay attention to text structure, or the way that the ideas in the text have been organized, as well as to special features intended to help readers as they read, such as pictures, graphs, size and type of font, headings, punctuation, and so on.

The two general types of texts that students are presented with most often are narrative texts, which tell a factual or fictional story, and expository texts, which provide and explain information. When students recognize the structure of a text, they begin to organize their thinking as they read to match the text structure. This makes comprehension easier.

Some techniques used by effective readers to help understand narrative and expository texts follow.

Check It Out!

National Geographic for Kids:
http://www.nationalgeographic.com/kids

Sports Illustrated for Kids:
http://www.sikids.com

World Wildlife Fund Kids' Stuff:
http://www.wwfcanada.org/satellite/wwfkids/

> ### Techniques to Support Comprehension of Narrative and Expository Texts
>
> - Story/text rebuilding
> - Story grammar
> - Nonfiction text features and structures

Story/Text Rebuilding

By rebuilding an unfamiliar piece of text that has been cut apart, students learn to recognize the organizational structures and elements of different kinds of texts. The piece might be a story, a chapter, or a section of informational text.

Implementing the Story/Text Rebuilding Technique

1. The teacher chooses a piece of text that is unfamiliar to students, copying and cutting it into meaningful segments and then modelling the text-rebuilding process.

2. The teacher chooses another piece of text that is unfamiliar to the students, copying and cutting it into meaningful segments.

3. The teacher distributes the segments to groups of three to five students each. All groups may work with the same piece of segmented text, or different groups may work with different texts, depending on the purpose of the activity.

4. Students work together to determine where their text parts fit into the sequence or organization of the whole piece.

5. Students share their thinking about why the segments go together in a particular order.

6. Once the text is rebuilt, students reread the completed text to determine if it makes sense and why. There is not necessarily a single correct way to rebuild the text. As long as the text makes sense grammatically (syntactically) and is meaningful (semantically) it is acceptable.

7. The teacher reads the original text aloud to the students. How do the students' versions compare with the original? Do they prefer their version? Why or why not?

Story Grammar

Story grammar consists of the various common elements of stories:

- setting—when and where the story takes place
- characters—who is in the story
- plot—what happens in the story and why
- problem—conflict, issue, disagreement
- solution—how the problem is solved

"Teaching students in grades 3–6 to identify and represent story structure improves their comprehension of the story they have read."

SNOW 2002, 33

When students use this technique, they are learning to identify and understand these elements. Fairy tales and fables are particularly well suited to demonstrating the story grammar technique.

Implementing the Story Grammar Technique

1. During shared reading time, the teacher helps students to identify and understand the elements of a story by first defining the key story-grammar terms (see the previous page).

2. The teacher reads a familiar story to the class.

3. Students are asked to use the story grammar definitions to identify the various parts of the story. The teacher records their responses in chart form on chart paper or an overhead (e.g., under Setting, "Calgary apartment building, summer 1997").

4. Students then apply this technique on their own after a read-aloud or an independent reading session, or in small groups after a guided reading lesson.

5. The teacher monitors students' understanding and use of this technique to support comprehension. Students could be asked to complete story grammar charts or to identify the elements of a story just read when in a reading conference.

BLM 8: Story Grammar

Nonfiction Text Features and Structures

Much of students' time in Grades 3 to 6 is spent reading nonfiction materials. This is because they spend more time throughout the day reading to learn. By learning how to read informational texts and nonfiction content in narrative texts across subject areas, students will develop the strategies needed to understand the concepts and information being presented.

This makes a great classroom chart or poster!

Text Features	
Captions	Labels
Charts	Lists
Descriptions	Maps
Diagrams	Photos
Directions	Procedures
Drawings	Table of contents
Glossary	Title
Graphs	Topic sentences
Headings	Varied print (bold
Index	and italics)

Teach Five Expository Text Structures to Help Students in Both Reading and Writing

Help students to: Graphic Organizers

- Describe

- Sequence

- Compare/Contrast

- Note cause and effect

- Recognize problem and solution

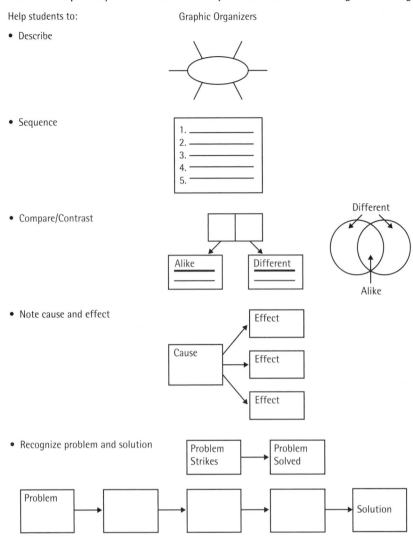

(Adapted from Tompkins 2000, 252–53)

Using Text Features to Help Students Preview Nonfiction Text

- During shared and guided reading, the teacher presents texts that include a variety of nonfiction text features.

- The teacher models for the students how to preview the text by looking at the text features, such as headings, subheadings, graphics, and the index. (For example, "The headings in this chapter of my math text tell me that the focus of the lessons will be on graphing, collecting data, and graphing with technology. I'm going to need some graph paper and will need to use the computer.")

- During guided reading, the teacher provides the students with many opportunities to practise their previewing skills using text features. Students may be encouraged to refer to a summary poster of text features or a shared reading/writing chart to help them identify and think about the purpose of each feature. They could also take turns adding the name of the book to a chart and checking off the text features found (see adjacent chart).

- The teacher also models writing using text features during shared writing.

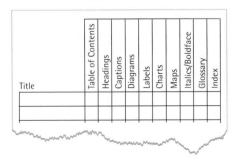

Beat the Clock

Beat the Clock is an engaging activity that gives students practice with finding and describing text features. Pairs of students or individuals are given a limited amount of time to review an informational text and to write down at least one example of every text feature they can find. The student or pair group who notes the most text features and explains their purposes within the time limit provided will "beat the clock."

Beat the Clock is a great activity to encourage partners to discuss the purposes of specific text features.

BLM 9: Beat the Clock

Visually Representing Text Using Graphic and Semantic Organizers

When students represent text visually, such as with a graphic organizer, they are prompted to remember what they have just read in a concrete, visual way. For many students, this strategy is a helpful method for organizing and remembering a text, which they may perceive as confusing and too abstract to readily recall and understand. Using graphic organizers also helps students to activate and organize prior knowledge around a topic.

Students benefit from using graphic organizers as a tool to support discussion and writing. Too often, however, students prepare a graphic organizer as an end product, not as a foundation for further thinking, discussion, and writing. The graphic organizer is just like the word processor on the computer—it is only a tool.

Graphic organizers, such as those described in this section, provide students with many different ways to represent and make sense of what they read. There are a wide variety of graphic organizers, including semantic maps, webs, charts, and frames.

Creating a graphic organizer must be a more valuable activity than simply more time spent reading.

Key Types of Graphic Organizers

- Plot organizers
- Semantic maps or webs
- Venn diagrams
- Story maps
- Story map comic strips

See also the diagram on the previous page for other graphic organizers not listed here.

Plot Organizers

Plot organizers are visual ways to organize and analyze story plots. They can be used to help students understand and summarize a text.

Graphic organizers help readers make sense of text. They are often aptly called "thinking tools."

Plot Organizer for Cinderella

Conflict: Cinderella wants to attend the ball, but her stepmother won't allow her to go.

Climax: Cinderella loses her glass slipper while fleeing the ball before the spell ends at midnight.

Rising Action: Fairy godmother casts magic spell on Cinderella so she can go to the ball.

Falling Action: Prince searches town for the girl who fits the glass slipper.

Introduction: Cinderella lives with stepmother and stepsisters, who are mean to her.

Resolution: Prince tries slipper on Cinderella. It fits, they marry, and live happily ever after.

Implementing Plot Organizers

1. As part of a shared or guided reading discussion, the teacher asks students to identify the elements of a story, which are recorded on chart paper or an overhead. If no one identifies the story's problem and solution, then the teacher identifies them for the students.

2. The teacher shows students the plot organizer and talks about how it can help them understand and remember the elements of a story.

3. The teacher reads a familiar story aloud and asks students to work in their group to complete the parts of the plot organizer. (Reading a familiar story enables students to focus on the strategy.)

4. Students use a plot organizer themselves or with a partner once they are familiar and comfortable with the strategy.

BLM 10: Plot Organizer

Semantic Maps or Webs

Semantic maps, or webs, provide students with a graphic way to organize, remember, and represent relevant information from a text or from a research project. Semantic mapping, or webbing, enables students to show relationships between or among many different story elements, such as characters, events, emotions, or settings. It also enables students to show relationships between or among facts, events, or ideas in a research project. This technique is equally useful for developing vocabulary and retrieving and organizing prior knowledge.

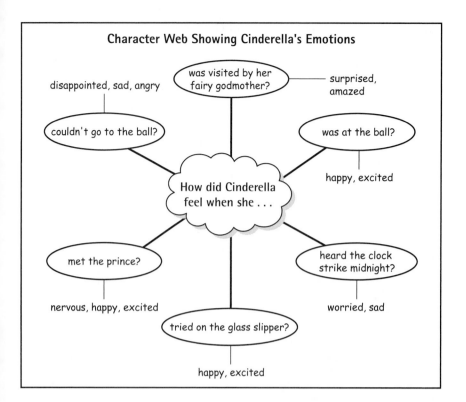

Character Web Showing Cinderella's Emotions

disappointed, sad, angry — couldn't go to the ball?

was visited by her fairy godmother? — surprised, amazed

was at the ball? — happy, excited

How did Cinderella feel when she . . .

met the prince? — nervous, happy, excited

heard the clock strike midnight? — worried, sad

tried on the glass slipper? — happy, excited

Using Semantic Maps or Webs

- The teacher uses chart paper or an overhead to create a semantic map or web with the class. If students are completing a web on their own or with a group, the teacher might provide them with a template (e.g., the Event Map that follows, or BLM 11: Main Idea and Supporting Details).

- The teacher reviews the students' work to ensure that they are able to sequence events, organize information, and make judgements and inferences from what they read.

What happened?

When did it happen?

Where did it happen?

Event Map

Who was involved?

How did it happen?

Why did it happen?

BLM 11: Main Idea and Supporting Details

Using Semantic Maps to Keep Track of Characters

Another type of semantic map involves drawing pictures (visuals) of characters and adding their names, nicknames, and roles. It is often difficult for students to keep track of numerous characters in more complex texts as the characters may appear infrequently.

Although it is a great read-aloud book, *Holes* by Louis Sachar tells three stories at once, which students may find confusing. In addition, the characters have nicknames, which can also lead to confusion. Creating a semantic map as the story is read aloud helps students to keep track of the characters and establish how they connect to one another.

Drawing pictures of the characters (visuals) and including the names, nicknames, and roles of each one helps students keep track of the characters during a read-aloud of *Holes*.

Venn Diagrams

A Venn diagram, often referred to as a compare/contrast diagram, is made up of two or more overlapping circles. Students describe, compare, and contrast attributes and characteristics of things, people, places, events, characters, stories, and nonfiction texts using a visual representation. The Venn diagram is a good way for students to see how ideas are related.

Check It Out!

More information on graphic organizers is available from http://www.graphic.org

If you want help creating a Venn diagram, visit http://www.readwritethink.org/materials/venn

Differences | Differences

Brown Bears
- brown fur
- hibernate during winter
- omnivore (vegetation main part of diet)
- live in forests and meadows
- most active at night

Similarities
- live alone for most of the year
- live for 20 to 25 years in the wild
- can survive without water or food for up to six months in winter
- native to North America

Polar Bears
- white or off-white fur
- only pregnant females hibernate in winter
- carnivore (seals are main part of diet)
- live in the Arctic and tundra
- most active in the morning and evening

Implementing Venn Diagrams

1. The teacher may introduce Venn diagrams by asking whether and how students have used them in mathematics (to show how objects are similar and how they are different).

2. The teacher explains that Venn diagrams in reading are used for the same purpose.

3. The teacher reads a familiar story with a number of key characters or different settings to the students. The teacher then works with the class to create a character or setting Venn diagram. Alternatively, the teacher could select a research theme, such as animals, and ask students to identify what is the same and what is different about each animal. The information is recorded using a Venn diagram.

4. Students may then be asked to create a Venn diagram on their own or with a partner after guided or independent reading. Students then have the opportunity to share and explain their diagrams to a small group or the whole class.

Story Maps

This technique requires students to create a pictorial or written representation of the settings in a story, the actions of the characters, and the conclusion of the story. Mapping the story allows students to visualize in sequence to see how the plot and characters are related to the setting. Story mapping is also a useful technique for helping students develop their organizational skills as they write their own stories.

Story Map

Title: *The Twits*
Author: Roald Dahl
Setting: The Twits' house, garden
Characters: Mr. and Mrs. Twit, Muggle-Wumps (monkeys), birds, Roly-Poly Bird
Problem: The Twits mistreat the birds and monkeys.
Actions:
• Mr. and Mrs. Twit are mean to everyone and everything.
• He covers the trees with glue to catch birds to eat, and forces his caged monkeys to do everything on their heads. She beats the monkeys if they don't obey.
• Roly-Poly Bird arrives on holiday and sets the birds and monkeys free.
• When the Twits leave to buy guns to shoot the birds, the monkeys and birds glue everything in the Twits' house to the ceiling.
• Birds swoop over the Twits' heads and paint them with glue, too.
Resolution: Finding everything in their house upside-down, the Twits stand on their heads as a temporary solution. But they get stuck to the floor forever and shrink until all that's left of them is a pile of clothes.

A story map is a tool intended to support students as they read and write. However, story maps used too frequently do not allow students the time needed to make sense of text through more personal and authentic ways, such as response journals and discussions.

Story Map Comic Strips

Creating story map comic strips provides students with a motivating and artistic way to demonstrate their understanding of a story and create a personal response to the text. A story map comic strip lesson plan for Grades 3 to 5 and tools to help students create their own strips are available from ReadWriteThink at http://www.readwrite-think.org/lessons/lesson_view.asp?id=236

BLM 12: Story Map

Retelling, Summarizing, Synthesizing, Inferring

Students' overall comprehension of text is improved when they are able to retell, summarize, synthesize, and infer. When students retell and summarize, they are doing more than just listing events; they are making decisions about what is and isn't important in a text, making inferences to draw conclusions about a text, and synthesizing concepts and ideas to pull their thinking together. Often, they are also adding their own personal connections to the text. "[S]ynthesis is as much about what a reader does during reading as it is about a coherent retelling after reading" (Keene and Zimmermann 1997, 176).

By Grade 3, most students will have experience in retelling stories and will be familiar with the retelling format; however, they may not have had experience with summarizing. Some students may find summarizing a difficult task. "[O]lder and more proficient readers summarize better than younger and less skilled readers" (Irvin 1998, 206). The techniques and activities that follow will improve students' skill and understanding and help to support their comprehension.

Techniques for Retelling and Summarizing

- Summarizing
- GIST procedure
- Book clubs and book talks, reviews, and recommendations (see relevant sections earlier in this chapter)
- Literary news reports
- Literature circles (see Chapter 5: In the Classroom: Making It Work)
- Readers Theatre
- Summarizing, Making Connections, Responding
- Who Wants But So (Then)
- Reciprocal teaching (See also Chapter 6: Supporting Struggling and Reluctant Readers.)

Summarizing

Being able to summarize what has been read is an important comprehension and study skills technique, but it is often difficult for students to do. Students have to learn how to select the most salient points of the text (the essence or the gist) and need to ensure that their summaries include inference, synthesis, and analysis. They may summarize orally or in writing.

Implementing the Summarizing Technique

1. The teacher provides students with a short story or an informational piece. The text either can be read aloud by the teacher or silently by the students.

2. After reading, students ask themselves one of these two questions: "What should I be able to tell someone else about this?" or "What are the most important points that were made in the text?" Students identify these important points.

3. The teacher reminds the students that a summary includes only essential information that readers need to remember. This information includes important ideas, events, details, and characters from the text.

One Approach to Summarizing

When students summarize a piece of text, they may find the following steps helpful.

Step 1: Delete unnecessary material. Eliminating information that is unnecessary or trivial is much easier than eliminating redundant material, even for students in Grades 4 and 5 (Pearson and Fielding 1991).

Step 2: Delete information that is repeated (redundant) and is not useful.

Step 3: Choose a word to replace a list of items. For example, the text may indicate that the character has bought peaches, pears, apples, cherries, and bananas. This would be summarized in one word—fruit.

Step 4: Choose a word to replace individual parts of an action. For example, the text may indicate that the character unlocked the car door, put the key in the ignition, looked behind him, and drove out of the parking lot. This idea could be summarized as, "The character drove out of the parking lot."

Step 5: Select a topic sentence if there is one.

Step 6: If there is no topic sentence, create one.

(Adapted from McNeil 1987, 157)

Less than one-third of nonfiction text has a topic sentence; fiction rarely has a topic sentence (McNeil 1987).

Students need to analyze their own summaries to ensure they have

- deleted unimportant or repeated (redundant) information
- replaced lists of words or events with a main heading or one word
- found or created a topic sentence

4. Through teacher modelling, as well as group and individual practice, students learn to apply the steps to create brief summaries of text.

5. The teacher records summary points in jot-note form so everyone can read them.

6. The class discusses and numbers these points.

7. In discussion with students, the teacher rewrites the points so they become full sentences. The class reviews the sentences and their order to ensure that a short summary of the information or story has been completed.

Studies conducted in upper elementary grades indicate that identifying the gist [of text] enhances the capacity to understand new text (Snow 2002, 33).

Check It Out!

New York Times Learning Network
http://www.nytimes.com/learning

Yahooligans
http://yahooligans.com

The GIST Procedure

A second approach to summarizing is the GIST procedure, developed by Patricia Cunningham. "In GIST, students create summaries of 15 or fewer words for increasingly large amounts of text, beginning with single sentences and working incrementally to an entire paragraph" (Duke and Pearson 2002, 221).

Teachers begin by working with the whole class to create a GIST summary. They then direct students to work in small groups, and finally have students create a GIST summary on their own.

Literary News Reports

Students learn to summarize when they turn stories into front-page news reports. They also learn what constitutes a news report. (See also the section titled Authentic Reasons to Write in Chapter 3.)

Implementing Literary News Reports

1. The teacher brainstorms with students the types of information that appear in a news report. Elements include headline, dateline, byline, and body of the report. A newspaper article or report is shown to students to demonstrate.

2. The class then identifies the order of the contents of a news report: the lead, the specific details arranged from most to least important, and the ending.

3. The teacher models the technique using a familiar story. The group then completes a literary news report together. For example, a headline for the story of Little Red Riding Hood might read, "Wolf captured!" The lead might be, "A quick-thinking hunter saved a grandmother and granddaughter from a hungry wolf yesterday in the forest outside of town."

4. Students work in pairs or small groups to create literary news reports based on a read-aloud, shared, or guided reading text. They then share their reports with other groups.

BLM 13: Literary News Report

Readers Theatre

Students dramatize a rehearsed story, poem, or story adaptation, using mainly their voices. Readers Theatre is generally performed without costumes or much movement. In bringing a piece of literature to life, students not only understand and summarize or retell a text, but they also interpret mood, character, and events.

Implementing Readers Theatre

1. Small groups of up to five students rewrite a story, poem, song, or chant as a short play with a narrator. This could be a piece that they've read together during shared or guided reading or through a read-aloud. They may add sound effects or music.

2. Students rehearse the selection until they are confident and comfortable about their parts. There may be times when the group combines their voices for special effects and other times when individuals speak alone. In some ways, Readers Theatre is like a musical composition.

3. Students perform their reading in front of an audience. Since there are few actions, the goal is for the audience to be able to visualize the story, based only on the reading performance.

For more information on Readers Theatre, see Chapter 5: In the Classroom: Making It Work.

Summarizing, Making Connections, Responding

This technique requires students to summarize what they know. They then make connections to personal experiences and memories, ideas, books, and so on. Finally, they respond or reflect by asking questions, wondering, and thinking about their reading and experiences.

Summarizing, making connections, and responding encourage students to make personal connections and inferences, thus improving their comprehension.

Implementing the Summarizing, Making Connections, Responding Technique

1. The teacher may model the technique after a read-aloud.

Teacher Model Based on *Silverwing* by Kenneth Oppel

Summarizing: This story traces the adventures of Shade, the runt of a silverwing bat colony, who becomes separated from his family during his first winter migration. In his struggle to return to his colony, Shade learns an important lesson about the dangers of reckless curiosity. But he also learns that within him are the instincts, intelligence, and courage to survive.

Making Connections: This story reminds me of the time I went shopping with my family and got lost because I decided to go look at something without telling anyone.

Responding: I wonder why people, even when they know something might be dangerous, do it anyway.

---

2. Students, working either in pairs or small groups, practise summarizing, making connections, and responding after a read-aloud, shared, or guided reading session.

3. The teacher encourages students to use this technique in their own personal responses to reading. They might choose a response journal, a book talk, or other form of response.

4. This activity also works with literature circles.

Who Wants But So (Then)

This simple technique can be used by students to quickly summarize the main conflict and resolution in fiction.

Implementing the "Who Wants But So (Then)" Technique

1. The teacher models the technique for students by completing a Who Wants But So chart for a familiar story.

Who Wants But So (Then) is a great technique for students to use when they come in from recess and have a problem to relate!

Story Title: Aladdin				Then
Who	**Wants**	**But**	**So**	the king's evil advisor Jafar, who seeks the power of the genie for himself, reveals Aladdin's identity and has him killed. But the genie saves Aladdin's life and together they save the kingdom from Jafar. Jasmine is permitted to marry Aladdin and they live happily ever after.
Aladdin, a poor street orphan,	to marry princess Jasmine	the law states that she must marry someone of royal blood	Aladdin has the genie grant him his wish of becoming a prince	

2. Students may then use this technique on their own when summarizing fiction by identifying
   - the character(s) (*Who*)
   - what the character(s) wants (*Wants*)
   - what is preventing the character(s) from achieving the goal; i.e., the problem (*But*)

- how the problem is solved (*So*)

Recently, a modification of this technique has been seen in classrooms. *Then* has been added to make the ending more complete.

(Adapted from Boyle and Peregoy 1990, 194–99)

Reciprocal Teaching

This indirect form of summarizing instruction involves four comprehension strategies: summarizing, asking important questions, clarifying unclear segments (monitoring comprehension), and predicting. This approach has proven very successful in improving text comprehension, especially for struggling comprehenders.

Implementing the Reciprocal Teaching Framework

1. The teacher prepares by selecting and reading the text that students will use.

2. The teacher thinks about how to help students predict what the selection or section will be about, or review or summarize what was read during the previous session. (See Using Prior Knowledge/Predicting later in this chapter.)

3. Students then read the text selection silently.

4. The teacher asks two or three questions to promote discussion of the text selection. Some of these questions should be "thick" questions (high level) or "off the page" questions. (See Thick and Thin Questions and Question–Answer Relationships (QAR) later in this chapter.)

5. Students are prompted to clarify any confusions (e.g., "Is there anything that doesn't make sense?"). Alternatively, the teacher uses a think-aloud to model a confusion and how it is clarified.

6. The teacher determines how to help students summarize the section of text read.

7. Steps 2 through 6 are repeated with the next section of the text.

The reciprocal teaching framework can be used during read-alouds, shared and guided reading, and literature circles. Students learn the strategies through teacher modelling and think-alouds so that they can eventually take turns coaching other students through the process. Following the Gradual Release of Responsibility Model, only when students understand and use the four comprehension strategies with support should they be expected to apply them independently.

Older struggling readers who use reciprocal teaching to support younger readers will themselves develop skill in

- generating and responding to questions
- making and checking predictions
- summarizing
- clarifying thoughts
- fluency

They will also develop confidence as readers!

See also Chapter 6: Supporting Struggling and Reluctant Readers for more information on the reciprocal teaching framework.

A review of numerous studies concluded that reciprocal teaching is effective at improving comprehension (Duke and Pearson 2002).

"The order in which the reciprocal teaching strategies are used is not fixed; it depends on the text and the reader."

OCZKUS 2003, 14

He who teaches learns.

Check It Out!

Lori D. Oczkus. *Reciprocal Teaching at Work: Strategies for Improving Reading Comprehension* (Newark, DE: International Reading Association, 2003). This superb book also has an accompanying video, published in 2005.

Steps in Reciprocal Teaching*

Predict
What will happen?

Question
Ask questions about the text being read.
- *who, what, when, where, why,* and *how* questions
- *thick* and *thin* questions
- *on the page* and *off the page* questions

Clarify
Clear up any confusion. Are there words or ideas that need to be explained?

Summarize
What are the most important ideas?

*The order of the steps may change, depending on the text and the reader.

If students are asked simple questions, simple thinking is often the outcome.

Ask fewer questions and give students more time to explain how they know.

In some classrooms three or four students give 95 percent of the answers.

Training Others in Reciprocal Teaching

Reciprocal teaching is also an ideal framework for supporting comprehension coaching. Volunteers, buddies, and paraprofessionals must have opportunities to see the framework modelled and to practise it with feedback before working independently.

- The teacher models the strategy several times. (I do it.)
- The coach is given several opportunities to work with the teacher in employing the framework with a group of students. (We do it.)
- The coach is then allowed to take the lead in assisting students using this technique. (You do it.)
- Feedback is provided as needed.

BLM 6: Intervention Lesson Framework: Reciprocal Teaching in Chapter 6

Generating Questions, Answering Questions

Both students and teachers need to ask questions. Teachers need to model questioning through think-alouds. They also need to model a variety of questions and techniques, such as thick and thin questions and question–answer relationships (QAR) (see later in this chapter). This will help students understand the process of questioning and how to find the answers. Research undertaken in Grades 3 to 5 indicates that "engaging students in elaborative questioning improves their comprehension of text read during instruction and their comprehension of new text read independently" (Snow 2002, 33).

When asking questions, effective teachers

- include open-ended questions
- focus on the thinking process, not a specific answer (students' responses need only be defensible). Teachers ask students further questions, such as "What makes you think so?" and "How do you know?"
- allow a wait time of at least 8 seconds. This may seem lengthy but it is important. Students need time to reflect on the question and to contemplate a meaningful response. Bombarding students with one question right after another may result in superficial answers (simply what comes into the student's head, with little or no reflection), and in the same students responding repeatedly.
- repeat or rephrase questions for the students who are struggling. When students understand that the teacher will persevere with them until they succeed, they become engaged in a different way and respond successfully (Bergman 1992).
- provide the response if the student continues to struggle, and then have the student repeat or paraphrase it

Do ...	Do not ...
• ask students to explain their thinking (e.g., "How do you know that?"); thinking aloud makes their thought processes public	• ask too many closed questions (e.g., simple *yes* or *no* questions); the quality of the response depends to a large degree on the quality of the question
• encourage students to self-question as they read (see Self-Monitoring Using Questions earlier in this chapter)	• follow-up any student response with "good"; this ensures that students who do not receive this affirmation do not interpret it to mean that their response was wrong or inferior

Students become active participants in the reading process by evaluating or making judgements about what they are reading. When students evaluate a text, they try to identify the author's viewpoint and purpose, distinguish fantasy from reality and fact from opinion, and make value judgements.

Students learn to evaluate texts by asking questions as they think about the meaning of the selection. Questions can be literally based, where students look for responses that are evident in the text, or inferentially based, where they read between the lines to determine the meaning of the text. However, students don't naturally know how to find the answers to questions. That skill has to be explained, modelled, and demonstrated.

Learning how to generate and answer questions is an important skill for students to learn. The following techniques will help students improve their skills in this area.

"Most children are interrogated after reading but have limited opportunity to receive instruction in the comprehension strategies needed to answer the questions posed."

ALLINGTON 1994, 22

- KWLM
- Question–Answer Relationships (QAR)
- Literature circles (see Chapter 5: In the Classroom: Making It Work)
- Questioning the Author (QtA)
- Questions that support critical literacy
- Self-monitoring using questions (see earlier in this chapter)
- Thick and thin questions

KWLM

KWLM is a good activity for generating many questions about an informational topic. This technique encourages students to

- think about what they know about the topic
- predict what they think they will learn or generate questions
- reflect on what they learn
- perhaps question and research further

> **KWLM Strategy**
> What I **know**
> What I **want** to know
> What I have **learned**
> What **more** do I want to learn?

KWLM Topic: _____	
What I **KNOW** 1. _____ 2. _____ 3. _____ 4. _____	What I **WANT** to know or think that I will learn 1. _____ 2. _____ 3. _____ 4. _____
What I have **LEARNED** 1. _____ 2. _____ 3. _____ 4. _____	What **MORE** do I want to learn? 1. _____ 2. _____ 3. _____ 4. _____

(Adapted from Ogle 1986, 564–70)

See Chapter 4: Literacy Learning Across the Curriculum for more information on the KWLM technique.

Question–Answer Relationships (QAR)

This technique involves teaching students how to create and then find answers to questions. Teachers often bombard students with questions, but don't often teach them how or where they might find the answers. QAR also helps students to learn to ask a variety of questions, including those that require higher-level thinking and promote self-questioning. Again, this is what effective comprehenders do naturally.

"The absence of comprehension is related to not knowing the relevant questions to ask, or not knowing how to find the relevant answers."

SMITH 1994, 53

There are two basic QAR divisions, which can be further subdivided, as the chart that follows shows.

In the Book (on the page)	In My Head (off the page)
Right There: The answer is in the text and stated clearly, usually within a single sentence. The words used to form the question and the words to answer it are "right there" in the book.	**On My Own:** The answer is not in the text. The reader comes up with the answer based on what he or she already knows.
• The answer is right there "in the book" and easy to find. It is usually found within a single sentence.	• The answer can only be found "in my head."
Think and Search (hidden): The answer is implied in the text but it is not directly stated. It is "hidden."	**Author and Me:** The answer is not in the text. The reader must think about what he or she knows and what the author says, and then put them together.
• The answer is in the text but it's not easy to find. It requires information from more than one sentence or paragraph.	• There is no answer unless the reader's knowledge and the author's information connect.

Question–answer relationships help students to understand that

- comprehension depends on both text (what is on the page) and reader (what is in the reader's head)
- there can be more than one right answer
- not all questions are answered in the text
- some questions will not have answers

During or after a read-aloud, it is a good idea to model all four question types for students using think-alouds.

Introducing QAR Using Visuals

QAR supports visual literacy, which involves making meaning from, or comprehending, visual stimuli. A great way to introduce the QAR technique is a mini-lesson during which students look very carefully at the details of a picture to make meaning.

Just like reading print, some pictures provide all the specific information needed to answer the question. In other cases, the information may be implied or the students may need to figure it out on their own. For many students, learning to "read pictures" using QAR is initially easier than applying the technique to print. And using the picture context is less threatening for many students, especially **ESL** students and those struggling with decoding print.

Implementing the QAR Technique

1. The teacher introduces QAR and the category terms and explains that there are two main categories of questions and answers:
   - In the Book (on the page): answers are stated in the text

Emma E. Cortese. "The Application of Question–Answer Relationship Strategies to Pictures." *The Reading Teacher* 57.4 (Dec. 2003/Jan. 2004), 374–80.

- In My Head (off the page): answers are not specifically stated in the text

The teacher then explains and models (using think-alouds) the two types of question–answer relationships for each category:

- In the Book = Right There and Think and Search
- In My Head = On My Own and Author and Me

2. Pairs of students are provided with a variety of questions to answer and then classify.

3. During read-aloud and guided reading, students are given opportunities to ask each kind of question.

4. Students formulate their own questions during guided reading. They work with a partner or a small group to first answer the questions. Then they classify the questions as "right there," "think and search," "on my own," or "author and me." Encourage students to engage in debates and discussions as they make their decisions about question types.

(Adapted from Raphael 1986, 516–22)

"[T]eaching students in grades 3–9 to self-question while reading text enhances their understanding of the text used in instruction and improves their comprehension of new text."

<small>SNOW 2002, 33</small>

Teachers can facilitate questioning by having students take part in a range of activities, such as

- KWLM (see earlier description)
- coming up with questions that correspond to supplied answers based on a familiar text
- taking turns asking one another questions about a small segment of text
- conducting in-role interviews in which partners take turns playing the interviewer and the interviewee

BLM 14: Question–Answer Relationships (QAR)

Questioning the Author (QtA)

When students use the Questioning the Author technique (QtA), they learn that it's important to ask questions as they read in order to think more deeply about their reading. They also learn to question what the author has said (or not said) or implied, and why.

Students who are struggling with comprehension often do not ask questions before, during, or after reading, listening, or viewing. They do not connect with the text, so they don't question what the author is saying or why it is being said. The QtA technique permits more student talk and less teacher talk. It is important for teachers to avoid asking too many questions before, during, and after reading. Rather, provide students with many opportunities to come up with the questions. Use of this technique during read-alouds, shared reading, guided reading, and independent reading results in improved listening and reading comprehension.

"[S]tudents become much more successful at higher order comprehension and monitoring their comprehension as a result of participating in Questioning the Author."

DUKE AND PEARSON 2002, 19

Implementing the QtA Technique

1. When reading aloud, the teacher promotes discussion by asking questions such as, "What is the author's message?" or "What is the author trying to tell us?"

2. The teacher further focuses students' attention on the author's message by saying, "This is what the author says, but what does it mean?" More discussion occurs.

3. The teacher then helps students link information by asking such questions as, "How does this new information connect with what the author has already told us? Does this make sense with what the author told us before?"

4. The teacher also helps students make inferences by asking, "Did the author tell us that? How do you know that if the author didn't tell us?"

(Adapted from Duke and Pearson 2002, 205–42, 230)

Reading Comprehension: Strategies That Work

Questions That Support Critical Literacy

Teachers scaffold critical literacy through the questions they ask during classroom discussions. The questions that follow help students to examine an author's perspective.

- "What is the topic? How is it presented? What themes are being expressed?"
- "How are the characters presented? Why are they presented in this way? How might you change a character(s) and why?"
- "What is the purpose of the text? What is it trying to make you think or feel?"
- "What wasn't said about the topic? Why was it left out? What would you add or delete if you were writing on this topic?"
- "Who is writing to whom? Whose positions are being expressed? Whose voices and positions are not heard?"

(Adapted from Luke, O'Brien, and Comber 2001,116)

Thick and Thin Questions

The terminology *thick and thin questions* has been cited by researchers such as Harvey and Goudvis (2000) and McLaughlin and Allen in *Guided Comprehension: A Teaching Model for Grades 3–8* (2002). The technique helps students to understand that questions have different depths ranging from strictly recall (thin) to complex and open-ended (thick). Students learn that the types of questions they ask themselves as they read affects the kind of meaning they make.

Implementing Thick and Thin Question Classification

1. The teacher explains the concept of thick and thin questions.
2. After reading aloud a text selection, the teacher asks a thick question and a thin question, and then labels each one to serve as a model.
3. The teacher reads the text selection aloud again, asks a series of questions, and then has the students classify the questions as thick or thin.
4. During the next read-aloud, the teacher has the students come up with questions, and then answer and classify one another's questions as thick or thin.
5. After guided reading, the teacher may have the students work in pairs to create thick and thin questions for one another to answer and classify.

Using Prior Knowledge/Predicting

In order to make sense of a text selection, students need to call on their background or prior knowledge. It is very difficult for students to understand material if they have little or no personal knowledge of the topic. Comprehension depends on readers, viewers, and listeners connecting what they already know with what the text is about. By using prior knowledge, students are able to draw on what they already know to help them confirm information and learn new ideas from the text. The techniques listed in the box that follows will help students identify what they already know before and as they read, listen, or view.

Techniques for Supporting Prior Knowledge/Predicting

- Anticipation guide
- Identifying, categorizing, and sorting
- Vocabulary prediction—Let's Predict
- Sort and predict
- KWLM (see earlier in this chapter and Chapter 4: Literacy Learning Across the Curriculum)
- SQ3R (Survey, Question, Read, Recite, Review)
- CATS (covers, author, title, skim)

Anticipation Guide

An anticipation guide, also known as a prediction guide, is a useful prereading and post-reading activity, best used with topics or themes about which students are likely to have different opinions and attitudes. It activates prior knowledge, prompts students to make predictions, and can be used to set a purpose for reading. It can motivate discussion and interest. After reading, it can also help some students focus on inaccuracies and misconceptions about a topic as they accept, reject, or modify their prior knowledge and predictions. This technique can be used with read-alouds, shared reading, and guided reading.

Implementing the Anticipation Guide Technique

1. Once the teacher decides whether to introduce the activity to the whole class, a large group, or a small group of students, he or she selects a fiction, nonfiction, or poetry text to work with.

2. The teacher identifies the main themes/ideas in the text by writing four to six statements related to them. These statements might be written on chart paper or an overhead, or distributed to students in the form of a handout. A few statements may come directly from the text.

3. Students respond to these statements orally or in writing, either agreeing or disagreeing with them. Their decisions should be based on what they know or think they know, and should be supported by reasons. "I believe this because...."

4. Students discuss the statements as a class, with a small group, or in pairs, being sure to justify their responses. They may then choose to revise their initial responses based on new information shared by peers.

5. Students read or listen to the text to confirm their predictions, and then revise their original responses to the statements where applicable.

6. The activity concludes with the teacher prompting discussion about what students have learned from the text by asking questions such as those that follow.
   - "What statements support your original opinions?"
   - "What statements contradict your original opinions?"
   - "Where have you changed your opinion?"
   - "Where you haven't changed your opinion, why do you still agree or disagree with the statements?"
   - "What would help you change your mind?"

BLM 15: Anticipation Guide

Identifying, Categorizing, and Sorting

Students use this technique to activate, expand, and revise prior knowledge by gathering information they already know about a topic or selection. Identifying can help them see the connections among ideas, concepts, and words. It is also a tool to help them see another's point of view and justify their decisions.

Implementing the Identifying, Categorizing, and Sorting Technique

1. The teacher asks students who are working in large or small groups an open-ended question about a specific topic or theme (e.g., "Which musical instruments can you name?").

2. The teacher records all responses on individual index cards without making any value judgements. If desired, the teacher may add further ideas.

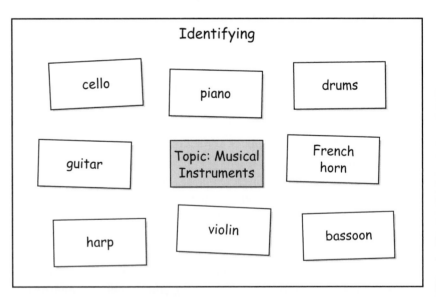

Identifying

cello · piano · drums · guitar · **Topic: Musical Instruments** · French horn · harp · violin · bassoon

3. Responses are then categorized and sorted. The teacher models the sorting of one or two cards and then distributes the remainder to students, who bring forward one card at a time. A student reads the card and the teacher begins to sort the cards into the categories identified by the students, encouraging debate and discussion.

4. If some words or ideas fit more than one category, the teacher makes duplicate cards.

5. After the sorting stage is complete, students reread the words in each category to ensure all cards are sorted appropriately.

6. The responses may be charted or organized as a semantic map, which may be used for note taking. (See Semantic Maps or Webs earlier in this chapter.)

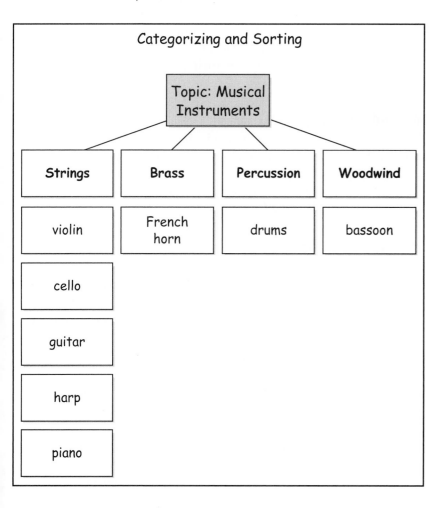

Bringing in actual items for the students to categorize and sort is especially helpful for students learning the language or for those weak in vocabulary or concept development.

7. Categorized and sorted words and ideas may remain posted in the classroom as the theme or topic is developed. They may also be added to students' personal word lists.

See also List–Group–Label in Chapter 1: Oral Language: Speaking, Listening, and Learning.

Vocabulary Prediction—Let's Predict

This partner activity is a good way to introduce a new book. It helps students to develop vocabulary as well as learn how to predict.

Implementing the Vocabulary Prediction Technique

1. From a new text, the teacher chooses 10 to 20 "strong words"; that is, words that elicit images and are key to comprehending the text selection. Students are asked to predict what the story might be about based on the words chosen.

2. Students work in pairs to discuss the vocabulary and to make pre-dictions. This step provides an excellent opportunity for purposeful

conversation, which often leads to new understandings of word meanings.

It is not critical for students to correctly predict how the words might be used in the story. What is important is the opportunity to reflect on what the words might mean in relation to one another.

3. Students share their predictions with others and then revisit their predictions after they have read the story. This step engages students in rich talk to enhance their comprehension of the text selection.

Sort and Predict

This activity uses 20 to 30 words, which students sort into categories and use for prediction. It supports prediction, categorization, and vocabulary development.

Implementing the Sort and Predict Technique

1. The teacher chooses 20 to 30 key words from the text and writes them on index cards for sorting purposes. The same words selected for Vocabulary Prediction—Let's Predict may be used.

2. The students work in pairs to sort the words into categories. The teacher may choose the number of categories or leave it open-ended. Students label index cards with the category names and manipulate the vocabulary words under their various categories.

3. Students walk around the classroom, looking at how other pair groups categorized the words and comparing how their categories are the same or different. The predictions about the content of the text selection may then be shared as a whole group.

4. The teacher then charts three or four predictions about the text and three or four questions the students may have. Students may also be asked to write their own predictions and questions. After reading, listening to, or viewing the text, students check their predictions. Were their questions answered?

An individual teacher or student chart may look like this:

Predictions	Confirmed (Yes/No)	Questions	Answered (Yes/No)

SQ3R (Survey, Question, Read, Recite, Review)

Use of this framework helps students effectively preview, read, and remember content-area reading information. It is a great study-skills technique.

Implementing SQ3R

- **Survey:** Students preview the selection by reading the first paragraph, headings, subheadings, last paragraph, and summary, if applicable, to predict what the text will be about.

- **Question:** Students are directed to come up with several questions that the selection might answer. They may choose to turn each heading into a question before reading the selection. This will result in more engagement with the text as students search for answers.
- **Read:** Students read each section of the text to answer their questions. New questions may be added as they read.
- **Recite:** Students ask the questions again and respond to them from memory, either orally or in writing. If they can't answer a question, they should reread the selection.
- **Review:** After the entire selection has been read, students summarize their responses to their questions.

See also SQRQCQ in Chapter 4: Literacy Learning Across the Curriculum. This strategy, which is modelled on the SQ3R reading strategy, supports learning in mathematics.

BLM 16: SQ3R Chart

CATS

CATS is a pre-reading activity that helps students to learn the before-reading strategies that most effective readers use. Effective readers preview the text before seriously beginning to read. They predict what the text will be about and decide if in fact they want to read any or all of the text.

Implementing the CATS Technique

It is important for teachers to model the CATS technique before read-alouds, as well as before shared and guided reading sessions. Encourage students to use CATS whenever they are choosing a new book.

C	What do the front and back **covers** tell us about the book?
A	What do we know about the **author** and other books he or she may have written?
T	What does the **title** suggest the text may be about?
S	**Skim** the text. Notice any pictures, charts, drawings, diagrams, and maps. Now, make your prediction.

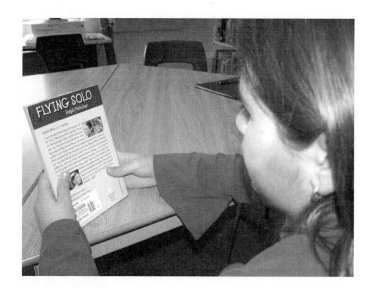

BLM 17: The CATS Technique

Using Mental Imagery (Visualizing)

Students who create mental images during and after reading understand the text with greater depth. The text becomes more memorable as students use these images to recall details from it and create their own interpretations of what they have read. Outlined below are suggested activities and techniques to help students learn to develop and use mental imagery to understand a text.

Techniques for Developing Mental Imagery

- Can you see it?
- Dramatic arts responses (interviews, tableaux)
- Visual arts responses (sketch to stretch, sketch a paragraph)

Can You See It?

This activity encourages students to visualize or paint a picture in their minds as they listen to a text being read aloud.

Implementing the "Can You See It?" Technique

1. The teacher might model the strategy first by describing orally or sketching on chart paper a picture that comes to mind after a student volunteer reads a text selection aloud.

2. Two students work together. One partner reads a text selection aloud while the other partner listens with eyes open or shut, visualizing what she or he is hearing. After the reading, the listener orally describes or sketches the image visualized.

   Alternatively, one student might read aloud a text selection to a small group while the rest of the group creates their sketches. Afterward, the group shares and discusses the sketches.

Dramatic Arts Responses

Using drama as a way of responding to a text enables students to deepen their understanding of situations, characters, problems, relationships, and concepts of a story, poem, or nonfiction piece. Interviews and tableaux are effective methods of dramatic response. Interviews provide opportunities for students to plan questions that enable them to delve deeper into what they are reading, hearing, or viewing. Students might interview each other in role as the author or illustrator, or as characters in factual, narrative, or poetic texts. Alternatively, they may create tableaux—frozen action shots or pictures that capture the essence of a text scene, historical event, or significant moment.

Implementing Interviews

1. Students plan in advance the questions they will ask, writing them down if necessary.

2. Working in pairs, one partner plays the interviewer while the other acts in role as the character (or other individual being interviewed). They then switch roles.

3. Character role-plays/interviews may also be presented to other groups of students.

Implementing Tableaux

1. Small groups of students read a story, poem, or other text and together consider what still picture they might create based on a scene or situation from the reading. Alternatively, the tableau could show what they think might have come before the situation in a text or what they think might happen next.

2. Before presenting the tableau, students plan how they will use their bodies and faces expressively. They may also use simple props and costumes to help create the scene. Positions should be held as long as is comfortable (about 30 seconds).

Visual Arts Responses

By using art to respond to a text, students can often provide greater detail and description than they might provide in an oral or written response. Sketch to stretch and paragraph sketches are two effective visual arts responses.

Implementing Sketch to Stretch

1. After a read-aloud, shared-reading, or guided-reading session, the teacher has students sketch an event or idea from the story. Some students may need prompting and could be asked to sketch what they learned or felt was the most important part.

2. Students are given about one minute to sketch after being reminded that a sketch is a quick doodle, not a finished piece of art.

3. Students share their sketches with a partner or small group. They describe the sketch's contents and explain why they decided to sketch this part of the text.

4. Students may decide to revise their sketches in response to ideas shared during the discussion that led to deeper understanding.

(Adapted from Seigel 1984, 178)

Implementing Sketch a Paragraph

1. After guided, shared, or independent reading of a descriptive paragraph, students interpret the content, mood, and characters by creating a quick drawing or sketch.

2. Students share their drawings, discuss their different interpretations, and make changes if they so choose.

Combining Strategies

Once students have been introduced to and understand the reading strategies outlined on the preceding pages, some of the strategies may be combined to encourage students to use and apply their comprehension skills in a more integrated way. Three of these combined strategies are Reciprocal Teaching, SQ3R, and SAIL (Students Achieving Independent Learning). For more on Reciprocal Teaching, see earlier in this chapter as well as Chapter 6: Supporting Struggling and Reluctant Readers. Information on the SQ3R strategy can also be found earlier in this chapter. The SAIL strategy is outlined below.

SAIL (Students Achieving Independent Learning)

The SAIL framework emphasizes predicting, visualizing, questioning, monitoring comprehension, making connections, and summarizing. After introducing these strategies individually, teachers should teach students how to integrate the strategies as they read across the curriculum.

Implementing the SAIL Strategy

1. The teacher selects a book, shows the cover to students, and asks them to predict what it will be about.

2. The teacher begins to read the book aloud, using think-aloud. For example, the teacher may think aloud a prediction or simply wonder aloud.

Check It Out!

Nell Duke and David Pearson discuss the SAIL strategy in *Effective Practices for Developing Reading Comprehension*, available at http://ed-web3.educ.msu.edu/reports/reports/ed%2Dresearchrep/03/march%5F03%5F3.htm

3. Students take turns reading aloud and are "cued" to apply various strategies when and as appropriate (e.g., "What do you think will happen next?"; "Summarize what you just read.").

4. The teacher encourages students to use strategies such as monitoring comprehension and visualizing.

5. When the reading is finished, the teacher prompts students to check their early predictions to determine how accurate they were.

Assessing Reading Comprehension Instruction

Nell Duke and David Pearson suggest that when teachers examine their own classrooms, they should consider whether students are being taught the full range of effective reading comprehension strategies.

For more practical techniques and mini-lessons to support comprehension, see Developing Comprehension and Metacognition in Chapter 4: Literacy Learning Across the Curriculum.

Are students being taught to

❑ identify their purpose for reading; preview texts before reading; make predictions before and during reading; and activate relevant background knowledge?

❑ use text structure to support comprehension and create visual representations to aid comprehension and recall?

❑ determine the important ideas and summarize what they read?

❑ generate questions for text?

❑ handle unfamiliar words?

❑ monitor comprehension and use appropriate fix-up strategies?

Does instruction about strategies include

❑ explicit description of the strategy and when to use it?

❑ modelling of the strategy in action?

❑ collaborative use of the strategy in action?

❑ guided practice using the strategy and the gradual release of responsibility to the student?

❑ independent practice using the strategy?

Teachers might also ask themselves the following questions:

❑ Are students being helped to orchestrate multiple strategies, rather than to use only one strategy at a time?

❑ Are texts used for instruction being carefully chosen to match both the strategy and the students being taught?

❑ Is there an active concern with student motivation to engage in literacy activities and apply newly learned strategies?

❑ Are students' comprehension skills being assessed regularly?

(Adapted from Duke and Pearson 2002, Fig. 10.6)

Closing Thoughts

"Comprehension involves what the reader knows as well as the nature of the text itself. It involves the type of text to be read—narrative, expository, poetry, etc." It involves the purpose for reading. And, it requires a variety of strategies to be shared with students.... In addition, as children progress in their reading development, comprehension becomes increasingly sophisticated. As they mature, readers need to become increasingly strategic in their ability to construct meaning from text" (Rasinski et al. 2000, 1).

To become increasingly strategic readers, listeners, and viewers, students need to have the strategies that work modelled, demonstrated, and explained to them. Think-alouds help to remove the mystery of what effective comprehenders do; the covert becomes overt.

Students need many opportunities to practise these strategies during authentic literacy experiences across all subject areas. They are required to do more than recall details; they need to know how to make personal connections as they think thoughtfully about the ideas, characters, and events in the texts they are engaged with. The ability to explain various strategies is not enough; students need to consistently and spontaneously select, apply, and synthesize the strategies that effective readers use to support comprehension.

When students have internalized the strategies described in this chapter, they will be metacognitive thinkers. They will negotiate text in its many forms, make meaning from it, and participate as thoughtfully literate members of our complex world.

> To support understanding means to ...
>
> - read widely, tenaciously pursuing ideas of interest, and remaining open to new interests
> - gain insight after struggling for meaning
> - read to reflect on ideas, remain open to new ideas, and consider multiple perspectives
> - extend existing knowledge, beliefs, and opinions, and understand how these change with learning
> - manipulate thoughts to understand more completely
> - engage in rigorous discourse about ideas
> - remember what we read
>
> (Adapted from Keene 2003)

The ultimate goal of all comprehension instruction is to develop proficient, thoughtful literacy learners; however, as effective teachers know, this does not happen by chance. Teachers have an important role to play in this development. Chapter 3: Writing: The Reading–Writing Connection demonstrates how writing becomes more important as students move through Grades 3 to 6 in supporting comprehension.

"We know a great deal about how to help students become more effective, more strategic, more self-reliant readers. It is time that we put that knowledge to work."

DUKE AND PEARSON 2002, 234

The endpoint sees that *"the proficient adult reader can read a variety of materials with ease and interest, can read for varying purposes, and can read with comprehension even when the material is neither easy to understand nor intrinsically interesting."*

SNOW 2002, XIII

"If we know that thinking about our own thinking and using the strategies that form this metacognitive foundation are associated with the tendency to read more deeply, critically, analytically, and independently, shouldn't comprehension strategy instruction be a major focus of our work with children who are learning to read and reading to learn?"

KEENE AND ZIMMERMANN 1997, 43

Chapter 2

BLACKLINE MASTERS

Character Pyramid

Name: _____ Grade: _____ Date: _____

Title: _____ Author: _____

Character's
Name

Physical Appearance

Character's Role

Character's Problems/Challenges

Character's Major Accomplishments

Character Trait Map

Name: _____ Grade: _____ Date: _____

Title: _____ Author: _____

Trait

Character's Name

Trait

Trait

Evidence from the Text

Evidence from the Text

Evidence from the Text

Keeping Track

Name: _____ Grade: _____

Texts I have completed (and why)

1.   Title: _____ Author: _____

       Genre: _____ Date: _____

       Why I completed reading this text: _____

       _____

2.   Title: _____ Author: _____

       Genre: _____ Date: _____

       Why I completed reading this text: _____

       _____

3.   Title: _____ Author: _____

       Genre: _____ Date: _____

       Why I completed reading this text: _____

       _____

4.   Title: _____ Author: _____

       Genre: _____ Date: _____

       Why I completed reading this text: _____

       _____

5.   Title: _____ Author: _____

       Genre: _____ Date: _____

       Why I completed reading this text: _____

       _____

Texts I gave up on (and why)

1.   Title: _____ Author: _____

       Genre: _____ Date: _____

       Why I did not complete reading this text: _____

       _____

2.   Title: _____ Author: _____

       Genre: _____ Date: _____

       Why I did not complete reading this text: _____

       _____

Home Reading

Date: _____

Dear Parents:

One of my major goals this school year is to help your child grow further as a reader, and you have a big role to play in achieving this. The best way for children to grow as readers is for them to read, so I encourage you to ensure that your child spends time reading after school *every day*.

Reading materials may range from short stories, novels, and magazines, to newspapers, recipes, and comics. Information may come from many sources, including the Internet. The most important goal is to "hook" your child on reading.

Two Great Web Sites

The Children's Choices Book Lists available from http://www.reading.org/resources/tools/choices.html are used in classrooms, libraries, and homes to help young people find books they will enjoy reading.

Pamphlets to help parents support their children's literacy learning are available in both English and Spanish from http://www.reading.org/resources/tools/parent.html.

Beyond having your child read, spend a few moments every day discussing the text. Doing so will give you insights into how well your child comprehends what she or he is reading. Also, occasionally listen to your child read aloud. To some extent, you will be able to gauge whether your child is selecting books that he or she can read fluently. When students read fluently, they read smoothly, without hesitation, and with expression. Generally, fluent readers find it easier to make sense of the text being read. Comprehension is, of course, the whole purpose of reading!

I look forward to working with you to make this a happy and successful year for your child.

Sincerely,

Choosing "Just Right" Books

Date: _____

Dear Parents:

Becoming a fluent reader means reading a lot both at home and at school. Sometimes though, children aren't reading as much as we think. Even though they are often given time and encouragement to read independently, they may be "faking it." Frequently, they pretend to read because the books they are using are too difficult for them. "Just right" books are books that interest children. These books are not so challenging that the children are solely occupied with figuring out the words, but not so easy that they are unlikely to learn anything new.

You can tell if your child has chosen a "just right" book by listening to him or her read a page or two. Your child should

• be able to read the text fairly smoothly

• have trouble with no more than three words on the first two pages

• be able to tell you what she or he read

• find the text interesting

Children's Favourite Picks
To find a current list of favourite books chosen by both teachers and students, visit www.readingonline.org/resources/tools/choices.html or www.cbcbooks.org. The latter site also provides parent tips and suggested reading activities.

If you are buying your child reading material for at-home reading, select texts that you know he or she can read now. Children need to experience the enjoyment and satisfaction that come from being able to read "just right" books fluently and independently. However, they also benefit from hearing and discussing more challenging texts read aloud.

Sincerely,

Book Review

Reviewer Name: _____ Grade: _____ Date: _____

Title: _____ Author: _____

Summary

_____

_____

_____

_____

_____

_____

_____

_____

Would you recommend this book? _____

Why or why not? _____

_____

_____

_____

_____

_____

_____

_____

_____

_____

_____

_____

Illustrate the setting or draw a picture of your favourite character.

Planning My One-Minute Book Talk

Name: _____ Grade: _____ Date: _____

Title: _____ Author: _____

Time* (in seconds)	Information
0 to 10	Catchy introduction: _____ _____ _____
11 to 21	Title, author, and genre: _____ _____ _____
22 to 45	What the text is about: _____ _____ _____ _____ _____ _____ _____
46 to 60	Who should read this book and why: _____ _____ _____ _____ _____ _____

*The times listed are only suggestions.

Story Grammar

Name: _____ Grade: _____ Date: _____

Title: _____ Author: _____

Characters (who):

Solution (how):

Plot

Setting (where and when):

Problem (what):

Beat the Clock

Name: _____ Grade: _____ Date: _____

Title: _____ Author: _____

Find as many text features as you can in the text you have chosen. List each text feature, the page you found it on, and the reason why it is useful.

Text Feature	Page	Purpose

Plot Organizer

Name: _____ Grade: _____ Date: _____

Title: _____ Author: _____

Climax (high point, turning point):

_____

_____

_____

Conflict (problem):   Falling Action:

_____   _____

_____   _____

_____   _____

_____   _____

Rising action
(tension increases)

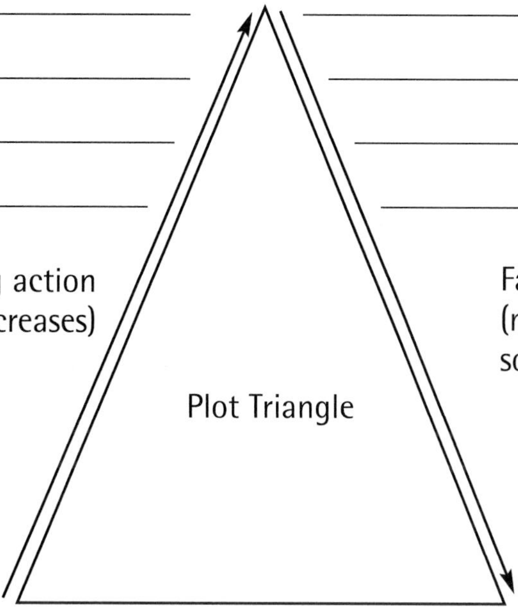

Falling action
(moves toward
solution)

Plot Triangle

Introduction (setting and characters):   Resolution:

_____   _____

_____   _____

_____   _____

_____   _____

_____   _____

Main Idea and Supporting Details

Name: _____ Grade: _____ Date: _____

Title: _____ Author: _____

```
┌────────────────────────────────────────────────────────────┐
│                                                            │
│                                                            │
│                                                            │
│                                                            │
│                                                            │
│                                                            │
│                                                            │
│                                                            │
│                                                            │
│                                                            │
└────────────────────────────────────────────────────────────┘
```

Main Idea

Detail 1   Detail 2   Detail 3

```
┌──────────────┐   ┌──────────────┐   ┌──────────────┐
│              │   │              │   │              │
│              │   │              │   │              │
│              │   │              │   │              │
│              │   │              │   │              │
│              │   │              │   │              │
│              │   │              │   │              │
│              │   │              │   │              │
│              │   │              │   │              │
│              │   │              │   │              │
│              │   │              │   │              │
└──────────────┘   └──────────────┘   └──────────────┘
```

(Pearson and Johnson 1978, 95)

Story Map

Name: _____ Grade: _____ Date: _____

Title: _____ Author: _____

Setting (where and when): _____

_____

_____

Characters (who): _____

_____

_____

Problem: _____

_____

_____

Actions:

- _____
- _____
- _____
- _____
- _____
- _____
- _____
- _____

Resolution: _____

_____

_____

_____

_____

Literary News Report

Name: _____ Grade: _____ Date: _____

Headline: _____

Byline: _____

Dateline: _____

Lead

_____

_____

_____

Main detail/event

_____

_____

_____

Next detail/event

_____

_____

_____

Other detail/event

_____

_____

_____

Ending (close)

_____

_____

_____

Question–Answer Relationships (QAR)

Name: _____ Grade: _____ Date: _____

Title: _____ Author: _____

In the Book QAR (on the page)	In My Head QAR (off the page)
Right There (answer is within one sentence in the text)	**Author and Me** (answer comes from the author and me)
Think and Search: Hidden (answer is hidden in more than one sentence)	**On My Own** (answer is not in this text but I know the answer)

(Raphael 1986, 516–22)

Anticipation Guide

Name: _____ Grade: _____ Date: _____

Directions

- Before you read the text, decide whether you agree or disagree with each numbered statement your teacher has provided. Then, check the appropriate box on the left.
- Explain why you agree or disagree.
- Read the text.
- Look at the statements again. Do you still agree with your answers? If not, check the appropriate box on the right.

Before Reading		Title:	After Reading	
Agree	Disagree		Agree	Disagree
		1. _____ _____ I believe this because _____ _____ _____		
		2. _____ _____ I believe this because _____ _____ _____		
		3. _____ _____ I believe this because _____ _____ _____		
		4. _____ _____ I believe this because _____ _____ _____		

SQ3R Chart

Name: _____ Grade: _____ Date: _____

Title: _____ Author: _____

Survey: Notice and record important information (headings, subheadings, charts, maps, pictures, diagrams, boldface, and italics). What do you predict this text will be about?

Question: Note questions that come to mind from the survey. You might want to make some of the headings into questions.

Read: Find the answers to your questions and write the responses.

Recite: At the end of each section, stop and try to answer your questions from memory. If you can't, reread the section.

Review: Create summary paragraphs based on the answers to your questions. Share what you have learned with a friend.

The CATS Technique

Name: _____ Grade: _____ Date: _____

Title: _____ Author: _____

Covers: What do the front and back **covers** tell you about the book?

_____

_____

_____

_____

Author: What do you know about the **author** and other books he or she may have written?

_____

_____

_____

Title: What does the **title** suggest the text may be about?

_____

_____

_____

Skim: **Skim** the text. Notice any photos, charts, drawings, diagrams, and maps. What clues do they give you?

_____

_____

_____

_____

What is your prediction?

_____

_____

_____

_____

Chapter 2

ASSESSMENT BLACKLINE MASTERS

Assessment BLM 1: Self-Assessment–Reading Attitude Survey

Assessment BLM 2: Self-Assessment–Reading Interests Inventory (Student)

Assessment BLM 3: Reading Interests Inventory (Class Tally)

Assessment BLM 4: Reading Interview

Assessment BLM 5: Fiction Retelling Scale

Assessment BLM 6: Nonfiction Retelling Scale

Assessment BLM 7: Reading Response or Summarizing Rubric

Assessment BLM 8: Think-Aloud Summary Sheet

Assessment BLM 9: Self-Assessment–Thinking Aloud

Assessment BLM 10: Informal Reading Conference

Assessment BLM 11: Self-Assessment–Making Connections

Assessment BLM 12: Comprehension Indicators During Literature Discussions

Assessment BLM 13: Self-Assessment–Independent Reading

Assessment BLM 14: Self-Assessment–When I Read

Self-Assessment—Reading Attitude Survey

Name: _____ Grade: _____ Date: _____

> For each statement, please check the box that best applies to you.
> Remember that this is your opinion. There are no "wrong" answers!

	I disagree	I agree a little	I agree	I strongly agree
1. I enjoy listening to someone read aloud.	❏	❏	❏	❏
2. I like to talk about ideas and information after I have read something.	❏	❏	❏	❏
3. I enjoy reading at home.	❏	❏	❏	❏
4. I think nonfiction is easier to read than fiction.	❏	❏	❏	❏
5. Other people think I am a good reader.	❏	❏	❏	❏
6. I read for enjoyment.	❏	❏	❏	❏
7. I often have trouble figuring out the words.	❏	❏	❏	❏
8. I only read to do schoolwork.	❏	❏	❏	❏
9. Reading is being able to say all the words correctly.	❏	❏	❏	❏
10. Reading is important for all subjects like science, social studies, art, and math.	❏	❏	❏	❏
11. After I have read a book, I like to read more books by the same author.	❏	❏	❏	❏
12. Reading is boring.	❏	❏	❏	❏
13. I read to find out about new things.	❏	❏	❏	❏
14. I choose books to read that other people have recommended.	❏	❏	❏	❏

Comments: _____

_____

_____

_____

Self-Assessment—Reading Interests Inventory (Student)

Name: _____ Grade: _____ Date: _____

Below is a list of reading materials and topics that you can read about. Show how interested you are in each by using the rating system that follows. Remember that there are no "wrong" answers!

| 1 = I don't really like this. | 2 = It's okay. | 3 = I like this a lot! |

Types of Reading Materials				Topics I Can Read About	
Fiction		**Nonfiction**			
	Rating		Rating		Rating
Fantasy		Magazines		Math	
Picture books		Biographies		Art	
Fables		Letters / E-mail		Games	
Novels		Maps		Music	
Legends		Fact books		History	
Poems		Autobiographies		Cars	
Adventure		Textbooks		Romance	
Folktales		Diaries / Journals		Relationships / Friendship	
Mysteries		Manuals		Crafts / Hobbies	
Myths		Experiments		Sports	
Comic books		Interviews		War	
Science fiction		Newspapers		Human body	
Humour		Recipes		Pets	
Riddles and Jokes		Other:		Wild animals	
Other:				Plants	
				Computers / Technology	
				Other:	

Comments: _____

_____

_____

_____

(Adapted from Doctorow, Bodiam, and McGowan 2003, 35)

Reading Interests Inventory (Class Tally)

Teacher: _____ Grade: _____ Date: _____

This tally sheet will assist with developing a classroom reading collection of interest to students. It might also be used to inform decisions regarding student groupings, theme development, and lesson focus.

Types of Reading Materials							Reading Topics		
Fiction			**Nonfiction**						
	Class Tally			Class Tally				Class Tally	
	Like a Lot	**Dislike**		**Like a Lot**	**Dislike**			**Like a Lot**	**Dislike**
Fantasy			Magazines				Math		
Picture books			Biographies				Art		
Fables			Letters / E-mail				Games		
Novels			Maps				Music		
Legends			Fact books				History		
Poems			Autobiographies				Cars		
Adventure			Textbooks				Romance		
Folktales			Diaries / Journals				Relationships / Friendship		
Mysteries			Manuals				Crafts / Hobbies		
Myths			Experiments				Sports		
Comic books			Interviews				War		
Science fiction			Newspapers				Human body		
Humour			Recipes				Pets		
Riddles and Jokes			Other:				Wild animals		
Other:							Plants		
							Computers / Technology		
							Other:		

Comments: _____

_____

_____

(Adapted from Doctorow, Bodiam, and McGowan 2003, 35)

Reading Interview

Name: _____ Grade: _____ Date: _____

Interview Questions and Student Responses

1. Do you think you are a good reader? How do you know?

2. When you are reading and you come to a word you do not know, what do you do?
   (Prompt if necessary: *Do you ever do anything else?*)

   Which of those strategies do you use most often?

3. How do you know when you don't understand what you are reading?

   What could you do to help your understanding?

4. Think of someone who is a good reader. What do you think makes that person a good reader?

   What do you think that person does when the text does not make sense?

5. Do you read any other language(s) at home or at school? Which one(s)?

6. What kind of reading do you do using technology (e.g., Web sites, e-mail, CD-ROMs)?

7. If someone were having difficulty reading a **story**, what could you suggest that might help?

8. If someone were having difficulty reading an **information article**, what could you suggest that might help?

9. How do you decide what to read?

   What do you like to read? Why?

10. As a reader, what would you like to do better?

Fiction Retelling Scale

Name: _____ Grade: _____ Date: _____

Title: _____ Author: _____

Minimally   **Fully**

Provides an overall unaided retelling

Begins with a story introduction

Names the characters

Identifies the problem

Identifies major events

Identifies the climax

Identifies the solution

Retells the story in sequence

States the main idea

Makes connections to the story

Comments: _____

_____

_____

Nonfiction Retelling Scale

Name: _____ Grade: _____ Date: _____

Title: _____ Author: _____

Minimally   **Fully**

Provides an overall unaided retelling

⟵―――――――――――――――――――――――――――⟶

Begins by introducing the topic

⟵―――――――――――――――――――――――――――⟶

States the main idea of the passage

⟵―――――――――――――――――――――――――――⟶

Uses vocabulary introduced in the text

⟵―――――――――――――――――――――――――――⟶

Explains concepts from the passage

⟵―――――――――――――――――――――――――――⟶

Refers to charts, maps, tables, captions, headings, and pictures

⟵―――――――――――――――――――――――――――⟶

Presents information in a logical order

⟵―――――――――――――――――――――――――――⟶

Makes connections to the text

⟵―――――――――――――――――――――――――――⟶

Comments: _____

_____

_____

_____

_____

Reading Response or Summarizing Rubric

Name: _____ Grade: _____ Date: _____

Categories / Criteria	Level 1	Level 2	Level 3	Level 4
• Demonstrates an understanding of the text by selecting and describing relevant information and ideas	• demonstrates a limited understanding of the text by selecting and describing a few ideas that may not always be relevant	• demonstrates some understanding of the text by selecting and describing some simple, but relevant, ideas and information	• demonstrates a general understanding of the text by selecting and describing most relevant ideas and information	• demonstrates a thorough understanding of the text by skillfully selecting and describing all or almost all relevant ideas and information
• Infers meaning	• demonstrates a limited ability to make and support simple inferences	• demonstrates some ability to make and support simple inferences	• demonstrates a general ability to make and support inferences of some complexity	• demonstrates a strong ability to make and support complex inferences
• Interprets and analyzes information from the text	• demonstrates a limited ability to interpret and analyze simple ideas and includes little or no supporting detail	• demonstrates some ability to interpret and analyze simple ideas with some supporting detail	• demonstrates a general ability to interpret and analyze ideas of some complexity with supporting detail	• demonstrates a strong ability to interpret and analyze complex ideas with extensive supporting detail
• Demonstrates an ability to explain, support, and apply what has been read	• demonstrates a limited ability to explain, support, and apply ideas and information	• demonstrates some ability to explain, support, and apply ideas and information	• demonstrates a general ability to explain, support, and apply ideas and information	• demonstrates a strong ability to explain, support, and apply ideas and information
• Demonstrates an ability to make connections among text, personal experiences, and life situations	• makes a few simple connections among text, personal experiences, and life situations	• makes some straightforward connections among text, personal experiences, and life situations	• makes connections of some complexity among text, personal experiences, and life situations	• makes complex and logical connections among text, personal experiences, and life situations

Think-Aloud Summary Sheet

Name: _____ Grade: _____ Date: _____

Title: _____ Pages: _____

Part ___ , page _____ to page _____	
	Monitors comprehension (realizes when it breaks down)
	Rereads or often uses other fix-up strategies
	Makes a prediction
	Makes a personal connection (text to self)
	Makes a connection to another text (text to text)
	Makes a connection to the world (text to world)
	Comments on text features or writing style
	Visualizes
	Asks questions
	Retells or summarizes
	Makes an inference and supports it

Part ___ , page _____ to page _____	
	Monitors comprehension (realizes when it breaks down)
	Rereads or often uses other fix-up strategies
	Makes a prediction
	Makes a personal connection (text to self)
	Makes a connection to another text (text to text)
	Makes a connection to the world (text to world)
	Comments on text features or writing style
	Visualizes
	Asks questions
	Retells or summarizes
	Makes an inference and supports it

Self-Assessment—Thinking Aloud

Name: _____ Grade: _____ Date: _____

Title: _____ Author: _____

This is what I think:	Page: _____

_____

_____

The evidence is:

On the Page	Off the Page
_____	_____
_____	_____
_____	_____
_____	_____
_____	_____
_____	_____

This is what I think:	Page: _____

_____

_____

The evidence is:

On the Page	Off the Page
_____	_____
_____	_____
_____	_____
_____	_____
_____	_____
_____	_____

Informal Reading Conference

Name: _____ Grade: _____ Date: _____

Title: _____ Author: _____

Ask the student to select a book that he or she has finished reading. Then, record the student's responses to the questions that follow.

Why did you decide to read this book?

Would you recommend this book to anyone else? Why or why not?

Did this book remind you of any other books you have read?

What personal connections did you make with this book?

Tell me something about the characters or individuals in the book.

Find some examples in the book where the author uses language to paint a picture. Read one of those examples to me.

Interviewed by: _____

Self-Assessment—Making Connections

Name: _____ Grade: _____ Date: _____

Title: _____ Author: _____

Text to Self	Phrase or Situation in Text	My Connections

Text to Text	Phrase or Situation in Text	My Connections

Text to World	Phrase or Situation in Text	My Connections

Comprehension Indicators During Literature Discussions

Teacher: _____ Grade: _____

- Used background knowledge to construct meaning

- Made reasonable predictions

- Used the text to support predictions

- Visualized

- Personally identified or made connections with the text (text to self)

- Evaluated or analyzed characters

- Questioned the author (to identify what was said or not said, implied or inferred, and why)

- Connected the book with other texts (text to text)

- Connected the book to what is understood in the world (text to world)

- Asked questions to further understand

- Used vocabulary effectively

- Inferred

- Retold/summarized

- Used context to identify unknown vocabulary

- Mentioned the book's theme

(Adapted from Evans 2001, 105)

Students' Names and Date																	

Self-Assessment—Independent Reading

Name: _____ Grade: _____ Date: _____

Title: _____ Author: _____

Check the description that applies to you.

Book Choice

❏ My book choice today was not right for me. The book was too easy or too hard. I did not find it interesting.

❏ My book choice today was slightly too easy or too hard; however, I still found the book interesting.

❏ My book choice today was neither too easy nor too hard; however, I did not find the book interesting.

❏ My book choice today was just right for me—neither too easy nor too hard. I found the book interesting.

Time Spent Reading

❏ I didn't spend much time reading today during silent reading.

❏ It took me some time to get started, but I read for most of the time.

❏ I began reading almost immediately and read for most of the time.

❏ I spent all of my time reading during silent reading time.

When I think about my reading, I know I can improve by _____

_____

_____

_____

_____

Self-Assessment—When I Read

Name: _____ Grade: _____ Date: _____

When I read I ...	Not Often	Sometimes	Usually
• choose "just right" books			
• make connections			
• make predictions			
• ask questions			
• make pictures or visualize in my head			
• am aware when I don't understand			
• use fix-up strategies			

Reading Goals

_____

_____

_____

_____

_____

Chapter 3

WRITING: THE READING–WRITING CONNECTION

Miriam Trehearne

"Learning to write assists children in their reading; in learning to read, children also gain insights that help them as writers. But writing is more than an aid to learning to read; it is an important curricular goal. Through writing children express themselves, clarify their thinking, communicate ideas, and integrate new information into their knowledge base."

CIERA 1998

Find Out More About Writing

Association for Supervision and Curriculum Development. *Writing! Educational Leadership.* Alexandria, VA: Volume 62 No. 2 October 2004.

Buss, Kathleen, and Lee Karnowski. *Reading and Writing Nonfiction Genres.* Newark, DE: International Reading Association, 2002.

Culham, Ruth. *6 + 1 Traits of Writing, The Complete Guide (Grade 3 and Up).* Portland, OR: Northwest Regional Educational Laboratory, 2003.

Dahl, Karin L., and Nancy Farnan. *Children's Writing: Perspectives From Research.* Newark, DE: International Reading Association, 1998.

Fletcher, R. *A Writer's Notebook: Unlocking the Writer Within You.* New York: Avon Books for Young Readers, 1996.

Fletcher, Ralph, and Joann Portalupi. *Craft Lessons: Teaching Writing K–8.* York, ME: Stenhouse Publishers, 1998.

Heffernan, Lee. *Critical Literacy and Writer's Workshop: Bringing Purpose and Passion to Student Writing.* Newark, DE: International Reading Association, 2004.

Lane, Barry. *After THE END: Teaching and Learning Creative Revision.* Portsmouth, NH: Heinemann, 1992.

McMackin, Mary C., and Barbara S. Siegel. *Knowing How: Researching and Writing Nonfiction, 3–8.* Portland, ME: Stenhouse, Publishers, 2002.

Olness, Rebecca. *Using Literature to Enhance Writing Instruction: A Guide for K–5 Teachers.* Newark, DE: International Reading Association, 2004.

Portalupi, Joann, and Ralph Fletcher. *Nonfiction Craft Lessons: Teaching Information Writing K–8.* Portland, ME: Stenhouse Publishers, 2001.

Portalupi, Joann, and Ralph Fletcher. *Teaching the Qualities of Writing.* Portsmouth, NH: Heinemann, 2004.

Routman, Regie. *Writing Essentials: Raising Expectations and Results While Simplifying Teaching.* Portsmouth, NH: Heinemann, 2004.

Spandel, Vicki. *Books, Lessons, Ideas for Teaching the Six Traits: Writing in the Elementary and Middle Grades.* Wilmington, MA: Great Source Education Group, 2001.

Spandel, Vicki. *Creating Writers Through 6-Trait Writing Assessment and Instruction.* 4th ed. New York: Pearson Education Inc., 2005.

Tiedt, Iris McClellan. *Tiger Lilies, Toadstools, and Thunderbolts: Engaging K-8 Students with Poetry.* Newark, DE: International Reading Association, 2002.

Tompkins, Gail E. *Teaching Writing: Balancing Process and Product.* Upper Saddle River, NJ: Prentice-Hall, Inc., 2000.

Vasquez, Vivian, Michael Muise, Susan Adamson, Lee Heffernan, David Chiola-Nakai, and Janice Shear. *Getting Beyond "I Like the Book": Creating Space for Critical Literacy in K-6 Classrooms.* Newark, DE: International Reading Association, 2003.

Research on Writing

Writing is tremendously important. People use writing for many purposes. They write for functional purposes such as sending letters and making lists. But they also write to help make sense of the world and who they are in that world. Talking and writing put words and thoughts into students' heads, allowing them to make new connections and thus new meanings (Elbow 2004). "Children develop meaning as they write. It's what we all do, especially when we're writing about something we don't fully understand or haven't figured out yet. It's what I do when I write a book. Writing makes us think harder" (Routman 2005, 126).

It takes years to develop the craft of writing. What happens in Grades 3 to 6 classrooms is a crucial part of this challenging but exciting journey.

Goals for Writers in Grades 3 to 6

It is important to have clear goals for students and to plan with the end in mind. Specifically, students must be helped to

- understand that people write for many authentic reasons
- understand how to write using the recursive writing process
- assess writing in different genres using the traits (qualities, characteristics, or key components) that define good writing across all subject areas
- use the appropriate language to talk about their writing and the writing of others
- think and organize their thoughts
- understand the differences between revising and editing and use both to improve their writing
- experience a sense of joy and satisfaction from writing, and want to write often
- use different genres (kinds of writing) for different audiences and different purposes
- think of themselves as writers
- become risk takers
- understand and deepen the reading–writing connection
- use writing to support reading, writing, listening, and viewing comprehension
- use the traits effectively across genres and subject areas
- develop a love of reading and listening to good literature
- become thoughtful and critical literacy learners

Students need to learn to read like a writer. When students read and hear text, they are taught to focus on more than what is being said. They are also focusing on how the writer is saying it (e.g., word choice, organization).

"Young children must learn to think like writers, to think that they are writers, and to believe that they have ideas to share with others."

CIERA, Topic 6 1998, 2

Writing not only helps to develop students' skills in phonological awareness, phonics, and word work, but it also helps to improve their thinking and their comprehension.

The traits are the qualities, characteristics, or key components that define good writing.

The Reality

The goals are clear and demanding. However, the reality is that many students start school seeing themselves as writers, or at least wanting to be writers, only to have their confidence and desire wane. They may decide that they don't like to write, are afraid to write (writing reveals one's inner self), or feel as though they have nothing worthwhile to say. Some students experience fine motor delays. Others become overly preoccupied with writing conventions, in particular spelling, and are fearful of taking risks.

How do teachers develop writing programs through which students develop as writers and really want to write? There is no magic answer. However, research indicates that there are certain factors associated with stronger writing programs and stronger writers.

Strong Writing Programs

The three components of strong writing programs are

- clear benchmarks
- time spent writing
- the reading–writing connection

Clear Benchmarks

Teachers must have clear and specific benchmarks in mind for their students. They must have a well-defined idea of what writing should look like by the end of each grade, which is then shared with students and their parents. (See the scoring guides provided on Assessment BLMs 1 to 3. Assessment BLMs 4 to 6 are designed for student self-assessment.)

Scoring guides are broken down trait by trait (ideas, content, organization, voice, word choice, sentence fluency, and conventions). "The scoring guides for each trait define good writing, whether it's for a third grader or an eleventh grader. In the trait of ideas, for example, you need a focused idea, details that matter, and a central theme to your writing, regardless of age ..." (Culham 2003, 273). That being

Let's take away the writing mystery by sharing the benchmarks with students and parents. "How different writing instruction—and assessment—can be when teachers of writing and their students share a common vocabulary that allows them to think, speak, assess, and plan like writers. Suddenly, there is no more mystery."

SPANDEL, CREATING WRITERS 2001, XIII

"Never forget, however, that a good paper has the same embedded qualities no matter what the age of the writer."

CULHAM 2003, 273

said, the level of writing maturity expected in Grade 3 is of course different from that expected in Grade 6, and vastly different from that expected in Grade 11.

To provide continuity and consistency across a school (and school district), teachers need to come up with anchor papers that they agree exemplify grade level standards for each trait. Because a single paper may be strong in conventions but weak in ideas, or vice versa, teachers must spend time examining a variety of student papers at all grade levels.

Benchmarks help students determine where they are strong and where they need to improve their craft. Benchmarks also help teachers plan the kinds of mini-lessons necessary to support student writing.

Assessment BLM 1: Scoring Guide—Ideas and Organization
Assessment BLM 2: Scoring Guide—Voice and Word Choice
Assessment BLM 3: Scoring Guide—Sentence Fluency and Conventions
Assessment BLM 4: Ideas and Organization
Assessment BLM 5: Voice and Word Choice
Assessment BLM 6: Sentence Fluency and Conventions

Time Spent Writing

Students learn to write in part by writing. It takes time. Writing involves thinking and planning, the actual writing, discussing, editing, revising, and sharing. However, research indicates that in most classrooms, students spend very little time actually writing extended text. And, they do not necessarily write every day.

Effective classroom management and student motivation are crucial to ensuring students remain engaged. The key to fitting everything in is to connect parts of the language arts block, integrate subject-specific curriculum content, and establish routines, structure, and expectations early in the year. Many teachers, for example, begin each day with a read-aloud or shared reading text that is connected to science, social studies, or math. When students are not involved in guided reading, which tends to be in place by the beginning of October, they spend their time independently reading or writing, often in response to the texts read.

With a structure and routines in place, most students should be spending at least 35 to 45 minutes of their literacy block writing independently. This may seem like a lot of time, but there is good reason for it. Writing requires more than putting pencil to paper; it requires thinking, talking, setting a purpose, and planning. If students just get started writing and there is a break or distraction (such as an intercom announcement), continuity takes time to re-establish. Providing long blocks of independent writing time daily, preferably with few interruptions, is central to students' writing development.

"As children progress and begin to master the fundamentals of spelling and text organization, nothing improves writing faster than providing lots of opportunities to write."

CIERA, *Topic* 6 1998, 4

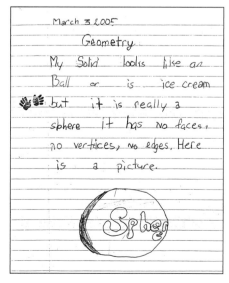

To establish a writing rhythm, students need frequent and predictable periods of time during which to write. According to Donald Graves, having students write only "one day a week will teach them to hate it. They'll never get inside writing."

FLETCHER AND PORTALUPI 2001, 8

"Children need fewer brief, shallow literacy activities and many more extended opportunities to read and write."

ALLINGTON 1994, 21

"The single most important thing you can do to help students become writers is to provide them with time to write, materials with which to write, and to demonstrate the process and the importance of writing to them."

CUNNINGHAM AND ALLINGTON 1994, 89

Sample Writing Workshop

■ Mini-Lesson – 5 to 10 minutes
■ Writing – 35 to 45 minutes
□ Share Time – 10 to 20 minutes

(Fletcher and Portalupi 2001, 11)

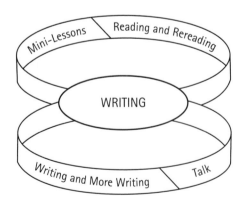

Mini-Lessons / Reading and Rereading / WRITING / Writing and More Writing / Talk

The Reading–Writing Connection

"Writing is the making of reading. If we know how to construct reading through writing, we will better understand how to take reading apart" (Graves 1994, 282). Students learn the craft of writing as they read, listen to, and discuss good literature. They fall in love with certain texts and genres and perhaps the works and style of certain authors. Fletcher and Portalupi (1998), among others, have stated that literature may be the most important influence of all for writing development. However, they also explain that simply enjoying good literature will not enable most students to become effective writers. It is through mini-lessons (craft lessons), reading and rereading, talk, and writing that students learn what effective authors do when they compose. Teachers may stimulate, encourage, and scaffold the talk as they prompt with questions such as the following:

- Who is the intended audience for this text? What makes you think so?
- What is the topic focus, or theme?
- Why do you think the author chose this setting?

- What are you visualizing? What details help you create this mental image?
- Whose voices are being expressed? Whose voices are not heard? Why?
- How did this text make you feel? What words did the author use to make you feel this way?
- What other text(s) does this remind you of? How are they similar? How are they different?

Reading and writing in the classroom "floats on a sea of talk."

James Britton in Fletcher and Portalupi 2001, 36

It is through talk that students become attuned to the techniques used by authors whose work they appreciate. The authors then become their mentors as students learn to read like a writer. And "the close attention that comes from rereading and talking about literature can help students become readers of their own writing" (Fletcher and Portalupi 1998, 12). It is also through this reading, rereading, and critiquing of their own writing and that of their peers that students develop both the skill and the confidence of effective writers.

"Wonderful literature can transport students to new realms of the imagination; it can also instruct them on issues of craft."

Fletcher and Portalupi 1998, 12

Why Do Some Students Never Finish a Piece of Writing?

Not all pieces need to (or should) be published, but there are some students who never finish a piece of writing. The research suggests several likely causes of incomplete writing:

- infrequent writing opportunities (writing that only occurs every few days causes students to lose the flow of their writing, and often their confidence)
- not enough uninterrupted writing time
- assigned topics (often boring to students)
- lack of awareness of the audience and purpose for writing
- unmanageable topic size
- inadequate time spent on the planning or prewriting stage
- lack of understanding of the writing process, especially revision

"Our students know best which topics and purposes for writing matter most to each of them. Letting them choose their own topics and set their own purposes makes it a lot more likely they'll be engaged and receptive."

Fletcher and Portalupi 2001, 10

Endangered Animals

They sadly watch their homes disappear,
They faithfully try to go on.
They try to picture their creeks that are dear,
They know that most will eventually be gone.

They miss their fellow friends,
They rely on us to help.
They think everything really depends,
They probably are quite mad at the world and yelp.

They shout angrily that we are mean,
They complain each day with great agony.
They really don't think we are very keen.

They are endangered, all of them,
so help them to stay alive,
It will make them happy, day by day
and hopefully they will thrive.

Vanessa

What to Write

Students do their best writing when they can choose what they are going to write and when there is an authentic purpose for writing (Fletcher and Portalupi 2001). They might write a letter to share exciting news, create a joke to tell a friend, or prepare a petition. What is important is that students experience different types of writing first hand and that their choice of mode is based on their audience and purpose for writing.

In the primary grades (Pre-K to 3), students spend the vast majority of their time reading and writing fiction. Beginning in the upper elementary grades, the reverse is true. Here, students spend much of their time reading and writing nonfiction (content-driven) text. This change in reading–writing focus is considered a contributing factor in the reading–writing slump that often begins around the fourth grade.

Students in Grade 3 and beyond learn how to write nonfiction by spending much time reading and discussing such text. They learn to write recipes and how-to text (procedural text), as well as magazine and newspaper articles and research reports. Teachers also model, demonstrate, and explain, often through think-alouds and mini-lessons, how to read and write both narrative and expository texts across all subject areas. (See Chapter 2: Reading Comprehension: Strategies That Work and Chapter 4: Literacy Learning Across the Curriculum for more information on expository text features and structures and report writing.)

Students in Grades 3 to 6 frequently enjoy both reading and writing poetry. Students who have difficulty writing extended text often find success in writing poetry. Unfortunately, little emphasis has been placed on poetry writing in most upper elementary classrooms; however, this situation is changing as teachers realize how poetry can be used effectively across all subject areas and in all four primary modes of writing that students encounter in Grades 3 to 6:

- narrative
- informational/expository/procedural
- persuasive
- descriptive

Some pieces of writing may be a combination of modes. For example, a book report (book talk) may be persuasive and descriptive.

Narrative Writing

Narrative writing tells a story and consists of a plot, characters, and setting. Although there is a sequence—beginning, middle (details), and some form of resolution or ending—narrative writing involves more than describing a sequence of events. Word choice, voice, ideas, and sentence fluency bring narrative writing to life. But while students tend to enjoy and spend much of their time composing stories, it is an extremely demanding mode of writing. For this reason, many narrative pieces go on and on and may remain unfinished.

It is important for students to learn that there are many other purposes for writing. In fact, the mastery of nonfiction writing is key to functioning successfully in society and many students actually prefer to read and write nonfiction.

Is the writing being taught and done representative of the various types of writing that are necessary in and outside of school?

Matthew

Save our Forests

The tropical rainforest is a wonderful place to see and explore. Even one of our greatest explorers, Christopher Columbus named the forest a beautiful place with its many trees and interesting animals. The rainforest can be used in many ways for each animal to adapt to such as for the frog. The forest holds many tall trees for frogs to lay their eggs in so the coral snakes don't eat them. Also, many Mia birds dig holes in the dead, rotting trees to build their nests. Military ants don't have a big part in the rainforest, but they keep the paper wasp colony from growing too much by eating their larvae. For snakes, they usually eat most of a frogs eggs so they don't grow too much. Even the trees help out the forest. When they die and rot, most of the tree dissolves and turns into food for many animals. Each year the rainforest gets at least 400 inches of rain which helps the trees grow tall and healthy and sometimes floods the rivers flowing through which can be a bad thing in some cases. It may drown many trees and animals, but it can soak the ground helping deep down roots grow and can give water to the underground animals. Even though the forest is home to many animals, people don't seem to care and just cut the trees down. All that is protected is 8%, and that can't hold every animal. By destroying the forest, people are also killing animals, and if people keep this up they may become extinct. All people want are more homes and buildings. This isn't fair to us nor to the animals. So think first before cutting down trees, how much do you need, don't just keep cutting and then say oops, too many cut down. Instead, don't just save the trees, save an entire rainforest, see what kind of change it can make.

See Linking Assessment to Instruction later in this chapter for more information on narrative writing.

Environmental issues provide a real reason to write. This is a great example of persuasive writing.

Informational/Expository/Procedural Writing

This mode of writing explains, teaches, gives information, shows how. Students are experts at many things and should be encouraged to share their expertise by relating, for example, how to skateboard, shoot a puck, skip rope, or play a video game.

More information on procedural writing is included later in this chapter. See also Chapter 4: Literacy Learning Across the Curriculum.

"Nonfiction is an important genre for helping children and ourselves to know an area particularly well. In this sense, nonfiction is probably the most usable kind of writing for school and a lifetime of work."

GRAVES 1994, 313

April

How to get a Horse ready for riding

To get a horse ready you first have to put the bridle on and the bite has to be in the horses mouth. Secound you have to put the sadle on. Third you have to put the gurth on. after sit on the horse and see if the sterups are the same length then you ride like the wind

---

Persuasive Writing

Persuasive writing involves stating an argument and is intended to convince the reader to take a specific action or adopt a particular belief. This form of writing is very appealing to students, who often select topics such as "Why summer holidays should be longer." Persuasive writing is often done in classrooms where critical or thoughtful literacy is encouraged. Students might write letters regarding social or moral issues, such as why smoking in public places should be banned, with the intent of trying to improve some aspect of the world.

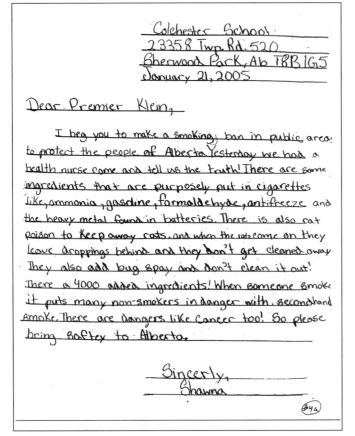

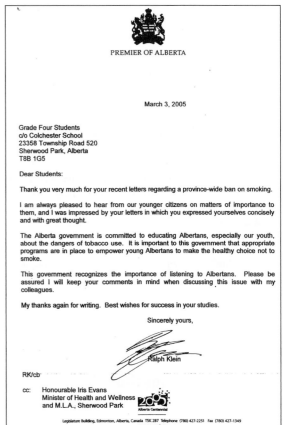

See later in this chapter for more information on persuasive writing.

Descriptive Writing

This mode of writing describes a person, place, or thing. Details bring the writing to life, enabling the reader to visualize what is being described. (See Descriptive Writing later in this chapter.)

The Six Traits or Characteristics That Define Good Writing

Traits are the characteristics or qualities that define good writing. In 1974, Paul Diederich began to clearly identify and describe the traits. In 1982, Donald Murray identified six traits. At approximately the same time, teachers in Oregon and Montana worked at clarifying the traits of effective writing. Teachers always knew that both ideas and

Check It Out!

Six-Trait Analytical Writing Assessment Guide
http://nwrel.org/assessment/toolkit98/traits/index.html
This is a superb site to gather information on the six traits of writing.

organization, for example, were important in good writing. Now, however, each trait is defined by clear criteria that explicitly identify what is most important and how that trait looks at various levels of performance. These traits are applicable across the genres. The criteria provide the language to make sense of the traits.

"[I]f we are to teach students to write, we must take writing apart— temporarily—in order to focus on one skill at a time. Thus, writing is described in terms of its key components, often called traits.*"*
Spandel, Creating Writers 2001, 26

The Traits Defined

Ideas convey a clear message; the content of the piece; the main theme or idea, together with the details that develop that theme.

The message makes sense!

Organization refers to the structure of the piece; i.e., the lead that grabs the reader, the logical ordering of the details, and an ending that is satisfactory or appropriate.

Well organized from beginning to end!

Voice expresses the heart and soul of the author; it is what captures the reader, making him or her "feel."

You can hear the author's voice!

Word choice refers to the use of rich, precise language (million-dollar words) that moves the reader. Through rich details, the reader is able to see (visualize), hear, smell, touch, or taste what is described. Strong verbs and phrases paint the picture, bringing the writing to life.

The words paint the picture!

Sentence fluency is the rhythm and flow of the writing. The beginnings and lengths of sentences vary, making the piece easy to read aloud.

It is smooth and easy to read aloud!

Conventions comprise the grammar and mechanics (the spelling, paragraphing, capitalization, and punctuation).

Editing!

Assessment BLM 1: Scoring Guide—Ideas and Organization

Assessment BLM 2: Scoring Guide—Voice and Word Choice

Assessment BLM 3: Scoring Guide—Sentence Fluency and Conventions

"I have become a teacher with a capital T.... Just as there are times when kids need a mirror, someone to reflect back their writing to them, there are times when they need an adult who will tell them what to do next or how to do it. Bottom line, what they need is a Teacher."
Atwell 1998, 21

Teaching Writing

Traditionally, writing instruction focused on spelling, mechanics, grammar, even penmanship; students rarely had the opportunity to actually write (Cunningham and Allington 1994). If this was the experience of many students' parents, they may overemphasize the importance of conventions. Although it is important for writing to be legible and spelling to improve over time, the heart of writing is determined by the other five traits: ideas, organization, voice, word choice, and sentence fluency. It is important for teachers to help parents understand why an undue emphasis on conventions alone can stifle a writer just as an overemphasis on phonics can stifle a reader.

Students, teachers, and parents need to share the same understandings and use the same language about writing.

BLM 6: Literacy Home Links: Surfing the Net

BLM 7: Literacy Home Links: Million-Dollar Words

BLM 8: Literacy Home Links: Assessing Writing

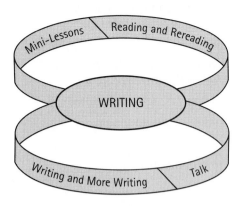

Teach students to take a snapshot—write small! Frequently students do not effectively limit their topic and their writing goes on and on.

We sat in the airport for a long time not really doing anything. When it was time to board I hugged each member of my family and told them I loved them. When I got to my dad he said in his deep raspy voice, "I'll miss you princess, I love you so much." I hugged him again. "I'll miss you too." I whispered. I didn't hold back my tears. I turned and handed the person behind the desk my boarding pass, looked at my family one more time, and went down the narrow hallway to the plane, waiting to take me away from my family.

No More Pendulum Swings

Although students do need to write extensively, they do not magically become effective writers simply by writing. They become strong writers by reading and rereading a great deal, talking about their writing and the writing of others, and through mini- or craft lessons. There is a craft to writing. Teachers need to model, demonstrate, and explain to students

- what strong writing looks like (i.e., the strategies used by effective writers)
- how to assess writing, both their own and that of others
- how to improve their writing through both revision and editing

Writing without strategy instruction doesn't work, just as immersing students in books without reading strategy instruction doesn't work.

Mini-lessons on the craft of writing focus mainly on one trait or writing characteristic at a time.

Mini-Lessons

Mini-lessons are short and focused. They tend to involve demonstrations of the qualities of good writing and the craft of writing through teacher read-alouds or shared reading of literature that exemplifies these qualities. Demonstrations also occur through modelled or shared writing. Teachers thinking aloud (writing aloud) help to take the mystery out of writing.

Mini-lessons may also involve writing share, during which students listen and respond to an author's work in a focused way. (See Writing Share later in this chapter.) Students then need the opportunity to develop the particular mini-lesson trait by writing themselves. The two most important questions students need to contemplate before writing are

- what is my purpose?
- who is my audience?

As teachers assess student writing, they determine appropriate mini-lessons. Possible mini-lessons include

- selecting or finding a topic
- prewriting ideas (incubating the topic or "panning for gold")
- revising, focusing on one trait
- editing
- responding to the writing of others

Read-Alouds: Teaching Students to Be Assessors

Read-alouds, and the student responses they generate, help to develop a community of learners. In addition, there is no better way to teach the craft of writing than through examining and enjoying literature and other texts. Students learn any craft or skill, such as riding a horse or playing the violin, from examining the strategies used by the experts. Learning to write follows the same process.

When selecting a read-aloud text, effective teachers consider

- how enticing it will be to students
- how it supports thoughtful literacy
- how it demonstrates a specific writing trait, for example, strong word choice
- how it might be used to demonstrate a number of traits, such as word choice and voice

Students also benefit from examining strong samples written by their peers. These samples can also serve as a source of new ideas for writing. Sometimes, it is equally effective to share weak writing with students so that it can be critiqued. Teachers and students discuss specifically how the text could be improved. An effective teaching strategy is to rewrite a piece together and compare the two versions.

Students also benefit when teachers use

- two texts—one fiction, one nonfiction—on the same theme and compare the two genres
- two texts of the same theme and genre but by different authors. How do the two authors provide different perspectives on the same topic or theme? (See Choosing Books to Teach the Traits later in this chapter.)

Read, Reread, and Talk!

Students who read a great deal often become stronger writers. They develop vocabulary (good word choice), ideas, a sense of sentence fluency, and text organization. However, reading alone is not enough. Students benefit from focused talk and mini-lessons. (See Talk and Writing and Explicit Strategy Instruction in Chapter 2: Reading Comprehension: Strategies That Work.)

Supporting Student Writers: Writing in a Comprehensive Literacy Program

Students learn to write through varying levels of teacher support, ranging from modelled writing (the most support) to independent writing (the least support).

Modelled Writing

Effective teachers model writing for students, using think-alouds while composing. These sessions allow teachers to make the writing process more obvious to students and provide an opportunity to convey an enthusiasm for writing. "I try to emphasize the writing process and show students every step of that process—from initially forming idea, to drafting, to revising and editing to publishing. Children learn from watching ..." (Polochanin 2004). Modelled writing is generally done with the whole class or a group.

Using think-alouds or write-alouds, teachers can demonstrate

- conventions
- how to find a word on the word wall or a chart
- how to reread to make sure that the writing makes sense
- how to create a good lead

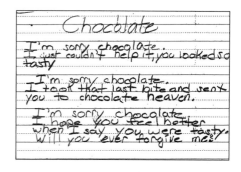

"We don't need literature to get students writing. We can hand them paper and pencils and simply say go. But we need to tap their experience as readers [and listeners] if we really want them to soar."

Fletcher and Portalupi 2001, 84

How much time do students spend on a daily basis just reading (using "just right" books)?

- how to make good word choices
- how to vary sentence length
- how to come up with ideas
- how and when to create a good title
- how to revise

Shared Writing

With shared writing, the teacher and students compose the text together. Students are supported by and can build on the knowledge and ideas of their classmates. The teacher is still doing the most work and thinking aloud. This process is very similar to shared reading and can be done with a small group or the whole class. When composing, the teacher guides the students in determining the content and organization of the message. "Teachers are writing models for their students. When they show excitement about writing and write with them, students will realize and respond to that energy" (Polochanin 2004).

Guided Writing

Similar to guided reading, guided writing occurs after students have had many opportunities to see demonstrations of teacher modelling and to participate in shared writing experiences with their classmates. The purpose of guided writing is to provide additional opportunities for students to apply specific writing skills and strategies prior to writing independently.

A small group of students with a common need is brought together for a mini-lesson (e.g., sentence leads). The students write in collaboration with the rest of the group and the teacher, with a focus on the strategy just taught. The teacher and group members respond to questions, extend students' thinking, and make suggestions as needed. In contrast to modelled and shared writing, the students create their own text.

Independent Writing

Independent writing time is a crucial component of a comprehensive literacy classroom. Students need a long block of uninterrupted time during language arts (at least 35 to 45 minutes daily) to write most effectively. "It is difficult for inexperienced writers to conceptualize and finish a piece that is left unattended for many days. Also, students build momentum and skill if they write consistently over time. They need to be able to use the feedback they get in conferences and sharing sessions while it is fresh. Finally, students must develop a 'routine' for writing; it is a daily activity, not a series of isolated assignments" (Fountas and Pinnell 2001, 19).

During independent writing, students might prepare journal entries, news articles, poems, or reports; create posters or comic strips; or develop Readers Theatre scripts. Any writing they do is often associated with the content area.

Writing Share (Author's Chair)

Students can learn a great deal from sharing and discussing their writing with their peers. Writing share is most effective when peers have something specific to focus on as they listen, and is a useful activity before, during, or after writing. For example, the student author might

- bring an unfinished piece to the group and point out where help is needed
- seek feedback on a finished piece to support revision

Student authors must also learn how to share effectively so everyone in the group can hear. Writing share generally works best when it is done for brief periods (10 to 20 minutes) and in small groups or with a partner.

Writing Conferences

Writing conferences are usually brief (less than five minutes) one-to-one discussions involving the teacher and a student. Either the teacher or the student may ask for a conference. Small-group conferences during which peers listen in (and sometimes provide feedback) also work.

To make the most of a writing conference, be sure to

- focus on one small area to help the student move forward. It is generally not the time to revise or edit a whole piece.
- encourage the student to talk about the piece (e.g., Where is feedback required? What trait does the student want to focus on?)
- have the student read aloud a portion of the piece so that he or she can "hear" it
- provide specific feedback and guidance. It is important to provide at least one element of praise immediately after students have

Ask ...
- What did you learn from this piece of writing?
- What did the author do well?
- What questions do you have?

Students benefit greatly from adult and peer feedback on their writing.

shared their work (e.g., "In this persuasive piece, your lead grabs me. Great!"). A prompt might then follow to assist students with identifying an area of weakness in their writing (e.g., "Read the last sentence aloud. Does the ending sound convincing?").

The next mini-lesson will be ideally based on a common need of a number of students. Providing students with specific individualized feedback on what they are doing well and one way to improve their writing is important.

Fitting It All In

"If you don't have clear expectations, how can your children know what to aim for? If you don't have the highest expectations, how do you know you're not underestimating what your students can do?"

MEM FOX IN SPANDEL, *CREATING WRITERS* 2001, 318

Even with a long block of uninterrupted time, it is not easy fitting it all in! Students need daily opportunities to write (independent writing/guided practice) and to see the teacher modelling writing. Generally, one or two students per day should also have the opportunity to share.

In a comprehensive language arts program, students need opportunities to

- observe modelled or shared writing (think-alouds and write-alouds)
- practise new skills during guided and independent writing
- share writing (author share or conferences to receive feedback)

Students and teachers must also constantly assess throughout the writing process, as assessment drives instruction, revision, and editing.

Assessment

Writing assessments are the bridge to revision that ultimately improves students' writing. "Direct assessment, the kind that requires students to actually write, is not about rights and wrongs. It is about writing to fit an audience, clarifying ideas, knowing when to shrink or stretch an idea, knowing how to begin and where to end, and so much more" (Spandel, *Creating Writers* 2001, 19). But before assessing student writing, teachers must establish clear expectations and ensure students understand what they are.

By setting specific criteria and communicating them to students and parents, teachers ensure their assessments are consistent and defensible.

Consistency in Assessing Writing

Writing assessment has often been very subjective. Two teachers teaching the same grade in the same school, looking at the same piece of writing, frequently end up giving it a very different grade. Clear grading criteria may or may not be evident. Often, the neatness of the piece and the correct use of conventions (spelling and punctuation) are the chief determinants. The teacher's perception of student effort also plays a role.

Conventions, neatness, legibility, presentation, and student effort are important, but writing is so much more. Teachers need to assess students' writing strengths and weaknesses to obtain the diagnostic information needed to develop mini-lessons, inform writing conferences, and drive guided practice. The traits and trait-based scoring guides take the mystery out of writing and assessing writing. "Do consider grade level as you score, but be careful not to overweight it. The traits do not change from grade to grade.... Ideas may become somewhat more sophisticated with experience and with living, but good writing always has detail, voice, internal structure, and fluency" (Spandel, *Creating Writers* 2001, 66).

Analytic versus Holistic Assessment

When writing is assessed using the traits, it is not assessed simply as a whole piece using a single grade. Instead, it is assessed diagnostically, on the basis of each trait(s) or writing characteristic(s). A student may have strong voice and great organization but weak conventions or vice versa. Students should know and be recognized for their writing strengths while still becoming aware of those areas that need work.

Self- and Peer Assessment

Students first learn about the traits of good writing from hearing good writing read aloud. As teachers draw students' attention to descriptive details and exceptional word choice through read-alouds, and through think-alouds during shared and modelled writing, students learn to be assessors or critics.

Teachers must find ways to limit bias. Their judgments must be defensible.

"When we present students with clear criteria, we turn on the lights."

SPANDEL, *CREATING WRITERS* 2001, 5

Check It Out!

Vicki Spandel, *Creating Writers Through 6-Trait Writing Assessment and Instruction, 4th edition* (New York: Pearson Education, 2005). This superb book, a must-read for teachers, provides both the theory and the practice of teaching and assessing the six writing traits.

"Feedback has been shown to improve learning when it gives each pupil specific guidance on strengths and weaknesses, preferably without any overall marks."

PAUL BLACK AND DYLAN WILLIAM IN SPANDEL, *CREATING WRITERS* 2001, 12

"We teach [children] how to read books, but not how to read their own writing. Unless we show children [how] to read their own writing, their work will not improve."

DONALD GRAVES IN SPANDEL, *CREATING WRITERS* 2001, 3

The journal entry at right is strong in voice.

> Apr. 1. 05
>
> I sat beside this really annoying kid today. He kept poking me and calling me fat: this from a kid who uses the vending machines at recess!
>
> My uniform that everybody has to wear at our school is way too tight. We have to wear a buttoned white shirt with a collar that restricts my breathing considerably and black pants that seem to come in only two sizes: fall-down-at-your-ankles-every-time-you-move size, and trip-and-fall-on-your-face-whenever-you-take-a-step-forward-because-you-have-the-flexibility-of-about-an-inch size.
>
> We do very extravagant science projects. Today my friend and I friend, Juko, built a battery-operated winch that could lift fourteen pounds!

When students self-assess, they become self-reflective. Their feelings about their writing do count. The whole purpose of self-assessment is to help students recognize what they have done well and how they can improve their writing. They, in collaboration with the teacher, can then determine where to go next. Assessment is not the end; it is the gateway to revision, and students often find assessing their own work and that of others motivating.

Students can read one another's work during the editing stage. However, when revising, it is important that they read aloud their work to others when eliciting feedback on organization, voice, and fluency in particular. Reading the work aloud enables the student author to "hear" the piece and note if it makes sense and flows. Students must also learn to read clearly and audibly (no mumbling), fluently, and with expression.

Sharing the writing aloud is important for revision.

Having one partner provide feedback is often less intimidating and more useful than sharing with a large group. But before the piece is read, the author needs to provide his or her partner with a reason or purpose for listening. Too much time is often spent with students sharing their writing in a manner that is both boring and inaudible, and feedback such as "I liked your story" serves little purpose. To make this time worthwhile, it is important for students to

- have a clear framework in mind. Both the author and his or her peer(s) must know their roles.
- have a specific focus for each sharing. This focus may follow in a mini-lesson (e.g., on leads, word choice, or voice) and be determined by the teacher. The focus may also be determined by the student author, who has identified the kind of help he or she needs (e.g., "I'd really like you to listen to my lead and tell me what you think.").

- know how to listen and respond appropriately. Role-play helps students understand what put-downs can do to a writer. Constructive criticism is appropriate—it is the way it is shared that counts.

Writing posters and other forms of environmental print can support self-assessment. However, students rarely use environmental print unless teachers provide specific activities.

These self- and peer-assessment blackline masters will assist students in identifying writing strengths and areas for improvement.

Assessment BLM 4: Ideas and Organization

Assessment BLM 5: Voice and Word Choice

Assessment BLM 6: Sentence Fluency and Conventions

Assessment BLM 7: Writing Attitude Survey

Assessment BLM 8: My Writing Ideas

Assessment BLM 9: Revising and Editing Checklist

Assessment BLM 10: Sharing My Writing with a Partner

Assessment BLM 3: Using My Portfolio to Reflect on My Learning in Chapter 4

Assessment BLM 9: Portfolio Tagging Sheets in Chapter 5

Assessment BLM 10: Portfolio Partners in Chapter 5

Which Traits to Assess

When assessing writing, it is important not to assess all traits for each writing sample. It also makes sense for the student to know before beginning the writing assignment which traits will be focused on. Sometimes the mode of writing influences the focus. In procedural writing (e.g., recipes, how-to guides), the most important traits to focus on are details (ideas) and organization so that the reader or listener can follow the procedure. Voice is more important in narrative and persuasive writing. The strong writer exhibits a clear point of view and cares deeply about the topic when trying to persuade the reader. In strong narrative writing, the author moves the reader. It is obvious that the piece is written with an audience in mind.

> Bananas
> What bananas? You know I hate bananas. If you have to buy them then you have to get all the stuff for a banana split. Or just buy strawberrys or chocolate bars instead. Only weird people like bananas

Even a response to a grocery list can have voice!

Providing Individualized Feedback

To provide individualized feedback, it is important for teachers to discover what young writers know, believe, and value about writing. This discovery can occur through a writing attitude survey, informal discussions, or writing conferences.

Teachers and students can use writing share and writing conferences as opportunities to provide assessment feedback. See earlier in this chapter for information on Writing Share (Author's Chair) and Writing Conferences.

"A student should come away from a conference not with a polished, ready-to-go draft, but simply with an idea of where to go next or, at the very least, a clear sense of a useful writing question to answer: Should I think about a different beginning? Can I make it shorter?"

SPANDEL, CREATING WRITERS 2001, 366

Assessment BLM 7: Writing Attitude Survey

Using Portfolios to Support Assessment

Portfolios are collections of student writing and other materials that reflect student reading and thinking as much as writing (Farr and Tone 1994). A portfolio is more than a place to store student work. It provides a means by which students and teachers can monitor and assess writing performance, set goals, and establish direction.

Portfolios are used to

• develop student skill in reflection (self-assessment)

• develop student skill in goal setting

• monitor student literacy development over time

• drive instruction

For more information on portfolios, see Chapter 4: Literacy Learning Across the Curriculum and Chapter 5: In the Classroom: Making It Work.

Assessment BLM 2: Assessing Portfolio Contents in an Integrated Unit in Chapter 4

Introducing the Writing Portfolio

Before students can begin to put together a writing portfolio and use it for self-assessment and reflection, they need to understand what a portfolio is, the criteria for selecting pieces to include, and the purpose (benefit) to the student, teacher, and parents.

Teachers need to consider

- the portfolio's design in terms of functionality, appearance, and organization
- possible contents
- criteria for choosing pieces to include
- how to manage portfolio size
- ways to share portfolio contents to support student reflection and self-assessment

Portfolio Design: How Important?

A writing portfolio is a tool to help students, teachers, and parents assess writing performance, set goals, and establish direction. The portfolio itself must be manageable and readable, and students should not spend a lot of time making the portfolio "beautiful." Their time is better spent reading through the portfolios, sharing with others, self-assessing, and planning where to go next.

It is very helpful for teachers to share an authentic portfolio with the class, whether it is their personal portfolio or that of a former student. (The latter may be difficult to come by as students may take them home at the end of the year, or may not grant permission to share them with others.)

The Writing Portfolio: What to Include

"The portfolio should include whatever the student and the teacher think will depict and promote that student's development as a language user" (Farr and Tone 1994, 49). Writing samples and student surveys reveal their skills, strategies, interests, and attitudes toward reading and writing. Just about anything can be included in a portfolio, such as

- free writing done at home and at school
- drawings
- letters, notes, memos
- reports
- journals
- fiction, nonfiction, poetry
- favourite works

"Getting the student to use his or her portfolio to develop self-analysis, assessment, and evaluation is the prime lesson for its existence, and if it accomplishes that, it is surely worth whatever time and trouble its development takes! Just creating the opportunity for the student to collect pieces of his or her writing and reactions to reading will affect the student's self concept as a reader and writer—provided the portfolio does more than act as a personal file cabinet collecting a few papers and a lot of dust."

FARR AND TONE 1994, 98

"Tying writing activities to reading, and vice versa, is a vital general instructional approach that should be reflected in assessment, so it is important that portfolios contain as many examples of student response to reading as possible."

FARR AND TONE 1994, 61

- not-so-favourite works
- student attitude surveys
- writers' notebooks
- portfolio reviews
- student responses to literature (reading–writing connections)

Teachers might direct students to include a certain number of pieces and certain genres in their portfolios. For each reporting period, for example, students might be required to add a specific number of fiction, nonfiction, and poetry pieces. However, such requirements may make portfolio work too stilted.

Teachers might also require students to include a certain number of pieces that they are proud of, as well as others that are not favourites. Students need to appreciate that writers do not have to like everything they write. The writing sample may be chosen because it demonstrates improvement or shows a degree of new learning (e.g., how to write a procedural piece).

Choosing Pieces for the Writing Portfolio

Portfolios are most effective when students, teachers, and parents have input into what gets included; however, it is the student who takes primary responsibility, or ownership. Students must learn to think carefully about, and be able to explain their reasoning behind, the pieces they select. Keeping a portfolio record helps students to track the contents and facilitates self-reflection.

Parents become part of the process at each reporting period—often during student-led conferences.

Using Tags (Entry Slips)

Teachers may require students to tag everything they put into their portfolios. Tags, or entry slips, are simply statements attached to the writing sample. They often explain why the piece was chosen and provide the reader with some background information.

However, tagging everything can become tedious and threaten the joy of keeping the collection (Farr and Tone 1994). If students are required to include only a limited number of pieces with tags, the task does not become onerous. Teachers may select categories to be tagged, such as "My favourite piece of fiction, nonfiction, poetry"; "My least favourite piece"; "The topic I am most interested in."

It is also important for both teachers and parents to tag each piece of writing that they include in students' portfolios. Doing so highlights for the student why the piece was chosen and draws their attention to different reasons for choosing pieces to include. Parents might provide brief explanations using such prompts as "I liked ...," "I think ...," and "I hope...."

Assessment BLM 9: Portfolio Tagging Sheets in Chapter 5

Portfolio Record for _____		
September • • •	October • • •	November • • •
December • • •	January • • •	February • • •
March • • •	April • • •	May • • •
June • • •	Possible Additions • • •	

Managing Portfolio Size

Teachers must consider whether they can limit the number of written pieces without stifling student enthusiasm. The portfolio should remain manageable, as students (and parents) will often give up reviewing it if it includes too many pieces. The portfolio is made more manageable if the student and teacher cull it at each reporting period, keeping some representative pieces and removing others. The pieces kept should represent

- different modes of writing in different genres
- growth over time

Culling the portfolio is an opportunity for the student and teacher to set future direction in writing. For example, students who are just writing on one topic or in one genre need to be encouraged to expand their repertoire. Completing a writing plan before writing helps students to write for different purposes using a variety of genres.

Sharing Writing Portfolios

It is important for teachers to first model for students how to share a portfolio. Students then practise the process with a buddy or partner.

Portfolios are often shared in roving conferences, which tend to take just a minute or two. But with large classes, it is difficult for the teacher to get to individual students as often as needed. One option is to implement small-group conferences during which students exchange ideas and learn from one another as they share their portfolios. Small-group conferences also support roving (on the run) conferences.

Student-led conferences involving parents and the teacher are another opportunity to share portfolios. Before a student-led conference, students need to first cull their portfolio, and then practise sharing its contents with a partner or buddy.

In addition to providing feedback on the contents of the portfolio, parents might be encouraged during the conference to select another piece to add and to write a note explaining why they chose it.

Assessment BLM 10: Portfolio Partners in Chapter 5

Writing: The Reading–Writing Connection |

Implementing Writing Portfolios

1. The teacher provides each student with a file folder or folders to use as a portfolio. Some teachers encourage students to decorate their folders right away to create a sense of ownership. Other teachers feel that the file folder art more naturally occurs as students begin to use their portfolios.

2. The teacher demonstrates how to choose pieces for the portfolio and how to explain the reasoning for including a piece using tagging or entry slips for at least some of the pieces.

3. The teacher then explains how to cull the portfolio for the reporting period.

4. Students are regularly given time to read through their portfolios, reflect on them, and share pieces with a partner.

5. While students are reading through their portfolios, the teacher circulates around the classroom, asking and responding to questions to promote student self-reflection. Teacher-generated questions focus on ideas that interest the student and that she or he connects to reading or writing (Farr and Tone 134). The questions should naturally develop into a conversation, not a grilling. Possible conversation starters include the following:

   • Tell me about a piece of writing.

   • How are you improving as a writer? Show me an example.

   • What other kinds of writing might you try next?

6. Students prepare for parent conferences at the end of a reporting period by culling the contents of their writing portfolio, updating their record sheets, and practising their presentation with a partner.

Partner Feedback on Writing

Title: _____

I think this piece of writing _____
_____
_____

This piece made me think about _____
_____

When I read or heard your writing, it made me feel _____
_____

I think you could improve this piece by _____
_____
_____

Assessment BLM 2: Assessing Portfolio Contents in an Integrated Unit in Chapter 4

Assessment BLM 3: Using My Portfolio to Reflect on My Learning in Chapter 4

Assessment BLM 10: Portfolio Partners in Chapter 5

Linking Assessment to Instruction

Students in Grades 3 to 6 are required to write a great deal on a daily basis across the curriculum and in a variety of genres. However, writing alone is not enough. Student writing improves with lots of reading and rereading, mini-lessons (craft lessons), talk, and writing. Students write to make meaning, not simply to maintain their existing understandings. Whereas meaning maintenance comes from simply recording meaning, meaning generation comes from discovering new connections among existing ideas (Harste, Short, and Burke 1988). Students make text-to-self, text-to-text, and text-to-world connections.

To become effective writers, students must learn and use

- the writing process (i.e., the steps in composing, which tend to be recursive rather than linear)
- the strategies used by effective writers and the traits of effective writing
- the modes and genres of writing (narrative, informational/expository/procedural, persuasive, descriptive, poetry) based on the purpose

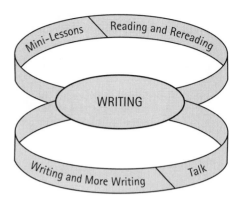

"When teachers share both their writing processing and their writing products with their students, they do the one thing non-writers need most: they demystify writing."

THOMASON AND YORK 2000, 5

The Writing Process

There has been much research on teaching and using the writing process. Although most writers follow the steps outlined in this section, the process used can change slightly to serve the content or the purpose for writing.

All parts of the writing process are interdependent and overlap. When teachers first introduce the writing process, they present, model, and discuss each step individually. As writers develop, the steps blend into one another and the process becomes more automatic.

It is important to begin with extensive modelling of each step in the writing process:

1. **Plan** (prewrite; find key questions; determine purpose, audience, and mode; gather information; discuss or rehearse ideas; outline, sometimes using graphic organizers; incubate ideas)
2. **Write or draft**
3. **Read** the piece aloud to yourself or to someone else and **revise**.
4. **Edit** (conventions)
   - capitals, punctuation
   - spelling
   - grammar and usage
   - paragraphing
5. **Publish**
   - make a "wow" copy
   - share it with others, in written or oral form

As students plan/prewrite, they are incubating ideas or panning for gold.

"Writers 'write' before they write."

MURRAY 1985, 17

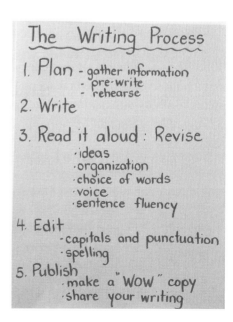

Feedback from peers can be useful. However, some students in Grades 3 to 6 may, for any number of reasons, prefer not to share their writing in a group. Writing is very personal and reading our writing aloud is like taking off our skin; it reveals who we are inside. Sharing with one other peer is often less intimidating.

Some students may feel pressured to write certain kinds of pieces to get a positive response (such as humorous pieces) if they know that they will have to share the piece aloud. Before sharing a piece, or part of a piece, it is important for the author to request the particular feedback wanted (for example, listening for word choice, lead, details, character description, or voice).

To allow more students to participate in writer's share, occasionally limit sharing to a favourite line, a strong character description, a great lead, or a million-dollar word.

Assessment BLM 7: Writing Attitude Survey

Assessment BLM 8: My Writing Ideas

Assessment BLM 9: Revising and Editing Checklist

Assessment BLM 10: Sharing My Writing with a Partner

Planning/Prewriting, Rehearsing, and Gathering Information

The stage involving planning/prewriting, rehearsing, and gathering information is the most important part of the writing process. It is a warm-up to writing in which writers generate ideas. "This is the time that the writer defines a purpose for writing (to inform, to persuade, to entertain), selects a topic, organizes and gathers, identifies an audience, and decides on the form of his or her writing (poetry, narrative, report)" (Buss and McLain-Ruelle 2000, 4). Often, this process unfolds as one thinks about the topic. Some of the best writing occurs in one's head, whether in the shower, on the way to school, or on a walk.

To warm up to writing, students might

- write a list of words or a question(s) to answer
- do a quick write (e.g., write a thought or quote)
- discuss an idea with a friend
- read/look at a book or poem
- draw pictures and then surround the pictures with words (see also Using Graphic Organizers During Prewriting later in this chapter)
- reread an old piece of writing
- examine a picture
- listen to a song or some music, or a story read aloud
- use a story map or graphic organizer
- view a film
- look out the window
- read through their writer's notebook

The two most important questions that need to be answered are
- what is my purpose for writing?
- for whom am I writing?

"Once they have words on the page, developing those words into longer pieces is not as intimidating as facing a blank sheet of paper."

ROMANO 2004, 20

THINKING PAGE

My topic: A Bully

Setting

this Setting is at the School and park of It is at A park

School   Park

Charcters

Bully looks like this

The victoms looks likes

Victomi brothers
name
danny

randy   donny   Camron.

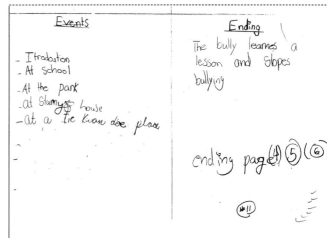

Events

- Itrodution
- At School
- At the park
- at Slumys house
- at, a lie kwan doe plase

Ending

The bully learnes a lesson and slopes bullying

ending page 4 5 (6)

#11

Overcoming Writer's Block

Some writers of any age go blank when trying to come up with a topic or begin a piece. The "Empty Your Head" technique (Schmidt 2004, 44) gets the writing started by getting some words down on paper.

1. Have students draw an outline of their heads on a sheet of paper.

2. Write all the words that come to mind related to a topic inside the head outline. Peter Elbow (in Romano 2004) suggests limiting the time to ten minutes and encouraging students not to let their pens stop moving. Alternatively, they can be encouraged to just keep writing until they are done!

3. Direct students to count the words they've written and to circle those that are most interesting.

4. Encourage students to connect the words that may go together. This works especially well with expository writing. Teachers might provide students with coloured markers to sort and connect the words. "This exercise reinforces the idea that although all the words in the Empty Head are related to the major topic, the linked words belong together in robust sentences or paragraphs. This activity helps visual/spatial and kinesthetic learners organize their ideas before they start writing" (Schmidt 2004, 44).

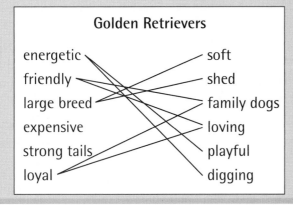

Golden Retrievers

energetic	soft
friendly	shed
large breed	family dogs
expensive	loving
strong tails	playful
loyal	digging

Writing Process
- plan
- write
- read and revise
- edit
- publish

Traits
- ideas
- organization
- voice
- word choice
- sentence fluency
- conventions

Modes
- narrative
- informational/expository/ procedural
- persuasive
- descriptive

Genres
- fiction
- nonfiction
- poetry

Using Graphic Organizers During Prewriting

Graphic organizers such as tables, charts, semantic maps, frames, webs, and storyboards are tools that support thinking. Graphic organizers rely on students' visual literacy to aid comprehension before, during, and after reading. They can also work as springboards for writing.

A circle organizer or map (see BLM 1) is an effective way to depict events that repeat themselves in a cycle, ending up back at the beginning. The song "There's a hole in my bucket" is a good example.

Graphic organizers demonstrate both *what* students are thinking and *how* they are thinking. They help students to clarify their thoughts and think about their own thinking (metacognition).

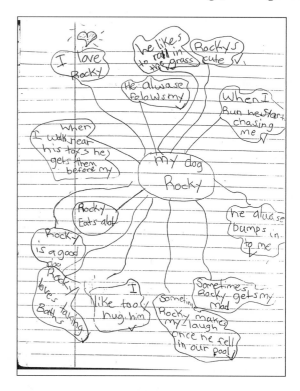

The purpose of completing a graphic organizer is not just to fill in the blanks. Graphic organizers "are interactive tools for constructing knowledge and generating understanding and new ideas. The ultimate goal is that students will independently create and use their own tools for learning" (Edmonton Public Schools 1999, 1). Using graphic organizers can be very helpful. However, students should not be made to feel locked into the organizer. "Rarely—except perhaps when doing a technical manual, recipe, or other step-by-step sort of writing—does a writer know where the trail will lead when he/she begins. It is important to have the mental freedom to follow an unexpected impulse" (Spandel, *Creating Writers* 2001, 136).

For more information on graphic organizers, as well as numerous reproducible templates for student use, see also Chapters 1, 2, 4, and 5.

BLM 1: Circle Organizer (Map)

Graphic Organizers and ESL Learners

"Lessons in which graphic organizers are constructed based on reading and then used as a basis for writing are particularly important and effective for children whose first language is not English" (Cunningham and Allington 1994, 97). Graphic organizers support both vocabulary development and discussion.

"Using ... graphic organizers lowers the language demands of the text for students for which English is a second language (ESL)."

EDMONTON PUBLIC SCHOOLS 1999, 3

The First Draft—Is a Sloppy Copy Acceptable?

Students should not think that anything goes with a first draft. "[S]ince writing is a recursive process, one in which I encourage students to do the best they can with each attempt, I don't call the first draft a 'rough' draft, or as some others say, 'a sloppy copy.' I call it a first draft. Nor do I call the most recent version the 'final draft.' It's the second draft, or third or fourth draft. Those other terms label the various phases with too much permanence, discouraging revision" (Polochanin 2004). If a sloppy copy is accepted as a first draft, if it is illegible with numerous spelling mistakes, then this kind of work often becomes habitual.

First drafts must be legible, have most words spelled correctly (especially high-frequency words), and contain appropriate punctuation and capitalization.

"I will not conference with a child until he or she has reread the paper and checked it for basic spelling and punctuation."

ROUTMAN 1993, 38

Revising

Many students do not revise simply because they don't know how. Rather than make changes to ideas, organization, word choice, and sentence fluency, many students instead recopy their work and correct spelling errors, tasks that are part of the editing process. But revision is about meaning. Its purpose is to improve the piece by

- clarifying ideas through adding or deleting information and details
- enhancing character development
- reordering content
- improving word choice
- varying sentence beginnings and/or lengths
- ensuring that the mode and genre (e.g., informational poem, historical fiction story) match the audience and purpose
- making the title, the lead, and/or the ending more effective

Through much teacher modelling, students learn what revision entails. "What students can assess they can revise" (Spandel, *Creating Writers* 2001, xiii). Students must be taught how to assess the traits in literature they read or hear, other written work (see Author Letters later in this chapter), and their own writing. Once they know how to assess, they will then know what they need to revise.

Rereading written work aloud and then to a partner is one of the best approaches to revision. Reading out loud helps students to hear the fluency of their sentences, the word choice, and the voice. It leads them to ask, "Does it make sense? Do I like what I hear?" Writers also benefit from considering suggestions. Focusing on revising only one small piece at a time, such as improving the lead or the verbs, makes the task more manageable.

"You should be the best expert in the world on your own writing, and the way to do that is by rereading it over and over as you write."

FLETCHER AND PORTALUPI 2001, 69

Check It Out!

Grammar Bytes
http://www.chompchomp.com

Guide to Grammar & Writing
http://grammar.ccc.commnet.edu/grammar/

These Web sites provide excellent information on writing conventions.

Remember:
If I can think about it,
    I can talk about it.

If I can talk about it,
    I can write about it!

Prompting students with some key questions when they think that they are finished can encourage them to revise.

- Does your lead pull in the reader?
- Does the piece say what you want it to say?
- Does the ending grow out of the piece or is it tacked on?
- What is your favourite part? Why?
- What is your least favourite part? Why?
- What would you like to write more about, either in this piece or another?
- Can you cut words, phrases, or ideas?
- Can you insert a snapshot, or "explode a moment"?
- Is there a better lead buried in this piece?
- Does the piece flow?

(Adapted from Lane 1993, 197)

Although most pieces should be revised, not all of them need to be taken to the publishing stage.

Assessment BLM 9: Revising and Editing Checklist

Assessment BLM 10: Sharing My Writing with a Partner

Editing

Capitalization, spelling, punctuation, paragraphing, and proper grammar should be modelled for students and discussed with them, not done for them.

Assessment BLM 9: Revising and Editing Checklist

Publishing

Most pieces should be revised and edited, but not all of them need to be published. Having students pick certain pieces to contribute to a class book or display is one great way to publish. For example, students may each complete an interview and write up the interview, perhaps as a news article. This activity limits the length of the piece and is manageable for all students.

Where Do Writers Get Ideas?

Too often teachers hear the refrain, "I have nothing to write." Some students may truly feel this way; others may simply wish to avoid writing. Posting a chart in the classroom of the many places from which writers get their ideas can serve as a helpful reference for students.

Students need to understand that their best writing will develop from

- topics that are important to them. *Ramona's World* by Beverly Cleary (New York: HarperCollins, 1999) is a great read-aloud to introduce this concept. In this novel, Ramona, a Grade 4 student, writes passionately and in detail about her baby sister, whom she deeply cares about. In contrast, Ramona's classmate writes: "My name is Susan. My favorite color is blue. My favorite food is...." This writing has few interesting details and no voice!

I can get ideas by ...

- reading my writer's notebook
- reading a book, newspaper, magazine, or poem
- looking at a picture
- talking with a partner
- reading my partner's writing
- listening to a story or poem
- drawing
- reading print around the school
- writing something down to help me remember to do something
- writing down a question I want answered

"The more we write and talk, the more we have to write and say."
ELBOW 2004, 13

When my partner is stuck
- we sit together in a quiet spot
- I share something that I am interested in
- my partner asks me questions
- my partner shares something of personal interest
- I ask my partner questions
- my partner comes up with a topic

If my partner is still stuck, we check the classroom chart for other ideas.

- topics about which they know something. In *Lilly's Purple Plastic Purse* (New York: Greenwillow Books, 1996), Kevin Henkes brings the everyday experience of Show and Tell to life! Expository writing on subjects about which students are "experts" is another option.

Non Fiction Topics to Write About

- space
- motorcycles
- baseball
- famous dancers or singers
- swimming
- racing cars
- interesting food
- bats
- insects
- the oldest person alive
- famous inventions
- popular pets
- dinosaurs
- popular video games
- popular movies
- the richest person in the world
- the coldest place on earth
- famous cartoonists
- gymnastics
- the Olympics

Check It Out!

Rotten Teeth by Laura Simms (New York: Houghton Mifflin, 1998) is a great companion read-aloud to *Lilly's Purple Plastic Purse*. The story shares what it takes to build one's confidence in public speaking. *Everybody Needs a Rock* by Byrd Baylor (New York: Aladdin Paperbacks, 1974) and *Miss Bridie Chose a Shovel* by Leslie Connor (New York: Houghton Mifflin, 2004) are great companion reads to *Wilfrid Gordon McDonald Partridge* by Mem Fox (Brooklyn, NY: Kane/Miller Book Publishers, 1985).

- objects that are important to them. *Wilfrid Gordon McDonald Partridge* by Mem Fox (Brooklyn, NY: Kane/Miller Book Publishers, 1985) explores memories and how treasured things connect people to their personal history, thoughts, hopes, and dreams (Spandel, *Books* 2001). What is important is not the object itself (which may simply be a leaf, rock, or ticket stub), but the recollections associated with the object. (See also Interviewing Community Members later in this chapter.)

- snapshots from their life—small topics that students can enlarge or "explode" to highlight the details. Instead of writing about their family, they might write about something funny or frightening that happened to one family member. It is the voice and the details of what happened that make the writing come to life for the reader. The student sample that follows makes effective use of both.

> I was staring out the window as my mom's car sped past the many buildings and shops in downtown Calgary. I looked down and noticed that my knees were shaking. I pulled down my skirt to cover them but that didn't help much. I felt a drop of sweat trickle down my forhead and then down my left cheek. I looked up and studied my mom's face, she was sweating to. Who doesn't when it's 32 degrees outside. Only I knew my sweat wasn't from the heat, to be honest I didn't really mind the heat. Nope, my sweat was from nerves. The most nerves I had ever felt in my entire life. Soon my mom turned the corner and I saw it. I was dreading this moment since Thursday. My mom pulled up to the curb and said, "Good Luck honey, I'll pick you up at 4:00." I stepped out onto the side walk and waved bye. When my mom's car was out of sight I slowly walked towards the big glass doors.

Using a Writer's Notebook

A writer's notebook is not a diary or simply a journal. It is a place to record reactions, thoughts, feelings, sensations, and opinions—things the writer notices or wonders about and doesn't want to forget.

"Notebooks are ... well, it's like you have sparks from a campfire that could start a fire. They haven't yet, but they could any time."

MICHAEL CICCONE (GRADE 1) IN FLETCHER 1996, 125

"Remember: It takes forty gallons of maple sap to make one gallon of maple syrup."

DON MURRAY IN FLETCHER 1996, 120

It takes lots of ideas and details to write effectively and it is the details that make writing come alive. "Maybe the single most important lesson you can learn as a writer is to *write small*. Use your writer's notebook to jot down the important little details you notice or hear about" (Fletcher 1996, 23).

Many writers keep lists of favourite books, words, names, things that bother them, and places they love. Their writer's notebooks also often include

- drawings
- artifacts (ticket stubs from sporting events, concerts, movies, vacations)
- photographs
- secrets
- favourite poems

Using Writing Prompts

In most cases, students should be encouraged to choose their own writing topics: topics that are interesting to them, that they care about, or about which they have some background knowledge (or can research). However, most large-scale assessments (e.g., provincial or state-wide assessments) require students to write from prompts and students sometimes enjoy writing from a prompt. Although there is nothing wrong with the occasional use of prompts, the particular prompt and how it is worded (text) or presented (visual) will greatly affect the quality of the writing.

Vicki Spandel (*Creating Writers* 2001, 32) shares the following prompts that have worked for her:

- Think of something you own that was not purchased in a store. Explain why it is important to you OR write a story connected to this object.
- Can very young and very old people be friends? This prompt would effectively support persuasive writing.
- Think of a place so important and special to you that you would like to return to it many times. Describe it so clearly that a reader can see, hear, feel, and smell just what it is like to be there.
- Think of a teacher (friend/family member) you will never forget. Describe this person. Why is he or she unforgettable?
- Sometimes it's fun to imagine what the world would be like if you were in charge for a day. What things would you change if you could be in charge for just one day?
- What if you won a time-travel contest and you could spend one day with any person, real or imaginary, from the past or present? Who would you choose? Why would you choose this person?

Spandel (*Creating Writers* 2001, 32–33) also reports some teachers having success with single-word prompts (e.g., "lost"; "key") or phrase prompts (e.g., "a time you were confused"; "You won't believe this, but ..."). Pictures also make excellent prompts.

"[No] prompt is perfect; no prompt will work for all students—or motivate all students."

Spandel, *Creating Writers* 2001, 31

Prompts are generally more effective if they

- motivate both the students and teacher
- are open-ended, allowing for individuality of response
- cannot be answered with a simple "yes" or "no"
- direct students to a particular genre (fiction, nonfiction, poetry)
- direct students to a particular mode of writing
  - narrative: tell the story; recount the time when …
  - informational/expository/procedural: explain; give directions
  - persuasive: convince; write an argument
  - descriptive: describe; give details that help your reader to picture

Using Patterns

Students often enjoy stories and songs written with patterns of rhyme, rhythm, or repetition. Using these patterns also helps to scaffold their writing. Using a familiar pattern provides security, boosts confidence, and often leads to success. Even experienced writers sometimes enjoy the opportunity to take a pattern and run with it. There are numerous books that lend themselves to pattern writing.

The important thing about a bottle is that it is breakable. You can put things in it. It is clear. It has a lid. But, the important thing about a bottle is that it is breakable.

Mini-Lesson: Using Patterns

1. The teacher shares *The Important Book* by Margaret Wise Brown (New York: HarperCollins Publishers, 1949) simply for enjoyment.

2. The teacher leads a choral reading of the last sentence, which is generally the same as the first.

3. The class works together to publish their own Big Book based on the writing pattern of *The Important Book* and following these steps:
   - brainstorm objects that might be used in the story
   - select one object for the purpose of creating a shared writing (e.g., a glass bottle)
   - brainstorm descriptive words (e.g., clear, lid, glass, breakable, dangerous)
   - choose one characteristic as the most important; this will make up the first and last line (e.g., "The most important thing about a bottle is that it is breakable.")
   - write three more sentences about the object (e.g., "You can put things in it. It is clear. It has a lid, but …")
   - repeat the first sentence as the last line: "The most important thing about a glass bottle is that it is breakable."

4. The product of the shared writing becomes the first page of the class Big Book. Students then work individually or in pairs to create more pages to add to the book.

Great Resources to Support Shared and Independent Writing

Byrd Baylor. *Everybody Needs a Rock.* (New York: Aladdin Paperbacks, 1974).

David Bouchard. *If You're Not from the Prairie.* (Vancouver: Raincoast Books, 1993).

Dr. Seuss. *My Many Colored Days.* (New York: Alfred A. Knopf, 1996).

Cynthia Rylant. *When I Was Young in the Mountains.* (New York: Dutton, 1982).

Marc Sutherland. *The Waiting Place.* (Waterbury, CT: Abrams, 1998).

Judith Viorst. *Alexander and the Terrible, Horrible, No Good, Very Bad Day.* (New York: Aladdin Paperbacks, 1972).

Judith Viorst. *If I Were In Charge of the World and Other Worries: Poems for Children and Their Parents.* (New York: Aladdin Paperbacks, 1981).

Authentic Reasons to Write

Students will understand what writing is about when they are writing for authentic reasons. Authentic writing introduces students to different writing forms—forms that have real-world applications, such as lists, invitations, letters, notes, and reports. Most adults rarely write stories, but they do write when they have something they want or need to share. Students write for similar reasons.

The types of authentic writing students in Grades 3 to 6 often enjoy both reading and writing include

- biographical accounts (personal narratives, autobiographies, and biographies)
- news stories
- interviews
- question-and-answer books
- New Year's resolutions
- journals
- learning logs
- letters (persuasive letters, e-mail, author letters)
- Web sites

Biographical Accounts

Personal narratives, autobiographies, and biographies are all forms of biographical writing that students both read and write in Grades 3 to 6.

Personal Narratives

The personal narrative is a common, familiar form of writing to most students. Beginning in the early elementary grades, students write about themselves and their experiences, often in the form of journal entries, but occasionally as more polished pieces of writing.

My fav sport is Soccer

Thur.15.2004

Im in a soccer team. I love soccer because because since I was little I wanted to be on a soccer team. I love soccer so much that when my dad said to go in a hockey team I would say N-O! In the team I am number nine. I run FAST. The team name is called the Newton Hawks. I kick with my left foot my dad said that lucky people can kick with there left foot. I love soccer.

Autobiographies

Like personal narratives, autobiographies are stories of a person's life written or told by that person. Reading aloud the autobiography of someone famous is often motivational for students and is a great way to introduce this writing form. The teacher might then introduce the concept of a Me Quilt (Tompkins 2000) as the basis for an autobiography.

Making a "Me Quilt"

1. Students draw a self-portrait in the middle of a large piece of craft paper.

2. The remainder of the page is divided into eight squares.

3. Students create eight pictures to represent important times in their life and paste the pictures into the eight squares on the craft paper.

4. Students then write a paragraph for each of the eight pictures. More advanced writers may prefer to write more extensive autobiographies, focusing individual chapters on different time periods or phases of their life. Timelines are another option for developing a piece of autobiographical writing.

5. Students share their Me Quilts.

Reading or listening to biographies is a great stimulus for journal writing. Students write a minimum of five journal entries in the role of the individual whose biography they have read or heard. They then share at least one of their entries and explain why that individual might have written such an entry.

Biographies

Biographies are accounts of a person's life written by someone else. Before writing a biography, students have to decide exactly what they want to know and share about the person. It is helpful for them to have the opportunity to read or listen to several biographies and come up with the general format for such writing. In addition, students benefit from comparing and contrasting two biographies written about the same person.

- In what ways do the portrayals differ?
- Why might each author have portrayed the individual in this manner?
- What was left out of one biography and not the other?
- What perspective of the individual was the author trying to portray?
- Which version is more believable? Why?

Students also find it interesting to select a line from a biography and provide evidence to support or oppose the statement.

Whether students choose to write about someone of particular interest to them personally, such as a family member, community leader, or favourite author (see Author Web Sites for Grades 3 to 6 later in this chapter for some ideas), or someone they learn about in their content area studies, the work they complete during the prewriting/planning stage will be key.

Before writing a biography, it is important for students to create an outline, which often includes a timeline. They gather details for their outline by conducting interviews with the person and/or with acquaintances (if possible); reading diaries, books, and letters written by the person; and researching information in newspapers, magazines, and on the Internet. Consulting at least three sources helps to ensure that the information is accurate.

Once the information is gathered and perhaps plotted on a timeline, it is then organized into paragraphs or chapters. It is best to encourage students to "write small" rather than to go on and on. Most students achieve success when they focus on developing no more than four or five paragraphs for their biographies.

- Paragraph 1: The Introduction. The introduction should grab the reader (see the mini-lesson on improving leads later in this chapter). Usually, the introduction names the individual and provides some background information, such as the place and date of birth and a detail about the individual or his or her family.
- Paragraphs 2 to 4: Main Events. Students need to focus on key points or events in the person's life. Some biographers include diagrams, maps, photographs, or drawings.
- Paragraph 5: The Conclusion. The ending to a biography should be interesting and convey how the student really feels about the person being profiled. It should be clear to the reader why the biographer chose to write about this particular individual.

Another authentic writing activity is for student biographers to prepare an All About the Author page. The information for this page could be researched, or could be based on an interview with the author. Some teachers allow students to interview classmates and take photographs of one another to include with this page. (See Interviewing an Author later in this chapter.)

This student chose to argue against Terry Fox's view of himself as "an ordinary guy."

Terry Fox
"Terry Fox an ordinary guy"

Terry fox was no ordinary guy. He had all the courage and determination it takes to be a hero. Having cancer and losing his leg didn't stop him from believing he could find a cure for cancer. He turned something life threatening into something positive that would help cancer researchers. Terry always thought about others, he wasn't selfish. It takes a special person to think about others, when your life depends on it. Not everyone could do what he did. He could have stayed at home studying on how to be a P.E. teacher. Terry's life could have been easier if he stayed at home but he believed he could make a difference. Terry was strong-willed. He decided to run everyday in any weather, rain or shine, sleet or snow to raise money for cancer. His goal was to run 42 km a day so Terry set out to accomplish it. Terry's courage and hope was what made him a true hero and we all wish to be like him.

Mandeep

All About the Author
My biography of _____
Paragraph 1: Introduction • strong lead • personal information
Paragraph 2: Main Event • key point • details
Paragraph 3: Main Event • key point • details
Paragraph 4: Main Event • key point • details
Paragraph 5: Conclusion

Newspaper exposure in school results in greater interest in news, politics, and lifelong reading. For further information about the Newspaper in Education Program, visit http://www.naa.org.

News Stories

A recent study revealed that "young adults who remembered using the newspaper in school were more likely to develop lifelong readership habits than those who said they had no exposure to newspapers in school" ("Study Finds Link ..." 2005, 35). Students enjoy and benefit from the opportunity to read and study newspapers, write news articles, and create class newspapers.

For more ideas on news writing with a focus on the traits, see Mini-Lesson: Shared Writing News Story later in this chapter.

Mini-Lesson: News Writing

1. The teacher shares news from a local paper, drawing students' attention to examples of
   - good news
   - bad news
   - entertainment news
   - business news
   - sports news
   - humorous news

2. No matter the type of news, the teacher points out
   - the headline—grabs the reader and captures the essence of the news story
   - the byline—identifies the writer and occasionally indicates his or her status with the newspaper, such as staff reporter, columnist, feature writer, or entertainment editor
   - the lead sentence(s)—tells who, what, where, when, why, and how, usually in a paragraph or two. This key information makes the reader want to read on.
   - the facts—outlines the details of what happened, in descending order of importance
   - the ending statement—leaves the reader with a specific idea to remember or consider

3. Students then write a news story about something they know about personally.

BLM 2: My News

Mini-Lesson: Shared Writing News Story

1. The teacher and students brainstorm classroom or school news on which to base their story. Together, they choose the topic for the story (e.g., school fundraiser for tsunami relief).

2. Through think-alouds, the teacher works with the class to outline the facts and details of the story: the who, what, when, where, why, and how. For example,
   - Indian Ocean tsunami hits parts of India, Indonesia, the Maldives, Sri Lanka, and Thailand on December 26, 2004
   - death toll 300 000
   - hundreds of thousands of homes destroyed; most coastal towns and cities wiped out
   - relief aid desperately needed to prevent more deaths from lack of food, clothing, shelter, and medicine
   - talent show to benefit tsunami relief held at Earl Grey Elementary School on January 28, 2005
   - many Grades 5 and 6 students perform
   - students donate money earned from doing extra chores at home
   - school raises $2200.00 for tsunami relief

3. Rather than work on the headline, the teacher might first encourage students to develop the lead (e.g., "A talent show put on by staff and students at Earl Grey Elementary School at the end of January raised a whopping $2200.00 for tsunami victim relief.")

4. After developing another paragraph or two outlining the remaining details of the story, a suitable ending is written (e.g., "The school is very glad to have been able to help the victims of this tragedy.").

5. The teacher then leads students in the creation of a headline (e.g., "One School, Big Difference!" or "Kids Helping Kids").

KIDS HELPING KIDS
Cathy & Courtney, Grade 5 students

On December 26, 2004 a terrible tragedy happened. There was a tsunami in Asia. This did not only hit Asia, but many other countries and cities as well. Many families and friends were separated and killed.

The students and staff at Earl Grey School decided to do something to help. So on January 28, 2005 we had a benefit talent show. Many of our grade 5 and 6 students participated to show their respect to fellow people that were part of the tsunami.

Teachers encouraged the students to do chores around the house to raise money. In each classroom there was a can for donations in which the students put the money they earned. As well, all the students at our school made little hearts with hopes and wishes written on them. These are displayed on our school bulletin board.

Earl Grey School successfully raised over $2,200. We are very glad that we were able to help all the victims.

Publishing in Newspapers and Magazines

Newspapers and magazines have become a favourite reading choice for adults and children alike. Writing a newspaper or magazine article can be very motivating for students, especially if they have the opportunity to get their work published.

Classroom newspapers (see the next subsection) provide a forum for students' writing, giving them an authentic reason to write. As a way of publishing students' work for a wider audience, Stone Soup, available at http://www.stonesoup.com, is an online publisher of work by students from around the world, aged 13 and under. The site also features links to other online publishers of the work of young writers.

For additional resources that publish student writing, see Supporting Poetry Writing in the Classroom later in this chapter.

Check It Out!

A strong collaborative writing venture is the Kids Are Authors competition at http://www.scholastic.com/kidsareauthors. This is a book-writing and illustrating contest for teams of K–8 students. The winning books are then published and distributed.

Implementing a Classroom Newspaper

Newspapers must appeal to a wide range of readers, which is why they contain different components, such as

- feature stories
- general news stories
- sports stories
- editorials (often persuasive writing)
- letters to the editor
- self-help columns
- comics
- display ads
- classified ads
- book, movie, concert, and television reviews

Photographs are also important to newspaper articles and can even stand on their own with little text.

1. Before creating their own newspaper, students will benefit from studying and revising work from real newspapers. They can examine headlines, leads, and details in the body and the ending, and can make revisions and debate the strength of each. This exploration provides the scaffolding for students to create their own news.

2. As with any form of writing, the items in the class newspaper must be written and compiled with a specific audience in mind. Students must consider who their readers are: fellow students (some younger, some older), parents, senior citizens, and so on.

Check It Out!

Web Sites:

Creating a Classroom Newspaper
http://www.readwritethink.org/
lessons/lesson_view.asp?id=249

The New York Times Learning
Network
http://www.nytimes.com/learning

Yahooligans
http://yahooligans.com

Books:

The Stone Age News by Fiona MacDonald (Boston: Candlewick Press, 1998).

Creating a Classroom Newspaper, edited by K. Buss and L. McClain-Ruelle (Newark, DE: International Reading Association. 2000).

Sharing Social Studies or Science Content as News

There are many creative ways for students to share what they are learning in the content areas without writing reports. Such information can be written in the form of an article for a school newsletter or a piece to be shared over the intercom. Again, these are real reasons to write.

Roller coasters on the Ring of Saturn

On Friday, January the fifth, 2005, local men from New York City were sent on a very urgent mission to Saturn. The reason for this mission was to find out what kind of unidentified animals were riding some sort of roller coasters on the ring of Saturn. (When thirty-year old Andrew Fitzerman, twenty-seven year old Bobby Huemes, thirty-two year old Clifford Berrymore, and twenty-five year old Simon Zitzback saw that the unidentified animals were a family of four aliens.) When the four local men landed on Saturn, they saw that the aliens had created a enormous theme park, which had two roller coasters, a few twisty and curvy slides and about three huge, long monkey bars. Once the aliens had seen that humans had landed on Saturn, they ran to their spaceship and possibly flew to another planet and supposedly they might start to make another theme park on another planet.

For more information on report writing, see Chapter 4: Literacy Learning Across the Curriculum.

Interviews

Interviews provide another opportunity for students to gain practice with a form of writing that has real-world applications.

A unique approach to interviewing is Paul Fleischman's "Interview with a Shrimp" in *When I Was Your Age, Volume Two: Original Stories About Growing Up*, edited by Amy Ehrlich (Cambridge, MA: Candlewick Press, 1999). The story is written from the perspective of Fleischman interviewing himself as a child troubled by Chronic Stature Deficiency (being short). Students might create an imaginary interview with themselves and write up the resulting biography.

Interviewing an Author

When students publish their own writing, a fellow classmate often interviews the student author, writes up the biographical information in the form of an All About the Author page, and takes the student author's photo (see Biographies, earlier in this chapter).

Before the interview occurs, the interviewer must determine the questions to be asked and put them in sequence. Questions are brainstormed and the teacher models the process. Students might consider questions such as the following:

- What makes you happiest?
- If you could change one thing in this world, what would it be?
- What do you like about yourself?
- If you could change anything about yourself, what would it be?
- What is your favourite subject or author?
- What made you write this particular piece?
- What do you enjoy doing most in your spare time?
- Tell me something interesting about yourself.
- What experience in your life was
  - the funniest?
  - the scariest?
  - the saddest?
  - the most intriguing?

Interviews are then written up as biographical sketches and included with the author's published work. Interviews might also be written up as news articles, featuring quotes from the interview.

Interviewing Community Members

Interviewing members of the community (including seniors in retirement or nursing homes) provides students with historical information and connections relevant to social studies. They also develop a better understanding of the concept of memories.

It is a good idea for students to first listen to a taped radio interview or read an interview in a magazine, newspaper, or online before discussing interviewing techniques and types of appropriate questions. Many author and illustrator Web sites feature the text of interviews they have done.

Check It Out!

Reading aloud *Wilfrid Gordon McDonald Partridge* by Mem Fox (Brooklyn, NY: Kane/Miller Book Publishers, 1985) will help students prepare for interviewing senior citizens in their community.

Check It Out!

The Stinky Cheese Man and Other Fairly Stupid Tales by Jon Scieszka and Lane Smith (New York: Viking Press, 1992) is a hilarious read. Numerous traditional tales are rewritten from other perspectives. From the cover to the back of the book, the artwork, presentation style, and humour ("Who is this ISBN guy?") make it a favourite among Grades 3 to 6 students.

Memories ... Pat Moore

In grade four we have been talking about the different memories that each of us have accumulated so far in our lives. Memories help us to understand ourselves and the world around us. Our memories are constantly changing and helping us to grow. We've chosen Pat Moore as our centennial project because we think that she has had a fascinating life and we wanted to share it with the world. We wanted to ask Mrs. Moore about some of her favorite memories. We picked a topic and then wrote questions relating to that topic. Later we had the opportunity to interview Mrs. Moore and ask her our questions.
This is what we found out:

Justin, Andrew, Dustin, Grant, Daniel

Mrs. Moore's favorite winter memories occurred during her childhood at the neighborhood skating rink. Almost everyday after school during the winter months, Mrs. Moore and her friends would rush home, get in their winter clothes, get their skates on and meet back at the rink. At the rink, they would have lots of fun together. There were mostly girls but a few boys would go. They would play games like Tag, Follow the Leader and Crack the Whip. They would skate until 6:00 and then go home for dinner. The weather didn't matter. Even if it was really cold outside, they would still skate. Sometimes it was so cold that when they took their skates off, their feet would be tingly. Mrs. Moore has many happy memories of winters spent at the neighborhood skating rink.

Guidelines for Conducting Interviews

- Ask questions for which you do not already know the answers.

- Ask questions that require more than a "yes" or "no" answer.

- Record direct quotes that you might include in the interview write-up to make it more interesting to read.

- Don't limit the interview to your preplanned questions. Listen carefully to the person you are interviewing and ask any new questions that may be sparked by his or her responses. Following up on such leads often makes the interview more interesting.

- Don't try to cover too much in one interview. Interesting details (quality) are more important than the number of details (quantity).

- Always be sensitive to the feelings of the person being interviewed.

- End the interview by thanking the person.

Interviewing Fictional Characters

It is important for students to understand that everything they read is written from a particular perspective or point of view. Shel Silverstein's poem "Point of View" from *Where the Sidewalk Ends* (New York: HarperCollins, 2004) might be used to introduce the concept of perspective to students. (For more on perspective, see Chapter 2: Reading Comprehension: Strategies That Work.) Conducting imaginary interviews with characters from the same text is another interesting way to examine different perspectives or viewpoints.

Mini-Lesson: Perspective

1. The teacher reads aloud *Voices in the Park* by Anthony Browne (London: A.E.T. Browne and Partners, 1998). This story is about two families who visit the same park but have very different perceptions of the experience. Alternatively, students might be reintroduced to the fairytale *Jack and the Beanstalk* or listen to a read-aloud of Jon Scieszka's *The True Story of the 3 Little Pigs* (New York: Viking Press, 1989).

2. Students imagine interviewing one of the characters in one of the stories to determine that character's perspective on the events.

3. The interview and the write-up that follows should help the reader to understand why the character perceived the events of the story in a particular way. The voice of the character should come through in the interview responses.

4. Students work with a partner or in small groups to act out their interviews.

5. Students might then rewrite the story or tale from the perspective of one of the characters, or write a letter in role as one of the fictional characters to one of the other characters.

6. Conducting imaginary interviews with other fictional characters and then rewriting the stories from different perspectives could culminate in a published classroom anthology of interesting alternative tales.

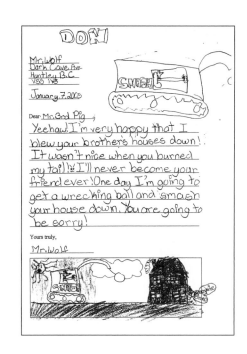

Question-and-Answer Books

What more authentic reason to write can there be than to pick a topic of interest to investigate? The key to success with this form of writing, however, is to limit the topic, or "write small." Students need support in taking a snapshot of the topic and using the details about that part of the topic to make their writing more interesting and compelling to read.

Many students wonder how certain everyday items came to be. They may be interested to learn that the yoyo, dry cleaning, coffee, correction fluid, microwaves, and bread were all invented by accident. Introducing students to *Accidents May Happen: Fifty Inventions Discovered by Mistake* by Charlotte Foltz Jones (New York: Delacorte Press, 1998) is a great way to stimulate topics to write about. As the author states on the back cover, "If you don't learn from your mistakes, there's no sense making them."

New Year's Resolutions

Self-reflection often sparks goal setting outside of the classroom. Students may have witnessed the adults in their lives making New Year's resolutions. Having students document their own New Year's resolutions is an authentic reason to write. The very act of writing down their goals makes them more concrete. Teachers, and especially students, revisit their resolution(s) in several months and determine how successful they are in adhering to them.

Check It Out!

Ask an Expert at http://www.askanexpert.com/ enables students to ask questions of experts in the fields of medicine, law, science, and computers.

These question-and-answer books might serve as models for students:

M. Berger and G. Berger. *How Do Flies Walk Upside Down?* (New York: Scholastic, 1999).

M. Meikle. *You Asked for It! Strange But True Answers to 99 Wacky Questions* (Toronto: Scholastic, 2000).

A. O'Neill. *I Wonder Why Snakes Shed Their Skin and Other Questions About Reptiles* (London: Kingfisher, 1996).

J.K. Wangberg. *Do Bees Sneeze? And Other Questions Kids Ask About Insects* (Golden, CO: Fulcrum, 1997).

Mini-Lesson: Writing Question-and-Answer Books

1. Students first pick a topic of interest; something they would like to know more about.

2. Once the topic is narrowed down, students develop a series of questions to guide their research. A graphic organizer, such as a KWLM chart, could assist them with this stage. (See Chapter 4: Literacy Learning Across the Curriculum for more on the KWLM strategy.)

3. Using a variety of resources to ensure consistency and accuracy, students research answers to their questions.

4. The final result is a book in which each question is followed by the answer.

Journals

The purpose of journal writing is for students to "record personal experiences, explore reactions and interpretations to books they read and videos they view, and record and analyze information about literature, writing, and social studies and science topics" (Tompkins 167).

Students can easily tire of journal writing, however. To guard against this, effective teachers limit journal writing to two or three times a week, scheduling other forms of writing in between. Having several journals for each student also adds variety: personal journals, dialogue journals, or reader response journals. Students rarely tire of dialogue journals when they know that they can expect a personal reply from the teacher, another adult, or a peer.

Personal Journals

In personal journals, students write about events or experiences in their own lives and about topics that interest them. The teacher may or may not ask questions or make comments.

Amelia's Notebook by Marissa Moss (New York: Tricycle Press, 1995) is a great introduction to journal writing. Amelia, aged 9, records her thoughts, feelings, and experiences—some humorous, some painful—during a cross-country move with her family. The book resembles an authentic child's journal, with drawings and text. Moss even points out that the copyright information "means this is my book."

Dialogue Journals

Dialogue journals are a means by which the student writer can converse with the teacher, another adult, or a peer on any topic.

Reader Response Journals

In reader response journals, students respond to what they have been reading—fiction, nonfiction, poetry. They may write, draw a picture or diagram, list million-dollar words, or write a few favourite lines from the text.

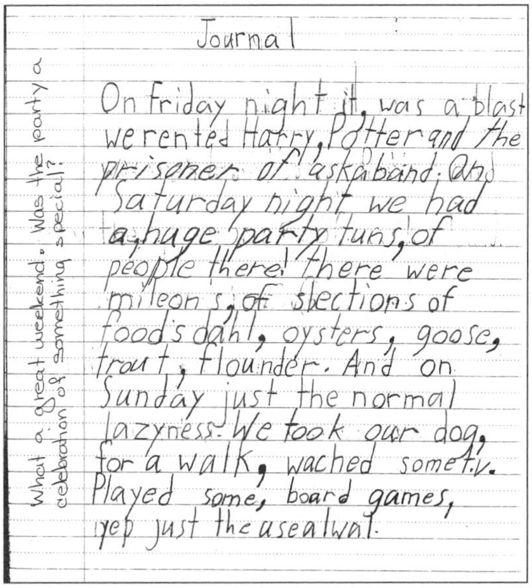

The handwritten journal entry:

> ## Journal
>
> *(left margin, written vertically: a party? Was the weekend something special? What a great weekend. celebration of something special?)*
>
> On Friday night it was a blast we rented Harry Potter and the prisoner of askaband. On Saturday night we had a huge party tuns, of people there! There were mileon's of slections of food's dahl, oysters, goose, trout, flounder. And on Sunday just the normal lazyness. We took our dog, for a walk, wached some t.v. Played some, board games, yep just the usealwal.

Note the dialogue between the teacher and the student.

Reader response journals allow students to

- gain a deeper understanding of a text they are reading
- make connections between the text and their own experiences
- express and support their personal thoughts
- practise their written communication skills
- make text-to-text connections
- become more critically literate

For more information on reader response journals, see Chapter 2: Reading Comprehension: Strategies That Work.

Prompts for Reader Response Journals

Some students initially benefit from writing prompts. As the year unfolds, however, students will likely initiate most of the writing.

Possible Prompts for Reader Response

• This is about....	• I wonder if ...
• I remember when ... because....	• It reminds me of ... because....
• I really liked when ... because....	• It was interesting when ... because....
• I didn't like when ... because....	• I was surprised when ... because....
• I found out....	• This makes me think of....
• I wonder why the author wrote it this way? (supports critical literacy)	• I think that this is the best line (or word) in the text ... because....

Other reader response prompts that help to develop students' critical-thinking skills and support critical literacy include the following:

- What was the story (novel, poem) about?
- _____ was my favourite character because....
- Why do you now think that the author picked the title?
- Talk about the illustrations. Do they match the text?
- Does this writing remind you of anything else you have read?

What is the title and how are the two texts similar?

- Which writing trait was the strongest (ideas, organization, word choice, voice, sentence fluency)? Provide an example from the text to support your opinion.
- Why did you pick this text to read? Explain why you are happy or unhappy with your decision.
- Write a note to one of the characters.

Assessing Reader Response Journals

The emphasis when assessing journal writing is on writing fluency and self-expression, rather than on correct spelling and neat handwriting (Tompkins 194). That being said, teachers have to walk a fine line. Students need to be encouraged to write as often as possible and to take risks in their writing. But illegible handwriting and careless spelling mistakes can become a habit. Journal writing should not simply increase the quantity of the writing, it should improve the quality. Writing, whether in journals or elsewhere, must be legible. And by the end of Grade 3, most words, especially high-frequency words, should be spelled correctly.

When assessing journals, teachers may want to consider the types and depth of student responses. Writing responses are only valuable if they serve a purpose by helping the student to reflect, make connections, comprehend more deeply, or enjoy more fully the texts they are reading.

In reviewing journals over time, it is important to observe if the student is

- making connections (text to self, text to text, text to world)
- activating prior knowledge and making predictions
- asking questions
- quoting and responding to words and passages
- identifying narrative and expository text structures and features (e.g., illustrations, charts, graphs, headings, glossary words, and so on)
- expressing opinions and confusions
- sharing new knowledge learned
- commenting on vocabulary or word choice
- connecting the text to such issues as social justice (critical literacy)

Learning Logs

Students use their learning logs to write or draw responses to what they are learning in a content area: social studies, science, music, math, health, art, and so on. The form of writing in a learning log can vary. For example, students might write a public service announcement for a nutrition unit in health, or a letter in role as a visitor to a

---

February 13, 2005

Dear Mom and Dad,

My trip to Japan so far has been wonderful. The Osaka Family has been very kind to me, especially Kimi.

Kimi and her family live in a traditional Japanese home. Their house is made out of wood and tatami mats are laid everywhere to keep the house clean. Each room is divided by sliding doors made out of wood and paper. The house also has a genkan. A genkan is a slightly sunken tiled area inside the front door where you put your shoes.

Here in Japan they eat out of bowls instead of plates like we do. They also use chopsticks instead of forks and spoons. It took me a while to learn how to use them, but I think I almost have got the hang of it.

See you in a week!

Swetha

---

country they are learning about in social studies. Letters provide students with an audience for their writing—real or imagined. This helps their voices to shine through.

Learning logs reveal to the teacher what knowledge students are assimilating and what personal connections they are making to the content.

Letters

Nothing develops or demonstrates an author's voice like a letter. Knowing there is a real audience and having the expectation of a response from that audience is a compelling reason to write. Most students enjoy writing letters. The range of flexibility in terms of content, voice, word choice, even length, makes the letter a highly accessible writing form for students in Grades 3 to 6.

An effective way to introduce letter writing to students is to share, through read-alouds, literature that makes use of this particular form of writing.

Letter Writing in Children's Literature

The Jolly Postman, or, Other People's Letters by J. Ahlberg and A. Ahlberg (Boston: Little, Brown, 1986) traces the delivery of postcards, letters, invitations, and thank-you notes to various fairy-tale characters (e.g., a letter of apology from Goldilocks, a postcard from Jack for the Giant, and so on). Students learn about different genres of mail as well as different letter formats: friendly, business, and persuasive.

Regarding the Fountain by Katie Klise (New York: Avon Books, 1998) focuses on a Grade 5 class who write letters, memos, telegrams, and postcards regarding a water fountain for their school. When they discover corruption, they end up researching their town's history by interviewing residents. (See Interviewing Community Members earlier in this section.)

Dear Mr. Blueberry by James Simon (New York: Simon and Schuster, 1991) links fiction, nonfiction, and voice! Emily writes to her teacher Mr. Blueberry about a whale that she imagines lives in her pond. In his response, Mr. Blueberry shares much factual information about whales.

Plantzilla by Jerdine Nolen (San Diego: Harcourt, 2002) demonstrates the power of voice and word choice as it looks at life through letters written from the perspective of a parent, Grade 3 student, teacher, and plant.

Dear Children From the Earth: A Letter From Home by Schim Schimmel (Minocqua, WI: North Wood Press, 1994) and the sequel *Children of the Earth ... Remember* (1998) may prompt students to research and write letters about environmental issues. In both books, Mother Earth writes a letter to students about caring for the planet and all the animals that inhabit it.

Check It Out!

Who's Got Mail? Using Literature to Promote Authentic Letter Writing

http://www.readwritethink.org/lessons/lesson_view.asp?id=85

Investigating Junk Mail: Negotiating Critical Literacy at the Mailbox
http://readwritethink.org/lessons/lesson_view_printer_friendly.asp?id=321

Check It Out!

A Genre Study of Letters with *The Jolly Postman*

http://www.readwritethink.org/lessons/lesson_view.asp?id=322

Check It Out!

As a follow-up to *Plantzilla*, students might join the Junior Master Gardener program at http://www.jmgkids.org. In addition to learning about plants and the environment, they can contribute to the online newsletter.

Check It Out!

Ramona's World by Beverly Cleary (New York: HarperCollins, 1999) highlights for young readers the importance of correct spelling. When Ramona asks, "What difference does spelling make if people know what you mean?", her teacher replies, "You wouldn't want people to think that you sat on a 'coach' instead of a 'couch' would you?"

Letters from Storybook Characters

Many students enjoy writing letters in role as a character in a story they have read. To introduce this approach to students, teachers might share *Dear Peter Rabbit* by Alma Flor Ada (New York: Aladdin, 1994). The book comprises a fascinating collection of letters written by, and addressed to, well-known storybook characters. The letters take the characters beyond their original stories; for example, one describes what happened to Goldilocks after her adventure.

Students might assume the role of both a character and the author of a story they have read and write letters back and forth. In their letters, characters might ask the author questions, complain about their role, or suggest how the book could be improved. The letters could be written occasionally, or chapter by chapter to serve as a summary of the story.

Persuasive Letters

Letters are written for a variety of purposes. Friendly letters reinforce and enhance personal connections. Business letters (to companies, organizations, newspapers, trustees, or politicians) generally acknowledge or demand some form of action. It is a great shared writing experience for a group of students or the whole class to work together on a letter to the principal, a newspaper editor, the mayor, or premier about an issue of importance to the school, city, or province. Students write such letters to ask for information, persuade, complain, or express thanks. (See Persuasive Writing in the Research on Writing section earlier in this chapter for a student-authored letter to a provincial premier and his response.)

Revising and Editing Letters

Student letters, especially business letters, often require revision and editing. This is a perfect time to discuss the importance of capitalization, punctuation, spelling, grammar, sentence fluency, word choice, organization, legibility, and ideas to ensure the letters not only make sense, but are also read.

A letter to a newspaper editor created through shared writing and including shared editing and revision, helps students to be part of the whole process. Spell check, although a useful tool, is limited in what it can do. Students have to learn to reread for the purpose of revision and editing, and must understand the difference between the two. A persuasive letter to the editor may need no editing, but it may be weak in content and fail to persuade anyone (see Persuasive Writing later in this chapter for more information).

Author Letters

Author studies are very popular with Grades 3 to 6 students. After reading one or more books by the same author, students often enjoy discovering what kinds of experiences led to the writing of a particular book or series, how difficult it was to get it published, or how the author came up with the title.

Students are also motivated to write when they are encouraged to critique a published author's style or particular work. This goes far beyond the usual questions authors receive, such as "When did you decide to become an author?" or "Do you like what you do?"

Before writing to an author, students must think critically about the text the author has composed. Students incubate their ideas or pan for gold as they consider and discuss with others such questions as the following:

- What is the topic? How is it presented? What themes are being expressed?
- How are the characters presented? Why are they presented in this way? How might you change a character(s) and why?
- What is the purpose of the text? What is it trying to make you think or feel?
- What wasn't said in the text? Why was it left out? What would you add or delete if you were writing on this topic?
- Who is writing to whom? Whose positions are being expressed? Whose voices and viewpoints are not heard?

(Adapted from Luke, O'Brien, and Comber 2001, 116)

Encouraging this type of thoughtful literacy enables students to provide more meaningful feedback, both positive and negative, to authors. They will have questions to ask but they will also have worthwhile comments and insights to share. They might even suggest a revision, such as to the title, lead, or perspective the text is written from, and send their ideas to the author. This has been described as respectfully "talking back to authors." What an authentic form of writing this is! (See Chapter 2: Reading Comprehension: Strategies That Work for more information on critical literacy.)

Students may choose to write the letter individually, with a partner or small group, or as a shared writing experience with the support of the teacher. Author letters should be sent via the publisher, the name and address for which is usually provided on the copyright page. It is important for students to understand, however, that not all authors are able or willing to respond to fan mail.

Students may also choose to contact authors by e-mail. Many authors and illustrators have Web pages, where students may learn a great deal about the author, read comments from other students, and find answers to frequently asked questions. Students may occasionally fill in Meet the Author cards, which can be posted on a bulletin board in the classroom.

E-mail

Technologies (computers, PDAs, cell phones, fax machines) enable students to discover and connect with their global community to acquire and share knowledge. Most students and teachers are able to communicate with e-mail pen pals (also called e-pals or key-pals), experts in an area of interest, other educators, and authors.

When students learn to analyze a published author's writing style and follow up with a written critique sent straight to the source, they suddenly regard writing as a powerful act (Lewin 2004). Being able to critique someone else's writing also helps students to critique their own.

Meet the Author

Name of Author:

Books by Author (minimum 3):

Common Themes:

How the Author Got Started Writing:

Other Interesting Facts:

By _____

Check It Out!

A superb read-aloud to introduce the concept of "talking back to authors" is Beverly Cleary's *Dear Mr. Henshaw* (New York: HarperCollins, 1983). As part of his Grade 6 author report, Leigh writes to Mr. Henshaw, who responds with a list of questions for Leigh to answer. Thus begins a correspondence and series of journal entries, which will resonate with students and help them to learn the qualities of effective writing.

Author Web Sites for Grades 3 to 6

Frank Asch	http://www.frankasch.com/
The Author Corner	http://www.carr.org/authco/
Marc Brown	http://pbskids.org/arthur/grownups/marc_brown/
Ann Cameron	http://www.childrensbestbooks.com/
Tomie dePaola	http://falcon.jmu.edu/~ramseyil/depaola.htm
Lois Ehlert	http://falcon.jmu.edu/~ramseyil/ehlert.htm
Denise Fleming	http://denisefleming.com/
Mem Fox	http://www.memfox.net/
Gail Gibbons	http://www.gailgibbons.com/
Kevin Henkes	http://www.kevinhenkes.com/
Carol Hurst's Children's Literature Site	http://www.carolhurst.com/index.html
I Spy	http://www.scholastic.com/ispy/
Internet School Library Media Center Index to Authors & Illustrators	http://falcon.jmu.edu/~ramseyil/biochildhome.htm
Ezra Jack Keats	http://www.ezra-jack-keats.org/
Kids Read Authors	http://www.kidsreads.com/authors/authors.asp
Gordon Korman	http://www.gordonkorman.com/
Leo Lionni (Grade 3 Author Study)	http://falcon.jmu.edu/~ramseyil/lionni
Arnold Lobel	http://www.eduplace.com/kids/hmr/mtai/lobel.html
Magic School Bus	http://www.scholastic.com/magicschoolbus/home2.htm
Bruce McMillan	http://www.brucemcmillan.com/
Katherine Patterson	http://www.terabithia.com/
Gary Paulsen	http://www.randomhouse.com/features/garypaulsen/
Patricia Polacco (Grade 4 Author Study)	http://www.patriciapolacco.com/
Faith Ringgold	http://www.faithringgold.com/
J.K. Rowling	http://www.scholastic.com/harrypotter/author/
Louis Sachar	http://www.louissachar.com
Maurice Sendak	http://falcon.jmu.edu/~ramseyil/sendak.htm
Shel Silverstein	http://falcon.jmu.edu/~ramseyil/silverstein.htm
Chris Van Allsburg (Grade 5 Author Study)	http://www.houghtonmifflinbooks.com/authors/vanallsburg/
Vera Williams	http://www.kidsreads.com/authors/au-williams-vera.asp
Yahooligans Author Site	http://www.yahooligans.com/School_Bell/Language_Arts/Authors/
Jane Yolen	http://www.janeyolen.com/

Some teachers send students a "message of the day" through e-mail and share responses to e-mails that have been sent as a class to others outside the school. Free electronic postcards and greeting cards are available on many Web sites and can be sent to mark special occasions.

Web Sites

School and classroom Web sites are another means of communicating with the world and give students an audience for their writing. Even very young students recognize the distinction of having a global audience and are provided with incentive to organize and present their work carefully. Through the World Wide Web, students can take

that concept of writing for their peers to peers all over the world. Many software programs, such as Microsoft Word, Dreamweaver, and FrontPage, give students Web publishing options, allowing them to add their learning and knowledge to that of other authors and researchers already on the Web.

Electronic field trips in real time enable students to share different cultural and environmental experiences. E-mail and telecommunications opportunities through the Internet facilitate direct communication and promote social interactions previously limited by the physical location of participating learners. One site that connects classrooms is ePALS, located at http://www.epals.com. This Web site has maps and language translators, and includes ideas for communication projects.

Students and teachers can also create Web sites to provide information for parents and for other students. The technology is easy to learn and the benefits are extraordinary.

Enhancing Critical Literacy Through Writing

"Ultimately, being successful at learning anything requires that we become interested in the activity to be learned and see doing it as enjoyable" (Cunningham and Cunningham 2002, 90). However, many students in Grades 3 to 6 prefer not to write and in fact write very little.

Check It Out!

Great ideas for creating a class Web site are available at
http://www.webyourclassroom.com/

Check It Out!

When I Was Your Age: Original Stories About Growing Up, Vol. 2, edited by Amy Ehrlich (Cambridge, MA: Candlewick Press, 2002) contains original stories about growing up, written by such well-known children's authors as Norma Fox Mazer, Jane Yolen, Paul Fleischman, Karen Hesse, and E.L. Konigsburg.

"Our rich conversations about social issues might be used as a resource—a springboard—for purposeful, provocative writing."

HEFFERNAN 2004, 24

When they do write, the product is often very flat or lacks voice. Voice requires students to know about the topic and have some vested interest in writing about it. Using big idea themes that facilitate critical literacy promotes enthusiasm, purposefulness, and voice in student writing.

Themes in the area of critical literacy (such as social issues) often hook students in Grades 3 to 6, especially when they can see connections to their own lives. "I think that reading books and finding books in which you might see an aspect of yourself is really important at this particular age. It can be incredibly cathartic. And because kids at this age don't always share a lot, this catharsis can be helpful" (Henkes 2005, 486).

Critical literacy provides a way of thinking that helps to uncover social inequalities and injustices, which may ultimately lead to social action and change. Students might effect positive change by writing persuasive letters to the editor or to the principal or school council chair. Through this process, students will ideally come to view writing "as a tool for disrupting the commonplace and taking social action" (Heffernan 2004, 18). Critical literacy brings the school and community together around real issues, making learning less insular.

Critical Literacy Themes Supported by Superb Literature and Writing

Teasing / Bullying	Ageism	Social Class / Differences	Displacement / Relocation	Growing Up / Social Issues
Crow Boy, Taro Yashima	*Wilfrid Gordon McDonald Partridge*, Mem Fox	*Olive's Ocean*, Kevin Henkes	*The Butterfly*, Patricia Polacco	*Ramona's World*, Beverly Cleary
Creativity, John Steptoe	*"The Little Boy and the Old Man,"* Shel Silverstein	*Voices in the Park*, Anthony Browne	*Number the Stars*, Lois Lowry	*Flying Solo*, Ralph Fletcher
Thank You Mr. Falker, Patricia Polacco	*How Does it Feel to Be Old?* Norma Farber	*Something Beautiful*, Sharon Dennis Wyeth	*They Came from the Prairies: How the Buffalo Were Saved from Extinction*, Neil Waldman	*The Sixth Grade Nickname Game*, Gordon Korman
Flying Solo, Ralph Fletcher	*Olive's Ocean*, Kevin Henkes	*Holes*, Louis Sachar	*So Far From the Sea*, Eve Bunting	*Dear. Mr. Henshaw*, Beverly Cleary
Millicent Min, Girl Genius, Lisa Yee	*Millicent Min, Girl Genius*, Lisa Yee	*The Story of the Seagull and the Cat Who Taught Her to Fly*, Luis Sepulveda	*One More Border*, Kaplan and Tanaka	*Fig Pudding*, Ralph Fletcher
My Secret Bully, Trudy Ludwig		*The Other Side*, Jacqueline Woodson	*Hana's Suitcase*, Karen Levine	*When I Was Your Age*, Amy Ehrlich, ed.
No Difference, Shel Silverstein			*Letters from Rivka*, Karen Hesse	*Holes*, Louis Sachar
Holes, Louis Sachar			*Baseball Saved Us*, Ken Mochizuki	*Olive's Ocean*, Kevin Henkes

Writing Responses That Work

Students may choose to respond in hundreds of ways. The most common, motivating, and meaningful methods include writing

- a journal entry regarding the text
- from the perspective of one of the characters
- a letter from one character to another and their response
- a letter from a character to the author of the text and the author's response
- an interview with a character
- letters from characters in one text to those in another text and their responses (text to text)
- a letter to the editor about a social issue such as homelessness (after much research and discussion on the issues affecting homelessness)
- a revision to the text using a prompt such as "What if ...?" For example, "What if most of the people in Europe during World War II had responded as the family in Patricia Polacco's *The Butterfly* did?" or "How could the ending of the story of Hana Brady as described in *Hana's Suitcase* be rewritten?"
- advertisements or posters regarding a social issue

Challenges Surrounding Critical Literacy

Using social justice issues or themes can sometimes be uncomfortable. Discussing difficult issues such as bullying, teasing, and stereotyping may result in students making connections to negative experiences. However, by dealing with these issues through reading, viewing, discussing, and writing, students will make connections to themselves, other texts, and the world. And it is big idea themes that motivate students to passionately discuss, read, write, and perhaps act.

"One of the best ways to increase student thinking ... is to make sure you have a curriculum that provides kids with things worth thinking about and that offers kids enough depth that they can actually think."

ALLINGTON IN PRELLER 2000, 1

How to Teach the Traits

It is crucial for teachers to highlight the importance of the traits and how students can use them to make their writing more effective. One approach is to first have students identify the characteristics through brainstorming and examples, and then to follow up with explicit instruction of each trait, one by one.

Have Students Identify the Traits

The teacher begins by asking the class how they know good writing when they hear or read it. Through brainstorming, students will likely identify most of the characteristics of effective writing. A shared writing chart of the traits is created and added to as the year goes on.

Students then find and share examples of the characteristics during guided, independent, and other types of reading in all subject areas. The shared writing chart will ideally be referenced when students are providing specific feedback to their peers about their writing. Comments such as "I liked (or didn't like) your writing" are really not helpful.

Good Writers

- use interesting million dollar words
- use just enough detail
- reread their writing to make sure it makes sense
- read their writing to a friend for feedback
- revise their writing to make it better
- use beginnings that grab the reader
- create titles after they have finished writing
- make sure that the title matches the topic
- have an audience in mind when writing
- know why they are writing
- write small (that is, they focus on a snapshot in time)
- use different types of sentences, beginnings or leads
- incubate their ideas before writing
- notice how authors that they enjoy write
- express their own thoughts and feelings
- care about what they are writing
- know lots about a topic
- write a lot! · read a lot!
- use a writer's notebook for ideas
- edit their writing for spelling, punctuation, capitalization
- often use humour
- reread their writing many times and sometimes out loud to decide how to make it better
- get ideas from other writers
- use an ending that ties everything together

Teach One Trait at a Time

The teacher introduces a trait by first explaining what it means and then reading aloud a literature selection to serve as a model. The language of the traits must be used during shared reading and read-alouds. Students can understand and identify the traits long before the traits consistently show up in their own writing (Spandel, *Creating Writers* 2001).

To ensure students actually hear the trait, it is recommended that the selection be read aloud twice: once for enjoyment, and again to highlight the trait. Students can enjoy the book on another level if asked to listen for voice or a million-dollar word, or to think about the picture the text makes in their heads (ideas).

Following the read-aloud, a discussion of the text, using the language of the traits, reinforces the characteristics of good writing. Students then identify and assess the trait in other writing and share their examples.

During modelled/shared writing (focused mini-lesson), students' attention is drawn to the use of the trait through teacher think-alouds. Students are then encouraged during guided or independent writing to focus on the trait taught. There are no surprises. Students know on which trait to focus during writing, and understand which trait will be assessed.

Choosing Books to Teach the Traits

It is most important that teachers share books that they themselves love. Reading with excitement and passion is contagious. Some books are better than others for teaching a specific trait. If teaching word choice, for example, a book full of million-dollar words such as William Steig's *Brave Irene* (New York: Farrar, Strauss, and Giroux, 1986) would be a great choice. In fact, most books by William Steig

It is important for the teacher, student, and parents to use the same language—the language of the traits.

are rich in word choice. It is important to use a good piece of literature more than once. Often the same book can be used to teach several traits at different times.

Reviewing books with a group of colleagues to create a list of titles that are particularly strong in one or more traits is an enjoyable task that saves everyone time in the long run!

The criteria for selecting texts vary depending on the trait to be taught.

Books for ideas: Is the main idea clear? Does the book have one central idea or an easy-to-follow story? Interesting details? Glorious images? Does it make "movies" flow through your mind?

Books for organization: Does the book have a powerful beginning? Does it have a strong or surprising conclusion? Is everything clearly linked to one main idea: bears, insects, whales, oceans, and so on? Does the book follow a pattern that student writers could imitate in their own writing?

Books for voice: Will I LOVE reading this book aloud? Will I enjoy reading it more than once? Can I hardly wait to share it? Would I give it as a gift? Does it make me laugh or cry?

Books for word choice: As I skim through, do I notice words or phrases I'd like students to know? Words I love myself? Are the words challenging without being too technical or difficult? Is the meaning clear from the context? Does the book contain some words likely to be new to students? Are everyday words used in creative ways?

Books for fluency: Does the text read like poetry? Are sentences highly varied in length and structure? Does it have a nice flow when read aloud? Does it have repeated rhythms or choruses where students could chime in?

Books for conventions: Does the book use a wide range of conventions so I could point some out to students? Does it make unusual use of any conventions—capitals, exclamation points, quotation marks, and so on?

(Adapted from Spandel, *Creating Writers* 2001, 343)

Check It Out!

For great ideas and suggestions, try Ruth Culham, Picture Books: *An Annotated Bibliography with Activities for Teaching Writing* (Portland, OR: Northwest Regional Educational Laboratory, 1998), or Vicki Spandel's *Books, Lessons, Ideas for Teaching the Six Traits: Writing in the Elementary and Middle Grades* (Wilmington, MA: Great Source Editing Group, 2001).

Using Focused Mini-Lessons to Teach the Traits

Good writing involves all the traits working together. However, it is helpful for students initially to learn one trait at a time. It sometimes takes at least three weeks with a focus on a particular trait before it is time to introduce the next one. As teachers read aloud, all traits are revisited daily. Ideas, the foundation of all writing, require a great deal of emphasis, often being the initial focus for many days.

Many teachers

- start with ideas (without good ideas, there is nothing to write)
- then focus on organization and voice
- follow by word choice and sentence fluency

Mini-Lesson: Shared Writing

Shared writing helps take the mystery out of writing.

1. The teacher selects a newspaper article of interest to the students. The title and byline (author) are shared before students begin predicting what the news story might be about. The teacher then reads the article aloud to the students.

2. From there, the teacher and the students pick a small part of the article (a stimulus or snapshot) and begin the process of constructing a text through shared writing. One teacher's explanation of the process and benefits of this shared writing experience follows.

Dear Miriam,

Just a note to provide you with some examples of shared writing with my students.

We used "the plot" from a newspaper as evidence that there are always "stories" and we can use those stories to shape fiction of our own.

The class created their own version of the plot provided for them.

We worked 15 minutes daily to create two pages of this text on chart paper. In all it took about 2 weeks. Along the way much was learned about the craft of writing ... as well as the ways in which writers solve problems.

As well our students learned about the thoughtfulness required of an illustrator. They figured out that titles are best constructed at the end of a story.

All of the students really felt ownership for this text. They read it to their parents during student-led conferences in March.

What we learn as teachers, as we model shared writing in this way, is how important such an activity is—to show children the writing process—rather than TELL THEM.

Best wishes,

Annie Davies

At the time of writing, Principal of Douglas Harkness Elementary, Calgary, Alberta.

The teacher later explained that the shared writing was completed on chart paper, but then word-processed. Each student received a copy. The results: Every child's published piece was unique, with his or her personalized titles and art.

One day Jill Miller was washing dishes after lunch. Duke, her German Shepherd puppy was tugging on her pant leg. He wanted to go for a walk.

"Stop, Duke! Stop! I guess you want to go outside?"

Duke started running to the back door. Jill went to get her house keys and the leash. "Okay Duke. Let's go. Let's go to the park."

They walked down the gravel-covered road to an off-leash area. When they got there Jill unclipped the leash, Duke zoomed off. He dashed into the bushes and he was soon out of sight. Jill called, "Duke! Duke! Where are you?"

Suddenly, she heard a terrifying yelp from the woods. Jill knew there was trouble. She raced with a feeling of panic in her heart. It was pounding so hard she was breathless. Reaching the bushes she saw Duke on the ground with a cougar sinking his teeth into the puppy's neck.

Luckily, Jill saw a rock on the ground. She grabbed it. Jill fired it right at the cougar's head. It hit him right between the eyes. The vicious cat leaped into the air in pain and escaped into the trees. Jill ran to Duke's side. She knelt down beside him, stroked him and checked for injuries. She saw two deep wounds that were pouring with blood. Scooping him up in her arms, she held him close. Slowly and carefully she walked back to the house whispering, "You're going to be okay boy. Don't worry. You're going to be okay."

Fifteen minutes later she picked up the phone and called the vet.

"Hello, how can I..."

"I have an emergency. My dog's bleeding to death. I'll be over right away! It's Jill Miller."

After a forty minute drive, Jill finally arrived at the vet's office. He was expecting them. "Come right into my ER," he said in a worried tone.

Jill put Duke on the operating table. She left the room while the vet put thirty stitches in her puppy's neck. After what seemed like hours, the vet came out and said, "Your dog's fine but be careful with his stitches. I've put a cone around his neck to protect them."

"Hi ice cream. You goofy guy. How about a big wet kiss?" said Jill as she rubbed Duke's back.

For two whole weeks Duke was bumping into everything because the cone was so large. Jill didn't mind a bit. She thought, I'm just happy he's alive.

by Ray...

A16   CALGARY HERALD   Sunday, November 30, 1997

MILLARVILLE

Area cautious of cougars

DARYL SLADE
CALGARY HERALD

Residents in the Millarville area are taking extra precautions after cougars killed — or stalked — several pets and livestock in the past couple of weeks.

John Seaborn, who has lived in the rural district for 15 years, said Saturday he had never seen cougars in the area before.

Last week he was twice stalked by a cat...

Other residents have reported horses, sheep and llamas killed by cougars.

But while cougars have done much damage lately, coyotes still are the primary concern, he said.

Seaborn said a Fish and Wildlife officer told him the cougar problem should diminish when hunting season starts Monday, because the animals will head to the hills.

A woman, who asked that her name not be used, said...

One student's title and cover.

So much was modelled, demonstrated, and shared. This teacher's students learned the traits used by effective writers.
- **Ideas:** picture and print match details and title
- **Organization:** sequencing the story; conclusion
- **Voice:** demonstrated in both the text and the art (e.g., "Oh my God!")
- **Word choice:** words paint a vivid picture (e.g., "Duke *zoomed* off," "*a feeling of panic in her heart*")
- **Sentence fluency:** beginning sentences in different ways; using a variety of sentence lengths
- **Conventions:** reflect the content and writing style (e.g., quotation marks, question marks, exclamation marks)

The students also learned
- how to read a newspaper article: title, byline, lead, conclusion
- how to own a piece of writing and to feel proud of their accomplishments. Through this shared writing experience and others, the students will be able to apply their understandings in guided and independent writing.

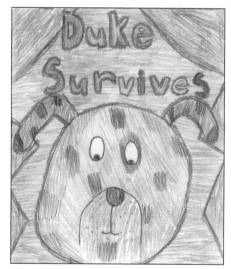

Class Shared Writing. Another student's title and cover.

Connecting the day from read-aloud to shared writing to independent and/or guided writing provides a sense of continuity. The day is not fragmented; time is used more efficiently.

It is important for students to understand that ideas and voice are not the same. A piece can have many ideas but limited voice. The mini-lesson that follows will help students to understand the difference between these two traits.

Ideas	Voice
What did you see, hear, smell?	What did you feel?

Mini-Lesson: Distinguishing Between Ideas and Voice

1. The teacher reviews the concept of ideas. Ideas are clear if the reader or listener can see, hear, feel, and/or smell what is being described. Ideas depend on the details chosen. It is not the number of details but the strength of the details. Too many or too few details don't present the audience with a clear picture. Voice, on the other hand, refers to feelings. It is the heart of the piece. It is what moves the reader.

2. The teacher selects a story that is strong in both details and voice so that students can distinguish the difference between the two traits. Books by Patricia MacLachlan such as *What You Know First* (New York: HarperCollins Books, 1995) are ideal.

3. After the teacher introduces the text selection, students simply listen to the read-aloud for enjoyment. After the read-aloud and a discussion, students contribute to a shared writing chart.

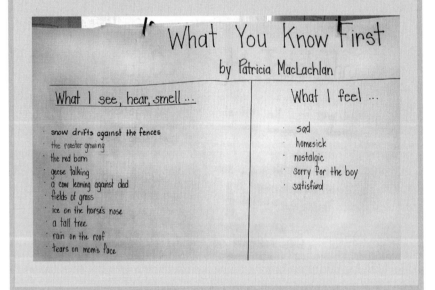

Teaching Revision

Many students in Grades 3 to 6 don't revise simply because they don't know how. When asked to revise, they often recopy the piece more neatly or correct some spelling errors. Frequently, they do not understand the difference between revising and editing. Through much teacher modelling, students learn what revision entails. Revision is about adding or subtracting information and improving word choice, sentence and paragraph organization and fluency, the lead, and the title—all to make the writing more effective. Before revising, writers generally benefit from reading the draft aloud and welcoming suggestions. Throughout the revision process, it is crucial that the author always keeps the audience in mind when asking two important questions:

- Who am I writing for?
- Why am I writing this?

See also Revising earlier in this chapter.

Assessment BLM 9: Revising and Editing Checklist

Main Ideas and Details

Often young writers need support in strengthening the ideas presented. The details that support the main idea(s) are what make this happen. Students may not include enough detail or they may include too much detail. Also, the quantity of details may be appropriate yet they may add very little new information, resulting in a boring piece of writing. Students discover that revising by

- adding details is the easiest
- changing the order comes next
- deleting information is one of the most difficult tasks

All writers like to be "done." It is difficult to decide what information should be deleted. Through mini-lessons, students learn that revision involves deleting information that is redundant, does not fit, and does not contribute any new information to the piece. The next three mini-lessons help students to focus on filling in details and pruning details.

Mini-Lesson: Filling in the Missing Details

1. The teacher first creates a story lacking in detail (and excitement). Students love if it is a true story that the teacher has experienced. Alternatively, use the following true story.

> I had quite the adventure. I had been working for a few days in Ontario and was trying to get home to Calgary. Because of the weather many of the planes were grounded. I really wasn't sure what to do. But I had to get home. After much negotiation I got home just a few minutes before the ceremony. The actual flight is another story! I learned two valuable lessons from this adventure. It was a close call.

---

2. The teacher asks students the following questions and records their responses:
   - Tell me what you learned from the story.
   - Do you wonder about anything, or have any questions or confusions?

3. Possible questions (and answers) based on the sample story above follow. The teacher records the answers as well for student reference during the rewriting stage.
   - Why did the author need to get home? (to attend a cousin's wedding)
   - What was the problem with the weather? (an ice storm combined with a lack of de-icing fluid grounded many planes at the airport)
   - Who did the author negotiate with? (the airline employees at the gate)
   - How was the problem solved? (the author got on another flight)
   - When did this happen? Where? (April 6, 2003, at Pearson International Airport in Toronto)
   - What adventure happened on the flight? (the author was seated next to two women wearing masks due to the SARS epidemic)
   - What lessons did the author learn? (persevere through difficulty; customer service is alive and well)

4. Model rewriting the story using the details that were uncovered during Step 3. A possible revision to the sample story follows.

Students who are floundering for details in their own writing will benefit greatly from being interviewed by the teacher or a peer. By fielding key questions targeted to their topic, students will come up with many details that they may not have thought of on their own.

Don't Take "No" for an Answer!

April 6, 2003, was the day that I learned not to take "no" for an answer. I had been working in the Sault for two days and was trying to get back to Calgary for my cousin's wedding on Sunday. Actually, I had been trying to get back to Calgary for two days but there was this little problem of no de-icing fluid at Toronto's Pearson International Airport, which meant that there were no planes landing or taking off. Everything was backed up. After finally landing in Toronto, I was lucky to get a reservation on Air Canada 117, Toronto to Calgary, leaving at 10:45 Sunday morning. This was to get me to Calgary by 10:45 AM Calgary time. I thought, "I should have lots of time to go home and get ready for the 5:00 p.m. wedding." Little did I know!

By 6:15 AM I was in line to check in. After we boarded, 60 minutes late, the captain came on and explained that there was a problem with the windshield and maintenance was looking at it. Thirty minutes later passengers were requested to deplane with all carry-on baggage. It was now

10:15 AM and departure was now slated for noon.

While off the plane, I checked the departure board. Another flight, Air Canada 107, was also slated to leave for Calgary at noon and it was just five gates away. At 11:45 AM an announcement was made: "Ladies and Gentlemen, Flight 117 is now slated to depart at 1:00 PM, perhaps 1:15." This did not sound promising. I dashed over to Gate 210 to try and get on Flight 107, which was about to leave.

"I have been trying to get to Calgary since Friday and I have a family wedding at 5:00 PM. Since Flight 117 is still out of commission, might I go standby on 107—the ice storm is not my fault," I begged! The agent explained that there was one empty seat but my bag was on the other airline. There was no discussion.

But there is a happy ending. Another agent took pity on me and provided me with the needed boarding pass. I dashed to the gate as the last passenger and boarded the plane to the cheers and congratulations of both passengers and employees—you would have thought that it was MY wedding. But the story is not yet over.

I was seated in the only empty seat—14D—next to two women wearing masks as a SARS precaution. I had to wonder whether the masks were to protect me or them! Lunch time was an adventure, watching them lift their masks for just a second to pop in a piece of chicken, and quickly lower the masks to chew. Drinking appeared more difficult. Oh well, it helped to pass the time.

I arrived in Calgary with just enough time to go directly to the wedding thanks to the kindness and sensitivity of one airline employee. There are still employees who care. My bag and Flight 117 arrived at 9:39 PM, long after the wedding. The moral of the story: There are times when refusing to take no for an answer works!

5. Compare the two versions. Which version do students prefer? Why? Have students provide specific examples of how the second version was improved.

Mini-Lesson: Pruning the Dead Wood

Pruned details include statements that give the reader no new or enticing information, such as "lightning can be dangerous" or "turtles move slowly." Sometimes, pruning involves removing information that really is not directly related to the topic being written about. Author thoughts may also stray from the topic.

1. Through a shared writing, the teacher models how details are pruned, and then reads aloud a first draft of a piece of writing that requires pruning. A sample follows, or another piece could be used instead.

Calgary, the Best Place to Live!

There's no doubt about it! Calgary is the best place in Canada to live. It was chosen by the United Nations as providing its citizens with one of the best qualities of life in the world. It has very clean air and water and is very close to the beautiful Canadian Rockies. There are many hiking trails and a natural, very hot, sulphur water pool in which to swim. Also the skiing is the best in the world. I love the mountains because I love to ski. I spend many weekends on the ski slopes. Boy, that gets expensive!

Calgary is a city of approximately one million people. Unlike larger cities it is still fairly easy to get from place to place, as long as you have a car. The traffic moves well even in rush hour. Calgary has a highway running all the way around it, making it easy to get from one side to the other. Although there is public transportation, a car is your best bet. The city is so spread out that public transportation often takes a very long time. Last week it took me 1.5 hours to get home on the bus!

Calgary's economy is very strong. Most people have work. The city is very fortunate to be the centre of the oil industry for Canada, have many other businesses and industries, and have a strong tourist trade. Calgary also has a very low unemployment rate. In addition, homes are still afford-able compared to many other large cities.

More and more people are moving to Calgary. I guess the secret is out! Calgary is the place to live.

2. Students receive a copy of the piece that was read aloud and work with a partner to determine what, if any, pruning is necessary. The students cross out details to be pruned.

3. Pairs share their revised piece followed by some class debate as to what should go (see the criteria for pruning listed above). The revision that follows has had eight details removed. Students discuss if the final revised piece is stronger and if there is another way to prune it. They then identify what was pruned and why.

Effective writers elaborate on a few details rather than on trying to describe everything.

Calgary, the Best Place to Live!
(revised)

There's no doubt about it! Calgary is the best place in Canada to live. It was chosen by the United Nations as providing its citizens with one of the best qualities of life in the world. It has very clean air and water and is very close to the beau-tiful Canadian Rockies. There are many hiking trails and a natural, very hot sulphur water pool in which to swim. Also, the skiing is the best in the world.

Calgary is a city of approximately one million people. Unlike larger cities it is still fairly easy to get from place to place. The traffic moves well even in rush hour. Calgary has a highway running all the way around it, making it easy to get from one side to the other.

Calgary's economy is very strong. The city is very fortunate to be the centre of the oil industry for Canada, have many other businesses and industries, and have a strong tourist trade. Calgary also has a very low unemployment rate. In addition, homes are still affordable compared to many other large cities.

More and more people are moving to Calgary. I guess the secret is out! Calgary is the place to live.

4. Students are encouraged to reread any writing they do to ensure that the details are strong and the dead wood is pruned!

Mini-Lesson: Improving Leads (Organization)

Good leads grab the reader and make them want to read more. It has been said that if a writer has a good lead, the rest will follow. A follow-up to any piece of modelled writing may involve a focus on beginnings (leads) and on endings.

1. Brainstorm the many types of leads that are used effectively. During daily shared read-alouds, the teacher has students identify great leads.

2. The teacher asks students' opinions on a lead such as, "My family had a camping adventure that we will never forget."

3. The teacher then provides students with other leads that might work. For example:
   - "Have you ever had a camping adventure? I sure have."
   - "Black bears are best seen from a long distance. I know this because ..."
   - "I have never been so frightened in my life...."
   - "Grrrrr.... Aaah ... a bear!"

4. Students vote on their favourite lead and, most importantly, explain why they chose the lead they did. How does the lead hook them into wanting to read more?

5. Each lead is then examined. Sometimes questions are effective, sometimes statements that show excitement or fear are effective.

6. The teacher tells the students a story. Have them do a quick write with a focus on creating an effective lead for the story.

7. Each lead is discussed as a class and classified as a setting, action, reflection, astonishing fact, sound effect, character, dialogue, or question.

8. Students are then encouraged to focus on leads during independent writing.

Mini-Lesson: Improving Titles

Ralph Fletcher talks about "Jazzing up Your Title" (Portalupi and Fletcher, 2001). Titles, both fiction and nonfiction, should really grab the reader. The title determines whether or not anyone will pick up the piece to read.

1. Joann Portalupi and Ralph Fletcher suggest students be taught three main techniques for writing effective titles (2001). These techniques are best introduced through read-alouds.

Effective titles may use ...	Examples
surprise	*Throw Your Tooth on the Roof* by Selby Beeler (New York: Houghton Mifflin, 1998)
humour	*My Little Sister Ate One Hare* by Bill Grossman (New York: Crown Publishers, Inc., 1996) *I Swim an Ocean in My Sleep* by Norma Farber (New York: Henry Holt and Co., 1997)
an adjective that starts with the same letter (alliteration) as the topic focus	*Some Smug Slug* by Pamela Duncan Edwards (New York: HarperCollins, 1996)

2. Another lesson involves revising a title, such as "Camping." Each student comes up with a title that either surprises the reader (e.g., "There's a Bear in My Sleeping Bag"), uses humour to entice, or uses alliteration. Again, there are many possible titles that are appropriate. The real learning occurs as the students defend their choices using the techniques suggested by Portalupi and Fletcher.

3. Students come up with titles for a shared writing and discuss and vote on their favourites.

Make sure that the title always matches the topic.

4. They then work together to title a piece that one student has written.

5. Focus on creating and sharing titles during independent writing.

Mini-Lesson: Improving Word Choice

Students need to understand that some words are overused or boring and need to be retired. One teacher actually involves her class in burying the boring words. Once buried, they can't be used anymore.

Lacklustre vocabulary might be brought to the students' attention by making lists of alternative words. Students love the term "million-dollar words" and enjoy brainstorming possible replacements for "tired" words. For example, alternatives to the word *walk* might include *stroll, race, saunter, lumber,* and so on. The lists then appear as wall charts and are referred to often by the teacher and students.

1. A text selection written by the teacher is critiqued to improve word choice. Alternatively, the teacher might take a paragraph from a literature selection and modify some of the stronger verbs, explaining to students that some of the original verbs have been changed.

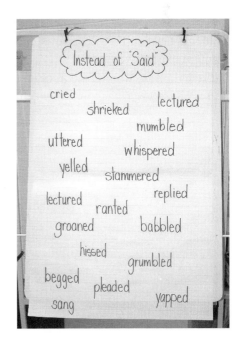

Silverwing by Kenneth Oppel (Toronto: HarperCollins Publishers, 1997) raises social and moral issues that support critical literacy. At a literal level, it is a fascinating story of bats and nature, which may stimulate some students to do more research.

This modified version of a paragraph from *Silverwing* by Kenneth Oppel (Toronto: HarperCollins Publishers, 1997) might be used.

> "He could barely breathe, the air *hitting* against his nostrils. The wind *blew* at his eyes like ice pellets, and he shut them tight. Even his mind's eye was nothing but pure blackness, sometimes *turning* into bright star bursts from the wind's howl in his ears."
>
> (Adapted from 207)

2. Students work in pairs to rewrite the paragraph to improve verb usage.

3. Students share their pieces with other pairs or small groups, who provide feedback on the verbs used.

4. The teacher shares his or her revised text selection, or the original author's paragraph. After discussing word choice, students decide which revisions they think were the strongest and why.

What follows is Oppel's original paragraph.

> "He could barely breathe, the air *smashing* against his nostrils. The wind *stabbed* at his eyes like ice pellets, and he shut them tight. Even his mind's eye was nothing but pure blackness, sometimes *blossoming* into bright star bursts from the wind's howl in his ears." (207)

Students develop their sense of story through exposure to, and participation in, storytelling in drama and art.

Narrative Writing

Students develop their concept of story by listening to, telling, and writing stories. They learn the elements of a story—the setting, introduction, main characters, problem or main goal, main events, and resolution (problem solved/goal achieved)—when their teacher or classmates point them out in literature. They are helped to recognize story elements by being taught how to retell a story and write a story, first as a shared writing, and then through guided and independent practice.

Students' understanding of story is further enhanced when they can recognize not only the story elements, but also the writing traits. For it is voice, word choice, organization, ideas, and sentence fluency that make stories come alive.

Linking narrative writing to the themes or concepts being taught in other subjects is an effective way for students to make sense of what they are learning. Using the material from such content areas as social studies, science, or math as the basis for a story not only demonstrates but also consolidates student knowledge.

Informational/Expository/Procedural Writing

Students must understand that not all reading is story reading and not all writing is story writing. Although many of the same strategies are used for reading fiction and nonfiction, there are some differences. (See Chapter 2: Reading Comprehension: Strategies That Work.) The same holds true for writing fiction and nonfiction.

The importance of linking reading with writing and vice versa cannot be overstated. "Children who write become better readers.... Children who read something knowing that they will write something are more likely to read with a clearer sense of purpose. Children who use information from their reading to write produce better writing because they have more to say" (Cunningham and Allington 1994, 94).

Students must have a reason to write, a purpose. It is easy for them to see a purpose when they write a persuasive letter to the principal, share a cookie recipe with a friend, or send a note to a pen pal describing their school. These are all forms of nonfiction writing.

Nonfiction Writing: Purposes and Forms

Here are some suggested ways to incorporate nonfiction writing into the Grades 3 to 6 classroom.

Purposes	Common Forms in Grades 3 to 6	
To describe	Personal description (Wanted posters, Missing posters, etc.) Poetry Scientific reports about animals, plants, and machines	Reports about countries Definitions Letters Illustrations Captions Labels
To explain	Scientific explanations of a phenomenon Personal narrative explanations Elaborations	Reports Letters Illustrations Captions Labels

Purposes	Common Forms in Grades 3 to 6	
To instruct	Recipes Rules (games, classroom) Directions Experiments Lists	Maps Letters Illustrations Captions Labels
To persuade	Debates Reviews Advertisements Petitions Book reports	Letters Posters Poetry Cartoons Illustrations
To retell information about a person or past event (nonfiction narrative)	Reports Autobiographies/ biographies Letters	Poetry Journals Scripts Historical retellings
To explore and maintain relationships with others	Cards Letters Questionnaires	Interviews Poetry

(Adapted from Stead 2002, 9)

Include surveys with questionnaires. Students enjoy and learn so much from surveying people about topics of personal interest or significance. They might conduct surveys about issues appearing in local or national newspapers. Students in one Grade 5 class decided to survey their parents, teachers, peers, community members, and politicians about whether smoking should be banned in all public areas. This survey occurred as part of a social studies current events unit. Such a ruling was being taken to a vote by the provincial legislature. Surveys often lead to the creation of petitions created as persuasive pieces strong in voice!

Procedural Writing

Procedural writing is used to explain or instruct, typically using a series of steps. Students are experts on many things and procedural writing affords them the opportunity to share their expertise with others. The two most important characteristics of procedural writing are

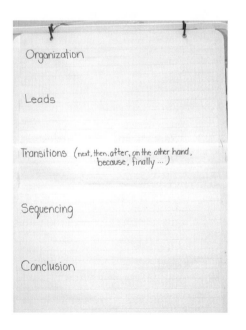

- the clarity of the ideas
  - the title must be clear and must state the goal (e.g., "Text Messaging in Three Easy Steps")
  - all the materials and quantities must be stated clearly
  - the instructions must be explicit (i.e., what to do when, where, and how)
- the careful sequencing of the text
  - linking or transitional words explicitly convey the process in a logical manner (e.g., "first," "then," "next," "after," "finally"). The steps are usually numbered.

– the reader or listener must be able to follow the instructions without assistance

Most procedural writing texts follow this structure:

Goal: This is usually stated in the title (e.g., "How to Make Pancakes")

Materials: This is often a listing of the equipment, utensils, ingredients, amounts, times, temperatures, or players—whatever is required in order to successfully achieve the goal.

Steps/Method: The explanation of what to do is usually provided in a series of short and clear numbered steps, beginning with short, clear words, such as "first," "then," "next," "after," and "finally." Some steps may include diagrams or pictures.

Evaluation: The goal is successfully achieved (e.g., the procedure results in the correct serving size of light and fluffy pancakes in the prescribed time frame). This stage is also an opportunity to identify why the goal may not have been achieved and to troubleshoot any problems in the directions (e.g., the pancakes were burned because the temperature wasn't specified).

One of the easiest ways to explain a procedure is to include diagrams and pictures.

Mini-Lesson: Creating a How-to Book

1. The teacher brainstorms with the class as many activities as the students know (or think they know) how to do. The list might include

   - playing a game
   - doing a science experiment
   - batting a ball
   - making a sandwich
   - feeding a baby
   - keeping busy on a long trip
   - doing a cartwheel
   - procedures for a substitute teacher

2. The teacher models the process by creating one page for a How-to book of games outlining the procedure for playing hopscotch. (For example, "To play hopscotch, first make squares, then throw in a marker into a square, and jump into the square. The game is finished after all of the squares have been used.")

3. Pretending they have never played hopscotch before, students evaluate the procedure by following the directions given. They then explain their findings.

4. Working with a partner, students rewrite the procedure. They determine what needs to change and whether the revised version works any better. This activity reinforces for students how difficult it is to write clear directions even for something as simple as a playground game or making a sandwich.

5. The teacher directs students to add a diagram to their procedure to see if it improves clarity.

6. Each pair group exchanges their revision with another pair group for feedback (e.g., "You might want to try ... to make it better.").

Check It Out!

Flying Solo by Ralph Fletcher (New York: Random House, 1998) is a superb read-aloud about what happens when a substitute teacher fails to show up to class. Gordon Korman's *The 6th Grade Nickname Game* (Toronto: Scholastic Canada, 1998) describes life with a substitute.

Check It Out!

KidsCom.com at http://www.kidscom.com features instructions for games that can be played online. It is a useful tool for helping students learn how to read and write instructional text.

7. Students try the directions that follow and compare the results to their revision. How is their procedure different from the one described below?

How to Play Hopscotch

Materials needed:

- Chalk (enough to draw eight squares on pavement). Each square has to be big enough to land in on one foot.

- A marker for each player (such as a bean bag, a flat stone, or a button).

Method/Steps (what to do):

1. First, using chalk, create the hopscotch court on pavement by creating the eight squares and numbering them as in the diagram below:

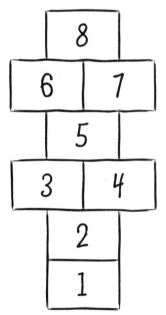

2. Then, the first player tosses his or her marker into the first square. The marker must land exactly within the square. If it lands on a line or bounces out, the turn is lost. It is then the next player's turn.

3. If the toss is successful, the player hops over the first square into the next square, and so on until he or she reaches the last square. With the side-by-side squares, the player puts one foot in each square. For single squares, either foot can be used for hopping. The player then turns around and hops back through the court in reverse order, stopping to pick up the marker. Once the marker is picked up, the player hops into that square.

4. The player continues playing by throwing the marker into the second square, continuing as described above.

5. If any player lands in a single square with two feet, steps on a line, misses a square, or loses balance and falls, the turn is lost. The player whose turn was lost must start the last sequence again on his or her next turn.

6. Finally, the winner is the player who finishes the course (all eight squares) first.

Evaluation (how it worked):

8. The class discusses what needs to be remembered about writing effective procedures. Students then contribute a page to a How-to book of games that younger students can play at recess. Their procedure might also include labelled diagrams.

9. Students self- or peer-assess by playing the games as if they had never played them before. Do the directions need to be modified so that they will be clear enough for younger students to follow?

Title: <u>How to</u> _____
Materials: _____
_____
Method/Steps:
1. First _____
2. Then _____
3. Next _____
4. After _____
5. Then _____
6. Finally _____

Evaluation (Partner Feedback):
This procedure makes sense:
    Yes / No (circle one)
You may want to _____
_____
_____
_____

Mini-Lesson: Linking Literacy and Math Through Procedural Writing

1. The teacher models for students how to build a structure using various geometric shapes (cones, cylinders, pyramids, rectangular prisms, cubes). The procedure is described through a think-aloud. For example, "I will start by placing a rectangular prism at the bottom. Then, I will place a cube in the middle of the rectangular prism. Next, a cylinder will go on top of the cube. Finally, I will place a cone on the top of the cylinder."

2. The teacher then writes the procedure on chart paper (i.e., Title, Materials Needed, Method/Steps, and Evaluation).

3. After dismantling the structure, the teacher, with the students' help, follows the written directions to rebuild the structure. Were the instructions clear enough and in the right order?

4. Working individually, students build a structure using three or four geometric shapes.

5. Once they have built their structure, they write down the procedure for someone else to follow.

6. After dismantling their structures, students find a partner who has not seen their final structure. The partner follows the student's written procedure to rebuild the structure.

7. The partner completes an evaluation of the student's procedure, making suggestions for improvement if the resulting structure does not match the original.

Persuasive Writing

Persuasive texts are written for many purposes:

- to put forward a point of view or justify a position
- to encourage people to purchase something, take part in a specific type of activity (such as exercise), or think in a certain way

(Stead 2002)

This writing form is particularly appealing to students, many of whom love to argue their point of view with both parents and teachers in an attempt to get (or get out of) something!

Persuasive writing gives students the opportunity to persuade others in many different ways, such as through signs, letters, book reports/reviews, advertising pamphlets, and petitions.

Teaching Persuasive Writing

It is enjoyable to introduce persuasive writing with one of two poems by Shel Silverstein. "Sick" from *Where the Sidewalk Ends* (New York: HarperCollins, 1974) is a poem about Peggy Ann McKay, who does not want to go to school and uses verse to try to convince her caregivers that she should stay home. "Little Abigail and the Beautiful Pony" in *A Light in the Attic* (New York: HarperCollins, 1996) is a poem about a girl who tries to convince her parents to buy her a pony. It ends with "This is a good story to read to your folks when they won't buy you something you want" (121).

To lay the foundation for the mini-lessons that follow, it is important to establish what a persuasive text is, and the characteristics that make it effective.

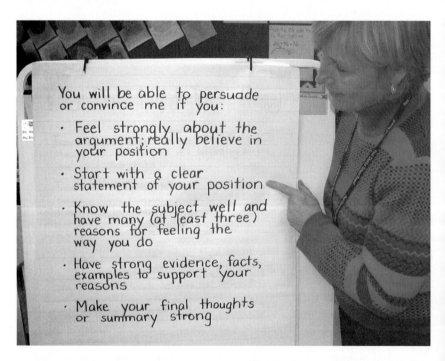

When modelling the writing of persuasive text, effective teachers emphasize

- using both facts and opinions. Students need to understand the differences between a fact and an opinion.
- doing research to find the facts needed to make a good argument. There should be at least three facts to support each argument.
- using connectives to defend the point of view (e.g., "because," "so," "therefore")
- using diagrams, drawings, and tables to make the points stronger
- keeping the audience in mind

The procedure for writing a persuasive piece, such as a report, article, or letter, is crucial to achieving the purpose for writing.

How to Write a Persuasive Piece

1. Pick a topic of personal interest.
2. Research the topic to find specific facts or details to support your argument.
3. Start with a strong beginning, stating your opinion.
4. Include at least three facts/details to support your opinion.
5. Make sure that the facts are written in an order that makes sense.
6. Use diagrams, drawings, and labels if they make the argument stronger.
7. End with a strong conclusion (usually a personal statement or summary explaining why you have this opinion).
8. Read the piece aloud. Does it sound convincing?

Possible Topics for Persuasive Writing

The best topics are those that students themselves feel strongly about. Persuasive writing fits naturally across the curriculum, particularly in social studies and health.

Some teachers have found the following topics effective:

- All smoking must be banned.
- Students in our school should wear uniforms.
- I learn more from reading than from watching TV.
- _____ are the most fantastic insects in the world.
- _____ is a Red Light story. You must read it! (See Book Reports, later in this chapter, for more information.)
- I really don't like _____ because....
- The most interesting sport is _____ because....
- Dogs make better pets than cats because....
- There should be no homework because....
- _____ pollutes and should be banned.
- _____ is the best city to live in. Create a pamphlet to prove it!
- Things I need are not always the same as things I want. An example is....

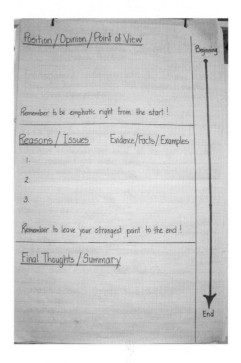

Check It Out!

For a variety of great lesson plans to support persuasive writing, visit

Can You Convince Me? Developing Persuasive Writing
http://www.readwritethink.org/lessons/lesson_view.asp?id=56

Persuasion Map
http://www.readwritethink.org/materials/persuasion_map/

All writing takes time. In writing a strong persuasive piece, students need time to come up with a topic they care about and to discuss and research it.

BLM 3: Planning My Argument

Sharing Persuasive Writing

Through sharing their pieces aloud, with a partner or a group, students hear their own voices coming through. Persuasive pieces especially must be shared with great passion and caring. Students can give feedback on the effectiveness of the piece and suggest ways to strengthen the argument. But they must first be given a focus for listening by the author (e.g., "Is my argument organized in a logical way?" "Does my voice come through in this piece?" "Have I provided enough facts to support my point of view?").

Some of the more enjoyable ways for students in Grades 3 to 6 to share their points of view include

- book reports, reviews, and commercials
- character and author business cards
- character résumés
- story map comic strips

Assessment BLM 11: Did I Persuade You?

Book Reports

Students often write and share book reports to try to entice or persuade a fellow student to read a particular book. Not all books turn out to be personal winners, however. Some books might be considered yellow-light books. Yellow means "Slow down and consider reading this book; it was okay." A green-light book means "I wouldn't recommend it, so proceed." A red-light book means "Stop and have a read!"

What is a green-light book to one student may be a red-light book to another. There is no right or wrong. What is important is being able to share and give reasons for opinions. After presenting their book reports orally, students write their name and the title of the book on a sticky note, which they have coloured red, green, or yellow. The sticky notes are placed on a classroom chart for student reference.

BLM 4: Red Light—STOP!

BLM 5: Book Review

BLM 6: Book Review in Chapter 2

BLM 7: Planning My One-Minute Book Talk in Chapter 2

Book Reviews

A book review is a wonderful writing activity that requires summarizing, but also includes personal reflections. Reviews may identify both strengths and weaknesses, touching on such aspects as character, setting, voice, subject matter, illustrations, details, and so on.

The greatest challenge in writing a summary is deciding what to include and what to leave out. It is often helpful for students to read

Check It Out!

These Web sites feature reviews written by students:

http://www.digisys.net/glaciergateway/bookindex.html

http://library.thinkquest.org/4155/brindex.html

http://www.threadsofreading.com/id35.htm

several reviews, written by adults or peers, of books they are familiar with. The book reviews are kept in a binder in the classroom or the library for others to enjoy.

BLM 5: Book Review
BLM 6: Book Review in Chapter 2

Book Commercials

Book commercials are another enticing way for students to share books they love. Because they are inundated with commercials on television, radio, and the Internet, students are very familiar with the form and often welcome the opportunity to create and present their own.

Students begin by watching or listening to several commercials, noting the techniques advertisers use. Students might also examine promotional summaries written by publishers. This activity supports media literacy: the ability to access, evaluate, analyze, and produce electronic and print media. (For more information on media literacy, see Chapter 4: Literacy Learning Across the Curriculum.) From the shared reading and listening experiences with commercials, a shared writing chart highlighting key techniques is developed.

Check It Out!

For teaching ideas to support media literacy, check out http://pbskids.org/dontbuyit/teachersguide.html

Key Techniques for Creating a Commercial

When creating a commercial

- provide a lead that gets the consumer's attention. Often this appears as a question, such as "Are you tired of boring books?"

- maintain the consumer's interest by promising a benefit, such as "Author Louis Sachar will have you spellbound!"

- include additional reasons to buy the book, such as "The illustrations are hauntingly beautiful."

- instruct the consumer on how to access the book and the cost (include shipping and handling and tax)

- keep the sentences short and to the point. A 30-second commercial contains approximately 75 words, a 60-second ad, 150 words.

- create an ending with impact. Some commercials leave the consumer hanging with an ending such as "To find out what really happened...."

Students might prefer to create a commercial for a well-loved author, rather than a book. See Author Web Sites for Grades 3 to 6 earlier in this chapter.

Students also enjoy presenting commercials. Videotaping the presentation allows for both self-assessment and peer assessment. The assessments are based on the criteria listed above.

BLM 2: Analyzing TV and Magazine Advertisements in Chapter 4

Character and Author Business Cards

For an alternative to the traditional book report or review, students might enjoy creating a business card for a character or an author. The

Check It Out!

Character and Author Business Cards
http://www.readwritethink.org/
lessons/lesson_view.asp?id=143

Check It Out!

Writing Resumes for Characters in
Historical Fiction
http://readwritethink.org/lessons/
lesson_view_printer_friendly.asp?
id=295

Check It Out!

Examining Story Elements Using
Story Map Comic Strips
http://www.readwritethink.org/
lessons/lesson_view_printer_
friendly.asp?id=236

size of the card forces students to be concise and give only essential information. Illustrations, colour, font, and so on, can also be used to convey information. Students might then trade their cards.

Character Résumés

Writing a résumé for one of the characters in a text encourages "writing small"—limiting the topic. In addition, writing résumés has real-world applications: many students are, or will soon be, looking for part-time jobs, such as babysitting, snow shovelling, or newspaper delivery.

Story Map Comic Strips

Students of all ages often enjoy reading comic strips. By creating comic strips using the elements of story grammar as a guide, students demonstrate their personal interpretations and perceptions of what they have read. They also learn how to capture the essence of a story in small pictures and few words.

BLM 8: Story Grammar in Chapter 2

Descriptive Writing

Descriptive writing is filled with details, enabling the reader to envision the person, place, or thing being described. The writing also appeals to the senses. The reader can hear, feel, smell, and/or taste it. Students need to understand the importance of strong descriptive words when writing and revising fiction, nonfiction, and poetry.

For more information, refer to the mini-lessons earlier in this chapter Filling in the Missing Details, Pruning the Dead Wood, and Improving Word Choice.

Mini-Lesson: Descriptive Words

1. The teacher chooses several items or categories and brainstorms with the class possible descriptive words and phrases for each one.

To describe ...	Students might suggest ...
size	as big as ...; larger; smaller; enormous; tiny
shape	square like a ...; oval; pointed
colour	bright yellow like the sun; crimson
number	seven; more than ...; fewer
Texture (how it feels)	rough as ...; silky; softer than ...
smell	smoky; like rotten garbage
taste	sweet as ...; salty
what it's made of	plastic; wood; synthetic
gender	woman; man; widower; stepsister
action	running; gliding like a ...; tiptoeing
sounds	loud; shrieking ...; whisper quiet
setting	a dark closet; a musty basement; an eerie cliff
age	older than ...; younger than ...; infant-like
direction	forward; left; above; beside; below; across
temperature	scorching; bone-chilling; as hot as ...

2. The teacher explains that writers can provide a specific word to describe something (*nine* children), or use a number of words to convey the same message in a different way (enough children for a baseball team). Students consider the statements "it tastes sweet" and "it tastes as sweet as a caramel," and then share which description they prefer and why.

Mini-Lessons: Describing the Setting

The setting is very important to both expository and narrative text. Often, the setting is simply mentioned without really developing a sense of place. Description develops this sense of place.

Lesson 1

1. The teacher reads aloud a passage that creates a strong setting or sense of place. *The Story of a Seagull and the Cat Who Taught Her to Fly* by Luis Sepulveda (New York: Scholastic Press, 2003) provides many such examples. The setting description that follows grabs the reader, compelling him or her to read on.

> "A heavy rain was falling over Hamburg, and the smell of wet earth was rising from the gardens. The asphalt streets were gleaming, and the neon signs were reflected, distorted, on wet sidewalks." (117)

2. The class examines each descriptive word or phrase in the passage read: *smell of wet earth, gleaming, reflected....*

3. The students then focus on using descriptive writing across the curriculum be it social studies, science, or any content area.

Lesson 2

1. The teacher then reads aloud another text selection that uses strong details to describe a place, such as *All the Places to Love* by Patricia MacLachlan (New York: HarperCollins Books, 1994).

2. Students describe, write, or draw the sights, smells, sounds, tastes, and textures the read-aloud evoked in them. A discussion of how the book appeals to the five senses might follow.

Lesson 3

1. To reinforce the importance of being specific in descriptive writing, the teacher writes and then reads a detailed description of a place known to most students. After reading, the teacher asks, "Where am I?" Students use the descriptive details to visualize and predict the location, and then share which details led to their predictions.

2. Students write their own description of a place and read it to a partner. The partner sketches what she or he visualizes from the read-aloud. Based on the sketch, each pair discusses whether the details in the description established a sense of place.

Check It Out!

The Web site http://www.encyclopedia.com contains information on many subjects, as well as links to dictionaries, almanacs, and thesauruses.

Check It Out!

The Story of the Seagull and the Cat Who Taught Her to Fly by Luis Sepulveda (New York: Scholastic Press, 2003) is a strong read-aloud, which supports many levels and themes. One key theme is the importance of being yourself even when this results in being different from friends and acquaintances.

Check It Out!

Home: American Writers Remember Rooms of Their Own edited by Sharon Sloan Fiffer and Steve Fiffer (New York: Random House, Inc., 1995) features clear descriptions of 17 rooms, each description written by a different well-known author. Reading a chapter from this book is a great way to introduce descriptive writing.

Poetry

Many students have an affinity for songs, verses, and rhymes, making poetry a natural fit (Tompkins 2000). "Poetry writing is the surest, easiest way I know to turn kids on to writing. Kids love it. Teachers love it. It's fun and easy for everyone (including the teacher).... Students love playing around with words and patterns in their head and on the page; they love the freedom to write as much or as little as they want; they love that a poem can be about anything at all" (Routman, *Kids' Poems* 2000, 5).

Why Poetry Writing Is a Hit

- may rhyme or not—free style
- may use simple phrases and words—not always sentences
- usually involves less writing
- may be about anything!
- often expresses personal feelings
- allows more freedom with punctuation, capitalization, and layout (the way the text is presented on the page)

"Read a lot and write a lot.... Like any skill, writing takes practice. Try different forms when you write: poetry, short stories, and plays. Have fun and experiment."

CREECH, "TEACH CREECH"

Check It Out!

Students (and teachers) may enjoy visiting these author Web sites:

Sharon Creech:
http://www.sharoncreech.com

Shel Silverstein:
http://www.shelsilverstein.com

For colour poetry, see
http://www.kyrene.k12.az.us/schools/brisas/sunda/sunkids4.htm

http://orchard.sbschools.net/users/pvandegraaf/colorpoems.htm

Color Poems: Using the Five Senses to Guide Prewriting
http://readwritethink.org/lessons/lesson_view_printer_friendly.asp?id=375

Inspiring Poetry Writing Through Read-Alouds

Some students in Grades 3 to 6 are reluctant to write poetry. It is important to recognize this reality and bring it to the fore. This can be accomplished through a great read-aloud: *Love That Dog* by Sharon Creech (New York: Harper Trophy, 2003). This fascinating novel is written in the style of a poem; most lines consist of just two to five words. Jack, who hates poetry and thinks only girls write it, shares his feelings in a series of journal entries. When his teacher introduces the class to the poetry of Robert Frost, Jack writes this journal entry (21):

> I think Mr. Robert Frost
> has a little
> too
> much
> time
> on his
> hands.

Jack expresses a range of emotions, from frustration, sadness, and anger, to humour and satisfaction as he eventually begins to feel good about writing poetry. Inspired by a Walter Dean Myers poem titled "Love That Boy," Jack writes a poem titled "Love That Dog" about his beloved pet Sky. It is easy for students to note Jack's voice in his poem. They learn that voice comes from writing about what you know and care about.

Poetry is often inspired by emotions and certain colours tend to evoke certain emotions in both writers and readers. *My Many Colored Days* by Dr. Seuss (New York: Alfred A. Knoff, 1996) is a superb picture book that leads to great discussions about the kinds of emotions associated with different colours.

Twilight Comes Twice by Ralph Fletcher (New York: Clarion Books, 1997) is a beautiful narrative poem. It describes two times of day: dusk and dawn. Fletcher's strong voice, word choice, and details, as well as the superb pictures, create vivid images in the mind of the reader. Drawing or painting a scene from this narrative poem might also inspire poetry.

The following prompts might inspire students to write and eventually get them hooked on poetry:

- choosing a headline from a newspaper or magazine as the title of the poem
- using a photo to inspire a poem
- getting ideas from listening to their peers' poems
- using poetry frames or formula poems

Using Poetry Frames or Formula Poems

It is important for the teacher to model each type of poetry frame or formula poem. Formula poems are an alternative (short form) to free verse that provides a helpful structure:

- **If I were ...** poems, in the same style as "If I Were in Charge of the World ..." by Judith Viorst.
- **Found poems,** made up of words (and phrases) that students have found elsewhere on a topic of their choice. Often, it is a good idea to put the words (e.g., from magazines and newspapers or shared readings) on cards. The cards can then be manipulated and ordered in different ways to create poems.
- **Acrostic poems,** using letters in a word or topic to begin each line of the poem. All of the words or phrases connect to the topic. The lines in acrostic poems begin with a capital letter (so, when read downward, the capital letters form the topic word), are short, and do not have to rhyme.
- **Limericks,** humorous, five-line poems. Usually the first, second, and last lines have the same rhyme. The third and fourth lines rhyme with each other.

How Does Poetry Fit with the Traits?

Poetry is often imaginative. It is condensed writing. It may or may not have a certain rhythm or rhyme. But it still involves a focus on the traits: ideas, voice, organization, word choice, fluency, and conventions. Words are chosen specifically for sound as well as meaning. Fluency is derived from the careful linking of words and phrases. Conventions, such as punctuation and capitalization, may be used (or not used) to convey a certain style or mood.

Blue is like
The Northern lites scattered across the sky.

Blue is like
Pencil crayons sketched upon paper.

Blue is like
Ice cream scooped on top of cones.

Blue is like
River fish flowing down a stream.

Blue is like
Cold lips freezing in a winter storm.

Blue is like
Easter eggs hid inside the house

And blue is like
Blue cheese inside of a refrigerator.

By Michael Schwebius + Patrick Quan

Runs at seagulls

On the ground he dies

Never is mean to Karana

Trots on the beach

Until the end they are friends

Why Rontu why Rontu did you have to die? Under the ground you will always lie. You would always chase the seagulls wherever they fly. But now you will watch over me high in the sky.

Check It Out!

Many superb Web sites publish student acrostic poems dealing with topics across the curriculum.

http://home.earthlink.net/~jesmith/Acrostic1.html

http://www.holycross.edu/departments/socant/dhummon/acrostics/acrostics.html

http://www.townwestss.qld.edu.au/StudentPages/Year5-6_files/rainforests/rainpoem.htm

---

Writing: The Reading–Writing Connection

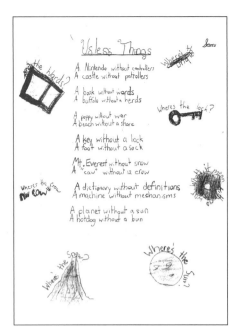

Check It Out!

The March issue of *The Reading Teacher* (http://www.reading.org) features poetry contests and classroom ideas.

See also
http://www.poets.org

http://www.kalwriters.com/kidswwwrite/index.html (English only)

http://poemes.csq.qc.net/index.htm (French only)

http://www.youngpoets.ca (bilingual)

Teaching Poetry

As with any other genre, teaching poetry requires

- read-alouds
- modelling/shared writing
- mini-lessons
- students writing and sharing
- lots of poetry in the classroom

Many students love rhyme, but they must understand that poems do not have to rhyme. Some students spend so much time trying to get lines to rhyme that the poem sounds contrived and makes little sense. Students need to hear teachers model writing free verse and to try it as a shared writing.

Supporting Poetry Writing in the Classroom

- Ensure that there are lots of books of poetry in the classroom.
- Initiate a "Poet of the Day," someone who shares one or two poems with the class.
- Create a classroom poetry anthology in a Big Book format.
- Record students' poems for others to enjoy.
- Encourage students to use poetry when writing in any subject area for any reason.
- Celebrate National Poetry Month in April.
- Encourage students to publish their poems online.

Poetry Across the Day

It is best when students begin to view poetry as a genre to choose any time they write. They can use poetry to respond, persuade, and describe, and to explore and share their feelings in various ways across the day. They might, for example, write a poem

- in response to literature (the student poem that follows was likely written in response to Shel Silverstein's *The Giving Tree*)
- in response to a unit of study or an issue in a content area
- to describe something, often a feeling or happening

Been through alot

I'm sorry tree,
We had to get some paper!
We had to keep the fire going
for we would have no heat!
I'm sorry tree
for climbing on your branches,
for building a tree fort.
I'm sorry tree
for leaving you in the rain,
i should have covered you up.
Will you ever forgive me?

By Chase

Poem fright

Too many words
hands are shaking
Playing with my sweater
knees are trembling
Stuttering
Watching their eyes as I speak
Listening to me
But now I'm done;
happy inside
Proud as I walk back to my seat
The relief from:
Poem fright

DECISIONS

Too much worrying
Will I make it?
Should I speak louder?
Should I do more actions?
Almost finished
Did I do well?
Decisions

English as a Second Language (ESL) and Writing

Research into the development of writing among English as a Second Language (ESL) students is showing that the writing process generally takes longer for those who lack literacy skills in their native language. Jim Cummins found (1999, 26–32) that students with a strong first-language foundation are more likely to develop high levels in their second language.

Using their first-language skills can help ESL students learn faster. Many have much to say and become frustrated with their limited ability to get it down on paper in English. They should be encouraged to get the ideas down in their own language first. Adults or peers who speak the second language (when available) are helpful supports.

Since vocabulary development is key to both reading and writing, ESL students need many oral language opportunities daily. They need to hear good language models. They need vocabulary to be intentionally taught. And they need to work on the same challenging writing assignments their peers are tackling.

As established earlier in this chapter, revision is one of the main ways to improve writing. It is important to help ESL students not to fixate on editing tasks but instead to focus on content (ideas), organization, and word choice. These students benefit greatly from revising their work with the support of a trained adult (paraprofessional or volunteer) or peer. Paraphrasing what they want to say before they write helps ESL students with word choice, syntax (sentence structure), and organization.

In general, the principles of effective teaching and learning for ESL students are the same as those for all learners:

- make learning relevant
- provide multiple demonstrations
- provide much guided practice
- promote and guide (scaffold) conversations
- provide lots of time to apply what's been taught
- keep the emphasis on communicating

(Routman 2005)

Simply put, good teaching is good teaching!

"Longitudinal studies have found that immigrant children, from advantaged families, who arrived in the United States at ages 8 or 9 with first-language literacy skills already developed, performed better in U.S. schools than younger children, ages 5 and 6, who came without first-language literacy skills."

Lenters 2005, 330

Remind those volunteers, peers, or paraprofessionals working with ESL students to focus on supporting revision not editing.

Supporting Struggling and Often Reluctant Writers

Before teachers can plan how best to support struggling and/or reluctant writers, they must first try to determine the cause of the problem. Profiles of these student writers often include delays in

- fine motor skills
- spelling
- self-confidence

- oral language
- organization
- understanding the writing process
- getting the writing started
- seeing a real reason or purpose for writing (motivation)

Struggling and/or reluctant writers need the same opportunities as any writer. In fact, they have a greater need to be guided through all the skills and stages of the writing process. They need plenty of uninterrupted writing time, and as many one-on-one or small-group writing opportunities and conferences as possible. They benefit from much modelled and shared writing, mini-lessons with teachers thinking aloud, and much guided practice afterward.

Like any student, struggling and/or reluctant writers need the opportunity to listen to and analyze and discuss the characteristics or traits of good writing in literature and in their own and peer writing. They also need to read a great deal of fiction, nonfiction, and poetry, at their own reading level.

For struggling writers, the time spent on prewriting or incubating ideas is especially important. Without a plan, much student writing remains weak even with revisions. They need to be reminded to keep in mind their purpose and audience. These students, especially, need to find authentic reasons to write (see Authentic Reasons to Write earlier in this chapter for numerous suggestions). They should be encouraged to write about what they know and are interested in, to write in the genre of their choice, and to write across the curriculum. The classroom environment must be made safe and welcoming for them; students and teachers must appreciate that everyone has worthwhile things to write and share.

Struggling and reluctant writers may be disinclined to revise, or may have trouble understanding the distinction between revision and editing. Again, they benefit from mini-lessons on both revision and editing, and from the opportunity to frequently support others in the revision process as well as revising their own writing. They must understand that this is their responsibility. If they are adept at keyboarding, students may find revising and editing on a computer easier.

Teachers need to have clear and high expectations for all students, and to share them with students and their parents. Struggling students should be encouraged to set their own goals in consultation with the teacher, and should be supported in reaching these goals by the teacher, parents, peers and, if available, trained volunteers or paraprofessionals. Effective teachers acknowledge that writing is hard work and requires lots of practice.

The support for struggling and/or reluctant writers described above is simply good teaching and learning. But there is nothing simple about it. Good teaching is good for all. Struggling students need the very best instruction and learning conditions to catch them up and to motivate them to believe in themselves as writers.

Showing students how one writes is much more effective than simply assigning writing.

"No one learns to swim by clinging to the side of a pool. Encourage your students to let go. They can float."

Spandel 2005, 373

"Just as there are times when kids need a mirror, someone to reflect back their writing to them, there are times when they need an adult who will tell them what to do next and how to do it. Bottom line, what they need is a Teacher."

Atwell 1998, 21

Reflecting on the Writing Program

Crafting writing is an art. So is effective writing instruction. Teachers need to be able to explain to themselves and to others not only how they support students' writing, but also why they do what they do. We do know that the most effective language arts programs see students spending most of their day engaged in interesting and meaningful reading and writing tasks. Students also need the scaffolding and the guided practice provided through mini- or craft lessons. Students need to see effective writing in action modelled by teachers and others. They also need many opportunities to discuss the traits or characteristics of good writing found in good literature, fiction, non-fiction, and poetry, as they read themselves or listen to literature being read aloud.

Teachers need to be confident in their abilities and parents need to be helped to understand how to support the effective teaching and learning happening at school. It is most helpful when teachers collaborate on school-wide writing programs so that teachers, parents, administrators, and students are all speaking the same language. Together they are then able to celebrate students' successes.

Developing Home–School–Community Partnerships

Students do better when teachers, parents, volunteers, and paraprofessionals work together to support writing. We all need to understand the process, the traits of writing, the different modes of writing, the writing goals, and how to effectively support student writers. Beyond the school walls, there is often a perceived slackness in the way teachers teach writing because they do not appear to focus on conventions such as spelling, capitalization, and punctuation. This perception needs to be dispelled. Through newsletters, parent conferences, evening workshops, and classroom visits, the school community can learn that

- there are clear writing goals for the students
- teachers do intentionally teach the craft of writing
- there are six traits or characteristics of writing, of which conventions is only one
- ideas are at the heart of writing
- editing and revision are both important but they are not the same
- students become better writers the more they read, reread, discuss, and write
- student writing is a focus in all subject areas, not just in language arts
- trained volunteers and paraprofessionals also play an important role in supporting student writing

Helping Parents to Support Their Child's Writing

Teachers need to communicate to parents the many ways in which they can help to improve their child's writing, such as by

- reading aloud to their child, no matter the age, and discussing the texts
- sharing fiction, nonfiction, and poetry
- encouraging daily reading
- listening to their child read aloud
- learning the terminology of the six traits of writing and using it when discussing their child's writing
- reading and responding to their child's first draft. This must be done with care and with a focus on listening and responding to the child's content as it is read aloud. The role of the parent (and teacher) is not that of editor. Students are taught spelling and editing strategies at school and they must take ownership of this stage of the writing process.
- encouraging their child to keep a writer's notebook and to discuss writing topics with others
- providing their child with real reasons to write: letters, notes, lists, invitations, thank-you notes, letters to the editor
- writing notes to their child, which may spark a written response
- allowing judicious use of the Internet. There are many safe sites where students can read student writing and submit their own writing.
- talking with their child about books, the news, their day, movies, television, and any other topics to help develop vocabulary and oral language skills
- framing reading and writing as enjoyable experiences, not punishments

BLM 6: Literacy Home Links: Surfing the Net
BLM 7: Literacy Home Links: Million-Dollar Words
BLM 8: Literacy Home Links: Assessing Writing
BLM 4: Literacy Home Links: How Families Can Support the "Talking" to "Reading and Writing" Connection in Chapter 1
BLM 10: Literacy Home Links: News from Room ___ in Chapter 5
BLM 11: Literacy Home Links: Supporting Your Reader at Home in Chapter 6

Closing Thoughts

"There is a synergy between reading and writing. Reading inspires and excites children about the possibilities awaiting them as writers, and acquaints them with the structure of text and books and the conventions of written language. Writing allows them to use what they've gleaned from reading as they craft their own stories, poems, and factual texts. And because of their writing efforts, children approach written text with a heightened awareness and understanding of print, text, and genre" (Taberski 2000, 176).

Students learn to write from understanding the traits, qualities, or characteristics used by authors in good literature that teachers share. Teacher read-alouds and write-alouds demystify writing. As teachers model, demonstrate, and explain, students are able to assess the qualities of good writing. They cannot revise until they understand the traits of good writing.

Students become good readers and writers by reading and writing a lot. They need to have the time to make this happen. They learn that there must be both a purpose for writing and an audience in mind. Nonfiction writing often provides that real purpose. Real reasons to write increase motivation. Students see themselves as writers with something worthwhile to say. As students read, reflect, and respond—orally and in written form—they improve both their vocabulary development and their comprehension.

Mini- or craft lessons are important tools in scaffolding writing: "Great teachers know only too well that writing is hard work—exhausting for students and massively time-consuming for teachers. But they also understand that if students are to make knowledge their own, they must wrestle with facts, struggle with details, and rework raw information into language that reaches their audience. Students need effective, bite-size opportunities to help them master writing skills" (Schmidt 2004, 45).

"Let's teach our students to identify the issues and questions that are worth writing about, whether for personal or socially significant reasons. Let's teach them to find information and to share their findings, not by piling up detached facts like logjams but by sifting, examining, synthesizing, and condensing. Let's help them see that all good writing has purpose: to teach, to provoke, to trouble, to question, to delight, to persuade or to entertain. The writer who knows a topic and audience well can choreograph their interaction like a well-timed dance. We can put this power into students' hands" (Spandel 2001, 387).

So little time, so much to do! The next chapter will demonstrate this "dance" as students learn literacy across the curriculum.

Chapter 3

BLACKLINE MASTERS

Circle Organizer (Map)

Name: _____ Grade: _____ Date: _____

```
┌─────────────────────────┐          ┌─────────────────────────┐
│                      6  │          │                      1  │
│  _____    │          │  _____    │
│                         │   ──→    │                         │
│  _____    │          │  _____    │
│  _____    │          │  _____    │
│  _____    │          │  _____    │
└─────────────────────────┘          └─────────────────────────┘
```

Title _____

_____

_____

_____

```
┌─────────────────────────┐          ┌─────────────────────────┐
│                      5  │          │                      2  │
│  _____    │          │  _____    │
│                         │          │                         │
│  _____    │          │  _____    │
│  _____    │          │  _____    │
│  _____    │          │  _____    │
└─────────────────────────┘          └─────────────────────────┘
```

```
┌─────────────────────────┐          ┌─────────────────────────┐
│                      4  │          │                      3  │
│  _____    │          │  _____    │
│                         │   ←──    │                         │
│  _____    │          │  _____    │
│  _____    │          │  _____    │
│  _____    │          │  _____    │
└─────────────────────────┘          └─────────────────────────┘
```

My News

Name: _____ Grade: _____ Date: _____

Planning the News

Who: _____

What: _____

When: _____

Where: _____

Why: _____

How: _____

My News

Headline: _____

Byline: _____

My Lead _____

The Facts

Fact	Fact	Fact

End (Closing) _____

_____

_____

_____

Planning My Argument

Name: _____ Grade: _____ Date: _____

Title: _____

My Strong Beginning:

_____

_____

_____

_____

Here Are the Facts:

_____

_____

_____

_____

Diagrams/Drawings

My Strong Ending:

_____

_____

_____

_____

Red Light—STOP!

Name: _____ Grade: _____ Date: _____

The title of the book I read is _____.

_____ is the author.

The illustrator's name is _____.

This book is: **(check one)**

❏ fiction

❏ nonfiction

❏ poetry

The book is about _____

_____

I think that you should stop and read this book because _____

_____

It has great: **(check one)**

❏ Ideas

❏ Organization

❏ Voice

❏ Word Choice

❏ Sentence Fluency

Here is a super example from the book: _____

_____

_____

_____.

This example can be found on page _____ .

Book Review

Name: _____ Grade: _____ Date: _____

The title of the book I read is _____.

_____ is the author.

The illustrator's name is _____.

This book is: **(check one)**

❑ fiction

❑ nonfiction

❑ other

This book is about _____

_____

_____

_____

_____

I think this book is a: **(check one)**

❑ green – go past

❑ yellow – slow down

❑ red – stop and read

The reason that I feel this way is because _____

_____

_____

_____

_____

Surfing the Net

Date: _____

Dear Parents:

Computers and the Internet can be effective tools to support literacy learning. Many Internet sites provide stories to read online or to print and enjoy off-line. Other sites encourage student book making and other forms of writing.

Encourage your child to surf, but make sure you support and supervise the activity. The International Reading Association recommends that families explore the following sites together:

• 700 Great Sites: Amazing Spectacular Mysterious Web Sites for Kids and the Adults Who Care About Them at http://ala.org/parentspage/greatsites/
• Kid News at http://www.kidnews.com publishes news, fiction, and poetry written by and for children from around the world.

Other sites worth checking out include

• Stone Soup at http://www.stonesoup.com, which also publishes writing by and for children.
• MidLink Magazine at http://www.ncsu.edu/midlink
• Surfing the Net with kids at http://www.surfnetkids.com/games/ provides students aged 8-17 with all sorts of games listed by type (crossword, jigsaw) and topic and a search engine for specific games.
• Ask an Expert at http://www.askanexpert.com allows students (aged 8-17) to contact real world experts in areas such as medicine, law, science, and computers.

Enjoy surfing together!

Sincerely,

Million-Dollar Words

Dear Parents: Date: _____

asked **bellowed** *sobbed*

roared

The students are being taught how important it is to make good word choices when writing. They are learning that picking the "just right" word will get the message across clearly and precisely; too often, they have relied on overused words, such as "said." They are coming to love the term *million-dollar words* and enjoy coming up with alternatives to tired, boring words.

Keep that in mind as you read aloud. Ask your child to listen for million-dollar words. If, for example, your child suggests that *yelled* rather than *said* is a million-dollar word, celebrate! Recognizing million-dollar words in books and in conversation and being able to explain why one word is preferable to another, will improve both your child's writing and vocabulary.

Families might also enjoy expanding their vocabularies by subscribing to A Word A Day at http://www.wordsmith.org. There is no charge to subscribe.

Sincerely,

mumbled

moaned

muttered

cried

yelled

shouted explained

Assessing Writing

Date: _____

Dear Parents:

Judging writing is often too subjective, but it doesn't have to be. We know that spelling, grammar, punctuation, and capitalization are important. Together, they are known as conventions. However, writing is more than simply conventions. Have you ever read a piece of writing with great conventions that put you to sleep?

In class we talk about the six traits, or characteristics, of good writing. One trait is conventions. But the other five are the heart of the writing.

Ideas: the message—the content—the reason for writing. The details support the main ideas. They are both interesting and important. The reader is able to imagine or picture the content.

Organization: how the piece is ordered or structured. Does the lead grab you? How are the details ordered? Does the ending bring closure?

Voice: the heart of the piece—the writer's personality coming through. Voice makes the reader "feel."

Word Choice: the choice of the "just right" words to make the message clear. The students use the term "million-dollar words." An example of a million-dollar word is "bellowed" rather than "said."

Sentence Fluency: the rhythm and sound of the writing—it is enjoyable to listen to when read aloud. Do the sentences start in different ways? Do they vary in length?

Your child is bringing home a piece of writing to share aloud with you. Before you hear it, have your child identify the trait that you should focus on. Then, compare your assessment of the writing with your child's assessment.

The traits take the mystery out of assessment. Enjoy discussing the piece.

Sincerely,

Chapter 3

ASSESSMENT BLACKLINE MASTERS

Scoring Guide—Ideas and Organization

Name: _____   Grade: _____   Date: _____

Title: _____

CATEGORY	LEVEL 1	LEVEL 2	LEVEL 3	LEVEL 4
Ideas	• The main idea is unclear. What is this writer trying to say? • The message/story lacks engaging moments. • The writer has a limited understanding of the topic. There is not enough information to make the writing interesting or helpful. • Details are very sketchy. The reader can only guess at the writer's meaning.	• The reader can discern the main idea. The topic is defined to some extent, but it needs to be narrower and more manageable. • The message/story has some engaging moments. • The writer has some understanding of the topic; more information is needed to make this writing more interesting or helpful. • The writing contains some interesting or unusual details.	• The reader can tell what the writer's main idea is. The topic is well-defined, and is small enough to handle in the scope of the paper. • The message/story has many engaging moments. • The writer knows enough about the topic to do a good job. • The writer has chosen many interesting details.	• The paper is clear and focused from beginning to end. The topic is small and very well-defined, so it's easy for the writer to manage. • The message/story is both engaging and memorable. • The writer seems to have a thorough understanding of the topic. • The writer is selective, sharing beyond-the-obvious details that are informing, entertaining, or both.
Organization	• Lack of order frequently leaves the reader feeling lost. • The organizational pattern is formulaic or seriously lacking. • Some transitions are attempted but are rarely effective. • The lead and conclusion are either missing or need a lot of work.	• The writer sometimes wanders from the main point, and this may distract or confuse. • The organizational pattern works some of the time, but it may be formulaic or hard to follow. • Transitions are sometimes present and effective, sometimes not. • The lead and conclusion are present; one or both need work.	• The writer seldom wanders from the main point. • The organizational pattern fits the topic, purpose, and audience. • Transitions adequately connect ideas. • The lead is appealing and the conclusion works.	• The writer focuses on the main message throughout the paper. • The organizational pattern is well suited to the topic, purpose, and audience; it enhances the reader's understanding of the text. • Transitions are smooth, clearly connecting sentences and ideas. • The lead is strong and compelling, and the conclusion is thoroughly satisfying.

(*Write Traits Ontario Rubrics 2003, 12 and 8*)

Scoring Guide—Voice and Word Choice

Name: _____ Grade: _____ Date: _____

Title: _____

CATEGORY	LEVEL 1	LEVEL 2	LEVEL 3	LEVEL 4
Voice	• This voice is difficult to identify or describe, or it's the wrong voice for the writing task. • Lack of voice makes this a piece the reader would not share aloud. • Energy and excitement are lacking. • The voice is missing, or inappropriate for the audience or purpose.	• This is a functional, sincere voice, though not especially distinctive. • The piece does not seem quite ready to be shared aloud. • Moments of passion, energy, or strong feelings are rare. The reader needs to look for them. • The voice may or may not seem acceptable for the purpose or audience.	• This voice is distinctive, though not unique. • The reader might share parts of this piece aloud. • There are frequent moments of passion, energy, or strong feelings. • The voice is acceptable for the audience and purpose.	• This paper stands out. The voice is recognizable if you know the writer. • The reader would likely share this piece aloud. • Moments of passion, energy, and strong feelings are evident throughout. • The voice is carefully selected to fit the purpose and audience.
Word Choice	• Many words and phrases are misused, vague, or unclear. The reader must guess at the writer's main message. • Strong verbs are lacking; the writing lacks energy. • Sensory language is minimal or lacking. • Word use may be skeletal or cluttered; either way, meaning is hard to determine.	• The writing is clear some of the time, but some words and phrases are vague, confusing, or inaccurate. • The writer uses some strong verbs, but relies too heavily on modifiers. • Sensory language is present, but adds little to the meaning or mood; or it may be overused. • The writing is concise in places, but is frequently wordy or cluttered.	• The writing is clear and often original. Words are generally used accurately. • The writer relies more on strong verbs than on modifiers to enrich meaning. • Sensory language, as appropriate, adds important detail or enhances mood. • The writing is generally concise; a word or phrase here and there could be cut.	• The writing is clear, striking, original, and precise. • The writer uses powerful verbs to give the writing energy. • Sensory language, as appropriate, greatly enhances meaning. • The writing is concise; each word counts.

(Write Traits Ontario Rubrics 2003, 10–11)

Scoring Guide—Sentence Fluency and Conventions

Name: _____ Grade: _____ Date: _____

Title: _____

CATEGORY	LEVEL 1	LEVEL 2	LEVEL 3	LEVEL 4
Sentence Fluency	• Choppy sentences, run-ons, or other problems make this piece difficult to read. • The writer uses little or no sentence variety to add interest to the text. • This piece is hard to read aloud, even with rehearsal. • Run-ons impair fluency. • Dialogue, if used, is hard to follow, or hard to separate from other text.	• The writing is sometimes easy to read. Choppy sentences or other problems may necessitate rereading. • Some sentences begin differently; there is some variety in sentence length. • Some rehearsal is necessary before reading this piece. • Some run-ons appear, but do not seriously impair fluency. • Dialogue, if used, does not quite echo the way people actually speak.	• The writing is smooth and quite easy to read. • Variety in sentence length is noticeable. • The piece is a pleasure to read aloud. • Run-ons, if present, are rare. • Dialogue, if used, sounds natural.	• The writing is smooth, natural, and easy to read. • Variety in sentence length and structure is highly effective. • The piece invites expressive oral reading that brings out the voice. • The writer avoids run-ons and repetition. • Dialogue, if used, sounds natural and conversational.
Conventions	• Serious, frequent errors make this text hard to read. • Though a few things are done correctly, serious errors impair readability. • This writer does not appear to be in control of many conventions appropriate for this grade level. • Thorough, word-by-word editing is required for publication.	• There are several minor errors, some of which may interfere with meaning or slow a reader down. • Errors in the use of conventions affect readability. • The writer uses some conventions appropriate for the grade level, but is not fully in control of them. • Thorough, careful editing is needed prior to publication.	• A few minor errors are noticeable. However, they do not affect the clarity. • The writer often uses conventions to enhance meaning or voice. • The writer shows control over most conventions appropriate for grade level. • This piece is ready to publish with minor touch-ups.	• If any errors remain, they are insignificant. Their impact on the text is minor. • The writer uses conventions skillfully to bring out meaning and/or voice. • The writer shows control over a wide range of conventions for this grade level. • This piece is ready to publish.

(*Write Traits Ontario Rubrics* 2003, 9 and 7)

Self-Assessment—Ideas and Organization

Name: _____ Grade: _____ Date: _____

Title: _____

CATEGORY	LEVEL 1	LEVEL 2	LEVEL 3	LEVEL 4
Ideas	• My main idea isn't clear. I don't know what I want to say. • I doubt my readers will want to finish reading my story/paper. • I don't know enough about this topic to write about it. My story/paper is not interesting. • I need better details. My readers won't be able to understand what I'm saying.	• My main idea is clear in some parts, but in others it's a little scattered. • Readers will enjoy some parts of my story/paper. • I know some things about this topic. I wish I knew more so that I could keep my readers interested. • Some of my details are interesting, but some of them are things most people already know.	• My main idea is clear and well thought out. • Readers will enjoy my story/paper. • I know enough about my topic to keep my readers interested. • My details make my topic interesting.	• My paper has plenty of details that make my main idea clear. • My readers will really enjoy and remember my story/paper. • Readers can tell that I know a lot about this topic. • I chose my details carefully. They are important and interesting.
Organization	• My paper is hard to follow. • I don't see any real pattern in my paper. • My ideas and sentences do not connect to each other. • My paper does not have a lead. I just started writing. I don't really have a conclusion. My paper just stops.	• My paper wanders off topic some of the time. • My paper follows a pattern some of the time. • Some of my ideas connect to my main point. Others do not. • My lead and conclusion are there, but they need to be livelier.	• My paper stays on topic most of the time. • My paper follows a pattern and grabs the reader's attention. • Most of my ideas and sentences connect to each other. • My lead is catchy and my conclusion fits my topic.	• My paper is logical and stays on topic. • My paper follows a pattern that makes sense for this topic and to the reader. • It's easy to see how things are connected to my main point. • My lead gets the reader's attention and my conclusion is just right!

(*Write Traits Ontario Rubrics 2003, 6 and 2*)

Self-Assessment—Voice and Word Choice

Name: _____ Grade: _____ Date: _____

Title: _____

CATEGORY	LEVEL 1	LEVEL 2	LEVEL 3	LEVEL 4
Voice	• My voice does not fit my topic well. It needs to be stronger or a completely different voice. • The reader won't want to read this paper aloud. • It doesn't sound as though I have any interest in this topic. • I don't hear my voice in this writing.	• I tried to make my voice fit my topic, but my writing is a little dull. • My paper needs more work. It's not ready to be read aloud. • This topic was okay, but I couldn't get excited about it. • My voice fits my topic in some ways.	• This paper shows who I am, but my writing is not that unusual. • The reader may want to share parts of this paper aloud. • I like this topic, and my interest in it is clear to the reader. • My voice is good for this topic.	• This paper is the only one of its kind and my writing clearly shows who I am. • The reader will definitely want to share this aloud with someone. • I love this topic, so lots of energy and strong feelings come through. • This is just the right voice for this topic.
Word Choice	• My words are used incorrectly so the reader has to guess what I'm trying to say. • My verbs are not powerful. I keep using the same ones. • I did not worry about helping the reader see, hear, touch, taste, or smell. I just used the first words I thought of. • I repeated words and used some words I did not need. It's hard to tell what I'm trying to say.	• At times my words are clear, but I have used some words incorrectly. • A few of my verbs are powerful, but some could use more force. • I helped the reader see, hear, touch, taste, and smell, but sometimes I had trouble doing it, and may have done it too much. • Sometimes my writing is understandable, but I often use unnecessary words.	• My words are clear and creative. I usually use my words in the right way. • My verbs are strong and really explain what I'm saying. • I used some words that help the reader see, hear, touch, taste, or smell. These words add to the mood of my writing. • My writing is mostly clear and to the point.	• Every word helps make my writing clear and interesting for the reader. • My verbs are powerful. They energize my writing. • I frequently used words that help the reader see, hear, touch, taste or smell so he/she can understand the mood of my writing. • I got rid of unnecessary words.

(*Write Traits Ontario Rubrics 2003, 4–5*)

Self-Assessment—Sentence Fluency and Conventions

Name: _____ Grade: _____ Date: _____

Title: _____

CATEGORY	LEVEL 1	LEVEL 2	LEVEL 3	LEVEL 4
Sentence Fluency	• My paper is hard to read, even for me. The reader can't tell one sentence from another. • All my sentences are the same length and they all begin in the same way. • Even with practice, the reader would have to work hard to read my paper aloud. • My writing contains many run-on sentences and these make it difficult to read. • If I used dialogue, it is hard to follow and gets mixed up with the rest of my writing.	• Some of my writing is smooth and easy to read. I have some choppy sentences or run-ons, though. • A few of my sentences begin differently and some are different lengths. • The reader will have to practise reading my paper aloud. • I used some run-on sentences, but my paper still makes sense. • If I used dialogue, it doesn't quite sound the way people actually speak.	• My writing is smooth and quite easy to read. • My paper contains many sentences that begin in different ways. It has a mix of long and short sentences. This style helps make my paper interesting. • The reader will enjoy reading my paper aloud. • I avoided using run-on sentences. • If I used any dialogue, it sounds natural.	• My writing is smooth, sounds natural, and is very easy to read. • Almost all of my sentences begin in different ways. Some are long and some are short. This style helps make my paper interesting. • The reader will love reading my paper aloud. It is very expressive. • I avoided using run-on sentences and repeating myself. • If I used any dialogue, it sounds like real people talking.
Conventions	• The reader will notice lots of errors. These errors make my meaning very hard to understand. • All of the errors make my paper very hard to read. • I did not check a lot of my spelling, punctuation, grammar, and capitalization. I did not really edit this at all. • My paper is far from being ready to publish. I have to reread it very carefully, one word at a time, and make all necessary corrections, before it will be ready to publish.	• The reader will notice some errors. These errors may make my meaning harder to understand. • I did a lot of things right, but I also made some errors. The reader might slow down once or twice because of the errors. • I checked my spelling, punctuation, grammar, and capitalization. I corrected things I knew were wrong, but I wasn't sure if some things were right or wrong. • I have to reread and carefully edit my paper before it will be ready to publish.	• I made a few minor mistakes that the reader will likely notice, but my meaning is still clear. • I used conventions correctly, and this helps the reader understand the meaning. • I checked my spelling, punctuation, grammar, and capitalization. I believe most of it is correct. • Once I make a few small changes, my paper will be ready to publish.	• A reader would have a hard time finding errors in my paper. If he/she does, those mistakes wouldn't change the meaning at all. • I used conventions correctly, which made the meaning very clear. • I checked the spelling, punctuation, grammar, and capitalization. They are all correct. • My paper is ready to publish.

(*Write Traits Ontario Rubrics 2003, 3 and 1*)

Self-Assessment—Writing Attitude Survey

Name: _____ Grade: _____ Date: _____

	Yes	Sometimes	No
1. I like to write. I feel this way because _____ _____ _____	❏	❏	❏
2. I think writing is hard work. I feel this way because _____ _____ _____	❏	❏	❏
3. I think I am a good writer. I feel this way because _____ _____ _____	❏	❏	❏

4. When I come to a word that I don't know how to spell, I _____

_____

_____

_____

5. I think _____ is a good writer because _____

_____

_____

_____

6. At home I write _____

_____

_____

_____

Self-Assessment—My Writing Ideas

Name: _____ Grade: _____ Date: _____

Title: _____

	Yes	No
1. Does my paper stick to the main topic or story?	❏	❏
All my sentences are about _____		
This is my topic. _____		
2. Did I use good information (details)?	❏	❏
I gave enough details	❏	❏
I gave too few details	❏	❏

Two details I gave are:

   1: _____

   2: _____

My details are interesting.	❏	❏
My details are boring.	❏	❏
It is clear that I know a lot about the topic.	❏	❏

3. I could improve the idea development of my piece by _____

_____

_____

_____

_____

Self-Assessment—Revising and Editing Checklist

Name: _____   Grade: _____   Date: _____

Title: _____

This is what I think of my writing:	Yes	No
Ideas: My writing …		
has a clear message and I stick to it	❑	❑
has enough detail (and not too much)	❑	❑
has details that are both important and interesting	❑	❑
Organization: My writing …		
has a good title	❑	❑
has a beginning, middle, end	❑	❑
tells the ideas in an order that makes sense	❑	❑
has a lead that "grabs" you	❑	❑
has an ending that ties everything together	❑	❑
Voice: My writing …		
has feeling	❑	❑
has "voice"—shows that I care	❑	❑
sounds like me talking	❑	❑
Word Choice: My writing …		
includes some million-dollar words, not boring or tired words	❑	❑
uses strong action words	❑	❑
does not include unnecessary words	❑	❑
Sentence Fluency		
I begin my sentences in different ways.	❑	❑
Some of my sentences are long; some are short.	❑	❑
My paper is easy to read aloud—it sounds smooth.	❑	❑
Conventions (Editing)		
My spelling is generally correct even on more difficult words.	❑	❑
My punctuation, capitalization, and grammar are appropriate and effective.	❑	❑
The paragraphing of this piece makes sense.	❑	❑

When I revise, I will improve my writing by _____

_____

_____

Sharing My Writing with a Partner

Name: _____ Grade: _____ Date: _____

Title: _____

Please listen to me read my piece to you. While I am reading, listen for this trait: **(pick one)**

❑ Ideas   ❑ Organization   ❑ Voice   ❑ Word Choice   ❑ Sentence Fluency

Now tell me what you think **(pick one)**	Yes	No
Ideas: Your writing …		
has a main idea and you stick with it	❑	❑
has enough detail (and not too much)	❑	❑
has details that are both important and interesting	❑	❑
Organization: Your writing …		
has a good title	❑	❑
has a beginning, middle, end	❑	❑
tells the ideas in an order that makes sense	❑	❑
has a lead that "grabs" you	❑	❑
has an ending that ties everything together	❑	❑
Voice: Your "voice" …		
sounds like you	❑	❑
shows that you care about the subject	❑	❑
makes me feel _____		
Word Choice		
Your writing uses some million-dollar words, not boring, tired words.	❑	❑
You use strong action words.	❑	❑
Your writing does not include unnecessary words.	❑	❑
Sentence Fluency		
You begin your sentences in different ways.	❑	❑
Some of your sentences are long; some are short.	❑	❑
Your paper is easy to read out loud.	❑	❑

_____

Signed, Your Partner

Did I Persuade You?

Name: _____ Grade: _____ Date: _____

Title: _____

	Yes	No
1. You started with a strong beginning.	❏	❏
2. You provided at least three facts to support your argument.	❏	❏
3. Your facts were all written in an order that makes sense.	❏	❏
4. You used diagrams or drawings to support your opinion.	❏	❏
5. You ended with a strong conclusion.	❏	❏
6. I could hear your "voice" coming through when you read this out loud.	❏	❏
7. You convinced me—I agree!	❏	❏

Suggestions to improve your writing:

_____

_____

_____

_____

_____

_____

_____

_____

_____

_____

Signed, Your Partner

Chapter 4

LITERACY LEARNING ACROSS THE CURRICULUM

Christine J. Gordon

To be literate in a content area is to be able to think, read, write, speak, listen, view, and represent with understanding in multiple ways the content of a discipline. Developing content literacy across the curriculum is not just about developing reading or writing across the curriculum. Such a definition would be far too limited for the 21st century. Understanding the literacy associated with the arts, or with technology, broadens the conventional definition of literacy. Development of multiple literacies (or multiliteracies) is a matter of good teaching in all of the content areas. However, it is important that multiple literacies complement rather than supplement reading and writing across the curriculum.

Find Out More About Literacy Across the Curriculum

Alvermann, Donna, Jennifer Moon, and Margaret Hagood. *Popular Culture in the Classroom: Teaching and Researching Critical Media Literacy*. Newark, DE: International Reading Association, 1999.

Anderson, William, and Joy Lawrence. *Integrating Music into the Elementary Classroom*. Belmont, CA: Wadsworth Thomson Learning, 2001.

Bruce, Bruce B., ed. *Literacy in the Information Age: Inquiries into Meaning Making with New Technologies*. Newark, DE: International Reading Association, 2003.

Checkley, Kathy. "The First Seven … and the Eighth: A Conversation with Howard Gardner." *Educational Leadership* 55.1 (1997): 8–13.

Considine, David, and Gail Haley. *Visual Messages: Integrating Imagery into Instruction*. Englewood, CO: Teacher Ideas Press, 1992.

Dreher, Miriam, Kathryn Davis, Priscilla Waynant, and Suzanne Clewell. *Easy Steps to Writing Fantastic Research Reports*. New York: Scholastic Professional Books, 2000.

Gordon, Christine J., and Dorothy MacInnis. "Using Journals as a Window on Students' Thinking Processes in Mathematics." *Language Arts* 70 (1993): 33–38.

Heffernan, Lee. *Critical Literacy and Writer's Workshop: Bringing Purpose and Passion to Student Writing*. Newark, DE: International Reading Association, 2004.

Hinchey, P.H. "A Crash Course in Media Literacy." *The Clearing House* 76.6 (2003): 295–97.

Livingston, N., C. Kurkjian, T. Young, and L. Pringle. "Nonfiction as Literature: An Untapped Goldmine." *The Reading Teacher* 57.6 (2004): 582–91.

Mantione, Roberta, and Sabine Smead. *Weaving Through Words: Using the Arts to Teach Reading Comprehension Strategies*. Newark, DE: International Reading Association, 2003.

Marzano, Robert, et al. *Handbook for Classroom Instruction That Works*. Alexandria, VA: Association for Supervision, Curriculum and Instruction, 2001.

Owens, R.F., J.T. Hester, and W.T. Teale. "Where Do You Want to Go Today? Inquiry-Based Learning and Technology Integration." *The Reading Teacher* 55.7 (2002): 616–39.

Piazza, C.L. *Multiple Forms of Literacy: Teaching Literacy and the Arts*. Upper Saddle River, NJ: Prentice Hall, 1999.

Post, Arden DeVries, Marilyn Scott, and Marilyn Theberge. *Celebrating Children's Choices: 25 Years of Children's Favorite Books*. Newark, DE: International Reading Association, 2000.

Rasinski, Timothy, et al. *Teaching Comprehension and Exploring Multiple Literacies: Strategies from The Reading Teacher*. Newark, DE: International Reading Association, 2000.

Richards, Janet C., and Michael C. McKenna. *Integrating Multiple Literacies in K–8 Classrooms: Cases, Commentaries, and Practical Applications*. Mahwah, NJ: Lawrence Erlbaum Associates, Publishers, 2003.

Sadler, Charlotte. *Comprehension Strategies for Middle Grade Learners: A Handbook for Content Area Teachers*. Newark, DE: International Reading Association, 2001.

Schurr, Sandra, Julia Thomason, and Max Thompson. *Teaching at the Middle Level: A Professional's Handbook*. Toronto: D.C. Heath and Company, 1995.

Stoll, Donald. *Magazines for Kids and Teens*. Glassboro, NJ: Educational Press Association of America; Newark, DE: International Reading Association, 1997.

Thomlinson, Carol A. *Fulfilling the Promise of a Differentiated Classroom*. Alexandria, VA: Association for Supervision and Curriculum Development, 2003.

Vasquez, Vivian. *Getting Beyond "I Like the Book": Creating Space for Critical Literacy in K–6 Classrooms*. Newark, DE: International Reading Association, 2003.

Wooten, Deborah. *Valued Voices: An Interdisciplinary Approach to Teaching and Learning*. Newark, DE: International Reading Association, 2000.

Yopp, Ruth, and Hallie Yopp. "Sharing Informational Text with Children." *The Reading Teacher* 53.5 (2000): 410–23.

Research on Literacy Across the Curriculum

Content literacy is reading to learn, writing to learn, speaking to learn, listening to learn, viewing to learn, and representing to learn. Students may respond visually through art; orally through song, drama, or performance; or linguistically through writing. They need to be able to function well "through multiple venues for expression" as well as having multiple venues for "receiving expression" (Kist 2000, 712). Content literacy includes a focus on multiple literacies, also called "multiliteracies," an umbrella term that includes mathematical literacy, scientific literacy, computer literacy, and so on.

The primary aim of content literacy is the development of learners who independently use their abilities to acquire new content or knowledge in the subject areas. Content literacy is not knowledge of content (although its aim is to learn content). It represents the skills and strategies that students need to acquire content and to represent their knowledge of that content. Some of these skills and strategies are general and can be used to learn across several subjects in the curriculum. Other skills and strategies are more specific to a subject area because of the nature of the subject matter itself (e.g., the specialized symbols and vocabulary in mathematics).

Research on Content Literacy

In the 1970s and 1980s, research findings on schema theory influenced content literacy instruction. Many classroom strategies for comprehending different kinds of texts were developed and validated (Vacca 2002, 184–204). These included such strategies and instructional frameworks as prior knowledge activation and mapping strategies, questioning strategies, graphic organizers, and KWL for improving content-area comprehension (Vacca 2002, 184–204). The influence of these approaches continues to be strong in the development of literacy across the curriculum. At the same time, constructivism is gaining ground (Vacca 2002).

Factors That Affect Content Literacy

To enhance students' content literacy, teachers must use multiple forms of representation, encompassing graphic art, music, drama, and movies, as well as print. In Informational Communication Technology (ICT), multiple ways of understanding and communicating are blended to form multimedia. Reinking (1994, cited in Richards and McKenna 2003, 126) clarifies the differences between printed texts and electronic texts.

- Electronic text is fluid, moving, and easily changed. Students need to know this so that they can deal with such matters as including or discarding ideas and changing font or size of type.
- Electronic text often incorporates other media, such as animation, hot links, sound, and art that flashes on the screen. Students need to develop the skills to be able to act purposefully when there are

We now understand literacy to be a concept of multiliteracies because we learn, understand, and represent in multiple ways (visual, oral, aural, print, digital/electronic) (Gardner 1983; Luke and Elkins 2002, 668–73).

"In order to read a poem, an equation, a painting, a novel, or a contract, each requires a distinctive form of literacy, when literacy means, as I intend it to mean, a way of conveying meaning through and recovering meaning from the form of representation in which it appears."

KIST 2000, 353, CITING EISNER 1997

Content literacy, or literacy across the curriculum, is a matter of best teaching practices in each subject area.

Being literate in the content areas means understanding or making sense of many kinds of texts, and representing one's knowledge through many kinds of texts. In elementary school in particular, textbooks are only one kind of text.

We have moved from learning from text to learning with text (Vacca 2002, 184–204).

such complex and varied choices. They need to decide quickly which features they need for learning and which features to avoid to limit confusion or distraction.

- Electronic text enables the learner to interact in many more ways than does printed text. Students need to know how to deal with deletions, revisions, copying and pasting, and the enhancements facilitated by multimedia features.

- Electronic text is not linear. It allows the learner to navigate various routes and to make different choices. The networks of choice are hypertexts. The main hypertext is the Internet itself, but other hypertexts include sidebars, online glossaries, and CD-ROM encyclopedias.

In any definition of reading and writing, teachers need to consider the following:

- Reading an electronic page is similar to reading a page in a printed text. Readers respond to the structure and layout of electronic illustrations and text, just as they do to pictures and print on a page in a book. Reading includes the ability to understand and interpret graphics, colour, sound, and video.

- The use of graphics, colour, sounds, and links to related screens enhances a writer's ability to communicate. Writing composition might include animation.

Different Forms of Literacy

Print literacy encompasses books, magazines, and other printed materials. **Visual literacy** involves such media as art, sculpture, artifacts, and film. **Oral literacy** may include discussion, conversation, guest speakers, music, or audiotapes. **Digital/electronic literacies**, the most recent to emerge, include computer texts (e-mail, computer games), the Internet, and CD-ROMs.

To continue developing a multiliteracy approach to learning, teachers must expand their understanding of the word "text" to include guest speakers, discussions, artifacts, lyrics, music scores, theatre performances, scripts, signs, riddles, pictures, films, computer screens, literature (fiction, nonfiction, and poetry), manuals, and textbooks (Wade and Moje 2000, 609–28). Any of these texts can be "read" and can enhance students' learning.

Effective Instructional Approaches to Promote Literacy Across the Curriculum

The following instructional approaches are complementary and provide positive results when used across the curriculum. To ensure students' success with literacy in the content areas, effective teachers

- promote active learning using the literacy processes (i.e., reading, writing, speaking, listening, viewing, and representing)
- foster affective as well as cognitive responses
- capitalize on multiple literacies and multiple intelligences
- use integrative approaches

- encourage collaborative learning
- support metacognitive learning
- link assessment to students' instructional needs

Promoting Active Learning

Active learning keeps students motivated and interested. Active learners are regularly engaged in predicting, questioning, inferring, reflecting, hypothesizing, connecting personally, applying relevant knowledge, interpreting, synthesizing, cooperating, and building their confidence.

It is important for students to become self-directed learners, to take ownership for their learning. In classrooms where self-directed, active learning is promoted, students

- discuss, read, write, view, and represent subject-specific content through a variety of literacies and texts (including those required for information and communication technology)
- learn many strategies and experience various instructional frameworks (such as KWLM, prompted journal writing, and graphic organizers) that involve several of these literacy processes. Each strategy emphasizes one or two processes.
- are taught that some strategies are more appropriate and effective in certain subject areas and that other strategies are transferable across a number of subject areas
- are shown how the strategies encourage them to think about their thinking, to track and guide their own learning and feelings: in other words, to think metacognitively. As they develop their metacognitive skills, students are better able to transfer strategies across subject areas.
- learn the importance of developing a repertoire of strategies to suit their individual learning needs, styles, and preferences

Fostering Affective Responses

Affective dimensions are likes, dislikes, choices, attention, preferences, moods, beliefs, values, feelings, associations, interests, attitudes, emotions, motivations, and personal associations (Krathwohl, Bloom, and Masia 1964). They are often inferred from behaviour. In the making of meaning, they exist along with cognitive dimensions (Mizokawa and Hansen-Krening 2000, 72–79).

Affective dimensions influence learning in several ways. They may serve as energizers (or de-energizers) that help learners to persist (or not) with literacy tasks. They set in motion such actions as self-questioning to satisfy curiosity. They also allow students to sustain and enjoy such literacy processes as reading, writing, speaking, viewing, and representing. Students will persevere in working on a topic or project in which they are deeply interested, even if the tasks are challenging.

Effective teachers

- provide students with informational texts that permit affective responses

"Whereas cognition is in the mind of the reader, and behaviour is of the body, affect is considered to emanate from the heart...."

Mizokawa and Hansen-Krening 2000, 4

Affect can be a way into a text and facilitate cognition and learning (Dreher and Singer 1986).

Check It Out!

"The ABCs of Performing Highly Effective Think-Alouds" by Cathy Collins Block and Susan E. Israel, *Reading Teacher*, 58(2), 154–67, 2004.

- encourage students to respond cognitively and affectively, and model how to do so through think-alouds (Block and Israel 2004).

- increase students' engagement in content learning by emphasizing strategies such as KWLRM, where R is the students' affective response (see Assessment later in this chapter)

For more information on think-alouds, see Chapter 2: Reading Comprehension: Strategies That Work.

Capitalizing on Multiple Literacies and Multiple Intelligences

Multiple texts (visual, oral, printed, electronic, and so on) serve as excellent resources in the classroom because they enable students to draw on their multiple literacies and multiple intelligences to learn new content across the curriculum.

Howard Gardner's Theory of Multiple Intelligences

- verbal–linguistic (the word player)
- logical–mathematical (the questioner)
- bodily–kinesthetic (the mover)
- visual–spatial (the visualizer)
- musical–rhythmic (the music lover)
- interpersonal (the socializer)
- intrapersonal (the individual)

More recently, a naturalistic intelligence has also been acknowledged.

(Gardner 1983; Checkley 1997, 8–13)

Multiple intelligences work together in complex ways in the learning process. Every student possesses all of them to a greater or lesser degree, and all can be assessed and developed to higher levels of competency. Specific teaching activities, teaching materials, and instructional strategies can be used to strengthen each type of intelligence.

Ideas for Strengthening Specific Intelligences

Intelligence	Teaching Activities	Teaching Materials	Instructional Strategies
Visual–Spatial (picture smart) • likes to read maps, charts, and diagrams • visualizes and creates images easily • draws clear, accurate representations of things • spends a lot of time engaged in art-related activities • is interested in machines and gadgets	• visual representations of concepts • mind mapping • visualization strategies • use of art or games to stimulate the imagination	• maps • videos • posters • picture books • cameras • graphs	• draw, map, colour • visualize it • see it at a museum, zoo, or science exhibit • see it on a Web site
Verbal–Linguistic (word smart) • likes to tell jokes and stories • has a good memory for names, places, and things • is interested in word games and puzzles • enjoys reading and writing	• talks • lectures • discussions • reading texts • writing in journals • word games	• books • CDs, audiotapes • word-processors	• read about it • talk about it • write about it • listen to it

Effective teachers meet the needs of many students by capitalizing on several multiple intelligences in any one lesson (see the sample lesson plan format that follows).

Logical–Mathematical	Verbal–Linguistic
How can I use numbers, calculations, classification, critical thinking, and logic?	How can I use the spoken and written word (reading, writing, and speaking)?

Visual–Spatial	Musical–Rhythmic
How can I use visual aids, colour, art, graphs, pictures, and visualization?	How can I include music, melodies, sounds, rhythms, and dance?

Objectives of Multiple Intelligences Lesson Planning

Intrapersonal	Bodily–Kinesthetic
How can I use private learning time, personal feelings, memories, and student choices?	How can I use movement, exercise, drama, crafts, and hands-on experiences?

Interpersonal	Naturalistic
How can I include small-group work, peer sharing, discussion, and collaborative or large-group learning?	How can I incorporate living things, living systems, and the environment?

(Adapted from Nelson 1999, Appendix IV, and Armstrong 2001, 40)

A lesson plan based on multiple intelligences allows teachers to draw from a variety of methods to assess students' needs and differentiate instruction. These include multiple-intelligence tests to get MI profiles (Thomlinson 2003); tests of learning styles or modalities, such as auditory, visual, tactile, and kinesthetic (Skowron 2001); interest inventories; and student interviews. A wider variety of options is then available to students for responding to texts and representing what they have learned in different subject areas.

Content, process, and product are important considerations when planning lessons for differentiation.

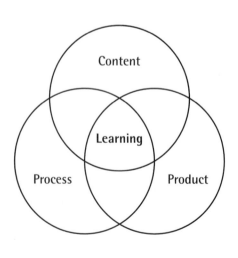

- Content might involve books on tape, the Internet, CD-ROMs, films, contracts, and so on.
- Process may involve different types/levels of assignments for different students, learning centres, paired learning, independent study, group work, or use of computers.
- Product might involve representations through art, songs, or poems on the computer screen; negotiated criteria (rubrics); or performance-based assessment.

Using Integrative Approaches

Integrated instruction is thought to be a more authentic, meaningful, and efficient way to implement curriculum (Gavelek et al. 2000, 587–608). Integrative (or interdisciplinary) approaches help students to make connections across the curriculum, breaking down walls that separate different subjects. They also enable students to connect content with process and with meaningful out-of-school literacies, such as Internet skills and personal writing.

Integration can take several main forms: integration of the communication processes, integration of content and process, and integration across several subject areas (Gordon, Sheridan, and Paul 1998).

- Integration of the *communication processes* means that the teacher has students combine several literacy processes (reading, writing, speaking, listening, viewing, or representing) in a task or activity. This could involve a KWLM strategy (see later in this chapter).

- Integration of *content and process* means that teaching and learning strategies are used to learn content. (The teacher might use KWLM to teach students about the life cycle of a frog.)

- Integration *across subject areas* means that the content of language arts, social studies, mathematics, science, and the visual and performing arts is taught within broad topics organized as thematic units, problem-based units, or inquiry-based projects throughout the whole school day. (For example, a number of topics from several curriculum areas might be studied under a theme like "the rainforest.") Subjects need not be segregated into separate time slots. Such integration is easily managed in Grades 3 to 6.

Subject areas can also be integrated through a curriculum-as-inquiry approach (Carr 2003, cited in Richards and McKenna 2003). "The shift from thematic units to curriculum as inquiry is a subtle change because the classroom does not look different on the surface–the same materials and activities are there. But many of the materials are now gathered up by the entire classroom community, not just the teacher; and the students set and create their own sites for exploration instead of only engaging in ... preplanned activities" (Richards and McKenna 2003, citing Short et al. 1996, 11).

Resources for Inquiry-Based Approaches to Integration Across the Curriculum

Print

Chapter 12: "Integrating Multiple Literacies with Curriculum as Inquiry" in *Integrating Multiple Literacies in K–8 Classrooms: Cases, Commentaries and Practical Applications*, edited by J.C. Richards and M.C. McKenna, 210–33. (Mahwah, NJ: Lawrence Erlbaum Associates, 2003).

Check It Out!

Deborah Wooten. *Valued Voices: An Interdisciplinary Approach to Teaching and Learning* (Newark, DE: International Reading Association, 2000).

William Anderson and Joy Lawrence. *Integrating Music into the Elementary Classroom* (Belmont, CA: Wadsworth Thomson Learning, 2001).

Susan Winebrenner. *Teaching Gifted Kids in the Regular Classroom* (Minneapolis, MN: Free Spirit Publishing, 2001).

Northwest Educational Technology Consortium, "It's a Wild Ride." (This 15-minute video shows the integration of mathematics, science, language arts, and technology through project work. A video field trip introduces the "It's a Wild Ride" project, which is described in detail on the Intel Innovation in Education Web site at www.intel.com/education.)

R.F. Owens, J.T. Hester, and W.H. Teale. "Where Do You Want to Go Today? Inquiry-Based Learning and Technology Integration." *The Reading Teacher* 55.7 (2002): 616–25.

Web Sites

http://inquiry.uicu.edu

http://www.saskschools.ca/curr_content/bestpractice/inquiry/index.html

http://www.galileo.org

Teachers can evaluate their own progress toward inquiry-based teaching practices using the rubric at http://www.galileo.org/research/publications/rubric.pdf

"Using the Internet to Promote Inquiry-Based Learning," available from Internet Innovations Incorporated at http://www.biopoint.com/ibr/Welcome.html

"Focus on Inquiry: A Teacher's Guide to Implementing Inquiry-Based Learning" available from Alberta Learning at www.LearnAlberta.ca

Encouraging Collaborative Learning

Students best develop their knowledge and understandings through social interaction. Working in collaborative groups is one of the best ways to encourage such interaction (Cambourne 2002). Strategies include talking-to-learn, paired or interactive writing, shared reading sessions, collaborative research, and report preparation or project opportunities.

Collaborative learning gives students the opportunity to

- personally construct meaning in group situations
- develop a positive attitude toward learning
- get help in solving problems as others provide their views, clarify, and explain
- engage in exploratory talk and writing
- take ownership for their learning

(Gordon, Sheridan, and Paul 1998)

Research shows that learning in cooperation improves student achievement, intergroup relationships, attitudes, and self-esteem (Brandt 1987; Kagan 1989–1990; Slavin 1990). Many studies have shown these positive effects for both high- and low-ability students (Wong and Wong 2001), shattering the myth that high-ability students will not progress if interacting with low-ability students.

Supporting Metacognitive Learning

Metacognitive students are independent, self-guided learners who

- strategically read, write, speak, listen, view, and represent, and are aware of their processing strengths and difficulties (and of a variety of strategies to overcome these difficulties)

"There is probably more evidence validating the use of cooperative learning than there is for any aspect of education."

Wong and Wong 2001, 254

- use the strategies from their repertoire to manage their thinking and to enhance their learning of subject area content (Garner 1987)
- monitor their feelings, emotions, attitudes, and other affective elements as they learn (Frager 1993, 616–22)

In this age of information explosion, teachers cannot teach students everything there is to know in the content areas; however, they can instill a desire in their students to *want* to learn. They can also provide them with strategies for learning independently by showing them *how* to learn. The critical facets in learning, teaching, and assessment are

- modelling of strategies
- student use of strategies under teacher guidance
- the gradual release of responsibility for using the strategies independently (modelled after Gordon 1985, 444–47; 1988)

For more information on the Gradual Release of Responsibility method, see Chapter 2: Reading Comprehension: Strategies That Work and Chapter 6: Supporting Struggling and Reluctant Readers.

Students who are strategic in their approach to learning content know *what* they know and don't know, *how* they need to go about learning or completing the task at hand, *when* to apply which strategies from a repertoire, and *why* it is important to exercise control over one's learning.

The Gradual Release of Responsibility
I do it.
We do it.
You do it.

Assessment

Assessment tells teachers what students have learned, are learning, and are ready to learn (Afflerbach 1995). It provides direct insight into the specific learning strengths of students.

Effective teachers make assessment an integral part of instruction. Rather than providing a wide scope of learning activities and hoping some students learn something, effective teachers target instruction, projects, and activities to meet the specific needs of individual students. Three essential questions guide assessment:

- How will students, teachers, and parents know that learning has taken place?
- How will they know what and how students still need to learn?
- How will assessment drive instruction?

Assessing the Development of Literacy Across the Curriculum

When assessing in the content areas, it is recommended that teachers first determine what to assess. For example,

- which range of literacy processes
- which attitudes, interests, and motivations
- what subject-area content to integrate into topics or interdisciplinary units

Teachers can then decide what tasks, texts, activities, and projects to use in assessing; that is, which range of techniques will be used to assess growth.

To obtain a profile of student learning, teachers often draw on

- performance standards, rubrics, and benchmarks
- performance-based assessments
- portfolios
- journals (including personal response and dialogue journals)
- observations/anecdotal records
- inventories and checklists
- cooperative assessment

A profile of student learning might also include assessments of

- affective dimensions
- the ability to be a critical learner
- interdisciplinary connections

Performance Standards, Rubrics, and Benchmarks

Performance standards, rubrics, and benchmarks detail specific learning criteria for students, teachers, and parents.

Rubrics are based on a scale that rates performance and can be developed in collaboration with students. This ensures that the language in the rubric is developmentally appropriate and understood by students (and by parents, to whom a child can explain the rubric).

Contextualized or situated assessment "refers to the gathering of information about students' learning within the learning experience."

McLaughlin and Vogt 1996, 105

Authentic assessment reflects "the actual learning and instructional activities of the classroom and out-of-school worlds."

Harris and Hodges 1995, citing Hiebert et al. 1994

"Varying the methods of gathering data will help them [teachers] appreciate the many facets of students' learning."

Luongo-Orlando 2003, 98

Check It Out!

Understanding by Design by G. Wiggins and J. McTighe (Alexandria, VA: Association for Supervision and Curriculum Development, 1998)

Understanding by Design Exchange
http://www.udbexchange.org/resources.html

Story Writing

SKILL	Level 1	Level 2	Level 3	Level 4
IDEAS	• main idea missing • not interesting • no details (few)	• idea is unclear • not very interesting • some details	• clear main idea • interesting • details	• very clear main idea • very interesting • lots of details
ORGANIZATION	• no plan • no problem or solution	• plan doesn't make sense • weak problem/solution	• plan makes sense • good beginning, middle & end	• plan is very clear • strong introduction, middle & conclusion
WORD CHOICE	• no dialogue • basic vocabulary • sentences unclear	• little dialogue • simple vocabulary • basic sentences	• use of dialogue • good vocabulary • ?'s, variety of sentences	• lots of dialogue • interesting vocabulary • sentences vary
VOICE	• not interesting • characters undeveloped	• somewhat interesting story and characters	• captures reader's interest • interesting characters	• strong voice • very interesting characters
GRAMMAR PUNCTUATION SPELLING	• poor spelling, punctuation & grammar - many errors • lots revision	• fair spelling, punctuation & grammar - some errors • moderate revisions	• good spelling, punctuation, grammar • few errors • minimal revisions	• excellent spelling, punctuation, grammar • no errors • no revisions needed

For more information on performance standards, rubrics, and benchmarks, see Chapter 2: Reading Comprehension: Strategies That Work, Chapter 3: Writing: The Reading–Writing Connection, and Chapter 5: In the Classroom: Making It Work.

Assessment BLM 1: Rubric for Assessing KWL Performance

Performance-Based Assessments

Performance assessment requires students to demonstrate what they know in a given subject area. Tasks, which are often related to real-world problems, can measure achievement in math, science, social studies, language arts, art, and drama.

The tasks for performance assessment might range from interviewing a parent and writing a short newspaper article on the parent's occupation to solving a mathematical problem with real-world applications; from writing a letter to the local newspaper editor about a headline or picture in the paper to scanning pictures to show understanding of the life cycle of a butterfly; from writing and sending an e-mail to someone in another country to illustrating weekly observations of changes in the growth of a plant. Tasks might also include writing an advertising jingle, making a short digitalized film, drawing a map showing the layout of the school or community, assembling a collage to reveal understanding of character, or creating a diorama of a key moment or event in history.

With performance-based assessment, students represent their understanding through art, drama, music, computerized technology, and so on, enabling them to capitalize on several intelligences.

Implementing a Performance-Based Assessment

1. The teacher first establishes the purpose for the assessment by determining the primary curricular goals. The learning objective(s) and audience are then identified.

2. Based on the learning objective(s), the teacher determines the type of performance task that will facilitate assessment of those objectives. Students' interests and individual needs are taken into

Check It Out!

A good interactive Web site for developing rubrics is http://www.rubistar4teachers.com.

Determine the Purpose
↓
Design the Task
↓

consideration. A format for the task is selected (or developed), and the learning materials, resources, equipment, and time required to complete the task are determined.

Identify the Tools and Criteria

↓

3. To measure achievement, assessment tools, scoring criteria, and procedures are developed collaboratively with students and perhaps with other teachers. Exemplars demonstrating levels of performance are obtained, or standards of excellence for performance are determined. The tools, criteria, procedures, and exemplars are then shared with students.

Implement the Curriculum

↓

4. The teacher identifies the essential content, skills, attitudes, and work habits that need to be taught to meet the task requirements. Integrated units of study or lessons are then developed to prepare students to meet the task requirements. Students must be provided with learning events and instructional activities designed to develop their knowledge of the content, processing skills, strategies, and habits needed for the task. Students' diverse needs must also be accommodated. Student progress during learning is monitored using a variety of assessments (e.g., checklists, observational/anecdotal records, and so on).

Administer the Task

↓

5. To successfully administer the performance task, sufficient time must be scheduled and adequate and appropriate resources and learning materials for the task must be provided. Before assigning the task, the teacher reviews the goal, learning objective(s), assessment tools, and scoring criteria with students. The task is explained and directions are given to guide students during the assessment.

Collect Data

↓

6. The teacher considers other evidence of student learning gathered throughout the integrated unit and on unit completion.

Encourage Student Reflection

↓

7. Students self-assess, reflect, and set goals, using a range of assessments.

Assess and Report

↓

8. The teacher assesses students' performance on the task using the tools and criteria previously established. Students' self-assessments are also taken into account. Results are shared with students, parents, and others through formats such as conferences and report cards, and are used to modify programs. The usefulness of the performance task itself is assessed. Along with information acquired during the planning and designing stages, this assessment is used to develop future performance tasks.

(Adapted from Luongo-Orlando 2003, 17)

Dear Editor,
   I read your article about allowing a grizzly bear hunt. I do not feel that this is right because grizzly bears are endangered animals. Tourists come to Alberta to look at the wildlife. One of the things that tourists are interested in is grizzly bears. If the Alberta Goverment wants tourists to keep coming to Alberta they should not allow people to hunt grizzly bears.
                    Yours truly,
                       Emily P.
                        Grade 4

Portfolios

The integrated-day concept in the elementary grades lends itself well to portfolio assessment across the curriculum. Ideally, each student will assemble only one portfolio (rather than a portfolio for each subject area).

Depending on the purpose of the portfolio, appropriate items might include

- written reports
- field experiences
- mathematical and scientific experiments
- scripts, notes, photos, and artifacts from drama productions

- pieces of sculpture or art
- taped oral readings or oral report presentations
- photographs of large completed projects
- anecdotal records or periodic teacher comments
- mathematical quizzes
- personal stories
- journal writing
- strategy checklists and attitude surveys
- self-assessments of knowledge
- works in progress
- pieces that show evidence of higher-level thinking

Portfolio assessment is one of the best means to represent multidimensional and continuous assessment; it is also good for collaborative assessment between teacher and student, or between peers.

For more information on portfolios, see Chapter 3: Writing: The Reading–Writing Connection and Chapter 5: In the Classroom: Making It Work.

In portfolio assessment, students are more able to display the use of their multiple intelligences (Hebert 1992, 58–61).

Assessment BLM 2: Assessing Portfolio Contents in an Integrated Unit
Assessment BLM 3: Using My Portfolio to Reflect on My Learning
Assessment BLM 9: Portfolio Tagging Sheets in Chapter 5
Assessment BLM 10: Portfolio Partners in Chapter 5
Assessment BLM 11: Assessing My Year in Chapter 5

Journals

Journal writing is a useful way to demonstrate learning in a subject area and to make connections across the curriculum. In prompted or structured journal writing, the teacher asks questions to give direction to students' writing. The teacher models responses so that students understand they are being assessed on knowledge of the content, rather than on knowledge of the task.

Nonfiction journal entries are sometimes dubbed "learnals."

AFFLERBACH 1995, 7

Implementing Journal Writing

1. The teacher discusses with the class what to include in each entry, beginning with "I learned about ...," or "I learned that...." The class brainstorms a list of key concept words from the topic to enable their writing.

2. The teacher prompts students to decide individually how they will represent (by writing, drawing, diagramming, charting, mapping, and so on) what they learned.

3. Once their entries are complete, the teacher invites students to share their responses with the whole group, a small group, or a partner.

4. The teacher discusses journal entries with the class in terms of the oral and written use of content-area vocabulary, understanding of concepts, questioning strategies, and higher-level thinking (Afflerbach et al. 1999).

When using journal writing for assessment purposes, effective teachers prompt students' writing using three sentence starters:

- I have enjoyed ...
- I have learned ...
- Next I would like to learn ...

(Fehring 2003, 79, citing Nelson 1999)

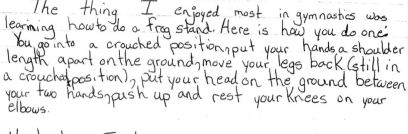

The thing I enjoyed most in gymnastics was learning how to do a frog stand. Here is how you do one. You go into a crouched position, put your hands a shoulder length apart on the ground, move your legs back (still in a crouched position), put your head on the ground between your two hands, push up and rest your knees on your elbows.

Next time I do gymnastics I would like to learn to be able to do a cartwheel better.

The teacher can then use the information derived from this form of assessment to guide the teaching of the remainder of a unit of study and to meet each student's individual learning needs.

For more information on journals, see Chapter 3: Writing.

Dialogue or Response Journals

The most useful type of journal in the content areas is the dialogue or response journal. As a communication tool between student and teacher, the journal provides an opportunity for students to sort out what they are learning in the content areas, what they do not understand, and what feelings, thoughts, and associations they bring to their learning. It also provides information on which to base instructional decisions.

If students are struggling with an unprompted journal in an expressive, free-writing format, the teacher might ask a series of questions to guide their writing (Gordon, Sheridan, and Paul 1998). Students' responses to these questions will pinpoint areas of difficulty they are experiencing in their learning.

- What did I learn in our unit work today?
- What was not clear to me?
- What questions do I have?
- What connections did I make?

Personal reactions may also be solicited through journal writing (Gordon, Sheridan, and Paul 1998). Exploring and discussing feelings enables teachers to gain insights into students' learning. For example, teachers might ask, "Why do you like science? What don't you like about it? What do you find hard about science? What makes science easy for you?"

Observations/Anecdotal Notes

To paint an even broader portrait of student learning in the content areas, teachers might document their observations and use their anecdotal notes to

- plan differentiated instruction based, for example, on multiple intelligences (MI) profiles (see later in this chapter)
- compile a record of student progress to inform students and parents
- generate further questions on a student's learning (Rhodes and Nathenson-Mejia 1999, 83–90)

Anecdotal notes can be as formal or as informal as the teacher wishes—there is no standard format. What is recorded depends on the student, the teacher (and the teacher's knowledge base/expertise), and the context. How students perform varies with the task or activity (Luongo-Orlando 2003). Further, during in-process assessment, students often show that they can learn in different ways and that they have skills and understandings that are not captured on final products and traditional tests.

> "Anecdotal records [or] notes are observations of children's learning processes, behaviours, and products. These notes capture growth as it happens, simultaneously with the experiences in which learning takes place."
>
> RHODES AND NATHENSON-MEJIA 1999, 83

> "These notes are used to record objective and subjective information, as well as affective information, such as engagement, curiosity, and motivational factors."
>
> BOYD-BATSTONE 2004, 230, CITING BAKER, DREHER, AND GUTHRIE 2000

Sample Anecdotal Note

Sam wanted help with finding more information for his science project. Didn't know why dinosaurs died out. Needed a mini-lesson on how to better use computer search engines. His main problem was coming up with appropriate descriptor words. He typed in "dinosaurs" which gave him too many hits/sources. He did not know what to do to limit the information to a narrower topic. I need to show students how to do that. Then I will show him (and others) how to do a library search. Also, better review some of the informational books on the extinction of dinosaurs.

Teachers need to organize anecdotal records for quick access, review, and use. A template, such as the one in the right-hand margin, provides for eight observational records per student. Teachers sort the observations into needs and strengths, make targeted instructional recommendations, and note accommodations for any special needs (Boyd-Batstone 2004).

Inventories and Checklists

Many teachers use inventories to assess students' underlying interests and attitudes toward learning in a content area. Such inventories can help to identify students' hobbies or collections; leisure or sports activities; favourite books, movies, and television programs; and emotional responses to school, learning, and specific subjects. Such inventories also help teachers identify the materials and activities best suited to each student.

> **Anecdotal Record Summary Form**
>
> Name: _____ Grade: _____
> Date: __ / __ / __   Date: __ / __ / __
> Date: __ / __ / __   Date: __ / __ / __
> Date: __ / __ / __   Date: __ / __ / __
> Date: __ / __ / __
> Date: __ / __ / __
> Needs and Strengths _____
> Teaching Recommendations _____
> Special Needs Accommodations _____
> _____

(Adaped from Boyd-Batstone 2004, 236)

Checklists enable more structured observations than do anecdotal records.

With checklists, teachers can systematically observe knowledge of specific content, behaviours, skills, strategies, and intelligences. A content-area observation checklist could be used to assess students' strategy use when reading informational content (Cohen and Weiner 2003, 118). Using a checklist of students' preferred intelligences as well as each student's need to strengthen other intelligences, teachers may differentiate instruction in a classroom. In specific content areas or in interdisciplinary units, a teacher may choose a variety of teaching materials/texts, teaching activities, and instructional strategies that will capitalize on and strengthen the different multiple intelligences of students.

Assessment BLM 8: Comprehension Strategy Use Across the Curriculum
Assessment BLM 9: Checklist for Assessing Students' Multiple Intelligences
Assessment BLM 1: Reading Attitude Survey in Chapter 2
Assessment BLM 2: Reading Interests Inventory (Student) in Chapter 2
Assessment BLM 3: Reading Interests Inventory (Class Tally) in Chapter 2
Assessment BLM 7: Writing Attitude Survey in Chapter 3
Assessment BLM 2: Attitude Survey in Chapter 5
Assessment BLM 3: Interest Inventory in Chapter 5

Cooperative Assessment

Cooperative assessment facilitates learning in several ways.

- It invites dialogue about the assessment process, the rubrics or criteria, the subject area content, the literacy processes, and the connections across the curriculum.
- It models self-assessment for students.
- It makes students more responsible for their own learning.
- It turns assessment situations into learning opportunities.

(Adapted from Valencia 1999, 113)

The collaborative bond that is established between teacher and student in cooperative assessment makes them *partners* in learning across the curriculum (Valencia 1999, 113–17).

Although portfolios offer numerous opportunities for interactive assessment by student and teacher, it is also important for students to interact with other students in assessment, paralleling interaction in learning situations. A new direction is collaborative testing (Gordon, Sheridan, and Paul 1998). This method can be difficult in a large classroom with young students, but teachers might consider it for

- problem-solving or computation tasks in subjects like mathematics
- co-writing of observations and findings in science experiments
- problem solving in social studies
- paired written responses in language arts

Students can be paired according to skill level, personality traits, strengths in multiple intelligences, or ability to work together without competition and domination. The paired activity, while viewed as a

Collaborative test taking shifts the focus from product to process and learning content.

test, is also viewed as a learning activity—peers learn from one another as content is addressed and tasks are completed.

In a mathematics arrangement, for example, one partner may talk aloud while the other may monitor the "thinking in the talk"; one partner will correct a miscalculation or a reasoning error while the other will share a test-taking strategy.

Assessing Affective Dimensions

The familiar KWL framework can be adapted to include an affective component which can be called Reaction (Mandeville 2000).

In the Reaction (R) category of KWLR, students respond to these questions:

- "What do I find interesting?" (Students reflect on their passions or interests.)

- "Why is this information important to me?" or "What difference does this make to me?" or "How does it help me to know this information?" (Students reflect on the value or importance of the information to themselves.)

- "How do I feel about what I have learned?" (Students reflect on their change in attitude.)

The strategy can be further expanded to have students consider what *more* (M) they want to learn on the topic. KWLRM is a comprehension-enhancing strategy that can be used for instructional/assessment purposes. BLM 1: KWLRM Chart links the affective and cognitive dimensions in instruction and assessment, and Assessment BLM 1: Rubric for Assessing KWL Performance can be used to assess the content, skills, and format of the student's completed KWLRM Chart.

K—What do I **know**?
W—What do I **want** to know?
L—What have I **learned**?
R—What is my **reaction**?
M—What **more** do I want to know?

An affective stance "assigns their [the students'] own relevance, interest and personal value to their learning experiences."

MANDEVILLE 2000, 21

BLM 1: KWLRM Chart

Assessment BLM 1: Rubric for Assessing KWL Performance

Critical literacy is the ability to stand back and ask critical questions about any text.

Critical analysis positions students to "see" what the content of texts does to their thinking; that is, they see the everyday through new lenses.

Check It Out!

Chris M. Worsnop, *Assessing Media Work: Authentic Assessment in Media Education* (Mississauga, ON: Wright Communications, 1999).

Assessing the Ability to Be a Critical Literacy Learner

"Everywhere outside of school, layering of information predominates" (Flood and Lapp 1997–98, 343). Therefore, students must have opportunities to work with "all forms of the communicative and visual arts from reading, writing, speaking, and listening to viewing and producing various modes of visual displays including dance, art, drama, computer technology, video, movies, and television, magazine and newspaper advertisements" (343). Students need to start learning how to explore the historical, social, cultural, and political meanings in those texts.

The development of critical literacy processes and skills includes:

- disrupting what appears to be commonplace
- knowing how to step back from stances taken in a text to see multiple viewpoints
- gathering information about social issues and practices (cultural/ethnic differences, materialism, and so on) to become aware of them
- questioning and changing perspective
- becoming more aware of possible courses of action to take, and taking some action

One way to introduce critical literacy in Grades 3 to 6 is through analyzing ads, songs, and children's literature. Teachers might also ask thought-provoking questions about stories, magazine and television advertisements, news broadcasts, Internet Web sites, scientific reports, or social studies texts. (For more information on questioning, see Chapter 2: Reading Comprehension: Strategies That Work.)

Questions may lead students to confront such issues as gender stereotyping, socio-economic level, body image, power, bias, and media influences. Teachers might ask,

- "What do you notice about most of the people in the story? Why do you think that might be?"
- "What do you notice about most of the people in magazines and advertisements?"

The same ends can be accomplished with activities such as the following (accompanied by discussion):

- Draw a different mother, father, king or queen, or hero than the one in the text.
- Draw and label some presents you might give mothers but would not see in Mother's Day sales catalogues or flyers. Make your own catalogue. Who do you think the catalogues are for?

Students' responses to these tasks provide information on their critical literacy development. During discussions, effective teachers make anecdotal notes to remember which students might need to be drawn into discussions more, find it difficult to think at this higher critical level, or feel uncomfortable in such situations.

BLM 2: Analyzing Television and Magazine Advertisements is an example of a tool to teach and assess critical literacy.

BLM 2: Analyzing Television and Magazine Advertisements

Assessing Interdisciplinary Connections

Multiple literacies fit well with an integrated curriculum. Why? Because multiple forms of representation are vehicles for communicating ideas—historical ideas, scientific and mathematical ideas, literacy ideas, and the range of human thoughts and emotions through the arts (Richards and McKenna 2003). It is, thus, advisable to monitor the extent to which students are making connections in their learning. Instruction to promote integration can take several forms: linking the interrelated communication processes (reading, writing, speaking, listening, viewing, and representing); linking learning at school with real life and personal experiences; linking the content of what is learned and the processes by which it is learned; and linking one topic to a related topic in another subject area.

To assess students' emerging abilities to make connections across the disciplines, the teacher asks questions that promote this kind of thinking. For example, in a study of the environment:

- "Why are scientists interested in the environment?"
- "Why do poets sometimes write about air pollution?"
- "How can a math professor help a scientist studying the hole in the ozone layer?"
- "What are our responsibilities in keeping our environment clean? How do we work to convince people this is an important thing for each of us to do?"
- "What does a health-care worker know that can help us tell other people why we should not put poisons from manufacturing plants in our rivers, streams, and oceans?"
- "How can an artist send messages about the environment? What kind of messages?"
- "What do we know from times past about how our environment is changing?"
- "Why are all these people important when we study the environment?"

To be successful in their learning, students will need different types of texts that vary in difficulty and sophistication of content; teacher guidance in the thinking process; a repertoire of strategies that they can use or discard as needs dictate; a climate of inquiry; a risk-taking classroom with engaging activities; and support and encouragement from their teachers, peers, and parents.

It is important for teachers to monitor the extent to which students are making connections across the curriculum (instead of viewing knowledge in different subject areas as belonging in different compartments).

Student Self-Assessment Across the Curriculum

Student self-reflection and self-assessment help create

- independent thinkers who improve their own learning
- a sense of ownership in the learning process
- an ability to take on more and more responsibility for learning
- a more complete portrait of the students' learning

Active engagement in learning means that students should play an active role in assessing their own work.

Varied activities and tasks can promote self-reflection and self-assessment. They include portfolio entries, checklists for students, prompted and other response journal entries, attitude inventories and other questionnaires (to document preferences, interests, and choices), conferences or conversations, and interviews.

Self-Assessment of Portfolios

Students may reflect on and reorganize the contents of their portfolios after

- using reflection tools to assess whether they have met learning goals in subject areas
- discussing their portfolios with peers or parents in small groups in an interdisciplinary unit
- conferencing with the teacher on the contents and quality of their portfolios, with teacher prompts enabling the reflective process (see Teacher Prompts on Portfolio Learning, below)

Teacher Prompts on Portfolio Learning

- "If you consider all the subject areas represented in your portfolio, what is your favourite piece?"
- "Explain why this piece is your favourite."
- "In what ways do you think your learning in the subject area (or unit) has improved?"
- "How can you improve your learning in the subject areas even more?"
- "How can I help you to improve your learning even more?"

(Adapted from Bergeron, Wermuth, and Hammar 1999, 129)

Refocusing Portfolio Contents	
Contents of my portfolio: • • •	What I like to write about: • • •
Favourite books read on topic: • • •	Favourite things I wrote in any subject area: • • •
What I want to read or view next:	What I want to write, draw, or create next:
What I want to work on next to learn more about:	

(Adapted from Farr and Tone 1994, 292, 308)

- completing written reflections (in response to a verbal or visual prompt) on what is known and not known about a content-area concept (shapes in mathematics, "community" in social studies, parts of a plant in science, and so on). Students might list "What I Learned" on the left side of the page and "What I Need to Learn or Do Better" on the right side.
- using concept/mind maps to depict their knowledge of topics and of relationships to other concepts studied
- revisiting and re-evaluating each content-area product based on the rubric that accompanied it
- self-assessing an oral research presentation (e.g., "Did I speak loudly and clearly? Did I make eye contact with my audience? Was my information interesting and well researched?")
- completing self-assessments of group presentations and collaborative work

Students might also include self-assessments of their ability to understand content. An effective way to assess content learning is by comparing and contrasting using a Think Sheet (see BLM 3). For example, students might compare and contrast flying insects (such as butterflies) and flying devices (such as airplanes) on characteristics such as wing design and means of landing.

For more information on portfolios, see Chapter 3: Writing: The Reading–Writing Connection and Chapter 5: In the Classroom: Making It Work.

BLM 3: A Think Sheet for Comparing and Contrasting
Assessment BLM 3: Using My Portfolio to Reflect on My Learning
Assessment BLM 4: Me as Part of a Group
Assessment BLM 9: Portfolio Tagging Sheets in Chapter 5
Assessment BLM 10: Portfolio Partners in Chapter 5
Assessment BLM 11: Assessing My Year in Chapter 5

Checklists, Inventories, and Surveys for Self-Assessment

Many kinds of checklists invite self-assessment of knowledge of content, skills and strategies, attitudes, interests, and feelings. Checklists can be complemented with interviews and conferences in one-on-one discussions, during which the teacher records student strengths, knowledge of content, skills and strategies shared, and plans for follow-up. Additionally, teachers can use a variety of observation checklists as ongoing records of learning and behaviour in the subject areas.

Assessment BLM 5: Checklist for My Research Report
Assessment BLM 6: My Informational Writing
Assessment BLM 1: Reading Attitude Survey in Chapter 2
Assessment BLM 2: Reading Interests Inventory (Student) in Chapter 2
Assessment BLM 7: Writing Attitude Survey in Chapter 3
Assessment BLM 2: Attitude Survey in Chapter 5

Other Assessment Tools

While it is important for students to complete self-assessment inventories and checklists, it is also imperative that teachers keep ongoing records of learning and behaviour, to be included in portfolios. Ways of doing so include

- short lists of cue statements on matters such as reading proficiency, ability to explain concepts orally, and willingness to ask questions for clarification (e.g., "My biggest problem with reading is …"; "What I know about photosynthesis is …"; "I ask questions when …")

- short lists of questions (e.g., "What do you understand [not understand] about osmosis?" "What vocabulary words can you spell without help?")

- incomplete sentences (e.g., "I know that osmosis takes place …"; "I have trouble with …")

- follow-up conferences and interviews that engage each student in one-on-one conversations

Assessment BLM 7: Conversational Interview on Informational Text

The linearity of checklists should not be interpreted to mean that learning occurs sequentially.

Linking Assessment to Instruction

Based on content literacy assessment, the teacher must determine what teaching and learning will look like. Three considerations must inform the development of all literacy skills across the curriculum: what materials to use, what teaching and learning approaches to take, and how to involve students in the learning.

Literature (particularly informational texts or nonfiction) is a wonderful resource and should be used in the content areas along with other types of texts (e.g., magazines, the Internet, music, pictures, films, and informational books including textbooks).

Some teaching/learning strategies work better in some subjects than others, and some transfer well across subject areas. The strategies and ideas presented below should be used where appropriate. Many integrate reading, writing, listening, speaking, viewing, and representing, and require students to use multiple literacies and multiple intelligences. They are organized by the literacy process emphasized in each strategy and by the main skill being developed (e.g., vocabulary, discussion, or comprehension). To a greater or lesser degree, the strategies involve the use of cognitive and affective processes, such as activating prior knowledge, summarizing, applying, organizing, visualizing, imagining, interpreting based on personal experiences, associating, and inferring.

Using Various Text Types and Genres

Careful thought must be given to materials. *Text* has been redefined to go beyond the printed word: it may be visual (e.g., videos, pictures, and artifacts), electronic and multimedia (e.g., the Internet), or aural (e.g., guest speakers). Understanding these texts requires multiple literacies.

Selecting Texts

Use of children's literature increases students' motivation and enjoyment, thus contributing to their development as lifelong readers. Literature can enhance students' understanding of content, deepen their aesthetic response to informational materials, and enable them to make personal and interdisciplinary connections.

Children's literature encompasses a wide range of materials, such as informational books, picture books, alphabet books, wordless books, high-quality fiction, and magazines. In addition to textbooks and materials published specifically for content-area learning (for example, materials from *Canadian Geographic*), children's literature should be a staple across the curriculum. Some of these materials are accompanied by audiotapes for students who benefit from listening and following along. Others lend themselves well to teacher read-alouds.

In choosing books, lists, annotated bibliographies, and book reviews are only beginning guides (Rhodes 1997). Effective teachers consider criteria relating to three elements: the readers, the books, and the curriculum.

In the content area classroom, children's literature is an "untapped goldmine."

LIVINGSTON ET AL. 2004, 582

Cognitive and affective stances play an important part in all content areas. The more cognitive stance involves reading for information while the more affective stance involves reading to relive experiences, to feel, and to associate to one's own life (Post, Scott, and Theberge 2000). Both stances are important when learning across the curriculum.

Check It Out!

R. Doiron. "Using Non-fiction in a *Read-Aloud Program.*" *The Reading Teacher* 47 (1994): 616–24.

P. Sudol and C.M. King. "A Checklist for Choosing Non-fiction Trade Books." *The Reading Teacher* 49 (1996): 422–24.

N. Livingston, C. Kurkjian, T. Young, and L. Pringle. "Nonfiction as Literature: An Untapped Goldmine." *The Reading Teacher* 57.6 (2000): 582–91.

For the annual Orbis Pictus Award for Outstanding Nonfiction for Children, see http://www.ncte.org/elem/awards/orbispictus/

To help students discover books, teachers must themselves first read them.

Guidelines for Selecting Children's Literature

Focus on the Readers

- Who are the readers?
- What are they interested in?
- What hobbies do they have?
- What are their special skills or talents?
- What topics in the curriculum do they enjoy?
- What are their favourite television documentaries?
- What type of videos do they favour?
- What reading background do they bring?
- Do they read willingly?
- Is reading a pleasurable activity for them?
- What genres have intrigued them?
- What types of books do they like?
- Do they prefer informational books or storybooks?
- Do they read series books on topic?
- Do they like books with appropriate illustrations?
- What books do they dislike?
- Do they avoid books that provide information?
- Do they avoid books that contain information within a story format?
- Do they avoid books dealing with social issues?
- What can they read independently?
- What can they handle emotionally?

Focus on the Books

- Do the books represent high literary quality?
- Will they engage the reader in the informational content?

- Are the books within students' reading ability?
- Are the books within their experiential background or their current learning?
- What books will extend their knowledge of the topic?
- What authors of informational books have they enjoyed?
- What books connect the information to their lives?
- Are stereotypes and sweeping generalizations avoided?

Focus on the Curriculum

- Do the text and the illustrations accurately portray the topic?
- Is the content of the book accurate?
- Is the level of detail appropriate for the students?
- Will the books capture the students' interest?
- Do the books present multiple perspectives?
- Do the books stimulate divergent responses?
- Will the books foster sharing of ideas, experiences, and thoughts?
- What aspects of the curriculum will be enhanced through the use of each book?
- How might the books expand the curriculum under study?
- How can the books be incorporated into the curriculum?
- What specific subject matter will be learned through reading the book?

(Adapted from Rhodes 1997)

Using Various Texts in Integrated Units

Classroom teachers and students can choose from a variety of texts for integrated units. (School librarians/teacher librarians, where available, often help to assemble these materials for teachers.) For example, on a theme titled "Canada," the study of relevant topics in social studies, science, mathematics, art, and the language arts curriculum can be improved by using materials such as the following:

O Canada: Our National Anthem by Scholastic Canada (Markham, ON: Scholastic Canada, 2003)

All About Series by Nelson Thomson Publishers (with numerous books in categories such as Canadian symbols, geographical regions, capital cities, attractions, animals, provinces and territories, communities, famous Canadians, and sports)

Under a Prairie Sky by Anne Laurel Carter (Victoria, BC: Orca Book Publishers, 2002)

M Is for Maple: A Canadian Alphabet by Mike Ulmer and Melanie Rose (Chelsea, MI: Sleeping Bear Press, 2001)

Canada from A to Z by Bobbie Kalman and Niki Walker (Niagara-on-the-Lake, ON: Crabtree Publishing, 1999)

Eh? to Zed: A Canadian ABeCEDARIUM by Kevin Major and Alan Daniel (Red Deer: Red Deer College Press, 2000)

The Inuksuk Book by Mary Wallace (Toronto: Maple Tree Press, 1999)

In Flanders Fields: The Story of the Poem by John McCrae by Linda Granfield and Janet Wilson (Toronto: Stoddart Kids, 1995)

Kurelek Country: The Art of William Kurelek by William Kurelek (Toronto: Key Porter Books, 1999)

Canada Invents by Susan Hughes (Toronto: Maple Tree Books, 2002)

Let's Call It Canada: Amazing Stories of Canadian Place Names by Susan Hughes (Toronto: Maple Tree Books, 2003)

Only in Canada! From the Colossal to the Kooky by Vivien Bowers (Toronto: Maple Tree Press, 2002)

One Is Canada by Maxine Trottier (Toronto: HarperCollins Publishers, 1999)

Using Various Texts to Build on Multiple Literacies

Various types of texts and multiple approaches can also help to improve students' knowledge of content.

One of the ways to build on students' multiple literacies is to use children's literature that reflects students' multiple ways of knowing (Crawford et al. 1995, 600–608).

Literature That Promotes Multiple Ways of Knowing

By relating to child authors	*Amber on the Mountain* by T. Johnston *Be a Friend: Children Who Live with HIV Speak* by L.S. Weiner, A. Best, and P. Pizzo *Papa's Stories* by D.F. Johnson
By using printed text to communicate	*The Gold Dust Letters* by J.T. Lisle *Truman's Aunt Farm* by J.K. Rattigan
By using language for word play	*The Alphabet Tale* by J. Garten *Meet Danitra Brown* by N. Grimes
By using talk and oral language in storytelling (oral literacy)	*Tiger Soup* by F. Temple *Zora Hurston and the Chinaberry Tree* by W. Miller
By connecting to history through story	*My Mama's Little Ranch in the Pampas* by M.C. Brusca *You Can Go Home Again* by J. Marton
Through musical literacy	*The Old Musician* by R. Törnqvist *Patakin: World Tales of Drums and Drummers* by N. Jaffe *The Singing Man* by A.S. Medearis

By promoting other ways of knowing	*Archibald Frisby* by M. Chesworth (mathematical literacy) *The Princess and the Painter* by J. Johnson (the artist's eye) *See the Ocean* by E. Condra (senses other than sight) *Sense Suspense: A Guessing Game for the Five Senses* by B. McMillan

(Adapted from Crawford et al. 1995, 600–608)

Teacher Resources

Numerous resources provide teaching ideas and activities: annotated bibliographies of children's books related to specific themes, topics, or concepts; lists of children's books for reading aloud in the subject areas; lists of books that have won awards, such as the Canadian Library Association Book of the Year Award; and lists of books, audio-visual materials, and articles about authors and illustrators.

Many of the resources that follow also contain other teaching ideas in the subject areas.

Teacher Resources for Using Literature Across the Curriculum

Bette Bosma and Nancy DeVries Guth, eds. *Children's Literature in an Integrated Curriculum: The Authentic Voice* (New York: Teacher College Press; Newark, DE: International Reading Association, 1995).

Robin Bright. *Read-Alouds for Young Children* (Newark, DE: International Reading Association, 2001). See Chapter 7 in particular.

The Children's Book Council Inc. *Kids' Favorite Books: Children's Choices 1989–1991* (Newark, DE: International Reading Association, 1992).

The Children's Book Council Inc. *More Kids' Favorite Books: A Compilation of Children's Choices 1992–1994.* (Newark, DE: International Reading Organization, 1995).

Children's Choices is now an annual listing of new books that children have picked as their favourites with reading levels, annotations, and bibliographies provided. This is a continuing project of the International Reading Association and The Children's Book Council Book Committee.

Bernice Cullinan, ed. *Fact and Fiction: Literature Across the Curriculum* (Newark, DE: International Reading Association, 1993).

Bernice Cullinan, ed. *Invitation to Read: More Children's Literature in the Reading Program* (Newark, DE: International Reading Association, 1992).

International Reading Association. *Teachers' Choices* (Newark, DE: International Reading Association, 2002; also 2003). This annotated list of trade books that classroom teachers have found to be excellent in curriculum use was developed by the Teachers' Choices Committee.

Mary Olson and Susan Homan, eds. *Teacher to Teacher: Strategies for the Elementary Classroom* (Newark, DE: International Reading Association, 1993). See Chapters 5 and 8 in particular.

Arden Post, Marilyn Scott, and Michelle Theberge. *Celebrating Children's Choices—25 Years of Children's Favorite Books* (Newark, DE: International Reading Association, 2000). This is an outstanding resource for teachers with teaching activities across the curriculum.

Judy Richardson. *Read It Aloud* (Newark, DE: International Reading Association, 2000). This resource is excellent! It contains read-aloud suggestions for science, mathematics, English language arts, music, art, physical education, as well as for ESL students and other special populations.

Judith Slaughter. *Beyond Storybooks: Young Children and the Shared Book Experience* (Newark, DE: International Reading Association, 1993). See especially Chapter 5.

Donald Stoll, ed. *Magazines for Kids and Teens* (Glassboro, NJ: Educational Press Association of America; Newark, DE: International Reading Association, 1997).

Iris McClellan Tiedt. *Teaching with Picture Books in the Middle School* (Newark, DE: International Reading Association, 2000). There are excellent sections on crossing the curriculum and introducing thematic studies.

Gail Tompkins, Robin Bright, Michael Pollard, and Pamela Winsor. *Language Arts: Content and Teaching Strategies* (Toronto: Prentice Hall, 2002). See especially Appendices A and B.

Ruth Yopp and Hallie Yopp. "Sharing Informational Text with Children." *The Reading Teacher* 53.5 (2000): 410–23.

In addition, *Teachers' Favorite Books for Kids—Teachers' Choices 1989–1993* and *More Teachers' Favorite Books for Kids—1994–1996*, both published by the International Reading Association, can be used across the curriculum in language arts, social studies, art, music, science and math. The first title is a useful resource for parents who wish to discuss or read aloud with their children at home. The second includes other useful items, such as notes on team teaching, using Teachers' Choice Books across the curriculum, and making use of poetry in teaching.

Developing Skills Across the Curriculum

Each subject requires particular skills to learn, some of which follow. Teachers need to monitor students' skills in these areas and plan activities to help develop them.

Physical Education: following directions; imaging/visualizing body movements; playing games and sports

Science: developing vocabulary; applying inquiry methods; making and testing hypotheses; observing; applying learnings; recalling accurately; engaging in cooperative learning; writing expository text; thinking about abstract phenomena; using resource material; using graphics and visual aids

Social Studies: developing vocabulary; developing critical literacy; using synthesis and analysis; note taking; writing expository text; using references (encyclopedia, Internet, informational books, almanacs, etc.); reading maps, charts, pictures, graphs, tables, and cartoons

(Adapted from Manzo, Manzo, and Thomas 2005, 300–301)

Planning Integrated Units

The first part of the unit-planning outline should identify both essential content and supplemental content. Teachers then need to outline what they want students to learn under each heading. The essential, or foundational, content is the vocabulary and content that students will be expected to remember and use long after a unit of study is finished. The essential content is often based on the essential questions being asked to enhance learning. The supplemental, or secondary, content is the vocabulary and content to which students will be exposed to provide them with some awareness of the depth and breadth of the topic.

A template for the part of a planning outline that focuses on essential skills, strategies, and processes, appears below. Teachers are encouraged to add specific skills and strategies as they wish.

Unit Planning Outline for Content

Essential Content:

Supplemental Content:

Adapted from Marzano, 2002.

Unit Planning Outline for Skills, Strategies, and Processes

Essential Skills, Strategies, and Processes: Students will be expected to perform these with fluency long after the unit is finished.

Supplemental Skills, Strategies, and Processes: Students will be exposed to these in order to gain some awareness of them and will use them under guidance.

Essential Skills, Strategies, and Processes

What learning experiences will be provided initially to introduce a new skill or strategy?

1. Describe to students the steps in the strategy.

2. Demonstrate the steps as you describe them.

3. As students watch, demonstrate the steps without a description of them.

---

4. Using a familiar content example, have students try out the strategy with step-by-step teacher guidance.

5. Have students try out the steps under teacher guidance using an example from the subject under study.

6. Have students try out the strategy themselves with little or no guidance.

How will I prepare students to enable them to better learn the new skill or strategy?

1. Provide a diagram, flow chart, or wall chart of the strategy.

2. Allow students to ask questions about the skill or strategy.

3. Ask students what they know and what more they want to know on the topic of study.

4. Preview important vocabulary.

5. Provide a brief summary explanation of what they are going to learn.

How will I help students synthesize and explain what they have learned about the new skill or strategy?

1. Have students orally summarize what they have learned.

2. Have students outline in writing the main points in the strategy.

3. Have students convert the strategy or skill into a diagram, chart, or other visuals using the content learned.

4. Have students compare the skill or strategy to another skill or strategy using the same content.

5. Have students brainstorm on what other strategy the newly learned strategy is like and why. For example, summary paragraphs are like concept maps because they put together the appropriate details with the main ideas.

How will I help students practise and apply the skill or strategy?

1. Have students practise the strategy to become fluent in its use.

2. Have students modify (adapt) the strategy and note what happens.

3. Have them use it independently in different contexts on different content and monitor their success.

4. If appropriate, have students use the strategy or skill for different purposes.

Supplemental Skills, Strategies, and Processes

(This section will be completed by the teacher as these are introduced.)

(Adapted from Marzano 2002)

Developing Oral Language Skills

Talking-to-learn strategies go hand in hand with the listening skills needed to take away information. (For more information, see Chapter 1: Oral Language: Speaking, Listening, and Learning.)

- Talk is part of active learning and promotes thinking and feeling.
- Talk is part of collaborative learning.
- Talk provides opportunities for cognitive and affective responses.
- Talk can be exploratory (depending on the purposes set for it); it allows students to sort through ideas, to question, to disagree, to clarify, or to negotiate meaning.

Since most students are fluent language users, talk is one of the best means of learning across the curriculum. Also, students with strong interpersonal intelligence benefit from opportunities for sustained talk and interaction as part of the learning process. Not only do students need opportunities for informal talk and discussion in the subject areas, they need to develop the in-school literacy of how to "talk-to-learn" through structured activities.

Effective teachers teach mini-lessons on

- different types of talk
- procedures for group work and talk
- strategies and skills to use to sustain talk on a topic (and to listen)

All the language arts strategies for holding conversations—discussing, listening in small groups, and so forth—described in Chapter 1: Oral Language: Speaking, Listening, and Learning transfer well into the study of thematic units in an interdisciplinary or integrated curriculum approach.

Some activities that promote purposeful talk in content-area learning are described below. They are structured to keep students focused on talking-to-learn, listening-to-learn, and staying on task. They also fit well with the effective instructional components outlined earlier.

> Talk is an important out-of-school and in-school literacy activity.

Discussion Following the KWLRM Procedure

The KWLRM strategy (described earlier in this chapter) can double as an instructional and an assessment strategy. It provides an excellent opportunity to encourage discussion of the cognitive and affective responses to a topic or theme. First, teachers will need to model

- types of reactions they may have to the information ("I didn't know that crocodiles were different from alligators.")
- their links to prior knowledge and real-life experiences ("Once when I was in Florida, I was too afraid to hold a baby alligator. But my friend did. I know that there are many alligators in Florida, but are there any crocodiles? I know there are crocodiles in Australia.")
- their associations with feelings ("I have never liked crocodiles and alligators because I am afraid to touch them. But I admire people who can work with them and not get hurt. Like the people on the television program *Crocodile Hunter*.")

> Personal reactions make content come alive and have a lasting value in developing and reinforcing content-area concepts.

Students may at first choose to mimic the teacher's responses. Eventually, by creating a risk-free environment and by teacher and peer modelling, the teacher will enable all students to share their own ideas. They will also construct new knowledge through an affective response and make content come alive.

(Adapted from Sadler 2001, 20)

BLM 1: KWLRM Chart

Using Questions to Sustain Talk

Questions stimulate thought and learning; questions help generate other questions for learning purposes.

Questions should centre on information to be learned in any text, whether it be visual, oral, printed, electronic, or other. For example, when looking at a photograph of Mt. Kilimanjaro, teachers or students may ask such questions as

- "How do you feel about Mt. Kilimanjaro?"
- "What picture do you have in your mind when you hear or read about it?"
- "What person, place, happening, or smell comes to you?"
- "What else does Mt. Kilimanjaro make you think of?"
- "How do you feel about someday climbing Mt. Kilimanjaro?"

Using Audio and Videotapes to Enable Talk

Some students are strong in comprehending material that they hear or see, but have difficulty reading content material. Such students would benefit from listening to the content on audiotapes (or CDs) or watching videotapes (or DVDs) before discussing it. The tape can be replayed several times to improve understanding. Sets of headphones and recorders with adjustable speeds allow audiotapes, in particular, to be used by individuals.

Implementing Oral Language Skills

1. The teacher guides a whole-class discussion on the topic or theme to access prior knowledge.

2. To guide the listening or viewing, the teacher provides several questions, some requiring higher-level thinking, some affective response, and so on.

3. The whole class watches or listens to the tape.

4. Individual students or small groups may listen to or view the tapes a second time in or out of class.

5. Students jot down answers to the guiding questions (all students will then have responses ready to use as a basis from which to contribute to discussion).

6. The teacher leads a class discussion on the content of the tapes.

7. Students are given the opportunity to add information and ideas to their responses following the discussion.

(Adapted from Sadler 2001, 68, citing Koskinen 1995)

Jigsaw Strategy

Jigsaw requires different students to read different parts of long informational or nonfiction texts (or different texts such as poems on the same theme or stories on the same topic). They then synthesize the information to share with their peers what they have learned. In this way, they become "experts" on one aspect of a topic.

Students can be "jigsawed" to different materials according to interest and ability. Jigsaw can be used in all content areas including physical education. For example, if students are learning a new game or sport in physical education or a specific skill in a sport, they could learn different aspects and then teach that to others.

Jigsaw is a collaborative strategy that focuses on speaking and listening while involving reading, viewing, and representing.

Implementing the Jigsaw Strategy

1. The teacher and student identify a number of texts related to the topic under study. These may include nonfiction, videos, magazines, newspaper accounts, CD-ROMs, encyclopedia selections, and popular books.

2. The teacher groups students into teams no larger than six, depending on the number of texts gathered. Each group member will be assigned a piece of text or choose one item to read or view within the subtopic.

3. The teacher asks students to read their selection or text independently. They may use sticky notes, jot notes, or graphic displays to collect the important ideas.

4. The teams then split up to join other students who were assigned the same text.

5. The new groups discuss important concepts in that text and compare the notes they made. They need to organize the information into a coherent set of notes, a graphic representation, a summary, or a mural.

6. The students move back to their original groups and present to that group the information they have learned.

(Adapted from Sadler 2001, 20, citing Aronson 1997; Hendrix 1999; also adapted from Buehl 2001, 73–74)

Think-Pair-Share/Think-Square-Share

This strategy allows students to work with a partner or in groups of four (squares) to share material they have read or viewed in any subject. (For more information on Think–Pair–Share, see Chapter 1: Oral Language: Speaking, Listening, and Learning.)

Implementing Think-Pair-Share/Think-Square-Share

1. Students read, view, and study a text on a topic.

2. The teacher asks students to pair (two students) or square (four students) to discuss what they know about the topic, what the reading material reminds them of, what new information they can add, and what might happen next (or what they need to do next). For example, in working to understand a poem about a boy's snail-paced approach to homework, questions to consider might be as follows:

   • "What do you know about a snail's pace?"

   • "What other things have you read, seen, heard, or written about snails in the past?"

   • "Where can we get more information on snails?"

   • "What is the boy's problem?"

   • "What might the boy in the poem have to learn to do?"

3. The paired or squared students share orally with the whole class, and add any new information that the large group may have offered to their notes.

(Adapted from Sadler 2001, 29, citing Banikowski and Mehring 1999)

Guided Imagery

Guided imagery, a strategy that triggers visual images as students activate their imaginations, adds depth and richness to learning. It prepares students for reading, viewing, writing, or listening to content and deepens understanding after reading, viewing, or listening to material not previously known. Guided imagery, which helps students remember, exposes students to a multiple sign system to learning and, in particular, engages their spatial/visual intelligence.

Implementing Guided Imagery

1. One good way to start is with a warm-up where students work in pairs. The teacher suggests one image—a lightning storm, an exotic animal, a pet, a sundae, a picnic, and so on. Students shut their eyes and let their imaginations roll. After giving them some time to elaborate on the image, the teacher asks students to describe to the partner what they have been seeing in their minds' eye (colours and all). The teacher suggests they can also use all their senses (touch, smell, hearing, and so on).

2. **Option A:** To introduce a unit about which students have some prior knowledge or experience, the teacher tells students to close their eyes and breathe deeply to relax. Students are invited to imagine sounds, sights, emotions, smells, and sensations. The teacher gives them some background on the image they will be asked to visualize. For example:

"[E]ffective readers ... are able to generate images for themselves as they read."

BUEHL 2001, 59

"It is impossible even to think without a mental picture."

MANTIONE AND SMEAD 2003, 43

"I always do my pictures first because then I can get looks at my picture to help me with my describing words. If I wrote my words first, I wouldn't be able to see my describing words in my pictures."

HANNAH, A GRADE 3 STUDENT QUOTED IN RICHARDS AND McKENNA 2003, 190

You are outside playing on a Saturday afternoon. Suddenly you notice that everything is very still. The birds have stopped singing and the buzz of insects is no longer heard. No wind is rustling in the leaves. As you glance around, you see no children in the playground next to your yard. There are no people anywhere. There are no vehicles driving by. You look up and you see a dark sky. You sense something is wrong, something is about to happen. The hair on the back of your neck begins to rise as if there was electricity in the air. Like a bolt of lightning, the stillness is broken with the sound of thundering footsteps and a shout of "A tornado coming!"

Option B: To prepare students for a guided imagery activity on a topic about which they have little knowledge, the teacher follows much the same process; however, before students are relaxed and alerted to use all their senses, they *preview* the text. They should look at all the visuals in the text and any other visuals collected to help with the imaging. (Following the guided imagery in Step 3, below, students might return to the text to compare their own images with the actual pictures.) Again, students are encouraged to use all their senses.

3. The teacher suggests an image to students, providing one sentence at a time with pauses in between so they can process the words and visualize.

4. Students share or discuss descriptions of their images with peers in the whole class or in small groups.

5. If possible, the teacher shows them photos of the phenomenon to which they can compare their descriptions; they can then add to them.

(Adapted from Buehl 2001, 59, citing Gambrell, Kapinus, and Wilson 1987)

Imaging: You Ought to Be in Pictures

This strategy invites students to imagine themselves in a photograph and thereby become personally engaged. It involves making closer examinations of photographs and visuals in various texts. This motivating strategy allows students to learn new things using mental imagery, and to use discussion to enhance learning.

"Photographs can evoke a sense of mood and convey meaningful information that communicates far beyond written description."
BUEHL 2001, 149

Implementing Imaging

1. The teacher looks for good photographs/pictures that relate to a themed unit or section of the curriculum. (For example, libraries may have archived pictures of the first efforts of humankind to fly.) Good sources are magazines, newspapers, posters, the Internet, and textbooks.

2. The teacher chooses appropriate photographs to introduce a unit or to underline certain important ideas in the unit. These can be made into overhead transparencies or scanned to create computerized images.

3. The teacher stimulates students' mental imagery when viewing the photograph by following the guided imagery exercise (see the preceding strategy). It is also good to suggest that students make personal connections to the picture by posing such questions as,

"What other pictures come to your mind from what you already know?" and "Looking at this picture, what particular things do YOU see in your mind's eye that you think are important?"

4. After the guided imagery, students jot down some thoughts in writing. The teacher may want to guide the writing with a prompt.

5. The teacher asks students to share their written entries and guides the discussion on the topic, attending to more details in the picture, if necessary.

(Adapted from Buehl 2001, 149–50)

Developing the Essential Vocabulary for Concept Development

Teachers must determine the essential topic- or theme-specific vocabulary to be taught. Programs of study are useful guides for determining the vocabulary central to understanding the topic.

Essential vocabulary can be taught directly, or indirectly by involving students in strategies that tap their multiple literacies and multiple intelligences. While all students benefit from vocabulary building, it is crucial for **ESL** students. Students will acquire other concepts and vocabulary from context through talk, reading, writing, viewing, and representing.

Working from Context Clues

Context clues include words, pictures, or charts and graphs from which students can glean meanings of words. A teacher think-aloud models how to determine word meanings from such contexts. In printed texts, meaning can be found by looking for a direct definition of a word, a synonym, an explanation, or an example. Meaning can also be found by looking at the pictures, charts, tables, and graphs that accompany the text (be it printed, visual, electronic, or an oral presentation with props and visuals).

If visuals alone are used, teachers need to model using clues in a picture to provide the meaning, or how the picture depicts the concept. Think-alouds also model finding the meaning of a word through context. (For more information on think-alouds, see Chapter 2: Reading Comprehension: Strategies That Work.)

Predicting Words in Definitions

This game-like prediction strategy teaches students reading skills, discussion skills, and skills for using a dictionary, glossary, and thesaurus. Elaborated by Olson and Homan (1993, 53), it is adaptable for use in all content areas.

Implementing the "Words in Definitions" Prediction Strategy

1. Groups of three to five students sit in a circle.

2. The teacher (or students) selects several words from the content areas in a themed unit (e.g., the word "settlement" from social studies).

Students need to be shown how text and visuals should be used together to determine meaning.

3. Starting with the first word, the teacher asks one of the students to provide a key word he or she predicts will be in the definition (e.g., the word "colony").

4. Play continues around the circle with no player able to predict a word already given. (Other students might predict such words as "fort," "homestead," "village," "town," "community," "neighbourhood," and "beehive.")

5. After the last prediction is given, the students look up the word in the glossary, thesaurus, and dictionary and a point is awarded to each person who made a correct prediction. Because word definitions differ from source to source, judgments need to be made as to which guesses are good ones and why, and which predictions are clearly inaccurate.

6. Students discuss word meanings in small groups.

7. Students then write down their understanding of the word's meaning. (Example: A *settlement* is a group of people living together, like a colony, village, or town in the pioneer days, or a town or city today.)

Alternatively, the whole class plays this game. Each student writes down guesses on a piece of paper and volunteers read out their predicted words.

Performing Skits and Plays on Content-Area Concepts

Skit, play, and puppet performances engage students cooperatively and draw on their bodily/kinesthetic intelligence. Many dramatic arts projects do not take much effort or elaborate planning (Richards and Goldberg 2003, 81).

Students read and discuss a text (informational book, film, information from the Internet, picture, words in a song) in social studies, language arts, science, or mathematics. During the discussion, the

Check It Out!

J. Ball and C. Airs. *Taking Time to Act: A Guide to Cross-Curricular Drama.* (Portsmouth, NH: Heinemann, 1995).

All drama is a laboratory for verbal and nonverbal language (Richards and McKenna 2003).

teacher lists the main concepts. Students write a short skit or play using the concepts. They then perform the skit or play to show their understanding of the concepts through vocabulary use and representation. For example, they might show the life cycle or stages of development of a butterfly, from egg through larva and pupa (cocoon) to butterfly. If the teacher finds the performance inadequate or inaccurate, then, after discussion, students modify their skit to clarify concepts. Assessment BLM 10: Skit Performance allows the teacher and students to discuss how well the performance showed the correct meaning of the concepts.

(Adapted from Sadler 2001, 25, citing Cochran 1993)

Assessment BLM 10: Skit Performance

Using the CONCEPT Strategy

In this strategy, CONCEPT refers to Convey-Offer-Note-Classify-Explore-Practise-Tie down. It works well at the beginning of an integrated unit or single-subject unit. Once the students understand the strategy, they practise the steps with other new concepts or vocabulary. Students indicate their understanding of the concept by providing new examples. Reading, viewing, and writing or representing are the main literacy processes involved.

The concept strategy can be taught to students using the Gradual Release of Responsibility method: I do it. We do it. You do it.

Implementing the CONCEPT Strategy

> The CONCEPT strategy works well for learning concepts in science, social studies, language arts, and mathematics.

C
O
N
C
E
P
T

1. The teacher **conveys** the concept by giving the topic of study (e.g., snakes).
2. The overall meaning of the concept is **offered** by describing what it relates to (e.g., snakes are cold-blooded living things, reptiles).
3. All the key words important to understanding the concept are **noted** ("vipers," "serpents," "venom," "poison," "fangs," "scales," "cold-blooded").
4. The key characteristics of the concept are **classified** (e.g., snakes are born live, not hatched; some are poisonous; they shed their skins; they are scaly and some are slippery; snakes swallow their prey whole).
5. Other examples are **explored** to see if they fit the definition (e.g., water snakes, ground snakes, tree snakes, garter snakes, rattlesnakes, diamond heads).
6. Students then **practise** with new examples under teacher guidance. (Students might go on to consider, for example, brown snakes from Australia, pythons, and cobras.)
7. Students **tie down** a definition. For example, students might determine that a snake is a long reptile with no legs, a slim and scaly body, and possibly a poisonous bite.

(Adapted from Sadler 2001, 56)

Teachers might use the CONCEPT strategy in tandem with concept mapping.

Concept Mapping

This strategy is a visual representation of the key elements in a definition: category, characteristics, and examples. Concept mapping enriches students' understanding of a word, allowing them to integrate prior knowledge and associations of a concept with new knowledge acquired from a text. It is one of the best strategies for learning the essential vocabulary in any subject area. The maps are also useful as a review or a study aid. (For more information using this and other graphic organizers, see Chapter 1: Oral Language: Speaking, Listening, and Learning.)

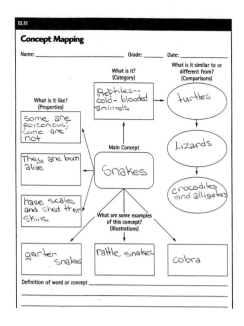

Implementing Concept Mapping

1. The teacher may use BLM 4: Concept Mapping initially as a direct instruction tool. With a concept blank map on the overhead projector, the teacher reviews the questions that a complete definition would answer:

   - What is it?
   - What is it like?
   - What are some examples?
   - How is it like or different from something else?

2. Using a familiar concept, the teacher models how to use the map by getting the information from students to complete it. If considering ice cream, students responding to "What is it?" might say it is a food, a dessert, a dairy treat. To "What is it like?", they might say it is frozen, made of cream and sugar, comes in many flavours, melts easily, gets drippy fast, and comes in different colours. To the question "What are some examples?", they might respond chocolate, vanilla, Neapolitan, low fat or regular, and mention specific brand names. Students might then compare ice cream to frozen yogurt.

3. After the demonstration, students complete concept maps on new concepts they are learning in the content areas. They could also complete comparison bubbles on their maps (Barton 2002). In a bubble, for example, it could be noted that snakes and lizards are both cold-blooded, but lizards have legs.

(Adapted from Buehl 2001, 41, 154)

Concept Definition

This learning task offers a way to go beyond concept mapping to gain a fuller definition of a concept.

Implementing the Concept Definition Technique

1. The teacher chooses a key term from the topic under study in a content area or integrated unit, and students work in pairs to develop a concept map for the new concept or term, which might range from rectangle, mineral, or government to grizzly bear, lacrosse, or haiku. Using a variety of texts, pictures or diagrams, examples, and artifacts, students construct the map.

2. Students then write a complete definition for the concept. The definition should consist of several sentences that include the

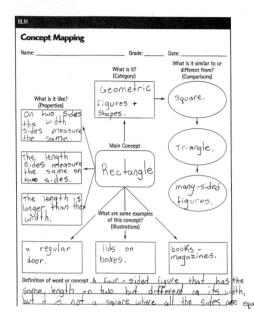

Concept Mapping

Name: _____ Grade: _____ Date: _____

What is it like?
(Properties)

What is it?
(Category)

What is it similar to or
different from?
(Comparisons)

Geometric
figures +
Shapes.

Square.

On two sides
the width
sides measure
the same.

Triangle.

The length
sides measure
the same on
two sides.

Main Concept

Rectangle

many-sided
figures.

The length is
longer than the
width.

What are some examples
of this concept?
(Illustrations)

a regular
door.

lids on
boxes.

books -
magazines.

Definition of word or concept: A four-sided figure that has the same length on two but different on its width, but it is not a square where all the sides are equal.

category of the word, its characteristics or properties, and several illustrations or examples. For example, "A *rectangle* is a figure with four straight sides. Each corner forms a right angle. A rectangle has the same length of sides on its width and the same length of sides on its length. Here is a picture of three different rectangles."

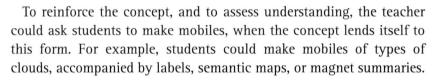

3. Once students have finished working in pairs, the teacher will require them to create concept or definition maps independently.

(Adapted from Buehl 2001, 154)

To reinforce the concept, and to assess understanding, the teacher could ask students to make mobiles, when the concept lends itself to this form. For example, students could make mobiles of types of clouds, accompanied by labels, semantic maps, or magnet summaries.

Magnet Summaries

The Magnet Summary is a strategy to identify key terms and concepts, and then organize these into summaries. This process makes a large amount of information manageable for comprehension and recall. It builds vocabulary, enhances comprehension, and teaches students how to write about the content.

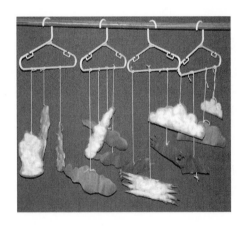

Implementing Magnet Summaries

1. The teacher begins by using the analogy of a magnet. A magnet attracts metal; magnet words attract information. (It would be a good idea to demonstrate how magnets work.)

2. Teachers guide students in looking for the magnets, or key terms/concepts in a short portion of the text. They explain that key words sometimes appear in headings and titles, or are bolded or italicized in text, but may not stand out.

3. The teacher solicits a magnet word from students and discusses why it can or cannot be considered a key concept.

4. Once the magnet word is written on the board, chart paper, or overhead transparency, the teacher asks students to recall important details from the text. The details are then written beside the magnet word.

5. Students write the magnet word and the details on index cards.

6. The teacher prompts students to reread the passage, looking for any important details that may have been missed.

7. Students work together in small groups to finish the reading and to note on index cards the magnet words in each paragraph or

section along with important information. (Decisions on words and information will be part of group discussion.) Each student will have about five cards when the group work is done.

8. The teacher models writing three or four summary sentences based on the information on each card.

9. Students construct sentences collaboratively in their groups. Each student writes sentences on the back of the index card, underlining the magnet word.

10. Students arrange sentences in the way they want their summaries to read.

Front of Card

when	where	who
what	STORY WEB	ending
	problem	solution

Back of Card

A good story has a problem or something the characters have to fix. At the beginning of the story, there is the when, where, who and what the problem might be. In the middle the characters try to slove the problem or problems. The important part is when the problem is sloved. The ending puts everything together so the story makes sense.

11. The teacher models inserting connectives (e.g., "and," "but," "also," "as well") so that the sentences are woven into a coherent whole.

12. Students may read their summaries aloud and make further revisions following peer feedback.

(Adapted from Buehl 2001, 80)

Keeping Personal Vocabulary Notebooks

Effective teachers encourage students to keep track of content-area words that they find difficult to understand. They ask students to jot down two words daily, and to meet in pairs or triads to discuss meanings and learn from one another.

Effective teachers also encourage students to look up the words in glossaries and dictionaries, and to use the context from a variety of texts to determine the meanings of the words. Once each pair or small group has decided on appropriate meanings, students compose definitions in their own words in their personal vocabulary notebooks.

Determining the Multiple Meanings of Words

Certain words can have very different, specialized meanings when they are used in subject areas such as social studies and science (e.g., "bank," "force," "fault," "revolution"). Olson and Homan (1993) suggest that teachers note specialized vocabulary before students read content-area texts. One good way to alert students to the multiple meanings of words is to question them about what each of the words would mean to people in various roles.

For more information on meaning (semantics), see Chapter 1: Oral Language: Speaking, Listening, and Learning.

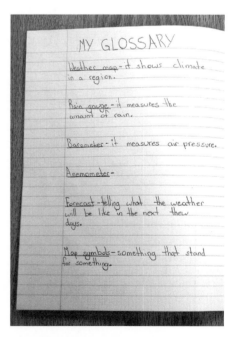

Having each student keep a list of vocabulary words personalizes learning.

Word Meanings from Different Perspectives

- What does the word "conductor" mean to a train passenger? a musician? an electrician?

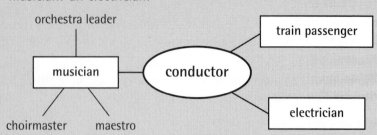

- What does the word "bank" mean to a businessperson? a roadway engineer? a race car driver? an environmentalist?

- What does the word "volume" mean to a librarian? a pharmacist? a drummer?

- What does the word "model" mean to a fashion designer? an architect or building contractor? a geneticist?

- What does the word "force" mean to a soldier? a physicist? a meteorologist? a *Star Wars* filmgoer?

- What does the word "charge" mean to a cashier? a police officer? a lawyer? a mechanic? a military commander? an electrician?

- What does the word "scale" mean to a fisher? a physicist? a teacher? a dieter? a mapmaker?

- What does the word "fault" mean to a geologist? a criminal? a jeweller? a judge?

- What does the word "revolution" mean to a historian? a physicist? a mathematician? a geologist?

(Adapted from Olson and Homan 1993, 59)

Building an Interest in Words in the Content Areas

Besides teaching effective learning strategies that students can use across the curriculum, teachers need to motivate students to learn vocabulary.

Effective teachers make vocabulary learning an integral part of classroom learning. They generate excitement about learning words with spontaneous word play and teachable moments. For example, teachers might use a variety of engaging resources, or bring in articles on word origins or new words to the language.

Effective teachers also demonstrate their own understanding of words in all classroom activities, tasks, and subjects. They show enthusiasm for subject-area vocabulary in discussions and other activities and provide a non-threatening and stimulating environment. Finally, they encourage reading, listening, and viewing activities in the content areas.

"The single most important factor in improving vocabulary is the excitement about words that teachers generate."

GORDON, SHERIDAN, AND PAUL 1998, 167

Developing Comprehension and Metacognition

Effective comprehenders switch from being cognitive to being metacognitive when comprehension breaks down or when a text is difficult for them—they take action to improve their comprehension. Basically, metacognition consists of two aspects. First, it means being aware of what one understands or does not understand. It means being aware of what one is doing. Second, it means being able to change the course of thinking and learning if needed. It means using strategies to improve comprehension.

Many research-based approaches and strategies are available to the content-area teacher for improving comprehension of informational texts: brainstorming and categorizing; generating and answering questions; visually representing text using graphic and semantic organizers; using reciprocal teaching, guided reading, and guided imagery; using text structures and features; predicting content; and retelling, summarizing, synthesizing, and inferring. Strategies to improve metacomprehension include

- KWLM
- autobiographical writing
- journal writing
- visual representation
- group investigation
- SQRQCQ

For much more information, see Chapter 2: Reading Comprehension: Strategies That Work.

KWLM

There are many useful variations of the KWL strategy, some of which are covered earlier in this chapter. KWLM extends the strategy to include generating questions for inquiry-based learning throughout a unit of study. It can be used in all subjects. In science, for example, students may use it to set up their own experiments.

The strategy

- sustains student interest and drives inquiry
- allows capable students to tap higher levels of thought
- provides a method for recording and then exploring answers to generate further questions
- activates prior knowledge (which may include affective components)
- encourages the selection and integration of ideas through such activities as brainstorming, discussion, writing, and graphic representation

(Adapted from KWLQ, Rasinski et al. 2000, 29)

Check It Out!

John Ayto. *Dictionary of Word Origins: The History of More Than 8,000 English-Language Words* (New York: Arcade Publisher, 1990).

Frank Oppel, ed. *Why Do We Say It? The Stories, Expressions and Clichés We Use* (Edison, NJ: Castle Books, 1985).

Marvin Terban. *Eight Ate: A Feast of Homonym Riddles* (New York: Clarion Books, 1982).

Marvin Terban. *In a Pickle and Other Funny Idioms* (New York: Clarion Books, 1983).

Most researchers would agree the difference between cognition and metacognition is that cognition is needed to perform a task, while metacognition is needed to understand how the task was performed (Schraw 2002, 3–16).

What do I KNOW?	What do I WANT to know?	What have I LEARNED?	What MORE do I want to know?
Students bring their personal knowledge to any text or topic of study.	Each student may read, view, and listen for different purposes. Once the student decides on a purpose, the related question, "Where do I find what I want to know?" arises.	Certain information is more useful to some students than others.	Students will have more questions that are uniquely their own. They will need to consider where they will find the information.

(Adapted from Bromley, Irwin-DeVitis, and Modlo 1999)

Parents might also be encouraged to use the KWLM strategy at home with their children. For guidelines, see BLM 5: Literacy Home Links: KWLM Strategy Use at Home.

BLM 1: KWLRM Chart
BLM 5: Literacy Home Links: KWLM Strategy Use at Home
Assessment BLM 1: Rubric for Assessing KWL Performance

Autobiographical Writing

Writing is a way to improve comprehension when reading and learning. Autobiographical writing enables students to connect personally with narrative texts in the language arts and other content areas. For example, before they listen to or read a story about an airplane ride, or before a field trip to the planetarium or airplane museum, students might be asked to write about related personal experiences. By writing in this way, they tie their prior knowledge at the outset to the topic under study.

Quick writes often serve the same purpose. Students jot down quickly everything that comes to mind on the topic.

After the text is read or the field trip is over, students write again for 10 or 15 minutes on how they felt, what they thought, what they did, what they saw, what they learned, and why they liked or did not like the experience. The quick writes could then be developed into autobiographical paragraphs. Eventually, students should be able to write autobiographical paragraphs without the need for prompts.

Prompts for Quick Writes
The teacher might guide a quick write with prompts such as

- "How did you feel?"
- "What were you thinking?"
- "What do you remember seeing?"
- "What did you learn?"
- "What did you like or not like about this experience?"

I was in an airplane when we went to Disney land. I felt like I was on top of the world looking down. I was always thinking look down, look down. There was no clouds so I could see the Grande Canyon. I learned you couldn't go see the pilate. I really liked how fast the plane went. My ears got plugged when we landed. I did not like the heart. I still don't know how a plane stays in the air.

Students derive many benefits from this writing strategy.

- They can better relate stories and other learning events to their own lives and interpret the content learning more personally.
- They tend to find learning events more interesting.
- They are better able to bring associations, images, feelings, and ideas as they "live through" the topic.
- They are more likely to stay on task.
- They have an informational base from which to enter into a discussion with confidence.

(Adapted from Gordon, Labercane, and McEachern 1993, 251)

> After I went to the airplane museum I had one of my questions answered. The man told us about lift and arrowdinamics I think it has to do with how air holds up the plane while they fly but airplanes have to be sleek to fly I was never scared in the airplane to Disney Land but now I feel even safer. I forgot what he said made my ears hurt, but I also learned how airplanes are youssed to take food, medicens and mail to people in the north.

Journal Writing

Journal entries are another effective way to bolster students' learning and comprehension across all subject areas.

It is important that journal writing is judged not on conventions but on ideas and organization. Students should, however, be expected to spell correctly high-frequency words, as well as vocabulary from word walls, classroom charts, or vocabulary lessons, and to make an effort at punctuation. Teachers may respond to each student's writing briefly to clarify misunderstandings, raise a question, assure, encourage, or reteach succinctly. Based on feedback in the journal entries, effective teachers teach mini-lessons to a group experiencing similar misunderstandings on a topic.

For much more information on journal writing, especially as it relates to language arts, see Chapter 3: Writing: The Reading–Writing Connection.

Journal entries in content areas enable students to heighten their understanding of the content as they attempt to explain the concepts in their own words (Gordon, Sheridan, and Paul 1998).

To gain from writing-to-learn activities such as journal writing, students have to think.

Journal Entry Ideas for Social Studies

The questions that follow might be used to prompt social studies journal entries:

- "If you had lived in pioneer times, what kind of school would you have gone to?"
- "What are some topics you might have studied?"
- "What were the books like in those days?"
- "What would you have worn to school?"
- "How would you have travelled to school?"

Ayesha

In pioneer times I have mostly gone to a one or two room school. There might be grades 1,2,3 in one room. The other bigger kids would be in another room grade 4 to 9. There might just be 5 or 6 kids in a grade. In grades 4 to 9 lots of kids would drop out to help on the farm. I would have studed subjects like writing, reading, anthematics, history, and science. My grandmother said they did lots of gramar in school, but they had fun doing art too. Har books had no coloured pictures. Somtimes no pictures at all! They made glue out of flour and water. For my cothes I would ware things my brother grew out of. Thesse were saved at school cothes. The kids chaged there cothes when they got home and had to work on the farm. If kids were close to the school house they would walk. Form far away, they rode on horse back in the winter in a little house built over a large selid. This was pulled by horses. This was called a caboose. There were little stoves in the caboues to keep people warm. I also saw some of this on a T.V program on the history chanel.

Hi Jessica,
I really enjoyed your journal about living in pioneer times. How wonderful, that you were able to talk to your grandmother to learn more about these times. It sounds like they had to study alot of subjects that are the same as we study. You mentioned 'grammar' as one subject. Do you know what she was learning? We study grammar too, but we call it something different. Do you know what we call it?
I'm glad that the TV documentary was so interesting and showed some of the things we had been studying. Do you think the caboose would be a very safe way to get to school? Lots of change and lots to think about!
Well done Jessica!

Mrs. Marcolini

My two friends and I have to divide ten cookies evenly between us. So we pased them out one by one. We each got three cookies but there was one left over. We try breaking it in three equal peices. So we each got one third and the desmae was .33. When we doubled the recipe it looked like this

1 cup butter (2 cups)
¾ cup brown sugar (1½ cups)
½ cup white sugar (1 cups)
1 tsp. Vanilla (2 tsp)
1½ cups flour (3 cups)
1 tsp salt (2 tsp)
1 tsp. baking soda (2 tsp)

Journal Entry Ideas for Mathematics

These writing suggestions may be passed on to students.

- "Write what you would say if you were explaining to another student how to add 24 to 5."

- "How would you explain to another student the difference between adding and subtracting?"

- "Why is 109 larger than 9?"

- "In what other school subject do you have to add or subtract? Why?"

- "You and two of your friends are going to your house after school for juice and chocolate chip cookies. Explain how you can divide 10 cookies evenly among all of you. Write out your answer in words. Read (or reread) Pat Hutchins's *The Doorbell Rang* (New York: HarperTrophy, 1989) and act it out with your classmates. Then, find a recipe for chocolate chip cookies and write it out in your journal. (You might get help at home when writing this journal entry.) Pretend you are having a party, and that you need twice as many cookies as the recipe will make. Double every ingredient in the recipe. Show your work."

Journal Entry Ideas for Science

In a science unit on sound, students might answer the following questions in their journals to demonstrate their learning:

- "How are sounds produced?"

- "How do we hear sounds?"
- "How are sounds different from one another? In other words, why is the buzz of a saw different from the bang of a hammer?"

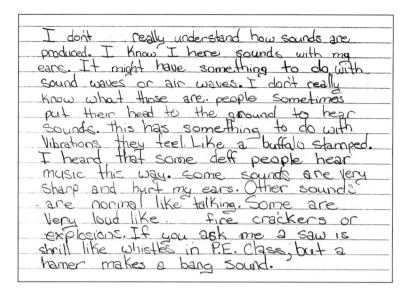

I don't really understand how sounds are produced. I Know I here sounds with my ears. It might have something to do with sound waves or air waves. I don't really know what those are. people Sometimes put their head to the ground to hear sounds. this has something to do with Vibrations they feel. Like a buffalo stamped. I heard that some deff people hear music this way. some sounds are very Sharp and hurt my ears. Other sounds are normal like talking. Some are Very loud like fire crackers or explosions. If you ask me a saw is shrill like whistles in P.E. Class, but a hamer makes a bang sound.

Visual Representation

Drawings, paintings, illustrations, and collages (which can be created from cut-out pictures) are ways students might demonstrate their personal understanding of texts read, viewed, listened to, or discussed. The teacher might ask content-related questions that students respond to in visual form, or provide guidelines that students can use to frame their representations. For example, teachers might require students to visually represent the main idea in a film (image, video, story, or speech), and add what they learned to their representation.

If vocabulary development is an important facet of the activity, the teacher would have students label their pictures with words, phrases, or sentences as captions. Students could also write short summary paragraphs to show their understanding of a text.

(Adapted from Sadler 2001, 71)

The teacher might assess the visual representation and summary paragraph with the student to ensure the representation of main ideas. If a visual is incomplete or inaccurate, the teacher might have the student re-examine the text, access additional information, and adjust the visual representation accordingly.

Students with strong spatial intelligence learn concepts and organize and represent their learning best through images.

There were sheep and chickens behind the barn. Altogether there were 14 legs. Please show how many could have been sheep and how many chickens.

$$2+2+2=6 \quad 4+4=8$$
$$6+8=14$$

There would be three chickens & two sheep.

Group Investigation

Group investigation is a good strategy to use in inquiry-based learning. Every student is responsible for some part of the information to be learned in language arts, science or social studies, or another subject area. In this way, a large amount of information can be covered. Students read, study, and research their portion of the material on a topic, and prepare written notes for an oral presentation. To learn about other aspects of the topic, students listen to presentations of their peers.

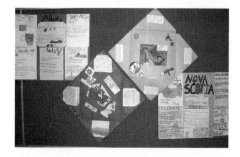

Implementing a Group Investigation

1. The teacher assigns students to groups of no more than six members.

2. Together, the class brainstorms elements of the main topic that might be covered in a unit of study. The teacher maps or webs the brainstormed ideas into subtopics. For example, in social studies, a main topic such as Canadian geography might be divided into regions of Canada as subtopics.

3. Each group chooses a subtopic related to the main topic, and each group member selects a small portion of that subtopic.

4. With teacher guidance, group members conduct appropriate research and report to their groups to be sure their portion has been well covered.

5. Each group then presents its information to the whole class.

6. The teacher assesses the accuracy of the content presented to the class and may also assess the students' ability to do oral presentations.

(Adapted from Sadler 2001, 19)

Assessment BLM 4: Me as Part of a Group
Assessment BLM 5: Checklist for My Research Report
Assessment BLM 11: How Did You Do with Your Report?
Assessment BLM 12: Presenting Our Report—How Did We Do?

SQRQCQ Strategy

The SQRQCQ strategy supports learning in mathematics.

The SQRQCQ strategy is modelled on the Survey, Question, Read, Recite, Review (SQ3R) strategy (see Chapter 2: Reading Comprehension: Strategies That Work). It is specifically designed to help students solve word problems in mathematics by

- guiding their reading
- providing a plan to find out what the problem is asking, which information is important, and what process to use to solve the problem

- asking students to "think about their thinking" and whether their solution makes sense

(Adapted from Barton 2002, citing Fay 1965)

To serve as student reference, teachers might post a wall chart outlining the steps in this strategy.

The SQRQCQ Strategy

Survey: Quickly read the problem to get the gist of it.

Question: Ask, "What is this problem asking me to do?"

Reread: Reread the problem carefully to find the essential facts, details, and other information.

Question: Question how to solve the problem. "What math operations are needed and in what order do I do them?" "Do I draw a model or picture to help me solve the problem?"

Compute: Do the computations, or come up with a solution to the problem.

Question: Ask yourself if the answer or solution seems to be correct. "Does the answer make sense?" "Is the answer reasonable?"

S
Q
R
Q
C
Q

Implementing SQRQCQ

1. The teacher models the strategy with a word problem. (I do it.) Students then carry out the steps under teacher guidance. (We do it.) Students solve the word problem in pairs. (You do it, in pairs.)

2. Next, the teacher models the strategy with a new problem. (I do it again.) Students carry out the steps under teacher guidance. (We do it.) They then use the strategy independently. (You do it.)

3. The teacher repeats the process with students as needed.

4. The teacher might periodically ask students to write an explanation of their thinking to solve the problem.

(Adapted from Barton 2002)

Assessment BLM 13: Math Problem-Solving Rubric

INSERT Strategy

INSERT (Interactive Notation System for Effective Reading and Thinking) is a comprehension monitoring system in the form of an interactive formalized activity. It is a way to encourage active reading and critical thinking.

As students read, they place sticky notes on the text to mark their reactions to specific parts. Effective teachers gradually introduce the INSERT strategy to students, beginning with the check mark (✓) and the X, and then moving on to the asterisk (*), and so on. Eventually, students learn that two notations can even be used for the same idea (Vaughan and Estes 1986, 138).

Using a strategy such as INSERT allows students to begin to understand how to "insert" their ideas, raise questions, argue or disagree with the text, acknowledge surprise, and so on.

After much use in the classroom (individually or in pairs), the teacher may turn the INSERT strategy into a card game, which will eventually require no teacher guidance and can be played by large groups of students. The procedure might be scripted on a wall chart for student reference.

Implementing the INSERT Strategy Card Game

1. Students meet in groups of six in the reading area. They arrange themselves in a circle, either on the floor or around a table.
2. The dealer (students take turns in this role) gives each group member one set of seven cards, as follows:

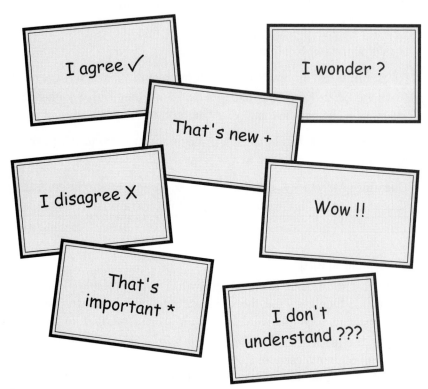

(Adapted from Vaughan and Estes 1986, 138)

3. The dealer then reads aloud a section of a content-area text. As students experience a response to the passage read, they put down a card from their deck to signal their desire to share.
4. The dealer goes around the circle, acknowledging each statement, comment, or question (according to the response card in front of the student) and asking that student to elaborate.
5. After each response, the student who shared picks up the card and places it back in his or her deck. The dealer monitors the discussion, and then someone else becomes the dealer and reads the next section in the text.
6. The process repeats until the whole text is read.

Developing Content-Area Writing Abilities

The writing demands of each subject area are different. Writing up a science experiment is different from writing a mathematics problem. Writing a story is different from writing an informational piece (non-

Not only do students need to use writing as a means of learning, but they also need to learn how to write subject-specific content, whether it be a math problem or a research report.

fiction) on the life cycle of a butterfly. Collecting and organizing information for a research report may be a similar task in several content areas, but the structure and style of the report may vary from one subject to another. Each subject has its specialized vocabulary, text structures (patterns), style, and formats, and follows a different logic in presentation.

Students find it interesting to write and illustrate their own informational books about what they are learning. To learn from a model, they can use an author's organization, patterns, and structures, and incorporate some of the vocabulary and phrasing.

Other suggestions for learning how to write content include

- paragraph frames
- writing sentences for pictures
- writing about art
- writing inspired by music
- integrating subject areas
- note taking
- report writing

Paragraph Frames

Based on the cloze procedure (see Chapter 2: Reading Comprehension: Strategies That Work), paragraph frames are a guided reading activity and writing activity that apply to informational text. They are designed to improve reading comprehension through use of text structures, connectives, and transition words. Paragraph frames are also an excellent way to help students learn to paraphrase information for report writing.

To construct a frame, the teacher provides a complete sentence at the beginning, follows it with relevant signal words and phrases, and concludes with a complete sentence. An example follows.

In 1981, the Canadarm was finished and had its first flight on the space shuttle *Columbia*. It was soon being used for two things: _____ and _____. Just like a human arm, this robot arm has _____. The "hand" at the end of the "arm" can lift _____. Since 1981, there has been a Canadarm on every space mission that has been flown by the United States outside of the earth's atmosphere. (Hughes 2002, 74)

Implementing Paragraph Frames

1. The teacher displays the frame and shows the students how to complete it by reading the text and filling in the blanks with them. While completing the frame, the teacher models the thinking process by using think-alouds.

2. Students read another paragraph or selection, preferably one with the same text structure, under teacher guidance.

3. In pairs or independently, students use the completed text frames as guides to comprehension or recall.

4. Eventually, students move from writing directly on the frames to writing paragraphs in their own words. They can also add information from other texts and from prior knowledge. Some students may choose to add illustrations to their compositions.

Writing Sentences for Pictures

Another effective way to develop content-area writing abilities is to capture the meaning of pages in wordless picture books. In language arts, students might learn to write descriptions of characters or to capture the action in a storyline. Using wordless nonfiction books, individual posters, or pictures, students in pairs might talk-to-learn to determine the meaning of the visual information on each page, or in each picture. They can then write summary sentences or short paragraphs to record their understandings.

This strategy is ideal for expanding students' experience from writing sentences to writing paragraphs, using organizational patterns such as description, sequence, compare and contrast, problem and solution, and cause and effect. Students may have initially learned these patterns through such activities as writing paragraph frames (see the preceding strategy).

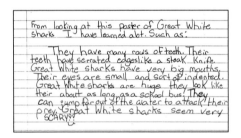

From looking at this poster of Great White sharks I have learned a lot. Such as:

They have many rows of teeth. Their teeth have serrated edges like a steak knife. Great White sharks have very big mouths. Their eyes are small and sort of indented. Great White sharks are huge they look like their about as long as a school bus! They can jump far out of the water to attack their prey. Great White sharks seem very SCARY!!

I had a problem because I had no place at home to do my homework. When I didn't do my homework, I got into trouble at school. I asked my mother what to do. She said you have to figure out how to solve that. But I will give you a hint. Clean up and organize your room. When I did I found a corner big enough to put an old desk that was in the basement. My problem is solved. Now my problem is I have no excuse and I have to do my homework.

Writing Pattern	Sample Prompt
Sequence	Write out the steps in planting a garden.
Description	Describe a spider.
Compare and Contrast	Write about the similarities and differences between cars and trucks.
Problem and Solution	Write about a problem you had and how you solved it.
Cause and Effect	Write about what causes plants to grow and what happens to plants when they lack these things.

It is important for teachers to first assess students' knowledge of these patterns. One way to obtain an authentic assessment is to have students write in each type of pattern based on a prompt.

On the basis of students' needs, the teacher explains and models the text structures or patterns (and cue words to signal each pattern).

Writing About Art

Art is often used in integrated units to improve students' comprehension of a concept or idea. Art can also be used to represent an understanding of concepts learned and to maintain motivation and interest in the work of an integrated unit. Teachers need to remember, though, that art must also be used to enhance students' understanding of art itself. Students might write about pieces of artwork, placing an emphasis on both cognitive and affective responses. Reproductions of paintings, sketches, or pieces of sculpture, whether created by a known or local artist, or by students themselves, can serve as the texts for art lessons or integrated units. Students might write a review in role as a newspaper art critic. They could capitalize on their spatial intelligence and other multiple literacies, or work to improve them through this activity.

Implementing Art-Inspired Writing

1. The teacher shows students a reproduction, piece of artwork, or sculpture, and provides some background information on the artist.
2. Students are prompted to study the piece with their eyes—for colour, feeling, interpretation, or any story or message it may elicit.
3. The teacher invites students to think about and respond to questions such as the following:
   - "What do you see?"
   - "How does this piece make you feel?"
   - "What do you think of the colours in this piece?"
   - "What message or story do you see in the piece?"
   - "What do you think the artist visualized when he or she created this piece?"
   - "What connections can you make between this piece and other learning in this subject (or integrated unit)?"
4. Students then form groups to discuss what they have written. Alternatively, they might create individual illustrations of their interpretation of the art viewed.

(Adapted from Olson and Homan 1993, 102–03)

Writing Inspired by Music

Music, too, can be used to stimulate students' writing. The teacher might ask students to listen to a piece of music, and then to illustrate their feelings by using felt pens, pencil crayons, or paint.

Alternatively, students might write content-area poems or songs. They need to review what they have been learning, or do more research, to make their creative work not only correct, but also alive

An effective and enjoyable way to improve students' understanding of science, mathematics, or social studies concepts or processes is to ask them to write a poem or a rap outlining what they have learned.

with detail. Writing a poem, song, or rap works well as a whole-class activity. Students select a concept, idea, or topic, such as changing from a tadpole to a frog (metamorphosis). The class brainstorms words and phrases to use and the teacher writes them on chart paper or the board. The students and teacher then arrange the words and phrases according to a simple rhyme scheme, song pattern, or beat (for rap), deleting or adding words to fit the melody or pattern. Often, understanding achieved in this way remains in memory for many, many years!

Check It Out!

W.M. Anderson and J.E. Lawrence. *Integrating Music into the Elementary Classroom, 6th ed.* (Belmont, CA: Wadsworth Thomson Learning, 2005). This resource also includes a CD.

From Poem to Rap: "Rappit the Frog"

What follows is an example of a content-area rap. Students need to play with the piece orally to get the beat; some words are held, others are cut short. Also, some phrases or sentences are sped up. A good way to start is to record the beat onto a tape recorder and play it while saying the rap. The way the piece is rapped orally is part of the creative process.

To be rapped to the continuous beat of
Boom, Boom-ching
Boom-Boom-Boom ... Ching
The *Boom, Boom* of the first line is equivalent in pace to the *Boom-Boom-Boom* of the second line.

Meta-Metamorph ...
(Boom ... Boom-ching)

Meta-morph-o-sis.
(Boom-Boom-Boom ... Ching.)

What does ... it mean?
(Boom ... Boom-ching)

Come on ... Come clean.
(Boom-Boom-Boom ... Ching.)

Starts with the egg.
Hatch into a tadpole.
Tadpole with a tail.
It's a tail of a tadpole.
Looks like a fish and
Swims with the otter
Breathes with gills and
Feeds on plants in water.
Two. Two weeks
Go, go, go ... by.
Loses its tail.
Gone, gone, gone ... jump!

Legs, back legs,
Front legs grow too.
Air. Swallows air,
With its lung times two.
It's, it's a what?
Frog, frog, frog ... hop.
Hops on land.
C'mon give 'em a hand.
The pond is its crib
Where it has its rugs,
Puts on a bib and
Eats all the bugs.
After some grub it
Sheds the skin it had
In its home
Called the "Lily Pad."
When it is time
Its eggs are laid
Then they hatch and
You know what they played?
Meta-Metamorph ...
Metamorphosis.

(Gordon and Gordon 2004)

An alternative is to have students write a song about content they have learned in an integrated unit or subject area. Motivation and participation tends to be high since many students enjoy or are at least familiar with nursery rhymes, poems, and simple songs associated with specific events. Students with musical and linguistic intelligence might serve as leaders for this activity.

(Adapted from Olson and Homan 1993, 103–04)

Integrating Subject Areas

Content-area writing abilities are readily developed on authentic tasks when subjects are integrated. When students are able to make connections among several content areas, writing becomes easier and more enjoyable.

Suggested Activity for Integrating Physical Education, Music, and Language Arts

Topic: Staying fit and active for life

1. Using a good picture of the outdoors (e.g., camping, whitewater rafting, fishing) and what you have been learning in physical education about being active to stay healthy, write a short poem that has no rhyme (free verse).

2. Write another poem that can be put to music or sung to a familiar jingle or nursery rhyme.

3. Shape the poem (by adding or taking away words) to fit the tune.

4. Be prepared to present your poem or jingle to the class.

(T. Gordon 2004, adapted from Olson and Homan 1994)

Note Taking

Note taking is an important skill for report and essay writing. One way to explicitly teach note taking is to divide a chapter, a book, or a research assignment into several important subtopics (e.g., place names in each of the 10 provinces and territories, or Canadian animals, birds, and plants) within the main topic of study (origins of names in Canada). The teacher models note taking by teaching how to recognize main ideas and details (see Chapter 2: Reading Comprehension: Strategies That Work) and how to reword and paraphrase. Students then work in groups of three with each student taking notes on one of the subtopics. Students find several interesting facts or ideas on their subsection and write their information on sticky notes. The teacher prompts students to share their notes with other members of the group. Based on contributions of each member, the group compiles one set of notes to share with the whole class.

(Adapted from Marshall 1999)

A graphic organizer can help students to record information gathered from various sources.

My notes on _____
                    Topic
Important Main Ideas (in my own words):
1. _____
2. _____
3. _____
Important Details (in my own words):
1. _____ 2. _____
3. _____ 4. _____
5. _____ 6. _____
7. _____ 8. _____
9. _____ 10. _____

Quotations: (Provide the author's exact words, the author's name, title of the text, and the page number on which the quotation is found.)
Bibliography: (Author name, title of the text, date of publication, and the publisher's name, or give the Web site.)

Check It Out!

Jean Dreher et al. *Easy Steps to Writing Fantastic Research Reports* (New York: Scholastic Professional Books, 2000).

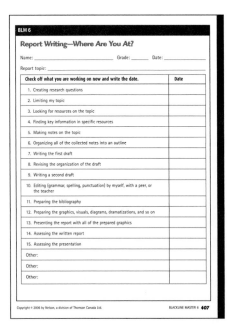

Following instruction on selecting main ideas and details, teachers introduce the RAAP note-taking strategy, which uses paraphrasing to improve comprehension and informational note taking.

The RAAP Strategy

Read the paragraph, or the text with which you are working.
Ask yourself, "What is the main idea in what I read?"
Ask yourself, "What are the important details?"
Put in writing the main idea and details in your own words.

(Adapted from Schumaker, Denton, and Deshler 1984)

Report Writing

Students need to learn how to prepare and present (in writing and orally) reports on topics they have been studying in the content areas or in integrated units. By guiding students through the research and writing stages of preparing a report, first through modelling, and then by scaffolding the process as they work collaboratively in groups, teachers lay the foundation for students to write individual reports.

Effective teachers use think-alouds to model for students how to summarize and paraphrase, and then provide many opportunities for students to practise the process through shared and guided writing sessions.

Teachers might then allow students to choose or assign to students working in small groups a subsection of a larger research question, instructing each group to research and write a report that will become part of a larger class report. Under teacher guidance, students compile the small-group reports into a class report and take turns orally presenting the class report to one another. Once students are comfortable researching, writing, and presenting whole-class or collaborative reports, they can then work with a partner and eventually on their own to assume responsibility for the entire process.

At every stage of the report-writing process, students must learn skills and strategies. A wall chart detailing the steps helps, as does a checklist handout (see BLM 6: Report Writing—Where Are You At?).

Planning, Preparing, and Presenting a Report

- **Narrow the topic.** Using a graphic organizer, subdivide a large topic into subtopics; brainstorm ideas and possible information to be collected.
- **Identify key questions.** Brainstorm questions from ideas, and then select two or three key questions to guide the research process.
- **Collect and organize information.** Identify and assess possible research materials (for example, encyclopedias, magazines, informational books, videotapes, experts, Web sites, CD-ROMs,

---

observations). Collect information using charts, jot notes, and so on, to answer each research question, maintaining a record of bibliographical information for all resources used. Then choose an organizational structure that will ensure the information is presented in a clear and interesting way.

- **Write, revise, and edit.** Prepare a rough draft, keeping in mind the audience and purpose for writing. Revise the draft based on peer and teacher feedback, and then edit the report for spelling, grammar, punctuation, and so on.

- **Add visuals.** Consider including charts, diagrams, models, illustrations, photographs, and so on.

- **Finalize the written report.** Include a bibliography.

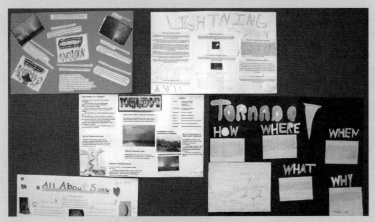

- **Rehearse the oral presentation.** Note key information on cue cards and collect suitable props, visuals, or models to integrate throughout the presentation. Videotape rehearsals to identify areas for improvement (self-assessment) or practise in front of a small group of classmates (peer assessment).

- **Present the report orally.** When reflecting on and assessing the oral presentation, teachers and students should consider audience enjoyment, presentation strengths, and what might be done differently next time to improve the presentation.

Chapter 3: Writing: The Reading–Writing Connection includes more information on the writing process and the traits that define good writing, in addition to checklists and rubrics for students and teachers.

Developing Skills for Learning, Remembering, and Studying Content

In many content areas, students have no prior personal experience with the content to be learned; thus, it is important that it be developed progressively to serve as a knowledge base for further learning.

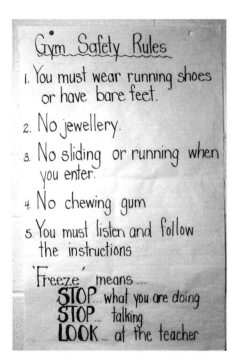

Gym Safety Rules

1. You must wear running shoes or have bare feet.
2. No jewellery.
3. No sliding or running when you enter.
4. No chewing gum
5. You must listen and follow the instructions

'Freeze' means...
STOP... what you are doing
STOP... talking
LOOK... at the teacher

Effective teachers use several techniques to review content with students and to show them how to remember information. The more learners understand and remember, the easier it will be to understand additional content.

"Read and Do" in Physical Education

In physical education, learning takes place through action and body movement, but also through the mind. In fact, mind and body are inseparable in physical education (Landers, Maxwell, Butler, and Fagen 2001, 343–50).

Upper elementary students more readily remember plays, steps, and games in a variety of sports if they are given basic instruction sheets to help them learn the content. Such sheets also teach them to follow instructions as in procedural writing (Manzo, Manzo, and Estes 2001). Instructional sheets will especially benefit students with linguistic intelligence who may have difficulty with a primary emphasis on kinesthetic intelligence.

Games to Review Content for Recall

Because games are so engaging for students, they should be used in all content areas to review information for recall purposes, and to assess students' understanding of specific information for reteaching purposes.

Although games require setting up teams, clarifying rules, and score keeping, they can be kept simple. For example, the teacher could divide the class into two teams and award one point for each correct answer. Alternatively, games to review content could be based on popular quiz-show formats, and students, perhaps working in pairs, might help to write some of the questions. However, effective teachers ensure that questions are not limited to just straight recall of facts. It is important to develop questions that involve higher-level thinking skills, such as inferring, evaluating, hypothesizing, analyzing, synthesizing, and critical thinking.

Chapter 2: Reading Comprehension: Strategies That Work includes detailed information on generating and answering questions, as well as question types.

Circle-Seat-Centre

This strategy accommodates and strengthens linguistic intelligence, spatial intelligence, and kinesthetic intelligence. It allows students to review material individually and in groups (hence, also involving interpersonal and intrapersonal intelligence). It is similar to the use of learning centres.

Implementing Circle-Seat-Centre

1. The teacher directs students to read or reread a text and, based on student needs, then divides the class into three groups. Each group is assigned to one of the following: Circle, Seat, or Centre.

- The Circle group works through the readings/content with teacher help.
- The Seat group works independently or with peers on study sheets or specific learning activities.
- The Centre group, individually or with peers, works on a project related to the information covered.

2. Students rotate to one of the other three groups after a given amount of time. In this way, students review content through a number of differentiated means.

(Adapted from Sadler 2001, 16)

Concept Maps as Review and Study Aids

Concept maps, whether they are called semantic maps, mind maps, or something else, are excellent ways for students to

- read for the essential concepts in texts
- find the relationships among the important ideas
- review and study

Concept mapping improves both comprehension and recall. It is a good idea for students to complete a concept map

- before reading to present all the information they know or have learned from a brainstorming session
- during reading to complete the map with information as they understand it and to add more subtopics and ideas
- after reading or rereading to add information they may have missed earlier or may have learned in discussion with peers

Before

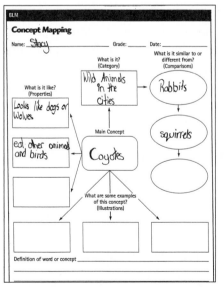

During

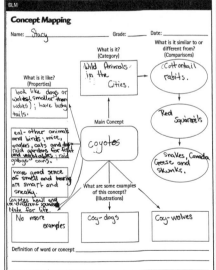

After

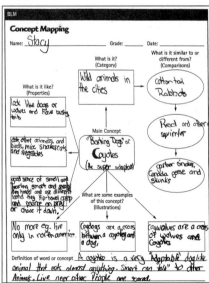

The maps then become excellent resources for whole-class discussion and still more information on the topic. They serve as notes for writing reports, oral presentation props, and review and study aids to help prepare students for more formal tests. In the absence of concept maps, most students do little more than reread whole selections.

(Adapted from Santa 1993, 245–62)

For more detailed information on concept and semantic mapping, see Chapter 1: Oral Language: Speaking, Listening, and Learning, and Chapter 2: Reading Comprehension: Strategies That Work.

Developing Critical and Media Literacy

Students should use their critical literacy skills

Critical literacy is looking at everyday things with "new eyes or new lenses" in the subject areas. It is "using text to get something done in this world."

HEFFERNAN 2004, VII

- when reading stories or watching films and videos
- when reading informational texts that may present a particular perspective on certain issues, or portray certain characters or events in ways students do not agree with or may question
- to analyze news reports and advertisements
- during writing in the content areas, to analyze the connection between personal lives and social structures

(Heffernan 2004)

The expanded meaning of text suggests that many different kinds of texts, including magazines, newspapers, videos, and the Internet, will be used in the classroom. Such texts increase the number of issues that may be faced and provide opportunities for discussions that will improve students' ability to become critically literate.

For more information on critical literacy, see Chapter 2: Reading Comprehension: Strategies That Work and Chapter 3: Writing: The Reading–Writing Connection.

Developing Critical Literacy

Critical literacy is the process of examining, questioning, and critiquing content-area texts and issues for multiple or different interpretations. Such literacy can be applied to any message delivered in any format—informational books, story books, documentaries, magazines, TV and magazine ads, pamphlets, action figures, posters, T-shirts, lunch boxes, hats, and political speeches (Thoman 2003).

Questioning is an effective starting point for promoting critical literacy in the classroom.

What to Ask About Any Media Message

Students first need to learn to ask these Five Key Questions about any media text:

1. Who created this message?

2. What techniques are used to attract my attention?

3. How might different people understand this message differently from me?

4. What lifestyles, values, and points of view are represented in, or omitted from, this message?

5. Why was this message sent?

(Center for Media Literacy 2005, 7)

I think the ending should be diffrent because girls today have jobs like teachers, bankers and they work in different kinds of stores. Or at home or going to the mall they wear jeans and mini Skirts.

Teachers might also ask more specific types of questions. Some examples follow:

- "What other kind of person could be a Cinderella?"
- "Why are boys often described as brave and strong? Can girls be brave and strong, too?"
- "What do we learn when we read *The Paper Bag Princess* by Robert Munsch (Toronto: Annick Press, 1980)?"
- "What is the problem with promoting $200 gifts for each member of a family?"
- "What causes pollution and how can we stop polluting the environment in today's society? How would that change our lives? Who has the power to pollute? Who has the power to stop pollution?"

Questions asked incidentally during the reading of texts on various topics might require students to put themselves in others' shoes, to take a different perspective, or to reposition themselves. Questioning can be used as a prompt to critical writing, especially after reading a text involving social issues (see BLM 7: Stepping Back from the Book). Critical writing could be about constructing or hypothesizing different endings to stories and other texts. For example, students might be asked to rewrite a fairy tale, or draw a different character for a story, explaining why that character should be different.

It is important for teachers to choose books on topics studied in the curriculum and on themes not too controversial to read aloud or to recommend for independent reading to students in a particular age group or in a particular community.

Books That Develop Critical Literacy

Books by and for young people

Cover Me by M. Tamaki (Toronto: McGilligan Books, 2000)

Crazy by B. Lebert (Vancouver, WA: Vintage International, 2000)

The Outsiders by S.E. Hinton (New York: Prentice Hall, 1997)

Yo Alejandro by A. Gac-Artogas, 2nd English edition (Fairview, NJ: Ediciones Nuevo Esacio, 1987)

Books that examine social issues

Ashok by Any Other Name by S. Yamate (Chicago: Polychrome Publications, 1992)

Check It Out!

An example of a six-session lesson guide to help teachers structure conversations on racial issues can be found in Chapter 3 of *Getting Beyond "I Like the Book": Creating Space for Critical Literacy in K–6 Classrooms* by Vivian Vasquez (Newark, DE: International Reading Association, 2003). The lessons deal with issues related to race and power using the picture book *Whitewash* by Ntozake Shange (New York: Walker and Company, 1997).

Another excellent teacher resource for developing critical literacy is Lee Heffernan's *Critical Literacy and Writer's Workshop: Bringing Purpose and Passion to Student Writing* (Newark, DE: International Reading Association, 2004), which includes sample writing lessons.

CML MediaLit Kit (Santa Monica, CA: Center for Media Literacy, 2005).

Bloomers by R. Blumberg (New York: Aladdin Publishers, 1996)

The Bobbin Girl by E.A. McCully (New York: Dial Publishers, 1996)

The Day the Earth Was Silent by M. McGufee (Bloomington, IN: Inquiring Voices Press, 1997)

Just Juice by K. Hesse (New York: Scholastic, 1998)

Our Brother Has Down's Syndrome by S. Cairo, J. Cairo, and T. Cairo (Chicago: Firefly, 1989)

Passage to Freedom: The Sugihara Story by K. Mochizuki (New York: Lee and Low, 1997)

Sarah, Plain and Tall by P. MacLachan (New York: HarperTrophy, 1987)

Whitewash by N. Shange, illustrated by M. Sporn (New York: Walker and Company, 1997)

Your Move by E. Bunting (New York: Harcourt Brace, 1992)

Books that describe social action

The Bus Ride by W. Miller (New York: Lee & Low, 1998)

Click, Clack, Moo: Cows That Type by D. Cronin (New York: Simon & Schuster, 2000)

Kids on Strike by S. Bartoletti (Boston: Houghton Mifflin, 1999)

Sweet Dried Apples: A Vietnamese Wartime Childhood by R. Breckler (Boston: Houghton Mifflin, 1996)

Books to prompt discussions about racism, power, and control

Follow the Leader by V. Winslow (New York: Delacorte Press, 1997)

Just One Flick of a Finger by M. Loribiecki (New York: Dial, 1996)

So Far from the Sea by E. Bunting (New York: Clarion Books, 1998)

White Socks Only by E. Coleman (Morton Grove, IL: Albert Whitman, 1996)

BLM 7: Stepping Back from the Book

> *"Media education has been called the perfect curriculum: it's timely, it's multidisciplinary, it's easily assimilated into the classroom, and it promotes critical thinking skills."*
>
> RICK SHEPHERD, ASSOCIATION FOR MEDIA LITERACY

Developing Media Literacy

Media literacy is a form of critical literacy.

A medium is anything that communicates a message—all forms of print (such as books, newspapers, magazines, brochures, flyers, and posters), TV, film, video, popular music, comic books, billboards, works of art, computer software, the Internet, video games, toys, T-shirts, labels, fashion, and so on. Media literacy is the ability to understand, assess, and evaluate the hidden messages, the intentions, and the targeted audience of a message, as well as who profits, how they profit, and why they profit from the message. It also refers to the effective use of oral, print, visual, multimedia, and mass media to communicate messages.

Most students have much exposure to different forms of media. They need to make informed decisions based on understanding the role of images (and styles, personalities, promotional techniques) in the portrayal of products, issues, policies, and reality in general.

Advertising Techniques

An important part of media literacy is understanding how advertisers promote the sale of products. What follows is an alphabetical list of some of the many techniques that advertisers use. Brainstorming real-world examples as a class can serve as reference for students when they come to create their own advertisements.

- **Attractive, but Vague:** The ad promotes the product based on its beauty or appeal, but gives few or no details about its features and benefits.
- **Bandwagon:** The ad aims to persuade the consumer that everybody is doing it, buying it, or thinking a certain way.
- **Fantasy Appeal:** The ad promises that the product will free people from their ordinary lives, offering excitement, wealth, or glamour.
- **Fear:** The ad is designed to make consumers believe that there will be consequences to not buying or using the product (e.g., their home may not be protected from a burglar).
- **Health or Environmental Benefits:** The ad boasts all-natural ingredients or emphasizes specific advantages from using it (e.g., better health, more energy, improved environment, and so on).
- **Humour:** The ad is funny. It makes people laugh or chuckle using, for example, funny, cartoon-like talking characters.
- **Novelty:** The ad suggests that the product is new or unique in some way and is designed to make consumers want to be among the first to have it.
- **Patriotism:** The ad wants consumers to believe that by buying the product, they are supporting a certain country, state, province, or territory.
- **Plain Folks:** Ordinary, honest, hardworking people are presented in the ad to make consumers believe that those using the product or believing in the idea are just average people like they are.
- **Price Appeal:** The ad promises buyers something free or at a discounted price (e.g., buy one, get another for half price).
- **Pride:** The ad appeals to consumers' desire to be more attractive, more popular, more fashionable.
- **Product Character:** The ad promotes the product based on all its good qualities.
- **Product Comparison:** Two similar, competing products are compared, leaving the audience with the impression that one or the other is better.
- **Product Slogan or Jingle:** The ad uses a familiar tune and recognizable jingle to sell a product.

Check It Out!

Media Awareness Network
http://www.media-awareness.ca

Media Education Foundation
http://www.mediaed.org/ and
http://www.mediaed.org/studyguides
(The above two Web sites offer critical media-viewing activities and study guides. The foundation also manages the Adbusters site and sponsors the Canadian Adbusters magazine.)

Media Ownership Chart
http://www.thenation.com/special/bigten.html

National Film Board
http://www.nfb.ca/e/

"Using Rubrics to Assess Media Work in the Classroom" by C.M. Worsnop
http://www.media-awareness.ca/english/resources/educational/teaching_backgrounders/media_literacy/using_rubrics.cfm

Check It Out!

D. Considine and G. Haley. *Visual Messages: Integrating Imagery to Instruction* (Englewood, CO: Teacher Idea Press, 1992).

C.M. Worsnop. *Screening Images: Ideas for Media Education* (Mississauga, ON: Wright Communications, 1999).

P.H. Hinchley. "A Crash Course in Media Literacy." *The Clearing House* 76.6 (July/August 2003): 295–97.

- **Repetition:** The ad repeats a message or tune so many times that it tends to stick in the mind.
- **Science and Statistics:** The ad suggests there is scientific evidence to prove that the product is better, or that more people like and use it.
- **Slice of Life:** The ad suggests that the product is somehow the basis of positive relationships with others. For example, the ad might show a loving couple, happy children, generous neighbours, or cheerful co-workers connecting in a positive way because of the product.
- **Status Appeal:** The ad appeals to consumers' desire to be special or better than everyone else.
- **Testimonials/Celebrity Approval:** Famous or popular people are used to promote a product as a way of convincing consumers to buy it.
- **Urgency:** The ad suggests that it is critical for consumers to act right away or they will miss out somehow (e.g., a limited-time or last-chance offer, a limited supply, and so on).

To assist students in thinking critically about the media, teachers need to ensure that students understand

- the nature of each medium
- how the media are produced
- what audience is being targeted

Raising the right questions in each category helps students to become media literate.

Understanding the Medium

Each specific medium has its own elements and forms that give meaning. For example, film uses sound effects, lighting, movement, different camera angles, and characters to carry meaning to the viewer. Visual art uses line, colour, shape, texture, size/scale, and perspective to convey meaning. Students need to determine

- the kind of medium
- how the medium communicates or tells a story
- what basic elements (e.g., colour, jingle) express its meaning
- what the obvious message is
- what the hidden message is
- what has been left out and why

Understanding How the Media Are Produced

Students need the opportunity to produce their own media. When students write advertisements, scripts, or newspaper articles, or make digitalized videos and storyboards, they come to understand the message that is played out. Producing their own messages is a hands-on way to understand how and why different media are put together. To develop their understanding of how a producer's choice of elements affects the video, photograph, or article, students need to consider

- who made or produced the piece

- where and why it was made
- what values or ideas the producer wanted the audience to see
- the relationship between the text and the intention of the piece
- the role language plays in the message the producer wants to convey
- how price affects the choice of medium and what it cost to produce the work
- how they might produce a similar work (e.g., what elements—sound effects, setting, and so on— would they include)

Understanding the Target Audience

Media works are designed to reach a target audience; that is, a specific group of people. Understanding the way each media work targets audiences will help students to better evaluate the messages, biases, and values in the works.

The intended audience determines how a movie, ad, or CD is produced. Different audiences will understand each work differently depending on their age, gender, beliefs, values, experiences, backgrounds, and critical literacy abilities. For example, teenagers will have a different understanding of, and response to, a song meant for young children. Knowing the characteristics of various audiences helps a media producer target a specific audience, or gear the work to a wider range of audiences.

Students need to determine

- the target audience for the piece (e.g., classmates, friends, relatives, pet owners, seniors)
- the elements of the piece that suggest the target audience
- what makes the piece appealing to the intended audience
- the technique used to get the audience's attention
- how the producer wanted the audience to feel
- what changes would make the piece appeal to a different audience
- whose point of view is presented and whose is omitted

Teachers might introduce students to critical media literacy by examining advertisements on television, in magazines, catalogues, flyers, posters, and on video and CD jackets. Advertisements can be analyzed first as a group, and then individually—with prompts if necessary (see BLM 2: Analyzing Television and Magazine Advertisements).

BLM 2: Analyzing Television and Magazine Advertisements

Representing or Producing Media Texts

After analyzing and assessing several advertisements with students, effective teachers involve students in producing media texts. Students could redesign an advertisement that they analyzed earlier, or invent a new product. They could begin by brainstorming what to invent, such as a bicycle that never needs repair, or an item of clothing that is never out of fashion. They could then write a magazine advertisement and illustrate it using one or more of the advertising techniques listed earlier in this chapter.

"Tell volunteers exactly what is expected of them and students."

TINGLEY 2001, 53

"Provide many opportunities for children to read during everyday activities. Let your child help cook by reading recipes and make crafts using directions. Read the newspaper together to find sales, to see how your favorite sports team is doing, or to enjoy the comics. Read about where you are going on vacation before you visit. Leave your child notes and send him cards."

INTERNATIONAL READING ASSOCIATION, *WHAT IS FAMILY LITERACY?*

Developing Home–School–Community Partnerships

It is important to partner with others when developing students' literacy across the curriculum. In particular, parents are the volunteers with the largest vested interest in their children's education. Their interest in and support of learning that occurs in the school means the "formal" learning does not stop when students exit the school building every day. In a reciprocal relationship, this continuity underlines for children that their parents place value on what is being learned in all subject areas. Parents demonstrate this not only when they volunteer in the classroom but also when they help their children with learning at home.

Effective teachers closely incorporate the assistance of paraprofessionals and volunteers (often parents) in the classroom and get to know their strengths. Putting their strengths to good use requires organization and detailed planning. For example, paraprofessionals often work hand in hand with the teacher in interdisciplinary/themed units; they handle specific activities assigned to them under the classroom teacher's supervision.

Although volunteers in schools are often parents, they may be high school, college, or university students interested in entering the teaching profession, or senior citizens who have expertise and free time to offer. Seniors, many of them retired teachers, may get involved in reading on various topics to students who are having difficulty with some of the informational materials or research. They may be able to share artifacts from previous decades, such as letters written during certain historical periods or important political events; look at and discuss an abacus or a slide rule for making calculations; examine early microscopes; talk about a pair of skates from the 1920s; or show a dress or a uniform worn many years ago.

In other collaborative learning situations, teachers may find it easy and useful to pair up students with buddies, both from their own grade and from higher and lower grades. The buddy system is most effective if the kinds of activities are mutually agreed upon by teachers and if the buddies have been taught how to work together. (See Chapter 5: In the Classroom: Making It Work for more information on buddies).

Enhancing Literacy Learning Through Home–School Links

There are many ways for teachers to establish home–school links to enhance the development of literacy learning across the curriculum. Some suggestions follow.

- Effective teachers invite parents to offer their expertise as guest speakers for themed units. Many parents possess a wealth of information and have expertise and talents in specific subject areas, including core subject areas and the arts. Teachers may also be able to capitalize on contributions from parents with different cultural and language backgrounds. For example, parents who speak the same language as ESL students may be able to help them work within the themed unit.

- Teachers might involve parents in shared reading of information books related to each interdisciplinary theme or integrated unit. They might also assemble related pamphlets, books, magazines, and newspaper articles for students to sign out to share with parents and siblings. Parents could read these to and with their children, and then document their follow-up discussions (see BLM 5: Literacy Home Links: KWLM Strategy Use at Home).

- At the end of a unit in the content areas, students might write their own personal comments and reflections on their work samples (Nelson 2003, 76–80). The samples of work, with the student's self-assessment annotations, could then be discussed during three-way conferences.

- Holding portfolio evenings allows students to communicate the story of their learning to their parents. These evenings are held on days other than interview days. After a student has given a portfolio presentation, parents might be asked to comment on one specific piece of work and on portfolio contents in general.

- Parents can be invited to respond to various forms or reports sent home. Students could write progress reports to take home, and then have parents respond and return them to school. Parents could also respond to questionnaires on students' interests and strengths. When each school year begins, parents could be asked to write a letter to the teacher commenting on their child's knowledge, interests, or learning in the content areas (Miller, 2003).

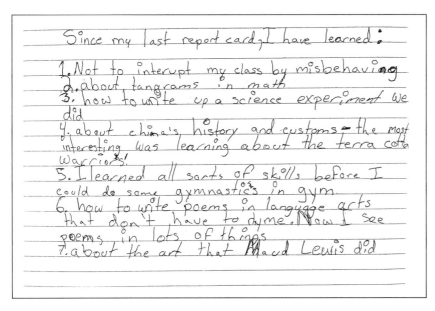

Since my last report card, I have learned:
1. Not to interupt my class by misbehaving
2. about tangrams in math
3. how to write up a science experiment we did
4. about china's history and customs - the most interesting was learning about the terra cotta warriors!
5. I learned all sorts of skills before I could do some gymnastics in gym.
6. how to write poems in language arts that don't have to rhyme. Now I see poems in lots of things
7. about the art that Maud Lewis did

- To maintain consistent literacy home links, it is a good idea to send a short newsletter home, outlining the work that is going to be done in the subject areas and describing work already completed and celebrated in the subject areas.

- Occasionally, teachers distribute to parents a calendar that outlines community events, television programs, and special events such as those in museums, science centres, arts centres, public libraries, and galleries, related to the themed unit under study. If field trips to 4-H events, concerts, local museums, botanical gardens, wetlands, and more are part of a unit plan, teachers might invite parents to accompany the students "to learn with them."

- Teachers might ask for parents' input when choosing themes for interdisciplinary units, and may create a reference list for students and parents to share on topics of study. This list would include fiction and nonfiction books, previewed Internet sites, films, and videos that parents and their children could read or view together. Parents might also be encouraged to add suitable items to the list.

Resources to Develop Home–School Links

The International Reading Association (IRA) has prepared numerous pamphlets, brochures, and larger resources to support family literacy. Copies of some of these can be downloaded from the Association's Web site at http://www.reading.org.

Pamphlets and Brochures

Family Literacy and the School Community: A Partnership for Lifelong Learning

I Can Read and Write! How to Encourage Your School-Age Child's Literacy Development

Library Safari: Tips for Parents of Young Readers and Explorers

Making the Most of Television: Tips for Parents of Young Viewers

Making the Reading–Writing Connection: Tips for Parents of Young Learners

Seeing the World on the Internet: Tips for Parents of Young Readers—and "Surfers"

Summer Reading Adventure! Tips for Parents of Young Readers

Books

Leslie Morrow, ed. *Family Literacy Connections in Schools and Communities.* (Newark, DE: International Reading Association, 1995).

Adele Thomas, Lynn Fazio, and Betty Stiefelmeyer. *Families at School: A Handbook for Parents.* (Newark, DE: International Reading Association, 1999).

See Chapter 5: In the Classroom: Making It Work for general information about what teachers might recommend to parents to support their children's learning and study habits.

BLM 5: Literacy Home Links: KWLM Strategy Use at Home
BLM 4: Literacy Home Links: How Families Can Support the "Talking" to "Reading and Writing" Connection in Chapter 1
BLM 4: Literacy Home Links: Home Reading in Chapter 2
BLM 5: Literacy Home Links: Choosing "Just Right" Books in Chapter 2
BLM 6: Literacy Home Links: Surfing the Net in Chapter 3
BLM 7: Literacy Home Links: Million-Dollar Words in Chapter 3
BLM 8: Literacy Home Links: Assessing Writing in Chapter 3
Assessment BLM 1: Literacy Home Links: Survey in Chapter 5
BLM 9: Literacy Home Links: Home Reading Program Log Sheet in Chapter 5
BLM 10: Literacy Home Links: News from Room ___ in Chapter 5
BLM 11: Literacy Home Links: Supporting Your Reader at Home in Chapter 6

Closing Thoughts

Content-area teachers have a direct role to play in the development of strategies that students need to be successful learners in all subject areas. As explored in this chapter, good teaching and learning practices across the curriculum encompass both visible and invisible dimensions. The visible dimension encompasses the explicit lessons on strategy development that help students to think and learn in the different subject areas. The invisible dimension is the dynamic underlying all of content learning. It is the understanding that strategy learning is as inseparable from content as the soul is invisible in the body (Vacca 2002, 184–204).

Both the visible and invisible aspects of teaching and learning across the curriculum have been incorporated into this chapter on developing multiple literacies across the curriculum. Teachers can help students use their multiple literacies to make sense of many kinds of texts and to represent knowledge via many kinds of texts to reach their learning goals in school and out of school.

Chapter 5: In the Classroom: Making It Work addresses how to make all this happen within the diversity and complexity of a classroom.

Chapter 4

BLACKLINE MASTERS

KWLRM Chart

Name: _____ Grade: _____ Date: _____

Topic: _____

K	What do I KNOW?

W	What do I WANT to know?

L	What have I LEARNED?

R	What is my REACTION?

M	What MORE do I want to know?

(Adapted from Mandeville 2000, 20–21)

Analyzing Television and Magazine Advertisements

Name: _____ Grade: _____ Date: _____

Medium: ❏ Television ❏ Magazine

What the ad is selling: _____

Target audience: _____

People in the ad: _____

What the people are doing: _____

Body language and facial expressions: _____

Setting: _____

Other actions in the ad: _____

Other objects in the ad: _____

Mood: _____

Jingle or song: _____

Language and catch phrases: _____

Sound effects: _____

Main message: _____

Advertising Techniques (Check all that apply and explain how you think each is used.)

❏ testimonial/celebrity approval
❏ bandwagon
❏ product comparison
❏ product character (qualities)
❏ product slogan/jingle
❏ repetition
❏ humour
❏ plain folks

❏ slice of life
❏ status appeal
❏ price appeal
❏ fear
❏ pride
❏ health or environmental benefits
❏ scientific or statistical evidence
❏ other: _____

Personal Response (Did the ad grab your interest? If so, how?) _____

_____

Persuasion Rating (circle one)

1	2	3	4	5
I'm asleep	Yawn	I'm somewhat interested	I like what I see/hear	I'm sold!

A Think Sheet for Comparing and Contrasting

Name: _____ Grade: _____ Date: _____

I will compare and contrast characteristics of _____

and _____.

Characteristic:	
Similarities (What is the same or alike?)	**Differences** (What is different?)

Characteristic:	
Similarities (What is the same or alike?)	**Differences** (What is different?)

Characteristic:	
Similarities (What is the same or alike?)	**Differences** (What is different?)

(Adapted from Raphael and Boyd 1997, 82)

Concept Mapping

Name: _____ Grade: _____ Date: _____

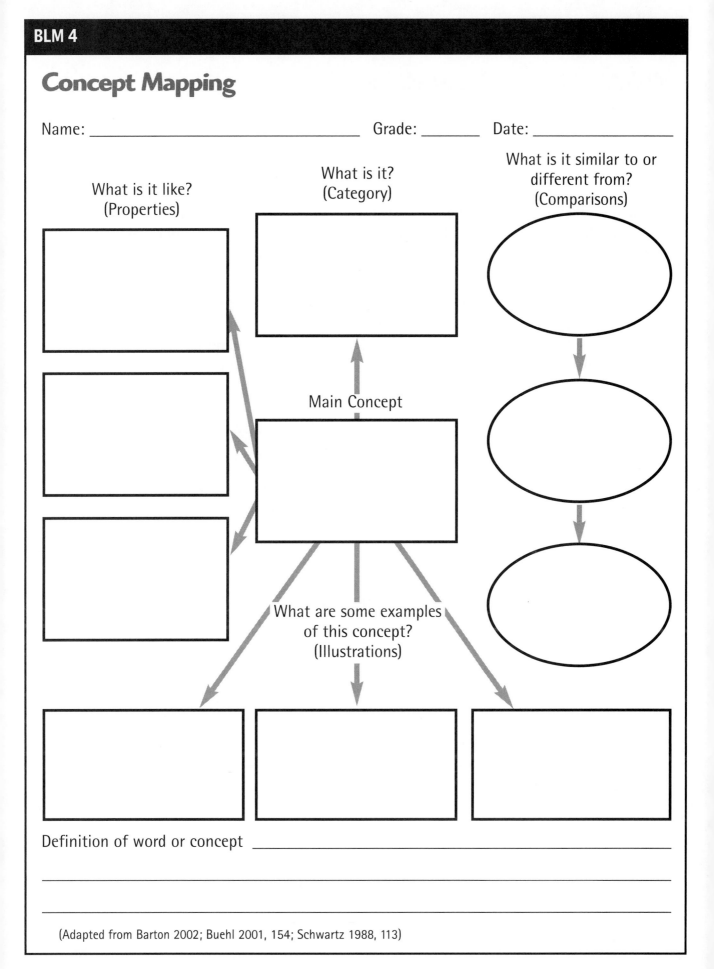

What is it like?
(Properties)

What is it?
(Category)

What is it similar to or
different from?
(Comparisons)

Main Concept

What are some examples
of this concept?
(Illustrations)

Definition of word or concept _____

_____

_____

(Adapted from Barton 2002; Buehl 2001, 154; Schwartz 1988, 113)

KWLM Strategy Use at Home

Date: _____

Dear Parents:

KWLM is a strategy that many teachers use to help students organize and remember information they have read or have had read to them. **K** stands for what your child already knows, **W** stands for what your child wants to know, **L** stands for what your child has learned, and **M** stands for what more your child still wants to learn. Your child is already familiar with this strategy from our work in the classroom.

You can help your child apply this strategy to connect information, to ask focusing questions, to learn to summarize, and to figure out what else he or she wants to know. When reading informational books together, use the guiding statements below and write down the comments made. Also, be sure to point out new things about the topic.

Sincerely,

- -

Name: _____ Grade: _____ Date: _____

We read _____ by _____

Before we began reading, you told me what you already **knew**. _____

_____

_____

You also told me that you had questions on the topic and what you **wanted** to learn. _____

_____

_____

After we finished reading, you told me the new things that you **learned**. _____

_____

_____

You also told me what **more** you wanted to learn. _____

_____

_____

Parent Comments (about the book or the KWLM strategy): _____

_____

(Adapted from Thomas, Fazio, and Stiefelmeyer 1999, 68)

Report Writing—Where Are You At?

Name: _____ Grade: _____ Date: _____

Report topic: _____

Check off what you are working on now and write the date.	Date
1. Creating research questions	
2. Limiting my topic	
3. Looking for resources on the topic	
4. Finding key information in specific resources	
5. Making notes on the topic	
6. Organizing all of the collected notes into an outline	
7. Writing the first draft	
8. Revising the organization of the draft	
9. Writing a second draft	
10. Editing (grammar, spelling, punctuation) by myself, with a peer, or the teacher	
11. Preparing the bibliography	
12. Preparing the graphics, visuals, diagrams, dramatizations, and so on	
13. Presenting the report with all of the prepared graphics	
14. Assessing the written report	
15. Assessing the presentation	
Other:	
Other:	
Other:	

Write or draw what you did today on the parts of the research process.

What was easy about what you did today?

_____

_____

_____

What was difficult about what you did today?

_____

_____

_____

What part of the research process would you like to learn more about through a lesson? Why?

_____

_____

_____

Today's date: _____

(Adapted from Dreher et al. 2000, 16)

Stepping Back from the Book

Name: _____ Grade: _____ Date: _____

Topic: _____

1. Something I noticed that I need to question: _____

_____

_____

2. Something that surprised me, that I did not expect, or that I took for granted: _____

_____

_____

3. Some questions I still have: _____

_____

_____

4. A connection that I can make to what is happening in my country today or somewhere else in the world: _____

_____

_____

_____

(Adapted from Heffernan 2004, 5)

Chapter 4

ASSESSMENT BLACKLINE MASTERS

Assessment BLM 1: Rubric for Assessing KWL Performance

Assessment BLM 2: Assessing Portfolio Contents in an Integrated Unit

Assessment BLM 3: Self-Assessment–Using My Portfolio to Reflect on My Learning

Assessment BLM 4: Self-Assessment–Me as Part of a Group

Assessment BLM 5: Self-Assessment–Checklist for My Research Report

Assessment BLM 6: Self-Assessment–My Informational Writing

Assessment BLM 7: Conversational Interview on Informational Text

Assessment BLM 8: Comprehension Strategy Use Across the Curriculum

Assessment BLM 9: Checklist for Assessing Students' Multiple Intelligences

Assessment BLM 10: Skit Performance

Assessment BLM 11: Self-Assessment–How Did You Do with Your Report?

Assessment BLM 12: Presenting Our Report–How Did We Do?

Assessment BLM 13: Math Problem-Solving Rubric

Rubric for Assessing KWL Performance

Name: _____ Grade: _____ Date: _____

Topic: _____

Category	0 Not Acceptable\Incomplete	1 Needs Improvement	2 Acceptable	3 Above Acceptable	4 Excellent
Content	• records incomplete information overall	• records few facts from prior knowledge, which are off topic, vague, or incorrect	• records some facts and some general ideas on topic	• records detailed facts but only general ideas on topic	• records detailed facts and specific ideas on topic
	• generates no questions or off-topic or incorrect questions	• generates few questions	• generates some basic questions on topic	• generates *how* and *why* questions on topic	• generates varied and complex higher-level questions on topic
	• records off-topic or incorrect information	• records off-topic or nonspecific information	• records some general information learned	• records new, but not detailed, information learned	• records new, detailed information learned
	• no evidence of new information accessed with or without help	• depends on teacher help to locate new information	• uses one new information source	• uses two sources of information	• uses three or more information sources
Skills	• unable or unwilling to share prior knowledge on topic	• limited attempt to share prior knowledge on topic	• shares some prior knowledge on topic	• shares some prior knowledge on topic and develops inquiry purpose	• shares specific prior knowledge on topic to develop purpose and inquiry/research plan
	• generates no questions	• generates a few simple questions on topic	• formulates basic questions to guide inquiry	• formulates different kinds of questions to guide inquiry	• formulates critical questions to guide inquiry

Rubric for Assessing KWL Performance

Name: _____ Grade: _____ Date: _____

Topic: _____

Category	0 Not Acceptable\Incomplete	1 Needs Improvement	2 Acceptable	3 Above Acceptable	4 Excellent
Skills (continued)	• information is not used	• all information is selected by the teacher	• identifies, with teacher help, some information sources, and then locates and records information	• identifies only some information sources, and then locates and records information	• identifies varied information sources, and then locates and records information
Format of Information on Chart	• incomplete	• in point form	• in point form with appropriate vocabulary	• in point form with specific vocabulary	• in point form with correct and precise vocabulary
	• scattered all over with no organization	• lacks some organization	• organized into columns	• organized into subheadings	• organized into subheadings and questions are classified
	• incomplete or inaccurate details	• lacking in many details	• complete with some details	• detailed and complete	• detailed, complete, accurate, unambiguous

Scoring Guide Content: _____ out of 4 Skills: _____ out of 4 Format: _____ out of 3 Total: _____ out of 10

(Adapted from Resource Development Services 1999, 153–54)

Assessing Portfolio Contents in an Integrated Unit

Name: _____ Grade: _____ Date: _____

	Most of the Time 4	Some of the Time 3	Rarely 2	Never 1
Versatility				
1. Are a variety of assignments, assessment forms (including self-assessments), and texts represented in several content areas?				
2. Are a variety of learning purposes or skills in the content areas being met by the forms, assignments, and so on?				
3. Is there evidence of group and independent work?				
Completeness/Responsibility				
4. Is the focus in the works sustained?				
5. Is there attention to the organization of the portfolio?				
6. Is there evidence of interest in the subject areas beyond the classroom?				
7. Is there evidence of use of multiple resources?				
8. Is there evidence of independence in learning?				
Carefulness				
9. Is there attention to grammar, spelling, and mechanics of language?				
10. Is there evidence of precise use of vocabulary in the content areas?				
11. Are organizational structures from the different subject areas known and used?				
12. Does the student show evidence of having mastered appropriate content in the subject areas?				
13. Is the student's knowledge of content represented in multiple ways (using a variety of intelligences and literacies)?				

(Adapted from Schurr, Thomason, and Thompson 1995, 371)

Self-Assessment—Using My Portfolio to Reflect on My Learning

Name: _____ Grade: _____ Date: _____

Date when I began my portfolio: _____

How well is my portfolio organized? _____

_____

What does my portfolio show about my reading and writing in the subject areas?

_____

_____

What does my portfolio show about my speaking, listening, and viewing in the content areas?

_____

_____

What does my portfolio show about my representing through art, drama, music, mathematics, technology, and other means?

_____

_____

_____

What is getting better about my work in the subject areas?

_____

_____

_____

(Adapted from Farr and Tone 1994, 300, 307)

Self-Assessment—Me as Part of a Group

Name: _____ Grade: _____ Date: _____

Use the Always–Never scale to rate your performance in a group.

1. I praise and encourage other members of my group.

◆———————————————————◆
ALWAYS   NEVER

2. I share my materials with others.

◆———————————————————◆
ALWAYS   NEVER

3. I listen without interrupting.

◆———————————————————◆
ALWAYS   NEVER

4. I check to make sure everyone in the group understands the directions and the work.

◆———————————————————◆
ALWAYS   NEVER

5. I am willing to help others and to receive help from others.

◆———————————————————◆
ALWAYS   NEVER

6. I accept responsibility for getting the work done.

◆———————————————————◆
ALWAYS   NEVER

Suggestions for the next time we work as a group:

_____

_____

_____

_____

(Adapted from Clarke, Wideman, and Eadie 1990, 105)

Self-Assessment—Checklist for My Research Report

Name: _____ Grade: _____ Date: _____

Research topic: _____

Presented as
- ❑ an interview
- ❑ an article
- ❑ a written report
- ❑ an art illustration
- ❑ a poster

- ❑ a videotape
- ❑ a brochure
- ❑ a book
- ❑ a chart
- ❑ other: _____

By writing my report, I learned how to ...	Yes	Somewhat	No
make a list of what I know			
write questions on what I still want to know			
add to the topic			
use the library to find resources			
use books and other resources to answer my questions			
locate other resources to use (the Internet, magazines, people)			
choose the best resources to use			
take notes to answer my questions			
summarize the information			
organize the information			
include a bibliography			
work alone on some tasks			
work with others			
be responsible			
prepare my presentation			
present the information orally			

When I work on my next topic, I want to improve _____

_____

_____

(Adapted from Fryar 2003, 39)

Self-Assessment—My Informational Writing

Name: _____ Grade: _____ Date: _____

Research topic: _____

1. What two things did you like best about this piece? _____

   _____

2. List two things you did very well. _____

   _____

3. What would you change if you were to write on this topic again? _____

   _____

4. Did this piece of writing tell what you know about the topic? Why or why not? _____

   _____

5. What could you have done to make this topic clearer to your audience? _____

   _____

	Did you ...	Yes	No
Ideas	include the most important ideas?		
	include important and interesting details?		
Organization	include a table of contents?		
	include an introduction (a paragraph that hooks your audience)?		
	organize your informational writing so that it made sense (for example, did you use description, problem and solution, or listing)?		
	organize your writing into subtopics?		
	include important and interesting details in each subtopic?		
	have an ending, summary, or conclusion to your writing?		
Conventions	use closing punctuation marks, such as periods and exclamation marks, at the end of sentences?		
	use commas where necessary?		
	begin each sentence with a capital letter?		
	check for misspelled words and correct any errors?		
	check that new paragraphs began clearly?		
Presentation	make your report legible?		
	include maps, photographs, labels, charts, diagrams, drawings, or other graphic aids to help others understand the information you presented?		

(Adapted from Cohen and Wiener 2003, 166)

Conversational Interview on Informational Text

Name: _____ Grade: _____ Date: _____

The aim of this interview is for the teacher to have a more natural, but structured conversation with a student. First, the teacher provides a prompt. An example follows.

"To find out more about something, we often read, watch television, or look for the information on the Internet. I remember a student of mine who read a lot of books and magazine articles on penguins to find out as much as she could about them. I would like to hear about some important information you have learned recently. So, let's start with a question or two to talk about it."

1. Think about something important that you learned, not from a teacher, but from a book or some other reading material, from television, or from the Internet. What topic did you learn about? (*Wait time.*) Tell me what you have learned.

   _____

   _____

   _____

   _____

   Further prompts: What else can you tell me? Is there anything else?

2. How did you know or find out about this topic? _____

   _____

   Further prompts: Was it assigned in school or did you choose it yourself? Where did you learn about it (in school or elsewhere)?

3. Why was this topic or informational text important and interesting to you? _____

   _____

(Adapted from Gambrell et al. 1999, 221–22)

Comprehension Strategy Use Across the Curriculum

Name: _____ Grade: _____ Date: _____

Observed by: _____

Observation Code AD = Adequate Development NH = Needs Help	First Observation Date: _____		Second Observation Date: _____	
1. Links previous knowledge to content studied				
2. Sets purpose for reading				
3. Uses titles, subtitles, illustrations, and other features to predict content				
4. Generates own questions for reading				
5. Determines importance and uses key ideas related to the concept				
6. Creates visual representations of main concepts during and after reading				
7. Makes summaries orally or in writing				

Additional Comments: _____

_____

_____

Mini-lessons: _____

_____

_____

(Adapted from Cohen and Wiener 2003, 123; citing Shearer and Homan 1994)

Checklist for Assessing Students' Multiple Intelligences

Name: _____ Grade: _____ Date: _____

Verbal–Linguistic Intelligence
❑ thinks in words
❑ spins tall tales or tells jokes and stories
❑ has a good memory for names, places, dates, or trivia
❑ enjoys playing with sounds in language and word games
❑ loves to read and write
❑ enjoys listening to the spoken word (stories, radio commentary, talking books)
❑ has a good vocabulary; spells accurately
❑ expresses self with precision in writing and speaking

Other Verbal–Linguistic Strengths: _____

_____

Logical–Mathematical Intelligence
❑ thinks conceptually, logically, and systematically
❑ enjoys working or playing with numbers and symbols
❑ enjoys identifying and solving problems
❑ finds math, science, and computer games and topics interesting
❑ enjoys playing strategy games (chess, checkers)
❑ enjoys working on logic puzzles or brainteasers
❑ likes to sort things by category, relationship, or pattern
❑ questions how things work and experiments

Other Logical–Mathematical Strengths: __

_____

Bodily–Kinesthetic Intelligence
❑ excels in one or more sports
❑ moves, twitches, taps, or fidgets while seated for a long time in one spot
❑ cleverly mimics the gestures or mannerisms of others
❑ likes to explore through touch and movement
❑ enjoys running, jumping, wrestling, or similar activities
❑ has excellent fine-motor coordination
❑ has a dramatic way of expressing herself or himself
❑ reports different physical sensations while thinking or working

Other Bodily–Kinesthetic Strengths: _____

_____

Visual–Spatial Intelligence
❑ thinks in images
❑ gets more from maps, charts, pictures, and diagrams than from text
❑ daydreams frequently
❑ enjoys art activities; doodles often
❑ makes perceptive representations
❑ likes to view movies, slides, or other visual presentations
❑ enjoys doing puzzles, mazes, or other visual activities (I Spy, Where's Waldo?)
❑ excels at building interesting, three-dimensional constructions (with blocks, Lego, Popsicle sticks)

Other Visual–Spatial Strengths: _____

_____

Musical–Rhythmic Intelligence
❑ thinks in sounds, rhythms, and patterns
❑ distracted by discord or music that is off-key
❑ immediately responds to music
❑ remembers songs and rhymes easily
❑ enjoys making and/or playing musical instruments
❑ has a rhythmic way of speaking and/or moving
❑ sings, hums, whistles unconsciously
❑ sensitive to environmental noises (e.g., crickets, rain)

Other Musical–Rhythmic Strengths: _____

_____

Interpersonal Intelligence
❑ enjoys socializing with peers; has many friends
❑ relates, cooperates, and communicates well
❑ excels at mediating conflicts
❑ seems to be street-smart
❑ belongs to clubs, committees, organizations, or informal peer groups
❑ enjoys coaching and mentoring
❑ is sensitive to and concerned for others
❑ is sought out by others

Other Interpersonal Strengths: _____

_____

Intrapersonal Intelligence
❑ displays a sense of independence or a strong will
❑ has a realistic sense of personal strengths and weaknesses
❑ is able to learn from personal failures and successes
❑ requires privacy; prefers working alone to working with others
❑ has a unique, personal style of living and learning
❑ has an interest or hobby that she or he doesn't talk much about
❑ can accurately express personal feelings
❑ has high self-esteem

Other Intrapersonal Strengths: _____

_____

Naturalist Intelligence
❑ enjoys pets or being around animals
❑ likes field trips in nature, to the zoo, museum, planetarium
❑ enjoys science topics and projects related to nature (plants, animals, weather)
❑ is concerned about environmental issues
❑ can distinguish birds, animals, insects, and so on
❑ actively pursues outdoor activities
❑ collects things in nature (insects, rocks, leaves)
❑ chooses books and television programs on nature topics

Other Naturalist Strengths: _____

Skit Performance

Names: _____

_____   _____

_____   _____

_____   _____

Topic of skit: _____ Grade: _____ Date: _____

Scoring Code
5 = Very Good   3 = Average   1 = Needs Improvement

Teacher   **Score**

1. Were the correct concepts displayed in the dialogue?   _____

2. Were the correct concepts displayed in the performance?   _____

3. Did the skit introduce the main concept correctly?   _____

4. Was the order/sequence correct in the process, event, or transformation?   _____

5. How well did the students dramatize or portray the subconcepts in the
   text of the skit?   _____

6. Were the essential details portrayed clearly enough?   _____

7. How well did the students use art/drawings to enhance their performance? _____

8. How well did the students work cooperatively?   _____

Do the students need to revise their skit?   ❏ Yes   ❏ No

Students

To revise the written dialogue, we need to _____

_____

_____

To revise our performance, we need to _____

_____

_____

Self-Assessment—How Did You Do with Your Report?

Name: _____ Grade: _____ Date: _____

Research topic: _____

Research Questions
1. Did you ask the right questions to help you research the topic?   ❏ Yes   ❏ No

   Why or why not? _____

2. Did you limit your topic so it was manageable? ❏ Yes   ❏ No

Information Sources
3. Where did you get your information? (check all that apply)
   - ❏ Informational books
   - ❏ Reference materials such as encyclopedias
   - ❏ Magazines (online or hard copy)
   - ❏ The Internet
   - ❏ Other printed materials: _____
   - ❏ CD-ROMs
   - ❏ Videos
   - ❏ Works of art
   - ❏ Posters, charts
   - ❏ Other materials: _____

Organization of Information
4. Did you make brief notes?	❏ Yes	❏ No
5. Did you take chunks of information from Web sites?	❏ Yes	❏ No
6. Did you use your own words (paraphrase information)?	❏ Yes	❏ No
7. Did you give credit for exact words/sentences (direct quotations) you used from the sources?	❏ Yes	❏ No
8. Did you include a strong introduction?	❏ Yes	❏ No
9. Did you use subheadings to organize information on subtopics in the body of the report?	❏ Yes	❏ No
10. Did you include a good concluding paragraph?	❏ Yes	❏ No

Report Writing
11. Did you gather enough information to write the whole report?	❏ Yes	❏ No
12. Did you include maps, pictures, charts, diagrams, and so on in your report to make it easier to understand?	❏ Yes	❏ No
13. Did you list all your sources in a bibliography?	❏ Yes	❏ No
14. Did you get the report done on time?	❏ Yes	❏ No

(Adapted from Fryar 2003, 38)

Presenting Our Report—How Did We Do?

Group Members

Date: _____

Title of Report: _____

_____

_____

Oral Presentation Features	Comments	Group Assessment		
		Good	**Average**	**Needs Improvement**
Content of Report				
Appropriate information				
Organization				
Knowledge of content for oral presentation				
Relationship with Audience				
Provided overview of report				
Made a clear introduction				
Used language audience understands				
Explained vocabulary				
Made eye contact with audience				
Oral Presentation Skills				
Expression				
Volume of voice				
Pace				
Presentation Strategies				
Used visual aids				
Used notes only for reference				
Made good use of each group member				
Provided answers to questions from audience				

(Adapted from Fryar 2003, 37)

Math Problem-Solving Rubric

Name: _____ Grade: _____ Date: _____

CATEGORY	LEVEL 1	LEVEL 2	LEVEL 3	LEVEL 4
Problem Solving	• completely misunderstood the task • generated inappropriate and unworkable strategy • made no connection to answer	• only partially understood the task • used appropriate strategy some of the time • provided some evidence of a plan, but it was unclear • made some connections to answer	• generally understood the task • generated a workable strategy • provided some evidence, but was unclear • made connections and applied the answer	• analyzed and easily understood the task • developed a workable strategy • showed clear evidence of carrying out the strategy • combined all elements to generalize a conclusion
Communication	• made inappropriate or unclear use of symbolism • made an incorrect representation • provided unclear explanations	• used appropriate language some of the time, but was not always clear • used some imprecise representation • provided clear explanations only in some parts	• used appropriate, accurate, and mostly clear language • made an accurate and appropriate representation • provided mainly clear and logical explanations	• used precise, clear, and correct mathematical language • used correct symbolism • made a precise representation using a chart, diagram, or graph • provided logical and appropriate oral and written explanations

(Adapted from http://www.nwrel.org/learns/resources/se)

Chapter 5

IN THE CLASSROOM: MAKING IT WORK

Charmaine Graves
Sue Jackson

"The first years of school establish the essential foundation of literacy that enables all future literacy achievement. In the intermediate grades [Grades 3 to 6], students use this foundation to develop a full, rich, wide-ranging facility. They assume the roles of readers and writers that will serve them throughout their lifetime."*

* Fountas and Pinnell 2001, 2

Find Out More About Making It Work in the Classroom

Allen, Janet. *On the Same Page: Shared Reading Beyond the Primary Grades*. Portland, ME: Stenhouse Publishers, 2002.

Allen, Janet. *Words, Words, Words: Teaching Vocabulary in Grades 4–12*. Portland, ME: Stenhouse Publishers, 1999.

Allington, Richard L. *What Really Matters for Struggling Readers*. Toronto: Addison-Wesley Educational Publishers, 2001.

Allington, Richard L., and Patricia M. Cunningham. *Schools That Work: Where All Children Read and Write*. Boston: Allyn and Bacon, 2002.

Allington, Richard L., and Peter H. Johnston. "What Do We Know About Effective Fourth-Grade Teachers and Their Classrooms?" In *Learning to Teach Reading: Setting the Research Agenda*. Cathy M. Roller, ed. Newark, DE: International Reading Association, 2001, 150–65.

Biancarosa, Gina. "After Third Grade." *Educational Leadership* 63.2 (October 2005), 16–22.

Calkins, Lucy McCormick. *The Art of Teaching Reading*. New York: Addison Wesley Longman, 2001.

Fountas, Irene C., and Gay Su Pinnell. *Guiding Readers and Writers, Grades 3–6: Teaching Comprehension, Genre, and Content Literacy*. Portsmouth, NH: Heinemann, 2001.

Hoyt, Linda. *Snapshots: Literacy Minilessons Up Close*. Portsmouth, NH: Heinemann, 2000.

Jensen, Eric. *Teaching with the Brain in Mind*. Alexandria, VA: Association for Supervision and Curriculum Development (ASCD), 1998.

Lesesne, Teri S. *Making the Match: The Right Book for the Right Reader at the Right Time, Grades 4–12*. Portland, ME: Stenhouse Publishers, 2003.

Marzano, Robert, Debra Pickering, and Jana Marzano. *Classroom Management That Works: Research-Based Strategies for Every Teacher*. Alexandria, VA: Association for Supervision and Curriculum Development (ASCD), 2003.

McQuirter Scott, Ruth, and Sharon Siamon. *Spelling: Connecting the Pieces*. Toronto: Gage Learning Corporation, 2004.

Reeves, Robyn, Laurence Swinburne, and Jack Warner. *Readers' Theater: Multiple Reading Levels in Each Play!* Austin, TX: Steck-Vaughn, 1999.

Routman, Regie. *Conversations: Strategies for Teaching, Learning, and Evaluating*. Portsmouth, NH: Heinemann, 2000.

Schwartz, Susan, and Maxine Bone. *Retelling, Relating, Reflecting: Beyond the 3 R's*. Toronto: Irwin Publishing, 1995.

Schwartz, Susan, and Mindy Pollishuke. *Creating the Dynamic Classroom: A Handbook for Teachers*. Toronto: Irwin Publishing, 2002.

Sibberson, Franki, and Karen Szymusiak. *Still Learning to Read: Teaching Students in Grades 3–6*. Portland, ME: Stenhouse Publishers, 2003.

Wilhelm, Jeffrey. *Reading IS Seeing: Learning to Visualize Scenes, Characters, Ideas, and Text Worlds to Improve Comprehension and Reflective Reading*. New York: Scholastic, 2004.

Worthy, Jo, Karen Broaddus, and Gay Ivey. *Pathways to Independence: Reading, Writing, and Learning in Grades 3–8*. New York: Guilford Press, 2001.

Research on Effective Classrooms

For most students, foundational literacy skills are established during the early elementary grades. By the time they enter Grade 3, the majority of students can communicate their thinking orally and in writing and have developed strategies to decode and encode text. However, to become strategic readers, writers, speakers, listeners, viewers, and representers students must develop their metacognitive skills.

Metacognition, or thinking about one's own thinking, is particularly important in the upper elementary grades, when students are exposed to more complex texts in a wider range of genres. To support students in developing their metacognitive skills, effective literacy teachers model and label their own thinking as they construct, deconstruct, and reconstruct understanding. They then provide students with explicit instruction and numerous opportunities for practice. The primary aim is for students to become confident, independent learners who are "more *strategic* in their approach to literacy, more *in control,* and more *automatic in skill and concept application*" (Soderman, Gregory, and O'Neill 1999, 125).

Grades 3 to 6 is a time when students "experience a shift toward more logical thinking and [the] ability to think abstractly about ideas and possibilities" (Soderman, Gregory, and O'Neill 1999, 130). They begin acquiring the essential skills of thoughtful literacy. As thoughtful literacy learners, they will be able to read, write, speak, listen, view, and represent in the complex and critical ways needed to succeed in a dynamic, evolving literacy world.

Chapter 2: Reading Comprehension: Strategies That Work and Chapter 6: Supporting Struggling and Reluctant Readers include much more information about metacognition and the strategies it comprises.

> "The ultimate goal of the literacy program is to enable students to learn how satisfying reading and writing are and to establish lifelong reading and writing habits. Teachers who themselves engage in reading and writing, and who examine their habits and attitudes as readers and writers, can best help students experience the power of their own literacy."
>
> Fountas and Pinnell 2001, 11

Key Goals in Literacy Development

There are three key goals in the literacy development of students in Grades 3 to 6.

- The first goal is to create effective readers, writers, speakers, listeners, viewers, and representers. Making meaning is at the heart of literacy. Students who can effectively articulate their ideas and derive explicit and implicit meaning from text are prepared for the world outside of school.

- The second goal is to foster in students a love of literacy. The literate learner regards reading and writing as pleasurable pastimes outside of school.

- The third goal is to expose students to a wide range of genres and text forms. The greater the range of exposure, the more likely students will understand and appreciate the power of the printed and spoken word.

Making Meaning

Love of Literacy

Power of Language

Literacy Skills in Grades 3 to 6

Students become effective literacy learners when they

- understand that reading, writing, speaking, listening, viewing, and representing are active, thinking processes
- use a well-developed vocabulary, prior knowledge, and personal experiences to comprehend text and as a springboard for writing, speaking, and representing
- know their purpose for reading, writing, speaking, listening, and viewing and their audience for writing, speaking, and representing
- read, write, speak, listen, view, and represent for a variety of purposes and on a wide range of topics
- monitor and adjust their reading, listening, and viewing to facilitate comprehension and apply a variety of strategies to help them make meaning of texts
- think critically before, during, and after reading, writing, speaking listening, and viewing
- understand and make use of style, technique, text features (e.g., headings, charts, diagrams, captions) and language conventions
- form opinions about print and media texts and authors, and recognize the strengths and weaknesses of a variety of formats (e.g., books, magazines, comics, films, television programs, posters, and so on)
- make effective use of information technology

"While reading, writing, listening, and speaking … [are] paramount, today's student must be able to decipher meaning and express ideas through a range of media. A literate person must not only excel in reading and writing text, but must also be able to listen and speak, and read and write fluently through text, images, motion video, charts and graphs, and hypertext across a range of media" (NCREL 2001).

Style is the way words, images, and phrases are used to create a feeling or convey a thought (Burke 2000).

Technique refers to elements of text used to produce a specific effect (e.g., foreshadowing, personification, comparison).

Elements of a Comprehensive Literacy Program

Effective literacy instruction in Grades 3 to 6 is a complex undertaking, founded on the following elements:

- teacher beliefs
- instructional approaches
- time for literacy development
- engagement in literacy development
- classroom environment (a "second teacher")
- materials
- establishment of a community of learners
- ongoing assessment that drives instruction
- intervention
- development of home–school–community partnerships

"The ability to read and write does not develop naturally without careful planning and instruction."

INTERNATIONAL READING ASSOCIATION
1998, 6

Teacher Beliefs

As Allington and Johnston (2001) confirm, teachers who believe in themselves as teachers of literacy are more effective practitioners in the classroom. They realize that they can make a difference. They know that their students are still learning to read, write, speak, listen, view, and represent, and appreciate the importance of explicit literacy instruction. To deepen students' level of engagement and comprehension, teachers provide ongoing guidance and support. They understand that, while students attain these skills at different rates and times, there are clear benchmarks to help measure growth and development. These benchmarks are used to group students, to plan for future learning, and to provide timely and skill-specific intervention.

Effective literacy teachers also believe that all students can become successful literacy learners and that attitude and motivation play a significant role in literacy acquisition. These teachers see their students as capable, competent, creative learners, and take every opportunity to instill these beliefs in their students. Consequently, their students not only see themselves as readers, writers, speakers, listeners, viewers, and representers, they believe that their skills will help them successfully accomplish any challenges that arise across the curriculum.

"Star teachers believe that, regardless of life conditions their students face, they as teachers bear a primary responsibility for sparking their students' desire to learn."

HABERMAN IN ALLINGTON AND JOHNSTON 2001, 154

Instructional Approaches

Instructional practices affect student success so it is important to incorporate varying approaches to scaffold new learning. Although students construct knowledge socially, they also need direct teaching involving models, demonstrations, and explanations.

Effective teachers consciously use a variety of strategies to explain information or guide students through a new process. They work with individual students or small groups to provide this instruction and are only occasionally in front of the class (Allington and Johnston 2001). They ask a variety of questions on several levels, taking care to provide "think" or "wait" time for students to process their thoughts and formulate a well-constructed response. After direct teaching, they provide students with multiple opportunities for practice, coupled with regular ongoing feedback and, if necessary, more instruction. By slowly moving from a high degree of support to independence, effective teachers gradually release the learning responsibility to their students. This entire process is highly interactive and interconnected. Therefore, by spending the majority of their day engaged in meaningful reading, writing, speaking, listening, viewing, and representing tasks, students are able to develop proficiency in these areas.

A comprehensive literacy program allows for this level of differentiated instruction and practice. Oral language and word study are intentionally scaffolded into reading and writing activities, and skills and concepts are generally taught in context. Each component is integrally connected to the other, offering teachers flexibility in approach, purpose, and engagement.

Frequent whole-class instruction is generally ineffective. It can be too easy for some and too hard for others. While it certainly has a place in shared reading and writing experiences, teachers must also incorporate small-group and individual instruction into their program.

"It is not just the presence of a variety of activities that makes a program of reading instruction effective or ineffective. It is the way in which its pieces are fitted together to complement and support one another, always with full consideration of the needs and progress of the readers with whom it will be used."

ADAMS 1990, 122

Time for Literacy Development

As curriculum demands increase over Grades 3 to 6, the timetable often becomes fragmented. However, significant research shows that time dedicated to literacy development remains important. Studies reported by Cunningham and Allington (1996) proved that students made the greatest gains in literacy skills when their teachers allocated more time to language arts instruction. Effective teachers strive to provide two hours of literacy time per day. Large blocks of time enable teachers to integrate the components of balanced literacy across subject areas and to promote longer and more sustained attention to tasks.

These large blocks of time must be free of interruptions and distractions. It may be necessary to have school-wide discussions to generate ways to ensure that assemblies, classroom visitors, or itinerant teachers do not erode instructional time. Once the decision has been made to dedicate a block of time for literacy, teachers may face specific organizational challenges. They will need to address such necessary but often time-consuming tasks as

- distribution and collection of materials and student work
- transitions from activities, recess, lunch, and so on
- collection of money, permission slips, and homework

Highly effective teachers integrate content-specific information and tasks with literacy instruction. This practice not only helps to motivate and engage students, but also lends coherence to the instructional day. It allows teachers the flexibility of where to schedule their explicit instruction and where to plan for practice and consolidation. Another critical factor is the task itself. Time spent on narrow, unconnected activities will fail to produce improved results (Allington and Cunningham 2002). Integration across subjects, time, and topics is more effective than a compartmentalized curriculum. The quality and rigour of the task, coupled with time, is what matters.

Engagement in Literacy Development

Effective literacy teachers know that the time their students spend engaged in purposeful reading, writing, viewing, representing and oral language activities is critical to their success. They understand that motivation and attitude are critical for engagement in a task and explicitly plan for it by

- establishing and following routines
- setting and sharing expectations and guidelines
- scaffolding new learning on prior knowledge
- allowing for student choice
- encouraging student independence
- creating doable tasks that provide interest and challenge
- using appropriate materials
- integrating subject matter
- providing opportunities for social interaction

"It makes sense that students in grades 3–6 need more instruction. The texts they are reading are becoming more complex and sophisticated.... We can't assume that the skills our students learned in grades K–2 will carry them through their lives as readers."

Sibberson and Szymusiak 2003, 2

Research indicates that the use of longer instructional blocks permits students to achieve more "productive and complicated student work."

Allington and Johnston 2001, 161

"Schools must become more efficient in their use of instructional time. Teachers need time to teach. Children need time to learn."

Allington and Cunningham 2002, 122

"Children need considerable time to practice and consolidate the skills they have learned so part of balanced reading is to provide students with a rich variety of texts and sufficient time to unify the skills and strategies so they can be used purposefully and selectively."

Burns 1999, 4

Allington and Cunningham (2002) support the importance of engagement. They cite task difficulty and task interest as the two factors that are likely to increase student involvement. In other words, students must see the task as purposeful, relevant, and doable.

Classroom Environment—A "Second Teacher"

Effective literacy teachers consciously develop and nurture the classroom environment. They address both the social and physical makeup of the classroom, often referred to as a "second teacher." Many decisions about the classroom environment are made before the school year begins. The physical layout of the classroom is organized to reflect the diversity of the program, the students, and the teaching strategies to be used. A comprehensive literacy classroom includes

- a writing-rich environment where all work is thoughtfully displayed (e.g., student work, word wall, rubrics, vocabulary charts, writing samples/exemplars, graphic organizers and writing frameworks, and shared reading charts)

- a large-group meeting area

- flexible furniture arrangements to promote interaction and purposeful talk, as well as individual work areas

- a comfortable and inviting reading area with a wide range of reading materials displayed in an inviting manner

- a conferencing area for use by student–teacher, student–student, and student–volunteer groupings

- a writing area with space for conferencing and publishing

- student response areas (e.g., research, writing, reading, drama, and science)

"The way we set up the classroom gives our students a clear message about the culture of the classroom, the kind of work they will do, and the expectations we have for them."
SIBBERSON AND SZYMUSIAK 2003, 29

Check It Out!

Susan Schwartz and Mindy Pollishuke. *Creating the Dynamic Classroom: A Handbook for Teachers* (Toronto: Irwin Publishing, 2002).

See this useful resource for more about classroom organization.

Map of a Classroom

When organizing classroom space, teachers must keep in mind the traffic flow and subject transitions as defined by their timetables. This awareness, combined with the setting of routines, will ensure that the majority of classroom time is focused on purposeful instruction and independent application of strategies and skills. Taking time at the

"I teach each day with a sense of urgency. Specifically, that means that I am very aware of the students in front of me, the opportunities for teaching and evaluating on the spot, the skills and strategies I need to be teaching, the materials I need, the amount of time available, and the optimal contexts and curriculum."
ROUTMAN 2003, 41–42

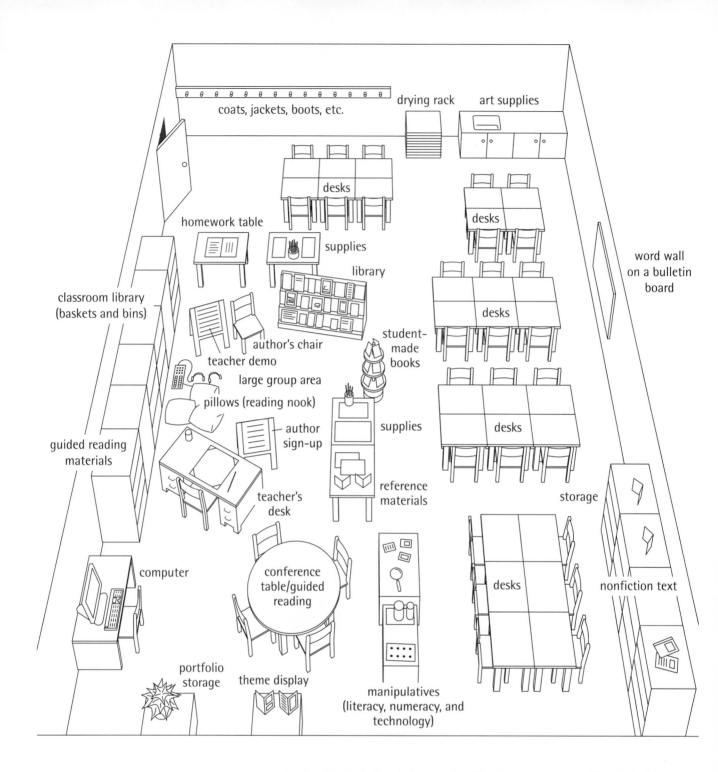

coats, jackets, boots, etc.

drying rack

art supplies

desks

homework table

supplies

library

desks

word wall
on a bulletin
board

classroom library
(baskets and bins)

author's chair

teacher demo

large group area

desks

pillows (reading nook)

author
sign-up

student-
made
books

supplies

guided reading
materials

teacher's
desk

reference
materials

desks

storage

computer

conference
table/guided
reading

desks

nonfiction text

portfolio
storage

theme display

manipulatives
(literacy, numeracy, and
technology)

beginning of the year to familiarize students with the classroom layout and procedures will result in the gain of valuable teaching time later.

While the classroom walls are usually reserved for student work and exemplars for learning, students' first impressions are critical. Effective teachers set the culture of thoughtful literacy through their use of wall space and bulletin boards. Wall displays for the beginning of the year might feature

- ways into books—"You might like this series if you ..."
- posters of book characters—"How many of these characters do you know?"

- enlarged copies of entertaining poems, such as "My Dog Ate My Homework" by Sara Holbrook
- enlarged copies of word games to promote active participation (e.g., crossword puzzles and word searches)

(Adapted from Sibberson and Szymusiak 2003, 31–34)

Throughout the year, teachers change wall displays often and involve students in displaying their efforts. If students have helped in the creation of classroom displays, they are more likely to view environmental print as useful rather than simply decorative.

Materials

Material-rich classrooms are necessary to allow for the range and variety required when addressing the components of a comprehensive literacy program. Students in Grades 3 to 6 benefit from a wide range of materials that span subject matters, interests, and skill levels. It is also important that these materials be personally and culturally relevant and appealing to the students.

Good management and organization of materials can significantly increase the time students actually spend reading and writing. If materials and supplies are not readily accessible, students waste considerable time trying to locate the tools they need. Creating easy retrieval and storage routines will maximize the time spent on practice and consolidation and build student independence.

During the first few weeks of school, or whenever new materials are introduced, effective teachers explicitly teach routines for accessing and returning materials and provide opportunities for practice. Doing so helps ensure that students know where, when, and how to retrieve and return publishing supplies, research materials, and resources from the class library, and where to store writing folders, portfolios, and work ready for teacher review.

Ready access to materials is also important for teachers. More time can be spent working directly with students when materials and supplies are close at hand. One efficient way of organizing teacher materials is

to use a rolling cart with compartments for materials such as highlighters, sticky notes, markers, whiteboards, individual chalkboards, chalk, clipboards, tape, pens, pencils, assessment materials, and paper of various sizes and colours. Not only does the cart keep teaching materials organized for whole-group and small-group sessions, it sets a good example for students.

The collection of reading materials is of utmost importance in the upper elementary classroom and should consist of at least 400 titles for independent student use. It should also provide a wide range of difficulty levels, genres, and topics. Another suggestion is for teachers to have access to 3200 additional books to support small-group instruction (Pinnell and Fountas 2002).

To stretch budgets and expand the breadth, depth, and scope of the classroom library, many teachers borrow resources from school and public libraries, central warehouses, and school bookrooms.

Assembling a Varied Classroom Collection

A classroom library must reflect students' needs, interests, and abilities, as well as the instructional strategies used. Therefore, classroom collections ideally consist of

- content-specific trade books, textbooks, and media supports
- reference material to support language and spelling conventions, vocabulary enrichment, and required content knowledge (e.g., print and/or multimedia versions of an encyclopedia, standard dictionary, and thesaurus)
- materials that reflect a wide range of text types and features (e.g., magazines, newspapers, textbooks, picture books, novels, manuals, graphical texts)
- levelled material for guided reading
- a wide range of materials suitable for read-alouds, shared reading, and independent reading, including at-home reading
- award-winning books
- collected works to support author, series, poetry, or theme-based study

When assembling the classroom library, it is important to consider how the titles will be displayed. "The best way to teach our students to choose appropriate books is to organize the classroom library thoughtfully" (Sibberson and Szymusiak 2003, 12). Using methods employed by bookstores will heighten interest and maximize book appeal for students.

To entice readers, bookstores try to

- display books of the same genre in the same section
- display books face out
- organize nonfiction by topic
- feature book recommendations prominently
- display popular titles next to not-so-well-known titles
- change their displays regularly

(Adapted from Sibberson and Szymusiak 2003, 13)

Using a variety of baskets and bins to organize the classroom library on shelves allows for easy retrieval and reorganization. Labelling the baskets enables all students to find an interesting "just right" book. While teachers may initially organize the classroom library, a good idea is to entrust this task to the students as the year progresses. Re-sorting and classifying the collection provides ongoing opportunities for students to share ideas, feelings, and opinions about the reading materials.

Book Basket Ideas

- Favourite Authors (labelled with author's name, photo, and mini-biography)
- Series (labelled with picture of main character)
- Nonfiction (organized by topic, such as animals, space, sports heroes, and so on)
- New Books
- Books We Have Read Together
- Class Picks
- Read-Aloud Connections
- Favourite Characters
- Letter/Journal Form
- If You Liked _____, You Might Like ...
- Award Winners
- Newspaper and Magazine Articles
- Topic Sets
- Read with a Friend

(Sibberson and Szymusiak 2003)

Check It Out!

These Web sites offer information about children's books:

PIKA Canadian Children's Literature Database
http://www.collectionscanada.ca/pika/index-e.html

American Library Association
http://www.ala.org.

International Reading Association
http://www.reading.org

Database of Award-Winning Children's Literature
http://www.dawcl.com

These titles are helpful for selecting texts for classroom use:

Best Books for Kids Who Think They Hate to Read by Laura Backes (New York: Prima Publishing/Random House, 2002).

Leveled Books for Readers, Grades 3–6 by Irene C. Fountas and Gay Su Pinnell (Portsmouth, NH: Heinemann, 2002).

The Read-Aloud Handbook, 5th edition, by Jim Trelease (New York: Penguin, 2001).

Magazines and newspapers that appeal to students include *Calliope: World History for Young People, National Geographic for Kids, Ranger Rick, Scholastic News, Sports Illustrated for Kids*, and *Time for Kids*.

Teachers are strongly cautioned to avoid organizing their classroom libraries using guided reading levels. By teaching students to select from an appropriate range of texts, teachers encourage students to take responsibility for selecting and reading "just right" texts.

Students May Enjoy ...	
Books by These Authors	**Books in These Series**
Judy Blume	Anastasia by Lois Lowry
Sharon Creech	Anne of Green Gables
Paula Danziger	by Lucy Maud Montgomery
Ralph Fletcher	Goosebumps by R.L. Stine
James Howe	Harry Potter by J.K. Rowling
Gordon Korman	Little House on the Prairie
Paul Kropp	by Laura Ingalls Wilder
Madeleine L'Engle	Poppy by Avi
Katherine Paterson	A Series of Unfortunate Events
Jack Prelutsky (poetry)	by Lemony Snicket
Jon Scieszka	Time Warp Trio by Jon Scieszka
Shel Silverstein (poetry)	
Eric Wilson	

Check It Out!

Many authors have their own Web sites:

http://www.sharoncreech.com
http://www.ralphfletcher.com
http://www.gordonkorman.com
http://www.paulkropp.com
http://www.lemonysnicket.com
http://www.jerryspinelli.com

An excellent book resource is *Meet the Authors and Illustrators: 60 Creators of Favorite Children's Books Talk About Their Work* by Deborah Kovacs and James Preller (New York: Scholastic, 1993).

Check It Out!

Jeanne Gibbs. *Tribes: A New Way of Learning Together* (Santa Rosa: Center Source Publications, 2001).

Barrie Bennett, Carol Rolheiser, and Laurie Stevahn. *Cooperative Learning: Where Heart Meets Mind* (Toronto: Educational Connections, 1991).

Barrie Bennett and Carol Rolheiser. *Beyond Monet: The Artful Science of Instructional Integration* (Toronto: Bookation Inc., 2001).

These books offer a wealth of information on cooperative learning.

After organizing the classroom space, it is important to ensure that the environment will be effective for literacy learning. The questions that follow will help teachers to reflect on the essential elements of their classroom's physical environment.

- Do I have a large classroom collection of books and magazines that represent a great range of readability and are engaging and interesting for students?
- Is my classroom organized to accommodate large- and small-group and individual activities?
- Do I have a print-rich classroom with a diverse selection of literature, word walls, exemplars, vocabulary charts, writing frameworks, displays of student work, and more?
- Do I have resources organized to facilitate independence?
- Do I have a balance of teacher, commercial, and student-generated materials to promote literacy?
- Do my students perceive their daily tasks and assignments as relevant and doable?
- Have I established and consistently reinforced expectations and procedures to ensure success for all students?
- Are my students able to articulate the classroom expectations and procedures?
- Are my students becoming more engaged and independent learners?
- As a result of this reflection, how will I change my classroom environment?

Establishment of a Community of Learners

In addition to creating a warm, inviting physical space, effective Grades 3 to 6 teachers spend much time cultivating a positive classroom climate. They understand that students succeed best in an environment that encourages risk taking and that honours them as independent readers, writers, speakers, listeners, and viewers. Successful teachers of thoughtful literacy develop a sense of community within their classrooms.

Clear expectations, order, and consistency of practice help to promote safe, caring, and purposeful classrooms. Brain researcher Eric Jensen in *Teaching with the Brain in Mind* (1998) suggests that many students come to school feeling anxious or unsafe. These emotions, in turn, often cause undue stress, a potential factor in poor academic performance. Thus, creating classroom climates that promote risk taking and a sense of belonging is of critical importance. When treated with respect, students are more likely to respect and value themselves and their peers. Teachers who honour what students know and can do and who set reasonable targets create communities of learners. Students in Grades 3 to 6 are very social and enjoy interacting with their peers. By providing ample opportunities for them to work collaboratively and cooperatively, teachers promote comprehension and thinking.

To develop and maintain a sense of community in the classroom, teachers might have students

- share their individual interests, strengths, and goals (Student of the Week)
- work cooperatively to establish classroom routines and behaviours (Setting Classroom Expectations)
- acknowledge acceptable behaviours (Caught in the Act)
- connect with their classmates at the start of each day (Morning Meeting)
- express opinions about classroom dynamics (Circle Meeting)
- share acquired knowledge and insights (Web of Learning)

Student of the Week

This activity highlights one student per week. At the beginning of each day, the Student of the Week talks about an item that is personally significant and may play a role in his or her future. The treasures (or a photo of the treasures) are displayed on a bulletin board reserved for Student of the Week.

Implementing "Student of the Week"

1. The teacher introduces this activity to the class during the first week of school.
2. The teacher reads aloud the poem "What's in the Sack?" by Shel Silverstein from *Where the Sidewalk Ends* (New York: Harper and Row, 1974).
3. Students generate questions that help to determine what might be in the sack (e.g., How large is the sack? Is he carrying the sack? Does the sack look full?)
4. The teacher shows a sack in which she or he has placed a personal treasure. The idea of a "personal treasure" is discussed with students.
5. The teacher then shares the treasure with students using a Tell, Relate, Reflect framework:
   - Tell about what the treasure is.
   - Relate or explain the treasure's personal significance.

Other great books to use with this activity include *Five Secrets in a Box* by Catherine Brighton (New York: Dutton, 1987), *Something Beautiful* by Sharon Dennis Wyeth (New York: Doubleday, 1998), and *Miss Bridie Chose a Shovel* by Leslie Connor (Boston: Houghton Mifflin, 2004).

- Reflect on how the treasure may affect your future (what you might wonder about).

6. The teacher continues to demonstrate the oral presentation throughout the first week of school.

7. At the end of the week, one student's name is drawn from a hat to be the next Student of the Week.

8. A parent information letter is sent home with the student explaining the Student of the Week process.

BLM 1: Student of the Week

Setting Classroom Expectations

Research by Allington and Johnston suggests that classroom organization and management have a direct effect on classroom instruction. By establishing clear classroom expectations and behavioural routines at the beginning of the year, and explicitly teaching them through modelling, demonstrating, and explaining, teachers ensure progress for all learners.

Expectations guide students as they work toward independence. Since they know what is expected, any surprises for them or their parents are avoided. While some teachers prefer to set the expectations, others see the value of involving students in the process, perhaps through a shared writing lesson. If the teacher is setting the expectations, each rule must be carefully explained and any confusion clarified. Ideally, a classroom should have no more than five rules. Once developed, the classroom rules or expectations should remain highly visible to enable teachers, students, and parents to refer to them throughout the year.

Implementing Classroom Expectations

1. The teacher shares the reasoning behind the need to have classroom rules.

2. Students are given some time to ponder what rules are needed.

3. The class then brainstorms ideas, which are recorded.

4. Ideas are categorized and students are divided into small groups.

5. One category is assigned to each group of students for the purpose of summarizing the ideas into one succinct statement.

6. Groups share their statement with the class and seek input from peers.

7. A classroom chart of rules is created and prominently displayed in the classroom.

Caught in the Act

For this activity, teachers and students identify behaviours in the classroom or around the school that promote a safe learning environment and develop responsible citizens. Such socially acceptable behaviours include taking turns, sharing equipment, including others, providing positive feedback, and following classroom procedures.

Implementing "Caught in the Act"

1. Teachers identify behaviours to "catch," and then create with the class a T-chart outlining what the behaviours look and sound like.

2. The T-chart is prominently displayed in the classroom.

3. Students are challenged to catch their classmates in the act of behaving responsibly.

4. The teacher provides blank Caught in the Act forms on which students record the classmate's name, a brief note about the behaviour observed, and the student's own signature.

5. Completed forms are posted in the classroom.

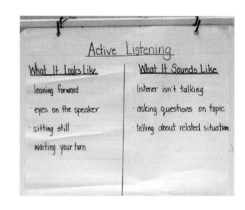

Morning Meeting

One way to build a sense of community within the classroom is to hold a Morning Meeting. Teachers gather the students together for a common purpose at the start of each day. During this time, they engage students in purposeful talk. They outline the expectations of the day and clarify questions or concerns. They set a safe and caring tone and try to instill a sense of fun. The Morning Meeting is also an opportunity to focus on social skills and to target a specific academic skill. Finally, teachers "defrazzle" students who may be feeling anxious, unsafe, or stressed.

"[F]or learning to take place, learners must feel safe. Morning Meeting helps to create a safety zone and maintain a climate of trust, respect and belonging."

BONDY AND KETTS 2001, 8

Implementing the Morning Meeting

The Morning Meeting usually lasts between 10 and 15 minutes and consists of four components.

1. **Greeting:** The teacher engages students in different ways of greeting their classmates (e.g., shaking hands, sharing greetings in other languages, and so on).

2. **Sharing:** The teacher selects two or three students each day to share something personal or to talk about a current event. The rest of the class is encouraged to offer empathy or ask questions.

3. **Group Activity:** Students are then engaged in a brief but involving activity (e.g., a word or mind game, chant, rap, or poetry reading).

4. **News and Announcements:** The teacher writes classroom news or expectations on chart paper or on the board and ensures the message is displayed for the remainder of the day.

Circle Meeting

This cooperative activity provides a forum for students to share ideas, feelings, and opinions about the workings of their classroom.

Implementing a Circle Meeting

1. With students seated in a large circle, the teacher first reviews the rules governing classroom discussion. For example:
   - Only one person speaks at a time.
   - Wait your turn—don't interrupt.
   - Listen attentively to other speakers.
   - If you disagree, do so in a polite and agreeable way.
   - Ask questions when you don't understand.
   - Encourage everyone to take part in the discussion.

   Alternatively, students generate rules collectively as a shared writing activity. When students "own" the rules, they are more likely to follow them.

2. The teacher then asks a question or provides a sentence stem for student responses. For example:
   - What did you do today to help our class work as a community of learners?
   - What other things can you do to help?
   - What was the best thing that you accomplished today?
   - What changes would you make to help yourself be more successful?

3. Encourage discussion etiquette.

4. Comment on class participation in the circle meeting.

The Web of Learning

This cooperative activity is best completed after students have had the opportunity to delve more deeply into a specific topic or concept. A large ball of string is all that is required.

Implementing the Web of Learning

1. Students form a large circle.

2. The teacher begins the web by citing one new idea, fact, or concept that the class has learned.

3. The teacher then calls out one student's name to receive the ball of string.

4. While holding on to the end of the string, the teacher gently tosses the ball to the student.

5. The student receiving the ball of string shares another idea, fact, or concept, and then calls out the name of another person to receive the string. Remind students to hold the string with one hand as they toss with the other.

6. Students may exercise the option of passing.

As students share their ideas and toss the ball of string, the web of learning is created. The fun comes at the end of the session when the string is rewound and its path is retraced.

Ongoing Assessment

The primary purpose of assessment is to acquire ongoing feedback to enhance teaching and learning. In fact, significant research supports the premise that assessment drives instruction. Effective teachers establish clear literacy goals and skills and use a variety of assessment tools to gather information about their students' learning. "The use of diagnostic, formative, and summative measures help to determine where ... students are, where they should be going, and how to get them there" (Schwartz and Pollishuke 2002, 170).

Diagnostic	Formative	Summative
• occurs at the beginning of the school year and whenever information about a student's prior learning is needed • determines the strengths, skills, and knowledge students have • used to make informed decisions about where to focus instructional time and effort	• similar to diagnostic assessment • occurs throughout the year • provides ongoing feedback to teacher and students about the effectiveness of instruction and learning • used to reflect on program structure and effectiveness, and to modify or adjust teaching as necessary	• occurs at the end of a unit, term, or year • provides feedback to students and parents about progress and achievement and demonstrates growth over time • used to determine program effectiveness and where improvements or interventions are required • used in evaluation

Collecting, analyzing, and evaluating assessment data, and then planning student instruction or intervention based on the results can be a formidable task. To facilitate the process, effective teachers

- use clear benchmarks
- embed assessment in instruction (e.g., conduct a record of oral reading during guided reading)
- implement a manageable system for record-keeping
- provide "authentic" reading and writing tasks (e.g., learning logs and literature circles)
- use a consistent set of assessment tools
- plan next steps for teaching using both individual and class results
- provide student self-assessment opportunities

Intervention

By Grades 3 and 4, most students have developed a foundation in reading, writing, and speaking and are successfully on their way to developing more complex understandings. Others, however, experience a "fourth-grade slump" (which may actually occur later, and may continue through high school). This slump may be due to the sudden complexity of text, the use of poorly written informational text, or an ineffective bank of decoding and comprehension strategies. Furthermore, students often enter Grade 4 with little nonfiction experience.

Research indicates that there are three key areas of difficulty for struggling readers:

- word identification (word reading in isolation and in context)
- meaning (comprehension and vocabulary)
- fluency (rate and expression)

What is interesting about the research is that most struggling students are not weak in all three areas (Valencia and Riddle Buly 2004, 520–31). Students who struggle with word identification generally also experience fluency and comprehension problems. These students may have a limited sight vocabulary, possibly combined with a lack of decoding skills, or limited decoding skills and a slow decoding speed. Therefore, effective intervention must target decoding and automatic word recognition.

Students who struggle with comprehension, however, may decode well and read fluently, and thus may go unnoticed. To provide appropriate intervention, teachers need to distinguish effective comprehenders from "word callers." The latter may be unaware that reading needs to make sense, or they may have limited self-monitoring strategies.

An effective comprehensive literacy program, coupled with the use of clear benchmarks, provides teachers with the strategies and data necessary for the provision of timely and skillful intervention. For some students, practice time is all that is required and teachers may arrange for adult volunteers or reading buddies to provide this additional practice. (For more details, see Developing Home–School–Community Partnerships toward the end of this chapter.) However, other students may require more direct instruction and ongoing assistance.

Teachers need support for their efforts to find intervention solutions that work. Reflecting on the classroom program as a whole may help teachers to find the answers. Sometimes, readjusting the classroom schedule provides more time for authentic reading and writing, as well as more opportunities for intervention. At other times, more resources and support staff may be necessary.

For more detailed information on intervention strategies, see Chapter 6: Supporting Struggling and Reluctant Readers.

Development of Home–School–Community Partnerships

Much research supports the notion that students experience greater success and are more likely to stay in school when their parents take an active role in their education. However, by Grades 3 and 4, many parents seem somewhat reluctant to read to and with their child; they

"Explicit instruction is especially important for struggling readers because it provides additional support and instruction before failure overwhelms the student."

Burns 1999, 8

"One substantial shift that is needed immediately in most schools is redesigning the use of instructional support personnel such that intensive interventions can be offered.... Rethinking how we design remedial and special education support is needed in most schools."

Allington 2001, 120

"Family involvement in a child's education is a more important factor in student's success than family income or education."

International Reading Association 2002, 2

are also less apt to volunteer in classrooms. By Grade 6, this reluctance increases dramatically. Therefore, the teacher often takes the initiative to provide encouragement and direction for parents. Ongoing communication through phone calls and newsletters may help parents feel more at ease and provide them with tips and strategies to help their child at home.

The use of parent or community volunteers in the classroom has a positive impact on the classroom environment, particularly when they receive direction and instruction. Spending time to train classroom volunteers results in teachers gaining more time to provide direct support and instruction to their students.

Paraprofessional support also makes a positive difference. Paraprofessionals take direction and guidance from the classroom teacher; they are not responsible for the explicit planning, delivery, or assessment of the program. After the teacher's lesson, a paraprofessional monitors and assists individuals or small groups by

- restating the concepts, ideas, and skills
- chunking the task or text
- asking guiding questions
- seeking clarification
- reviewing basic skills
- scribing for the student

See Developing Home–School–Community Partnerships later in this chapter for more information.

Assessment

Effective literacy teachers use a variety of assessment strategies to determine whether literacy goals are being met and students are acquiring the skills and strategies needed to become fluent readers, writers, speakers, listeners, viewers, and representers. They know that the assessments they use provide them with the evidence and knowledge needed to make informed instructional decisions about new learning and to report to students and parents about strengths and areas for improvement. They begin by collecting baseline data and, through ongoing assessments, chart growth and development. At certain points throughout the year, they check their students' progress using summative assessment tools. Their aim is to ensure students reach the appropriate benchmarks and achieve their goals.

Assessment tools, from informal observations to detailed rubrics, measure student growth and development. The results of these varied assessments are used to provide new and ongoing opportunities for students to maximize their learning.

Assessment enables teachers to measure both process and product and to plan for future work. Although teachers plan and conduct most assessments, students benefit greatly when meaningfully engaged in the assessment process. The more students understand what will be assessed and why, the better able they are to attain the

"An extraordinary amount of information can be gathered informally and unobtrusively as teachers watch their students participating in daily activities."

BURNS 1999, 257

The Assessment–Instruction Connection

What do I need to know?
- students' prior knowledge of, and understanding about, reading, writing, vocabulary, and use of oral language
- students' interests and attitudes toward reading and writing
- strategies students use to read, write, listen, speak, and view
- appropriate benchmarks, expectations, and outcomes

How will I find out?
- gather data using observations, work samples, checklists, self-assessments and reflections, surveys, inventories, and interviews

What will I do with the information?
- analyze and reflect on the data
- share results with students (and with parents as necessary)
- engage students in setting goals
- use results to plan future learning experiences
- gather and use appropriate resources and texts
- use a variety of teaching approaches and strategies
- provide meaningful activities
- weigh results against benchmarks
- provide timely and effective intervention
- regroup students

targets. Therefore, peer- and self-assessments should be part of the data collected and used by teachers. Having varied assessments is also useful when reporting to parents.

Parental assessment can also help to document student progress. Interest surveys, student–parent conferences, and feedback forms are useful ways to involve parents in the assessment process.

Assessment BLM 1: Literacy Home Links: Survey

Understanding what students know and are able to do enables teachers to plan for future learning, group students appropriately, and provide specific, effective, and timely intervention. Being familiar with the learning stages and benchmarks of development helps teachers direct, or in some cases redirect, their instruction. Effective teachers make assessment purposeful and directly linked to learning experiences to ensure that reliable and valid data are collected.

Assessing Students' Strengths and Needs

It is important to note that not all of these assessments need to be completed with every student.

To determine students' ...	Consider using ...
views/beliefs of reading and writing	• observations of choices students make and reactions to activities • teacher–student interviews • student self-assessment of reading and writing progress • learning logs
attitude toward reading and writing	• observations • parent survey (Assessment BLM 1) • student self-assessment of attitudes and interests (Assessment BLMs 2 and 3) • book choices on reading log • interviews with student and/or family member
listening comprehension	• observations during discussions, literature circles, and so on • listening comprehension assessments
level of appropriate text	• records of oral reading/comprehension • benchmark books
use of reading strategies (See Chapter 2: Reading Comprehension: Strategies That Work)	• reading conferences (Assessment BLM 4) • observations during guided, shared, and independent reading (Assessment BLM 5) • records of oral reading—use of fix-up strategies • think-alouds • benchmark books • oral questions or surveys • miscue analyses/running records • student self-assessments • developmental continua
reading comprehension (See Chapter 2: Reading Comprehension: Strategies That Work)	• retellings—oral and written for fiction and nonfiction (Assessment BLMs 6 and 7) • reading conferences • Question–Answer Relationships (right there, on my own, think and search, author and me)

	• observations of text-to-self, text-to-text, and text-to-world connections • cloze activities • comprehension strategy checklists • student self-assessments of comprehension strategies • records of oral reading—use of fix-up strategies • benchmark books • response activities (e.g., journals, story maps, book talks, drama, art) • observations during literature circles, book clubs, read-aloud discussions, and think-alouds • developmental continua
response to literature	• response journals • reading logs • observations during guided and independent reading • observations during read-aloud discussions
oral reading fluency rate	• benchmark books • timed records of student reading • miscue analyses/running records
word identification	• observations during shared and guided reading and writing, classroom activities, and games • cloze activities • records of oral reading • high-frequency word assessment (Assessment BLM 8)
use of writing strategies (See Chapter 3: Writing: The Reading–Writing Connection)	• observations during shared, guided, and independent writing • samples from writing performance tasks • writing conferences • skills/writing traits checklists • student self-assessments of writing strategies
acquisition of vocabulary and oral language (See Chapter 1: Oral Language: Speaking, Listening, and Learning)	• observations of students speaking informally to peers and formally to a partner, small group, or entire class • answers to questions • retellings—oral and written • writing samples • teacher–student interviews • drama activities (e.g., role-playing a character) • developmental continua
growth over time	• goal setting (Assessment BLMs 9 and 11) • portfolio samples (Assessment BLMs 9 and 10)
metacognition	• student think-alouds • conferences and interviews • portfolios (Assessment BLM 9) • student self-reflection activities • learning logs • goal setting

Developing an Assessment Plan

The following charts outline an assessment plan that could be used throughout the year in Grades 3 to 6 classrooms. It is important to note that not all assessments need to be completed for all students. Those marked with an asterisk (*) are explained in more detail under Assessment Strategies.

Diagnostic Assessment (Baseline Data)

While diagnostic assessment is used throughout the school year, baseline data is generally collected during the first five weeks of school.

Teacher/Student	Student	Parent
• informal reading conference* • benchmark book* that includes oral reading, retell or summary, and interpretation of book • listening comprehension assessment • writing task • high-frequency word assessment* (if concerned about fluency)	• attitude survey • interest inventory • goal setting • portfolio*	• home survey

Assessment BLM 1: Literacy Home Links: Survey

Assessment BLM 2: Attitude Survey

Assessment BLM 3: Interest Inventory

Assessment BLM 4: Informal Reading Conference

Assessment BLM 8: High-Frequency Word Assessment

Check It Out!

Regie Routman, *Conversations: Strategies for Teaching, Learning, and Evaluating* (Portsmouth, NH: Heinemann, 2000).

Regie Routman, *Invitations: Changing As Teachers and Learners K–12* (Portsmouth, NH: Heinemann, 1994).

Irene C. Fountas and Gay Su Pinnell, *Guiding Readers and Writers, Grades 3–6: Teaching Comprehension, Genre, and Content Literacy* (Portsmouth, NH: Heinemann, 2001).

Lucy McCormick Calkins, *The Art of Teaching Reading* (New York: Addison Wesley Longman, 2001).

These books have strong chapters on assessment.

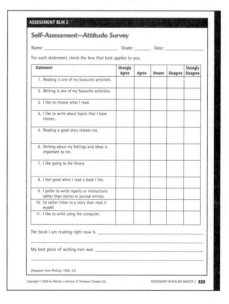

"Our classroom-based system of assessment should wreak havoc with any instructional plan that doesn't allow us the elasticity and breadth necessary to teach the full range of readers. Our assessments should nudge us, as teachers, to look at all our children and their work, and to look at ourselves and our work."

CALKINS 2001, 157

Formative Assessment (Ongoing)

This form of assessment is used throughout the school year.

Teachers gather this data to develop a profile of each student. By determining the skills, knowledge, attitudes, and interests that students already possess, teachers better target needs and plan activities that both challenge and support their students.

"An important prerequisite for providing engaging instruction is to find out more about your students as readers and writers, to investigate their reading and writing habits, interests, and attitudes. One way to do this is to ask students to respond to a reading interview in writing or to ask them ... survey type questions in an interview."

FOUNTAS AND PINNELL 2001, 9

Teacher/Student	Student	Parent
• observation • reading/writing conference • record of oral reading* • questions and answers (literal, inferential, critical, evaluative) • reading records/logs* • cloze activities • high-frequency word assessment*	• self-reflection • peer assessment • conferences • review of goals • portfolio samples • learning log/journal • reading records/logs* • exemplars	• conferences • feedback/response forms • questionnaires

Assessment BLM 9: Portfolio Tagging Sheets

Assessment BLM 10: Portfolio Partners

Summative Assessment (Culminating)

This form of assessment is completed at the end of a term, unit of study, or year.

Teacher/Student	Student	Parent
• benchmark book* • record of oral reading* • writing task • portfolio* • performance tasks	• self-reflection on portfolio,* goal achievement, reading records/logs*	• portfolio assessment

Assessment BLM 11: Assessing My Year

For many other assessment tools specifically related to oral language, reading comprehension, writing, and literacy learning, see Chapters 1 through 4.

Assessment Strategies

Effective teachers use the data obtained from both informal and formal assessment opportunities to plan and guide instruction, ensuring it is meaningful for all students and assists them in achieving their goals. Although teachers can use many strategies to identify students' unique strengths and needs, much research supports in particular the value of

- informal reading conferences
- high-frequency word assessments
- records of oral reading
- benchmark books
- oral and written retellings
- reading records or logs (student self-assessment)
- portfolios (student self-assessment)

Informal Reading Conferences

In this type of conference, teachers engage one student in a brief, informal conversation to gain greater insight into that student's reading skills and strategies. The focus of the discussion may differ with each individual student, with the teacher asking questions to clarify aspects of the student's performance. The conference also allows students to express thoughts, feelings, and opinions about the text they are reading or have read.

Studies have shown that "there exists a potent relationship between volume of reading and reading achievement. The recent correlational data from the NAEP [National Association of Elementary Principals] studies suggest that volume may be critically important in developing thoughtful literacy proficiencies" (Allington 2001, 33). Informal conferences allow teachers to monitor students' reading materials, ensuring they are at an independent level (95 percent accuracy rate or higher with comprehension).

Informal reading conferences provide information about a student's
- ability to select appropriate text
- retelling or summarizing skills
- oral reading fluency (expression, phrasing, speaking rate, and accuracy rate) and behaviours
- literal, inferential, critical, and reflective comprehension
- awareness and use of comprehension strategies
- ability to set realistic goals

Implementing Informal Reading Conferences

1. Students bring to the conference the text being read during independent reading. *(Is the student able to select texts he or she can read and understand?)*

2. The teacher asks the student to explain the choice of text. *(Does the student take recommendations from peers? Is this a favourite author or series? Is the student relying too much on being able to read all the words?)*

3. The student tells what the text is about so far. *(Can the student give an adequate retelling that reveals an understanding of the gist of the text?)*

4. The teacher prompts the student to read part of the text orally or

A reading conference may simply be an informal conversation about what is being read.

silently, and then observes the reading strategies or behaviours. If fluency is a concern, the teacher notes the time the student begins and ends the reading to determine an approximate reading rate. If the student is reading orally, the teacher records any miscues. *(During oral reading, does the student reread, seem to use illustrations and visuals, understand the humour, skip over difficult vocabulary? Does the student subvocalize during silent reading?)*

If oral reading is a problem, the teacher helps the student select a more appropriate text for independent reading.

5. The teacher has the student retell what was just read. *(If the text is fiction, does the student understand character motivation and behaviour? If the text is nonfiction, does the student use charts, photos, and graphs to get information? Is the student going beyond literal events in the retelling?)*

6. The teacher engages the student in a discussion about reading strengths and areas for growth. The student is then asked to state one or two goals that resulted from the conference. *(Is the student able to set realistic goals for reading?)*

(Adapted from Routman 2000, 115–16)

For more information, see Reading Conferences—Having a Conversation! in Chapter 2: Reading Comprehension: Strategies That Work.

Assessment BLM 4: Informal Reading Conference
Assessment BLM 10: Informal Reading Conference in Chapter 2

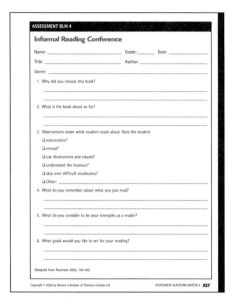

High-Frequency Word Assessments

This assessment strategy is used when teachers are concerned about a student's reading fluency. Readers who can quickly recognize most words in text are more able to focus on the meaning of the text. High-frequency word assessments enable teachers to determine the student's ability to accurately and effortlessly recognize many words as whole units (automaticity).

The comprehension of text requires rapid and fluent word identification. Many high-frequency words are considered irregular because they do not follow the commonly taught sound–symbol relationships and often have little meaning. However, these words affect the flow and coherence of text. Research has shown that students need to read a great deal at their independent reading level to develop automaticity of high-frequency words (Beck and Juel 1995, as cited in Blevins 2001).

High-frequency word assessments provide information about a student's
- sight-word proficiency and automaticity
- decoding strengths and areas for growth

Implementing High-Frequency Word Assessments

1. The teacher makes two copies of the high-frequency word sheet: one for the student and one for recording the student's responses.

2. The teacher sets a stopwatch for 90 seconds and directs the student to read as many words as possible in that time.

3. The teacher analyzes the results by counting the number of words the student read correctly, and identifying any patterns of mispronounced or skipped words.

Assessment BLM 8: High-Frequency Word Assessment

Records of Oral Reading

To create a record of oral reading, the teacher listens as the student reads aloud. As the student reads, the teacher uses a set of symbols to transcribe the student's reading. Teachers often refer to this procedure as taking a running record or performing a miscue analysis. This strategy enables teachers to systematically record what a student does while reading and assists in determining a student's independent, instructional, or frustrational reading level.

Studies by Allington and Cunningham (1996) indicate that students reading at less than a 90 percent rate of accuracy often cannot readily understand a text and tend to rely on less efficient strategies to decode and comprehend. Conversely, some students can decode text accurately, but not comprehend it, while a few very weak decoders still manage to make sense of the passage. Students need to read materials within an appropriate range to continue to develop reading skills and strategies.

Readers Theatre is a great way to improve students' fluency rates. As students practise rereading the text, they improve automaticity and fluency. (More information on Readers Theatre appears later in this chapter.)

A record of oral reading provides information about a student's
- use of cueing systems (semantic, syntactic, and graphophonic) and reading strategies to decode and comprehend text
- timed reading rate
- phrasing, fluency, intonation, and comprehension

Implementing Records of Oral Reading

1. The teacher explains the purpose of the reading record and provides a brief introduction to the text. Students may read familiar text (e.g., independent reading material) or unfamiliar text (e.g., a benchmark book).

2. As the student reads the text orally, the teacher takes note of fluency and uses a set of symbols to record everything the student says or does while reading. If fluency is a concern, the teacher may use a stopwatch to time the reading.

3. The teacher then has the student retell or simply discuss the text to check comprehension.

4. After praising the student's reading, the teacher scores and analyzes the record to determine the student's strengths and areas for growth.

Check It Out!

These books are helpful when completing a record of oral reading: Irene C. Fountas and Gay Su Pinnell, *Guiding Readers and Writers, Grades 3–6: Teaching Comprehension, Genre, and Content Literacy* (Portsmouth, NH: Heinemann, 2000).

Mary Shea, *Taking Running Records* (New York: Scholastic Professional Books, 2000).

To calculate oral reading fluency and for a range of adequate reading rates by grade level, see Reading Rate under Assessment in Chapter 6: Supporting Struggling and Reluctant Readers. See also the Scale for Oral Reading Fluency in Chapter 2: Reading Comprehension: Strategies That Work.

Benchmark Books

Benchmark books enable teachers to track a student's reading progress over time. Each book in a set of benchmark books has specific text features and characteristics. Within a set, such as PM Benchmarks, books progress in level of difficulty.

This assessment strategy assists teachers in monitoring a student's growth in reading skills (e.g., fluency and comprehension) and proficiency with the strategies that effective readers use. It also helps teachers determine the range of text suitable for a student's independent and guided reading (instructional) level.

Skill is the ability to perform a task; **strategy** is a conscious knowing of when, how, and why to use the skill.

Benchmark books provide information about a student's

- oral reading fluency (expression, phrasing, speaking rate, and accuracy rate) and behaviours
- predicting skills
- independent reading level
- retelling or summarizing skills
- literal, inferential, critical, and reflective comprehension
- awareness and use of comprehension strategies
- appropriate text level

Implementing Benchmark Books

1. The teacher identifies a book that is at the student's instructional level (90–95 percent accuracy).

2. The teacher introduces the selected text by reading the title and discussing the cover.

3. The student reads the text aloud as the teacher records what the student says and does while reading.

4. The student then completes a retelling.

5. The teacher asks additional questions to check for understanding, to address any gaps in the retelling, or to extend the student's thinking.

6. The accuracy rate and level of understanding are calculated using a comprehension rubric. (These rubrics usually accompany the benchmark book.) If accuracy is 90–95 percent and the level of understanding is appropriate, then the book is at the student's instructional level.

7. The teacher identifies the student's strengths as a reader and determines the next steps in reading instruction.

Oral and Written Retellings

Oral and written retellings enable the teacher to determine a student's overall comprehension of material read. They also provide information about the student's literal and inferential interpretation of text.

Studies indicate that, through the use of retelling, students come to understand that reading requires critical thinking and the construction of meaning (Benson and Cummins 2000, 7). When students anticipate having to retell the text, reading engagement is often heightened; they read actively and project themselves into the text. Research has also shown that retelling reveals when struggling readers have difficulty determining the main idea, linking pieces of information, and making personal connections.

Oral and written retellings provide information about a student's

- understanding of the main idea, events, characters, setting, and important details in a text
- ability to logically sequence events, procedures, or directions
- use of vocabulary or phrases from fiction or factual text
- literal recall
- ability to make personal connections

Implementing Oral and Written Retellings

1. The teacher predicts that the student can recognize 95 percent or more of the words in the text to be read and is aware that a retelling will be required once the reading is complete.

2. The teacher uses an unaided retelling, providing prompts only if the student is experiencing difficulty.

Prompts for Fiction Retells	Prompts for Nonfiction Retells
• Can you tell me who else was in the story? • Where else does the story take place? • What other events occurred in the story? • How did the story end? • How was the problem solved? • In what way did the main character change?	• What else did you discover when reading the text? • What new or surprising information did you learn? • What other steps were part of the procedure? • What other words were used to describe ... ? • What term or definition was given to ... ?

For more information on assessing comprehension, see Chapter 2: Reading Comprehension: Strategies That Work.

Assessment BLM 6: Retelling/Interpreting Checklist—Narrative Text

Assessment BLM 7: Retelling/Interpreting Checklist—Informational Text

Reading Records or Logs (Student Self-Assessment)

A reading record or log is completed by the student during or after independent reading. The information recorded includes any or all of the following:

- title and author of text
- genre
- pages read per day
- average number of pages read per book
- personal response

An analysis of a student's reading log enables the teacher and the student to see the range and quantity of text read over a given period of time. This information is used to help students balance their reading diet, set personal reading goals, and match their interests with books. Increased reading does not necessarily result in reading proficiency, however. Students must be able to understand what they are reading, which is why it is so critically important that their reading material is at an independent level (95 percent accuracy rate or higher).

Reading records or logs provide information about
- the number of books read by the student
- the difficulty level of the books read
- the range of genres, authors, and types of text read
- the student's reading preferences and interests
- the frequency and length of time spent reading
- the reading rate

Implementing Reading Records or Logs

1. The teacher demonstrates how to complete a reading record or log.

2. Using a form distributed by the teacher or a designated notebook page, students record the title and author of each text read, the genre, the date each text was completed, and a personal rating of or response to the text. The teacher reminds students to record the title and author each time they begin a new reading selection and, when finished, to complete the other sections of the log.

3. The teacher scans each student's reading record during a reading conference or while circulating throughout the classroom. Anecdotal notes are made about the quantity, breadth, and difficulty level of the texts the student has read.

4. Using the log and anecdotal notes, the teacher works with the student to examine and then provide text suggestions to expand the student's reading diet.

For more information about reading logs, see Chapter 2: Reading Comprehension: Strategies That Work.

BLM 3: Keeping Track in Chapter 2

Portfolios (Student Self-Assessment)

A student literacy portfolio demonstrates growth over time. By reflecting on the contents of their portfolios, students are able to set goals and focus on their learning strengths, styles, and needs.

Literacy portfolios may feature both reading and writing selections. Suggestions related to reading include reading logs, response journal entries, charts of books read, and audiotapes of oral readings and retellings. Suggestions related to writing include personal journal entries about writing tasks and written pieces in various stages, such as draft.

Electronic portfolios provide an efficient way for students to collect and organize their work samples. They are easily stored and provide students with further options to demonstrate growth in literacy. The inclusion of video clips, scanned images, oral presentations, multimedia projects, and digital photos ensures a more complete record of progress over time.

The use of literacy portfolios as a self-assessment tool has been well documented by researchers and classroom teachers. "Student portfolios contain the valuable evidence needed by the teacher, the student and the parents to readily measure progress and growth. The portfolio provides tangible evidence to support the report card mark. When students self-assess to make selections for their portfolios, it leads to self-reflection and goal setting" (Easley and Mitchell 2003, 21).

Check It Out!

This Web site explains the creation and use of electronic portfolios: http://www.ash.udel.edu/ash/teacher/portfolio.html

Portfolios provide information about a student's
* personal growth and development over time
* ability to self-assess and reflect on thinking (metacognition)
* progress on meeting goals and actions taken
* strengths and areas for improvement

Implementing Portfolios

1. The teacher develops a plan for the possible contents of the literacy portfolio and devises a management strategy.

2. The teacher introduces students to the concept of portfolios. Parents are also informed of the portfolio process through newsletters or portfolio nights.

3. The teacher demonstrates how criteria provide the opportunity to assess work and develop goals from the assessment information.

4. Working collaboratively, the teacher and students develop criteria to assist in the selection of work samples. The teacher then collects baseline samples.

5. The teacher schedules times for students to select and reflect on their portfolio samples, using the criteria as the basis for self-assessment. Students complete a written reflection and attach it to the samples.

How to Assess Your Portfolio

1. Write your name, grade, and date on the appropriate tagging sheet.

2. Look at your sample and the criteria for this subject area. Use these questions to guide your thinking:
   a) What does this sample tell about your strengths (e.g., what you do well; what you have learned)?
   b) What could you do to improve in this subject area?
   c) What else would you like to learn?

3. Complete the tagging sheet by recording your response to question (a).

4. Using your responses to questions (b) and (c), write a realistic goal about what you plan to accomplish next.

6. Students are provided with the opportunity to work with a partner to present portfolio contents.

7. The teacher conducts portfolio conferences with students. Portfolios are also shared during parent–teacher or student-led conferences.

8. Students continue to select portfolio samples in various areas of literacy, reflecting on their progress and setting further goals.

For more information on portfolios, see Chapter 3: Writing: The Reading–Writing Connection and Chapter 4: Literacy Learning Across the Curriculum.

Assessment BLM 9: Portfolio Tagging Sheets
Assessment BLM 10: Portfolio Partners
Assessment BLM 11: Assessing My Year
Assessment BLM 2: Assessing Portfolio Contents in an Integrated Unit in Chapter 4
Assessment BLM 3: Using My Portfolio to Reflect on My Learning in Chapter 4

Linking Assessment to Instruction

Daily, ongoing collection and analysis of data ensure that professional, informed decisions are made regarding instruction, student groupings, appropriate resources, and the modifications necessary to meet the needs of all learners.

An effective, comprehensive literacy program is driven by assessment and comprises the following elements:

- oral language
- read-aloud
- shared reading
- guided reading
- literacy activities (involving lots of independent reading and writing)
- balanced writing
- word study

It is structured to move students from high teacher support and student dependence to low teacher support and student independence, with a balance among whole-group, small-group, and individual teaching approaches.

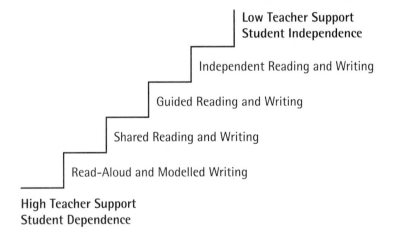

**Low Teacher Support
Student Independence**

Independent Reading and Writing

Guided Reading and Writing

Shared Reading and Writing

Read-Aloud and Modelled Writing

**High Teacher Support
Student Dependence**

It is also important for a comprehensive literacy program to be organized and managed effectively and to foster partnerships with the home, the school, and the community at large.

Oral Language

Oral language is the foundation of all literacy learning. It is often linked to reading and writing and occurs naturally and intentionally across the whole day. Therefore, purposeful oral communication should provide the foundation for all language activities. Effective teachers explicitly model and teach oral communication skills in meaningful contexts. Students then apply their skills as they problem solve their way through reading and writing.

"Assessment and evaluation are the foundations upon which you build your classroom program. They are integral components of the teaching/learning process. Essentially, assessment and evaluation are what drive your program, setting the direction and flow of your curriculum and actions."

SCHWARTZ AND POLLISHUKE 2002, 169

For a detailed look at oral language research, assessment, and instruction in Grades 3 to 6, see Chapter 1.

Read-Aloud

Teachers read aloud material that their students may not choose to read, or may be unable to read independently. They also read aloud material that they think will entice students to read on their own. They model fluent reading and think-alouds while their students listen.

Think-Alouds

Think-alouds enable teachers to demonstrate for students the reading process. As the text is read aloud, the teacher articulates the thought processes used to comprehend the text. By modelling the strategies proficient readers use before, during, and after reading, teachers demonstrate how effective readers interact with a text.

Comprehension strategies such as monitoring comprehension, making connections, asking questions, visualizing, inferring, finding the important ideas, and synthesizing information can be made explicit for students through the think-aloud process. Before reading, teachers decide on a strategy focus and the book that best facilitates the chosen strategy. While reading the text, the teacher stops at strategic points to model the think-aloud for students. A helpful approach is to write thoughts on a sticky note and place these at the strategic points. This preplanning ensures clarity and succinctness and guards against interrupting the flow of the text.

The sentence stems and picture books suggested under During Reading later in this section may prove useful when demonstrating through think-alouds.

For more information on think-alouds, see Chapter 2: Reading Comprehension: Strategies That Work.

"Because sustaining comprehension and interest throughout an entire book is often a challenge for students at this age, read-aloud time is a great way to model and teach the strategies that promote persistence and stamina."

SIBBERSON AND SZYMUSIAK 2003, 79

Read-alouds in Grades 3 to 6 are planned-for experiences that allow teachers to

- promote a love of reading
- introduce students to new authors and genres
- encourage an appreciation for authors and illustrators
- model proficient, fluent reading and think-alouds
- engage students in thoughtful discussions about texts
- assist students in constructing meaning of texts that are beyond their current reading level
- stimulate an interest in words and in the ways authors use them
- help students learn the traits of good writing
- expand spoken and written vocabulary
- present more formal syntax and structures of book language

Planning for Read-Alouds
Frequency and Grouping
Ideally, read-alouds are scheduled daily for a minimum of 15 minutes per session. They can involve either the whole class or a small group.

Materials
A variety of texts can be used for a read-aloud:

- well-crafted picture books, short stories, poetry, informational and persuasive text, novels, science fiction, fantasy, articles, and biographies
- books that evoke strong emotions, encourage critical thinking and critical literacy, and promote thoughtful conversations (e.g., books by Chris Van Allsburg, Eve Bunting, Patricia Polacco, Sharon Creech, Cynthia Rylant, Jane Yolen, and Phyllis Reynolds Naylor)
- books with strong plots and subplots
- books that support integration (e.g., social studies, science, math)

Many fiction and nonfiction authors have numerous works that captivate young readers. Introducing students to a particular author encourages them to read other books by the same author.

Captivating Authors for Grades 3 to 6	
Linda Bailey	Ted Harrison
Fiona Bayrock	James Howe
Judy Blume	Joanna Hurwitz
Tonya Bolden	E.L. Konigsburg
Lisa Burby	Gordon Korman
Beverly Cleary	Madeleine L'Engle
Joanna Cole	Lois Lowry
Roald Dahl	Katherine Paterson
Mem Fox	Gary Paulsen
Gail Gibbons	Jon Scieszka
Patricia Reilly Giff	Shelley Tanaka

Implementing Read-Alouds
Before a Read-Aloud

1. The teacher selects a text that students will enjoy and records the title on a form such as BLM 2: A Week-at-a-Glance Planner to monitor the range of genres. The teacher then practises reading the text before reading it aloud to the students.

2. The teacher establishes the focus for the read-aloud by determining if the text is
   - connected to a unit of study, for example, in science or social studies
   - an example of a text form that the students will be writing next
   - part of an author or genre study
   - a model for richness of language or the author's literary techniques

3. The students gather together in a comfortable place. During the first few months of school, students are reminded about behaviour expectations during read-alouds (e.g., listening actively).

Check It Out!
The following Web sites recommend great read-aloud picks:

Jim Trelease's Picks of Recent Read-Aloud Novels
http://www.trelease-on-reading.com/whatsnu_novels.html#pagetop

Kids Love a Mystery
http://www.kidsloveamystery.com/

Booktalks Quick and Simple:
http://www.nancykeane.com/booktalks/

Carol Hurst's Children's Literature Site
http://www.carolhurst.com/

"We read aloud to immerse students in terrific literature as well as to teach reading comprehension strategies. Occasionally, we worry that efforts to design reading strategy lessons around trade literature might ruin a great picture book. We know the last thing kids need is a monotonous litany of comprehension lessons every time their teacher picks up a great book to read to them. We need to remember to share books for the sheer joy of reading as well as for strategy instruction."

HARVEY AND GOUDVIS 2000, 32

4. The teacher shares the title, author, and illustrator of the text. If appropriate, the teacher provides connections or background knowledge, and asks students to make predictions about the text.

BLM 2: A Week-at-a-Glance Planner

During a Read-Aloud

1. The teacher reads the text with good phrasing, intonation, and volume, stopping at strategic points (so as not to interrupt the flow) to ask questions, think aloud, or provide clarification.

2. Illustrations, if applicable, are shared.

3. The teacher engages students with such metacognitive strategies as making text-to-self, text-to-text, and text-to-world connections, predicting, generating and answering questions, visualizing the text, and so on.

Strategies and Sentence Stems	Helpful Picture Books
Making Connections: Effective readers connect what happens in a text to personal experiences, other texts, and what they know about the world. **Sentence Stems** This reminds me of ... It made me think of ... I read another book where ...	*Amazing Grace* by Mary Hoffman (New York: Penguin, 1991). *The Pain and the Great One* by Judy Blume (New York: Bradbury/Paperback Dell, 1974). *Rose Blanche* by Roberto Innocenti (Mankoto, MN: Creative Editions, 1996). *Up North at the Cabin* by Marsha Chall (New York: Lothrop, Lee & Shepard, 1992). *Thank You, Mr. Falker* by Patricia Polacco (New York: Philomel, 1998).
Generating Questions: Effective readers ask themselves questions before, during, and after reading. **Sentence Stems** I wonder if ... I wonder why ... I wonder about ... What is ...	*The Wednesday Surprise* by Eve Bunting (New York: Clarion Books, 1989). *The Stranger* by Chris Van Allsburg (New York: Houghton Mifflin, 1986). *Something Permanent* by Cynthia Rylant (San Diego: Harcourt/Brace, 1994). *Brave Irene* by William Steig (New York: Farrar Straus & Giroux 1986). *Charlie Anderson* by Barbara Abercrombie (New York: Aladdin, 1995).

Visualizing: Effective readers use all of their senses to create mental images that represent the words in a text. **Sentence Stems** I visualized ... I can see (smell, hear, taste) ... I can picture ...	*Fireflies* by Julie Brinkloe (New York: Macmillan, 1985). *Twilight Comes Twice* by Ralph Fletcher (New York: Clarion, 1997). *Greyling* by Jane Yolen (New York: Putnam, 1991). *I'm in Charge of Celebrations* by Byrd Baylor (New York: Simon and Schuster, 1986). *A Lucky Thing* by Alice Schertle (New York: Browndeer/Harcourt Brace, 1999).
Identifying the Key Ideas: Effective readers distinguish important information from unimportant information to identify the key ideas. **Sentence Stems** The most important ideas are ... So far, I have learned that ... Based on my knowledge of _____, I now know ...	*Hungry, Hungry Sharks* by Joanna Cole (New York: Random House, 1986). *The Unhuggables* (Washington, DC: National Wildlife Federation, 1988). *Magic School Bus* series by Joanna Cole (New York: Scholastic).
Synthesizing: Effective readers demonstrate an understanding of the text by summarizing what they have read. **Sentence Stems** Now I understand that ... I have learned that ... This gives me an idea that ...	*Oliver Button Is a Sissy* by Tomie dePaola (New York: Harcourt Brace Jovanovich, 1979). *Smoky Night* by Eve Bunting (New York: Harcourt, 1995). *The Table Where Rich People Sit* by Byrd Baylor (New York: Simon and Schuster, 1994). *Tea with Milk* by Allen Say (Boston: Houghton Mifflin, 1999). *For Every Child a Better World* by Louise Gikow (New York: Muppet Press/Golden Book, 1993).
Inferring: Effective readers combine their own experiences with clues from the text to make sense of, and gain deeper insights into, the text. **Sentence Stems** With the clue on page __ and what I already know, I think ... Based on what I know ... I think that ...	*Encounter* by Jane Yolen (New York: Harcourt Brace Jovanovich, 1992). *Tight Times* by Barbara Shook Hazen (New York: Viking Penguin, 1983). *The Mysteries of Harris Burdick* by Chris Van Allsburg (Boston: Houghton Mifflin, 1984). *Bull Run* by Paul Fleischman (New York: Harper Trophy, 1993). *Fly Away Home* by Eve Bunting (New York: Clarion, 1991).

After a Read-Aloud

Effective teachers engage students in thoughtful conversations after the read-aloud. These conversations may take the form of a teacher-led discussion, literature circles, or book clubs. This "talk time" allows students to discuss teacher-demonstrated strategies and behaviours, or to react to the book, share insights, and clarify their thinking.

Once students have had the opportunity to talk, teachers may engage the class in after-reading activities. Depending on the purpose for the read-aloud, the time may be used to explicitly teach or to enable students to make connections. Recording read-aloud texts on a class reading log enables students to make connections to other texts. Students might create story maps or complete graphic organ-

"An interactive classroom that promotes conversation can provide opportunities for our students to raise the level of their thinking, to dig deep into texts, and to grow as readers."

SIBBERSON AND SZYMUSIAK 2003, 87

izers, such as Venn diagrams; retell or summarize; create timelines or complete plot organizers; write character sketches; develop tableaux; create artistic interpretations; or simply write responses. However, it is important to remember that the read-aloud experience can be ruined if a follow-up activity is always required!

Sample Read-Aloud Lesson

The purpose of this sample lesson is to demonstrate and reinforce the importance of rereading a text. *The Wretched Stone* by Chris Van Allsburg is ideally suited to this lesson; it requires critical inference on the part of the reader. Written in the form of a ship's log, *The Wretched Stone* documents the strange behaviours of crew members during a voyage.

This lesson, which can be readily applied to various texts, works particularly well when implemented near the beginning of the school year.

Sample Read-Aloud Lesson: Day 1

1. The teacher introduces the text to the students. After discussing the title and the cover of the book, students make predictions about the story.

2. The teacher informs students that the text will be read several times to assist them with understanding the author's message. First, the book is read for enjoyment. On the second and third readings (Days 2 and 3), students listen for answers to any questions they may have and try to clarify their understanding.

3. The teacher tells students that they will be expected to respond in their reading journals after the read-aloud.

4. The teacher then reads aloud the entire text without interruption.

5. Students write a personal response in their journals. (See Chapter 2: Reading Comprehension: Strategies That Work and Chapter 3: Writing: The Reading–Writing Connection for more information on response journals, including possible writing prompts.)

Sample Read-Aloud Lesson: Day 2

1. Students share their personal responses to the story with a partner. (See Chapter 1: Oral Language: Speaking, Listening, and Learning for information on Think–Pair–Share.)

2. Students then share any questions they have or note parts of the text that didn't make sense to them. The teacher records the questions or points for clarification on chart paper.

3. The teacher asks students how their listening might change for the second reading.

4. The entire text is read again without interruption.

5. Students discuss whether their understanding has changed or their questions have been answered.

6. The teacher directs students to respond to the text in their journals.

Sample Read-Aloud Lesson: Day 3

1. Students share their personal responses with a partner.

2. Referring to the chart of questions/uncertainties from Day 2, the teacher invites students to share their new understandings with the class.

3. Students explain how rereading helped them understand the text.

4. If students still have unanswered questions, the teacher rereads the text again.

Sample Read-Aloud Lesson: Follow-Up

The rereading strategy is then reinforced in both guided and independent reading. In guided reading, the teacher directs students to reread and to respond orally. During independent reading, students are reminded to reread when they encounter questions or when they find the text confusing or unclear. Marking those sections of the text with sticky notes is a good idea. Students might also reread an entertaining or thought-provoking passage, documenting where in the text these passages are and why they chose to reread them.

Shared Reading

Shared reading is a direct instructional component of a comprehensive literacy program. The use of large print materials that everyone can see clearly enables teachers to explicitly teach reading skills and strategies in whole-group or small-group settings. A safe environment for oral reading is also established as all students read or "chime in" together. In addition to allowing teachers to make speaking and writing connections for students, shared reading is also an opportunity for teachers to teach or reinforce the traits of good writing.

Shared reading enables teachers to

- provide opportunities for students to read a whole text or parts of a text in a supported, low-risk environment

- demonstrate a variety of comprehension strategies (e.g., word-solving, fix-up strategies, and so on)

- explicitly teach think-alouds (See Think-Alouds earlier in this chapter and in Chapter 2: Reading Comprehension: Strategies That Work.)

- observe students' reading behaviours and skills and note those that require further attention in guided reading

- make the reading process visible

- make reading and writing connections; help students to recognize the traits of good writing

- support a less able reader to function as a reader with both peer and teacher support

- examine text structures to assist reading and writing comprehension

- introduce skills and strategies required for the grade level, but possibly beyond the reach of some readers

- demonstrate reading as a writer and the writer's craft (See Chapter 3: Writing: The Reading–Writing Connection.)

"Shared reading is an important missing piece in many reading programs.... [W]hen teachers shift their attention to give more time to shared reading, guided practice is more meaningful and efficient, and teachers don't have to work so hard in small reading groups. Also, and this is very important, teaching reading becomes much more enjoyable."

Routman 2003, 130

"Through developing familiarity with the text, each rereading becomes easier and leaves more cognitive energy for the related aspects of analyzing, synthesizing and extending knowledge."

Allen 2002, 31

Planning for Shared Reading
Frequency and Grouping

Ideally, shared reading occurs daily for a minimum of 15 to 20 minutes per session, and involves either the whole class or small groups of students.

Materials

To facilitate shared reading, teachers might use either enlarged text that has clear print (e.g., Big Books, charts, or overhead transparencies), or individual copies of the text (e.g., newspaper articles or anthology selections).

When selecting a text for shared reading, teachers might consider any of the following criteria:

- a captivating story line
- rich language to develop vocabulary
- degree of student interest or enjoyment, especially to facilitate personal connections
- challenge to students' thinking to enlarge their world
- text type and genre (e.g., narrative, essay, poetry, information, visual, musical) to enable students to find a genre that is accessible and engaging
- multiple text sources for key concepts or themes
- inclusion of divergent or unique points of view
- accessibility of language and context

(Adapted from Allen 2002)

Implementing Shared Reading
Before Shared Reading

1. The teacher reads the text and determines how and where the text best supports the teaching of the strategies and skills needed by the students. The most salient information and features of the particular text are chosen.
2. The teacher establishes the discussion that will follow the first reading.
3. The text and focus for each shared reading lesson is recorded on a weekly planner (such as BLM 2: A Week-at-a-Glance Planner).

"With shared reading offering students the opportunity to read a text multiple times, they can return to familiar texts when they encounter various challenges of the language arts."

ALLEN 2002, 119

Check It Out!

These two books by Janet Allen are valuable professional resources:

On the Same Page: Shared Reading Beyond the Primary Grades (Portland, ME: Stenhouse Publishers, 2002).

Yellow Brick Roads: Shared and Guided Paths to Independent Reading 4–12 (Portland, ME: Stenhouse Publishers, 2000).

The following Web site contains links to ideas for shared reading lessons and texts:
http://www.teachers.net/cgi-bin/lessons/sort.cgi?searchterm=Reding

---

Instructional Focus for Shared Reading

The instructional focus for shared reading is based on the skills and strategies outlined in the curriculum, as well as on the assessment of students' needs. Comprehension strategies, word solving, and possible text obstacles are among the many areas that may be addressed in shared reading experiences. Ideally, each shared reading lesson within the three- to five-day plan will have a new focus, such as

---

Comprehension Strategies	• Monitoring comprehension
	• Activating prior experiences and background knowledge
	• Predicting and confirming
	• Generating and answering questions
	• Using graphic organizers
	  – main idea/supporting details
	  – cause and effect
	  – sequence
	  – comparison and contrast
	  – topic/subtopic
	  – problem/solution
		• Making connections (text to self, text to text, and text to world)
		• Visualizing (creating mental images during and after reading)
		• Using fix-up strategies
		• Visually representing text
		• Summarizing or retelling
		• Drawing inferences
		• Generalizing or drawing conclusions
		• Synthesizing what was read

Word Solving	• Finding out what is known in the word (chunks, blends, smaller words, word families, prefixes, suffixes) • Breaking the word into syllables • Rereading what comes before the word • Reading on and then revisiting the word • Thinking about the root word	• Using bolded text, which may be in the glossary • Using margin text to find word definition • Checking word charts or a dictionary • Substituting a word to see if it makes sense in the same context • Asking a friend

Possible Text Obstacles	• Unfamiliar concepts, vocabulary, and settings
	• Complicated sentence patterns
	• Unstated emotions
	• Unusual time patterns (e.g., flashbacks)
	• Unexpected change of narrators and characters
	• Organizational patterns, if unfamiliar
	  – cause and effect
	  – sequence
	  – comparison and contrast
	  – topic/subtopic
	  – problem/solution
		• Graphic aids
		  – maps
		  – graphs
		  – charts
		  – diagrams
		• Textual aids
		  – preview sections
		  – summary sections
		• Uninterrupted plot or disjointed information

During Shared Reading

For guidance with implementing a four/five day plan, see BLM 3: Shared Reading Lesson Planner.

BLM 3: Shared Reading Lesson Planner

Day 1: Introducing the Text

1. The teacher introduces the text by drawing on students' prior knowledge or by supplying information about the topic, genre, or format. (See Chapter 2: Reading Comprehension: Strategies That Work.)

2. The teacher sets the purpose for reading the text, and then introduces the selection by identifying the title, author, and illustrator.

3. Students make predictions about, or connections to, the title/cover of the text selection.

4. The teacher reads the text fluently with appropriate phrasing, intonation, and expression as students follow along.

5. During reading, the teacher stops, where appropriate, to affirm predictions or demonstrate think-alouds.

6. The text is then reread with the students.

7. The teacher elicits students' initial reactions to the text and possibly records them for future reference.

Days 2, 3/4: Working with the Text

1. The teacher rereads the appropriate section(s) each day before working on a teaching point. Students either take turns as the teacher, pointing to the text, or participating together as the lead voice.

2. Connections are made, where appropriate, to read-aloud texts, discussions, or response activities.

3. The targeted comprehension strategies, word study skills, writing techniques, formats, or forms are then taught using the text.

4. The teacher poses questions to enable students to talk about the targeted strategies, skills, techniques, formats, or forms. The discussion might take place in pairs or small groups.

The reading experiences of the students combined with the genre and purpose for the lesson will determine whether the whole text is reread each day.

Story Map

Title: _____

Author: _____

Setting: _____

Characters: _____

Problem: _____

Actions:

• _____

• _____

• _____

Resolution: _____

_____

Questions to Promote Discussion

• Was there anything else that intrigued you about ...?

• Can you find another example of ...?

• What enabled you to make that connection?

• Did you notice ...?

• Do you think the author intended ...?

• Did you agree or disagree with ...?

• Can you find additional support for ...?

(Adapted from Allen 2002)

Tableaux are still images created by groups of students posing in response to a theme, situation, or story. Students plan the tableau and take up positions and attitudes to highlight one significant moment in the text.

5. The teacher provides opportunities for the students to respond to the text in various ways: through further reading, graphic organizers, word study activities, character analysis, story maps, plot summaries or retells; tableaux (group poses); or Readers Theatre. To deepen students' understanding, it is important for the response activities to be appropriate for the text shared.

Suggestions for reading response activities are included in Chapter 2: Reading Comprehension: Strategies That Work and Chapter 4: Literacy Learning Across the Curriculum.

After Shared Reading
Days 4/5: Closure
What happens on Days 4/5 is determined by the age and maturity of the readers and their experience with the genre or text form. For example, teachers may have students reread the entire text, demonstrating fluent, expressive reading; share tableaux; or perform Readers Theatre. They may ask students to refer back to their initial reactions to the text and compare understandings—a valuable exercise—or compare the text to another text read that week. Another option is to have students explain how multiple readings improved their understanding of the text.

Assessment Strategies
Making anecdotal records of observations and using a checklist of skills are effective ways to assess shared reading. Assessment BLM 5: Assessing Shared Reading is presented as a checklist.

Assessment BLM 5: Assessing Shared Reading

Developing the Reading-Writing Connection in Shared Reading
Shared reading is a prime opportunity to help students make reading and writing connections. As students read and study the work of an author, they learn valuable lessons that they may apply to their own writing.

When revisiting a shared reading text, teachers can heighten students' awareness of the techniques used by the author to engage readers. The following chart lists some picture books that help teach a variety of literary devices.

Literary Device	Helpful Picture Book
Alliteration (phrases or sentences in which many of the words have the same initial sound)	*Feathers and Fools* by Mem Fox (New York: Harcourt Brace, 1996)
Flashback (an interruption in the main action that takes the reader to a time or an event preceding the main action)	*Miss Rumphius* by Barbara Cooney (New York: Viking, 1982)
Foreshadowing (clues given by the author about what will happen in the text)	*Just Plain Fancy* by Patricia Polacco (New York: Bantam, 1990)
Inference (what the author implies in the text)	*Mirette on the High Wire* by Emily Arnold McCully (New York: Scholastic, 1992)
Metaphor (a word or phrase that ordinarily means one thing, but is used to describe another in order to suggest a likeness between the two)	*The Stranger* by Chris Van Allsburg (Boston: Houghton Mifflin, 1986)
Personification (attributing human qualities or characteristics to inanimate objects)	*Sylvester and the Magic Pebble* by William Steig (New York: Simon and Schuster, 1969)
Simile (a comparison using like or as)	*The Girl Who Loved Wild Horses* by Paul Goble (New York: Atheneum, 1979)

(Adapted from Allen 2002, 233–36)

Sample Shared Reading Lesson: A Five-Day Plan for Grade 6

The poem "Hot Like Fire" in *Rimshots: Basketball Pix, Rolls, and Rhythms* by Charles R. Smith Jr. (New York: Dutton Children's Books, 1999) provides an enjoyable read for students, especially sports enthusiasts. It may be used to teach imagery, inference, and word study, as well as themes such as harassment, bullying, and ethics. (See the author's Web site at www.charlesrsmithjr.com for additional teaching ideas using the author's books, poems read aloud by the author, and ways to contact the author.)

This shared reading lesson might be scheduled within a language arts block or linked to physical and health education studies.

Sample Shared Reading Lesson: Day 1

To introduce the poem "Hot Like Fire," teachers engage students in activating prior knowledge and making predictions.

Before Shared Reading: Day 1

1. Using BLM 4: Word Sort for "Hot Like Fire," the teacher prepares word sort pieces for each student and puts the pieces in small sandwich bags.

2. After distributing the word sort pieces to each student, the teacher instructs students to independently sort the words into at least two categories.

3. Students then share their categories and reasoning with a partner.

4. The teacher asks students to make predictions about the text based on their knowledge of the words from the text. For example, "Is the text expository or narrative? What might be the major theme? What questions do you hope to have answered?"

5. The teacher reads the title of the poem and asks students if their predictions have changed or remain the same with this added information.

For more information on word sorts, see List–Group–Label in Chapter 1: Oral Language: Speaking, Listening, and Learning, and Sort and Predict in Chapter 2: Reading Comprehension: Strategies That Work.

BLM 4: Word Sort for "Hot Like Fire"

During Shared Reading: Day 1

1. The teacher reads "Hot Like Fire" aloud once.

2. Students' reactions to the poem and the accuracy of their predictions are then discussed.

3. The teacher and students read the poem several times together.

After Shared Reading: Day 1

1. Students return to their word sort and are prompted to consider how they would arrange the words now, after having read the poem.

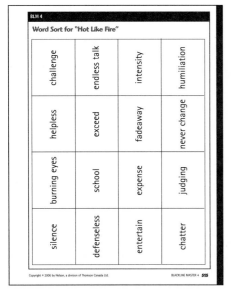

BLM 4

Word Sort for "Hot Like Fire"

challenge	endless talk	intensity	humiliation
helpless	exceed	fadeaway	never change
burning eyes	school	expense	judging
silence	defenseless	entertain	chatter

Copyright © 2006 by Nelson, a division of Thomson Canada Ltd.

BLACKLINE MASTER 4 **515**

2. Students re-sort the words and discuss the categories and their rationale with a partner.

3. The teacher asks students to consider what theme they think is emerging.

Sample Shared Reading Lesson: Day 2

This part of the lesson has students working directly with the text of the poem and focusing on imagery.

Before Shared Reading: Day 2

The teacher engages students in a discussion of how authors use imagery to create a vivid picture for the reader.

During Shared Reading: Day 2

1. The teacher and students reread the poem together. Students listen for examples of poetic imagery (e.g., "I am on fire").

2. Students record examples of imagery in the poem as they reread it independently.

After Shared Reading: Day 2

1. The teacher creates a chart listing the examples of imagery students found in the poem.

2. Students explain what each word or phrase means within the context of the poem.

3. The teacher challenges students to find examples of imagery in their independent reading texts and to share one of those examples with a partner.

Sample Shared Reading Lesson: Day 3

Students continue to work directly with the text of the poem, this time with a focus on word study.

Before Shared Reading: Day 3

The teacher reviews with students the terms "root word" and "suffix."

During Shared Reading: Day 3

1. Students read through the poem silently.

2. The teacher instructs students to note down words in the poem with suffixes, and then to compare their findings with a partner.

3. The teacher directs students to read each word in its context (e.g., "The only competition....").

4. The teacher creates a chart of root words and suffixes, looking at the root word's part of speech and the meaning of the suffix.

After Shared Reading: Day 3

Students work with a partner to complete a word web showing other examples of words with *-less* or *-tion* endings.

Sample Shared Reading Lesson: Day 4

The focus of this part of the lesson is on inferences in "Hot Like Fire."

Before Shared Reading: Day 4

1. The teacher reviews ways in which readers make inferences.

2. The teacher explains how readers interpret what a character says or does to make inferences about that character's personality, motives, and decisions. The author doesn't state things specifically; rather, readers use what they know about people and the clues left by the author to infer the character's personality.

During Shared Reading: Day 4

1. Students reread "Hot Like Fire," looking for insights into the character's personality and noting actions that might also provide clues.

2. The teacher models how to use the information from this rereading to complete the following chart:

Author Clues	What I Know About People	What I Think the Author Meant

After Shared Reading: Day 4

Teachers direct students to use the chart to make two inferences about a character from their independent reading text.

Sample Shared Reading Lesson: Day 5

Depending on the nature of the text and the strategies or skills chosen for instruction, a fifth day working directly with the text may not be necessary. The sample shared reading lesson for "Hot Like Fire" outlined in this section requires only four days of instruction.

Guided Reading

Guided reading is an instructional approach that may be used in any subject area. Teachers work with small groups to provide individual and small-group instruction, as well as ongoing support. Pre-, during, and post-reading activities are used to heighten the reading experience for all students.

Texts used for guided reading are at the students' instructional level (90 to 95 percent accuracy). Most students will be able to make sense of the majority of the text but will still face some challenges. The text challenges allow the teacher an opportunity to observe the students' use of reading strategies and their reading behaviours. Teachers take advantage of "teachable moments" to check for individual understanding and to provide timely feedback and encouragement. The small-group setting also facilitates ongoing assessment.

Because it is the bridge between shared and independent reading, guided reading in Grades 3 to 6 classrooms focuses primarily on comprehension. Guided reading enables teachers to

- match texts to readers
- provide students with guided opportunities to read a variety of genres

The main purpose of guided reading is to improve reading comprehension.

- provide individual attention and instruction before, during, and after reading
- support readers as they deal with unfamiliar vocabulary, text, or concepts
- chunk text or provide guiding questions
- observe students' behaviours, skills, and strategies
- seize the "teachable moment"
- provide introductions and follow-up to text to support word study, vocabulary development, and text comprehension
- engage students in meaningful discussions about the text
- help students understand a text that provides some challenges for them
- reinforce effective strategies, skills, and behaviours that students are already using
- build on students' current strategies, skills, and behaviours

During guided reading, the teacher introduces the text and then individual students read the text independently. This is very different from the traditional practice of round-robin reading during which students take turns reading the text aloud. Guided reading ensures all students actively employ strategies to process and interact with the text.

While guided reading is important for all students, it is particularly helpful for struggling readers. These students benefit from reading material exactly at their instructional level, receiving individual and small-group attention, and practising a range of teacher- and peer-modelled strategies.

Planning for Guided Reading
Frequency and Grouping

A minimum of three 15- to 20-minute sessions per week per guided-reading group is ideal; however, this may not be feasible with a large class, and not all groups need this level of support. Nevertheless, it is important for struggling readers to receive guided-reading group lessons daily.

Guided reading groups generally comprise six to eight students each. When grouping students for guided reading, teachers consider needs, abilities, interests, and text level, which is why the groupings tend to be flexible.

The small-group setting for guided reading is less intimidating for struggling readers. These students can be drawn into discussions without feeling threatened, and can be heard even if they are quiet or less confident.

Grouping Students for Guided Reading Instruction

When grouping students for guided reading instruction, teachers might ask the following questions:

- What are the specific needs not addressed in whole-group lessons?
- Which students need help with transferring skills to independent reading?

- Can students with the same needs be grouped together for a short period?
- How long will each group meet?
- Does level matter?
- How will groupings benefit each student?
- Which students would not benefit from working in a small group at this time?

(Adapted from Sibberson and Szymusiak 2003, 64)

Materials

A guided reading lesson requires

- chart paper and stand, chalkboard, or whiteboard
- multiple copies of a range of levelled material that is unfamiliar to students (e.g., newspaper articles, magazines, poetry, content text, short stories, and picture books). These reading materials may be housed in a levelled text room.
- sticky notes, highlighters, markers, or pencils

Preparing for Guided Reading

To ensure a successful guided reading lesson, teachers are encouraged to do some initial preparation.

1. Teachers identify the needs of students through authentic assessment, using tools and techniques such as
   - running records/miscue analyses
   - comprehension checks (e.g., retellings, questions, or journal entries)
   - anecdotal records
   - writing samples
   - reading behaviours checklists
2. Teachers group six to eight readers with similar reading behaviours; however, these groupings are flexible and will change often as students develop new skills.
3. Guided reading groups are matched to text that is unfamiliar to them. The materials chosen should be within the range of students' instructional level and be well crafted and appealing to the group.
4. Students continue to practise classroom procedures and routines so that they can work independently on literacy-building activities.
5. The teacher establishes a management system and schedule for guided reading groups (see Putting the Pieces in Place for Guided Reading, on the following page).
6. A daily planning sheet ensures that the lesson maintains focus to make the most of time spent with students.

Putting the Pieces in Place for Guided Reading

Step 1
- Establish routines and expectations for working independently.

Step 2
- Develop purposeful and meaningful literacy-building activities.
- Introduce activities to students, and reinforce behaviour and expected responses.
- Provide multiple opportunities for students to practise each literacy activity, especially reading and writing.
- Record literacy activities on a weekly planning sheet (see BLM 2: A Week-at-a-Glance Planner).

Step 3
- Create groupings of students based on assessment data.

Step 4
- Develop a schedule for guided reading groups (struggling readers should be seen daily).

Step 5
- Begin guided reading with one group per day.
- Record the guided reading group number, text, and focus on a lesson planning sheet (see BLM 5: Guided Reading Lesson Planner).
- Discuss with the rest of the class how things are going when they are working independently.

Step 6
- Introduce a second guided reading group per day.
- Monitor how the rest of the class is doing before and after each guided reading group session.

Step 7
- Continue to practise routines and expectations.
- Continue to monitor and assess students and change groupings as necessary. (Anecdotal observations of individual students might be recorded on BLM 6: At-a-Glance Guided Reading Observations.)

Check It Out!

Here are some great professional resources for guided reading:

Teri S. Lesesne, *Making the Match: The Right Book for the Right Reader at the Right Time, Grades 4–12* (Portland, ME: Stenhouse Publishers, 2003).

Irene C. Fountas and Gay Su Pinnell, *Guiding Readers and Writers, Grades 3–6: Teaching Comprehension, Genre, and Content Literacy.* (Portsmouth, NH: Heinemann, 2001).

Irene C. Fountas and Gay Su Pinnell, *Leveled Books for Readers, Grades 3–6* (Portsmouth, NH: Heinemann, 2002).

Karen Szymusiak and Franki Sibberson, *Beyond Leveled Books* (Portland, ME: Stenhouse Publishers, 2002).

Franki Sibberson and Karen Szymusiak, *Still Learning to Read* (Portland, ME: Stenhouse Publishers, 2003).

Michael Opitz and Michael Ford, *Reaching Readers: Flexible & Innovative Strategies for Guided Reading* (Portsmouth, NH: Heinemann, 2001).

Linda Hoyt, *Snapshots: Literacy Minilessons Up Close* (Portsmouth, NH: Heinemann, 2000).

BLM 2: A Week-at-a-Glance Lesson Planner

BLM 5: Guided Reading Lesson Planner

BLM 6: At-a-Glance Guided Reading Observations

Before Guided Reading

1. The teacher introduces the selection with the aim of motivating the students to read and make predictions. The introduction is short enough to maintain interest.

In *What Really Matters for Struggling Readers*, Richard Allington (2001) shows that students will read the remainder of the text independently with greater fluency and fewer misread words when teachers begin the reading.

2. When the teacher activates background knowledge, students share prior knowledge and experiences. Making connections helps them put the text in context and makes reading more relevant. (See Chapter 2: Reading Comprehension: Strategies That Work for more information on using prior knowledge.)

3. The group discusses features of the text, such as title, author, illustrations, charts, diagrams, tables, photos, and layout.

4. The teacher presents unfamiliar vocabulary, proper names, technical terms, or expressions that may provide difficulty. A group discussion follows, during which students may ask questions.

5. Once the text has been introduced, the teacher sets a reading task or focus, ensuring that students understand the reading purpose. Students build expectations.

6. The teacher presents a new skill or strategy, or reinforces those explicitly taught in shared reading.

7. The teacher develops possible tasks for students who finish quickly to ensure they do not distract group members who are still reading. Possible tasks include rereading, generating more questions, recording ideas to focus questions, recording page references to support answers, marking text that poses difficulty, highlighting "million-dollar words," using a graphic organizer to make sense of the text, and sketching. (See Chapter 3: Writing: The Reading–Writing Connection for more about "million-dollar words.")

During Guided Reading

1. As students read the whole text or a unified part to themselves, they actively engage in the reading process, self-monitoring and self-correcting as they go. They read silently or in a quiet voice. The teacher listens in by observing the students' silent reading behaviours and making note of any strategies they are using. The teacher may also choose to work with one student while the others are reading silently.

2. Students read chunks of text determined by the teacher. These chunks range from two or three paragraphs to two or three pages in length. Students mark confusing parts or unknown vocabulary with sticky notes, but also read to find clarification or support in the text.

3. After reading one chunk, the group stops for discussion, working with guiding questions to ensure comprehension.

4. The teacher asks a range of questions to address literal, inferential, critical, and evaluative comprehension. (See Chapter 2: Reading Comprehension: Strategies That Work.) The teacher also models for students what questions to ask themselves as readers.

5. When needed, students request help in problem solving and share their problem-solving strategies with peers. The teacher confirms students' problem-solving attempts and successes.

6. Students may pause to ask questions or discuss focus questions. The teacher provides clarification or intervenes with individual students when necessary, taking advantage of any teachable moment.

When observing silent reading, look for

- subvocalizing
- eye movement
- finger tracking or pointing to areas of difficulty
- highlighting words with sticky notes
- rate of reading
- use of graphical features (e.g., illustrations and diagrams)

After Guided Reading

1. The teacher and students talk about the text, with the teacher inviting responses.

2. The teacher asks a range of questions to address literal, inferential, critical, and evaluative comprehension.

3. The teacher prompts the group to revisit the text for one or two specific reasons, such as finding evidence, confirming predictions, talking about the craft of writing, or discussing word-solving techniques.

4. Students may engage in activities to respond to and extend the text, such as writing in their reading response journals or creating dramatic or visual arts responses. (See Chapter 2: Reading Comprehension: Strategies That Work for more about responding to texts through drama and visual arts.) They may also check earlier predictions, reread text to a partner, or reread independently.

5. The teacher assesses and records students' understanding of what they have read, and then considers what was learned about the students.

6. Finally, the teacher reflects on the session and makes modifications to groupings, the weekly plan, the lesson focus, and so on, as necessary. The focus for the next guided reading lesson is determined. Students apply acquired skills and strategies to their independent reading.

Talk

Ask

Revisit

Engage

Assess

Reflect

Reflecting on Guided Reading

When reflecting on a guided reading lesson, it is important to address the following diagnostic assessment questions:

- How well did the students understand the text?
- What did you notice about their responses to the text during the discussion?
- Were there any surprises?
- What did you learn about the students?
- Do you need to make changes to your weekly plan for this group of students?
- What reading strategies or behaviours will you focus on next time?

Literacy Activities: What Is the Rest of the Class Doing?

For the teacher to focus attention on the shared or guided reading group, the rest of the class must be productively involved in literacy-building activities. Because students need to read a great deal to become good readers, they should be spending this time reading texts and writing, often by responding to their reading.

Research indicates that students learn best when they are challenged, actively engaged, and self-reflective. It is busy work, not hard work that turns students away (Spandel 2004).

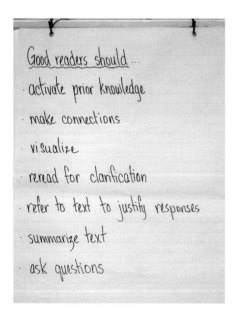

Good readers should ...
- activate prior knowledge
- make connections
- visualize
- reread for clarification
- refer to text to justify responses
- summarize text
- ask questions

The goal of independent work is not to keep students busy. The motivating work assigned should address a wide range of interests, learning styles, skill levels, and student needs, and provide opportunities for students to refine and extend the skills, strategies, and behaviours that they have learned in shared and guided reading lessons. Teachers may assign activities or allow students to choose.

Managing the Classroom for Independent Work

Establishing routines and expectations for independent work is key to ensuring effective small-group instruction. It is important to demonstrate the expectation that students can and should work independently and that learning will occur without the teacher being directly involved. Providing many opportunities to learn and practise routines is critical for the development of student responsibility and independence. During the first six weeks of school, effective teachers model the following routines and procedures and ensure that students practise them regularly:

- how to work in small groups
- how to read with a partner
- how to locate, use, and replace materials and equipment
- what to do when finished with a task
- when and how to move to another activity
- how to move about in the classroom
- how to maintain an acceptable noise level
- what to do when assistance is required

Charts outlining directions, as well as task cards, word walls, and word charts, guide students to independence.

Creating engaging activities for students is also critical in facilitating small-group instruction. The goal is for students to view these activities as purposeful and doable, yet challenging and interesting. When students are actively engaged, their time is spent focused on the task at hand.

Teachers may find it useful to develop with students a list of expectations for independent work. This list might then be prominently displayed in the classroom to serve as a reminder for students.

Independent Work	
What It Looks Like	**What It Sounds Like**
• concentrating on completing the assigned task • working cooperatively with a partner or small group • solving problems on my own • sharing materials and resources • discussing ideas with others	• speaking in quiet voices • asking a friend for help ("Could you please help me … ?") • politely reminding classmates to follow the procedures • using words like "Please" and "Thank you"

Planning and Organizing Independent Work

During small-group instruction, teachers may have the rest of the class involved in a single activity, such as independent reading, response journals, writers' workshop, shared reading responses, research project, or book club. Another option is to divide the rest of the class into two groups. While one group completes the follow-up activity from their guided reading lesson, the balance of the class works on a single activity. Yet another option is to have the rest of the class working on different activities.

Students not involved in guided reading spend the majority of this independent work time on authentic reading and writing tasks. These activities, designed to address a wide range of interests, learning styles, skill levels, and student needs, give students the opportunity to practise the reading, writing, speaking, listening, and viewing skills they have learned.

"Kids need to read a lot if they are to become good readers. The evidence of this point is overwhelming.... The cornerstone of an effective school organizational plan is allocating sufficient time for lots of reading and writing."

ALLINGTON 2001, 43

In addition to establishing clear expectations and routines for working independently, it is recommended that teachers

- create heterogeneous groupings to promote cooperation and independence, and change the groups regularly

- plan tasks that directly link to the skills being taught during shared reading, guided reading, and writing

- develop a manageable number of activities that can be quickly and easily changed

- introduce each task and demonstrate expectations for behaviour and use of materials

- develop a rotational system and tracking method

- create task cards, signs, and charts to provide direction and necessary information

- introduce and demonstrate problem-solving strategies to build independence

- instruct students to manage their own behaviour, and to interrupt teaching sessions only in an emergency

- involve students in assessing what is and is not working

"Continually ask yourself when planning work for students, How is this activity helping my students become more independent as readers, writers, and thinkers? *If it's not, set it aside."*

ROUTMAN 2003, 205

Worthwhile literacy activities that many students in Grades 3 to 6 find engaging include

- independent reading
- response journals
- literature circles
- Readers Theatre
- independent writing (retellings, author studies)
- word work
- research projects

Independent Reading

"Independent reading ... is the time students can begin to take responsibility for their reading habits and behaviors: learning to make good choices; learning when to abandon a book; discovering how to find books that support their author, genre, or theme tastes; and more important, how to find books that will help them know they are truly readers" (Allen 2000, 101). Independent reading not only provides students with the opportunity to invest quality time with a particular text, but it also ensures that students clock many hours reading a range of text.

Teachers might guide students in their choice of reading selection, ensuring they can read at 95 percent accuracy or higher with sufficient comprehension. Or, they occasionally assign "just right" materials to students.

What Is "Just Right"?

"Just right" reading materials are not so challenging that students are solely occupied with figuring out how to decode the words, and not so easy that they are unlikely to learn anything new. Because these selections pose little, if any, decoding difficulty, students are able to concentrate on refining and extending the comprehension strategies and reading behaviours previously taught. "Just right" materials also allow students to build their volume of text read and their repertoire of reading experiences.

In-class independent reading time enables teachers to

- increase the amount of time students spend truly engaged in reading
- provide students with the opportunity to monitor and record what they read, and to practise specific reading skills and strategies previously taught and reinforced in shared and guided reading
- acquire information to plan for instruction by observing the skills and strategies students use while reading a variety of texts
- offer students enough time to "become lost" in a book
- share ways of selecting texts, introduce new authors, and model book talks (e.g., looking at everyone and speaking loudly enough to be heard, as well as piquing the listeners' curiosity by reading a small part of the book)

How to Select a Text

1. Select a genre from your reading log that you haven't read.
2. Browse through the topic, author or series bins.
3. Check out the "New Titles" bulletin board.
4. Check out the "Class Recommendations" list.
5. Read a book published by a classmate.
6. When you have selected your book, be sure to use the "five-finger rule" to make sure the book is "just right."
7. Find a comfortable place to sit.

Enjoy your reading!

More proficient readers in the upper elementary grades might prefer to apply the Five-Finger Rule to select appropriate materials for independent reading.

Planning for and Implementing Independent Reading

Frequency and Grouping

It is important to allow 30 to 40 minutes of classroom time daily for independent reading. This time might be used to engage the whole class in independent reading, or as a way of facilitating small-group instruction (i.e., allowing the teacher time to focus on a shared or guided reading group while the rest of the class reads silently).

Materials

Ensuring their students are actively engaged with reading is a challenge many Grades 3 to 6 teachers face. It can be helpful to have students complete an attitude survey and an interest inventory (see Assessment BLMs 2 and 3), reading log, or response journal. (See Chapter 2: Reading Comprehension: Strategies That Work for more information on student surveys, reading logs, and response journals.)

To facilitate student engagement with independent reading, effective teachers

- create attractive displays of fiction and nonfiction materials from the classroom library
- provide a comfortable, inviting reading environment (e.g., carpeted area, extra large pillows, beanbag chairs)
- offer a wide range of reading materials that reflect the independent reading levels, interests, and cultural diversity of all students
- feature selections published by the class or individual students, as well as books that have been read during read-alouds
- set up a classroom listening station with books on tape and provide access to computers and interactive CD-ROMs
- post strategy charts in the classroom, such as ways to choose books, to serve as student reference. (See also the section titled Before I Read, I Can ... in Chapter 1: Oral Language: Speaking, Listening, and Learning.)

> ### Ways to Choose Books
>
> - Pick a favourite author
> - Ask a friend for a recommendation
> - Read the front and back covers
> - Scan the illustrations
> - Read the first few pages
> - Pick another book in a series
> - Ask your teacher or the librarian
> - Find a book that has been read aloud
> - Look in the "Great Books" basket

Assessment BLM 2: Attitude Survey

Assessment BLM 3: Interest Inventory

Assessment BLM 1: Reading Attitude Survey in Chapter 2

Assessment BLM 2: Reading Interests Inventory (Student) in Chapter 2

Assessment BLM 3: Reading Interests Inventory (Class Tally) in Chapter 2

Before Independent Reading

1. Students complete one or more self-assessment surveys indicating their attitudes toward reading, as well as their particular areas of interest.

2. The teacher determines the independent reading level of students and stocks the classroom library using information from the student surveys. Ideally, title selections will accommodate a wide range of reading levels and interests.

3. The teacher instructs students on strategies for self-selecting "just right" texts. The Three-Finger Rule is an initial strategy for text

selection. (For more information on the Three-Finger Rule, see Chapter 1: Oral Language: Speaking, Listening, and Learning.) Mini-lessons on ways to choose books might also be conducted.

The Three-Finger Rule

The Three-Finger Rule is a quick method for selecting a "just right" text.

- The student chooses a book and reads the first page or two.
- While reading, the student counts the words that he or she (i) can decode and (ii) can decode but does not understand.
- Three or more challenging words means that the book is likely too difficult. In this case, the student might select another book for independent reading, or may take the first choice home to read with a family member.
- If the student knows all the words, the book may be too easy, but the student is still allowed to select it.

The purpose of **book talks** is to share great books and compelling authors, tweak an interest in books, and present new genres. It is important for teachers to select a book that complements the interests, age, and cultural diversity of the class, and to read it prior to talking about it. (For more information about book talks, see Chapter 2: Reading Comprehension: Strategies That Work.)

4. After the teacher introduces and explains the purpose of maintaining a reading log, students begin to record pertinent information in their logs.

5. The teacher prepares book talks, which may focus on authors, genres, or use of literary devices; presents strategies for selecting a book; or explains how and why to persevere with a book and when to abandon it.

6. Students choose independently or with teacher help appropriate reading materials following the Three-Finger Rule.

7. After establishing and reviewing the classroom expectations for independent reading, the teacher decides what the response activity, if necessary, will be. Paired discussion, group response, response journal entries, literature circles, or Readers Theatre are among the many response activities teachers might assign. (See Literature Circles and Readers Theatre later in this chapter.)

8. Students are reminded of the reading strategies and behaviours that they should apply to their independent reading. They might also participate in mini-lessons as they arise.

BLM 2: Before I Read I ... in Chapter 1

BLM 3: Before I Read I ... Bookmark in Chapter 1

During Independent Reading

1. Students read for a sustained period of time, applying strategies learned during shared and guided reading sessions, and monitoring their understanding. They self-assess their use of reading strategies.

2. While students read independently, the teacher might
   - conduct a guided reading lesson

- assess individual students through timed reading or retells, checking for fluency
- hold reading conferences with individuals or small groups
- observe student choices and reading behaviours
- observe students during literature circles, book talks, and book clubs

Teacher observations inform future book talks, subsequent shared or guided reading lessons, and what to model in read-alouds.

3. Students make notes or pose questions to assist with their reading response activity. If they are participating in a literature circle, they think about and record ideas related to their role.

After Independent Reading

1. The teacher provides time for students to respond to their reading if an activity was assigned. Students might prepare and present their responses, if appropriate, or participate in relevant discussions.

2. The teacher reminds students to update their reading logs, if they haven't already done so. (For more information on reading logs and a sample template, see Chapter 2: Reading Comprehension: Strategies That Work.)

3. Students reflect on their reading experience and create a reading plan (e.g., The next book I plan to read is....").

Teachers clearly establish the purpose and nature of an expected response. Students are not expected to complete long or complex responses every time they read independently. It is important that they not view responses as "busy work."

Assessment BLM 13: Independent Reading in Chapter 2

Assessment BLM 14: When I Read in Chapter 2

Response Journals

Reading response journals (or reader's notebooks) are records of students' thoughts about their reading. Students might prepare written responses such as letters, diagrams, mind maps, or sketches to demonstrate their understanding of what they read. Or, they might choose to relate the text to their own experiences or to other texts they have read. (See Chapter 2: Reading Comprehension: Strategies That Work for more detailed information on response journals.)

Literature Circles

Literature circles are small, literary discussion groups that meet regularly to share views, ideas, and understanding of a text. The groups comprise five or six students, all of whom have read the same text. Students take complete ownership of their learning while the teacher acts as the facilitator. Predetermined roles are assigned by the teacher or group members to maximize discussion.

Literature circles give students the opportunity to

- experience quality literature
- be part of a community of readers
- take ownership of their learning
- share views, questions, ideas, and understandings of a common text in a supported environment

- build communication skills
- experience the power and exhilaration that comes from a focused conversation about a text

Materials

Texts for literature circles might include

- short stories
- articles
- poetry

It is important to select high-quality literature that can be used to explicitly teach the roles, and to provide a copy of the text for each group member.

Before Literature Circles

1. The teacher introduces the concept of literature circles and explicitly teaches the roles. Ideally, students will participate in developing and outlining the responsibilities for each role. Detailed information about each role, including appropriate sentence stems or questions, is then posted in the classroom. (See BLM 7: Literature Circle Role Cards for sample task criteria.)
2. The teacher assigns students to specific roles or groups. Alternatively, group members determine their roles together.

Literature Circle Roles and Responsibilities

Discussion Director: Selects one or two questions from a class-created list to initiate and guide the group discussion.

Connector: Makes text-to-self, text-to-text, and text-to-world connections.

Illustrator: Finds or creates one or two images that show what readers might visualize as they read the text.

Literary Luminary: Locates a brief passage in the text that warrants rereading and further discussion by the group and leads the discussion.

Vocabulary Enricher: Selects and clarifies for the group vocabulary that might have special importance or that posed some difficulty.

Summarizer: Prepares a brief summary of the day's reading to share with the group.

---

3. Before the group meets, the teacher establishes routines and behaviour expectations.
4. A time frame for the entire activity is determined and opportunities for in-class reading are provided. Group members discuss the time frame and set a reading schedule. The teacher posts the timetable for student reference.
5. Either the teacher or the literature circle group members select the text to be read.

During Literature Circles

1. Students complete the tasks associated with their roles. (See BLM 8: Literature Circle Group Results, a copy of which can be given to each group and then cut apart for students to record text information related to their roles.) When necessary, the teacher redirects students to the role information posted in the classroom. Roles may change for the next discussion.

2. Students engage in meaningful discussion, sharing ideas, predictions, questions, opinions, connections to the text, and more. They apply the rules of conversation. The teacher listens to their conversations and acts as a facilitator, redirecting conversations or groups as needed.

3. Students self-monitor their group to ensure maximum participation and individual accountability. The teacher assesses individuals or groups using anecdotal observations or checklists. The criteria for a teacher, peer, or self-assessment rubric might focus on preparation, planning, participation, depth of response, and so on.

4. Students set a reading schedule for the next circle.

After Literature Circles

1. The teacher provides opportunities for reflection. Students assess their own contributions and the performance of their groups. The teacher reinforces exemplary behaviour and quality responses.

2. Using their in-class reading time, students read the next predetermined chunk of text.

3. Students fulfill the tasks associated with their roles.

BLM 7: Literature Circle Role Cards

BLM 8: Literature Circle Group Results

Assessment BLM 12: Comprehension Indicators During Literature Discussions in Chapter 2

Check It Out!

Harvey Daniels, *Literature Circles: Voice and Choice in the Student-Centered Classroom* (Portland, ME: Stenhouse Publishers, 2002).

Harvey Daniels, *Literature Circles: Voices and Choice in Book Clubs and Reading Groups* (Portland, ME: Stenhouse Publishers, 2002).

Jeni Pollack Day, Dixie Lee Spiegel, Janet McLellan, and Valerie B. Brown, *Moving Forward with Literature Circles: How to Plan, Manage, and Evaluate Literature Circles That Deepen Understanding and Foster a Love of Reading* (New York: Scholastic, 2002).

Marcia C. Huber, *Literature Circles: Using Student Interaction to Improve Reading Comprehension* (Huntington Beach, CA: Creative Teaching Press, 2001).

Readers Theatre

Readers Theatre is a planned-for dramatic presentation of a script by a group of readers. Unlike a formal stage production, Readers Theatre relies mainly on the readers' voices to convey the meaning of the text; the words, not the actions, are the focus.

Students assume the role of the characters in the text, and then communicate the theme, plot, and mood by using their voices and facial expressions with limited action. Memorization is not necessary; however, rehearsal provides for a stronger performance. Readers Theatre serves as an interpretive activity for all students in the classroom. Readers bring the characters and action to life to enable the listeners to visualize the text.

Readers Theatre provides an opportunity for students to

- read rich literature repeatedly
- improve reading fluency through rehearsal
- interpret the meaning of a text
- develop positive attitudes toward reading
- link reading and writing activities
- examine the differences between two genres: story and script
- collaborate with group members and participate in decision making

Materials

Suitable texts for a Readers Theatre performance include short, published plays, as well as student adaptations of stories, poems, chants, songs, and nonfiction material. Narratives chosen for adaptation will ideally have compelling plots, plenty of dialogue, several characters, actions that can be relayed by a narrator, and short, descriptive passages.

> Readers Theatre is a particularly effective way for students, especially struggling readers, to develop fluency and text interpretation skills.

Check It Out!

The following are great Web sites for Readers Theatre:

http://www.aaronshep.com

http://www.eplaybooks.com/browse.htm

http://hometown.aol.com/rcswallow/index.html

Possible Books for Script Adaptation

Grades 3 and 4

Anastasia Krupnik by Lois Lowry (Boston: Houghton Mifflin, 1979).

Cam Jansen and the Mystery of the Stolen Corn Popper by David A. Adler (New York: Viking Press, 1982).

Charlotte's Web by E.B. White (New York: Harper and Brothers, 1952).

The Stinky Cheese Man and Other Twisted Tales by Jon Scieszka and Lane Smith (New York: Viking, 1992).

Any of Robert Munsch's books (various).

Grades 5 and 6

Cinderellis and the Glass Hill by Gail Carson Levine (New York: HarperCollins, 2000).

Crispin: The Cross of Lead by Avi (New York: Simon and Schuster, 2003).

Dog Breath: The Horrible Trouble with Hally Tosis by Dav Pilkey (New York: Blue Sky Press/Scholastic, 1994)

Harry Potter and the Sorcerer's Stone by J.K. Rowling (New York: Scholastic, 1997).

Love That Dog by Sharon Creech (New York: HarperCollins/Joanna Cotler Books, 2001).

No More Dead Dogs by Gordon Korman (New York: Hyperion, 2000).

Wayside School series by Louis Sachar (New York: HarperCollins, various years).

Implementing Readers Theatre

1. The teacher selects a suitable script or a text that can be adapted. If adapting a text, the teacher demonstrates how to compose the script by using story dialogue for characters and by rewriting descriptive passages or action scenes to be read by a narrator.

2. The teacher also models how to prepare scripts by labelling or highlighting parts for each reader. Students label or highlight their own parts.

3. Students read the script and discuss how to express each character.

4. The readers rehearse the selection, paying particular attention to

   - fluency
   - enunciation
   - voice projection
   - pronunciation
   - characterization
   - responding on cue

5. Students may sit or stand in front of an audience to perform their script.

6. The teacher assesses the script adaptation, if applicable (see Assessment BLM 12: Readers Theatre Script Rubric). In assessing students' individual performances, consideration is given to fluency (expression, phrasing, and rate), character development

Check It Out!

More great Readers Theatre resources:

Susan Hill, *Readers Theatre: Performing the Text* (Winnipeg: Peguis Publishers, 1990).

Robyn Reeves, Laurence Swinburne, and Jack Warner, *Readers' Theater* (Austin, TX: Steck-Vaughn, 1998).

Neill Dixon, Anne Davies, and Colleen Politano, *Learning with Readers* (Winnipeg: Peguis Publishers, 1996).

Jacqui Farley, Elaine Sishton, and Peter Beere, *Readers' Theater Level 2 (Grades 3–7)* (Grand Rapids, MI: Instructional Fair, 2001).

Suzanne I. Barchers, *Multicultural Folktales* (Englewood, CO: Teacher Ideas Press, 2000).

(alters voice to portray character, uses appropriate facial expression), and voice (volume and enunciation).

7. Students reflect on their individual performances, noting strengths and areas for improvement (see Assessment BLM 13: Readers Theatre Performance).

Assessment BLM 12: Readers Theatre Script Rubric

Assessment BLM 13: Readers Theatre Performance

Independent Writing

Retellings and author studies are two authentic writing activities that students might complete independently in response to texts read. Using graphic organizers, such as story maps, students prepare a retelling of the text or a section of the text. This written work could become the basis of a Speakers Theatre presentation, where students are encouraged to paraphrase, improvise, and weave their own knowledge and personality into an oral retelling. (For more on Speakers Theatre, see Chapter 1: Oral Language: Speaking, Listening, and Learning. Chapter 2: Reading Comprehension: Strategies That Work features numerous graphic organizers that students might use to plan their retelling.)

Through author studies, students develop a greater understanding of the writer's craft. Writing letters to favourite authors is a particularly enjoyable activity for students. By thinking critically about the text read, students are able to give the author meaningful feedback, and to come up with questions that target specific aspects of the writer's craft.

Chapter 3: Writing: The Reading–Writing Connection contains detailed information on many more authentic writing activities.

Word Work

Literacy activities that focus on reinforcing word-solving strategies are another effective way for students to spend their independent work time in the classroom.

Materials

Most of the items needed to facilitate students' working with words are readily accessible in any comprehensive literacy classroom. Such items include

- whiteboards, chalkboards, or magnetic boards
- markers, chalk
- word cards
- spelling lists
- dictionaries
- thesauruses
- graphic organizers
- activity worksheets (e.g., crossword puzzles, word searches, and scrambled words)
- individual letters (magnetic, wood, or paper)

Suggested Activities

The number of vocabulary-building and reinforcement activities suitable for independent work is limitless. Students might, for example,

- identify and record three-, four-, five-, and six-syllable words in a text they have read
- develop or complete crossword puzzles and word searches
- unscramble high-frequency or content-specific vocabulary
- write alliterative sentences or stories
- sort word cards by parts of speech (e.g., adjectives, adverbs, nouns, and verbs)
- generate word lists with like prefixes and suffixes
- list million-dollar words to describe a photo from a magazine
- illustrate the meaning of homographs and homophones
- build words from a finite number of letters (see Magic Square, below, and Making Words later in this chapter)

Great Books for Alliteration

Faint Frogs Feeling Feverish and Other Terrifically Tantalizing Tongue Twisters by Lillian Obligado (New York: Viking Press, 1983).

The Z Was Zapped: A Play in Twenty-Six Acts by Chris Van Allsburg (Boston: Houghton Mifflin, 1987).

Sample Magic Square Activity

Use the Magic Square letters to make as many words as you can!

e	s	f
w	a	r
i	m	l

Make words that have …

- 1 letter
- 2 letters
- 3 letters
- 4 letters
- 5 letters
- More than 5 letters

Now try using some of the words in sentences. See how many of your words you can use in just one sentence!

Check It Out!

These Web sites have some great word activities:

Puzzlemakers
http://puzzlemaker.School.discovery.com/Wordsearchsetupform.html

Virtual Thesaurus
http://www.plumbdesign.com/thesaurus/

See Word Study later in this chapter for other vocabulary-building activities.

Research Projects

Students might work independently to research and organize information on assigned or self-selected topics. The topics may be of personal interest related to social science units, themes, or genres.

Materials

To facilitate research in Grades 3 to 6, students require access to

- a variety of nonfiction texts on topics of interest
- materials such as maps, graphs, charts, photographs, and diagrams
- various graphic organizers (e.g., comparison charts, semantic maps, Venn diagrams, cause–effect charts, timelines)

- writing materials (e.g., various sizes of paper, crayons, markers, rulers, stapler)
- computers and software (e.g., Encarta, Inspiration, and Kidspiration)
- list of appropriate Internet sites

Suggested Activities

Students might work independently on any of the research-based activities that follow.

- Record information on an appropriate graphic organizer, such as a Gathering Grid.
- Create a speech that identifies the main topic and three important facts about the topic.
- Write a magazine article using the information discovered about the topic.
- Read information about the next science or social studies topic.
- Create a list of "fast facts" about a topic.
- Develop questions and find answers for a class trivia activity.

For more information on research projects, refer to Chapter 3: Writing: The Reading–Writing Connection and Chapter 4: Literacy Learning Across the Curriculum.

Gathering Grid

Topic: _____

Questions	1st Source _____	2nd Source _____

Balanced Writing

The writing program in a comprehensive literacy classroom parallels the structure of the reading program: students progress from a position of high teacher support and dependence to low teacher support and independence.

The process of writing, when taught with a focus on creating meaning, significantly increases students' reading achievement. As students explore a range of texts, they learn to think about how writers communicate their ideas to the reader. When constructing their own literary works, students heighten their attention to text structure, language, and literary techniques; when reading the work of others, they tend to look for the writing lessons that authors can teach.

Effective teachers use a variety of methods and strategies to teach students the information they need to know about writing. Both beginning and advanced writers require knowledge of the writing process, specific elements and conventions of writing, and the structure of different text forms. Modelled, shared, and guided writing help students read and write for meaning, think on a higher level, and see reading and writing as complementary processes.

For a detailed look at effective writing, see Chapter 3: Writing: The Reading–Writing Connection.

Word Study

In the upper elementary grades, the focus of word study is on building vocabulary and understanding how words work (word solving). Word study can enhance students' reading and writing development and strengthen their vocabulary, spelling, and grammar skills (Bloodgood and Pacifici 2004), particularly when it is embedded in the reading, writing, speaking, listening, viewing, and representing tasks completed throughout the day.

Of course students will not be able to learn every word associated with a concept or unit of study. Teachers must determine how important the word is, how often the students will encounter it in the unit, and whether they will need to use it in other areas. Teachers might ask themselves these ten questions:

1. Which words are most important to understanding the text?
2. How much prior knowledge will students have about this word or its related concept?
3. Is the word encountered frequently?
4. Does the word have multiple meanings?
5. Is the concept significant, and does it, therefore, require preteaching?
6. Which words can be figured out from the context?
7. Are there words that could be grouped together to enhance understanding of a concept?
8. What strategies might help students integrate the concept (and related words) into their lives?
9. How might repeated exposures to the word/concept be productive and enjoyable?
10. How can students be helped to use the word/concept in meaningful ways in multiple contexts?

(Adapted from Allen 1999)

> *"Vocabulary acquisition is crucial to academic development. Not only do students need a rich body of word knowledge to succeed in basic skill areas, [but] they also need a specialized vocabulary to learn content area material."*
>
> BAKER, SIMMONS, AND KAMEENUI 1995B, 35

Activities to Build Vocabulary

A wide range of activities can assist students in remembering key concepts and vocabulary, including

- vocabulary tableaux
- word charts
- ABC books

For other vocabulary-building and concept-reinforcement activities, refer to Developing Oral Language Across the Curriculum and Developing Phonological Awareness Through Word Study in Chapter 1: Oral Language: Speaking, Listening, and Learning, and to Weak Decoders with Limited Comprehension in Chapter 6: Supporting Struggling and Reluctant Readers.

Vocabulary Tableaux

In this activity, students work in small groups to create a visual representation of an assigned or group-selected word. This visual representation may take the form of a mural, a drawing on the board, a static pose, a dance, a statue (possibly with a commentary or epitaph), clip art, video clips, or PowerPoint presentations.

For example, students might show their understanding of the word "metamorphosis" by demonstrating the key stages in the life cycle of a butterfly (egg, larva, pupa, butterfly).

Word Charts

Building vocabulary is the primary use for word charts in Grades 3 to 6. These charts may contain content-specific vocabulary, synonyms and antonyms, or word families with prefixes or suffixes. Unlike word walls, word charts focus on a particular theme, idea, or word strategy. Shared reading provides the perfect opportunity to create word charts based on the teaching focus for the text chosen. Students can assist in collecting and charting words or phrases that

- convey humour
- evoke smells, sights, sounds, and strong emotions
- paint mental pictures
- make noise
- express action, hurt, or conflict
- are associated with experts
- show/not tell
- imply change
- suggest peace

(Allen 1999)

During independent reading, students may continue to find words to add to the class-created word charts.

ABC Books

Students write the letters of the alphabet on a page and list the unit's key words, concepts, and ideas under them. This activity works well at the end of a unit to help students remember key concepts, ideas, and vocabulary (Bromley 2002). Working with a partner, students

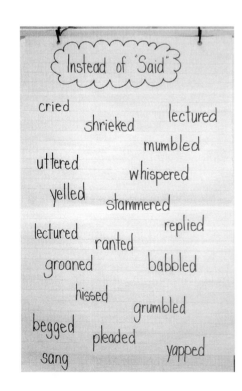

Instead of "Said"

cried
shrieked   lectured
                 mumbled
uttered
                 whispered
yelled
        stammered
lectured   replied
        ranted
groaned   babbled
        hissed
                 grumbled
begged
        pleaded
sang   yapped

compare lists and record new ideas, where appropriate. Finally, the teacher calls out key words and students check their lists for accuracy, recording more words as necessary. As an extension, students may take one word each to illustrate, define, and explain why it is important to the unit. Their sheets might then be compiled into a book for the class library.

Activities to Activate Prior Knowledge

The activities that follow activate prior knowledge particularly well. Effective teachers examine the word associations and determine what key vocabulary needs to be explicitly taught. For more suggested activities, refer to the section on using prior knowledge/predicting under Effective Comprehension Strategies in Chapter 2: Reading Comprehension: Strategies That Work.

Word Solving

Word solvers decode in reading and encode in writing. By engaging students in frequent opportunities to analyze words, teachers reinforce sound–symbol relationships. Knowing word-solving strategies enables students to concentrate on comprehension.

The most successful word study programs focus on learning words in context and do not require students to memorize rules. When selecting these words, teachers focus only on those that are critical to the text or that can be clustered around a concept or strategy. Challenging students to use a more sophisticated vocabulary elevates their speaking and writing level.

Generating and posting lists of synonyms and antonyms provides students with the words they need to clarify, strengthen, and improve their message. Once posted, these lists of words remain in prominent view. While students use these lists as a reference tool for spelling accuracy and vocabulary enhancement, teachers may use these words to teach such concepts as syllabication and affixes.

When students get stuck on a word during guided reading or writing, they can be helped to get on with their task through teacher prompts, such as those that follow:

- Try reading that again.
- Make sure that sounds right.
- Look for a chunk you already know. Use your finger to cover part of the word.
- Start the word again. Say the beginning sound and read the rest of the sentence.
- I will start the word for you to help you figure it out.
- Read the word without the vowel. See what would make sense there.
- Does that look right?
- What word would make sense?
- Here's a word you already know that is like this one.
- Skip the word and read on. Go back. What word fits?
- Look at the picture (chart/diagram/figure) to help you.

"Making vocabulary study meaningful and useful for students has always been the difficult part. As teachers, we must help students incorporate new words into their existing language in ways that don't seem phony."

ALLEN 1999, 40

To increase vocabulary development, students with poor vocabularies need to learn the meaning of new words and be given the chance to use them often (Baker, Simmons, and Kameenui in Allen 1999).

(Adapted from Allen 1999, 23)

- Make sure that sounds right.
- Does that make sense?
- I liked the way you tried to help yourself.
- I noticed you tried ... when you had trouble. That's what good readers do.
- You worked out the hard part. I saw you checking....
- Try reading that sentence again.
- The word is....

Mnemonic Devices

Mnemonic devices aid memory and may be used to help students remember a concept or aid in the spelling of multisyllabic or difficult words. Acronyms, rhymes, and so on, are just some of the methods for activating prior knowledge.

Mnemonic Device	Examples
Acronyms	radar = **ra**dio **d**etecting **a**nd **r**anging NAFTA = **N**orth **A**merican **F**ree **T**rade **A**greement
Rhymes	**i** before **e** except after **c**, or when it says **ay** as in **neighbour** and **weigh** When two vowels go walking, the first one does the talking (e.g., **e**at, b**o**at).
Word Endings	The princi**pal** is your pal. A fri**end** is there in the end.
Order	**Planets: M**y **v**ery **e**mbarrassed **m**onkey **j**ust **s**pat **u**p **n**ine **p**eanuts. (Mercury, Venus, Earth, Mars, Jupiter, Saturn, Uranus, Neptune, Pluto) **Operations: P**lease **e**xcuse **m**y **d**ear Aunt **S**ally. (parentheses, exponents, multiplication, division, addition, subtraction)

Students might also enjoy playing with language using puns, palindromes (e.g., Madam, I'm Adam), portmanteau words (e.g., brunch = breakfast + lunch), eponyms (e.g., teddy bear, derived from Teddy Roosevelt), onomatopoeia (e.g., splatter, zipper), common Latin and Greek roots (e.g., auto, tri, rupt), and so on.

Great Books for Playing with Language

The Word Detective: Solving the Mysteries Behind Those Pesky Words and Phrases by Evan Morris (New York: Penguin, 2001).

Demonic Mnemonics (800 Spelling Tricks for 800 Tricky Words) by Murray Suid (New York: Fearon Teacher Aids/Simon and Schuster, 1981).

A Cache of Jewels and Other Collective Nouns by Ruth Heller (New York: Putnam Juvenile, 1998).

> *Fantastic! Wow! And Unreal! A Book About Interjections and Conjunctions* by Ruth Heller (New York: Putnam: 1998).
>
> *Get Thee to a Punnery* by Richard Lederer (Charleston, SC: Wyrick & Company, 1988).
>
> *The Dictionary of Wordplay* by Dave Morice (New York: Teachers & Writers Collaborative, 2001).
>
> *Go Hang a Salami! I'm a Lasagna Hog!* by Jon Agee (New York: Farrar Strauss Giroux, 1991).
>
> *A Hog on Ice and Other Curious Expressions* by Charles Earle Funk (New York: HarperResource, 2002).

Word Sorts and Word Webs

The sample shared reading lesson earlier in this chapter for the poem "Hot Like Fire" demonstrates how word sorts can be used to activate prior knowledge and make predictions. For other word sort and word web activities, see Developing Phonological Awareness Through Word Study in Chapter 1: Oral Language: Speaking, Listening, and Learning. See also Identifying, Categorizing, and Sorting; Vocabulary Prediction; and Sort and Predict activities in Chapter 2: Reading Comprehension: Strategies That Work.

Word-Solving Strategies to Assist Independent Reading

Students need to be explicitly taught a variety of word-solving strategies to help them when reading independently. Once the strategies have been taught, they can be added to the list permanently on display in the classroom. The checklist for word solving under Activities to Build Vocabulary (see the preceding section) outlines approaches teachers might take.

Once the activities have been taught and practised, they can become the basis for independent literacy tasks, as well as tools to teach spelling. (See Word Work earlier in this chapter.)

Making Words

Making as many words as they can from a set number of letters is a fun and worthwhile activity for students. Students begin by making two-letter, three-letter, and four-letter combinations until they eventually use all of the letters that make up one mystery word. (For more information on making words, as well as a list of some of the books in the Making Words series by Patricia Cunningham, see the section Weak Decoders with Limited Comprehension in Chapter 6: Supporting Struggling and Reluctant Readers.)

Root Words

Upper elementary students and teachers often enjoy word study activities that involve creating word lists derived from a specific Greek or Latin root (Bloodgood and Pacifici 2004). At the beginning of each day, the teacher writes a root word on the board, for example, the Latin word *specere*. (The English form of the Latin root *specere* is

Check It Out!

Root words and their meanings can be found in most dictionaries. Other great resources include the following:

E. Fry, D.L. Fountoukidis, and J.K. Polk, *The New Reading Teacher's Book of Lists* (Englewood Cliffs, NJ: Prentice-Hall, 1985).

K. Ganske, *Word Journeys: Assessment-Guided Phonics, Spelling, and Vocabulary Instruction* (New York: Guilford, 2000).

D. Bear, M. Invernizzi, S. Templeton, and F. Johnston, *Words Their Way: Word Study for Phonics, Vocabulary, and Spelling Instruction.* 2nd ed. (Englewood Cliffs, NJ: Prentice-Hall, 2000).

spec or *spect*.). Students are encouraged to add words derived from this root to the list throughout the day (e.g., *inspect, spectator, respect,* and so on). At the end of the day, students determine the meaning of the root word based on the words they have listed. In this case, *specere* means "look."

Word Walls

Word walls in Grade 3 may be systematically organized lists of high-frequency words that students need to read and write automatically and fluently. Some teachers refer to these words as "no excuses" words based on an expectation that they will be read and written correctly and automatically.

During modelled and shared writing sessions, teachers demonstrate how to use a word wall effectively to assist with spelling. It is important to note that having a word wall is not the same as using a word wall. Students will more readily use a word wall when provided with activities that require them to do so. The creation and use of a personal word wall is helpful for many struggling students.

Beyond Grade 3, word walls usually focus on content-specific words that students will encounter in a single unit of study or throughout the year. They appear as subject-area word charts (e.g., science, mathematics, or social studies) and are often generated by teachers and students together. The words, which are also organized systematically, help struggling readers and writers interpret text and record their thoughts. (See also the material under Word Charts earlier in this section, as well as Content Word Boards in Chapter 1: Oral Language: Speaking, Listening, and Learning.)

Spelling

Exemplary spelling instruction enables students to explore and master the graphophonic aspect of language. In other words, students match letters to sounds and learn the few rules that govern how those sounds are represented. Effective teachers embed spelling instruction in meaningful reading, writing, and word-study tasks, and focus on

- language structures (root words, word origins, affixes, and compound words)
- specialized vocabulary from cross-curricular studies and high-frequency "no excuses" words
- spelling strategies to address multiple learning styles (auditory, visual, kinesthetic)
- spelling patterns and generalizations
- word exploration
- multisyllabic words

(Adapted from Tarasoff 1990)

Assessing Spelling Skills

Effective literacy teachers use many methods to collect information about students' growth in spelling. One method is to analyze individual writing samples. From these ongoing assessments, teachers are able to

Using word walls regularly throughout the year enables teachers to assist students in word mastery through the repetition of previously learned principles (Allen 1999).

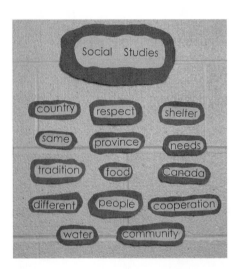

Check It Out!

Jo Phenix, *The Spelling Teacher's Book of Lists* (Markham, ON: Pembroke Publishers, 1994).

Ruth McQuirter Scott and Sharon Siamon, *Spelling: Connecting the Pieces* (Toronto: Gage Learning Corporation, 2004).

Mary Tarasoff, *Spelling Strategies You Can Teach* (Victoria, BC: Active Learning Press, 1990).

- start with what students already know about spelling conventions
- plot students on a developmental continuum (see below)
- create individual or class profiles
- target specific skills
- group students by strength, need, or strategy
- match strategies to learners

Prephonetic	Phonetic	Patterns Within Words	Syllable Juncture	Meaning Derivation
• scribbles in horizontal lines • eventually writes from left to right • readable by student only, right after it is written • letters are not linked with sounds • may include number symbols as part of the spelling of a word • often mixes upper- and lower-case letters	• direct letter-to-sound matches (e.g., *u* for *you*) • omits many short vowels and ambiguous consonants (e.g., *jup* for *jump*) • *m* and *n* often omitted before a final consonant (e.g., *stap* for *stamp*) • pattern of short vowel substitutions • long vowels spelled by the vowel letter alone (e.g., KAK for *cake*)	• silent "marking" vowel for long vowels (e.g., RANE for *rain*) • more correctly spelled words • regular appearance of correctly spelled short vowels • patterns of letters can represent a sound (e.g., *boat, boil*) • use of consonant blends and digraphs (e.g., spl*ash*, pl*uck*, th*at*)	• doubles consonants to mark the short vowel (e.g., *hopped*) • properly applies doubling principle to long vowels (e.g., *hope/hoping* vs. *hopeing/hopping*) • conventional rules and generalizations about spelling beginning to be applied	• homophones are spelled correctly more consistently • sees relationship between words with common roots (e.g. *sign/signal*) • uses simple prefixes and suffixes

(Adapted from McQuirter Scott and Siamon 2004, 9)

Weekly spelling tests do not provide an accurate measure of how well students spell. Effective teachers know that many students do well on these memory tests, but struggle with spelling in their day-to-day work. Weekly spelling tests remain controversial. While many parents see them as vital to developing good spellers, no research supports this belief. However, some literacy teachers see a place and a purpose for weekly tests in a comprehensive literacy program. Acting on the advice of such experts as J. Richard Gentry, Louisa Moats, and Edmund Henderson, these teachers have modified the way lists are generated and tests are administered by

- using pretests, which allows teachers to pare down the lists to focus on the words that students do not know
- teaching the words through word study, such as word sorts
- creating spelling lists from students' writing, specialized or technical vocabulary needed for cross-curricular studies, and word lists
- allowing students to make multiple attempts to spell each word
- having peers administer pre- and post-tests
- posting spelling words on a word wall
- giving multiple clues to students, such as showing the shape of the word, breaking the word into syllables, giving a word history, or sharing related words

Check It Out!

Donald R. Bear, et al., *Words Their Way* (Englewood Cliffs, NJ: Prentice-Hall, 2000).

J. Richard Gentry and Jean Wallace Gillet, *Teaching Kids to Spell* (Portsmouth, NH: Heinemann, 1992).

Rebecca Sitton, *Spelling Sourcebook 1* (Upper Saddle River, NJ: Globe Fearon Educational Publisher, 1998).

Diana Rees and Judith Rivalland, *First Steps Spelling Developmental Continuum* (Toronto: Heinemann, 1997).

Diana Rees, Kay Kovalevs, and Alison Dewsbury, *Spelling Resource Book* (Melbourne: Rigby Heinemann, 1997).

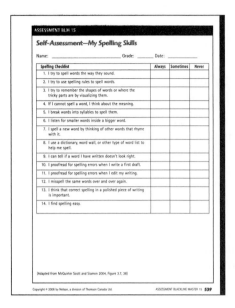

However, the true spelling test appears daily in authentic student writing experiences such as reader response and science or math journals. It is important for teachers to examine spelling attempts or approximations to assess each student's level of word knowledge, to identify what word-solving strategies the student has adopted, and to determine appropriate instruction. Equally important is ensuring that the words chosen to teach through word study "have a connection and are not just random words thrown out to them [students] to memorize" (Bloodgood and Pacifici 2004, 252).

Encouraging students to assess their own spelling abilities will enable them to identify their strengths, pinpoint strategies that require practice, and set individualized spelling goals.

Assessment BLM 14: Spelling Rubric
Assessment BLM 15: My Spelling Skills
Assessment BLM 3: Scoring Guide—Sentence Fluency and Conventions in Chapter 3
Assessment BLM 6: Sentence Fluency and Conventions in Chapter 3

Spelling Strategies

Self-confidence is critical to student success. Students who recognize that spelling is doable will be more apt to persevere when faced with an unfamiliar word. Also, students fortified with a wide range of strategies will have a larger bank of automatic words and will be more inclined to include words they are unsure of in their writing.

Matching strategies to the way students most easily learn is one way of helping students become better spellers. (For more information on learning styles and multiple intelligences, see Chapter 4: Literacy Learning Across the Curriculum.)

Check It Out!

Teacher Spelling Toolkit (MECC) is a software resource that allows students to input and save word lists from their reading. It has a variety of interesting practice options.

Learning Style	Strategies	Examples
Auditory	Sounding out, sound–symbol matching	**d** – **d**og li**d**
	Exaggerating hard-to-hear sounds	surprise probably February
	Pronouncing silent letters	We**d**nesday cu**p**board of**t**en
	Spelling words out loud	M-i-s-s-i-s-s-i-p-p-i r-h-y-t-h-m
	Listening for rhyming patterns	**b**attle **c**attle **r**attle
	Clapping or tapping syllables	Sask át chew an *clap* *CLAP* *clap* *clap*
Visual	Highlighting tricky letters	c|ough| bri**ght** de**C**ide
	What looks right?	because ~~beeuase~~ ~~beeuse~~
	Add a letter	E _ _ _ _ _ Eg _ _ _ Egy _ _ Egyp _ Egypt!
	Shape/configuration	▌▍▐ blink judge

	Sorting words by visual pattern	**gh**ost **gh**astly **gh**oulish
	Personal word walls	**Aa** **Bb** Akim Bart apple baby after buy
	Cloze	su _ pri _ e bec_ _ _ e Feb_ _ a _ y
Tactile/ Kinesthetic	Using a keyboard or chalkboard	
	Sorting word cards or playing word games	
	Making words with letter cards	
	Making illustrated words	
	Making words with a group	
	Sorting words in hoops	

(Adapted from McQuirter Scott and Siamon 2004, 131, 134, 138)

Using Meaning Strategies to Improve Spelling

The three main strands of spelling include alphabet, pattern, and meaning. The alphabet strand targets the sound–symbol relationship; the pattern strand targets such letter groups as *ough* and the consonant–vowel–consonant pattern that has a short vowel sound. "The meaning strand weaves in and out of the other two; it expands words in an ever-widening pool as students understand that the spelling of many words is linked to meaning" (McQuirter Scott and Siamon 2004, 142).

Check It Out!

These Web sites support spelling and vocabulary development:

Education by Design: Learning to Spell
http://www.edbydesign.com/spelling.html

Vocabulary Enhancement Strategies
http://www.smsu.edu/ids117/new/vocabulary.html

Vocabulary Learning Strategies
http://www.public.asu.edu/~ickpl/learningvoc.htm

Vocabulary University
http://www.vocabulary.com/

Meaning Strategies	Examples
Forms of Base Words	**colour** colouring coloured colourful
Borrowed Words	**beau**tiful "beau" = "good looking" in French
Homophones	rode road threw through
Word History	The **k** in **knight** was once pronounced in English. The word **holiday** comes from "holy day."
Prefixes	**trans** = across **trans**fer **trans**portation **trans**mit
Suffixes	**ation** circul**ation** transport**ation** conver**sation**
Sorting Related Words (see also Chapter 1: Oral Language: Speaking, Listening, and Learning)	sign signal signature assign
Word Webs/ Word Explosions	thrilled ecstatic glad — **happy** — joyful cheerful

(Adapted from McQuirter Scott and Siamon 2004, 143)

Organizing and Managing an Effective Literacy Program

A comprehensive literacy program requires time for explicit teaching and demonstrations through modelled, shared, and guided sessions. As well, students require much time for practice through independent reading and writing. They also need many opportunities for talk. To meet these requirements, teachers need to schedule large blocks of uninterrupted time. In this way, they are able to promote longer and more sustained attention to tasks. Planning daily activities that blend reading, writing, and oral language allows students to see and make connections among the components of a literacy program and across the curriculum. Many of the components listed in the chart on the following page can be readily incorporated into other curriculum areas. (See also Chapter 4: Literacy Learning Across the Curriculum.)

Suggested Time Requirements for Comprehensive Literacy		
Components	Frequency	Duration per Session
Oral Language	Integrated daily	Ongoing
Read-Aloud	Daily	15–20 minutes
Shared Reading	Daily	15–20 minutes
Guided Reading	Two or three sessions per group per week	15–20 minutes
Literature Circles/ Book Clubs*	One or two texts per term	20–30 minutes
Independent Reading	Daily	30–40 minutes
Modelled/ Shared Writing	Daily	10–15 minutes
Independent Writing	Daily	30–40 minutes
Word Study**	Daily	10 minutes

* Literature circles or book clubs may meet at the same time as guided reading groups, or may be substituted for guided or independent reading.

** Word study is best taught in context and is often embedded in the instruction and practice of reading, writing, and oral language.

(Adapted from Toronto District School Board 2000)

Regularly assessing their literacy program enables teachers to make modifications as necessary.

Reflecting on My Literacy Program

- Have I collected a diverse selection of literature for read-aloud? Shared reading? Guided reading? Independent reading?

- Do I select texts for instruction based on both the strategies the students need and their interests?

- Do I plan opportunities for regular, purposeful demonstrations of before-, during-, and after-reading strategies, skills, or behaviours during read-aloud, shared, and guided reading sessions?

- Do my students spend most of their time engaged in authentic reading and writing tasks?

- Do I ensure that my students read/listen to a variety of genres, including nonfiction and poetry?

- Do I attempt to connect what my students are reading to what they are writing?

- Do I explicitly teach both decoding and comprehension strategies for fiction and nonfiction?

- Do I provide opportunities for my students to respond to literal, inferential, critical, and evaluative types of questions?

- Do I provide opportunities for my students to read material that they have selected themselves, as well as material that I have chosen?
- Do I integrate reading and writing instruction with the teaching of content subjects?
- Do I provide opportunities for my students to discuss their reading and writing with partners, in small groups, and as a class?
- Do I provide students with ongoing assessment and feedback to enable them to improve their decoding and comprehension skills?
- Do I provide opportunities for students to monitor and self-assess their reading?

As a result of this reflection, what change(s) will I make to my program?

Timetabling for Effective Instruction

Effective teachers keep in mind that timetables may change throughout the year to accommodate student needs.

Maintaining flexibility is crucial to capturing teachable moments. Flexibility further enables teachers to give students the time they need to complete a more complex task. However, it is important to keep in mind that students thrive on predictable structures, routines, and stability; finding that balance is critical for student success.

As stated earlier, integration of language arts skills and strategies with cross-curricular content (e.g., social studies, science) is crucial to fitting in the large blocks of time students need for authentic reading, writing, speaking, listening, and viewing. (See Chapter 4: Literacy Learning Across the Curriculum.)

Effective teachers consider whether

- the curriculum expectations/outcomes, the diversity of a comprehensive literacy program, and the needs of students are reflected
- students spend most of their time engaged in authentic reading and writing activities
- they have established a long uninterrupted block of time for literacy learning
- other subject-area content has been integrated with language arts, where possible
- the same strategies used in language arts are being used across the curriculum

Weekly Planning

Many teachers find that a week-at-a-glance organizer enables them to see the variety and range of strategies, behaviours, and texts explicitly taught and practised. This road map helps teachers see where students have been and where they need to go.

"In creating your timetable, remain flexible and open to changes. Expect to make adjustments to your timetable as you plan your program, establish routines, and encourage independence and confidence in your students."

SCHWARTZ AND POLLISHUKE 2002, 21

A Week-at-a-Glance: Language Instruction

Component	Monday	Tuesday	Wednesday	Thursday	Friday
Shared Reading/ Word Study (20 min.) • word-solving and comprehension strategies • phrasing and fluency	**Text:** *Should There Be Zoos?* **Focus:** introduce persuasive form	**Text:** *Should There Be Zoos?* **Focus:** persuasive vocabulary	**Text:** *Should There Be Zoos?* **Focus:** reading with phrasing and fluency	**Text:** *Should There Be Zoos?* **Focus:**	**Text:** **Focus:**
Modelled or Shared Writing (10 to 15 min.)	**Modelled:** write the introduction to a persuasive letter	**Modelled and Shared:** continue persuasive letter			
Independent Reading/ Literacy Activities (30 to 40 min.)	**1. Reading Corner:** independent reading **2. Writing Centre:** text innovation	**3. Word Study:** compound words **4. Research:** info on zoos	**5. Readers Theatre:** script		
Guided Reading (15 to 20 min.) (other students engaged in independent reading/literacy activities)	Group # _3_ **Text:** appropriate "just right" text **Focus:** chunking of text with guided questions	Group # _1_ **Text:** appropriate nonfiction "just right" text **Focus:** features of text (e.g., glossary, index)	Group # ____ **Text:** **Focus:**	Group # ____ **Text:** **Focus:**	Group # ____ **Text:** **Focus:**
Reflection (5 min.)		What did you learn about yourself as a reader or writer? Where else can you use this information?			
Read-Aloud (15 min.)	**Text:** *Zella, Zach, and Zodiac* (half of story) **Focus:** modelling think-aloud strategy	**Text:** *Zella, Zach, and Zodiac* (rest of story) **Focus:** partner discussion—animals in wild vs. captivity	**Text:** *Dr. Doolittle* (Chapter 1) **Focus:** using your imagination	**Text:** **Focus:**	**Text:** **Focus:**
Independent Writing (30 to 40 min.) (guided writing/ mini-lessons during this time)	**Focus:** begin writing book reviews introduced in last week's shared reading and shared writing	**Focus:** conference with peer/self regarding appropriate vocabulary	**Focus:**	**Focus:**	**Focus:**

BLM 2: A Week-at-a-Glance Planner

Developing Home–School–Community Partnerships

Research shows that involving parents and other community members in the classroom has a positive impact on students' literacy development. However, as students move through the upper elementary grades, parents become more passive about their role in the learning process and less inclined to volunteer. While it is important for teachers to ensure parents remain actively engaged in their children's learning, inviting community volunteers such as senior citizens, as well as paraprofessionals and reading buddies into the classroom, can do much to enhance the learning environment.

For more information on developing home–school–community partnerships, see Chapter 4: Literacy Learning Across the Curriculum.

Home–School Partnerships

Effective literacy teachers realize the importance of the home–school partnership in scaffolding the literacy development of their students. Because most students in Grades 3 to 6 are reading and writing, parents tend to believe that reading and writing to and with their child are unnecessary. However, students are never too old to be read to and benefit greatly from hearing fiction, nonfiction, and poetry read aloud and from taking part in discussion afterwards. To encourage and support parental participation in their children's literacy development, teachers rely on various communication and educational tools.

To initiate the home–school connection, teachers might send each student a letter in late August or early September to

- introduce him- or herself to the students and parents
- welcome the students to the new grade
- provide a general orientation to the year
- outline some of the upcoming activities
- invite each student to bring a favourite book or a magazine to class to share

Fostering the Home–School Connection

Parents have a vested interest in their child's success, so it is essential that the methods for maintaining open, ongoing communication between the school and home, and vice versa, are established early on. The mutual exchange of information, support, and encouragement benefits all those who have a stake in students' literacy development: the parents, the teachers, the school, the community, and most importantly, the students themselves.

Some of the methods that follow require parents to provide feedback to the teacher; others involve teachers conveying information to parents.

Dear _____
            (Student Name)

Hello! My name is _____ and as your teacher for the new school year, I am writing to welcome you to my class.

I hope you had a fun summer. My summer was wonderful, but I am looking forward to returning to school next week. I bet you are excited, too! It is always great to see old friends and to meet new ones.

During the school year, we will be learning about many interesting things. We will read a lot, write in many forms, solve math problems, study the world around us, and make good friendships. If any questions or problems come up for you, please make sure you ask for my help.

To begin our reading program, please bring to school your favourite book or magazine from home or the public library. We will be sharing something about the text and discussing why you enjoyed reading it. Talking about your choice will also let class members get to know you better.

See you on _____!
              (First Day of Fall Term)

                    Sincerely,

Parent Survey

Ideally, a parent survey is sent home at the beginning of the school year and at least once more during the school year. The purpose of this communication tool is to determine parents' understanding of their child's literacy skills, attitudes, and interests.

Assessment BLM 1: Literacy Home Links: Survey

Home–School Journal or Student Agenda

Many schools have implemented a home–school journal or student agenda system as a convenient way for

- students to record daily homework requirements and school business, such as field-trip reminders and library book due dates
- teachers to provide suggestions for parental support at home
- parents to connect with the classroom, monitor homework, and record questions or comments about the progress of their child

Homework

Daily at-home reading is the most important homework students can do, with additional homework assigned as required. At-home reading enables parents to become involved in their child's reading program and provides students with more time to become lost in a book (magazine, poem, comic book). Homework in general gives students the opportunity to practise skills and strategies; however, the tasks must be relevant, meaningful, and connected to the classroom program. Homework also enriches background knowledge and understandings, and helps to convey to parents what learnings teachers value.

"Homework is often seen as a window into the classroom as it acquaints parents with their children's in-school learning experiences."

SCHWARTZ AND POLLISHUKE 2002, 156

BLM 9: Literacy Home Links: Home Reading Program Log Sheet

BLM 4: Literacy Home Links: How Families Can Support the Talking to Reading and Writing Connection in Chapter 1

BLM 4: Literacy Home Links: Home Reading Program in Chapter 2

BLM 5: Literacy Home Links: Choosing "Just Right" Books in Chapter 2

Volunteer Programs

Inviting parents and other community volunteers to become directly involved in supporting literacy learning at school is another effective way to develop the home–school–community partnership. Parents and volunteers might participate daily, weekly, or as often as possible. Research shows, however, that trained volunteers feel more useful in the classroom and provide more effective support for students than if not trained.

Parent–Teacher or Student-Led Conferences

These more formal, face-to-face meetings typically occur after a scheduled reporting period. They provide an opportunity to discuss student progress, celebrate achievement, voice specific concerns, and establish goals or next steps. Informal parent–teacher conversations may also be conducted over the phone or via e-mail throughout the year as necessary.

Sharing Literacy Information with Parents

Letters, notes, monthly newsletters and calendars, and even scheduled school events are just some of the ways specific information about literacy can be shared with parents.

Classroom Sharing

Students in Grades 3 to 6 are becoming fluent readers and writers, but benefit from parental support. Parents, however, need advice and suggestions for working with their children to further enhance their literacy skills. Teachers may wish to share with parents

- the importance of the parents' role in literacy development and school success
- pertinent research
- developmental stages of reading and writing
- appropriate books to read aloud to students in Grades 3 to 6
- other ideas for reading materials and writing formats
- the definition of "just right" books
- tips on how to read to, and with, children
- ways to listen to children reading aloud
- suggestions for the family to monitor all the many ways that members read and write at home during the week, including newspapers, e-mail messages, the family bulletin board, and shopping lists
- tips on how to study spelling words with spelling strategies that work
- exemplars of reading and writing, provided during interviews or conferences
- suggestions for improving or enhancing comprehension
- the definition of reading as meaning making, which goes beyond decoding
- information about the reading process and how reading is taught
- the role of spelling, grammar, and phonics

Teachers might communicate this information to parents in a variety of ways, from personalized letters or notes outlining specific suggestions for individual students to monthly classroom newsletters and calendars.

Parents are more likely to read a newsletter if it showcases their child in some way.

BLM 10: Literacy Home Links: News from Room _____

A monthly newsletter outlines the emphasis for that month and features samples of student work. This format enables parents to see what writing in Grades 3 to 6 looks like and how it improves over time. A section could be set aside to address questions from parents. The monthly newsletter also provides an authentic purpose and audience for student writing, thus demonstrating the functionality of writing.

BLM 7: Literacy Home Links: Million-Dollar Words in Chapter 3

BLM 8: Literacy Home Links: Assessing Writing in Chapter 3

Grade 4 News

"Working with our community for a better future"

5 Ways To Encourage Reading At Home

1. Read at home! It is important to let children see "real" people read. Continue reading to your child even when they can read themselves. Reading books out loud that are too difficult for your child to read will help add new words to their vocabulary. Let your child know that you value reading as a worthwhile leisure time activity.

2. Talk about reading with your child! Encourage your child to talk about things he or she has read. Be genuinely interested in the books your child brings home. Discuss the books and stories your child is reading or has completed. Have your child read to you, if only for 10 minutes a day.

3. Build a home library! On special occasions give books and magazines as gifts. Visit your local library regularly with your child.

4. Use family games! Games can help develop your child's vocabulary and comprehension in reading. Provide a family reading time as well.

5. Monitor television! Limit the television time to one hour or less on school days. Instead, encourage reading or other activities.

Why should I read to my children?

- When you hold children and give them attention, they know you love them.
- Reading to children will encourage them to become readers.
- Children's books today are so good that they are fun — even for adults.
- Books are one way of passing on your moral values to children. Readers know how to put themselves in other's shoes.
- A province-wide assessment of Grade 9 students in Ontario found that youngsters who had stories read to them when they were growing up tended to outperform those who did not. (Macleans, November 1994.)

At home activities to develop your child's number sense skills:

☺ Practise counting by 2, 3, 4, 5, 6, 7, 8, 9, and 10's starting from any number. E.g., Count by 4's starting from 13.

☺ Spend time looking for and reading numbers in the newspaper or magazines. E.g., *3552 Left Homeless By Hurricane Jeanne* (3552 = three thousand five hundred fifty-two)

☺ At the store, estimate the total cost of a few items. Calculate the approximate change. Go to http://www.funbrain.com/cashreg/index.html for more practice making change.

☺ Review basic addition and subtraction facts using flashcards, computer or board games.

☺ Have your child practise telling the time of family activities using an analog clock (not digital).

☺ Try the games *Sum and Difference*, and *Make a Number* at http://demo.granada-learning.com/maths2000/#

October's Highlights

Mississauga Public Library visits Kindree on October 7th. Students will learn about the services available at the public library. Students who return a completed application form by Oct. 1st will receive a library card entitling them to borrow materials from any Mississauga Library location.

The Science Demonstration Centre is booked for the week of October 17th. Each Grade 4 class will visit for 2 days. After learning how to reduce the amount of force required to lift a load, students will design and construct a device using both a gear and pulley.

> "Learning is a treasure that will follow its owner everywhere."
> **Chinese Proverb**

Special Events

Teachers within a division or a school often plan special events to support and educate parents about literacy. These sessions are generally more formal and take careful planning to succeed.

- Reading/Writing Information Night: Only parents attend these sessions.
- Family Reading/Writing Night: Parents and children attend these sessions together.
- Literacy-Focused School Assemblies: Families are invited to attend Readers Theatre performances, dramatic presentations, and so on.

As not all parents are able to attend these special events, many schools implement other methods for reaching out to them, such as

- establishing a Parent Shelf in the school library, from which parents sign out books or videos
- publishing literacy information on the school's Web site or in the school newsletter
- publishing a home literacy newsletter
- creating literacy bulletin boards, perhaps on a Meet the Author theme
- setting up an information booth at a local fair

Community–School Partnerships

Many communities can boast a rich resource of adult volunteers willing to assist with school literacy programs, act as mentors, and provide in-class support. Students in Grades 3 to 6 are in a similar position. Because they are becoming more fluent readers and writers, they may act as reading buddies and scribes for younger students—a beneficial arrangement for students at both grade levels and a way for teachers to further strengthen the literacy environment.

Younger students gain enthusiastic reading and writing models when they participate in a buddy program. They have an opportunity to develop speaking and listening skills outside of their classroom and to

experience different learning arrangements. Together, buddies celebrate reading and writing successes, and positive relationships between grades, and between the school and the community are strengthened.

Student Reading Buddies

The reading buddy arrangement has many literacy benefits for older students, too. Not only do they engage in authentic reading experiences, but they are also able to practise reading skills and behaviours. During reading buddy time, older students who struggle with fluency are free to practise reading easier material without feeling judged. Comprehension skills and reading strategies are highlighted when, as mentors, they discuss the text and ask questions of their young buddies. As older students scribe for their younger partners, they develop punctuation, spelling, and grammar skills. Their self-esteem improves and their interpersonal skills develop.

Prior to reading with their buddy, older students who struggle with fluency are encouraged to reread the text their buddy has chosen.

Characteristics of Successful Buddy Programs

- Teachers of both grades meet frequently to review the expectations for the reading and writing experiences.
- Frameworks for the buddy sessions are developed, modelled, and often reviewed by the classroom teachers.
- Ongoing training sessions are held so the older buddy understands how to work with the younger student. Students are provided with opportunities to share what is working and what is not. This allows for the improvement of the buddy experience.
- Students are matched on strengths, needs, similarities, or interests.
- Older buddies are made aware of the strategies, skills, or behaviours to model or encourage.
- The purpose of the reading or writing session is clear to both students.
- Buddy sessions generally last between 20 and 40 minutes. This allows buddies enough time to read and explore a text together.
- The older buddy completes a reading log for texts that are shared together. Both students rate the text and write a brief response.
- Teachers supervise and assess the validity of the reading or writing experience.

Closing Thoughts

Literacy remains at the heart of all classroom learning. It is the foundation upon which all other learning occurs. Scaffolding instruction, making connections, and using "just right" materials all help to support students on their journey to become effective readers, writers, speakers, listeners, and viewers. Classrooms that recognize and celebrate cultural diversity and have clear, realistic structures and expectations are more apt to create critical and creative problem solvers and risk takers.

Teachers who use a wide repertoire of effective assessment tools and teaching strategies, who embrace a comprehensive literacy framework, who teach literacy across the curriculum, and who engage parents, volunteers, and paraprofessionals in the learning process benefit their students' literacy learning. When students spend most of their time involved in authentic reading and writing experiences, they generally thrive. However, some students will require additional support and timely intervention to move them along the literacy continuum. Intervention strategies and frameworks are the focus of Chapter 6.

Chapter 5

BLACKLINE MASTERS

BLM 1: Student of the Week
BLM 2: A Week-at-a-Glance Planner
BLM 3: Shared Reading Lesson Planner
BLM 4: Word Sort for "Hot Like Fire"
BLM 5: Guided Reading Lesson Planner
BLM 6: At-a-Glance Guided Reading Observations
BLM 7: Literature Circle Role Cards
BLM 8: Literature Circle Group Results
BLM 9: Literacy Home Links: Home Reading Program Log Sheet
BLM 10: Literacy Home Links: News from Room ___

Student of the Week

Dear Parent,

Your child has been selected as next week's "Student of the Week." Through this activity, our class is getting to know one student better each week. A major benefit is a stronger sense of community within the classroom.

As "Student of the Week," your child will be responsible for sharing some personal treasures, or items of personal significance with the class. Your child is expected to follow this framework:

> **Tell:** Explain what the treasure is.
> **Relate:** Share why the item is meaningful.
> **Reflect:** Discuss how the item may affect his or her future.

The treasures or pictures of the treasures will be displayed in the classroom.

Please help your child make wise choices about what to bring to school. Also, it would be helpful to encourage your child to rehearse the framework for each treasure; this will result in a better presentation. Thank you for assisting with this activity.

If you have any questions or concerns, please contact me at the school.

Sincerely,

A Week-at-a-Glance Planner

Grade: _____ Week of: _____

Component	Monday	Tuesday	Wednesday	Thursday	Friday
Shared Reading/Word Study (20 min.) • word-solving and comprehension strategies • phrasing and fluency	Text: Focus:	Text: Focus:	Text: Focus:	Text: Focus:	Text: Focus:
Modelled or Shared Writing (10 to 15 min.)					
Independent Reading/Literacy Activities (30 to 40 min.)					
Guided Reading (15 to 20 min.) (other students engaged in independent reading/literacy activities)	Group # ___ Text: Focus:	Group # ___ Text: Focus:	Group # ___ Text: Focus:	Group # ___ Text: Focus:	Group # ___ Text: Focus:
Reflection (5 min.)	What did you learn about yourself as a reader or writer? Where else can you use this information?				
Read-Aloud (15 min.)	Text: Focus:	Text: Focus:	Text: Focus:	Text: Focus:	Text: Focus:
Independent Writing (30 to 40 min.) (guided writing/mini-lessons during this time)	Focus:	Focus:	Focus:	Focus:	Focus:

Shared Reading Lesson Planner

Text selected: _____

Purpose/focus for using this text: _____

When text will be used (e.g., language arts, science, or social studies block): _____

Day 1: Introducing the Text   Date: _____

Possible activities and questions for introducing the text:

Day 2: Working with the Text   Date: _____

Teaching point:

Comprehension focus:

      Reread: ❏ Whole Text   ❏ Targeted Section _____

Day 3: Working with the Text   Date: _____

Teaching point:

Comprehension focus:

      Reread: ❏ Whole Text   ❏ Targeted Section _____

Day 4: Working with the Text   Date: _____

Teaching point:

Comprehension focus:

      Reread: ❏ Whole Text   ❏ Targeted Section _____

Day 5: Extending the Text (optional)   Date: _____

Possible activity to deepen students' understanding of the text read:

Word Sort for "Hot Like Fire"

challenge	endless talk	intensity	humiliation
helpless	exceed	fadeaway	never change
burning eyes	school	expense	judging
silence	defenseless	entertain	chatter

Guided Reading Lesson Planner

Students (Group #)	Date: _____
	Title: _____
	Author: _____

Purpose/Comprehension Focus

Before Reading

During Reading

After Reading

At-a-Glance Guided Reading Observations

Text: _____   Author: _____

Observations might focus on
- word-solving strategies used
- comprehension strategies used (making connections, monitoring comprehension, using text structures, generating and answering questions, visualizing, predicting, retelling, summarizing, making inferences, synthesizing, relating, reflecting)

Student:	Date:	Student:	Date:
Student:	**Date:**	**Student:**	**Date:**
Student:	**Date:**	**Student:**	**Date:**
Student:	**Date:**	**Student:**	**Date:**

Literature Circle Role Cards

Discussion Director

Come up with one or two questions that you think will encourage members of your group to talk. Be sure to jot down your answers to share with the group.

Connector

Look for connections between you and the text. Look for connections between the text and what's happening in your world (for example, in the classroom, at school, or in the community). Think about connections you can make between this text and other texts. Record the connections (visually or in words), and be prepared to share them with the group.

Illustrator

As you read the text, what pictures popped into your head? Select one or two of those images and re-create them for your group. Remember that you can use magazines, photos, or labels to help you. Listen carefully to the conversation and share your images with the group at the most appropriate time.

Literary Luminary

Reread the text, looking for a memorable event, a thought-provoking or puzzling idea, or a humorous quote. Note the page number and location of the passage and the reason why you selected it. Determine what you would like the group to discuss. Read the passage aloud (or have another group member read it), explain why you chose it, and then lead the discussion.

Vocabulary Enricher

Look for words that might have special importance in the text. Note unfamiliar words and words that the group may have trouble with. Find words that are used in a different way than usual or that have peculiar patterns. Share your words and the reasons for choosing them with your group. Be sure to have definitions, parts of speech, and phonetic spellings ready.

Summarizer

Prepare a brief summary of the day's reading for the group. Be sure to include main ideas, plot highlights, or new character development. You may write in paragraphs or point form. Be sure to read over your summary before sharing it with the group.

Literature Circle Group Results

Group Members

Date: _____

Title: _____

Author: _____

Pages _____ to _____

Role A: Write two to three questions that you think will engage your group in an interesting discussion. (Make sure your questions cannot be answered in one or two words.) Generate a possible response for each question.

Question 1: _____

_____

Response: _____

_____

Question 2: _____

_____

Response: _____

_____

Question 3: _____

_____

Response: _____

_____

Role B: Think about the connections that can be made between the text and you, the world around you, and other texts. Note places in the text where you made a connection and briefly explain each one.

Connection 1: _____

_____

Connection 2: _____

_____

Literature Circle Group Results

Role C: Reread the text, looking for a memorable event, a thought-provoking or puzzling idea, or a humorous quote. Note the page number of the passage and explain why you selected each passage. Practise reading the passage aloud.

Page number: _____ Reason for selection: _____

_____

Page number: _____ Reason for selection: _____

_____

Role D: Look through the text for words that have special importance, may pose difficulty, are unfamiliar or are used in a different way, or have a peculiar pattern. Select two or three words. For each word, complete the information that follows.

Word: _____ Phonetic Spelling: _____

Part of Speech: _____

Definition: _____

Reason for selection: _____

Word: _____ Phonetic Spelling: _____

Part of Speech: _____

Definition: _____

Reason for selection: _____

Word: _____ Phonetic Spelling: _____

Part of Speech: _____

Definition: _____

Reason for selection: _____

Role E: Write a brief summary of the pages read for this discussion group. Be sure to include main ideas, plot highlights, and new character development.

_____

_____

_____

_____

Home Reading Program Log Sheet

Name: _____ Grade: _____ Date: _____

This month, I have agreed that I am going to read for at least
_____ minutes at home every day.

Date	Title	Type of Text	Pages	Signature

News from Room _____

News from Room ___

Dear Parents,

Welcome to a new school year! I am looking forward to a busy and enjoyable time with your child and the rest of the class. Already, I have planned many exciting learning experiences for the students.

In the meantime, please take note of the following important items.

Monthly Calendar: To keep you informed of activities planned, I will be sending home a monthly calendar full of information and reminders. Please have your child check the calendar daily so that he or she is prepared for each day. On the back of the calendar, you will find suggestions about how to help your child at home.

Homework: On most evenings, your child will have a short homework assignment to complete and return to school the next day. Since research has shown that students do better in school when their parents support their learning, please take an active role. Talk with your child about the day's events at school and help with homework as your child requires. Remember that the most important homework is daily reading and discussion. You can make a big difference!

Volunteers: Having volunteers serve in the classroom is very beneficial for students. Adult family members and friends are invited to help students practise the literacy skills and strategies used by strong literacy learners. If you are available to contribute to the class's learning experiences, please let me know.

I look forward to meeting you during the school year. If you have any questions or concerns, or if there is anything that you would like to share with me about your child, please call me.

Sincerely,

Chapter 5

ASSESSMENT BLACKLINE MASTERS

Assessment BLM 1: Literacy Home Links: Survey
Assessment BLM 2: Self-Assessment—Attitude Survey
Assessment BLM 3: Self-Assessment—Interest Inventory
Assessment BLM 4: Informal Reading Conference
Assessment BLM 5: Assessing Shared Reading
Assessment BLM 6: Retelling/Interpreting Checklist—Narrative Text
Assessment BLM 7: Retelling/Interpreting Checklist—Informational Text
Assessment BLM 8: High-Frequency Word Assessment
Assessment BLM 9: Self-Assessment—Portfolio Tagging Sheets
Assessment BLM 10: Portfolio Partners
Assessment BLM 11: Self-Assessment—Assessing My Year
Assessment BLM 12: Readers Theatre Script Rubric
Assessment BLM 13: Self-Assessment—Readers Theatre Performance
Assessment BLM 14: Spelling Rubric
Assessment BLM 15: Self-Assessment—My Spelling Skills

Survey

To the Parents of: _____

From: _____ Grade: _____ Date: _____

To help me to know your child better and to devise effective programming, please complete the survey that follows. Your answers will be most useful and appreciated.

1. How do you think your child views himself or herself as a reader?

   _____

   _____

2. How do you think your child views himself or herself as a writer?

   _____

   _____

3. What type of reading material does your child prefer? (Check all that apply.)

   ❑ novels or chapter books   ❑ comic or cartoon books

   ❑ magazines   ❑ poetry

   ❑ newspaper articles   ❑ information on Internet sites

   ❑ nonfiction books (information)   ❑ instructions and directions

4. What does your child like to write?

   _____

   _____

5. Does your child enjoy ...

   • listening to books being read?   ❑ Yes   ❑ No

     Please explain: _____

   • discussing books, magazines, or movies?   ❑ Yes   ❑ No

     Please explain: _____

   • writing?   ❑ Yes   ❑ No

     Please explain: _____

6. What advice would you give your child to help his or her reading or writing?

   _____

   _____

Self-Assessment—Attitude Survey

Name: _____ Grade: _____ Date: _____

For each statement, check the box that best applies to you.

Statement	Strongly Agree	Agree	Unsure	Disagree	Strongly Disagree
1. Reading is one of my favourite activities.					
2. Writing is one of my favourite activities.					
3. I like to choose what I read.					
4. I like to write about topics that I have chosen.					
5. Reading a good story relaxes me.					
6. Writing about my feelings and ideas is important to me.					
7. I like going to the library.					
8. I feel good when I read a book I like.					
9. I prefer to write reports or instructions rather than stories or journal entries.					
10. I'd rather listen to a story than read it myself.					
11. I like to write using the computer.					

The book I am reading right now is _____

_____

My best piece of writing ever was _____

_____

(Adapted from Phillips 1999, 53)

Self-Assessment—Interest Inventory

Name: _____ Grade: _____ Date: _____

1. What after-school activities do you enjoy? (Check as many as apply to you.)

   ❏ Reading   ❏ Playing games or sports

   ❏ Using the computer   ❏ Playing a musical instrument

   ❏ Watching TV   ❏ Taking lessons

   ❏ Other (specify) _____

2. If you could do anything you wanted this weekend, what would you choose? _____

   _____

3. Do you take lessons, belong to a team, or belong to a club or group?   ❏ Yes   ❏ No

   If "yes," tell what you do and why you like these activities. If "no," what activities would you like
   to do. Why? _____

   _____

   _____

4. What is your favourite subject in school? Why? _____

   _____

5. What subject is the most difficult for you? Why? _____

   _____

6. When learning something new, which ways are the most helpful for you?

   ❏ Reading a book, magazine, or article

   ❏ Watching a movie, video, DVD, or television program

   ❏ Reading information on the Internet

   ❏ Talking to a friend, the teacher, or an expert

   ❏ Listening to an audiotape or CD

   ❏ Working with objects

   ❏ Working with a group of peers

7. What topic would you like to learn more about? _____

   _____

Informal Reading Conference

Name: _____ Grade: _____ Date: _____

Title: _____ Author: _____

Genre: _____

1. Why did you choose this book?

   _____

   _____

2. What is the book about so far?

   _____

   _____

3. Observations made while student reads aloud. Does the student

   ❑ subvocalize?

   ❑ reread?

   ❑ use illustrations and visuals?

   ❑ understand the humour?

   ❑ skip over difficult vocabulary?

   ❑ Other: _____

4. What do you remember about what you just read?

   _____

   _____

5. What do you consider to be your strengths as a reader?

   _____

   _____

6. What goals would you like to set for your reading?

   _____

   _____

(Adapted from Routman 2003, 104–05)

Assessing Shared Reading

Does the student ...	Student Names and Dates				
• share background knowledge and personal experiences during prereading discussions?					
• participate in the reading of the text?					
• make accurate predictions about the content of text?					
• demonstrate knowledge of word-solving and comprehension strategies?					
• share text-to-self connections during group discussions?					
• share text-to-text connections during group discussions?					
• share text-to-world connections during group discussions?					
• form opinions about the text and support opinions with evidence?					
• use ideas from text in personal writing?					
• demonstrate thoughtful responses to text?					

Retelling/Interpreting Checklist—Narrative Text

Name: _____ Grade: _____ Date: _____

Criteria for Retelling	Unassisted	Assisted	Comments
Includes main characters			
Includes secondary characters			
Includes time and place orientation			
Sequences events correctly and includes supporting details			
Summarizes logically			
Identifies the problem in the story			
States how the problem was solved			
Uses the language of the story			
Shows awareness of the audience through the use of an expressive, clear voice			

Criteria for Interpreting	Unassisted	Assisted	Comments
Interprets author's message			
Connects to other texts, authors, personal experiences, and knowledge of world			
Assesses text			

(Adapted from Shea 2000, 83)

Retelling/Interpreting Checklist—Informational Text

Name: _____ Grade: _____ Date: _____

Criteria for Retelling	Unassisted	Assisted	Comments
Identifies the topic of the text			
Summarizes the main idea			
Uses key vocabulary from text in retell			
Sequences information logically			
Interprets charts, tables, and pictures			

Criteria for Interpreting	Unassisted	Assisted	Comments
Draws conclusions			
Connects information in the text to real-life applications/experiences			

(Adapted from Shea 2000, 81)

High-Frequency Word Assessment

For Grade 3

about	enough	journal	schools	want
again	especially	knew	something	was
almost	everybody	know	sometimes	wear
also	everything	laughed	terrible	weather
always	except	let's	that's	went
another	exciting	lovable	their	we're
anyone	favourite	myself	then	were
are	first	new	there	what
beautiful	friendly	no	they	when
because	general	off	they've	where
before	getting	one	thought	whether
buy	governor	our	threw	who
by	have	people	through	whole
can't	hidden	prettier	to	winner
community	hole	prettiest	too	with
confusion	hopeless	pretty	trouble	won
could	I'm	probably	two	won't
countries	impossible	question	unhappiness	wouldn't
didn't	independent	really	until	write
discover	into	recycle	usually	your
doesn't	it's	right	vacation	you've
don't	its	said	very	

For Grades 4 and Up

a lot	crazier	hopeless	probably	to
accident	delicious	I'm	professional	too
adventure	depression	impossible	really	transportation
again	didn't	indescribable	relative	treasure
all right	different	into	reporter	two
almost	disagreement	irresponsible	restaurant	unfriendly
always	discourage	it's	said	until
amazing	doesn't	know	something	usually
another	employee	let's	sometimes	want
apologize	endurance	misunder-	substitute	went
beautiful	especially	standing	supervisor	we're
because	everybody	nonsense	swimming	were
biggest	everyone	off	that's	when
biologist	everything	our	their	where
buy	except	outrageous	then	which
caught	favourite	outside	there	whole
communities	finally	overwhelmed	they	would
competition	friend	people	they're	write
confidence	happiness	predictable	thought	you're
confusion	heard	prettier	through	

(Hall and Cunningham 1999, 124–125)

Self-Assessment—Portfolio Tagging Sheets

Portfolio Tag—Writing

Name: _____ Grade: _____ Date: _____

This writing sample shows that I can

- _____

- _____

- _____

This writing sample is an example of ❑ narrative ❑ expository ❑ poetry

My goal is to _____

_____

_____

_____

_____

_____

Portfolio Tag—Reading

Name: _____ Grade: _____ Date: _____

This is an example of _____

I chose this for my portfolio because _____

_____

My goal is to _____

_____

_____

_____

_____

_____

Portfolio Partners

Name: _____ Grade: _____ Date: _____

Portfolio Partner: _____

1. When you are being presented with the contents of your partner's portfolio, listen carefully and look closely at the work samples.

2. Think about the questions that follow. Record your ideas using positive statements.

   a) What do you think the portfolio shows that your partner can do well?

   _____

   _____

   _____

   _____

   b) What do you think your partner has learned?

   _____

   _____

   _____

   _____

   c) Has your partner set a realistic goal? What suggestions would you give your partner about that goal?

   _____

   _____

   _____

   _____

3. Share your comments with your partner. Use examples from the portfolio to support your comments.

Self-Assessment—Assessing My Year

Name: _____ Grade: _____ Date: _____

1. I finished Grade _____! This year, I learned to _____

_____

_____

_____

2. When I began this grade, I didn't know how to _____

_____

_____

but now I can _____

_____

3. I reviewed all of the samples in my portfolio. The sample that makes me the most proud is

_____

_____

_____

because _____

_____

_____

4. Next year, I want to learn to _____

_____

_____

_____

5. My advice to a student in this class next year would be _____

_____

_____

_____

Readers Theatre Script Rubric

Name: _____ Grade: _____ Date: _____

Level 1	Level 2	Level 3	Level 4
• script is uninteresting and does not hold the reader's attention	• script is satisfactory and occasionally holds the reader's attention	• script is interesting and usually holds the reader's attention	• script is enticing and holds the reader's attention
• adaptation of original text is not evident	• adaptation of original text is partial	• adaptation of original text is good	• adaptation of original text is excellent
• script is very awkward and difficult to read	• script is awkward in parts	• script is clear	• script is very clear and smooth
• script consists entirely of narration; dialogue is not evident	• script consists mostly of narration; dialogue is limited	• script demonstrates a solid balance between dialogue and narration	• script demonstrates an excellent balance between dialogue and narration

(Adapted from Alberta Assessment Consortium 1997, 13)

Self-Assessment—Readers Theatre Performance

Name: _____ Grade: _____ Date: _____

Script Title: _____

Use the questions that follow to help you reflect on your performance during your Readers Theatre presentation. Then, share your reflections with the rest of your Readers Theatre group.

During the Readers Theatre presentation ...	Yes	No
• was my voice loud and clear?		
• did I use expression in my voice?		
• was my reading fluent?		
• did I come in at exactly the right moment?		
• were my movements and actions appropriate?		
• did I do the best job I could with my part?		

The strength of my performance was _____

_____

_____

I could improve my performance by _____

_____

_____

(Adapted from Alberta Assessment Consortium 1997, 15)

Spelling Rubric

Name: _____ Grade: _____ Date: _____

Knowledge	LEVEL 1	LEVEL 2	LEVEL 3	LEVEL 4
Patterns	• uses phonics or inadequate memory strategies to spell without thought to word structure, meaning, or families of words; often spells the same word different ways	• uses phonics awareness when reminded; needs assistance to understand word structure and meaning as they relate to spelling; uses mnemonics at times to recall words studied	• regularly uses phonics, awareness of word structure, awareness of meaning, and personal mnemonics to spell accurately	• consistently uses phonics, awareness of word structure, awareness of meaning, and mnemonics to spell accurately
High-Frequency Words	• spells few high-frequency words correctly	• spells some high-frequency words correctly	• spells most high-frequency words correctly	• spells a wide range of high-frequency words correctly
Spelling Consciousness	• approaches spelling randomly and not as a system	• simply or incompletely articulates how he or she spells	• can usually articulate how he or she spells	• articulates how he or she spells and views spelling as a system that can be controlled

Strategies	LEVEL 1	LEVEL 2	LEVEL 3	LEVEL 4
Range	• focuses primarily on a single spelling strategy (e.g., sounding out words)	• uses a limited range of spelling strategies	• usually uses a range of spelling strategies (e.g., sound, visual, meaning)	• consistently uses a range of spelling strategies (e.g., sound, visual, meaning)
Appropriateness	• uses one or two simple strategies for all words regardless of the nature of the word (e.g., sounds out all words; tries to remember what words look like)	• sometimes chooses appropriate strategies to learn the spelling of words (e.g., sounds out patterned words; memorizes irregular words)	• usually chooses appropriate strategies (e.g., – sound strategies for words that fit sound patterns – visual strategies or memory tricks for irregular words – word-building strategies for longer words)	• consistently chooses appropriate strategies (e.g., – sound strategies for words that fit sound patterns – visual strategies or memory tricks for irregular words – word-building strategies for longer words)

(Adapted from McQuirter Scott and Siamon 2004, Figure 3.13, 46–47)

Spelling Rubric

Name: _____ Grade: _____ Date: _____

Strategies	LEVEL 1	LEVEL 2	LEVEL 3	LEVEL 4
Proofreading	• experiences difficulty both in detecting errors and in correcting them	• uses some simple proofreading strategies to detect and correct spelling errors	• usually uses effective proofreading strategies to detect and correct spelling errors	• consistently uses effective proofreading strategies to detect and correct spelling errors
Use of Secondary Sources	• seldom consults other sources in proof-reading, or uses them ineffectively	• relies on a small number of sources to aid proofreading	• usually makes appro-priate use of sources, such as dictionaries, spell checks, word walls, and personal word lists, in proofreading	• independently makes effective use of sources, such as dictionaries, spell checks, word walls, and personal word lists, in proofreading
Attitudes				
"Spelling Conscience"	• sees little connection between correct spelling and good writing	• views correct spelling as a requirement set by the teacher	• views correct spelling as a component of good writing	• views correct spelling as an important aspect of clear communication
Responsibility	• proofreads own writing only when required to do so	• proofreads own writing with some direction	• increasingly assumes responsibility for proofreading own writing	• assumes responsibility for proofreading own writing
Views of Spelling	• approaches words randomly without looking for patterns or consistency	• approaches some spelling tasks system-atically, but often just tries to memorize words	• demonstrates a growing comfort level with the spelling system; approaches spelling systematically	• views spelling as a system that can be controlled; is confident in ability to become a mature speller
Interest in Words	• shows little interest in words or how they work	• occasionally shows an interest in word-study activities	• often shows an interest in word-study activities that are gen-erated by the teacher	• displays a keen interest in words—their meaning, struc-ture, usage, spelling

(Adapted from McQuirter Scott and Siamon 2004, Figure 3.13, 46–47)

Self-Assessment—My Spelling Skills

Name: _____ Grade: _____ Date: _____

Spelling Checklist	Always	Sometimes	Never
1. I try to spell words the way they sound.			
2. I try to use spelling rules to spell words.			
3. I try to remember the shapes of words or where the tricky parts are by visualizing them.			
4. If I cannot spell a word, I think about the meaning.			
5. I break words into syllables to spell them.			
6. I listen for smaller words inside a bigger word.			
7. I spell a new word by thinking of other words that rhyme with it.			
8. I use a dictionary, word wall, or other type of word list to help me spell.			
9. I can tell if a word I have written doesn't look right.			
10. I proofread for spelling errors when I write a first draft.			
11. I proofread for spelling errors when I edit my writing.			
12. I misspell the same words over and over again.			
13. I think that correct spelling in a polished piece of writing is important.			
14. I find spelling easy.			

(Adapted from McQuirter Scott and Siamon 2004, Figure 3.7, 38)

Chapter 6

SUPPORTING STRUGGLING AND RELUCTANT READERS

Deidre McConnell

"The pedagogical clock for students who are behind in reading and literacy development continues to tick mercilessly, and the opportunities for these students to advance or catch up diminish over time."*

A major need for students reading below grade level in grade three and above is to help them accelerate their reading as quickly as possible. **

* Kameenui in Allington 1998, 12
** Allington and Walmsley 1995

Find Out More About Supporting Struggling and Reluctant Readers

Allen, Janet. *Yellow Brick Roads: Shared and Guided Paths to Independent Reading 4–12.* Portland, ME: Stenhouse Publishers, 2000.

Allington, Richard L. *What Really Matters for Struggling Readers: Designing Research-Based Programs.* New York: Addison-Wesley, 2001.

Balajthy, Ernest, and Sally Lipa-Wade. *Struggling Readers: Assessment and Instruction in Grades K–6.* New York: Guilford Press, 2003.

Blachowicz, Camille, and Donna Ogle. *Reading Comprehension: Strategies for Independent Learners.* New York: Guilford Press, 2001.

Falba, C. J., and R. E. Reynolds. "Strategies to Accelerate Reading Success (STARS) in the Middle Grades." In *Bridging the Literacy Achievement Gap Grades 4–12,* edited by D. S. Strickland and Donna D. Alvermann, 109–25. New York: Teachers College Press, 2004.

Harvey, Stephanie, and Anne Goudvis. *Strategies That Work: Teaching Comprehension to Enhance Understanding.* York, ME: Stenhouse Publishers, 2000.

Ivey, Gay, and Marianne Baker. "Phonics Instruction for Older Students? Just Say No." *Educational Leadership* 61 (2004): 35–40.

Klenk, Laura, and Michael Kibby. "Re-mediating Reading Difficulties: Appraising the Past, Reconciling the Present, Constructing the Future." In *Handbook of Reading Research: Volume III*, edited by M. L. Kamil, P. B. Mosenthal, P. D. Pearson, and R. Barr, 667–90. Mahwah, NJ: Lawrence Erlbaum Associates, 2000.

McCormack, Rachel L., and Jeanne Paratore, eds. *After Early Intervention, Then What? Teaching Struggling Readers in Grades 3 and Beyond.* Newark, DE: International Reading Association, 2003.

Sibberson, Franki, and Karen Szymusiak. *Still Learning to Read: Teaching Students in Grades 3–6.* Portland, ME: Stenhouse Publishers, 2003.

Tovani, Cris. *Do I Really Have to Teach Reading? Content Comprehension, Grades 6–12.* Portland, ME: Stenhouse Publishers, 2004.

Worthy, Jo, Karen Broaddus, and Gay Ivey. *Pathways to Independence: Reading, Writing, and Learning in Grades 3–8.* New York: Guilford Press, 2001.

Research on Intervention

Ideally, the majority of students arrive in Grades 3 to 6 as motivated and successful readers and writers. However, the reality is that about 30 percent of students will have fallen off-track in their acquisition and application of literacy skills (Spear-Swerling and Sternberg 1998)—they will be struggling readers and writers. Teachers need to be aware not only of struggling students, but also of students who experience difficulty for the first time, especially as literacy demands, particularly with informational texts, increase (Allington and Johnston 2002). Both groups of students require effective intervention in order to support and accelerate their ongoing literacy learning.

The priority of intervention for struggling and reluctant readers in Grades 3 to 6 is accelerated learning that is congruent and aligned with effective classroom instruction. Research also tells us that no single program is going to work for all students. A successful intervention will be designed and implemented based on excellent teaching practice and the needs of the individual student. It is important to know that retention of students who struggle with literacy in Grades 3 to 6 is not a viable option. Repeating a grade with no change of instruction or intervention tends to be more of a detriment to students (academically, socially, and emotionally) than "socially promoting" them. Neither option—social promotion without significant support or retention—is viable.

Why Students Need Literacy Intervention

Students need literacy intervention for many reasons. Some reasons are historical; for example, not being identified for early intervention, having a history of transience, or showing the effects of inadequate early instruction. Other students may require intervention for the first time as they begin to experience the effects of "the fourth-grade slump."

The fourth-grade slump is not isolated to Grade 4 and can occur at any time in Grades 3 to 6. It refers to a time when students may experience a drop in both their reading performance and their interest in reading. One possible cause of this slump is the significant shift that occurs in the upper elementary grades from narrative texts to non-fiction texts (Kuhn and Morrow 2003, 172–89). The increased challenges and demands of texts may also diminish motivation and interest in reading. In turn, levels of motivation and reading engagement have a significant impact on student achievement in the upper elementary grades.

Motivation

Student motivation for reading and learning is important to continued success in Grades 3 to 6. However, research shows that just when students need it most, motivation for learning and reading begins to decline (Pressley 2002). This decline in motivation is even more critical for struggling and reluctant readers who are also

"The consequences of not learning to read at a level commensurate with one's peers are substantial."
McCormack and Paratore 2003, 118

"We ... believe that for most students the intermediate years [Grades 3 to 6] provide the last opportunity to address the prevention of continued failure in reading and writing. These years are a critical bridge to middle school, where the tendency is to be less personalized and focused on individual needs."
Strickland, Ganske, and Monroe 2002, ix

"Reading instruction effectiveness lies not with a single program or method but, rather, with a teacher who thoughtfully and analytically integrates various programs, materials, and methods to best meet student needs."
Duffy and Hoffman 1999, 11

"There is reason for concern when children are so turned off by an activity as important as reading."
Pressley 2002, 292

beginning to feel the cumulative impact of years of struggle and failure with literacy tasks. In addition, these readers are often being presented with reading texts and assignments across the curriculum that they find too difficult and that leave them feeling unsuccessful and frustrated. Over time, students begin to feel that they are incapable of learning and they become disengaged masters of avoidance (Pressley 2002).

Lack of motivation to read creates the Matthew Effect (Stanovich 1986, 360–406). The Matthew Effect derives from the concept that the rich get richer and the poor get poorer. Students who enjoy reading read more and continue to develop and improve their reading skills. Students who struggle with reading and do not enjoy it read less and continue to fall behind their peers in reading and other literacy tasks. The severity of the Matthew Effect is heightened when a continuing pattern of failure develops and reading is avoided.

Reading less has a negative impact on vocabulary development, word recognition, decoding, fluency, and comprehension skills. As a result of deficits in these areas, struggling readers read less. Not surprisingly, reading more has the opposite effect. Strong readers, whose skills in these areas consistently improve the more they read, tend to read more. Without intervention, the gap widens. Struggling readers need support and encouragement to read. They need to be matched with books and placed in learning experiences where they can be successful and will want to read. A positive attitude toward reading motivates a student to keep going and face different types of reading challenges (Irvin 1998).

Reading Engagement

The number one indicator of success in reading is the amount of reading that students do both in and out of school. For struggling readers, it is important to provide them with opportunities to read as much as possible and to ensure that the texts are at the right level in order to close the huge gap between themselves and other students (Moats 2001, 36–40).

> *"[T]he grade-3 student who has not yet learned to read interprets his or her failures to date as strong evidence of a lack of ability to read, undermining attempts to make additional efforts to learn to read."*
>
> Pressley 2002, 298

We know from research that the amount of reading is important and students who read more gain more background knowledge and learn more vocabulary words than struggling readers (Klenk and Kibby 2000, 667–90).

> *"Practice makes perfect. In learning to read it is true that reading practice –just reading– is a powerful contributor to the development of accurate, fluent, high-comprehension reading."*
>
> Allington 2001, 24

This understanding highlights the importance of having classrooms filled with books that students can and want to read and having literacy programs that emphasize reading. Teachers need to know who the struggling and reluctant readers are in their classrooms in order to assist these students with selecting "just right" books. "Just right" books are not so challenging that students are solely occupied with decoding the words and not so easy that they are unlikely to learn anything new. "Just right" books motivate or hook readers because they offer interesting text that students can read and understand.

"Our role as teachers is to make sure that the right books are in students' hands at all times."

Sibberson and Szymusiak 2003, 12

Reluctant Readers

Most reluctant (aliterate) readers are capable of reading, but choose not to. However, some reluctant readers also struggle with reading. In either case it is important for teachers to

- establish a clear purpose for reading
- determine reader interests
- carefully match books to readers

When trying to "hook" reluctant readers, motivation and engagement are key factors for teachers to address.

Struggling and/or reluctant readers require support not only to become engaged, but also to remain engaged with text. Teachers need to carefully monitor struggling and/or reluctant readers during DEAR (Drop Everything and Read) or SSR (Sustained Silent Reading) times. Effective teachers ensure that students are selecting and reading appropriate books and not just pretending to read books they wish they could read but are not yet able to.

The Importance of Intervention

Early identification and intervention are critical to helping struggling readers become successful, independent learners able to close the achievement gap. Struggling readers are at a disadvantage because they do not learn at the same rate as their peers (McCormack and Paratore 2003). The longer these students go without intervention, the larger the gap becomes. Research shows that older struggling readers can make progress when they have the opportunity to learn under the right instructional conditions (Lyon 2002, 3–6). However, even when students make academic gains with intervention, there is still some question about whether their progress will be enough for them to catch up with their peers (Snow, Burns, and Griffin 1998).

Research on instruction and intervention in Grades 3 to 6 is receiving more attention. The research reveals that beyond high-quality, differentiated classroom instruction, struggling readers often benefit from literacy intervention designed to accelerate student learning (Falba and Reynolds 2004, 109–25). Successful intervention does not replace high-quality classroom instruction; rather, it complements it.

Effective Intervention

Struggling readers in Grades 3 to 6 need effective classroom instruction and intensive intervention designed to accelerate learning. Most reluctant and struggling readers do not require instruction that is substantially different from what their more successful peers receive; they just require a greater intensity (Snow, Burns, and Griffin 1998). Therefore, it is important to examine the instructional program in the classroom before designing an intervention program. Congruence between classroom instruction and intervention is critical for maximizing student learning.

Intervention that is provided by the classroom teacher helps build curriculum congruence. Connecting classroom instruction and intervention provides the consistency that students need to transfer and apply new strategies in different contexts. It also helps reduce the confusion and frustration of "catch-up" work that students may experience when being pulled out of class (Richeck and Glick 1998, 100–106).

Intervention, whether it occurs in small groups or one-on-one, is more effective when students have access to intensive daily sessions. Offering students ten weeks of daily intervention two or three times per year will have a more significant impact on student achievement than two sessions a week over an entire school year (Allington 2001).

Elements of Effective Intervention Programs

There is no quick fix for struggling readers at any grade. These students need a comprehensive, responsive, and flexible intervention plan delivered by a knowledgeable professional.

Effective intervention programs comprise six key components:

- expertness
- intensity
- explicit instruction
- responsiveness/scaffolded learning
- involvement in meaningful literacy activities
- congruence

Expertness

Accelerated student progress is only possible if students receive intervention from the most knowledgeable professionals. In most schools, this will be the classroom teacher; in some settings, it will be the classroom teacher in collaboration with a resource teacher or reading specialist. Expert instruction from trained professionals is important for struggling students because they require carefully scaffolded lessons that involve them in authentic reading and writing experiences.

"Research has consistently shown that even when academic progress of struggling readers is accelerated as a result of remedial programs, these gains are difficult to maintain unless there is congruence between intervention and regular class instruction."

Gaskins 1998, 537

"It is important that students have a coherent and congruent reading program, and communication between those responsible for providing reading instruction is of critical importance."

IRA Board of Directors 2000

"The role of an insightful teacher who understands the individual child's thinking and processing as a result of long-term observation and interaction—a function we call instructional assessment—is critical."

Balajthy and Lipa-Wade 2003, 164

Intensity

Student–teacher ratio, the teacher's professional expertise, the pacing of instruction, and the amount of time that can be devoted to reading and writing all have an impact on the intensity of instruction. For intervention to be successful, it must be provided either in very small groups or one-on-one and take place daily. Intervention sessions should maintain a fast pace that takes advantage of every instructional minute and maximizes student engagement.

Explicit Instruction

It is particularly important for struggling students to have new concepts and strategies explained in clear, concise language. With explicit instruction the teacher never assumes students know something. Teachers make the hidden obvious by showing (often through think-alouds) and by telling students what they are thinking when they read and write.

Responsiveness/Scaffolded Learning

Successful intervention, like successful instruction, is highly responsive to the needs of the student. The teacher gains insight into learning by actively observing students as they work through literacy tasks. The teacher is able to respond immediately to student behaviour with either praise or a prompt. Daily observations of student learning assist in setting the direction for future lessons. Struggling readers will make the accelerated progress necessary if they receive carefully scaffolded instruction that meets their needs.

Scaffolded learning is critical for successful intervention. It is a procedure for gradually reducing the level of teacher participation and increasing the student's responsibility (Roller 1996). New concepts, strategies, or skills are first introduced with explicit teacher modelling and demonstration; teacher participation is high and student participation low. Over time, as students gain experience and confidence with new learning, the teacher gradually releases responsibility to the students. The goal for students is to eventually be able to successfully apply and monitor new strategies independently. The goal for teachers is to successfully offer varying levels of support to scaffold student learning.

See Chapter 2: Reading Comprehension: Strategies That Work for more information on the Gradual Release of Responsibility model.

Involvement in Meaningful Literacy Activities

Worksheets and out-of-context skill and drill activities do not help struggling readers make the academic gains needed to close the reading gap. Students who have been identified for intervention need to read and write far more than their classmates if they are to catch up.

Congruence

Congruence between classroom instruction and intervention sessions is critical to student success, regardless of who provides the intervention—a paraprofessional, the classroom teacher, a resource

Struggling readers need to make accelerated progress, or they will fall further behind with every school year. Teacher response is critical to their future (Worthy, Broaddus, and Ivey 2001).

"The explicit teaching of reading is about making the hidden obvious; about exposing and explaining what is taken for granted; about demystifying mental processes; about bringing embedded ideas, values, and cultural norms to the surface; and about letting children in on the information and strategies that will enable them to become powerful literacy users."

WILKINSON 1999, 7

In scaffolded or mediated learning, the teacher carries out a variety of roles. "These roles include modeling, encouraging, reminding, hinting, questioning, challenging, correcting, directly teaching, reteaching, reviewing, and, when necessary, just letting the learner be."

KLENK AND KIBBY 2000, 681

"Educational methods that attempt to teach content or skills in isolation, without connections to past learning or to authentic literacy experiences of reading and writing, will fail to make real differences in students' lives."

BALAJTHY AND LIPA-WADE 2003, 198

It is important for effective Grades 3 to 6 teachers to believe that all students can learn and that students learn to read and write by reading and writing (Allington and Johnston 2002).

"Massive reading does increase fluency, and thus there is something to be said for having students read a great deal in order to increase comprehension."

PRESSLEY 2002, 277

Wednesday, October 10, 2005

8:35 – 9:00	Word Study
9:00 – 9:45	Modelled and Independent Writing
9:45 – 10:30	Nonfiction Literature Circles
	Guided Reading — Group 3
Recess	

Students need more structured modelling, demonstrating, and coaching and less assigning. This involves more work with small, flexible groups based on student need and interest (Allington and Cunningham 1996).

teacher, or a reading specialist. As stated earlier, intervention that is provided by the classroom teacher helps build curriculum congruence between classroom instruction and intervention. This connection provides the consistency that students need to transfer and apply new strategies in different contexts. It also helps reduce the confusion and frustration of "catch-up" work that students may experience when being pulled out of class (Richeck and Glick 1998, 100–106). When intervention is provided by someone other than the classroom teacher, it is important that it be planned collaboratively to develop and implement a quality, research-based intervention plan to meet student needs (IRA Board of Directors 2000).

Effective Literacy Programs

Effective classroom instruction is key to supporting learners across the school day and the best way to prevent reading failure (Snow, Burns, and Griffin 1998). Effective literacy programs are based on beliefs, time, teaching, engagement, materials, comprehensiveness, and home–school connections.

Beliefs

Teachers who believe that every student can read and progress may have a major impact on the attitudes and motivation of struggling readers. Teachers must also have confidence in themselves as knowledgeable and effective literacy teachers. Such teachers believe in and support the continued importance of teaching and extending students' literacy learning skills within language arts and across the curriculum.

Time

Research shows that the students of teachers who allocate more time to reading and language arts instruction show the greatest gains in literacy development (Allington and Cunningham 1996). Students in Grades 3 to 6 are still learning how to read and write, honing their literacy skills. Effective Grades 3 to 6 literacy programs incorporate large blocks of literacy learning time, which gives students the opportunity to read, reflect, and respond without interruption.

Teaching

Working with small, flexible groupings of students allows for instruction that meets diverse learner needs and interests within a classroom. Students in Grades 3 to 6 continue to benefit from a classroom environment where learning is scaffolded through direct instruction, teacher modelling, and demonstration, as well as through guided and independent practice that leads to independent application.

Engagement

The amount of time that students are engaged in learning is the most potent predictor of literacy learning (Allington and Cunningham 1996). It is essential for struggling readers in Grades 3 to 6 to take part in meaningful literacy activities that engage them and keep them on task. Because students' perception of task interest and task difficulty have a significant impact on their engagement, instruction and assignments must be interesting, motivating, and perceived as doable. Students become frustrated when the activities are too difficult and bored when they are too easy.

Materials

Schools and classroom teachers encourage wider reading when they develop collections that contain a rich assortment of appropriate reading materials and build time into every day for students to actually sit and read (Allington 2001). Class libraries filled with all kinds of books, at a variety of reading levels, and across genres, promote successful reading experiences (Beers 2003). Informational texts, including magazines, on topics related to student interest and subject content should also be part of these collections. Environmental print, such as posters, charts, and word walls, continues to be important. Effective teachers guide struggling readers in using environmental print and remind them to use it across the day.

> *"Successful reading experiences lead to more enjoyment of reading, and thus to more reading. All students should have access to materials they can read independently—materials that provide success and enjoyment."*
>
> WORTHY, BROADDUS, AND IVEY 2001, 32

Comprehensiveness

An effective literacy program incorporates a variety of activities provided consistently across the timetable. Students engage in reading and writing within the context of a comprehensive curriculum that meets individual literacy needs and allows them to practise strategies and enjoy authentic reading and writing. Shared and guided reading and writing are incorporated into daily lessons. Students are also provided with ample time for independent practice with reading and writing. Read-alouds from narrative and informational text remain an important part of daily instruction. Oral language continues to be important in these grades as well, and students need opportunities to build and extend their oral language skills. These activities need to occur not only within the language arts or literacy block but also across the content areas.

For an excellent discussion of the role of teacher language in shaping the learning environment and influencing students as learners, see Peter Johnston, *Choice Words: How Our Language Affects Children's Learning* (Portland, ME: Stenhouse Publishers, 2004).

"We strongly believe that well educated, thoughtful classroom teachers who engage in continued learning can and should provide appropriate best instruction for students who struggle in their classrooms."

WORTHY, BROADDUS, AND IVEY 2001, 253

"Teaching all children to read requires that every child receive excellent reading instruction, and that children who are struggling with reading receive additional instruction from professionals specifically prepared to teach them."

IRA BOARD OF DIRECTORS 2000

"What appears to be most effective is for the reading specialist's instruction to support, supplement, and extend excellent classroom teaching."

PIKULSKI IN IRA BOARD OF DIRECTORS 2000

Chapters 1 through 5 of this resource contain detailed information on strategies and activities related to the development of oral language, reading comprehension, writing, and multiple literacies across the curriculum, as well as relevant blackline masters for assessment.

Home–School Connections

Involving parents in their child's education is important at all grades. Parents want to support their children in learning new content and in improving developing literacy skills. Home–school communication and teamwork are particularly important in supporting struggling readers. (See Enhancing the Home–School Connection toward the end of this chapter for more information. Refer also to those sections under Linking Assessment to Instruction in Chapters 2 through 5 that relate specifically to promoting and maintaining links between home and school.)

BLM 11: Literacy Home Links: Supporting Your Reader at Home

BLM 4: Literacy Home Links: Home Reading in Chapter 2

BLM 5: Literacy Home Links: Choosing "Just Right" Books in Chapter 2

Who Best Supports Struggling Learners?

When classroom teachers provide the intervention, students are more likely to benefit from incidental teaching and reinforcement of previously taught skills throughout the day (O'Shaughnessy and Swanson 2000, 257–75). Also, teachers can effectively schedule intervention opportunities into their daily timetable.

In-school specialists (resource teachers and reading specialists) who have received professional training related to reading difficulties are a valuable resource for classroom teachers. Specialists are able to support the teacher in providing effective literacy programming across the day for all students. They also offer expertise related to the prevention and remediation of reading difficulties (IRA Board of Directors 2000). Working with a specialist may be necessary for a few students who require a higher level of intervention than is available in the classroom.

Paraprofessionals and volunteers, if trained and given a structure to follow, can provide additional support to struggling learners. However, maximum benefit for struggling readers will come from working with the most experienced and knowledgeable professionals. (See Training Buddies, Volunteers, and Paraprofessionals later in this chapter, as well as related sections under Linking Assessment to Instruction in Chapters 2 through 5.)

Scheduling

In many schools, intervention is provided during class time with the rest of the class present. When planning for daily intervention, the teacher carefully examines the daily timetable for scheduling possibilities. If a teacher has organized for learning using a comprehensive literacy approach (see Chapter 5: In the Classroom: Making It Work), then there will be many opportunities for intervention. The teacher may work with an intervention group during the language arts block, providing extra support to struggling readers through guided and shared reading sessions, or during independent reading. The neediest students in the class may require additional brief moments of intervention throughout the school day (for example, a daily five-minute reading conference during independent reading time).

Home reading is another way for struggling students to gain extra reading practice. By working closely with students and parents to monitor and support home reading, teachers ensure congruence with classroom instruction and intervention.

In the Classroom or Pullout?

What matters most for struggling readers is the quality of the intervention they receive, not the location. Teachers often wonder if there is a difference between the effectiveness of in-class and pullout intervention. Both models have proven to be effective (Bean 2004). In-class interventions reduce lost transition time and eliminate the stigma sometimes felt by students who leave the room for intervention. A specialist coming into the class to work with students provides opportunities for demonstration, discussion, and learning with the classroom teacher (Bean 2004). On the other hand, pullout removes students from the noise and activities of a classroom, which they may find distracting, and helps them to better focus on what they are learning.

Determining Which Students Are at Risk

Teachers begin by observing students at the start of the school year to identify those who are struggling with, or are unmotivated by, literacy tasks. These students may exhibit difficulty with engagement in reading, decoding, fluency, and basic comprehension of grade-level material (Lapp and Flood 2003, 10–24). Many struggling readers lack fluency, which is defined as reading smoothly, without hesitation, and with comprehension (Harris and Hodges 1995).

The teacher follows up initial observations with more detailed assessments to create a profile of student strengths and areas for growth. This information becomes the starting point for instruction. Students who are performing below their grade placement are flexibly grouped for intervention based on their needs.

Check It Out!

Irene C. Fountas and Gay Su Pinnell. *Guiding Readers and Writers: Grades 3–6* (Portsmouth, NH: Heinemann, 2000).

Jo Worthy, Karen Broaddus, and Gay Ivey. *Pathways to Independence: Reading, Writing and Learning in Grades 3–8* (New York: Guilford Press, 2001).

Richard L. Allington. *What Really Matters for Struggling Readers* (New York: Addison-Wesley, 2001).

Rachel L. McCormack and Jeanne R. Paratore, eds. *After Early Intervention, Then What? Teaching Struggling Readers in Grades 3 and Beyond* (Newark, DE: International Reading Association, 2003).

These resources provide ideas and information on scheduling for intervention.

"Good reading instruction is more important than who provides the instruction or where it takes place."
Mason and Schumm 2003, 6

"The improvement of reading fluency is considered a major goal, if not the major goal, of programs of intensive intervention in reading."
Klenk and Kibby 2000, 672

Assessment

Assessment is key to effective, targeted instruction for readers who are struggling, reluctant, or both. The assessment of reading fluency and comprehension in Grades 3 to 6 must be thorough and in-depth for intervention to effectively accelerate student learning and close the achievement gap. In addition, the progress of students involved in intervention must be closely monitored to ensure adjustments are made when and where necessary.

The purpose of assessment is to design and implement targeted lessons that will enable students to develop the skills and strategies needed to accelerate their learning. For assessment information to effectively guide instruction, it must be carefully and thoroughly analyzed. A score or mark may provide some clues about student strengths and weaknesses, but most of what an effective teacher knows about student literacy comes from observing a student during instruction, not from giving tests (Rhodes and Dudley-Marling 1996). The patterns of errors or student attempts at problem solving need to be analyzed in detail. A comprehensive analysis shows specifically what strengths students have and where the points of weakness or confusion are. Finding the trends or patterns in student reading behaviour helps teachers make inferences about student literacy, which, in turn, guides instruction and intervention.

Once the teacher has analyzed the information, an instructional plan is developed. When planning for instruction the teacher answers the question, "What does this student need to learn or experience next based on the results of assessments and observations?" (Rhodes and Shanklin 1993). With the instructional plan formulated, the teacher begins instruction with the confidence that student needs are being addressed.

Assessments for Developing a Student Profile

A comprehensive student profile consists of assessment information gathered before, during, and after instruction. As a start, students requiring intervention can be identified using diagnostic assessment activities that focus on the following:

- listening comprehension
- oral reading
  - reading fluency
  - decoding and strategy use
  - reading comprehension and strategy use
  - metacomprehension
- writing samples
- spelling (in daily writing across the curriculum)

After the teacher has reviewed the assessment information for areas of strength and improvement, a profile of the student as a reader may begin to emerge. The profile of a struggling reader may fit into one of the following categories: weak decoders who generally experience comprehension problems, strong decoders with comprehension problems, and reluctant readers who may or may not be struggling. Once the general profile is established, the teacher then plans to complete further assessments that will provide specific information about that student as a reader.

Listening Comprehension

Administering a listening comprehension assessment provides valuable information about a student's ability to understand text that is read aloud. A listening comprehension assessment also provides information about a student's potential for growth in reading comprehension. For example, if a student reads at an independent level that is significantly below grade level, but comprehends passages at or above grade level, this indicates that with the right instruction and intervention there is potential for improvement (Johns and Lenski 2001).

To administer a listening comprehension assessment, the teacher uses short graded passages. The teacher begins with a passage at the student's instructional level, reading the passage to the student and then asking the student to retell the story and answer questions. The teacher moves up the grades until the student reaches a frustration level. The highest passage before the student experiences this level determines the listening comprehension level or the potential reading comprehension level.

Oral Reading

Listening to students read provides teachers with a window into their reading processes. Oral reading is the only way to assess reading fluency. To assess it, the teacher may use an Informal Reading Inventory or a passage from a narrative or informational text that seems to be at the student's instructional level. As the student reads, the teacher takes a running record or a modified miscue analysis. (See Running

"Because assessment is intended to inform and guide instruction, it needs to be pursued in an ongoing manner, not only for evaluation at the beginning and end of the school year. The most informative kind of assessment occurs on a daily basis during everyday reading and writing in the classroom."

RHODES AND SHANKLIN 1993, 23

Records or Miscue Analyses under Assessment in Chapter 2: Reading Comprehension: Strategies That Work.) After reading, the student retells what was read and may be asked to respond to questions about the text. An oral reading assessment provides valuable information about a student's

- reading fluency
- decoding and strategy use
- reading comprehension and strategy use
- metacomprehension (self-monitoring for understanding)

Reading Fluency

The main goal of reading intervention is improved fluency (Klenk and Kibby 2000, 667–90). As students move through the grades, silent reading tends to displace oral reading. Reading fluency, although often overlooked, is still key. Some students, for example, do not "read the punctuation," resulting in limited comprehension.

When readers can read smoothly, without hesitation, and with expression, they have more mental capacity to apply to making meaning from the text than readers struggling to decode, pronounce, and recognize new words (Lyon 1998, 14–18). (See the Scale for Oral Reading Fluency under Assessment in Chapter 2: Reading Comprehension: Strategies That Work.)

Proficient oral reading does not always result in effective comprehension, though. Some students who read smoothly and expressively are only word calling and gain minimal understanding from the text. These students tend to think that reading is all about reading fast rather than making meaning. Others may realize when their comprehension breaks down, but don't know how to use fix-up strategies.

In Grades 3 to 6, many students make the transition from purposeful decoding to fluent reading. For some students, however, this transition will not be smooth, and they will need explicit instruction and scaffolded experiences targeted to improve fluency (Worthy, Broaddus, and Ivey 2001). It is important for teachers to consistently include reading fluency instruction in classroom literacy activities using both narrative and informational texts.

Fluency is affected by the rate, smoothness, expression, phrasing, and prosody in oral reading. Fluency directly contributes to increased comprehension. Although there are exceptions, disfluent readers usually have difficulty understanding what they read. A student who reads disfluently will require further assessment to identify the causes. The base of the problem could be limited phonological skills, limited sight vocabulary, difficulty of text, and/or lack of exposure to fluent models of reading.

See Chapter 2: Reading Comprehension: Strategies That Work for more information on fluency.

Decoding and Strategy Use

When listening to a student read, it is important for the teacher to observe and record how easily the student recognizes words and uses strategies to decode new words in text. Poor word recognition and decoding skills undermine fluency and comprehension.

Reading fluency "consists not only of rate, accuracy and automaticity, but also of phrasing, smoothness, and expressiveness."

WORTHY AND BROADDUS 2002, 334

"Although silent reading tends to be faster and can facilitate students' comprehension, struggling readers are likely to be hindered in their silent reading by a lack of fluency."

STRICKLAND, GANSKE, AND MONROE 2002, 120

The ability to decode has a significant impact on oral reading fluency and comprehension (Pressley 2002).

Improving decoding abilities will help to improve reading fluency. When students have a limited sight vocabulary and are unable to decode words quickly, their reading rate and automaticity in processing text suffer. As a result, reading sounds slow, choppy—disfluent.

Reading Levels

	Word Recognition	Comprehension
Independent	95–100%	90–100%
Instructional	90–94%	75–89%
Frustration	Less than 90%	Less than 75%

Reading Comprehension and Strategy Use

Comprehension assessments measure students' understanding of text read. Comprehension and use of comprehension strategies can be assessed through retellings, cloze procedures, discussion, responses to questions, and observations of the strategies used to make sense of the text as it is read aloud. For example, a student who self-corrects reveals an awareness of

- a breakdown in comprehension
- where in the text comprehension broke down
- the need to use fix-up strategies to make sense of the text

Independent, instructional, and frustration levels for comprehension can be determined by the percentage of questions answered correctly. (See the Reading Levels chart, above.)

For more information on retellings, cloze, and other methods for assessing comprehension, see Chapter 2: Reading Comprehension: Strategies That Work.

"It has become clear that work on isolated skills does not help disabled readers become more proficient. They need to focus their attention on comprehension and learn strategies for understanding text."

IRVIN 1998, 54

Teachers may find the following assessment blackline masters from Chapter 2 useful.

Assessment BLM 5: Fiction Retelling Scale

Assessment BLM 6: Nonfiction Retelling Scale

Assessment BLM 7: Reading Response or Summarizing Rubric

Assessment BLM 8: Think-Aloud Summary Sheet

Assessment BLM 10: Informal Reading Conference

Assessment BLM 12: Comprehension Indicators During Literature Discussions

Chapter 5: In the Classroom: Making It Work also features blackline masters for assessing comprehension.

Assessment BLM 4: Informal Reading Conference

Assessment BLM 5: Assessing Shared Reading

Assessment BLM 6: Retelling/Interpreting Checklist—Narrative Text

Assessment BLM 7: Retelling/Interpreting Checklist—
Informational Text

See also Assessment BLM 8: Comprehension Strategy Use Across
the Curriculum in Chapter 4.

Metacomprehension

Metacomprehension is an important component of reading comprehension. It means having an awareness of one's own understanding.
Readers demonstrate metacomprehension when they apply strategies
such as rereading, self-monitoring, and self-correcting as they read.
When listening to a student read, it is important for teachers to record
any evidence of self-monitoring for comprehension. For example, the
student might pause and self-question ("Does that make sense?") or
reread parts of the text and self-correct.

It is important for readers to be able to recognize when comprehension has broken down and to take appropriate steps to resolve the problem.

The Metacomprehension Strategy Index (MSI) is a useful, informal
questionnaire for determining which strategies students use before,
during, and after reading. (More information on MSI can be found
under Assessments for Fine-tuning a Student Profile later in this
chapter.)

Assessment BLM 1: Metacomprehension Strategy Index

Assessment BLM 2: Metacomprehension Strategy Index Scoring Sheet

Writing Samples

Reading and writing are interconnected processes. Usually a student
who struggles with reading will also struggle with writing. When creating a learner profile for intervention, the effective teacher completes a writing assessment. Analysis of a student writing sample
provides valuable information about organization, vocabulary for
writing, sentence fluency, and use of conventions and spelling. (See
also Chapter 3: Writing: The Reading–Writing Connection and
Chapter 4: Literacy Learning Across the Curriculum.)

Assessment BLM 1: Scoring Guide—Ideas and Organization in
Chapter 3

Assessment BLM 2: Scoring Guide—Voice and Word Choice in
Chapter 3

Assessment BLM 3: Scoring Guide—Sentence Fluency and
Conventions in Chapter 3

Spelling Assessments

Many students who struggle with decoding also struggle with spelling
(Beers 2003). Improving decoding skills generally improves spelling,
and improving spelling skills usually improves decoding. It is important for teachers to know that effective spelling instruction is based
on an understanding of how students learn to read and spell and
where students are working on this developmental continuum
(Worthy, Broaddus, and Ivey 2001).

For more information on spelling, see Chapter 3: Writing: The Reading–Writing Connection and Chapter 5: In the Classroom: Making It Work.

| Assessment BLM 14: Spelling Rubric in Chapter 5 |
| Assessment BLM 15: My Spelling Skills in Chapter 5 |

Assessments for Fine-tuning a Student Profile

Listening to a student read provides an initial baseline of information on what strengths and strategies the student uses when reading. A review of student performance and teacher observations will determine an individual's reading profile. Based on the student profile, further assessment may be completed to gain more detailed information on student strengths and needs. The three common profiles for students needing intervention are as follows:

- weak decoders who generally experience comprehension problems
- strong decoders with limited comprehension
- reluctant readers who may or may not be struggling

Weak Decoders Who Generally Experience Comprehension Problems

Students in this profile are characterized either by a limited sight vocabulary, which may be combined with a lack of decoding skills, or by limited decoding skills and a slow decoding speed. In order to develop an effective intervention, assessments that target decoding and automatic word recognition need to be administered. These include

- reading rate—the speed, smoothness, and phrasing of reading
- sight word assessments
- decoding assessments

Reading Rate

Reading rate measures speed, or the number of words per minute a student reads. Fluency is significantly limited when students read either too slowly or too quickly. Some students perceive that being a good reader is being a fast reader. These fast readers may be word calling and lack an awareness of when comprehension breaks down; as a result, their comprehension is limited.

Reading rate is affected by automaticity with high-frequency words and decoding skills, and can be calculated as follows:

1. Count the number of words in the passage, then multiply by 60 seconds.
2. Using a stopwatch, record the number of seconds it takes the student to read the passage.
3. Calculate the words per minute (WPM).

$$\text{Words per minute} = \frac{\text{Words in passage} \times 60 \text{ seconds}}{\text{Seconds taken by student}}$$

Typical Reading Rates for Grades 3 to 6

Grade	Oral	Silent
3	80–110 wpm	90–120 wpm
4	95–120 wpm	110–140 wpm
5	110–140 wpm	140–170 wpm
6	110–150 wpm	160–190 wpm

(Blachowicz and Ogle 2001, 69)

Sight Word Assessments

High-frequency, or sight, words are words that occur frequently in written English. Proficiency with these words helps students read more fluently (automaticity) and focus their energies on comprehending the text. Graded word lists, such as the Jerry John's or the San Diego Quick Word, may be used to determine a student's basic sight word vocabulary. Sight vocabulary assessments also provide insight into the graphophonic strategies a student uses to solve new words. (See Chapter 5: In the Classroom: Making It Work for more information.)

Assessment BLM 8: High-Frequency Word Assessment in Chapter 5

Decoding Assessments

The most effective way to assess decoding skills is to listen to students read connected text aloud. The teacher, while completing a running record, notes which cueing systems—graphophonic, syntactic, and semantic—are being used and whether the student is self-monitoring and self-correcting.

An additional assessment is the Names Test (Cunningham 2000). It can be used to measure students' decoding of words that they may have in their listening vocabularies, but are not likely to be part of their sight words. As students read and decode the names on the list, teachers observe and record which letter sounds, consonant blends, phonograms, affixes, and word parts students recognize and use to solve words. The results show students' decoding strengths and areas of need. This assessment is best used with students who demonstrate a significant weakness in decoding words due to an apparent lack of phonics knowledge.

Assessment BLM 3: Names Test for Decoding

Assessment BLM 4: Names Test for Decoding—Teacher Tracking Sheet

Strong Decoders with Limited Comprehension

Strong decoders with limited comprehension decode well and may read smoothly and with expression but lack comprehension of the texts read. Students who fall into this category often go unnoticed because their reading sounds fluent. It is important that teachers not only consistently listen to students read, but also follow up with a comprehension check. Students who may fit this profile include word callers, students who do not realize that reading needs to make sense, students with limited self-monitoring strategies, and English as a second language (**ESL**) students.

Metacomprehension Strategy Index (MSI)

One way to assess the reading strategies that students use or perceive that they use is the Metacomprehension Strategy Index (MSI). This assessment can also be helpful when creating reading groups. The MSI (Schmitt 1990) is an informal assessment that can be used with an individual, small groups, or an entire class, and is designed to find out what strategies students know and use before, during, and after reading. Information from this assessment provides a specific starting point for strategy instruction and grouping of students.

Assessment BLM 1: Metacomprehension Strategy Index
Assessment BLM 2: Metacomprehension Strategy Index Scoring Sheet

Reluctant Readers Who May or May Not Be Struggling

The main characteristic of reluctant readers is that they prefer not to read. They may or may not struggle with reading. The best way to determine which category reluctant readers fall into is through observation. Some reluctant readers will need intervention and some just need to be reconnected with the joy of reading. Consideration of students' reading engagement is an important step in getting them hooked on books, magazines, comics, and other texts.

The Importance of Reading Engagement

One of the most important factors to consider when working with struggling or reluctant readers is how to significantly increase their volume of reading (Allington 2001). Research shows that increasing reading volume, or the amount of time students are truly engaged in reading, will increase reading achievement. Struggling and reluctant readers need to engage in reading more actively. To encourage this, teachers create classroom environments that are filled with books that students can and want to read. Encouragement and monitoring need to be consistently provided to ensure that students make appropriate book choices at their independent levels and truly read.

Struggling and reluctant readers in Grades 3 to 6 need to read books that they can read, but also books that align with their ages and interests. Motivation, attitude, and student interests have a significant impact on reading engagement in these grades. The teacher may gather information on reading engagement and what affects it through

- interviews and interest inventories
- reading logs

Interviews and Interest Inventories

Conducting one-on-one interviews with students is an effective and personal way to find out about their interests, attitudes, perceptions, and reading habits. Interviews provide more information than an

"Aliterate students are those students who can read, but choose not to read. These reluctant readers range from students who will read if we find them that one good book to students who claim to have never read a book in their lives."

BEERS 2003, 11

"Providing books that span the content areas, match students' reading levels, and encompass a variety of formats and genres is nonnegotiable if we want struggling readers to improve."

IVEY AND BAKER 2004, 37

inventory or checklist, and serve as an opportunity for the teacher to gain insight into an individual student through discussion.

It is extremely important that the teacher discovers what struggling and reluctant readers want to read and gets those books into their hands. Interest inventories allow the teacher to find out what interests, genres, and authors appeal to students. The teacher revisits interest inventories throughout the year as student needs change.

Assessment BLM 1: Reading Attitude Survey in Chapter 2
Assessment BLM 2: Reading Interests Inventory (Student) in Chapter 2
Assessment BLM 3: Reading Interests Inventory (Class Tally) in Chapter 2
Assessment BLM 4: Reading Interview in Chapter 2
Assessment BLM 2: Attitude Survey in Chapter 5
Assessment BLM 3: Interest Inventory in Chapter 5

Reading Logs

Reading logs for at-school and at-home reading are a valuable tool for monitoring what and how much students read. They enable the teacher to determine whether the books the students are selecting are good matches. The logs also help the teacher assess how much reading students are doing and in which genres, such as poetry, comics, and informational text. The logs provide the teacher with a glimpse into the personal connections the students are making. It is recommended that home reading continue to be an expectation in Grades 3 to 6, especially for struggling readers.

For more information on at-home reading and reading logs, see Chapter 2: Reading Comprehension: Strategies That Work and Chapter 5: In the Classroom: Making It Work.

Linking Assessment to Instruction

"Without assessment and evaluation, instruction is a hit-or-miss affair" (Worthy, Broaddus, and Ivey 2001, 22). The information gathered from assessment is the information that teachers use to guide instruction. Once teachers identify what is working, they can determine more easily how to instruct and provide intervention (Beers 2003). Struggling learners will make accelerated progress when intervention is specific and targeted to areas of need. Effective intervention is also matched to each student's developmental reading level so students can master the necessary skills to move to the next stage. Assessment information also helps teachers determine whether to intervene in small groups or one-on-one.

"Not being able to read can mean a range of things, depending on the student's strengths and weaknesses."
BEERS 2003, 24

Designing Effective Intervention Programs

In effective intervention programs, struggling readers receive instruction that will support them in accelerating their literacy skills. This, in turn, will help them become successful and independent learners. Intervention programs are not a substitute for high-quality classroom instruction; rather, they complement and support effective classroom instruction.

"Sending a 'fixed' student back into 'broken' classrooms just means that the student will likely need fixing again."
ALLINGTON 2001, 121

Features of Effective Intervention in Grades 3 to 6

- occurs daily (minimum 30 minutes) in small groups or one-on-one for at least a 10-week period
- is provided within the regular classroom, with the classroom teacher, whenever possible
- is intensive and responsive, and involves modelling, demonstrating, explaining, and guided practice
- includes a strong assessment component that targets and groups students (one-on-one or small groups) to maximize instructional time
- features ongoing monitoring of progress
- consists of instruction that is meaningful and generally within the context of authentic reading and writing activities
- offers multiple opportunities to engage in reading and rereading of "just right" materials to develop fluency
- provides access to a variety of materials students can and want to read
- provides opportunities for writing and/or word study
- coordinates and connects with regular classroom instruction
- encourages daily home reading
- fosters ongoing communication with parents
- supports ongoing professional development for intervention teachers

Grouping to Accelerate Learning

Because intensity of instruction is a key factor in accelerating student learning, intervention groups should ideally comprise four or fewer students with similar needs. The degree of student need determines whether intervention is best provided one-on-one or in small groups.

One-on-One Intervention

One-on-one tutoring, with an experienced and knowledgeable teacher, is the most powerful form of instruction for struggling readers (Allington 2004, 22–25). Working one-on-one provides intensive instructional opportunities. It enables the teacher to modify the pace and content of lessons to directly target student needs. Research shows that teachers who have tutored one-on-one have a better understanding of literacy processes, are more aware of the needs of students in their classrooms, and incorporate materials and strategies from tutoring into small-group and whole-class instruction (Worthy, Broaddus, and Ivey 2001). However, one-on-one intervention is not always viable in today's classrooms.

Small-Group Intervention

Small-group intervention is the type of intervention most likely to be used with struggling readers. While some students require one-on-one intervention, many students make significant gains through small-group work (Falba and Reynolds 2004, 109–25). As stated earlier, the key to successful intervention groups is to keep them small (four or fewer students) and flexible, and to create groups of students with similar needs. This allows for lessons paced to maximize every learning opportunity.

> *"I will suggest that the more expert the tutor the greater the likelihood of progress in the greatest number of struggling readers. Thus, whenever possible, tutorial support should be offered by teachers, ideally, expert teachers."*
>
> ALLINGTON 2001, 76

Forming Intervention Groups

Teachers form intervention groups based on information obtained through assessment. Students requiring similar instruction or reading at the same grade levels will be grouped together. Students may require intervention to scaffold any or all of the following:

- fluent reading
- decoding/word work
- comprehension

Explicit instruction combined with a great deal of teacher modelling, demonstration, and think-alouds are necessary to scaffold learning opportunities.

Developing Fluent Readers

Teachers of Grades 3 to 6 need to recognize the importance of fluency for improving comprehension and for school and home reading assignments (Rasinski 2003). All students, especially those who are struggling readers, need classroom instruction and practice to improve their reading fluency. Fluency lessons, either for classroom instruction or intervention, need to include a variety of activities to motivate and engage students.

Effective teachers ensure students understand that fluency means more than reading fast. They talk with students about what fluency is and why it is important; they also explain and model what it looks and sounds like. Before focusing on specific components, teachers establish in older students an understanding that fluency helps develop ease, rate, and comprehension during silent, independent reading (Worthy and Broaddus 2002, 334–43). Students who feel that they control their own learning and who understand why they need to be fluent will likely engage in activities that will allow them to improve their fluency (Worthy, Broaddus, and Ivey 2001).

The top two ways to develop fluent readers are

- explicit instruction using modelling and think-alouds
- reading and repeated reading (often with feedback and guidance)

See Chapter 2: Reading Comprehension: Strategies That Work for much more detail on these topics.

Explicit Instruction Using Modelling and Think-Alouds

Explicit instruction through modelling and think-alouds effectively helps struggling students learn and apply the skills needed to read fluently. Features of text, punctuation, and phrasing can all be directly taught and demonstrated. For example, students may not understand punctuation such as commas, semi-colons, and dashes. With explicit instruction, the teacher explains the function of each mark, models how to read the text with the punctuation, and then has students read the text, applying what they have just learned. Students may know other punctuation (period, question mark, exclamation mark, and quotation marks), but may not know how to "read the

"If children fail to make the transition to fluent reading, they will encounter significant difficulties in constructing meaning from text. To develop fluency, students need teacher-directed lessons in which children spend the maximum amount of time engaged in reading connected text."

STAHL AND KUHN 2002, 582

"Existing scientific research on reading fluency indicates that it is an important factor in reading education and thus should be part of any comprehensive and effective reading curriculum."

RASINSKI 2004, 50

punctuation." Again, the teacher explains that when encountering a question mark in reading, the voice needs to rise up. The teacher demonstrates reading a question mark, prompts students to practise, and provides feedback.

Once the skill has been introduced and practised, it can then be prompted: "Remember what you need to do when you see that punctuation?" Or, it can be reinforced: "Excellent! You read that like the character would say it in real life." It is also important for the teacher to model and demonstrate fluent reading for students using both fiction and nonfiction texts. Students need to understand that reading rate can and will vary based on the text they are reading.

Repeated Reading

All students improve reading fluency through reading and rereading text, often with adult assistance and feedback. Rereading for fluency development works best with short sections of text that are familiar to students and are at an instructional or independent reading level. Rereading also helps to improve student word recognition, comprehension, phrasing, and transfer of fluency improvement to new material (Worthy, Broaddus, and Ivey 2001). Repeated reading may benefit students who find it difficult to decode, as well as students who decode accurately but slowly.

BLM 1: Repeated Reading with a Paraprofessional, Volunteer, or Buddy
BLM 2: Intervention Lesson Framework for Fluency: One-on-One

Oral or Silent Repeated Reading?

Repeated silent reading can be effective as long as students are reading books at their level and not pretend-reading books they wish they could read. Repeated oral reading to a partner, to an adult, or into a tape recorder ensures that students are truly reading. They will also benefit from feedback from more proficient readers.

The Importance of "Just Right" Text

For some students the first key to fluency is to be matched to appropriate reading materials at their independent or instructional level. In fact, many students would increase their reading fluency just by reading more books at their "just right" level (Worthy, Broaddus, and Ivey 2001). Struggling readers may require extra time, teacher assistance, and ongoing support to select "just right" books. In addition to reading level, it is important to consider student interest.

Effective teachers include nonfiction titles as part of student reading because for many students in Grades 3 to 6 reading informational text is a priority. Struggling readers will also benefit from being introduced to series and thematically related books (Worthy, Broaddus, and Ivey 2001). A familiar vocabulary, story structure, and writing style makes reading easier and improves fluency.

> "[Repeated reading] is a deceptively simple yet powerful technique based on the automaticity theory. This theory suggests that fluent readers are those who decode text automatically leaving attention free for comprehension. Repeated reading in all its simplicity works!"
>
> DOWHOWER 2002, 85

> "In our survey of over 1,700 sixth graders, independent reading was named as a favorite activity in reading/language arts class more times than any other activity."
>
> WORTHY, BROADDUS, AND IVEY 2001, 100

Popular Series for Engaging Readers

Fiction

Amber Brown, by Paula Danziger (Penguin Putnam Books for Young Readers)

Cam Jansen, by David Adler (Penguin Putnam Books for Young Readers

Captain Underpants, by Dav Pilkey (Blue Sky Press/Scholastic)

The Danger Guys, by Tony Abbott (HarperTrophy)

Hank Zipzer, by Henry Winkler (Penguin Putnam Books for Young Readers)

Horrible Harry, by Suzy Kline (Puffin Books)

Joey Pigza, by Jack Gantos (HarperTrophy)

Marvin Redpost, by Louis Sachar (Random House)

A Series of Unfortunate Events, by Lemony Snicket (HarperCollins)

Time Warp Trio, by Jon Scieszka (Penguin Putnam Books)

Nonfiction

Eyewitness, by various authors (DK Children)

I Spy ..., by Jean Marzollo (Scholastic)

Look Inside Cross-Sections, by various authors (DK Children)

The Magic School Bus, by Joanna Cole (Scholastic)

Check It Out!

Jo Worthy, Karen Broaddus, and Gay Ivey. *Pathways to Independence: Reading, Writing, and Learning in Grades 3–8* (New York: Guilford Press, 2001).

Dorothy Strickland, Kathy Ganske, and Joanne Monroe. *Supporting Struggling Readers and Writers: Strategies for Classroom Intervention 3–6* (Portland, ME: Stenhouse Publishers, 2002).

Kylene Beers. *When Kids Can't Read, What Teachers Can Do: A Guide for Teachers 6–12* (Portsmouth, NH: Heinemann, 2003).

Timothy Rasinski. *The Fluent Reader* (New York: Scholastic, 2003).

These resources offer more information on fluency instruction.

Small-Group Fluency Intervention Lessons

Effective fluency intervention lessons are 15 to 20 minutes long and structured into three parts, as follows:

- explicit instruction using teacher modelling and think-alouds
- guided practice and repeated reading
- independent practice

Intervention Framework 1: Assisted Reading

Short instructional level material works best for assisted reading lessons. Brief articles or short passages of informational text are easy to find and match to student interest. Picture books, poetry, and joke books may also be used.

Implementing an Assisted Reading Mini-Lesson

1. The teacher sets the purpose for the reading: observing and reading punctuation, expression, phrasing, and/or increased speed.
2. The teacher models the reading for students.
3. The teacher then debriefs the reading. For example, "When I saw these bold words I changed my voice to match." "How did my voice change when there was a question mark at the end of the sentence?"
4. Reading is assigned. When using articles or short informational pieces, the reading can be divided up with a section for each student to practise and read.

"Reading fluency contributes to comprehension and enjoyment, but is not commonly taught beyond the primary [early elementary] grades."
WORTHY AND BROADDUS 2002, 334

Explicit Instruction

Guided Practice

5. The teacher or students time the first reading.

6. Students then practise reading silently before their final reading to a partner.

7. The teacher or partner times the final reading, recording, comparing, and commenting on improvement (speed and accuracy of reading). (See the last section of BLM 2 for a sample repeated reading record.)

8. The teacher debriefs the lesson, commenting on improvements noted.

(Adapted from Stahl and Kuhn 2002, 582–87)

BLM 2: Intervention Lesson Framework for Fluency: One-on-One

Intervention Framework 2: Reading Performance

Reading performance is one instructional activity that combines several effective research-based practices and that students find motivating and engaging (Worthy and Broaddus 2002, 334–43). It includes poetry, jokes, stories, or Readers Theatre scripts at the student's instructional level that students rehearse and perform. Picture books can also be used; students can read them to, or make book tapes for, kindergarten to Grade 2 students. Reading performances can be easily incorporated into content-area studies. With whole-class reading performances, struggling readers often lack self-confidence to perform or are simply not given significant speaking parts. However, using reading performance as the basis of an intervention lesson, provides struggling readers with an opportunity to select, rehearse, and perform a text at their instructional level, which they can then share confidently with others.

See Chapter 5: In the Classroom: Making It Work for more information on Readers Theatre.

Check It Out!

The Web site www.aaronshep.com provides teachers with tips for using Readers Theatre in the classroom, as well as a wide variety of downloadable and ready-to-use scripts.

Implementing a Reading Performance

1. As a component of explicit instruction, the teacher provides an explanation of what a reading performance should sound like. The teacher reviews expression, tone, volume, and fluency.

2. The teacher then models fluent reading.

   For Readers Theatre, the teacher reads aloud part of a script, then talks about the voices, expression, and phrasing that should be used.

   For individual text selections, the teacher reads aloud a poem or picture book similar to what students will be working with and debriefs with students.

3. Students practise their text or part by reading and rereading silently. Then, they work with a partner or with a small group to rehearse parts or texts. Group members give one another feedback.

4. Students continue to rehearse independently. When ready, the group performs before a small group and receives feedback.

Teacher Explanation

Teacher Modelling

Guided Practice

Small-Group Performance

Assessment BLM 12: Readers Theatre Script Rubric in Chapter 5

Assessment BLM 13: Readers Theatre Performance in Chapter 5

Intervention Framework 3: Fluency Development Lesson

The Fluency Development Lesson (FDL), presented by Timothy Rasinski, is another beneficial lesson framework. Students read and reread short, manageable text selections, such as poems, monologues, dialogues, speeches, and other performance pieces. Fluency Development Lessons are usually 20 to 25 minutes long.

Implementing a Fluency Development Lesson

1. Students reread a familiar passage from the previous lesson to the teacher or a partner, who checks for accuracy and fluency.

2. The teacher introduces a new short text and reads it to the students two or three times while the students follow along.

3. The students and teacher discuss the nature and content of the passage.

4. The students and teacher read the passage chorally several times.

5. The teacher organizes students into pairs. Each student practises the passage three times while his or her partner listens and provides feedback.

6. Individuals and groups of students perform their reading for the class or other audience.

7. The students and the teacher select three or four words from the text to add to the word bank or word wall.

8. Students use the words for word study activities, such as word sorts, flashcards, word bingo, or other word games.

9. The students take home a copy of the passage to practise.

10. The next day students read their passages to the teacher or to a partner who checks for accuracy and fluency.

(Adapted from Rasinski 2003)

The Neurological Impress Method has been effectively used with older buddies, volunteers, paraprofessionals, and parents acting as coaches.

One-on-One Fluency Intervention

Paired reading is a collaborative activity between a student and an adult or peer. It is an excellent way to support and improve reading fluency. Reading aloud gives students the opportunity to hear what fluent reading sounds like and to participate in guided practice. It can also be supported at home.

Struggling readers benefit from the structure and support provided in paired reading. Teachers may adopt any of the following paired reading formats:

- Neurological Impress Method (NIM)
- modelled reading
- nudge or tap reading

Neurological Impress Method (NIM)

The theory behind the Neurological Impress Method (NIM) is that modelling correct patterns impresses them on a less fluent reader's mind and replaces incorrect word identification (Balajthy and Lipa-Wade 2003, 190). Each NIM session is 15 to 20 minutes long. A student and a coach, either an adult or a more proficient reader, read aloud together using a shared copy of the text.

Implementing a NIM Session

1. A piece of instructional level text is chosen that the student reads slowly and laboriously, but with at least 90 percent accuracy. The text can be narrative or expository based on student interest.

2. The coach and the student sit side by side. They preview and discuss the text before starting to read.

3. The coach and the student read the text aloud at the same time. The coach reads louder and slightly ahead of the student, modifying the pace of reading as needed.

4. The coach holds the text selection and tracks the words (moves a finger underneath the words) as the text is read.

5. Since continuous reading is important, the coach does not stop to help the student with words or to correct errors. If the student gets stuck or stops reading, the coach points to where they are on the page and continues reading.

6. If time permits, the text is reread.

(Adapted from Heckelman 1969, 277–82)

BLM 3: Working Together Using NIM

Modelled Reading

Modelled reading helps improve rate, accuracy, phrasing, and expression. It also assists students in reading and engaging in texts they could not manage on their own (Worthy, Broaddus, and Ivey 2001). With modelled reading the student listens and follows along as the teacher reads from text. The student may read along with the teacher (choral reading) or repeat the text after the teacher has finished (echo reading). Reading one paragraph or section at a time generally works best. Modelled reading is easily supported within the classroom while the other students are engaged in independent reading.

Nudge or Tap Reading

Nudge or tap reading is a motivating way to support and engage struggling readers both in school and at home. The coach and the student alternate reading out loud. The support from the coach allows the student to hear and become familiar with the language of the text. The coach models fluent reading and helps the student to progress through the text selection at a faster rate than possible in independent reading. Using this technique at the beginning of independent reading time helps a student get into the text. In an intervention session, the student and teacher read independent level text together for 15 to 20 minutes.

Implementing Nudge or Tap Reading

1. The student and teacher preview and discuss what the text is about.

2. The teacher reads first and the student follows along. Up to one page of text is read.

3. The teacher taps or nudges the student when it is time for the student to read.

4. The student reads and the teacher follows along. The student controls how much or how little he or she reads, but is not allowed to stop in the middle of a sentence or paragraph. The student taps or nudges the teacher to read again.

5. The teacher takes a turn reading, then taps or nudges the student to take over. The process is repeated.

6. After reading, the teacher and the student discuss what was read.

7. The student takes home the text selection for additional reading practice.

Nudge or tap reading is a great way to make reading at home more motivating and enjoyable for parents and their children.

These 13 words make up about 25 percent of all words used in school texts.

a	in	of	to
and	is	that	was
for	it	the	you
he			

(Johns and Lenski 2001, 155)

Check It Out!

When Kids Can't Read, What Teachers Can Do: A Guide for Teachers 6–12, by Kylene Beers (Portsmouth, NH: Heinemann, 2003), provides teachers with a list of the top one thousand high-frequency words.

Weak Decoders with Limited Comprehension

Weak decoders with limited comprehension struggle so much with figuring out the words on the page that they cannot attend fully to the message in the text (CIERA 1998). Their decoding difficulties limit their comprehension for both oral and silent reading. Students who fit this profile frequently need to be matched to books at their independent level. Reading texts with fewer unfamiliar words will help fluency and improve comprehension. These students will also benefit from intervention designed to teach them strategies for working out big words.

Small-Group Reading Intervention: Decoding and Word Work

The ability to decode words quickly and efficiently becomes more important as text difficulty increases and students encounter more multi- or polysyllabic words in texts. Careful assessment of students who struggle with oral reading fluency will determine what impact limited sight vocabulary (high-frequency words) and weak decoding skills have on their reading. Intervention lessons may need to focus on

- high-frequency sight words
- word families (phonograms)
- affixes

High-Frequency Sight Words

Supporting struggling readers to build their base of instantly recognizable sight words contributes to increased fluency and comprehension. Research shows that about 100 words account for 50 percent of the words that students will encounter in reading and writing (Johns and Lenski 2001). The challenge in learning these words is that they tend to be phonetically irregular and do not follow regular sound-to-letter patterns. This makes them difficult to remember and impossible to sound out (Worthy, Broaddus, and Ivey 2001). (For more information on high-frequency sight words, see Chapter 5: In the Classroom: Making It Work.)

Assessment BLM 8: High-Frequency Word Assessment in Chapter 5

Word Families (Phonograms)

Teaching common word families, or phonograms, will enable students to move from decoding letter by letter to quickly recognizing chunks or word parts. This will speed up the decoding process with smaller words and provide a strategy for solving polysyllabic words. As students become familiar with different rimes, they begin to look through words for familiar chunks or combinations of letters. This shift helps significantly speed up word recognition. Grades 3 to 6 students need not systematically learn all the phonograms; instead, the teacher focuses on those students do not know. Once students have mastered the 37 core phonograms (as identified by Wylie and Durrell and highlighted on BLM 4: 50 Common Rimes), the teacher encourages them to learn others as appropriate.

Words consist of onsets and rimes. **Onset** refers to the sounds before the vowel; **rime** refers to the sounds from the vowel to the end of the word (the part of the word that rhymes). It is the part usually referred to as the "word base" or "word family."

Word	Onset	Rime
fine	f	ine
block	bl	ock
sprinkle	spr	inkle

When students can orally segment words into onsets and rimes automatically, their word solving for reading and spelling becomes more efficient and effective.

BLM 4: 50 Common Rimes

Affixes

Instruction in prefixes, suffixes, and root words is important for two reasons. First, it provides students with one more strategy to use when working out a new word. Students learn to look through a word to identify the root word and then look for prefixes or suffixes. Second, knowing how prefixes and suffixes change the meaning of words helps students understand more vocabulary. For example, teaching students that the prefix "un" means *not* will help them understand words such as *unreasonable, undone,* and *unbalanced.*

Most Frequent Prefixes and Suffixes	
Prefixes	un-, re-, in-, im-, il-, ir-, dis-, en-, em-, non-, over-, mis-, sub-
Suffixes	-s, -es, -ed, -ing, -ly, -er, -or, -ion, -tion, -ation,-ition, -able, -ible, -al, -ial, -y, -ness

(Adapted from Stahl 2001)

Making Word Work Meaningful

Contextualized word study will help struggling readers develop greater proficiency in identifying, pronouncing, and comprehending unfamiliar words in their reading and spelling words in their writing (Ash 2002). Word work is effective when it is taught and reinforced within the context of authentic reading and writing. When introducing new skills, effective teachers ensure the skills match the students' developmental level so that new learning can be connected to what they already know (Strickland, Ganske, and Monroe 2002). When skills are taught in isolation, students do not internalize them and, therefore, do not transfer them into their work. Effective teachers complete word work in intervention sessions before the reading to complement and support the reading (Spear-Swerling and Sternberg 1998). That is, they first focus on a word or word family and then reinforce it as students encounter the word in text.

"Isolated-skills work should be the 'warm-up,' and the contextualized activities—such as reading in context, meaningful writing, and listening comprehension—should be the main events."

SPEAR-SWERLING AND STERNBERG 1998, 206

An interactive and connected approach, such as word study, enables students to manipulate key words from their reading and begin extending generalizations to unfamiliar words, thereby strengthening not only reading skills, but also writing and spelling skills (Bear, Invernizzi, Templeton, and Johnston 2003)

Some struggling readers need to think more about the structure of words (Ivey and Baker 2004, 35–40). The purpose of word study is not only to teach students to sound out words, but also to give them strategies for recognizing words quickly and automatically (Tyner 2004). To determine what a student already knows about word parts and sounds, the teacher administers a phonics assessment (see earlier in this chapter). Running records help to determine where comprehension breaks down as the student decodes new words. Intervention and support for students who struggle with decoding should always be embedded and connected with meaningful reading activities (Spear-Swerling and Sternberg 1998).

Chapter 5: In the Classroom: Making It Work includes other ideas for learning words.

Reading Big Words—Word Detectives

Struggling readers often lack not only skills, but also confidence when attempting to decode multisyllabic words. Word Detectives (Gaskins 2004) is a less-intimidating, collaborative process that encourages students to use their collective knowledge to figure out new words. Students apply what they know from familiar words to solve more complex, new words.

Implementing a Word Detectives Lesson

1. The teacher selects three or four words for the lesson from student reading, content-area text, or demonstrated student needs.
2. The teacher writes one word on chart paper or on an overhead transparency.
3. Students are asked to look at the word and identify parts of the word they recognize.
4. Students work together, with the teacher scaffolding, to correctly identify the word. The teacher may need to clarify the meaning of some words.

> Students might make the following connections for the word "destination."
> - "I see the word 'in' in the middle of the word."
> - "I know that *tion* says /shun/."
> - "The first part looks like *best* but it starts with the letter 'd' so it must say /dest/. If I know *best*, then I can figure out *dest*."
> - "Now I have it: *dest • in • a • tion!*"

5. The teacher provides feedback on the strategies students used to figure out the word.
6. The teacher repeats the sequence for the rest of the words chosen for the lesson.
7. Students may add the words from each lesson to their personal word banks for ongoing review and practice.

(Adapted from Gaskins 2004, 70–73)

Making Big Words

Making Big Words is a classroom activity that is also effective for small-group intervention. This hands-on, interactive activity supports students' discovery of sound–letter relationships and familiar patterns in words. The words selected for each 15- to 20-minute lesson are based on demonstrated student need. (See Chapter 5: In the Classroom: Making It Work for more information on Working with Words.)

Word Sorts

Word sorts help students increase their understanding of words and word patterns. Word sorts actively engage students both physically (manipulation of word cards) and mentally (discussing their ideas about categorizing the words). Word sorts can be closed or open. With a closed sort, students sort the words according to preset categories. With an open sort, students independently identify and label the categories, and then sort the words accordingly.

Word sorts are motivating and engaging for struggling students because the activity is developed around knowledge they already have, and the words used are words that they can read. Using words that students can read with minimal assistance helps them to concentrate on how words work rather than on what they say (Strickland, Ganske, and Monroe 2002). Word sorts can be easily designed to meet specific learner needs. Words for this activity might come from the students' personal word banks, Word Detective lessons, Fluency Development lessons, and Making Big Words activities.

Developing Phonological Awareness Through Word Study in Chapter 1: Oral Language: Speaking, Listening, and Learning features examples of closed and open word sorts. See also Using Prior Knowledge/Predicting under Linking Assessment to Instruction in Chapter 2: Reading Comprehension: Strategies That Work.

Check It Out!

Making Words: Multilevel, Hands-on Spelling and Phonics Activities

Making More Words: Multilevel, Hands-on Spelling and Phonics Activities

Making Big Words: Multilevel, Hands-on Spelling and Phonics Activities

Making More Big Words: Multilevel, Hands-on Spelling and Phonics Activities

Making Words: Lessons for Home and School

Patricia Cunningham developed all of the useful resources listed above (from Carthage, IL: Good Apple).

Word Hunts

Word hunts are a more explicit activity to help students learn and practise spelling patterns. The teacher determines the categories for the word hunt based on the students' identified needs. Students then look through familiar texts to locate and list words that have the identified pattern.

Small-Group Reading Intervention: Building Sight Vocabulary

Automaticity, or being able to recognize words quickly during reading, is important for both fluency and comprehension. Automaticity is developed through much time on task in reading and through forms of practice that emphasize accuracy, expression, and smoothness (Gerdes 2001 in Balajthy and Lipa-Wade 2003). Students with limited sight vocabulary need a higher number of exposures to a word, sometimes as many as 75 to 100, to move the word into long-term memory (Balajthy and Lipa-Wade 2003). Effective intervention lessons for developing sight vocabulary are 15 to 20 minutes long. Students build sight vocabulary through

- increased reading
- word banks
- Visual–Auditory–Kinesthetic (VAK) approach
- word bingo and other word games

Increased Reading

One of the best ways to help students improve their sight vocabularies is to increase the amount of time they spend reading "just right" books both in school and at home. Assisted reading, repeated reading, and reading performance, as in Readers Theatre, help students increase and improve their sight word banks.

Word Banks

A word bank is a collection of words that students know how to read. At the most basic level, it would focus on helping students develop automaticity with the 100+ most frequent sight words.

Once these are mastered, other sight words, specialized content-area vocabulary, and tricky words may be added. Students may develop personalized word banks by identifying words that challenge them from their own reading and writing. It is important that they frequently review mastered words in their word banks to ensure retention over time.

Creating a Word Bank

One way to create an individualized student word bank is to use three legal-sized envelopes, hole-punched in the upper left-hand corner, and held together with a ring. The envelopes are labelled New, Learning, and Mastered. Students move words from envelope to envelope as they are learned.

One approach for introducing new words follows.

"A student who reads at home for recreation will have a larger sight-word vocabulary than a student who does not read outside of the school setting."

Balajthy and Lipa-Wade 2003, 84

1. The teacher selects a word for instruction and writes it on chart paper or on an overhead transparency.

2. The teacher tells students the word and explains its meaning, if necessary.

3. Students identify any tricky parts of the word.

4. Students generate and share a simple sentence using the word.

5. Students write the word on a word card. They may use a different colour of ink to highlight tricky parts.

6. On the back of the word card students write a simple sentence using the word, and then underline the word in the sentence.

7. The steps are repeated as necessary.

Words added to the bank are filed in the envelope labelled "New." Students frequently review the words and move them to the next envelope when appropriate. If a student incorrectly reads a word in the Learning or Mastered envelope, it is moved back to the previous envelope. When the Mastered envelope is full, the easiest words are removed.

Visual–Auditory–Kinesthetic (VAK) Approach

The Visual–Auditory–Kinesthetic approach is a multisensory technique for learning words. VAK lessons are typically 20 to 25 minutes long.

Implementing the VAK Approach

1. For each VAK lesson, the teacher selects four to five words for instruction.

2. The teacher introduces one word in context by saying it in a sentence and discussing its meaning.

3. On chart paper, the teacher shows the word written in a sentence, with the target word written in a different colour.

4. Students are shown the word in isolation and pronounce it.

5. The teacher asks the students questions about the word. "What are the easy parts?" "What are the tricky parts?" "How will you remember the word?"

6. Students close their eyes and visualize the word.

7. Students practise writing the word on paper. The teacher prompts them to say the word parts (sounds) as they write it.

8. Students write the word on a word card. They may use different colours to highlight the tricky parts.

9. Students may use their word cards to create personal word banks.

10. The teacher repeats the process with the rest of the words selected for the lesson.

(Adapted from Balajthy and Lipa-Wade 2003, 176)

Word Bingo and Other Word Games

Word bingo, played in pairs or small groups, is a fun and motivating way for students to increase their sight vocabularies. It is important that the words presented on the game cards are carefully matched to

A three-ring pencil case, with word cards made to fit it, can also be used for student word banks. Each time words are reviewed, a checkmark for a correct response or a question mark for an incorrect response is recorded on the word card.

"Instruction to facilitate word knowledge begins with high interest, easy reading and pulls high-utility words directly from the pages of students' current texts."

Ivey and Baker 2004, 38

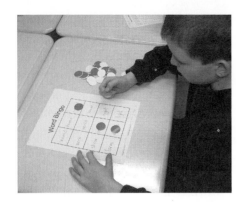

student needs. Bingo cards can be created to develop students' recognition of high-frequency words, word families, content vocabulary, and words in the students' personal word banks. Word bingo cards might also be placed in literacy centres for others to use during guided reading or for practice during free time in class.

See Chapter 5: In the Classroom: Making It Work for more information on word games.

Comprehension and Intervention

For all students, comprehension instruction is important if they are to become confident and competent readers able to independently comprehend an increasing range of text. Comprehension, or making meaning of what is read, is what reading is all about. In fact, in the upper elementary grades, improving comprehension is arguably "the most important challenge" that teachers and students face (Strickland, Ganske, and Monroe 2002, 141). By the time students reach Grades 3 to 6, many of them have developed adequate word recognition skills and are in need of comprehension instruction (Spear-Swerling and Sternberg 1998).

Strong Decoders with Limited Comprehension

Strong decoders with limited comprehension are known as word callers. Word callers decode words quickly and accurately and may read fluently and with expression; however, they often make little meaning of text and have difficulty remembering what they have read (Valencia and Riddle Buly 2004, 520–31). **ESL** or ELL students often fit this type of reading profile. It is difficult to identify these students just by listening to them read. Retelling, questioning, and discussion are needed to quickly and informally assess a student's comprehension.

For these students, it is important to emphasize that reading is an interactive, meaning-making activity. Students need to learn to monitor their understanding and to select and apply appropriate fix-up strategies as needed. Word callers benefit from explicit strategy instruction along with many supported opportunities to apply the strategies through authentic reading and writing tasks, repeated readings, and conversations.

Teaching Comprehension Strategies Effectively

Comprehension demands change as students move through the grades. Students are expected to read narrative texts with deeper understanding. They also have to read and understand a variety of content-area materials. Generally, struggling readers are not very strategic readers and tend to understand material at a literal level (Pressley 2002).

For comprehension strategies to be successfully taught, instruction needs to be explicit and scaffolded so students learn to use the strategies automatically and seamlessly (Pressley 2002).

The Gradual Release of Responsibility Model (Pearson and Gallagher 1983) is an effective way to introduce a new comprehension strategy. Teachers

- describe the strategy and when to use it
- model the strategy, often using a think-aloud
- enable collaborative use of the strategy
- provide opportunities for guided practice with specific feedback
- encourage individual practice with the strategy

For more information on scaffolded learning and the gradual, guided release of responsibility, see Explicit Strategy Instruction in Chapter 2: Reading Comprehension: Strategies That Work.

BLM 5: Intervention Lesson Framework: Reading Comprehension

What Strategies to Teach

Metacognition, or thinking about one's own thinking, is an umbrella term given to the following eight strategies for improving text comprehension.

- monitoring comprehension
- using narrative and expository text structures
- visually representing text using graphic and semantic organizers
- retelling, summarizing, synthesizing, inferring
- generating questions
- answering questions
- using prior knowledge/predicting
- using mental imagery (visualizing)

Teaching of strategies should be explicit and scaffolded, with a variety of opportunities for students to practise and receive feedback. Effective teachers introduce the strategies one at a time, allowing students to practise using them with a variety of texts. Struggling readers will require ongoing monitoring and feedback about when and how to apply the strategies successfully.

See Chapter 2: Reading Comprehension: Strategies That Work for more detailed information on each of the eight metacognitive strategies for improving text comprehension.

Small-Group Reading Intervention: Comprehension

Small-group intervention is an efficient and effective way for teachers to model and support the introduction of the eight metacognitive strategies. Think-alouds enable teachers to provide direct and explicit modelling, which is then followed up with guided practice.

Two other techniques that can be used during small-group intervention sessions and that are highly effective for developing comprehension skills are Question–Answer Relationships (QAR) and Questioning the Author (QtA). Chapter 2: Reading Comprehension: Strategies That Work contains detailed information on QAR and QtA.

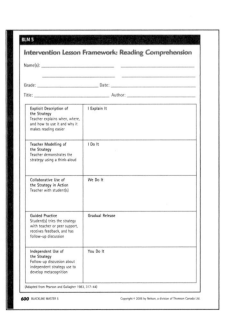

BLM 5: Intervention Lesson Framework: Reading Comprehension

Check It Out!

Reciprocal Teaching at Work: Strategies for Improving Reading Comprehension by Lori D. Oczkus (Newark, DE: International Reading Association, 2003) is an excellent resource.

The following phrases can be introduced to students as the language for predicting:

I think ...	I imagine ...
I'll bet ...	I suppose ...
I wonder if ...	I predict ...

(Oczkus 2003)

Reciprocal Teaching

Reciprocal teaching (Palincsar and Brown 1984, 117–75) is a social process that engages students in reading appropriate fiction and non-fiction texts by using strategies that effective comprehenders use. Research shows that this instructional framework significantly improves comprehension and accelerates student learning (Oczkus 2003). It works particularly well with students who are strong decoders with limited comprehension. The half-hour procedure involves predicting, questioning, clarifying, and summarizing.

Reciprocal teaching builds on the cooperative nature of learning (Oczkus 2003). As students work together through the four strategies, they develop a better understanding of the text and self-monitor their comprehension.

The four strategies of reciprocal teaching are best introduced through teacher modelling and think-alouds. Students need many opportunities to learn and apply each strategy with support before they can use it consistently on their own. Teacher support is gradually withdrawn as students gain confidence with the process and the strategies. The goal is for students to be able to apply all four comprehension strategies automatically and flexibly when reading. While reciprocal teaching works well with narrative text, it is also highly effective for use with informational texts. Much more information on reciprocal teaching can be found in Chapter 2: Reading Comprehension: Strategies That Work.

BLM 6: Intervention Lesson Framework: Reciprocal Teaching

Predicting

Predicting is an important comprehension strategy that struggling readers need to know and use independently. It involves previewing the text to activate background knowledge and making appropriate predictions about what might be learned from reading the text. When previewing and predicting become part of a student's prereading routine, decoding and fluency are improved. An effective preview of pictures, headings, subheadings, and graphics activates background knowledge and provides important information about content. Predicting alerts the teacher to limited student background knowledge, which can then be addressed prior to reading. Students must be taught to continue making predictions as they read the complete text.

Questioning

Teaching students to ask questions before, during, and after reading helps them set a purpose for reading, maintain focus while reading, and monitor for understanding or misunderstanding as they read (Oczkus 2003). In addition, developing question-generating skills significantly improves comprehension (Lubliner 2004, 430–38). Teacher modelling and think-alouds about generating and asking questions allow students to hear and understand different types of questions and support them in making the transition from literal to higher-order questions.

Clarifying

Clarifying involves identifying confusions about text, vocabulary, or unknown words. Struggling readers need to learn to clarify their understanding of text as they read. They benefit from learning to monitor their own reading and to recognize when their comprehension starts to break down. Initially, the goal is for students to identify and discuss confusions within the group. As lessons progress, the teacher encourages students to talk about strategies they used while reading to clear up confusion.

Teaching students to clarify develops and reinforces self-monitoring strategies that are critical for improving comprehension. Students need to know how to monitor reading for meaning, recognize when understanding breaks down, and apply appropriate fix-up strategies to get back on track. A simple way to engage students in monitoring for understanding is to introduce the following three prompts:

- Does it look right? (graphophonic)
- Does it sound right? (syntactic)
- Does it make sense? (semantic)

Once students realize that comprehension has broken down, they need to know which fix-up strategies may help get them back on track.

Encourage students to use sticky notes to mark places in the text where they decide to create great questions. This keeps them focused on their purpose, engaged in the text, and motivated to read.

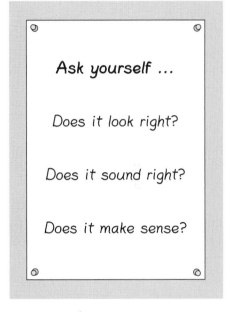

Ask yourself ...

Does it look right?

Does it sound right?

Does it make sense?

To effectively monitor and clarify comprehension, students must

- be aware of what they understand
- be aware of where and when their understanding breaks down
- use the appropriate fix-up strategies to restore comprehension

"A reader's repertoire of fix-up strategies needs to be flexible enough to solve comprehension problems with words, sentences and overall meaning."
Harvey and Goudvis 2000, 19

Strategies for Clarifying Text

- Look back—reread. ←
- Look forward—skip ahead. →
- Slow down (or occasionally speed up).
- Reread, paying close attention to punctuation.
- Reread out loud.
- Ask questions and look for answers.
- Explain to a friend what is understood so far.
- Use pictures, graphs, and charts.
- Discuss the confusing part with someone.
- Visualize—make a picture in your head.
- Ask for help.

Prompts to think about for summarizing

> The most important ideas in the text are ...
> This part was about ...
> This book was about ...
> First, ...
> Next, ...
> Then, ...
> Finally, ...
> The story takes place ...
> The main characters are ...

Students need to learn that the four strategies of reciprocal teaching—predicting, questioning, clarifying, and summarizing—can be applied in any order depending on the text and the purpose for reading (Oczkus 2003).

"True comprehension goes beyond literal understanding and involves the reader's interaction with text. If students are to become thoughtful, insightful readers, they must extend their thinking beyond a superficial understanding of the text."

HARVEY AND GOUDVIS 2000, 8

For more information on fix-up strategies, see Chapter 2: Reading Comprehension: Strategies That Work under Linking Assessment to Instruction.

Summarizing

The ability to summarize is an important comprehension and study skills strategy, but it is often very difficult to master. The goal of summarizing is to present the gist or essence of a text. It is a step beyond retelling and therefore more challenging. Retelling involves recalling and arranging the main ideas from a text to create a sequenced and detailed account. Summarizing requires students to select the most important points in the text, whether narrative or informational, and may involve making references to personal experiences or other texts (Oczkus 2003). Inferring, synthesizing, and analyzing are other aspects of summarizing that students need to practise. (Chapter 2: Reading Comprehension: Strategies That Work includes detailed information on summarizing.)

Implementing Reciprocal Teaching

Elements of reciprocal teaching include scaffolded learning, teacher and student think-alouds, metacognition, and cooperative learning to maximize student success. Shorter pieces of text are easier to work with when the strategy is being introduced.

1. The teacher prepares by selecting and reading the text that students will use.

2. The teacher thinks about how to help students predict what the selection or section will be about, or review or summarize what was read during the previous session.

3. Students then read the text selection silently.

4. The teacher asks two or three questions to promote discussion of the text selection. Some of these questions should be "thick" questions (high level) or "off the page" questions. (See Thick and Thin Questions and Question–Answer Relationships in Chapter 2: Reading Comprehension: Strategies That Work.)

5. Students are prompted to clarify any confusions (e.g., "Is there anything that doesn't make sense?"). Alternatively, the teacher uses a think-aloud to model a confusion and how it is clarified.

6. The teacher determines how to help students summarize the section of text read.

7. Steps 2 through 6 are repeated with the next section of the text.

The reciprocal teaching framework can be used during read-alouds, shared and guided reading, and literature circles. Students learn the strategies through teacher modelling and think-alouds so that they can eventually take turns in the role of teacher. Following the Gradual Release of Responsibility Model, only when students understand and use the four comprehension strategies with support should they be expected to apply them independently.

BLM 6: Intervention Lesson Framework: Reciprocal Teaching

Framework for Reading Intervention: Small Group or One-on-One

The framework of Marie Clay's Reading Recovery program has served as the basis for many successful interventions developed for use with students in Grades 3 to 6 (Falba and Reynolds 2004, 109–25). Intervention frameworks for students in these upper elementary grades have the same basic elements as a Reading Recovery lesson: rereading familiar text, word work, introducing and reading new material, and writing. Lessons provide direct, intense instruction designed to accelerate student learning over time. Assessments throughout the lessons guide instruction in subsequent lessons.

Ideally, the intervention period runs from 10 to 15 weeks, with sessions scheduled daily (or a minimum of four times per week) for at least 30 to 40 minutes. Each session focuses on developing essential literacy components: fluency, word work, strategic reading skills, comprehension, and written expression. To make the necessary gains to catch up with their peers, struggling students need intensive, expert instruction that meets them where they are at and systematically and responsively moves them along the literacy continuum.

An effective intervention session is structured as follows:

- rereading familiar text (5 to 10 minutes)
- word work (5 to 10 minutes)
- introducing new text (10 minutes)
- responding to text/writing (5 to 10 minutes)

BLM 7: Basic Framework for Small-Group or One-on-One Intervention

BLM 8: Blank Framework for Small-Group or One-on-One Intervention

> "A framework serves as a scaffold, a planning document, a way for teachers to apply their own personal, professional, and practical knowledge to the observed needs of their students."
>
> ASH 2002, 5

Part 1: Rereading Familiar Text

For the first 5 to 10 minutes of each session, the students revisit or reread the text from the previous lesson. Students may choose to read independently or with a partner. The rereading of familiar text helps them improve speed and accuracy, word recognition, fluency, and comprehension (Worthy and Broaddus 2002, 334–43).

During this time the teacher conferences and completes a running record for one or two students. As a student reads, the teacher observes and records the student's reading behaviours, noting progress and areas that need to be addressed either with that student or with the group. The teacher reviews the running record with students so they hear positive comments about their reading and receive quick and responsive feedback to individual areas of need.

> "Rereading familiar material is intended to build confidence and fluency, two important aspects of reading that troubled readers may rarely have experienced."
>
> LEE AND NEAL 1992, 278

Part 2: Word Work

The next 5 to 10 minutes of the session are spent on word work. The purpose of this part of the lesson is to help students increase their knowledge of high-frequency words, word patterns, and affixes, and develop new vocabulary. Direct and explicit instruction in these areas provide students with the skills and strategies needed to become more efficient word detectives. The focus of instruction for each lesson will come from identified student needs or from new vocabulary in the student reading for that day. During this part of the lesson, students may learn sight words and new phonograms, do word solving with multisyllabic words or word sorts, or review word bank words.

For more information on decoding, word work, and building sight vocabulary, see earlier in this chapter, as well as Chapter 5: In the Classroom: Making It Work.

Part 3: Guided Reading of New Text

Reading new texts supports students in developing strategies for reading. In this part of the lesson, students learn to use and develop strategies with teacher assistance, allowing them to focus on constructing meaning (Falba and Reynolds 2004, 109–25). A guided reading framework works well for this part of the lesson and enables the teacher to address before-, during-, and after-reading comprehension strategies. Short instructional level texts, either narrative or informational, are best suited for use in intervention lessons.

- Before reading, the students are guided through previewing, predicting, and generating questions about the text to be read. New vocabulary or concepts are discussed.

- The teacher then reads a section of the text aloud as the students follow along. Next, the students are given time to read the text silently. Students are expected to monitor reading for any areas of confusion or clarification that need to be discussed after reading.

- After reading, the students and teacher discuss the text, confirming their predictions, answering questions, and clarifying confusions.

Part 4: Responding to Text/Writing

Writing is part of every intervention session, serving to help students develop spelling skills, improve their use of writing conventions, and remind them of the connection between reading and writing. Students will also improve their comprehension if they are engaged in writing-to-learn activities, such as recording questions about, or developing summaries of, what they have read.

"Explicit instruction in the components of fluency should be combined with opportunities to practice oral reading fluency using manageable texts."

WORTHY, BROADDUS, AND IVEY 2001, 127

"When the teacher begins the reading of a text, with the students following along in their own texts, the students read the remainder of the story with greater fluency and fewer missed words."

ALLINGTON 2001, 79

"Writing can be a very powerful way to teach reading skills, especially for struggling readers who need to become more resourceful word solvers."

CALKINS 2001, 165

Intervention for Reluctant Readers

Students need access to text they are interested in reading. It is part of every teacher's job to ensure that the right books are in students' hands at all times (Sibberson and Szymusiak 2003). The key to intervention for reluctant readers, struggling readers, and fluent readers alike is hooking them on reading. Engaging reluctant readers depends on finding texts that they want to read and that is at their reading level.

Reading Preferences of Grade 6 Students

Scary books
Comic books and cartoon collections
Science fiction
Adventure stories
Fantasy
Popular magazines
Sports biographies and stories
Joke and riddle books
Information texts
Guinness Book of World Records and other almanacs
Current fiction or nonfiction series
Humorous picture books

(Worthy, Moorman, and Turner 1999, 13–27)

"What we find in schools, however, is that there is often a glaring mismatch between what students like to read and what schools provide, which is especially marked for reluctant readers."

WORTHY, BROADDUS, AND IVEY 2001, 53

Check It Out!

The following Web sites feature great book recommendations for reluctant readers:
Rip-Roaring Reads
www.srv.net/~gale/rrr.html

GUYS READ
www.guysread.com

"Technology has a motivational factor that will frequently interest students who would be reluctant to learn in other ways."

BLACHOWICZ AND OGLE 2001, 169

Supporting Struggling and Reluctant Readers with Technology

Instructional technology has the potential to support struggling readers in ways that traditional print-based materials can't (Kuhn and Morrow 2003, 172–89). Available programs provide a variety of technical modifications, with varying degrees of reading support in the areas of fluency, vocabulary, and comprehension.

- **Fluency:** Talking books on CD-ROM provide students with the opportunity to see the text while listening to the read-aloud. Some programs also highlight meaningful phrases so students can see how to read the text and then practise rereading on their own.

- **Vocabulary:** Many books on CD-ROM include a feature that provides immediate assistance with potentially unfamiliar or difficult words. In some programs, difficult words may already be highlighted; with others, clicking on the word will show its meaning.

- **Comprehension:** The Internet is a valuable tool for helping students access information and build background knowledge. The visual and audio elements that accompany the text on many Web sites make it easier to understand and more engaging than traditional text.

"Educational researchers and practitioners alike assert that the potential of new technologies for learning is likely to be found not in the technologies themselves but in the way in which they are used as tools for learning."

HOLUM AND GAHALA 2001, 1

"Providing training for paraprofessionals and volunteers seems essential, but even then their instructional roles must necessarily be limited."

Allington 2002, 277

Providing access to computers and other technologies in the classroom can motivate and engage struggling and reluctant readers. However, technology cannot replace the expertise and interaction of a teacher. Struggling students still need highly scaffolded instruction and ample opportunities across the day to read interesting, appropriately levelled texts. Effective teachers use technology as a complement to, rather than a substitute for, instruction and intervention.

Developing Home–School–Community Partnerships

Extensive research confirms that the preferred person to provide intervention to struggling learners is the classroom teacher. However, buddies, volunteers, and paraprofessionals can make effective contributions when they are given training and ongoing support (Fitzgerald 2001, 28–47).

Training Buddies, Volunteers, and Paraprofessionals

Effective training begins with an orientation outlining the time commitment required, the range of activities involved, and the level of student support to be provided. Interested individuals then take training sessions, including interpersonal, management and preparation skills (Rekrut 2000, 290–95). For maximum efficiency, this training is followed up through conversations, mentoring, or an ongoing training component. Having volunteers and paraprofessionals work with the same students over time also contributes to successful intervention (Invernizzi, Juel, and Rosemary 1998, 276–84).

Using Buddies Effectively

Working with a buddy is often a very successful and rewarding experience for struggling learners. It is particularly effective when struggling or reluctant readers function as peer tutors for younger students. Research shows that the benefits from cross-age tutoring include reinforcement of reading strategies and metacognition, increased motivation and engagement in reading, and improved reading ability and self-esteem (Rekrut 2000, 290–95).

A buddy system gives struggling readers the opportunity to

- read picture books aloud
- record books on tape
- tutor through paired reading

Reading Picture Books Aloud

The actual book-sharing time provides an opportunity for the older student to have a positive and rewarding reading experience and to feel like an expert reader. Sharing narrative and informational picture books with younger students legitimizes the reading of "baby books." Students preparing to read like professionals will have to read and reread a book several times in order to achieve fluency and intonation. They will also gain experience with previewing, questioning, and responding to the book, all strategies that support comprehension.

Recording Books on Tape

Recording audio- or videotapes of books is another way to engage older students in reading picture books (Worthy, Broaddus, and Ivey 2001). The students select a picture book appropriate for younger students and practise reading it until they have a polished performance on tape or video. The finished products can be given to the kindergarten or early elementary classrooms, or added to the audio-visual section of the school library.

Tutoring Through Paired Reading

With this approach, the struggling reader can either act as the tutor or receive tutoring. Paired reading helps students develop fluency, accuracy, and self-monitoring in their reading. Instructional level narrative or informational text is used. Parents, volunteers, and para-professionals may serve as tutors.

Each paired reading session has four components.

- **Preview:** The tutor and student preview and then discuss the cover, title, and illustrations of the reading selection, as applicable, to activate background knowledge. The focus is on the question, "What do you think this text is about?"

- **Pause:** The tutor and student begin reading the text orally together. When the student feels ready to read independently, he or she taps the table or desk and the tutor stops reading. If the student experiences difficulty, the tutor waits three to five seconds to allow the student to apply appropriate fix-up strategies.

- **Prompt:** If the student has not solved the problem within the three- to five-second time frame, the tutor provides a strategic prompt to guide thinking. If the student successfully solves the problem, the tutor offers specific praise about the strategy used and the reading resumes.

- **Praise:** Positive feedback is provided for the appropriate use of strategies throughout the reading process. After the reading, the student and tutor share their favourite parts of the text read.

BLM 9: Paired Reading: Preview, Pause, Prompt, Praise—Fluency Mini-Lesson

---

BLM 10: Paired Reading: Pause, Prompt, Provide Praise (PPPP)—Flow Chart

---

Check It Out!

Cathy Roller. *So What's a Tutor to Do?* (Newark, DE: International Reading Association, 1998).

Using Volunteers and Paraprofessionals Effectively

Many schools now recognize that their volunteers and paraprofessionals can provide assistance and support beyond preparing materials and performing miscellaneous classroom tasks. Frequently they attend and participate in teacher professional development activities. Some schools even provide specially designed professional development opportunities. In addition to their more traditional contributions, trained volunteers and paraprofessionals can support classroom intervention by

- monitoring the class
- reading with students to develop fluency
- serving as mentors or reading role models
- leading small-group intervention or post-intervention groups

Monitoring the Class

When scheduling intervention time, a teacher faces the challenge of what to do with the rest of the class. One solution is to have an adult who has been appropriately trained monitor the class. Once class routines and expectations are clearly established, the paraprofessional or volunteer can help students select new books; supervise independent reading, literature circles, and literacy centre activities; read aloud to the class; or facilitate other instructional activities.

Reading with Students to Develop Fluency

Paraprofessionals and volunteers who have been trained in paired reading, the Neurological Impress Method, and repeated reading have the confidence and skills needed to provide meaningful and effective intervention for struggling students.

Because paraprofessionals and volunteers are frequently asked to read with students, they require specific training in carefully matching books to readers, selecting books, prompting and praising students, and questioning and responding. Talking with students about the books and stories that have been read is important for checking their understanding and developing comprehension skills. Untrained volunteers and paraprofessionals will have limited strategies for working with students and supporting reading intervention (for example, they may rely heavily on the "sound it out" strategy).

"Make sure the support staff or volunteers who provide extra help to struggling readers and writers work closely with you, so that your most vulnerable students do not receive mixed messages."

Fountas and Pinnell 2001, 113

BLM 1: Repeated Reading with a Paraprofessional, Volunteer, or Buddy

---

BLM 3: Working Together Using NIM

Serving as Mentors or Reading Role Models

Motivation has a significant impact on struggling readers. One factor, particularly for boys, may be the lack of a positive reading role model (Peterson 2004, 33–38). Having male volunteers share their reading experiences and favourite authors, or serve as reading mentors, can be extremely motivating for some students (Cunningham and Allington 1994).

Gains in students' reading skills have been documented once parents are shown how to better respond and interact with their children during shared reading at home (Snow, Burns, and Griffin 1998).

Check It Out!

The International Reading Association has a fabulous parent section on its Web site at www.reading.org/resources/tools/parent.html.

Leading Small-Group Intervention or Post-Intervention Groups

Research tells us that, with training and ongoing support, paraprofessionals and volunteers can successfully provide both one-on-one and small-group interventions (Fitzgerald 2001, 28–47). Schools willing to invest time, money, and human resources will develop a cadre of highly trained individuals available to provide additional support for struggling learners. Research shows that such extended support helps students maintain gains over time (MacKenzie 2001, 222–34).

Enhancing the Home–School Connection

Parental involvement in their children's education is important at all grade levels, especially for struggling or reluctant readers. Research shows that students generally experience more success in school if parents are involved in their education (Cunningham and Allington 1994). Parents are powerful partners in the intervention process because they provide teachers with valuable information about students' interests, development, and educational histories. They are also key in supporting literacy learning at home.

Most parents want to help their children and know that they should, but don't know how (Cunningham and Allington 1994). Teachers need to provide some form of education to help parents learn how to better support struggling learners at home. They may provide tips through information letters, parent in-services, educational articles, and videos.

Effective teachers support parents by explaining and, when possible, demonstrating what home reading should look and sound like. Parents need to know and understand the importance of "just right" reading material so they are not expecting their child to read grade-level books that are too difficult. They also need to hear that it is perfectly acceptable for their children to read magazines, comics, picture books, and information texts that they find interesting. Talking with parents about the value of having students reread texts is important as well.

Teachers know that as students progress through Grades 3 to 6 there are increased demands for reading in the content areas. For some struggling and reluctant readers, the amount and difficulty of the reading is just too much. Parents reinforce learning in the content areas when they stay informed about what their child is studying and offer support at home. They may assist with reading textbook material, perhaps even reading it aloud, gather other trade books on the topic from the library, rent videos or watch TV programs, talk about the topic, and make connections to newspaper or magazine articles. The conversation and exposure at home will help build the child's background knowledge and confidence with the topic.

BLM 11: Literacy Home Links: Supporting Your Reader at Home

Closing Thoughts

There is hope that intervention will enable struggling and reluctant readers to accelerate their learning and narrow the achievement gap. Effective intervention plans for students take into consideration four key elements: ongoing assessment, which drives instruction, quality classroom instruction, high-quality intensive intervention, and congruence across the school day.

Assessment is critical to developing successful interventions for struggling and reluctant readers. This is because not all struggling or reluctant readers face the same challenges. Some students struggle with fluency, some with decoding, some with both fluency and decoding, others only with comprehension, and some in all areas of reading. Reluctant readers may be struggling, but may also be skilled readers who are not yet hooked on reading. Only through assessment do teachers learn what is and isn't working with a student; they can then propose a plan for providing instruction and intervention for that student.

Integral to successful intervention for a student is the quality and organization of classroom instruction. High-quality classroom instruction provides support to struggling and reluctant readers. Intervention is of little benefit if students are sent back to "broken" classrooms (Allington 2001). Teachers need to identify the struggling and reluctant readers in their classrooms so they can adapt and modify classroom expectations and assignments appropriately to meet the students where they are. They will thereby replace anxiety and frustration with enjoyment and success.

Congruence between what is happening in the classroom and what happens during intervention is also critical for success. Whenever possible, a trained teacher, preferably the classroom teacher, provides the intervention. The quality of the intervention, rather than quantity, is another important consideration. Interventions that engage students in meaningful reading, writing, and thinking activities will have a greater impact than interventions that take more of a worksheet approach.

To accelerate student learning, intervention sessions must be fast paced, intense, explicit, responsive, and targeted to meet the specific needs of the learner. If designed with these principles in mind, small-group intervention can be just as effective as one-on-one intervention in accelerating learning with many students.

Finding ways to support and extend learning from intervention sessions across the school day calls for creativity. Providing additional intervention opportunities for struggling students is one way to extend learning. For example, effective teachers make it a priority to briefly meet one-on-one with students during independent reading time. They use this conference time to ensure that struggling students are "matched" to a book, to listen to students read aloud, to have them practise rereading parts of text, and to talk about the reading.

If properly trained, parents, paraprofessionals, volunteers, and buddies may also support struggling and reluctant readers.

With time, intensive instruction, and motivational techniques, struggling readers in Grades 3 to 6 can overcome their difficulties, especially if teachers are well prepared, supported, and able to provide comprehensive intervention programs (Moats 2001).

"From our experience, we believe that middle-grade [Grades 3 to 6] struggling readers gain tremendous benefit from explicit instruction in fluency, comprehension, written expression, and word knowledge, especially if this instruction is accompanied by teacher modelling and scaffolding."

GASKINS, GENSEMER, AND SIX 2003, 154–55

The goal of intervention is to support struggling and reluctant readers in becoming lifelong independent learners. It is important to remember that teachers not only support students in improving and developing their cognitive skills, such as word recognition, fluency, decoding, and comprehension, but they also support the affective aspects of reading, such as motivation, enjoyment, and engagement (Beers 2003). Students are unlikely to experience long-term gains from intervention if they don't come to like reading.

Finally, and perhaps most importantly, successful intervention depends on having teachers who believe that literacy learning is crucial, that all students can learn when given the right instruction, and that they can make a positive difference in their students' lives.

Chapter 6

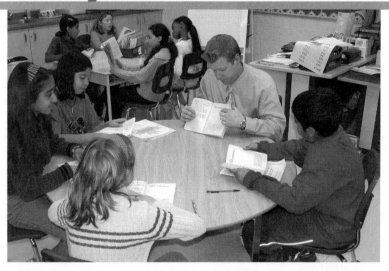

BLACKLINE MASTERS

Repeated Reading with a Paraprofessional, Volunteer, or Buddy

Name: _____ Grade: _____ Date: _____

Title: _____ Author: _____

The student...	First Reading		Second Reading	
	Yes	No	Yes	No
• previewed the text				
• read smoothly and with expression				
• "read" the punctuation				
• read with 95 percent or better accuracy				
• used fix-up strategies while reading, asking				
– does it look right?				
– does it sound right?				
– does it make sense?				
• understood what was read				
– by talking about it				
– by answering questions				
– by making connections				

Comments: _____

_____

_____

_____

_____

_____

Completed by: _____

Intervention Lesson Framework for Fluency: One-on-One

Name: _____ Grade: _____ Date: _____

Title: _____ (90–94 percent accuracy)

Author: _____ Completed by: _____
(teacher, paraprofessional, volunteer, buddy)

Procedure

1. Preview the text with the student, breaking it into chunks of 100 to 200 words each.

2. Consider reading the text aloud to serve as a model for the student.

3. Have the student silently read through the first chunk of text.

4. Direct the student to read the first chunk of text aloud while you time the reading.

5. Note miscues, misread punctuation, or other behaviours that affect fluency, and then provide feedback on the reading.

6. Record the reading time on the Chart for Repeated Reading (below).

7. Repeat this procedure two more times using the same chunk of text.

- -

Chart for Repeated Reading

Name: _____ Grade: _____ Date: _____

Title: _____ Author: _____

Time in Seconds	First Reading	Second Reading	Third Reading
120			
110			
100			
90			
80			
70			
60			
50			
40			
30			
20			
10			

Working Together Using NIM

Procedure for Volunteers or Paraprofessionals

1. Use a short text provided by the teacher, or select one that the student can read, but reads very slowly with at least 90 percent accuracy.

2. Sit beside the student and hold the text. Explain the process by saying, "We will read this text aloud together. If you don't know a word, just say what I say as I read with you. Keep your eyes on the words as my finger guides you across the page. Read aloud with me, not after me."

3. To begin, review what the text is about.

4. Point to the words as you read at a comfortable speed—slightly faster than what the student can read independently.

5. When you finish a line, move your finger from the end of that line to the beginning of the next.

6. If the student gets stuck or stops reading, motion him or her to join in by indicating where you are on the page. Don't stop. Just keep reading. Never stop to correct errors.

7. Discuss the text.

8. If time permits, reread the text with the student.

(Adapted from Heckelman 1969, 277–82)

50 Common Rimes

–ab	–ew
–ace	–ice
–ack	–ick
–ade	–ide
–ail	–ight
–ain	–ill
–ake	–im
–ale	–in
–all	–ine
–ame	–ing
–an	–ink
–ank	–ip
–ap	–it
–ash	–ob
–at	–ock
–ate	–oke
–ave	–old
–aw	–op
–ay	–ore
–eam	–ot
–eat	–ub
–ell	–uck
–ent	–ug
–est	–ump
–et	–unk

(Highlighted rimes referenced by Wylie and Durrell)

(Strickland, Ganske, and Monroe 2002, 96)

Intervention Lesson Framework: Reading Comprehension

Name(s): _____   _____

_____   _____

Grade: _____ Date: _____

Title: _____ Author: _____

Explicit Description of the Strategy Teacher explains when, where, and how to use it and why it makes reading easier	I Explain It
Teacher Modelling of the Strategy Teacher demonstrates the strategy using a think-aloud	I Do It
Collaborative Use of the Strategy in Action Teacher with student(s)	We Do It
Guided Practice Student(s) tries the strategy with teacher or peer support, receives feedback, and has follow-up discussion	Gradual Release
Independent Use of the Strategy Follow-up discussion about independent strategy use to develop metacognition	You Do It

(Adapted from Pearson and Gallagher 1983, 317–44)

Intervention Lesson Framework: Reciprocal Teaching

Name(s): _____   _____

_____   _____

Grade: _____   Date: _____

Title: _____   Author: _____

What We Know	
Our Predictions	
Our Questions Before During After	
Clarify Words Understanding	
Summary of What We Read	
Next Steps	

Basic Framework for Small-Group or One-on-One Intervention

Rereading 10 minutes	• Student(s) review reading from the day before in preparation for the discussion.
	• The teacher listens to one or two students read and takes a running record.
	• The teacher leads a discussion of the reading from the previous session, applying the four reciprocal teaching strategies—summarizing, clarifying, questioning, and predicting—in an order that complements the purpose for reading as well as the text selection.
Word Work 5 to 10 minutes	• The teacher selects a high-frequency word, word family, word part, or affix that the individual or group needs to learn and writes it on chart paper or an overhead transparency to facilitate instruction.
New Text/ Guided Reading 10 to 15 minutes	• Activate background knowledge.
	• Preview text.
	• Introduce key words or concepts.
	• Generate questions and predictions.
	• The teacher may begin the read-aloud to support fluency.
	• Student(s) reads the section of text independently, and then discusses the reading.
	• Student(s) takes the text for home reading, which becomes familiar text for the next lesson.
Writing/ Responding 10 minutes	• The teacher guides the student's(s') writing with a question or prompt in response to the reading.
	• The student(s) rehearses (thinks before writing), writes, and then checks response.
	• The teacher praises observed strategic behaviour and scaffolds any edits or revisions.
	• The sequence for responding is repeated for two or three more sentences (depending on time).

Blank Framework for Small-Group or One-on-One Intervention

Name(s): _____   _____

_____   _____

Grade: _____   Date: _____   Lesson#: _____

Text(s): _____

Familiar Text 10 minutes	Summary: _____ Possible Items to Clarify: _____, _____ Running Record with: _____ Read-Aloud: _____, _____
Word Work (select one) 5 minutes	Target Word: _____ Phonograms: 1. _____ 2. _____ 3. _____ Prefix/Suffix: _____ _____ Review:
New Text 10 minutes	Vocabulary: _____, _____, _____ Key Strategy:
Writing 10 minutes	Focus: _____ Reminders: _____ Work with: _____

Paired Reading: Preview, Pause, Prompt, Praise— Fluency Mini-Lesson

Date: _____

Dear _____

Thank you for doing a paired reading with _____.

The text you will use today is _____.

Please follow the mini-lesson framework below.

1. **Preview:** Discuss the title and cover of the text selection, if applicable. Ask the student, "What do you think this is about?"

2. Read the text together. Ask the student to tap the table or desk when he or she wants to carry on reading alone.

3. **Pause:** If the student gets stuck on a word or reads inaccurately, pause for at least three seconds and let the student try to solve the problem.

4. **Prompt:**

   • If the student remains stuck and does not self-correct, say to the student, "Let's read that again."

   • If the student is stuck and the miscue does not make sense, prompt with clues about how it should sound by asking the student, "Does that make sense?"

   • If the student is stuck and the miscue does not sound right, prompt with clues about how it should sound. Ask the student, "Does that sound right?"

   • If the student is stuck and the miscue makes sense and sounds right, prompt with clues about how it looks. Ask the student, "Does that look right?"

5. If the student is still stuck after two prompts, tell the student the word.

6. **Praise:** If the student tries to self-correct, figures out the word, or even realizes that something is not right, offer praise.

7. Continue to read together. Ask the student to tap when she or he wants to continue to read aloud independently.

8. After reading, discuss the text. You may choose to ask the student to share his or her favourite part and explain why it was the favourite. Share your favourite part, too!

Have fun!

(Adapted from Allington 2001, 76)

Paired Reading: Pause, Prompt, Provide Praise (PPPP)— Flow Chart

If the student gets stuck or miscues (reads inaccurately),
pause at least three seconds to give the student a chance to solve the problem.

↓

If the student remains stuck and does not self-correct,
prompt with, "Let's read that again."

↓

If the student is still stuck and the

miscue does not make sense	miscue does not sound right	miscue makes sense and sounds right
↓	↓	↓
prompt with, "Does that make sense?"	prompt with, "Does that sound right?"	prompt with, "Does that look right?"

↓

If the student does not read the word correctly after two prompts,
provide the word by saying, "The word is _____ ."

↓

Praise the student when he or she
• realizes the need to self-correct
• attempts to self-correct
• self-corrects after prompting
• self-corrects on his or her own

(Adapted from Allington 2001, 76)

Supporting Your Reader at Home

Dear Parents:

Did you know that reading with your child remains as important in Grades 3 to 6 as it was in the earlier grades? As with hockey, dancing, or playing a musical instrument, practice makes perfect. Following are some tips that you may find helpful to support your reader at home.

• Encourage your child to read at home daily for at least 30 minutes. When possible, be a role model and read as well.

• Books, magazines, comics, and nonfiction books are *all okay* to read! The important thing to remember is that whatever your child chooses to read must be at his or her **independent** reading level. *Independent material is text that can be read with 95 percent accuracy and comprehension.* The goal is for your child to enjoy reading, not be frustrated!

• Silent reading is okay. You do not always have to listen to your child read aloud, but you *do* have to listen to them read to check that the material is at the appropriate level.

• When listening to your child read, resist the urge to give away the word or to point out a mistake right away. Allow a wait time of three to five seconds before helping out. Children need time to monitor their reading and realize that they have made a mistake.

• When your child is stuck on a word, help him or her to work it out, *not* sound it out. The first prompt to use should be, "Try that again." Ask your child to have a good look at the word. Find out what parts of the word are known. Tell your child the unknown parts and then see if she or he can put the parts together to say the word.

• If your child does not realize when an error has been made, stop and ask for a rereading of the sentence or paragraph. If there is no attempt to self-correct, use these three questions to guide your child's thinking:
 – Does what you read sound right?
 – Does what you read look right?
 – Does what you read make sense?

 Using these three questions will help your child to become a more strategic reader.

• Read aloud with your child. Children of this age still love adults to read to them! Read picture books, novels, magazine articles, nonfiction texts—read anything. Children need to hear what fluent reading sounds like. Read-alouds also help them to experience and enjoy text that they may be unable to read independently. Listening to audiobooks is another great option.

• Talk with your child about reading. Share what books and authors you enjoyed reading as a child or enjoy now as an adult. Talk about times when reading was hard for you; children need to know that reading is not always easy. Just as in a book club, read and discuss a book together with your child.

Happy reading!

Chapter 6

ASSESSMENT BLACKLINE MASTERS

Self-Assessment—Metacomprehension Strategy Index

Name: _____ Grade: _____ Date: _____

I. In each set of four, circle the one statement that tells a good thing to do to help you understand a story better before you read it.

1. Before reading, it is a good idea to
   a) See how many pages are in the story.
   b) Look up all of the big words in a dictionary.
   c) Try to guess what will happen in the story.
   d) Think about what has happened so far in the story.

2. Before reading, it is a good idea to
   a) Look at the pictures to see what the story is about.
   b) Decide how long it will take me to read the story.
   c) Sound out the words I do not know.
   d) Check to see if the story is making sense.

3. Before reading, it is a good idea to
   a) Ask someone to read the story to me.
   b) Read the title to see what the story is about.
   c) Check to see if most of the words have long or short vowels in them.
   d) Check to see if the pictures are in order and if they make sense.

4. Before reading, it is a good idea to
   a) Check to see that no pages are missing.
   b) Make a list of the words I am unsure about.
   c) Use the title and pictures to help me predict what will happen in the story.
   d) Read the last sentence so I will know how the story ends.

5. Before reading, it is a good idea to
   a) Decide why I am going to read the story.
   b) Use the difficult words to help me guess what will happen in the story.
   c) Reread some parts to see if I can figure out what is happening if things are not making sense.
   d) Ask for help with the difficult words.

6. Before reading, it is a good idea to
   a) Retell all of the main points that have happened so far.
   b) Ask myself questions that I would like to have answered in the story.
   c) Think about the meanings of words that have more than one meaning.
   d) Look through the story to find all of the words with three or more syllables.

7. Before reading, it is a good idea to
   a) Check to see if I have read the story before.
   b) Use my questions and guesses as a reason for reading the story.
   c) Make sure I can pronounce all of the words before I begin.
   d) Come up with a better title for the story.

8. Before reading, it is a good idea to
   a) Think of what I already know about what I see in the pictures.
   b) Count how many pages are in the story.
   c) Choose the best part of the story to read again.
   d) Read the story aloud to someone.

9. Before reading, it is a good idea to
   a) Practise reading the story out loud.
   b) Retell the main points to make sure I can remember the story.
   c) Think of what the characters in the story might be like.
   d) Decide if I have enough time to read the story.

10. Before reading, it is a good idea to
    a) Check to see if I understand the story so far.
    b) Check to see if the words have more than one meaning.
    c) Think about where the story might be taking place.
    d) List all of the important details.

II. In each set of four, circle the one statement that tells a good thing to do to help you understand the story better while you are reading it.

11. While reading, it is a good idea to
    a) Read the story very slowly so I do not miss any important parts.
    b) Read the title to see what the story is about.
    c) Check to see if the pictures are missing anything.
    d) Check to see if the story is making sense by seeing if I can tell what has happened so far.

12. While reading, it is a good idea to
    a) Stop to retell the main points to see if I understand what has happened so far.
    b) Read the story quickly so I can find out what happened.
    c) Read only the beginning and end of the story to find out what it is about.
    d) Skip the parts that are too difficult for me.

13. While reading, it is a good idea to
    a) Look up all of the big words in the dictionary.
    b) Put the story away if it is not making sense and find another one.
    c) Remember the title and pictures to help me figure out what will happen next.
    d) Keep track of how many pages I have left to read.

14. While reading, it is a good idea to
    a) Keep track of how long it is taking me to read the story.
    b) See if I can answer any of the questions I asked before I began reading.
    c) Read the title to see what the story is going to be about.
    d) Add any missing details to the pictures.

15. While reading, it is a good idea to
    a) Have someone read the story to me.
    b) Count how many pages I have read.
    c) List the story's main characters.
    d) Figure out if my predictions are right or wrong.

16. While reading, it is a good idea to
    a) Check to see that the characters are real.
    b) Make a lot of guesses about what is going to happen next.
    c) Stop looking at the pictures because they might confuse me.
    d) Read the story to someone else.

17. While reading, it is a good idea to
    a) Try to answer the questions I asked myself.
    b) Try not to confuse what I already know with what I am reading about.
    c) Read the story silently.
    d) Check to see if I am saying new vocabulary words correctly.

18. While reading, it is a good idea to
    a) Try to see if my guesses are going to be right or wrong.
    b) Reread to be sure I haven't missed any of the words.
    c) Decide on why I am reading the story.
    d) List what happened first, second, third, and so on.

19. While reading, it is a good idea to
    a) See if I can recognize new vocabulary words.
    b) Be careful not to skip any parts of the story.
    c) Check to see how many of the words I already know.
    d) Think about what I already know about the ideas in the story to help me figure out what will happen.

20. While reading, it is a good idea to
    a) Reread some parts or read ahead to see if I can figure out what is happening if things are not making sense.
    b) Take my time reading so I can be sure I understand what is happening.
    c) Change the ending so it makes sense.
    d) Check to see if there are enough pictures to help me make the story ideas clear.

III. In each set of four, circle the one statement that tells a good thing to do to help you understand a story better after you have read it.

21. After reading, it is a good idea to
    a) Count how many pages I read without mistakes.
    b) Check to see if the story had enough pictures to make it interesting.
    c) Check to see if I met my purpose for reading the story.
    d) Underline the causes and effects.

22. After reading, it is a good idea to
    a) Underline the main idea.
    b) Retell the main points of the story to see if I understood it.
    c) Reread the story to make sure I said all of the words correctly.
    d) Practise reading the story aloud.

23. After reading, it is a good idea to
    a) Read the title and look over the story to see what it is about.
    b) Check to see if I skipped any of the vocabulary words.
    c) Think about what made me make good or bad predictions.
    d) Make a guess about what will happen next in the story.

24. After reading, it is a good idea to
    a) Look up all of the big words in the dictionary.
    b) Read the best parts aloud.
    c) Have someone read the story to me.
    d) Think about how the story reminded me of things I already knew before reading it.

25. After reading, it is a good idea to
    a) Think about how I would have acted if I were the main character in the story.
    b) Practise reading the story silently for practice of good reading.
    c) Look at the story title and pictures to see what will happen.
    d) List what I understood most in the story.

(Adapted from Schmitt 1990, 454–61)

Metacomprehension Strategy Index Scoring Sheet

Name: _____ Grade: _____ Date: _____

I. Before Reading	II. While Reading	III. After Reading	
1. C	11. D	21. C	
2. A	12. A	22. B	
3. B	13. C	23. C	
4. C	14. B	24. D	
5. A	15. D	25. A	
6. B	16. B		
7. B	17. A		
8. A	18. A		
9. C	19. D		
10. C	20. A		
Totals / 10	/ 10	/ 5	/ 25

Comments:

(Adapted from Schmitt 1990, 454–61)

Names Test for Decoding

Jay Conway	Chuck Hoke	Kimberly Blake
Homer Preston	Cindy Sampson	Ginger Yale
Stanley Shaw	Glen Spencer	Flo Thornton
Grace Brewster	Ron Smitherman	Vance Middleton
Bernard Pendergraph	Floyd Sheldon	Austin Shepherd
Neal Wade	Joan Brooks	Thelma Rinehart
Tim Cornell	Yolanda Clark	Roberta Slade
Gus Quincy	Chester Wright	Patrick Tweed
Wendy Swain	Fred Sherwood	Dee Skidmore
Ned Westmoreland	Troy Whitlock	Zane Anderson
Shane Fletcher	Dean Bateman	Bertha Dale
Jake Murphy	Gene Loomis	

Procedure

1. Type the names on a sheet of paper or print them on individual index cards.

2. Ask the student to pretend that he or she is a teacher on the first day of school and it is time to take attendance. Say that you will be unable to help with difficult names, and encourage the student to guess when necessary.

3. As the student reads the list of names, use a record sheet to keep track of the names pronounced correctly (see Assessment BLM 4). Also, keep track of student attempts by recording the phonetic spellings of any mispronounced names.

4. Count the number of names pronounced correctly, regardless of syllable emphasis (e.g., *Yo' lan da* or *Yo lan' da*). Next, analyze the names that were mispronounced for patterns indicative of decoding strengths and weaknesses.

(Adapted from Cunningham 2000, 137–38)

Names Test for Decoding—Teacher Tracking Sheet

Name: _____ Grade: _____ Date: _____

Teacher: _____ School: _____

Jay Conway	_____	Chuck Hoke	_____
Kimberly Blake	_____	Homer Preston	_____
Cindy Sampson	_____	Ginger Yale	_____
Stanley Shaw	_____	Glen Spencer	_____
Flo Thornton	_____	Grace Brewster	_____
Ron Smitherman	_____	Vance Middleton	_____
Bernard Pendergraph	_____	Floyd Sheldon	_____
Austin Shepherd	_____	Neal Wade	_____
Joan Brooks	_____	Thelma Rinehart	_____
Tim Cornell	_____	Yolanda Clark	_____
Roberta Slade	_____	Gus Quincy	_____
Chester Wright	_____	Patrick Tweed	_____
Wendy Swain	_____	Fred Sherwood	_____
Dee Skidmore	_____	Ned Westmoreland	_____
Troy Whitlock	_____	Zane Anderson	_____
Shane Fletcher	_____	Dean Bateman	_____
Bertha Dale	_____	Jake Murphy	_____
Gene Loomis	_____		

Observations:

(Adapted from Cunningham 2000, 137–38)

Final Thoughts

A Grade 6 student says it best!

I sit in my room all by myself,
Oblivious to you or anyone else.
No one can bother me during this time,
For as you can see, this time is mine.
I'm reading you see.
For while reading I can be honestly me.
There's no need to pretend to be someone
I'm not,
There's no need to have my stomach tied
in knots,
For I only need one thing to put me at
ease,
A book you see,
My refuge, my peace.

Gabriella Fialkow
Calgary, Alberta

"The major prevention strategy ... is excellent instruction."

Snow et al. 1998, 172

It's fitting to end where we began. Literacy learning in elementary school must be the priority of every teacher, parent, school, and school district.

To quote the motto of the International Reading Association, "Reading is a right that we must guarantee for all children, not a privilege to bestow on some." Yet this right is not the current reality. "Scientists now estimate that fully 95 percent of all children can be taught to read. Yet, in spite of all of our knowledge, statistics reveal an alarming prevalence of struggling and poor readers that is not limited to any one segment of society" (American Federation of Teachers 1999, 7). "When children perform poorly, it is attributed to their delayed development or disability, rather than to the paucity of experiences and opportunities to explore written language and literary understandings" (McGill-Franzen 1992, 57). It is important for teachers to revise their instruction, not their expectations for learning, when children are not progressing. Effective intervention is also crucial.

And too many students who appear to be keeping up with their peers in the early elementary grades lose ground in Grades 4 to 6. In addition, many students are *aliterate*: they *can* read but choose not to.

In a 1998 study (Baumann et al. 1998, 648), teachers identified their greatest challenges in improving the quality of classroom reading instruction:

- trying to provide for the wide range of reading levels
- lack of time
- not enough money for materials
- teaching struggling readers
- parent support and involvement
- class size
- accommodating diverse student needs

These are still major areas where teachers need support. They also need effective staff development, the heart of good teaching—teachers can't teach what they don't know. Pendulum swings have disenfranchised many children. P. David Pearson describes how it is important to "reclaim the centre" rather than taking an extreme perspective. "I'd rather be in the radical middle going somewhere, than in the far left or right in the ditch going nowhere" (1999). The reading wars must be over!

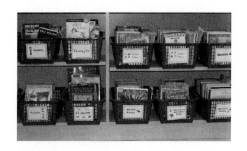

The most effective teachers base their teaching on sound research verified by carefully examined practice. The International Reading Association provides a research-based description of the six distinguishing qualities of excellent reading teachers.

1. They understand reading and writing development, and believe all children can learn to read and write.

2. They continually assess children's individual progress and relate reading instruction to children's previous experiences.

3. They know a variety of ways to teach reading, when to use each method, and how to combine the methods into an effective instructional program.

4. They offer a variety of materials and texts for children to read.

5. They use flexible grouping strategies to tailor instruction to individual students.

6. They are good reading "coaches" (that is, they provide help strategically).

(International Reading Association, *Excellent Reading Teachers* 2000)

"Both Ferguson (1991) and Snow et al. (1991) found that nothing was as powerful as the quality of the teacher in predicting the achievement of children. Neither parents nor socioeconomic status of the family was as powerful as good instruction in shaping the academic futures of students."

ALLINGTON 2006, 142

In addition, excellent reading teachers share the characteristics of good teachers in general. They have strong content and pedagogical knowledge, manage classrooms so that there is a high rate of encouragement, use motivational strategies that encourage independent learning, have high expectations for students' achievement, and help those who are having difficulty (International Reading Association, 2000).

Teaching Reading Is Rocket Science (American Federation of Teachers 1999)

"Children need time to read [and write] in school. We continue to organize the school day such that most children have little opportunity to actually read or write."

ALLINGTON 1994, 20

"We cannot simply stop teaching reading skills and strategies after fourth or fifth grade if we want students to continue to develop as readers. Without continued reading instruction into the high school years, we will continue to observe the 'middle school hump' in that too many successful elementary school readers exhibit little growth in reading proficiency during the middle school years."

ALLINGTON 2006, 175, CITING SNOW ET AL. 1991

"You never judge a [school] system by those who succeed in it. Those people will likely succeed in any system. You judge it by those it fails."

HAMILTON 1995, 94, CITING HAROLD ROSEN

Thoughtful literacy teaching and learning is the heart of strong classrooms. Studies indicate that teachers who promote thoughtful literacy have students who routinely produce superior achievement in varied forms of assessment, including standardized tests. In addition, their students read and write more and differently from students in more typical classrooms. They talk more and make more connections across texts and across conversations.

(Allington 2006)

Teachers need to *teach*. Most students do not learn to read magically. "Students need more structured modeling, demonstrating and coaching and less assigning" (Allington 1996). "All children need instruction, but some children need incredible amounts of close, personal instruction, usually clear and repeated demonstrations of how readers and writers go about reading and writing" (Allington 1994, 23, citing Duffy, Roehler, and Rackliffe 1986).

Students spend a great deal of time doing "activities." One must ask if these activities are as valuable as time spent in authentic reading and writing.

Enhancing the home–school connection is crucial. Most parents are willing to help their children learn to read and write. With the few who can't or won't, it is important not to blame the "victim" (the student) nor to lower expectations. These students, especially, depend on schools. Catherine Snow's research, summarized in the table that follows, provides dramatic evidence that classroom teachers can make it happen even for at-risk students.

Percentage of Children Who Are Successful with Varying Levels of Home and Classroom Support

	High Home Support	Low Home Support
Consistent High Classroom Support	100%	100%
Mixed Classroom Support	100%	25%
Consistent Low Classroom Support	60%	0%

Allington 1996, 66, citing Snow et al. *Unfulfilled Expectations*, 1990

Reading and writing open up the world of learning. Effective teachers take students from where they are in their literacy development and scaffold instruction. For all elementary school teachers who teach all content areas, there is nothing more exciting than seeing each student develop both the necessary literacy strategies and skills and the confidence and enthusiasm of a successful literacy learner.

"Read! A book can be as delicious as a hot-fudge sundae, as exciting as a roller-coaster ride, and as beautiful as a spring morning."

JUDITH VIORST IN DODSON AND DODSON 1997

"Being able to read enhances everyone's life. Not only will it open many doors for you, but it will also broaden your horizons. It's an adventure every time you open a book."

CAL RIPKEN, JR. (RETIRED ALL-STAR SHORTSTOP, BALTIMORE ORIOLES) IN *KIDS LITTLE INSTRUCTION BOOK*

BIBLIOGRAPHY

Adams, Marilyn Jager. *Beginning to Read: Thinking and Learning about Print.* Cambridge, MA: Center for the Study of Reading, 1990.

Adams, T.L. "Reading Mathematics: More Than Words Can Say." *The Reading Teacher* 56.8 (May 2003): 786–96.

Afflerbach, Peter. "Teachers' Choices in Classroom Assessment." *Reading Assessment: Principles and Practices for Elementary Teachers.* Shelby, J. Barrantine, ed. Newark. DE: International Reading Association, 1995, 68–72.

Alberta Education. *Senior High English Language Arts Teachers' Resource Manual.* Edmonton: Alberta Education, 1991.

Alberta Learning. *Program of Studies for Elementary English Language Arts.* Edmonton: Alberta Learning, 2000.

——. *Researching and Making Presentations: Grades 5–11, English Language Arts* (CD-ROM). Edmonton, AB: Alberta Learning, 2001.

Allan, Karen Kuelthau, and Margery Staman Miller. *Literacy and Learning in the Content Areas: Strategies for Middle and Secondary School Teachers.* New York: Houghton Mifflin, 2005.

Armstrong, Thomas. Alberta Teachers' Association. *Exploring Multiple Intelligences.* Edmonton, AB: The Alberta Teachers' Association, 2001.

Allen, Janet. *On the Same Page: Shared Reading Beyond the Primary Grades.* Portland, ME: Stenhouse Publishers, 2002.

——. *Words, Words, Words: Teaching Vocabulary in Grades 4–12.* Portland, ME: Stenhouse Publishers, 1999.

——. *Yellow Brick Roads: Shared and Guided Paths to Independent Reading 4–12.* Portland, ME: Stenhouse Publishers, 2000.

Allen, L. *First Steps: Oral Language Resource Book.* Toronto: Irwin Publishing, 1994.

Allington, Richard L. "Research on Reading/Learning Disability Interventions." *What Research Has to Say About Reading Instruction*, Alan E. Farstrup and S. Jay Samuels, eds. Newark, DE: International Reading Association, 2002, 261–90.

——. "The Schools We Have, the Schools We Need." *The Reading Teacher* 48.1 (1994): 14–29.

——. "Setting the Record Straight." *Educational Leadership* 61.8 (2004): 22–25.

——. *What Really Matters for Struggling Readers: Designing Research-Based Programs.* New York: Addison-Wesley Educational Publishers, 2001.

——. *What Really Matters for Struggling Readers: Designing Research-Based Programs.* 2nd ed. Boston: Allyn & Bacon, 2006.

Allington, Richard L., ed. *Teaching Struggling Readers.* Newark, DE: International Reading Association, 1998.

Allington, Richard L., and Patricia M. Cunningham. *Schools That Work: Where All Children Read and Write.* New York: HarperCollins College Publishers, 1996.

——. *Schools That Work: Where All Children Read and Write.* 2nd ed. Boston: Allyn & Bacon, 2002.

Allington, Richard L., and Peter H. Johnston. *Reading to Learn: Lessons from Exemplary Fourth-Grade Classrooms.* New York: Guilford Press, 2002.

——. "What Do We Know About Effective Fourth-Grade Teachers and Their Classrooms?" *Learning to Teach Reading: Setting the Research Agenda.* Cathy M. Roller, ed. Newark, DE: International Reading Association, 2001, 150–65.

Allington, R.L., and S.A. Walmsley, eds. *No Quick Fix.* New York: Teachers College Press, 1995.

Anders, Patricia L. "Toward an Understanding of the Development of Reading Comprehension Across the Grade Levels." *Comprehensive Reading Instruction Across the Grade Levels.* Cathy M. Roller, ed. Newark, DE: International Reading Association, 2002, 111–32.

Anderson, R.C., and P.D. Pearson. "A Schema-Theoretic View of Basic Processes in Reading." *Handbook of Reading Research.* P.D. Pearson, et al., eds. White Plains, NY: Longman, 1984, 255–91.

Anderson, R.C., P.T. Wilson, and L.G. Fielding. "Growth in Reading and How Children Spend Their Time Outside School." *Reading Research Quarterly* 23 (1988): 285–303.

Anderson, William, and Joy Lawrence. *Integrating Music into the Elementary Classroom.* Belmont, CA: Wadsworth Thomson Learning, 2001.

Armbruster, B.B., F. Lehr, and J. Osborn. *Put Reading First: The Research Building Blocks for Teaching Children to Read.* Jessup, MD: National Institute for Literacy, 2001.

Armstrong, Thomas. Alberta Teachers' Association. *Exploring Multiple Intelligences.* Edmonton, AB: The Alberta Teachers' Association, 2001.

Arrington, H. "Using Storytelling to Engage Middle Level Students with Content Area Literacy." IRA Conference, May 2004.

Ash, Gwynne Ellen. "Teaching Readers Who Struggle: A Pragmatic Middle School Framework." Reading Online. 2002. 29 June 2003. www.readingonline.org.

Association for Supervision and Curriculum Development. "Writing!" *Educational Leadership* 62.2 (2004).

Atwell, Nancie. *In the Middle: New Understandings about Writing.* 2nd ed. Toronto: Irwin Publishing, 1998.

Baker, S.K., D.C. Simmons, and E.J. Kameenui. *Vocabulary Acquisition: Synthesis of the Research.* Technical Report No 13. University of Oregon: National Center to Improve the Tools of Educators, 1995.

Balajthy, Ernest, and Sally Lipa-Wade. *Struggling Readers: Assessment and Instruction in Grades K–6.* New York: Guilford Press, 2003.

Ball, J., and C. Airs. *Taking Time to Act: A Guide to Cross-Curricular Drama.* Portsmouth, NH: Heinemann, 1995.

Barcher, Suzanne. *Readers Theatre for Beginning Readers.* Englewood, CO: Teacher Ideas Press, 1993.

Barton, Mary Lee. *Literacy: Practical Ways to Achieve Success—Teaching Reading in Mathematics.* Workshop presented in Mississauga, Ontario, January 30–February 1, 2002.

Bauer, Caroline Feller. *Presenting Readers Theatre: Plays and Poems to Read Aloud.* New York: H.W. Wilson Co., 1987.

Baumann, James F., James V. Hoffman, Jennifer Moon, and Ann M. Duffy-Hester. "Where Are Teachers' Voices in the Phonics/Whole Language Debate? Results from a Survey of U.S. Elementary Classroom Teachers." *The Reading Teacher* 51.8 (1998): 636–50.

Bean, Rita M. *The Reading Specialist: Leadership for the Classroom, School, and Community.* New York: Guilford Press, 2004.

Bear, D., M. Invernizzi, S. Templeton, and F. Johnston. *Words Their Way: Word Study for Phonics, Vocabulary, and Spelling Instruction.* 2nd ed. Englewood Cliffs, NJ: Prentice-Hall, 2000.

——. *Words Their Way: Word Study for Phonics, Vocabulary, and Spelling Instruction.* 3rd ed. Englewood Cliffs, NJ: Prentice Hall, 2004.

Beck, I., and C. Juel. "The Role of Decoding and Learning to Read." *American Educator* (Summer 1995).

Beck, I.L., M.G. McKeown, R.L. Hamilton, and L. Kucan. *Questioning the Author: An Approach for Enhancing Student Engagement with Text.* Newark, DE: International Reading Association, 1997.

Beck, I., M. McKeown, and L. Kucan. *Bringing Words to Life: Robust Vocabulary Instruction.* New York: Guilford Press, 2004.

——. "Taking Delight in Words." *American Educator* (Spring 2003): 36–47.

Beers, Kylene. *When Kids Can't Read, What Teachers Can Do.* Portsmouth, NH: Heinemann, 2003.

Bell, Nanci. *Visualizing and Verbalizing for Language Comprehension and Thinking.* Paso Robles, CA: Academy of Reading Publications, 1991.

Benson, Vicki, and Carrice Cummins. *The Power of Retelling: Developmental Steps for Building Comprehension.* Bothell, WA: The Wright Group, 2000.

Bergeron, Bette, Sarah Wermuth, and Rebecca Hammar. "Initiating Portfolios Through Shared Learning: Three Perspectives." *Reading Assessment: Principles and Practices for Elementary Teachers.* Shelly Barrantine, ed. Newark, DE: International Reading Association, 1995, 118–30.

Bergman, Janet L. "SAIL—A Way to Success and Independence for Low Achieving Readers." *The Reading Teacher* 45.8 (1992): 598–602.

Biemiller, A. "Teaching Vocabulary: Early, Direct, and Sequential." *American Educator* 25 (Spring 2001): 24–28.

Blachowicz, Camille, and Donna Ogle. *Reading Comprehension: Strategies for Independent Learners.* New York: Guilford Press, 2001.

Block, C.C., and S.E. Israel. "The ABCs of Performing Highly Effective Think-Alouds." *The Reading Teacher* 58.2 (2004): 154–67.

Block, C.C., and M. Pressley, eds. *Comprehension Instruction: Research-Based Practices.* New York: Guilford Press, 2002.

Bloodgood, Janet, and Linda C. Pacifici. "Bringing Word Study to Intermediate Classrooms." *The Reading Teacher* 58.3 (2004): 250–63.

Bondy, Elizabeth, and Sharon Ketts. "Like Being at the Breakfast Table: The Power of Morning Meeting." *Responsive Classroom: A Newsletter for Teachers* 13.4 (2001): 48.

Booth, David. *Classroom Voices.* Toronto: Harcourt Brace and Co., 1994.

——. *Literacy Techniques for Building Successful Readers and Writers.* Markham, ON: Pembroke Publishers, 1996.

Booth, David, and C. Thornley-Hall, eds. *The Talk Curriculum.* Portsmouth, NH: Heinemann, 1991.

Bosma, Bette, and Nancy DeVries Guth, eds. *Children's Literature in an Integrated Curriculum: The Authentic Voice.* New York: Teacher College Press/Newark, DE: International Reading Association, 1995.

Boyd-Batstone, Paul. "Focused Anecdotal Records Assessment: A Tool for Standards-Based Authentic Assessment." *The Reading Teacher* 58.3 (2004): 230–39.

Boyle, O., and S. Peregoy. "Literacy Scaffolds: Strategies for First- and Second-Language Readers and Writers." *The Reading Teacher* 44.3 (November 1990): 194–99.

Brandt, Ron. "A Conversation with Spencer Kagan." *Educational Leadership*, 47.4 (1989/90): 8–11.

——. "On Cooperation in Schools: A Conversation with David and Roger Johnson." *Educational Leadership* 45.3 (1987): 14–19.

Bright, Robin. *Read-Alouds for Young Children.* Newark, DE: International Reading Association, 2001.

British Columbia Ministry of Education. "Learning Through Representing." *Primary Program: A Framework for Teaching.* Victoria: Government of British Columbia, 2000.

Britton, James. *Language and Learning.* Urbana, IL: The National Council of Teachers of English, 1970.

Broaddus, Karen, and Janet W. Bloodgood. "We're Supposed to Already Know How to Teach Reading: Teacher Change to Support Struggling Readers." *Reading Research Quarterly* 34 (1999): 426–51.

Bromley, Karen. *Stretching Students' Vocabulary.* New York: Scholastic Professional Books, 2002.

Bromley, Karen, Linda Irwin-DeVitis, and Marcia Modlo. *50 Graphic Organizers for Reading, Writing and More.* New York: Scholastic Teaching Resources, 1999.

Brownlie, F., C. Feniak, and V. McCarthy. *Instruction and Assessment of ESL Learners.* Winnipeg: Portage and Main Press, 2004.

Bruce, Bruce B., ed. *Literacy in the Information Age: Inquiries into Meaning Making with New Technologies.* Newark, DE: International Reading Association, 2003.

Buehl, Doug. *Classroom Strategies for Interactive Learning.* Newark, DE: International Reading Association, 2001.

Burke, Jim. *Reading Reminders: Tools, Tips, and Techniques.* Portsmouth, NH: Boynton/Cook Publishers, 2000.

Buss, K., and L. Karrowksi. *Reading and Writing, Nonfiction Genres.* Newark, DE: International Reading Association, 2002.

Buss, K., and L. McClain-Ruelle, eds. *Creating a Classroom Newspaper.* Newark, DE: International Reading Association, 2000.

Calkins, Lucy McCormick. *The Art of Teaching Reading.* New York: Addison-Wesley Longman, 2001.

Cambourne, Brian. "Holistic, Integrated Approaches to Reading and Language Arts Instruction: The Constructivist Framework of an Instructional Theory." *What Research Has to Say About Reading Instruction.* Alan Farstrup and S.J. Samuels, eds. Newark, DE: International Reading Association, 2002, 25–47.

Canadian Magazine Publishers Association. "Industry Facts." 2005. http://www.cmpa.ca/index.cfm/ci_id/1319/la_id/1.htm.

Carr, Kathryn. "Integrating Multiple Literacies with Curriculum as Inquiry (Overview)." *Integrating Multiple Literacies in K-8 Classrooms: Cases, Commentaries and Practical Applications.* Janet Richards and Michael McKenna, eds. Mahwah, NJ: Lawrence Erlbaum Associates, 2003, 210–15.

Center for Advancement of Learning. "Reading Comprehension." *Learning Strategies Database.* http://www.muskingum.edu/~cal/database/general/reading.html#Background.

Center on English Learning & Achievement (CELA). *English Update* (Spring 2000). Albany, NY: The National Research Center on English Learning & Achievement, University at Albany, 2000.

Centre for the Improvement of Early Reading Achievement (CIERA). *Every Child a Reader: Topic 1—Oral Language and Reading.* Ann Arbor, MI: University of Michigan, 1998.

——. *Every Child a Reader, Topic 2—Concepts of Print, Letter Naming and Phonemic Awareness.* Ann Arbor, MI: University of Michigan, 1998.

——. *Every Child a Reader, Topic 4—High-Frequency Words and Fluency.* Ann Arbor, MI: University of Michigan, 1998.

——. *Every Child a Reader: Topic 5—Strategic Comprehension.* Ann Arbor, MI: University of Michigan, 1998.

——. *Every Child a Reader, Topic 6—Reading and Writing.* Ann Arbor, MI: University of Michigan, 1998.

——. "How Do I Teach Reading to English Language Learners?" *Teaching Every Child to Read: Frequently Asked Questions.* Ann Arbor, MI: University of Michigan, 2001.

Center for Media Literacy. *Five Key Questions That Can Change the World— Part II, CML MediaLit Kit™.* Santa Monica, CA: Center for Media Literacy, 2005, 7.

Chall, Jeanne S. *The Academic Achievement Challenge.* New York: Guilford Press, 2000.

——. *Stages of Reading Development.* New York: McGraw-Hill, 1993.

Chall, Jeanne S., and Vicki A. Jacobs. "Poor Children's Fourth-Grade Slump." *American Educator.* http://www.aft.org/pubs-reports/american_educator/spring2003/chall.html.

Chall, Jeanne S., Vicki A. Jacobs, and L.E. Baldwin. *The Reading Crisis: Why Poor Children Fall Behind.* Cambridge, MA: Harvard University Press, 1990.

Checkley, Kathy. "The First Seven ... and the Eighth: A Conversation with Howard Gardner." *Educational Leadership* 55.1 (1997): 8–13.

Ciardiello, A. Vincent. "Democracy's Young Heroes: An Instructional Model of Critical Literacy Practices." *The Reading Teacher* 58.2 (October 2004): 138–47.

Clarke, Judy, Ron Wideman, and Susan Eadie. *Together We Learn*: Scarborough, ON: Prentice-Hall, 1990.

Clemmons, J., et. al. *Portfolios in the Classroom: A Teacher's Sourcebook.* New York: Scholastic, 1993.

Close, Elizabeth. "CELA Researchers Describe Some Essential Features of Effective Fourth-Grade Teachers and Their Classrooms." Center on English Learning and Achievement, Spring 2001. http://cela.albany.edu/newslet/spring01/betty.htm.

Cohen, Judith, and Roberta Wiener. *Literacy Portfolios: Improving Assessment, Teaching, and Learning.* Upper Saddle River, NJ: Merrill Prentice Hall. 2003.

Colker, Laura J. *When Children Read Because They Want To, Not Because They Have To.* Reading Is Fundamental, Inc., 2005. http://www.rif.org/coordinators/articles/WhenChildrenRead.mspx.

Considine, David, and Gail Haley. *Visual Messages: Integrating Imagery into Instruction.* Englewood, CO: Teacher Ideas Press, 1992.

Cooper, J.D., and N.D. Kiger. *Literacy Assessment: Helping Teachers Plan Instruction.* Boston: Houghton Mifflin, 2001.

Cornett, Claudia E. "Beyond Retelling the Plot: Student-Led Discussions." *Teaching Comprehension and Exploring Multiple Literacies.* T. Rasinski, et al., eds. Newark, DE: International Reading Association, 2000, 56–58.

Cortese, Emma E. "The Application of Question–Answer Relationship Strategies to Pictures." *The Reading Teacher* 57.4 (Dec. 2003/Jan. 2004): 374–80.

Crawford, Kathleen, et al. "Exploring the World Through Multiple Literacies." *The Reading Teacher,* 48.7 (1995): 600–608.

Creaghead, Nancy. "Classroom Interactional Analysis/Script Analysis." *Best Practices in School Speech–Language Pathology: Descriptive/Nonstandardized Language Assessment.* Wayne A. Secord, ed. New York: The Psychological Corporation, Harcourt Brace Jovanovich, Inc., 1992: 65–72.

Crilly, Ruth. *Three Stages of Reading.* Commonwealth of Australia: My Read, 2002. http://www.myread.org/guide_stages.htm.

Culham, Ruth. *6 + 1 Traits of Writing: The Complete Guide (Grades 3 and Up).* Portland, OR: Northwest Regional Educational Laboratory, 2003.

——. *Picture Books: An Annotated Bibliography with Activities for Teaching Writing.* Portland, OR: Northwest Regional Educational Laboratory, 1998.

Cullinan, Bernice, ed. *Fact and Fiction: Literature Across the Curriculum.* Newark, DE: International Reading Association, 1993.

——. *Invitation to Read: More Children's Literature in the Reading Program.* Newark, DE: International Reading Association, 1992.

Cummins, Jim. "Alternative Paradigms in Bilingual Education Research: Does Theory Have a Place?" *Educational Researcher* 28.7 (1999): 26–32.

Cunningham, P.M. *Phonics They Use: Words for Reading and Writing.* New York: HarperCollins, 1995.

——. *Phonics They Use: Words for Reading and Writing.* New York: Longman, 2000.

Cunningham, Patricia M., and Richard L. Allington. *Classrooms That Work: They Can All Read and Write.* New York: HarperCollins, 1994.

Cunningham Patricia M., and James W. Cunningham. "What We Know About How To Teach Phonics." *What Research Has to Say About Reading Instruction.* 3rd ed. Alan E. Farstrup and S.J. Samuels, eds. Newark DE: International Reading Association, 2002, 87-109

Dahl, Karin, and Nancy Farnam. *Children's Writing: Perspectives from Research.* Newark, DE: International Reading Association, 1998.

Daniels, H. *Literature Circles: Voice and Choice in the Student-Centered Classroom*. Portland, ME: Stenhouse Publishing, 1994.

Davey, B. "Think Aloud: Modeling the Cognitive Processes of Reading Comprehension." *The Journal of Reading* 27.1 (1983): 44–47.

Doctorow, R., M. Bodiam, and H. McGowan. *CASI 4–6 Reading Assessment Teacher's Guide*. Toronto: Thomson Nelson, 2003.

Dodge, Ellen Pritchard. *CommunicationLab 1*. E. Moline, IL: LinguiSystems, 1994.

Dodson, Jim, and Steve Dodson. *KIDS Little Instruction Book*. New York: Troll Communications, 1997.

Doiron, R. "Using Non-Fiction in a Read-Aloud Program." *The Reading Teacher* 47 (1994): 616–24.

Dowhower, Sarah L. *Evidence-Based Reading Instruction: Putting the National Reading Panel Report into Practice*. Newark, DE: International Reading Association, 2002.

——. "Supporting a Strategic Stance in the Classroom: A Comprehension Framework for Helping Teachers Help Students to Be Strategic." *The Reading Teacher* 52 (April 1999): 672–88.

Dreher, Mariam Jean. "Motivating Children to Read Nonfiction." *Motivating Recreational Reading and Promoting Home–School Connections*. Timothy Rasinksi et al., eds. Newark, DE: International Reading Association, 2000, 18–22.

——. "The Role of Affect in the Reading Process." *Literacy: Issues and Practices*, 7 (1990): 20–27.

Dreher, Mariam, Kathryn Davis, Priscilla Waynant, and Suzanne Clewell. *Easy Steps to Writing Fantastic RESEARCH REPORTS*. New York: Scholastic Professional Books, 2000.

Dreher, M.J., and H. Singer. "Affective Processes Involved in Reading Comprehension." Paper presented at the Eleventh World Congress in Reading. London, England: 1986.

Duffy, G.G., and J.V. Hoffman. "In Pursuit of an Illusion: The Flawed Search for a Perfect Method." *The Reading Teacher* 53 (1999): 10–16.

Duke, N.K., and P.D. Pearson. "Effective Practices for Developing Reading Comprehension." *What Research Has to Say About Reading Instruction*. 3rd ed. Alan E. Farstrup and S.J. Samuels, eds. Newark DE: International Reading Association, 2002, 205–42.

——. *How Can I Help Children Improve Their Comprehension?* Ann Arbor, MI: Center for the Improvement of Early Reading Achievement (CIERA), Michigan State University, 2001.

Durkin, Delores. "What Classroom Observations Reveal About Reading Comprehension Instruction." *Reading Research Quarterly* 14 (1978–79): 481–533.

——. "Matching Classroom Instruction with Reading Abilities: An Unmet Need." *Remedial and Special Education* 11.3 (1990): 23–28.

Easley, Shirley-Dale, and Kay Mitchell. *Portfolios Matter: What, Where, When, Why and How to Use Them*. Markham, ON: Pembroke Publishers, 2003.

Edmonton Public Schools. *The Toolkit: Curriculum Summaries; Assessment Tasks*. Third edition. Edmonton, AB: 1998.

Education Department of Western Australia. *First Steps: Writing Resource Book and Developmental Continuum*. Melbourne, Victoria: Longman Publishing, 1996.

Edwards, Pamela Duncan. *Some Smug Slug*. New York: HarperCollins, 1996.

Elbow, Peter. "Writing First!" *Educational Leadership* 62.2 (2004): 8–13.

Essex, G., and B. Raban. *Professional Development for Teachers: Speaking and Listening*. Melbourne: Pearson Education Australia, 1999.

——. *Teaching Speakers and Listeners in the Classroom, Stage 3, Early Years Literacy Program*. Melbourne: State of Victoria Department of Education/Pearson Education Australia, 2000.

Evans, Janet. *First Steps: Oral Language Developmental Continuum*. Toronto: Irwin Publishing, 1994.

——. *Writing in the Elementary Classroom: A Reconsideration*. Portsmouth, NH: Heinemann, 2001.

Evans, Karen S. *Literature Discussion Groups in the Intermediate Grades: Dilemmas and Possibilities*. Newark, DE: International Reading Association, 2001.

Falba, C.J., and R.E. Reynolds. "Strategies to Accelerate Reading Success (STARS) in the Middle Grades." *Bridging the Literacy Achievement Gap Grades 4–12*. D. Strickland and D. Alvermann, eds. New York: Teachers College Press, 2004, 109–25.

Farr, Roger, and Bruce Tone. *Portfolio Performance Assessment: Helping Students Evaluate Their Progress as Readers and Writers*. Orlando, FL: Harcourt Brace College Publishers, 1994.

Farstrup, Alan E., and S. Jay Samuels, eds. *What Research Has to Say About Reading Instruction*. 3rd ed. Newark, DE: International Reading Association, 2002.

Fay, K., and S. Whaley. *Becoming One Community: Reading and Writing with English Language Learners*. Portland, ME: Stenhouse Publishers, 2004.

Fehring, Heather, ed. *Literacy Assessment: A Collection of Articles from the Australian Literacy Educators' Association*. Newark, DE: International Reading Association, 2003.

Fehring, Heather, and Pam Green, eds. *Critical Literacy: A Collection of Articles from the Australian Literacy Educators' Association*. Newark, DE: International Reading Association, 2001.

Fiderer, Adele. *40 Rubrics & Checklists to Assess Reading and Writing*. New York: Scholastic, 1999.

Fielding, Linda G., and P. David Pearson. "Reading Comprehension: What Works." *Educational Leadership* (February 1994): 62–68.

Fiffer, Sharon Sloan, and Steve Fiffer, eds. *Home: American Writers Remember Rooms of Their Own*. New York: Random House, Inc., 1995.

Fink, Lisa Storm. "Book Report Alternative: Examining Story Elements Using Story Map Comic Strips." http://www.readwritethink.org/lessons/lesson_view_printer_friendly.asp?id=236.

Fitzgerald, Jill. "Can Minimally Trained College Student Volunteers Help Young At-Risk Children Read Better?" *Reading Research Quarterly* 36 (2001): 28–47.

——. "Literacy and Students Who Are Learning English as a Second Language." *The Reading Teacher* 46 (May 1993): 638–47.

Fitzpatrick, Jo. *Phonemic Awareness: Playing with Sounds to Strengthen Beginning Reading Skills*. Cypress, CA: Creative Teaching Press, 1997.

Fletcher, R. *What a Writer Needs*. Portsmouth, NH: Heinemann, 1993.

——. *A Writer's Notebook: Unlocking the Writer Within You*. New York: Avon Books for Young Readers, 1996.

Fletcher, Ralph, and Joann Portalupi. *Craft Lessons: Teaching Writing K–8*. Portland, ME: Stenhouse Publishers, 1998.

——. *Writing Workshop: The Essential Guide*. Portsmouth, NH: Heinemann, 2001.

Flood, James, and Diane Lapp. "Broadening Conceptualizations of Literacy. The Visual and Communicative Arts." *The Reading Teacher* 51 (1997/98): 342–44.

Fountas, Irene C., and Gay Su Pinnell. *Guiding Readers and Writers Grades 3–6: Teaching Comprehension, Genre, and Content Literacy*. Portsmouth, NH: Heinemann, 2001.

——. *Voices on Word Matters: Learning About Phonics and Spelling in the Literacy Classroom*. Portsmouth, NH: Heinemann, 1999.

——. *Word Matters: Teaching Phonics and Spelling in the Reading/Writing Classroom*. Portsmouth, NH: Heinemann, 1998.

Frager, A.M. "Affective Dimensions of Content Area Reading." *Journal of Reading* 36 (1993): 616–22.

Freppon, P.A., and K.L. Dahl. "Balanced Instruction: Insights and Considerations (Theory and Research into Practice)." *Reading Research Quarterly* 33.2 (1998): 240–51.

Fry, E., D.L. Fountoukidis, and J.K. Polk. *The New Reading Teacher's Book of Lists*. Englewood Cliffs, NJ: Prentice-Hall, 1985.

Fryar, Ros. "Students Assess Their Own Reporting and Presentation Skills." *Literacy Assessment: A Collection of Articles from the Australian Literacy Educators' Association*. Heather Fehring, ed. Newark, DE: International Reading Association, 2003, 36–39.

Gajewski, N., P. Hirn, and P. Mayo. *SSS: Social Skill Strategies (Book A)*. Eau Claire, WI: Thinking Publications, 1989.

Gambrell, Linda, et al. "Assessing Motivation to Learn." *Reading Assessment: Principles and Practices for Elementary Teachers*. Shelby Barrentine, ed. Newark, DE: International Reading Association, 1999, 215–32.

Ganske, K. *Word Journeys: Assessment-Guided Phonics, Spelling, and Vocabulary Instruction*. New York: Guilford Press, 2000.

Gardner, Howard. *Frames of Mind: The Theory of Multiple Intelligences*. New York: Basic Books, 1983.

Garner, Ruth. *Metacognition and Reading Comprehension*. Norwood, NJ: Ablex, 1987.

Gaskins, Irene. "There's More to Teaching At-Risk and Delayed Readers Than Good Reading Instruction." *The Reading Teacher* 51 (1998): 534–47.

——. "Word Detectives." *Educational Leadership* 61 (2004): 70–73.

Gaskins, Irene, Eleanor Wiley Gensemer, and Linda M. Six. "Tailoring a Middle School Language Arts Class to Meet the Needs of Struggling Readers." *After Early Intervention, Then What? Teaching Struggling Readers in Grades 3 and Beyond*.

R.L. McCormack and J.R. Paratore, eds. Newark, DE: International Reading Association, 2003, 137–57.

Gavelek, James, et al. "Integrated Literacy Instruction." *Handbook of Reading Instruction*, Vol. 3. Michael Kamil, et al., eds. Mahwah, NJ: Erlbaum, 2000, 587–608.

Giffin, P., and P. Smith, "Assessing Student Language Growth: Kirsten's Profile." *Talking Classrooms: Shaping Children's Learning Through Oral Language Instruction*. Patricia G. Smith, ed. Newark, DE: International Reading Association, 2001.

Gordon, Christine, J. "Modeling Inference Awareness Across the Curriculum." *Journal of Reading* 28 (1985): 444–47.

——. "Modeling Teaching Strategies." *New Directions in Reading Instruction*. Joy Monahan and Bess Hinson. Newark, DE: International Reading Association, 1998.

Gordon, Christine J., George Labercane, and William R. McEachern. *Elementary Reading: Process and Practice*. Needham Heights, MA: Ginn Press, 1993.

Gordon, Christine, J., and Dorothy MacInnis. "Using Journals as a Window on Students' Thinking Processes in Mathematics." *Language Arts* 70 (1993): 33–38.

Gordon, Christine J., Mary Sheridan, M, and W. James Paul. *Content Literacy for Secondary Teachers*. Toronto: Harcourt Brace Canada, 1998.

Gordon, Christopher, and Christine Gordon. *Rappit the Frog: A Rap on the Developmental Stages of a Frog*, 2004.

Gordon, Dale. "Practical Suggestions for Supporting Speaking and Listening in the Classroom." *Talking Classrooms: Shaping Children's Learning Through Oral Language Instruction*. Patricia G. Smith, ed. Newark. DE: International Reading Association, 2001, 72.

Government of Tasmania. "English Learning Area: Critical Literacy." 10 May 2004. http://www.education.tas.gov.au/english/critlit.htm.

Graves, Donald. *A Fresh Look at Writing*. Portsmouth, NH: Heinemann, 1994.

——. *Writing: Teachers and Children at Work*. Portsmouth, NH: Heinemann, 1983.

Graves, Michael F., Paul Van den Broek, and Barbara M. Taylor, eds. *The First R: Every Child's Right to Read*. New York: Teachers College Press, 1996.

Hall, Dorothy, and Patricia Cunningham. "Multilevel Word Study: Word Charts, Word Walls and Word Sorts." *Voices on Word Matters: Learning About Phonics and Spelling in the Literacy Classroom*. Irene C. Fountas and Gay Su Pinnell, eds. Portsmouth, NH: Heinemann, 1999, 114–30.

Hamilton, Sharon Jean. *My Name's Not Susie: A Life Transformed by Literacy*. Portsmouth, NH: Heinemann, 1995.

Hansen, Jane. *When Writers Read*. Portsmouth, NH: Heinemann, 1987.

Harris,T.L., and R.E. Hodges. *The Literacy Dictionary*. Newark, DE: International Reading Association, 1995.

Harste, J.C., K.G. Short, and C.L. Burke. *Creating Classrooms for Authors: The Reading–Writing Connection*. Portsmouth, NH: Heinemann, 1988.

Harvey, Stephanie, and Anne Goudvis. *Strategies That Work: Teaching Comprehension to Enhance Understanding*. Portland, ME: Stenhouse Publishers, 2000.

Hebert, E.A. "Portfolios Invite Reflection–From Students *and* Staff." *Educational Leadership* 49.8 (1992): 58–61.

Heffernan, Lee. *Critical Literacy and Writer's Workshop, Bringing Purpose and Passion to Student Writing.* Newark, DE: International Reading Association, 2004.

Henkes, Kevin. "Evocative Books: Books That Inspire Personal Response and Engagement." *The Reading Teacher* 58.5 (2005): 480–88.

Hibbing, Anne Nielsen, and Joan L. Rankin-Ericson. "A Picture Is Worth a Thousand Words: Using Visual Images to Improve Comprehension for Middle School Struggling Readers." *The Reading Teacher* 56.8 (2003): 758–70.

Hill, Bonnie Campbell, Cynthia Ruptic, and Lisa Norwick. *Classroom Based Assessment.* Norwood, MA: Christopher-Gordon Publishers, 1998.

Hill, Peter, and Carmel A. Crevola. "The Role of Standards in Educational Reform for the Twenty-First Century." *ASCD Yearbook.* Alexandria, VA: Association for Supervision and Curriculum Development, 1999.

Hirsch, E.D., Jr. "Reading Comprehension Requires Knowledge of Words and the World." *The American Educator* (Spring 2003): 10–29.

Holum, Ann, and Jan Gahala. *Critical Issue: Using Technology to Enhance Literacy Instruction.* North Central Regional Laboratory, 2001.

Hoyt, L. *Making It Real: Strategies for Success with Informational Texts.* Portsmouth, NH: Heinemann, 2002.

——. *Revisit, Reflect, Retell.* Portsmouth, NH: Heinemann, 1999.

——. *Snapshots: Literacy Minilessons Up Close.* Portsmouth, NH: Heinemann, 2000.

Hoyt, L., and C. Ames. "Letting the Learner Lead the Way." *Primary Voices* 5 (1997): 16–29.

International Reading Association (IRA) "Comprehension Strategies." *Evidence-Based Reading Instruction: Putting the National Reading Panel Report into Practice.* Newark, DE: International Reading Association, 2002, 137–38.

——. *Evidence-Based Reading Instruction: Putting the National Reading Panel Report into Practice.* Newark, DE: International Reading Association, 2002.

——. *Excellent Reading Teachers: A Position Statement of the International Reading Association* (pamphlet). Newark, DE: International Reading Association, 2000.

——. *Family Literacy and the School Community: A Partnership for Lifelong Learning* (pamphlet). Newark, DE: International Reading Association.

——. *Family-School Partnerships: Essential Elements of Literacy Instruction in the United States: A Position Statement.* Newark, DE: International Reading Association, 2002.

——. *I Can Read and Write! How to Encourage Your School-Age Child's Literacy Developmen*t (booklet). Newark, DE: International Reading Association, 1999.

——. *Learning to Read and Write: Developmentally Appropriate Practices for Young Children.* Newark, DE: International Reading Association, 1998.

——. *Library Safari: Tips for Parents of Young Readers and Explorers.* Newark, DE: International Reading Association, 1999.

——. *Making the Most of Television: Tips for Parents of Young Viewers.* Newark, DE: International Reading Association, 1998.

——. *Making the Reading–Writing Connection: Tips for Parents of Young Learners.* Newark, DE: International Reading Association, 1999.

——. *Seeing the World on the Internet: Tips for Parents of Young Readers and "Surfers."* Newark, DE: International Reading Association, 1998.

——. *Summer Reading Adventure! Tips for Parents of Young Readers* (pamphlet). Newark, DE: International Reading Association, 1998.

——. "Study Finds Links Between Newspaper Use in School and Young Adult Readership." *Reading Today* (February/March 2005): 35.

——. *Teachers' Choices.* Newark, DE: International Reading Association, 2002.

——. *Teachers' Choices.* Newark, DE: International Reading Association, 2003.

——. *Teaching All Children to Read: The Roles of the Reading Specialist. A Position Paper of the International Reading Association.* Newark, DE: International Reading Association, 2000.

——.*What Is Evidence-Based Reading Instruction? A Position Statement of the International Reading Association* (brochure). Newark, DE: International Reading Association, 2002.

——. *What Is Family Literacy? Getting Involved in Your Child's Literacy Learning* (pamphlet). Newark, DE: International Reading Association.

Invernizzi, Marcia, Connie Juel, and Catherine A. Rosemary. "A Community Volunteer Tutorial That Works." *Teaching Struggling Readers.* Richard Allington, ed. Newark, DE: International Reading Association, 1998, 276–84.

Irvin, Judith L. *Reading and the Middle School Student: Strategies to Enhance Literacy.* Meeham Heights, MA: Allyn & Bacon, 1998.

Ivey, Gay, and Marianne Baker. "Phonics Instruction for Older Students? Just Say No." *Educational Leadership* 61 (2004): 35–40.

Jensen, Eric. *Teaching with the Brain in Mind.* Alexandria, VA: Association for Supervision and Curriculum Development (ASCD), 1998.

Johns, Jerry, and Susan Davis Lenski. *Improving Reading: Strategies and Resources.* Dubuque, IO: Kendall/Hunt Publishing, 2001.

Johnston, Peter. *Choice Words: How Our Language Affects Students' Learning.* Portland, ME: Stenhouse Publishers, 2004.

Juel, C., and R. Deffes. "Making Words Stick." *Educational Leadership* 61 (2004): 30–34.

Kagan, Spencer. "The Structural Approach to Cooperative Learning." *Educational Leadership* 47.4 (1989/90): 12–15.

Kameenui, Edward J. "Diverse Learners and the Tyranny of Time: Don't Fix Blame; Fix the Leaky Roof." *Teaching Struggling Readers.* Richard Allington, ed. Newark, DE: International Reading Association, 1998, 10–18.

Kamil, Michael L., Peter B. Mosenthal, P. David Pearson, and Rebecca Barr, eds. *Handbook of Reading Research, Volume III.* Mahwah, NJ: Lawrence Erlbaum Associates, 2000.

Katz, L.G., and S.C. Chard. *Engaging Children's Minds: The Project Approach.* 2nd ed. Westport, CT: Ablex, 2000.

Keene, Ellin. "Ways to Demonstrate Independence in Use of Comprehension Strategies." Mosaic Listserve Tools, 2003. http://www.u46teachers.org/mosaic/tools/tools.htm.

Keene, Ellin, and Susan Zimmermann. *Mosaic of Thought: Teaching Comprehension in a Reader's Workshop.* Portsmouth, NH: Heinemann, 1997.

Kist, W. "Beginning to Create the New Literacy Classroom: What Does the New Literacy Look Like?" *Journal of Adolescent and Adult Literacy* 43.8 (2000): 710–18.

Klenk, Laura, and Michael W. Kibby. "Re-Mediating Reading Difficulties: Appraising the Past, Reconciling the Present, Constructing the Future." *Handbook of Reading Research, Volume III,* Michael L. Kamil et al., eds. Mahwah, NJ: Lawrence Erlbaum Associates, 2000, 667–90.

Klinger, J.K., S. Vaughan, and J.S. Schumm. "Collaborative Strategic Reading During Social Studies in Heterogeneous Fourth-Grade Classrooms." *Elementary Journal* 99.1 (1998): 3–22.

Krathwohl, D.R., B.S. Bloom, and B.B. Masia. *Taxonomy of Educational Objectives–Handbook II: Affective Domain.* New York: David McKay, 1964.

Kuhn, Melanie, and Lesley Mandel Morrow. "Taking Computers Out of the Corner: Making Technology Work for Struggling Intermediate-Grade Readers." *After Early Intervention, Then What? Teaching Struggling Readers in Grades 3 and Beyond.* R.L. McCormack and J.R. Paratore, eds. Newark, DE: International Reading Association, 2003, 172–89.

Kuhn, Melanie R., and Steven A. Stahl. *Fluency: A Review of Developmental and Remedial Practices.* Ann Arbor, MI: CIERA, 2000.

Landers, Daniel, et al. "Developing Thinking Skills in Physical Education." *Developing Minds: A Resource Book for Teaching Thinking.* Arthur Costa, ed. Alexandria, VA: ASCD, 2001, 343–50.

Lane, B. *After THE END: Teaching and Learning Creative Revision.* Portsmouth, NH: Heinemann, 1993.

Lapp, Diane, and James Flood. "Understanding the Learner: Using Portable Assessment." *After Early Intervention, Then What? Teaching Struggling Readers in Grades 3 and Beyond.* R.L. McCormack and J.R. Paratore, eds. Newark, DE: International Reading Association, 2003. 10–24.

Lee, Nancy G., and Judith C. Neal. "Reading Rescue: Intervention for a Student 'At Promise.'" *Journal of Reading* 36.4 (1992): 276–82.

Lenters, Kimberly. "No Half Measures: Reading Instruction for Young Second-Language Learners." *The Reading Teacher* 58.4 (Dec. 2004–January 2005): 328–35.

Lewin, Larry. "Talking Back to Authors." *Educational Leadership* 62.2 (2004): 58–63.

Lewison, M., A.S. Flint, and K. van Sluys. "Taking on Critical Literacy: The Journey of Newcomers and Novices." *Language Arts* 79.5 (2002): 382–92.

Livingston, N., C. Kurkjian, T. Young, and L. Pringle. "Nonfiction as Literature: An Untapped Goldmine." *The Reading Teacher* 57.6 (2004): 582–91.

Lubliner, Shira. "Help for Struggling Upper-Grade Elementary Readers." *The Reading Teacher* 57 (2004): 430–38.

Luke, Alan, and John Elkins. "Towards a Critical, Worldly Literacy." *Journal of Adult and Adolescent Literacy,* 45.8 (2002): 668–73.

Luke, A., J. O'Brien, and B. Comber. "Making Community Texts Objects of Study." *Critical Literacy: A Collection of Articles from the Australian Educators' Association.* H. Fehring and P. Green, eds. Newark, DE: International Reading Association. 2001.

Luongo-Orlando, Katherine. *Authentic Assessment: Designing Performance-Based Tasks.* Markham, ON: Pembroke Publishers, 2003.

Lyon, G.R. "Reading Development, Reading Difficulties, and Reading Instruction: Educational and Public Health Issues." *Journal of School Psychology* 40 (2002): 3–6.

MacKenzie, Karla K. "Using Literacy Booster Groups to Maintain and Extend Reading Recovery Success in the Primary Grades." *The Reading Teacher* 55 (2001): 222–34.

Mandeville, Thomas, F. "KWLA: Linking the Affective and Cognitive Domains." *Teaching Comprehension and Exploring Multiple Literacies: Strategies from The Reading Teacher.* Timothy Rasinski, et al., eds. Newark, DE: International Reading Association, 2000.

Mantione, Roberta D., and Sabine Smead. *Weaving Through Words: Using the Arts to Teach Reading Comprehension Strategies.* Newark, DE: International Reading Association, 2003.

Manzo, Anthony, Ula Manzo, and Thomas Estes. *Content Area Literacy: Interactive Teaching for Active Learning.* New York: John Wiley & Sons, Inc., 2001.

Manzo, V., U.C. Manzo, and M.W. Thomas. *Content Area Literacy: Strategic Teaching for Strategic Learning.* Hoboken, NJ: John Wiley & Sons, Inc., 2005.

Marshall, P. *How to Study and Learn: Your Practical Guide to Effective Study Skills.* Philadelphia, PA: Trans-Atlantic Publications, 1999.

Marzano, Robert. *Classroom Management That Works.* Alexandria, VA: Association for Supervision and Curriculum Development (ASCD), 2003.

——. *Literacy: Practical Ways to Achieve Success–Classroom Instruction That Works.* Workshop presented in Mississauga, Ontario, January 30 to February 1, 2002.

Marzano, Robert, et al. *Handbook for Classroom Instruction That Works.* Alexandria, VA: Association for Supervision, Curriculum and Instruction, 2001.

Marzano, R.J., B.B. Gaddy, and C. Dean. *What Works in Classroom Instruction.* Aurora, CO: Mid-Continent Research for Education and Learning, 2000.

Mason, Pamela A., and Jeanne Shay Schumm. *Promising Practices in Urban Reading Instruction.* Newark, DE: International Reading Association, 2003.

McCormack, Rachel L., and Jeanne Paratore, eds. *After Early Intervention, Then What? Teaching Struggling Readers in Grades 3 and Beyond.* Newark, DE: International Reading Association, 2003.

McGill-Franzen, Anne. "Early Literacy: What Does 'Developmentally Appropriate' Mean?" *The Reading Teacher* 46.1 (1992): 56–58.

McLaughlin, Maureen, and Mary Beth Allen. *Guided Comprehension in Action Lessons for Grades 3–8*. Newark, DE: International Reading Association, 2002.

——. *Guided Comprehension in the Primary Grades*. Newark, DE: International Reading Association, 2003.

McLaughlin, Maureen, and MaryEllen Voyt. *Portfolios in Teacher Education*. Newark, DE: International Reading Association, 1996.

McMackin, Mary C., and Barbara S. Siegel. *Knowing How: Researching and Writing Nonfiction 3–8*. Portland, ME: Stenhouse Publishers, 2002.

McNeil, John D. *Reading Comprehension: New Directions for Classroom Practice*. Glenview, Il: Scott Foresman, 1987.

Merkley, Donna G. "Modified Anticipation Guide." *Teaching Comprehension and Exploring Multiple Literacies*, T. Rasinski, et al., eds. Newark, DE: International Reading Association, 2000, 59–63.

Merritt, D., and B. Culatta. *Language Intervention in the Classroom*. Toronto: Nelson Thomson Learning, 1998.

Miller, Debbie. *Reading with Meaning: Teaching Comprehension in the Primary Grades*. Portland, ME: Stenhouse Publishers, 2002.

Mizokawa, Donald, and Nancy Hansen-Krening. "The ABCs of Attitudes Toward Reading: Inquiring About the Reader's Response." *The Reading Teacher* 44.1 (2000): 72–79.

Moats, Louisa C. "Teaching Reading IS Rocket Science. What Expert Teachers of Reading Should Know and Be Able To Do." Washington, DC: American Federation of Teachers, 1999.

——. "When Older Students Can't Read." *Educational Leadership* 58 (2001): 36–40.

Moline, Steve. *I See What You Mean: Children at Work with Visual Information*. Markham, ON: Pembroke Publishers, 1996.

Morrow, Lesley Mandel. "Oral Strategies to Promote Comprehension, Fluency, and Retelling." Presented at The International Reading Association World Congress, Edinburgh, Scotland, July 2002.

Murray, Donald. *A Writer Teaches Writing*. 2nd ed. Boston, MA: Houghton Mifflin, 1985.

The National Reading Panel Report. *Teaching Children to Read: An Evidence-Based Assessment of the Scientific Research Literature on Reading and Its Implications for Reading Instruction*. Washington, DC: National Institute of Child and Human Development and the Department of Education, 2000.

NCREL (North Central Region Education Laboratory). EnGauge Project: 21st Century Skills. http://www.ncrel.org. 2001.

Nelson, Anne. "Authentic Assessment and System Accountability." *Literacy Assessment: A Collection of Articles From the Australian Literacy Educators' Association*. Heather Fehring, ed. Newark, DE: International Reading Association, 2003, 76–80.

Nelson, Kristen Nicholson, *Developing Students' Multiple Intelligences (Grades K–8)*. Jefferson City, MO: Scholastic Professional Books. 1999.

Northwest Regional Educational Laboratory. *Seeing with New Eyes*. Portland, OR: 1999.

Oczkus, Lori D. *Reciprocal Teaching at Work: Strategies for Improving Reading Comprehension*. Newark, DE: International Reading Association, 2003.

——. *Reciprocal Teaching Strategies at Work: Improving Reading Comprehension, Grades 2–6* (video). Newark: DE: International Reading Association, 2005.

Ogle, D.M. "K-W-L: A Teaching Model That Develops Active Reading of Expository Text." *Reading Teacher* 39 (1986): 564–70.

O'Keefe, V. *Speaking to Think, Thinking to Speak: The Importance of Talk in the Learning Process*. Portsmouth, NH: Heinemann, 1995.

Olness, Rebecca. *Using Literature to Enhance Writing Instruction, A Guide for K–5 Teachers*. Newark, DE: International Reading Association, 2005.

Olson, Mary, and Susan Homan. *Teacher to Teacher: Strategies for the Elementary Classroom*. Newark, DE: International Reading Association, 1993.

Ontario Ministry of Education. *Early Reading Strategy. The Report of the Expert Panel on Elementary Reading in Ontario*. Toronto: Ontario Ministry of Education, 2003.

Opitz, Michael F., and Roger G. Eldridge, Jr. "Remembering Comprehension: Delving into the Mysteries of Teaching Reading Comprehension." *The Reading Teacher* 57.8 (2004): 772–73.

O'Shaughnessy, Tam E., and H. Lee Swanson. "A Comparison of Two Reading Interventions for Children with Reading Disabilities." *Journal of Learning Disabilities* 33 (2000): 257–75.

Owens, R.F., J.T. Hester, and W.T. Teale. "Where Do You Want to Go Today? Inquiry-Based Learning and Technology Integration." *The Reading Teacher* 55.7 (2002): 616–39.

Padak, Nancy, et al. *Developing Reading and Writing Connections*. Newark, DE: International Reading Association, 2000.

Palincsar, A.S., and A.L. Brown. "Interactive Teaching to Promote Independent Learning from Text." *The Reading Teacher* 39.6 (1986): 564–70.

Palincsar, A.S., and L. Klenk. "Fostering Literacy Learning in Supportive Contexts." *Journal of Learning Disabilities* 25.4 (1992): 211–25.

Paris, Scott G., and Robert D. Carpenter. "FAQs About IRIs." *The Reading Teacher* 56.6 (March 2003): 578–80.

Pearson, P.D. "Reclaiming the Center." *The First R: Every Child's Right to Read*. Michael F. Graves, Paul Van den Broek, and Barbara Taylor, eds. New York: Teachers College Press, 1999, 259–74.

Pearson, P.D., and N.K. Duke. "Comprehension Instruction in the Primary Grades." *Comprehension Instruction: Research-Based Best Practices*, C.C. Block and M. Pressley, eds. New York: Guilford Press, 2002, 247–58.

Pearson, P.D., and L. Fielding. "Comprehension Instruction." *Handbook of Reading Research, Volume II*. M. Kamil, et al., eds. White Plains, NY: Longman Publishing, 1991, 815–60.

Pearson, P.D., and M.O. Gallagher. "The Instruction of Reading Comprehension." *Contemporary Educational Psychology* 8 (1983): 317–44.

Pearson, P.D., and D.D. Johnson. *Teaching Reading Comprehension*. New York: Holt, Rinehart and Winston, 1978.

The Pennsylvania System of State Assessment Reading Instructional Handbook. Revised 1997. http://www.pasd.com/PSSA/reading/rihand1.htm.

Peterson, Shelley. "Supporting Boys' and Girls' Literacy Learning." *Orbit* 34 (2004): 33–38.

Phillips, Linda. *Assessment Handbook 3*. Scarborough: Prentice Hall Ginn Canada, 1999.

Piazza, C.L. *Multiple Forms of Literacy: Teaching Literacy and the Arts*. Upper Saddle River, NJ: Prentice Hall, 1999.

Polochanin, David. "Teacher as Author: Modeling the Writing Process." *Classroom Leadership* 8.3 (November 2004). http://www.ascd.org/publications/class_lead/200411/polochanin.html.

Portalupi, Joann, and Ralph Fletcher. *Nonfiction Craft Lessons: Teaching Information Writing K–8*. Portland, ME: Stenhouse Publishers, 2001.

——. *Teaching the Qualities of Writing*. Portsmouth, NH: Heinemann, 2004.

Post, Arden Devries, Marilyn Scott, and Marilyn Theberge. *Celebrating Children's Choices: 25 Years of Children's Favorite Books*. Newark, DE: International Reading Association, 2000.

Powell, Janet L. *How Well Do Tests Measure Real Reading? ERIC Digest*. Bloomington, IN: ERIC Clearinghouse on Reading and Communication Skills, June 1989. http://www.ericdigests.org/pre-9211/real.htm.

Preller, Paula. "Fostering Thoughtful Literacy in Elementary Classrooms." *English Update* (Spring 2000). Albany, NY: The National Research Center on English Learning & Achievement, University at Albany.

Pressley, M. "Comprehension Instruction: What Makes Sense Now, What Might Make Sense Soon." *Reading Online* 5.2 (2001): http://www/readingonline.org/.

——. "Metacognition and Self-Regulated Comprehension." *What Research Has to Say About Reading Instruction*. 3rd ed. Alan E. Farstrup and S. Jay Samuels, eds. Newark, DE: International Reading Association, 2002, 291–309.

Pressley, Michael. *Reading Instruction That Works*. 2nd edition. New York: Guilford Press, 2002.

——. "What Should Comprehension Instruction Be the Instruction Of?" *Handbook of Reading Research, Volume III*. Michael H. Kamil, et al., eds. Mahwah, NJ: Lawrence Erlbaum Associates, 2000, 545–61.

Pressley, M., and K.R. Harris. "What We Really Know About Strategy Instruction." *Educational Leadership* (1990): 31–34.

Pressley, M., and K. Helden. *How Can Children Be Taught to Comprehend Text Better?* Paper presented at the University of Calgary, 2 February 2002.

Pressley, M., and R. Wharton-McDonald. "Skilled Comprehension and Its Development Through Instruction." *School Psychology Review* 26.3 (1997): 448–66.

Pressley, M., R. Wharton-McDonald, J.M. Hampston, and M. Echevarria. "The Nature of Literacy Instruction in Ten Grade 4/5 Classrooms in Upstate New York." *Scientific Studies of Reading* 2 (1998): 159–91.

Raphael, T. "Teaching Children Question–Answer Relationships, Revisited." *The Reading Teacher* 39.6 (1986): 516–22.

Raphael, T., and F. Boyd. "When Readers Write: The Book Club Connection." *The Book Club Connection*. Susan McMahon and Taffy Raphael, eds. New York: Teachers College Press, 1997, 69–89.

Raphael, T., and S. Englert. "Writing and Reading: Partners in Constructing Meaning." *The Reading Teacher* 43.6 (1990): 388–400.

Rasinski, Timothy. "Creating Fluent Readers." *Educational Leadership* 6 (2004): 46–51.

Rasinski, Timothy. "The Fluency Development Lesson (FDL)." Presented at the International Reading Association, 48th Annual Convention, in Orlando, FL., May 2003.

Rasinski, Timothy. *The Fluent Reader*. New York: Scholastic, 2003.

Rasinski, Timothy, et al., eds. *Teaching Comprehension and Exploring Multiple Literacies*. Newark, DE: International Reading Association, 2000.

Red, Suzy. "Ten Reasons to Teach an Integrated Curriculum." 2003. http://suzyred.com/integratedten.htm.

Reithaug, Dawn. *Orchestrating Academic Success by Adapting and Modifying Programs*. West Vancouver, BC: Stirling Head Enterprises, 1998.

Rekrut, Martha D. "Peer and Cross-Age Tutoring: The Lessons of Research." *Struggling Adolescent Readers: A Collection of Teaching Strategies*. D.W. Moore, D.E. Alvermann, and K.A. Hinchman, eds. Newark, DE: International Reading Association, 2000, 290–95.

Resource Development Services. "Rubric for K-W-L Chart." Edmonton, AB: Edmonton Public Schools, 1999.

Rhodes, Carole S. "Evaluating and Selecting Quality Children's Books." *Teachers' Choices Committee: More Teachers' Favorite Books for Kids: Teachers' Choices 1994–1996*. Newark, DE: International Reading Association, 1997, S5–S10.

Rhodes, Lynn K. *Literacy Assessment: A Handbook of Instruments*. Portsmouth, NH: Heinemann, 1993.

Rhodes, Lynn K., and Curt Dudley-Marling. *Readers and Writers with a Difference: A Holistic Approach to Teaching Struggling Readers and Writers*. Portsmouth, NH: Heinemann, 1996.

Rhodes, Lynn K., and Nancy L. Shanklin. *Windows into Literacy: Assessing Learners K–8*. Portsmouth, NH: Heinemann, 1993.

Rhodes, Lynn, and Sally Nathenson-Mejia. "Anecdotal Records: A Powerful Tool for Ongoing Literacy Assessment." *Reading Assessment: Principle and Practices for Elementary Teachers*. Shelby Barrentine, ed. Newark, DE: International Reading Association, 1999, 83–90.

Richards, Janet C., and Michael McKenna. *Integrating Multiple Literacies in K–8 Classrooms: Cases, Commentaries, and Practical Applications*. Mahwah, NJ: Lawrence Erlbaum Associates, Publishers, 2003.

Richardson, J.S., and R.F. Morgan. *Reading to Learn in the Content Areas*. Belmont, CA: Wadsworth, 2000.

Richek, Margaret Ann, and Linda Conviser Glick. "Coordinating a Literacy Support Program with Classroom Instruction." *Teaching Struggling Readers*. Richard Allington, ed. Newark, DE: International Reading Association, 1998, 100–106.

Roller, Cathy M., ed. *Comprehensive Reading Instruction Across the Grade Levels*. Newark, DE: International Reading Association, 2002.

——. *Learning to Teach Reading: Setting the Research Agenda*. Newark, DE: International Reading Association, 2001.

Roller, Cathy. *Variability, Not Disability: Struggling Readers in a Workshop Classroom*. Newark, DE: International Reading Association, 1996.

Romano, Tom. "The Power of Voice." *Educational Leadership* 62.2 (2004): 20–23.

Roser, Nancy L., and Miriam G. Martinez, eds. *What a Character! Character Study as a Guide to Literary Meaning Making in Grades K–8*. Newark, DE: International Reading Association, 2005.

Routman, Regie. *Conversations: Strategies for Teaching, Learning and Evaluating*. Portsmouth, NH: Heinemann, 2000.

——. *Invitations: Changing as Teachers and Learners, K–12*. Portsmouth, NH: Heinemann, 1994.

——. *Kids' Poems: Teaching Second Graders to Love Poetry*. New York: Scholastic, 2000.

——. *Reading Essentials: The Specifics You Need to Teach Reading Well*. Portsmouth, NH: Heinemann, 2003.

——. "The Uses and Abuses of Invented Spelling." *The Instructor*. (May/June 1993): 36–47.

——. *Writing Essentials: Raising Expectations and Results While Simplifying Teaching*. Portsmouth, NH: Heinemann, 2005.

Sadler, Charlotte Rose. *Comprehension Strategies for Middle Grade Learners: A Handbook for Content Area Teachers*. Newark, DE: International Reading Association, 2001.

Samuels, S. Jay. "Reading Fluency: Its Development and Assessment." *What Research Has to Say About Reading Instruction*. 3rd ed. A. Farstrup and S. Jay Samuels, eds. Newark, DE: International Reading Association, 2002, 166–83.

Santa, Carol. "Comprehending and Studying the Content Subjects." *Elementary Reading: Process and Practice*. Christine Gordon, George Labercane, and William R. McEachern, eds. Needham Heights, MA: Ginn Press, 1993, 245–62.

Sarroub, L., and P.D. Pearson. "Two Steps Forward, Three Steps Back: The Stormy History of Reading Comprehension Assessment." *The Clearing House* 72.2 (1998): 97–105.

Schmidt, Laurel. "Is There a Hemingway in the House?" *Educational Leadership* 62.2 (2004): 42–45.

Schmitt, Maribeth. "A Questionnaire to Measure Children's Awareness of Strategic Reading Processes." *The Reading Teacher* (March 1990): 454–61.

Schraw, G. "Promoting General Metacognitive Awareness." *Metacognition in Learning and Instruction*. H. Hartman, ed. Dordrecht: Kluwer Academic Publishers, 2002, 3–16.

Schumaker, J.B., P. Denton, and D.D. Deshler. "The Paraphrasing Strategy." E.S. Ellis and B.K. Lenz. "A Component Analysis of Effective Learning Strategies for LD Students." *Learning Disabilities Focus* 2 (1984): 94–107.

Schurr, Sandra, Julia Thomason, and Max Thompson. *Teaching at the Middle Level: A Professional's Handbook*. Toronto: D.C. Heath and Company, 1995.

Schwartz, Susan, and Maxine Bone. *Retelling, Relating, Reflecting: Beyond the 3 R's*. Toronto: Irwin Publishing, 1995.

Schwartz, Susan, and Mindy Pollishuke. *Creating the Dynamic Classroom: A Handbook for Teachers*. Toronto: Irwin Publishing, 2002.

Scott, Ruth McQuirter, and Sharon Siamon. *Spelling: Connecting the Pieces*. Toronto: Gage Learning Corporation, 2004.

SEDL (Southwest Educational Development Laboratory). "The Cognitive Elements of Reading: Reading Comprehension." 2000. http://www.sedl.org/reading/framework/elements.html#reading

Seigel, M. "Sketch to Stretch." *Reading, Writing and Caring*. O. Cochrane, ed. New York: Richard C. Owen Publisher, 1984, 178.

Shea, Mary. *Taking Running Records*. New York: Scholastic Professional Books, 2000.

Sibberson, Franki, and Karen Szymusiak. *Still Learning to Read: Teaching Students in Grades 3–6*. Portland, ME: Stenhouse Publishers, 2003.

Silverstein, Shel. "The Little Boy and the Old Man." *A Light in the Attic*. New York: HarperCollins, 1981.

Skowron, J. *Powerful Lesson Planning Models: The Art of 1000 Decisions*. Arlington Heights, IL: Skylight Professional Development, 2001.

Slaughter, Judith. *Beyond Storybooks: Young Children and the Shared Book Experience*. Newark, DE: International Reading Association, 1993.

Slavin, Robert. *Cooperative Learning: Theory, Research and Practice*. New York: Prentice-Hall, Inc., 1990.

Smith, F. *Understanding Reading*. 5th ed. Hillsdale, NJ: Lawrence Erlbaum Associates, 1994.

Smith, Patricia G., ed. *Talking Classrooms*. Newark, DE: International Reading Association, 2001.

Snow, Catherine. *Reading for Understanding: Toward an R&D Program in Reading Comprehension*. Prepared for the Office of Educational Research and Improvement, U.S. Department of Education. Santa Monica, CA: RAND Education, 2002.

Snow, Catherine C., M. Susan Burns, and Peg Griffin, eds. *Preventing Reading Difficulties in Young Children*. Washington, DC: National Academy Press, 1998.

Snowball, D., and F. Bolton. *Spelling K–8*. York, ME: Stenhouse Publishers, 1999.

Soderman, Anne K., Kara M. Gregory, and Louise T. O'Neill. *Scaffolding Emergent Literacy: A Child-Centered Approach for Preschool Through Grade 5*. Needham Heights, MA: Allyn & Bacon, 1999.

Spandel, Vicki. *Books, Lessons, Ideas for Teaching the Six Traits: Writing in the Elementary and Middle Grades*. Wilmington, MA: Great Source Education Group, 2001.

——. *Creating Writers Through 6-Trait Writing Assessment and Instruction*. 3rd ed. New York: Addison-Wesley Longman Inc., 2001.

——. *Creating Writers Through 6-Trait Writing Assessment and Instruction*. 4th ed. New York: Pearson Education Inc., 2005.

Stahl, Steven A. *How Can I Help Children Crack the Code?* Ann Arbor, MI: CIERA 2001.

Stahl, Steven A., and Melanie R. Kuhn. "Making It Sound Like Language: Developing Fluency." *The Reading Teacher* 55.6 (2002): 582–87.

Stanovich, Keith. "Matthew Effects in Reading: The Consequence of Individual Differences in the Acquisition of Literacy." *Reading Research Quarterly* 21 (1986): 360–407.

State of Wisconsin. Wisconsin Governor's Literary Education and Reading Network. http://www.wilearns.com/apps/default.asp?cid-27.

Stead, Tony. *Is That a Fact? Teaching Nonfiction Writing K–3.* Portland, ME: Stenhouse Publishers, 2002.

Stoll, Donald. *Magazines for Kids and Teens.* Glassboro, NJ: Educational Press Association of America/Newark, DE: International Reading Association, 1997.

Strickland, Dorothy S., Kathy Ganske, and Joanne K. Monroe. *Supporting Struggling Readers and Writers: Strategies for Classroom Intervention 3–6.* Portland, ME: Stenhouse Publishers, 2002.

Sudol, P., and C.M. King. "A Checklist for Choosing Non-fiction Trade Books." *The Reading Teacher* 49 (1996): 422–24.

Tarasoff, M. *Reading Instruction That Makes Sense.* Victoria, BC: Active Learning Institute, 1994.

——. *Spelling Strategies You Can Teach.* Victoria, BC: Active Learning Press, 1990.

Thoman, E. *Skills and Strategies for Media Education,* 2003. http://www/medialit.org/reading_room/pdf/CMLskillsandstrat.pdf©2003. Center for Media Literacy. http://www.medialit.org/.

Thomas, Adele, Lynn Fazio, and Betty Stiefelmeyer. *Families at School: A Guide for Educators.* Newark, DE: International Reading Association, 1999.

Thomason, Tommy, and Carol York. *Write on Target: Preparing Young Writers to Succeed On State Writing Achievement Tests.* Norwood, MA: Christopher-Gordon Publishers, 2000.

Thomlinson, Carol A. *Fulfilling the Promise of a Differentiated Classroom.* Alexandria, VA: Association for Supervision and Curriculum Development, 2003.

Thompson, Dr. Lesley. "Reading Assessment and Instruction Go Hand in Hand." Interview by Northwest Regional Educational Laboratory. *Northwest Report* (February 1999). (Online, updated September 2001; cited February 2005). http://www.nwrel.org/nwreport/feb99/article2.html.

Tingley, Jennifer. "Volunteer Programs: When Good Intentions Are Not Enough." *Educational Leadership* 58.7 (2001): 53–55.

Tompkins, Gail E. *Teaching Writing: Balancing Process and Product.* 3rd ed. Upper Saddle River, NJ: Prentice-Hall Inc., 2000.

Toronto District School Board. *Teaching Children to Read and Write.* Toronto: Toronto District School Board, 2000.

Tovani, Cris. *Do I Really Have to Teach Reading? Content Comprehension in Grades 6–12.* Portland, ME: Stenhouse Publishers, 2004.

Trehearne, M., et al. *Kindergarten Teacher's Resource Book.* Toronto: ITP Nelson Publishing, 2000.

Trehearne, M., et al. *Language Arts Grades 1–2 Teacher's Resource Book.* Toronto: Thomson Nelson, 2004.

Tyner, Beverly. *Small-Group Reading Instruction: A Differentiated Teaching Model for Beginning and Struggling Readers.* Newark, DE: International Reading Association, 2004.

Vacca, Richard. "Making a Difference in Adolescents' School Lives: Visible and Invisible Aspects of Content Area Reading." *What Research Has to Say About Reading Instruction.* A.E. Farstrup and S.J. Samuels, eds. Newark, DE: International Reading Association, 2002, 184–204.

Vacca, R.T., and J.L. Vacca. *Content Area Reading: Literacy and Learning Across the Curriculum.* 7th ed. Boston: Allyn & Bacon, 2001.

Valencia, Sheila. "A Portfolio Approach to Classroom Reading Assessment: The Whys, Whats, and Hows." *Reading Assessment: Principles and Practices for Elementary Teachers.* Shelby Barrentine, ed. Newark, DE: International Reading Association, 1999, 113–17.

Valencia, Sheila W., and Marsha Riddle Buly. "Behind Test Scores: What Struggling Readers *Really* Need." *The Reading Teacher* 57.6 (2004): 520–30.

Vasquez, Vivian. *Getting Beyond "I Like the Book": Creating Space for Critical Literacy in K–6 Classrooms.* Newark, DE: International Reading Association, 2003.

Vaughan, J.L., and Thomas Estes. *Reading and Reasoning Beyond the Primary Grades.* Toronto: Allyn & Bacon, 1986.

Wade, Suzanne, and Elizabeth Moje. "The Role of Text in Classroom Learning." *Handbook of Reading Research,* Vol. 3. Michael Kamil, et al., eds. Mahwah, NJ: Lawrence Erlbaum, 2000, 609–28.

Walker, Barbara J. "Discussions That Focus on Strategies and Self-Assessment." *Lively Discussions! Fostering Engaged Reading.* L.B. Gambrell and J.F. Almasi, eds. Newark, DE: International Reading Association, 1996, 286–96.

Walker, Catherine, and Dana Antaya-Moore. *Thinking Tools for Kids: Practical Organizers.* Edmonton, Alberta: Resource Development Services, Edmonton Public Schools, 1999.

Westby, Carol. "Learning to Talk–Talking to Learn: Oral Literate Language Differences." *Communication Skills and Classroom Success.* C. Simon, ed. Eau Claire, WI: Thinking Publications, 1991, 334–55.

Wiggins, G., and J. McTighe. *Understanding by Design.* Alexandria, VA: Association for Supervision and Curriculum Development, 1998.

Wilhelm, Jeffrey. *Action Strategies for Deepening Comprehension: Role Plays, Text Structure Tableaux, Talking Statues, & Other Enrichment Techniques That Engage Students with Text.* Toronto: Scholastic, 2002.

——. "Getting Kids Into the Reading Game: You Gotta Know the Rules." *Voices from the Middle* 8.4 (2001): 25–36.

——. *Improving Comprehension with Think-Aloud Strategies.* Toronto: Scholastic, 2001.

——. *Reading IS Seeing.* New York: Scholastic, 2004.

Wilhelm, J., T. Baker, and J. Dube. *Strategic Reading.* Portsmouth, NH: Heinemann, 2001.

Wilkinson, Louise C., and Elaine R. Silliman. "Classroom Language and Literacy Learning." *Reading Online* 4.7 (February 2001). http://www.readingonline.org/articles/art_index.asp?HREF=/articles/handbook/wilkinson/index.html.

Wilkinson, Lyn. "An Introduction to the Explicit Teaching of Reading." *The Explicit Teaching of Reading.* J. Hancock, ed. Newark, DE: International Reading Association, 1999, 1–12.

Wilks, Susan. *Critical and Creative Thinking Strategies for Classroom Inquiry.* Portsmouth, NH: Heinemann, 1995.

Winebrenner, Susan. *Teaching Gifted Kids in the Regular Classroom.* Minneapolis: Free Spirit Publishing, 2001.

Wisconsin Literacy Education and Reading Network Source. http://www.wilearns.com/apps/.

Wong, H, and R. Wong. *How to Be an Effective Teacher: The First Days of School.* Mountain View, CA: Harry Wong Publications, 2001.

Wooten, Deborah. *Valued Voices: An Interdisciplinary Approach to Teaching and Learning.* Newark, DE: International Reading Association, 2000.

Worthy, Jo. "What Makes Intermediate-Grade Students Want to Read?" *The Reading Teacher* 55.6 (March 2002): 568–69.

Worthy, Jo, Karen Broaddus, and Gay Ivey. *Pathways to Independence: Reading, Writing, and Learning in Grades 3–8.* New York: Guilford Press, 2001.

Write Traits Ontario Rubrics. 2003, 1–12.

Yopp, H.K., and R.H. Yopp. "Supporting Phonemic Awareness Development in the Classroom." *The Reading Teacher* 54.2 (2000): 130–43.

INDEX

fluency and, 104-5, 121-22, 139, 554
genres and, 105
graphic organizers, 110, 158
guided reading and, 472-73
Informal Reading Inventories (IRI)
    and, 118
instruction, 18, 576-77
Internet and, 583
intervention for, 596
learning of, 101-2
listening, 115, 553
mental imagery and, 182-84
monitoring, 33, 109, 147-48
of narrative texts, 155-56
oral language and, 18
oral responses and, 118
phonics and, 140
predicting and, 113, 176-79
prior knowledge and, 113, 176-79
questioning and, 112-13, 170-76
read-alouds and, 118
reading and, 135-39, 544, 576
reading as, 99
reading strategy use and, 555
reciprocal teaching and, 169-70, 184
release of responsibility and, 144-45
responding and, 167-68
retelling and, 110-11, 117-18, 164
rubrics, 454
SAIL strategy, 184-85
say something technique, 150
self-monitoring for, 119, 147-48, 150-
    51, 556, 576
semantic organizers and, 110
shared reading and, 467
small-group reading intervention in,
    577
SMART technique for, 153-55
strategies, 146-47
strategy use across curriculum, 420
and struggling readers, 444
students' reading attitudes and, 102-3
summarizing and, 110-12, 117-18,
    164-70
talk and, 106, 140
teaching of, 114
text structures and, 109-10, 155, 156
think-alouds and, 33, 121, 144, 145-
    46, 186, 460
as thoughtful literacy, 99-100
visualizing and, 113, 182-84
vocabulary and, 103-4
world knowledge and, 103-4
writing and, 107, 140, 305
Comprehension assessment, 115-30
    arts-based responses and, 126-27
    through conversation, 122-23
    of fluency in oral reading, 122
    by listening in, 127-28
    through literature discussions, 127-
        28, 217-18
    miscue analysis and, 119
    retelling and, 117-18, 164
    running records and, 119-20

self-assessment in, 128-29
summarizing and, 117-18
think-alouds and, 121
written responses and, 123-26
Concept definition technique, 369-70
Concept development, 28-29, 62
Concept Ladder graphic organizer, 66,
    87
Concept maps, 369, 405
    as study aids, 389-90
Concepts, new, 32
CONCEPT strategy, 368
Conferences
    parent, 244
    parent-teacher, 505
    reading, 122-23, 138, 215, 451-52, 527
    roving, 243
    small-group, 243
    student-led, 243, 505
    writing, 235-36, 240
Confirming, 32
Connecting/connections, 43
    complex sentences and, 35
    comprehension and, 167-68
    for ESL students, 78
    questioning and, 118
    in read-alouds, 462
    self-assessment of, 216
    with social issues, 272
    synthesizing and, 111
    to texts, 106
Content literacy, 331. See also
    Curriculum
    comprehension in, 373
    factors affecting, 331-32
    home-school links and, 396-99
    instructional approaches to, 332-39
    newsletters on, 397
    oral language in, 361-66
    parents and, 396-99
    partnerships in, 396
    self-assessment of, 349-52, 351
    talk and, 361
    teacher resources for, 356-57
    vocabulary learning and, 366-72
    writing abilities development in, 380-
        87
Content literacy assessment, 340-52
    benchmarks, 340
    instruction and, 353
    journals in, 343-44
    performance standards, 340
    portfolios in, 342-43
    rubrics, 340
Content Word Boards, 74
Context
    cues, 366
    words in, 28, 63-64, 82, 571
Conventions
    books for, 275
    defined, 231
    editing of, 245
    in home-school-community partner-
        ships, 303

in journal writing, 375
modelling of, 277
scoring guide for, 320
self-assessment of, 323
Conversation, 47, 140
    after read-alouds, 463
    assessment through, 122-23
    classroom, 18
    of parents, 61
Cooperative assessment, 346-47
Cooperative learning, 106-7, 578
Critical literacy, 130-34
    assessment of ability in, 348
    books for, 391-92
    critical thinking and, 100-1
    development of, 390-92
    media literacy for, 392
    questioning and, 176, 390-91
    reader response prompts and, 265-66
    teaching of, 100, 101-2
    voice and, 272-73
    writing and, 271-73
Critical thinking
    critical literacy and, 100-1
    and letters to authors, 269
    reader response prompts and, 265-66
Cues
    cards, 54
    ESL students and, 40
Curriculum. See also Content literacy
    comprehension strategy use across,
        420
    congruence with intervention, 546,
        547-48
    integrated, 135, 349, 432
    narrative writing across, 286
    new concepts in, 32
    oral language across, 15, 62-73
    skills development across, 358-60
    writing across, 245
Curriculum-as-inquiry approach, 337

D
DEAR (Drop Everything and Read), 136,
    545
Decoding
    and accuracy rate of reading, 453
    assessment of, 558, 609-10
    and repeated reading, 564
    and sight vocabulary, 444
    in small-group intervention, 570
    in struggling readers, 553, 554-55
    and volume of reading, 544
Descriptive writing, 230, 296-97
Differentiated instruction, 345
Digital/electronic literacies, 332
Directions, 32
Distractions, 25, 48, 432, 476
Diversity. See also ESL students
    pragmatics and, 26-27
Does Not Fit columns, 77
Drafts
    of reports, 387
    of writing, 245, 249

engagement in, 103, 544-45, 559-60
expository texts, 105
fluency, 446, 452, 544, 554. *See also*
  Fluency
guided. *See* Guided reading
home, 85, 138-39, 191, 521, 551, 602
hooking students on, 136-37
independent. *See* Independent reading
interest in, 543
interests inventory, 116-17, 207, 208
interviews, 117, 209
journals, 124, 143-44
listening and, 115
and literacy development, 15
logs, 124, 143-44, 456-57, 463, 483,
  521, 560
modelled, 568
motivation in, 587
narrative texts, 105
nudge, 569
opportunities for, 138
and oral language development, 54-
  61
paired, 585-86, 600-1
parents and, 138-39, 588
performance, 543, 566-67
perseverance in, 134
poetry, 228
rate, 104-5, 557-58
Red Light—STOP!, 311
repeated, 139, 564, 587, 592
role models, 587
round-robin, 473
shared. *See* Shared reading
silent, 476
silent vs. oral, 554, 564
SQ3R technique, 180-81
strategy use in, 554-55
tap, 569
teachers of, 103
thinking during, 108
time for, 103, 574
and vocabulary development, 544
volume of, 451
and word recognition, 544
writing and, 85, 226-27, 233, 287,
  305
Reading aloud. *See also* Oral reading
fluency and, 139
modelling through, 139
of persuasive writing, 294
self-monitoring of, 119
think-alouds and, 120
of writing, 238, 246, 249
Reading comprehension. *See*
  Comprehension
Reading conferences, 122-23, 138
informal, 215, 451-52, 527
Rebuilding, of text, 156
Reciprocal teaching, 169-70, 184, 578
intervention for, 597
summarizing in, 580
in think-alouds, 577
Reciting (SQ3R technique), 180-81

Red Light—STOP!, 311
Reluctant readers, 545, 559-60. *See also*
  Struggling students
independent reading by, 103
interest inventories, 559-60
intervention for, 583-84
reading engagement of, 559-60
Reports
book, 294
oral, 69-71
persuasive, 70
writing, 386-87, 407-8
Rereading, 564, 581
and revision of writing, 249
Research projects/reports, 489-90
presentation, 425
self-assessment, 417, 424
Response(s)
activities after reading, 61
affective, 333-34
and comprehension, 167-68
dramatic arts, 127, 183
journals, 344, 483
linguistic, 331
oral, 331
question-based, 124-25
reader journals. *See* Reader response
  journals
rubric for, 212
supporting, 125
visual, 331
visual arts, 127, 184
written, 582
Résumés, 296
Retelling, 455-56
and comprehension, 110-11, 117-18
fiction, 210
in independent writing, 488
of informational texts, 530
of narrative text, 529
of nonfiction, 211, 455
and oral reading records, 453
in reading conferences, 451, 452
and semantic knowledge, 32
summarizing compared to, 580
Reviewing (SQ3R technique), 180-81
Revision, 237, 238, 245, 249-50
editing vs., 302
ESL students and, 301
of letters, 268
of reports, 387
self-assessment of, 326
teaching of, 279
and traits of writing, 305
Rewriting, 233, 280-81
Rhyme awareness, 37
Rimes, 37, 595
Role-plays, 71-72
Roving conferences, 243
Rubrics. *See also* Scoring guides
comprehension, 454
content literacy assessment, 340
for KWL performance, 412-13
math problem-solving, 426

Readers Theatre script, 535
reading response, 212
spelling, 454
summarizing, 212
Running records, 119-20, 453, 553-54,
  572, 581

S
SAIL (Students Achieving Independent
  Learning), 184-85
Say something technique, 150
Scaffolded learning, 547, 548
Scanning, 152-53
Schema, 28-29, 331
School(s)
community and, 261-62, 272, 303,
  396-99
language of, 16-18
Web sites, 270-71
Science
content as news, 260
journal entries for, 376-77
skills development in, 359
Scoring guides. *See also* Rubrics
for conventions, 320
ideas and organization, 318
Metacomprehension Strategy Index
  (MSI), 608
trait-based, 224-25, 237
for voice, 319
for word choice, 319
Self-assessment, 342
of attitudes, 525
checklists, 351
in comprehension assessment, 128-29
of connections, 216
of content literacy, 349-52, 351
of conventions, 323
cooperative assessment and, 346
of editing, 326
of group participation, 416
for ideas, 321
of independent reading, 219
of informational writing, 418
of interest inventories, 526
inventories for, 351-52
of listening skills, 95
Metacomprehension Strategy Index
  (MSI), 604-7
of oral language, 38, 43
of oral presentations, 351, 425
for organization, 321
portfolios and, 38, 257-58, 350-51,
  415, 532
of Readers Theatre, 536
of reading attitudes, 206
of reading interests, 116-17, 207
with reading logs, 456-57
of research projects/reports, 417, 424
of revision, 326
of sentence fluency, 323
of speaking skills, 94
of spelling, 498, 539
surveys for, 351-52

conferences, 235-36, 240
in content areas, 380-87
conventions. *See* Conventions
craft of, 232
critical literacy and, 271-73
deletion of, 279
descriptive. *See* Descriptive writing
drafting of, 245, 249
environmental print, 239
and ESL students, 301
expository, 105, 229
feedback on, 238, 240, 246
fiction, 228
first drafts, 249
fluency in, 266
goals for, 223
guided. *See* Guided writing
home-school partnerships in, 303-4
ideas for, 250-52, 325
independent. *See* Independent writing
in integrated subject areas, 385
interviews in, 261-63
journal, 255, 256, 264-66, 375-77
leads, 284
letters, 267-71
life snapshots, 252
and literacy development, 15
literature and, 226
main ideas vs. details in, 198, 279-81

mini-lessons, 226, 232, 279-81, 303, 305
modelling of, 233-34, 236, 303
motivation and, 225, 305
about music, 383-85
narrative. *See* Narrative writing
nonfiction. *See* Nonfiction
about objects, 252
oral language development through, 73-74
parent support for, 304
patterns in, 254
by peers, 233
personal, 337
persuasive. *See* Persuasive writing
planning of, 245, 246
poetry, 228, 298-300
procedural. *See* Procedural writing
process of, 245-46
programs, 224-27
prompts for, 253-54
purposes for, 223, 228, 287-88, 305
reading aloud of, 232, 246, 249, 305
reading and, 85, 226-27, 233, 287, 305
of reports, 386-87, 407-8
of responses, 273
rough drafts, 249
samples, 556

self-expression in, 266
sentences for pictures, 382-83
shared. *See* Shared writing
shared reading and, 232
sloppy copy, 249
"small", 257, 263
strong vs. weak, 233
talk and, 227
teaching, 231-33, 303
think-alouds in, 232-33
time for, 225-26, 302
titles, 284-85
topics, 227, 228, 250-52
traits. *See* Traits, writing
unfinished, 227
and vocabulary development, 140, 305
workshops, 226
Writing assessment, 237-44
analytic vs. holistic, 237
choice of traits for, 239
consistency vs. subjectivity in, 237
large-scale, 253
peer assessment in, 238-39
portfolios in, 240-44
reading aloud in, 238
self-assessment in, 237-38
trait-based, 237
Writing share, 232, 235, 240

LITERARY CREDITS

This page constitutes an extension of the copyright page. We have made every effort to trace the ownership of all copyrighted material and to secure permission from copyright holders. In the event of any question arising as to the use of any material, we will be pleased to make the necessary corrections in future printings. Thanks are due to the following authors, publishers, and agents for permission to use the material indicated.

Introduction. Quotes from Richard L. Allington and Patricia M. Cunningham, *Schools That Work: Where All Children Read and Write*, (New York, NY: Harper and Row Publishers, 1996), p. viii, 4, 118, published by Allyn and Bacon, Boston, MA, copyright © 1996 by Pearson Education are reprinted by permission of the publisher. **7:** Allington, Richard L. and Peter H. Johnston. "What do we know about effective fourth-grade teachers and their classrooms?" In *Learning to Teach Reading Setting the Research Agenda.* (Newark, DE: International Reading Association, 2001), p. 160. Copyright © 2001 by the International Reading Association. **8:** Allington, Richard L. and Peter H. Johnston. "What do we know about effective fourth-grade teachers and their classrooms?" In *Learning to Teach Reading Setting the Research Agenda.* (Newark, DE: International Reading Association, 2001), p. 157. Reprinted with permission of Richard L. Allington and the International Reading Association. **12:** From the Random House Book of Poetry for Children (Random House: 1983), p. 117. Reprinted with permission by Jack Prelutsky.

Chapter 1. 18: King Features Syndicate **30:** BORN LOSER © reprinted by permission of Newspaper Enterprise Association, Inc. **30:** Table 1 from Adams, Thomasenia Lott. (2003 May). "Reading mathematics: More than words can say." *The Reading Teacher,* 56(8), 786–795. Reprinted with permission of Thomasenia Lott Adams and the International Reading Association. All rights reserved. **31:** Table 1 from Adams, Thomasenia Lott. (2003 May). "Reading mathematics: More than words can say." *The Reading Teacher,* 56(8), 786–795. Reprinted with permission of Thomasenia Lott Adams and the International Reading Association. All rights reserved. **54:** Adapted from Dawn Reithaug, *Orchestrating Academic Success by Adapting and Modifying Programs* (West Vancouver, BC: Stirling Head Enterprises Inc., 1998), 71. Reprinted with permission. **60:** Reprinted by permission from *When Kids Can't Read: What Teachers Can Do* by Kylene Beers. Copyright © 2003 by Kylene Beers. Published by Heinemann, a division of Reed Elsevier, Inc., Portsmouth, NH. All rights reserved. **64:** Adapted from Janet Allen, *Words, Words, Words: Teaching Vocabulary in Grades 4–12,* (Portland, ME Stenhouse, 1999), 140. Copyright © 1999. Reprinted with permission of Stenhouse Publishers. **65:** From *Stretching Students' Vocabulary* by Karen Bromley. Published by Scholastic Professional Books/Scholastic Inc. Copyright © 2002 by Karen Bromley. Reprinted with permission. **66:** Adapted from Janet Allen, *Words, Words, Words: Teaching Vocabulary in Grades 4–12,* (Portland, ME Stenhouse, 1999), 131. Copyright © 1999. Reprinted with permission of Stenhouse Publishers. **67:** From *Stretching Students' Vocabulary* by Karen Bromley. Published by Scholastic Professional Books/Scholastic Inc. Copyright © 2002 by Karen Bromley. Reprinted by permission. **82:** Adapted from Janet Allen, *Words, Words, Words: Teaching Vocabulary in Grades 4–12,* (Portland, ME Stenhouse, 1999), 140. Copyright © 1999. Reprinted with permission of Stenhouse Publishers. **83:** Adapted from Dawn Reithaug, *Orchestrating Academic Success by Adapting and Modifying Programs* (West Vancouver, BC: Stirling Head Enterprises Inc., 1998), 71. Reprinted with permission. **84:** Adapted from Dawn Reithaug, *Orchestrating Academic Success by Adapting and Modifying Programs* (West Vancouver, BC: Stirling Head Enterprises Inc., 1998), 71. Reprinted with permission. **86:** Adapted from Janet Allen, *Words, Words, Words: Teaching Vocabulary in Grades 4–12,* (Portland, ME Stenhouse, 1999), 19. Copyright © 1999. Reprinted with permission of Stenhouse Publishers. **87:** Adapted from Janet Allen, *Words, Words, Words: Teaching Vocabulary in Grades 4–12,* (Portland, ME Stenhouse, 1999), 131. Copyright © 1999. Reprinted with permission of Stenhouse Publishers.

Chapter 2. Quotes from Richard L. Allington, *What Really Matters for Struggling Readers: Designing Research-Based Programs,* (Boston: Allyn & Bacon, 2001), pp. 87, 89, 106, 110 are adapted by permission of the publisher, copyright © 2001 by Pearson Education. **Quotes** from Richard L. Allington and Patricia M. Cunningham, *Schools That Work: Where All Children Read and Write,* (New York, NY: Harper and Row Publishers, 1996), p. 97, 161 published by Allyn & Bacon, Boston, MA, copyright © 2006 by Pearson Education are reprinted by permission of the publisher. **Quotes** from Nell K. Duke and P. David Pearson, "Effective Practices for Developing Reading Comprehension" in *What Research Has to Say About Reading Instruction,* edited by A. E. Farstrup and S. J. Samuels, pages 205–42, (Newark, DE: International Reading Association, 2002), p. 221, 234, copyright © 2002 by the International Reading Association are reprinted with permission. **Quote** from Karen S. Evans, *Literature Discussion Groups in the Intermediate Grades: Dilemmas and Possibilities,* (Newark, DE: International Reading Association, 2001), p. viii, copyright © 2001 by the International Reading Association is reprinted by permission. **Quotes** from Regie Routman, *Reading Essentials: The Specifics You Need to Teach Reading Well,* (Portsmouth, NH: Heinemann), 2002, pp. 83, 84, 93, 125, 129 are reprinted with permission from Heinemann, copyright © 2003 by Regie Routman, published by Heinemann, a division of Reed Elsevier, Inc., Portsmouth, NH. All Rights Reserved. **Quotes** from Catherine Snow, *Reading for Understanding: Toward an R&D Program in Reading Comprehension,* prepared for the Office of Educational Research and Improvement, U.S. Department of Education, (Santa Monica, CA, RAND Education, 2002), pp. *xiii,* 5, 33, 236 are reprinted with permission. **99:** Adapted from Snow, Catherine. *Reading for Understanding: Toward an R&D Program in Reading Comprehension,* Figure S-1, p.xiv. Prepared for the Office of Educational Research and Improvement, U.S. Department of Education. Santa Monica, CA: RAND Education, 2002. Reprinted with permission. **106:** Material adapted from State of Wisconsin, Wisconsin Governor's Literary Education and Reading Network at http://www.wilearns.com/apps/default.asp?cid-27. Reprinted with permission. **115:** British Columbia Ministry of Education. "Learning Through Representing," in *Primary Program: A Framework for Teaching.* Victoria: Government of British Columbia, 2000, p. 35. Copyright © Province of British Columbia. All rights reserved. Reprinted with permission of the Province of British Columbia. www.ipp.gov.bc.ca. **119 (left):** Doctorow, R., M. Bodiam, and H. McGowan. *CASI 4: Reading Assessment Scoring Guide 4 Errata Sheet,* (Toronto: Thomson Nelson), 2003, p. 40. © 2003. Reprinted with permission of Nelson, a division of Thomson Learning: www.thomsonrights.com. Fax 800-730-2215. **119 (right):** Doctorow, R., M. Bodiam, and H. McGowan. *CASI 4: Reading Assessment Scoring Guide 4 Errata Sheet,* (Toronto: Thomson Nelson), 2003, p. 8. © 2003. Reprinted with permission of Nelson, a division of Thomson Learning: www.thomsonrights.com. Fax 800-730-2215. **126 (top):** Adapted from Lynn K. Rhodes and Nancy L. Shanklin, *Windows into Literacy: Assessing Learners K–8.* (Portsmouth, NH: Heinemann, 1993), 90. Copyright © 1993 by Lynn Rhodes and

Nancy Shanklin. Published by Heinemann, a division of Reed Elsevier, Inc. Portsmouth, NH. All rights reserved. **126 (bottom):** Adapted from Wayne Andrew, Andrew Griffin, and Wendy Mader, *InfoCanada: Geographical Regions–The Arctic.* (Toronto: Nelson, 2004), p. 44. Reprinted with permission of Nelson, a division of Thomson Learning: www.thomsonrights.com. Fax 800-730-2215. **128:** Adapted from Karen Evans, *Literature Discussion Groups in the Intermediate Grades: Dilemmas and Possibilities* (Newark, DE: International Reading Association, 2001), 105. Copyright © 2001 by the International Reading Association. **129:** Regie Routman, *Reading Essentials: The Specifics You Need to Teach Reading Well* (Portsmouth, NH: Heinemann, 2002), 125. Copyright © 2003 by Regie Routman. Published by Heinemann, a division of Reed Elsevier, Inc., Portsmouth, NH. All rights reserved. **135:** Adapted from Suzy Red, "Ten Reasons to Teach an Integrated Curriculum." Kids' Wings: 2003 http://suzyred.com/integratedten.htm. Reprinted with permission. **145:** Adapted from P. David Pearson and Linda Fielding, "Comprehension Instruction," in *Handbook of Reading Research, Volume II,* edited by R. Barr, M. Kamil, P. Mosenthal, and P. David Pearson. (White Plains, NY: Longman Publishing), 1991, pp. 815–60. Published by Allyn and Bacon, Boston, MA. Copyright © 1991 by Pearson Education. Reprinted/adapted by permission of the publisher. **146:** Adapted from B. Davey, "Think Aloud: Modeling the Cognitive Processes of Reading Comprehension" *Journal of Reading* 27.1 (1983): 44–47. Copyright ©1983 by the International Reading Association. **149:** Zwiers, Jeff. *Building Reading Comprehension Habits in Grades 6–12: A Toolkit of Classroom Activities.* Newark, DE: International Reading Association, 2004, p. 134. Copyright © 2004 by the International Reading Association. **151:** Allington, Richard L. *What Really Matters for Struggling Readers: Designing Research-Based Programs.* Boston: Allyn & Bacon, 2001, p. 105. Copyright © 2001 by Pearson Education. Adapted by permission of the publisher. **154:** Rhodes, Lynn K., and Nancy L. Shanklin. *Windows into Literacy: Assessing Learners K–8.* Portsmouth, NH: Heinemann, 1993, p. 256. Reprinted by permission. Copyright © 1993 by Lynn Rhodes and Nancy Shanklin. Published by Heinemann, a division of Reed Elsevier, Inc., Portsmouth, NH. All rights reserved. **158:** Adapted from Gail E. Tompkins, *Teaching Writing: Balancing Process and Product,* 3rd edition (Upper Saddle River, NJ: Prentice-Hall, Inc., 2000), 252–53. Copyright © 2000. Adapted by permission of Pearson Education, Inc., Upper Saddle River, NJ. **165:** Adapted from John D. McNeil, *Reading Comprehension: New Directions for Classroom Practice* (Glenview, IL: Scott Foresman, 1987), 157. Published by Allyn and Bacon, Boston, MA. Copyright © 1987 by Pearson Education. Reprinted by permission of the publisher. **168:** Adapted from Owen Boyle and Suzanne Peregoy, "Literacy Scaffolds: Strategies for First- and Second-Language Readers and Writers," *The Reading Teacher 44* (November 1990): 194–99. Copyright © 1990 by the International Reading Association. **172:** Ogle, D.M. "K-W-L: A Teaching Model That Develops Active Reading of Expository Text," *Reading Teacher 39* (1986): 564–70. Copyright © 1986 by the International Reading Association. **173:** Adapted from Taffy Raphael, "Teaching Question and Answer Relationships, Revisited," *The Reading Teacher 39.6* (1986): 516–22. Copyright © 1986 by the International Reading Association. **175:** Duke, Nell K., and P. David Pearson. "Effective Practices for Developing Reading Comprehension." In *What Research Has to Say About Reading Instruction,* edited by A. E. Farstrup and S. J. Samuels, pages 205–42. Newark, DE: International Reading Association, 2002, p. 230. Copyright © 2002 by the International Reading Association. **185:** Duke, Nell K., and P. David Pearson. "Effective Practices for Developing Reading Comprehension." In *What Research Has to Say About Reading Instruction,* edited by A. E. Farstrup and S. J. Samuels, pages 205–42. Newark, DE: International Reading Association, 2002, p. 235. Copyright © 2002 by the International Reading Association. **198:** P. David Pearson and Dale D. Johnson, *Teaching Reading Comprehension.* (New York: Holt, Rinehart and Winston, 1978), 95. **201:** Adapted from Taffy Raphael, "Teaching Children Question-Answer Relationships, Revisited," *The Reading Teacher 39* (1986): 516–22. Copyright © 1986 by the International Reading Association. **207:** Doctorow, R., M. Bodiam, and H. McGowan. *CASI 4: Reading Assessment Scoring Guide 4 Errata Sheet,* (Toronto: Thomson Nelson), 2003, p. 35. Copyright © 2003. Reprinted with permission of Nelson, a division of Thomson Learning: www.thomsonrights.com. Fax 800-730-2215. **208:** Doctorow, R., M. Bodiam, and H. McGowan. *CASI 4: Reading Assessment Scoring Guide 4 Errata Sheet,* (Toronto: Thomson Nelson), 2003, p. 35. Copyright © 2003. Reprinted with permission of Nelson, a division of Thomson Learning: www.thomsonrights.com. Fax 800-730-2215. **217:** Adapted from Karen Evans, *Literature Discussion Groups in the Intermediate Grades: Dilemmas and Possibilities* (Newark, DE: International Reading Association, 2001), 105. Copyright © 2001 by the International Reading Association.

Chapter 3. Quotes from Vicki Spandel, *Creating Writers Through 6-Trait Writing Assessment and Instruction,* 3rd Edition (New York, NY: Addison Wesley Longman Inc.: 2001), pp. 5, 19, 26, 27, 31, 32, 136, 343, 366 published by Allyn and Bacon, Boston, MA, copyright © 2001 by Pearson Education are reprinted/adapted by permission of the publisher. **Quote** from Richard L. Allington, *What Really Matters for Struggling Readers: Designing Research-Based Programs,* (New York, N.Y: Addison-Wesley Educational Publishers, 2001), p. 21, published by Allyn and Bacon, Boston, MA, copyright © 2001 by Pearson Education is reprinted/adapted by permission of the publisher. **277:** "Area Cautious of Cougars" reprinted with permission of The Calgary Herald. **287:** Adapted from Stead, Tony. *Is That a Fact? Teaching Nonfiction Writing K–3.* Portland, ME: Stenhouse Publishers, 2002, p. 9. Copyright © 2002, with permission of Stenhouse Publishers.

Chapter 4. Quotes from Doug Buehl, *Classroom Strategies for Interactive Learning* (Newark, DE: International Reading Association, 2001), p. 59, 149 copyright © 2001 by the International Reading Association are reprinted with permission. **Quote** from Katherine Luongo-Orlando, *Authentic Assessment: Designing Performance Based Tasks* (Markham, ON: Pembroke Publishers, 2003), 98 is reprinted with permission. **341:** Adapted from Katherine Luongo-Orlando, *Authentic Assessment: Performance-Based Tasks* (Markham, ON: Pembroke Publishers, 2003), 17. Reprinted with permission. **345 (top):** Adapted from Rhodes and Nathenson-Mejia "Anecdotal Records: A Powerful Tool for Ongoing Literacy Assessment" (pp. 83–90). In Shelby Barrentine (Ed.), *Reading Assessment: Principle and Practices for Elementary Teachers.* (Newark, DE: International Reading Association, 1999), 86. Copyright © 1999 by the International Reading Association. **345 (bottom):** Adapted from Boyd-Batstone, Paul. "Focused Anecdotal Records Assessment: A Tool for Standards-based Authentic Assessment," *The Reading Teacher, 58.3,* p. 236, Table 4, 2004. Copyright © 2004 by the International Reading Association. **350 (left):** Adapted from Roger Farr and Bruce Tone, *Portfolio and Performance Assessment: Helping Students Evaluate Their Progress As Readers and Writers* (Fort Worth, TX: Harcourt Brace and Company, 1994), 292, 308. Reprinted with permission of Wadsworth, a division of Thomson Learning: www.thomsonrights.com. Fax 800-730-2215. **350 (right):** Adapted from Bette Bergeron, Sarah Wermuth, and Rebecca Hammar, "Initiating Portfolios Through Shared Learning: Three

Perspectives." In *Reading Assessment: Principle and Practices for Elementary Teachers–A Collection of Articles from The Reading Teacher*, edited by Shelby Barrantine, 118–30 (Newark, DE: International Reading Association, 1999), 129. Copyright © 1999 by the International Reading Association. **354:** Rhodes, Carole S. "Evaluating and Selecting Quality Children's Books," *Teachers' Choices Committee: More Teachers' Favorite Books for Kids: Teachers' Choices 1994–1996*, (Newark, DE: International Reading Association, 1997), pp. S5–S10. Copyright © 1997 by the International Reading Association. **355:** Adapted from Crawford, Kathleen, Caryl Crowell, Gloria Koffman, Barbara Peterson, LaFon Phillips, Jean Schroeder, Cyndi Giorgis, and Kathy Short. "Exploring the World Through Multiple Literacies." *The Reading Teacher, 48.7.* 600–608, 1995. Copyright © 1995 by the International Reading Association. **359:** Manzo, Anthony, Ula Manzo, and Thomas Estes. *Content Area Literacy: Interactive Teaching for Active Learning.* (New York: NY: John Wiley & Sons, Inc, 2001), pp. 300–301. Reprinted with permission of John Wiley & Sons, Inc. **360:** Adapted from Robert Marzano, "Classroom Instruction That Works." Workshop presented at the Literacy: Practical Ways to Achieve Success conference in Mississauga, ON. January 31-February 1, 2002. Reprinted with permission from the Mid-Continent Regional Educational Laboratory. **365:** Adapted from Buehl, Doug. *Classroom Strategies for Interactive Learning.* Newark, DE: International Reading Association, 2001, p. 59. Copyright © 2001 by the International Reading Association. **365:** Adapted from Buehl, Doug. *Classroom Strategies for Interactive Learning.* Newark, DE: International Reading Association, 2001, pp. 149–150. Copyright © 2001 by the International Reading Association. **369:** Adapted from Buehl, Doug. *Classroom Strategies for Interactive Learning.* Newark, DE: International Reading Association, 2001, pp. 41, 154. Copyright © 2001 by the International Reading Association. **370:** Adapted from Buehl, Doug. *Classroom Strategies for Interactive Learning.* Newark, DE: International Reading Association, 2001, p. 154. Copyright © 2001 by the International Reading Association. **371:** Adapted from Buehl, Doug. *Classroom Strategies for Interactive Learning.* Newark, DE: International Reading Association, 2001, p. 80. Copyright © 2001 by the International Reading Association. **372:** Adapted from Mary Olson and Susan Homan, *Teacher to Teacher: Strategies for the Elementary Classroom* (Newark, DE: International Reading Association, 1993), 59. Copyright © 1993 by the International Reading Association. **383:** Adapted from Mary Olson and Susan Homan, *Teacher to Teacher: Strategies for the Elementary Classroom* (Newark, DE: International Reading Association, 1993), 102–3. Copyright © 1993 by the International Reading Association. **385 (top):** Adapted from Mary Olson and Susan Homan, *Teacher to Teacher: Strategies for the Elementary Classroom* (Newark, DE: International Reading Association, 1993), pp. 103–4. Copyright © 1993 by the International Reading Association. **390:** "Five Key Questions that Can Change the World – Part II," CML MediaLit Kit ™, Center for Media Literacy: Santa Monica, CA 2005, p. 7. Reprinted with permission of Elizabeth Thoman, Center for Media Literacy. **402:** Adapted from Thomas Mandeville, "KWLA: Linking the Affective and Cognitive Domains." In *Teaching Comprehension and Exploring Multiple Literacies: Strategies from The Reading Teacher*, edited by Timothy Rasinski et al., pp. 20–21 (Newark, DE: International Reading Association, 2000). Copyright © 2000 by the International Reading Association. **404:** Adapted from Taffy Raphael and Fenice Boyd, "When Readers Write: The Book Club Writing Connection." In *The Book Club Connection*, edited by Susan McMahon and Taffy Raphael, 69–88. (New York: Teachers College Press, 1997), 82. Material adapted by permission of the publisher. Copyright © by Teachers College, Columbia University. All rights reserved. **406:** Adapted from Adele Thomas, Lynn Fazio, and Betty Stiefelmeyer, *Families at School: A Guide for Educators* (Newark, DE: International Reading Association, 1999), p. 68. Copyright © 1999 by the International Reading Association. **407:** Adapted from Jean Dreher, et al. *Easy Steps to Writing Fantastic Research Reports.* (New York: Scholastic Professional Books, 2000), 16. Copyright © 2000 by K.A. Davis, Priscilla Wayant, Suzanne Clewell, Jan Dreher et al. Reprinted by permission of Scholastic Inc. **409:** Adapted from Lee Heffernan, *Critical Literacy and Writer's Workshop: Bringing Purpose and Passion to Student Writing.* (Newark, DE: International Reading Association, 2004), p. 5. Copyright © 2004 by the International Reading Association. **415:** Adapted from Roger Farr and Bruce Tone, *Portfolio and Performance Assessment: Helping Students Evaluate Their Progress as Readers and Writers*, 1st edition (Fort Worth, TX: Harcourt Brace and Company, 1994), pp. 300, 307. Copyright © 1994. Reprinted with permission of Wadsworth, a division of Thomson Learning: www.thomsonrights.com. Fax 800-730-2215. **416:** Adapted from Judy Clarke, Rone Wideman, and Susan Eadie, *Together We Learn.* (Scarborough, ON: Prentice-Hall Inc., 1990), p. 105. Reprinted with permission of Pearson Education Canada, Inc. **417:** Adapted from Ros Fryar, "Students Assess Their Own Reporting and Presentation Skills." In *Literacy Assessment: A Collection of Articles from the Australian Literacy Educators' Association* edited by Heather Fehring, 36–39. (Newark, DE: International Reading Association, 2003), 39. Reprinted with permission from the Australian Literacy Educators' Association. **419:** Adapted from Linda Gambrell et al., "Assessing Motivation to Learn" in *Reading Assessment: Principles and Practices for Elementary Teachers–A Collection of Articles from The Reading Teacher*, edited by Shelby Barrentine, (Newark, DE: International Reading Association, 1999), 221–22. Copyright © 1999 by the International Reading Association. **420:** Adapted from *Linking Reading Assessment To Instruction* by Shearer/Homan, St. Martin's Press, © 1994, p. 155. Reprinted with permission by Lawrence Erlbaum Associates, Inc. Publishers. **424:** Adapted from Ros Fryar, "Students Assess Their Own Reporting and Presentation Skills." In *Literacy Assessment: A Collection of Articles from the Australian Literacy Educators' Association*, edited by Heather Fehring. (Newark, DE: International Reading Association, 2003), p. 38. Reprinted with permission from the Australian Literacy Educators' Association. **425:** Adapted from Ros Fryar, "Students Assess Their Own Reporting and Presentation of Reports," in *Literacy Assessment: A Collection of Articles from the Australian Literacy Educators' Association*, edited by Heather Fehring, (Newark, DE: International Reading Association, 2003), 37. Reprinted with permission from the Australian Literacy Educators' Association.

Chapter 5. Quotes from Janet Allen, *On the Same Page: Shared Reading Beyond the Primary Grades*, (Portland, ME: Stenhouse Publishers, 2002), p. 31, 119 copyright © 2002, are reprinted with permission of Stenhouse Publishers. **Quote** from Janet Allen, *Words, Words, Words: Teaching Vocabulary in Grades 4-12*, (Portland, ME: Stenhouse Publishers, 1999), p. 40, copyright © 1999, is reprinted with permission of Stenhouse Publishers. **Quotes** from Richard L. Allington, *What Really Matters for Struggling Readers: Designing Research-Based Program*, (Boston, MA: Allyn and Bacon, 2001), pp. 33, 120, 43, copyright © 2001 by Pearson Education are reprinted/adapted by permission of the publisher. **Quotes** from Irene C. Fountas and Gay Su Pinnell, *Guiding Readers and Writers, Grades 3-6: Teaching Comprehension, Genre and Content Literacy*, (Portsmouth, NH: Heinemann, 2001), p. 2, 9, 11, 14, copyright © 2001 by Irene C. Fountas and Gay Su Pinnell, published by Heinemann, a division of Reed Elsevier, Inc., Portsmouth, NH, all rights reserved, are reprinted with permission. **Quotes** from Regie Routman, *Reading Essentials: The Specifics You Need to Teach Reading Well,* (Portsmouth, NH: Heinemann, 2003), pp. 41–42, 130, 205, copyright © 2003 by Regie Routman, published by Heinemann, a division of Reed Elsevier, Inc., Portsmouth, NH, all rights reserved, are reprinted with permission. **Quotes** from Franki Sibberson and Karen Szymusiak, *Still Learning to Read: Teaching Students in Grades 3–6,* (Portland, ME: Stenhouse Publishers, 2003) p. 2, 12, 29, 31–34, 79, 87, copyright © 2003, are reprinted with permission of Stenhouse Publishers. **436:** Sibberson, Franki, and Karen Szymusiak. *Still Learning to Read: Teaching Students in Grades 3–6.* Portland, ME: Stenhouse Publishers, 2003, p. 13. Copyright © 2003. Reprinted with permission of Stenhouse Publishers. **437:** Sibberson, Franki, and Karen Szymusiak. *Still Learning to Read: Teaching Students in Grades 3–6.* Portland, ME: Stenhouse Publishers, 2003, p. 13–20. Copyright © 2003. Reprinted with permission of Stenhouse Publishers. **466:** Allen, Janet. *On the Same Page: Shared Reading Beyond the Primary Grades.* Portland, ME: Stenhouse Publishers, 2002, p. 9. Copyright © 2002. Reprinted with permission of Stenhouse Publishers. **469:** Adapted from Allen, Janet. *On the Same Page: Shared Reading Beyond the Primary Grades.* Portland, ME: Stenhouse Publishers, 2002, p. 233–36. Copyright © 2002. Reprinted with permission of Stenhouse Publishers. **473:** Adapted from Sibberson, Franki, and Karen Szymusiak. *Still Learning to Read: Teaching Students in Grades 3–6.* Portland, ME: Stenhouse Publishers, 2003, p. 64. Copyright © 2003. Reprinted with permission of Stenhouse Publishers. **491:** Adapted from Janet Allen, *Words, Words, Words: Teaching Vocabulary in Grades 4–12.* (Stenhouse Publishers: Portland, ME), 1999, p. 23. Copyright © 1999. Reprinted with permission of Stenhouse Publishers. **491:** Allen, Janet. *Words, Words, Words: Teaching Vocabulary in Grades 4–12.* Portland, ME: Stenhouse Publishers, 1999, p. 7. Copyright © 1999. Reprinted with permission of Stenhouse Publishers. **491:** Allen, Janet. *Words, Words, Words: Teaching Vocabulary in Grades 4–12.* Portland, ME: Stenhouse Publishers, 1999, p. 7. Copyright © 1999. Reprinted with permission of Stenhouse Publishers. **492:** Allen, Janet. *Words, Words, Words: Teaching Vocabulary in Grades 4–12.* Portland, ME: Stenhouse Publishers, 1999, p. 262–63. Copyright © 1999. Reprinted with permission of Stenhouse Publishers. **494:** Allen, Janet. *Words, Words, Words: Teaching Vocabulary in Grades 4–12.* Portland, ME: Stenhouse Publishers, 1999, p. 23. Copyright © 1999. Reprinted with permission of Stenhouse Publishers. **499:** Scott, Ruth McQuirter, and Sharon Siamon. *Spelling: Connecting the Pieces.* Toronto: Gage Learning Corporation, 2004, p. 131, 134, 138. Reprinted with permission of Nelson, a division of Thomson Learning: www.thomsonrights.com. Fax 800–730–2215. **500:** Scott, Ruth McQuirter, and Sharon Siamon. *Spelling: Connecting the Pieces.* Toronto: Gage Learning Corporation, 2004, p. 143. Reprinted with permission of Nelson, a division of Thomson Learning: www.thomsonrights.com. Fax 800–730–2215. **525:** Adapted from Linda Phillips, *Assessment Handbook 3.* (Scarborough, ON: Prentice Hall Ginn Canada, 1999), p. 53. Reprinted with permission by Pearson Education Canada, Inc. **527:** Routman, Regie. *Reading Essentials: The Specifics You Need to Teach Reading Well.* Portsmouth, NH: Heinemann, 2003, p. 104–105. Copyright © 2003 by Regie Routman. Published by Heinemann, a division of Reed Elsevier, Inc., Portsmouth, NH. All rights reserved. **529:** Adapted from Mary Shea, *Taking Running Records* (New York: Scholastic Professional Books, 2000), p. 83. Published by Scholastic Teaching Resources/Scholastic Inc. Copyright © 2000 by Mary Shea. Reprinted by permission. **530:** Adapted from Mary Shea, *Taking Running Records* (New York: Scholastic Professional Books, 2000), p. 81. Published by Scholastic Teaching Resources/Scholastic Inc. Copyright ©2000 by Mary Shea. Reprinted by permission. **531:** Dorothy P. Hall and Patricia M. Cunningham, "Multilevel Word Study: Word Charts, Word Walls and Word Sorts" In *Voices on Word Matters: Learning About Phonics and Spelling in the Literacy Classroom,* edited by Irene C. Fountas and Gay Su Pinnell (Portsmouth, NH: Heinemann, 1999), pp. 121, 122. Copyright © 1999 by Heinemann. Published by Heinemann, a division of Reed Elsevier, Inc., Portsmouth, NH. All rights reserved. **535:** Adapted from Alberta Assessment Consortium, Grade 2, Readers Theatre, Summer 1997, p. 13. Reprinted with permission. **536:** Adapted from Alberta Assessment Consortium, Readers Theatre, Grade 2, Summer 1997, p. 15. Reprinted with permission. **539:** From Ruth McQuirter Scott and Sharon Siamon. *Spelling: Connecting the Pieces* (Toronto: Gage Learning Corporation, 2004), p. 38. Copyright © 2004. Reprinted with permission of Nelson, a division of Thomson Learning: www.thomsonrights.com. Fax 800–730–2215.

Chapter 6. Quotes from Richard L. Allington, *What Really Matters for Struggling Readers: Designing Research Based Programs,* (New York: Addison-Wesley, 2001), pp. 22, 24, 76, 79, 121, published by Allyn and Bacon, Boston, MA, copyright © 2001 by Pearson Education are reprinted/adapted by permission. **Quotes** from Dorothy S. Strickland, Kathy Ganske, and Joanne K. Monroe, *Supporting Struggling Readers and Writers: Strategies for Classroom Intervention 3–6,* (Portland, ME: Stenhouse Publishers, 2002), pp. ix, 14, 90, 120, 146, copyright © 2002, are reprinted with permission of Stenhouse Publishers. **558:** Blachowicz, Camille, and Donna Ogle. *Reading Comprehension: Strategies for Independent Learners.* New York: Guilford Press, 2001, p. 69. Reprinted with permission. **594:** Adapted from Robert G. Heckelman, "Neurological Impress Method of Reading Instruction," *Academic Therapy 44:* 277–82. Copyright © 1969 by PRO-ED, Inc. Adapted by permission. **595:** Adapted from Strickland, Dorothy S., Kathy Ganske, and Joanne K. Monroe. *Supporting Struggling Readers and Writers: Strategies for Classroom Intervention 3–6.* Portland, ME: Stenhouse Publishers, 2002, p. 96. Copyright © 2002. Reprinted with permission of Stenhouse Publishers. **596:** Adapted from Pearson and Gallagher, *Contemporary Educational Psychology,* 8, 1983, pp. 317–44. Copyright © 1983, with permission of Elsevier. **600:** Adapted from Allington, Richard L. *What Really Matters for Struggling Readers: Designing Research Based Programs.* Boston: Allyn and Bacon, 2001, p. 76. Published by Allyn and Bacon, Boston, MA. Copyright © 2001 by Pearson Education. Adapted by permission. **601:** Adapted from Allington, Richard L. *What Really Matters for Struggling Readers: Designing Research Based Programs.* Boston: Allyn and Bacon, 2001, p. 76. Published by Allyn and Bacon, Boston, MA. Copyright © 2001 by Pearson Education. Adapted by permission of the publisher. **607:** Schmitt, Maribeth Cassidy. "A questionnaire to measure children's awareness of strategic reading processes." *The Reading Teacher,* 43(7), 454–461. Reprinted with permission of Maribeth Cassidy Schmitt and the International Reading Association. All rights reserved. **608:** Schmitt, Maribeth Cassidy. "A questionnaire to measure children's awareness of strategic reading processes." *The Reading Teacher,* 43(7), 454–461. Reprinted with permission of Maribeth Cassidy Schmitt and the International Reading Association. All rights reserved. **609:** Patricia M. Cunningham, *Phonics They Use: Words for Reading and Writing.* 3rd edition. (New York: Longman, 2000), 136–37. Copyright © by Pearson Education. Reprinted by permission of the publisher. **610:** Patricia M. Cunningham, *Phonics They Use: Words for Reading and Writing.* 3rd edition. (New York: Longman, 2000), 136–37. Copyright © by Pearson Education. Reprinted by permission of the publisher.

Final Thoughts. Quotes from Richard R. Allington, *What Really Matters for Struggling Readers,* Second Edition, (Boston, MA: Allyn and Bacon, 2006), p. 142, 175, published by Allyn & Bacon, Boston, MA, copyright © 2006 by Pearson Education are reprinted/adapted by permission of the publisher. **614 (top):** Allington, Richard R. *What Really Matters for Struggling Readers,* Second Edition, Boston, MA: Allyn and Bacon, 2006, p. 45. Published by Allyn & Bacon, Boston, MA. Copyright © 2006 by Pearson Education. Adapted/reprinted by permission of the publisher. **614 (bottom):** Allington, Richard L., and Patricia M. Cunningham. *Schools That Work: Where All Children Read and Write.* New York, NY: Harper and Row Publishers, 1996, p. 66. Published by Allyn and Bacon, Boston, MA. Copyright © 1996 by Pearson Education. Adapted/reprinted by permission of the publisher.